GEOFF HAMILTON'S

COTTAGE GARDENS

GEOFF HAMILTON'S

COTTAGE GARDENS

BBC BOOKS

$\mathcal{M}$y thanks for adding greatly to my knowledge of cottage gardening and to my enjoyment of the pleasant task of making the television series go to the following participants in the programmes, many of whom also allowed us to photograph their beautiful gardens for the book: Arthur Robinson of The Ancient Society of York Florists; Hannah Hutchinson, Owl Cottage, Isle of Wight; Anne Liverman, Dove Cottage, Derbyshire; Malcolm and Carol Skinner, Eastgrove Cottage Nursery, Worcestershire; Peter Herbert and Lindsay Shurvell, Gravetye Manor, West Sussex; George Flatt, Thatch Cottage, Suffolk; Alex Pankhurst, Malt Cottage, Essex; Roger and Margaret Pickering, Barwell, Leicestershire; Leslie Holmes, Camp Cottage, Gloucestershire; Rose Goodacre, Upton, Cambridgeshire; Pat Mansey, East Lode, Norfolk; The National Trust, Blaize Hamlet, Bristol, and Moseley Old Hall, Wolverhampton; Lynne Raynor, The Herb Garden, Derbyshire; Kim Hirst, The Cottage Herbery, Worcestershire; Richard Palethorpe and Bob Holman, The Weald and Downland Museum, West Sussex; John Scarman, Cottage Garden Roses, Staffordshire; Elizabeth Braimbridge, Langley Boxwood Nursery, Hampshire; Dina Penrose, Northfield, Birmingham; Yvonne Bell, Peterborough, Cambridgeshire; Ron Racket, Isle of Wight; Tom Pope, Haddon Hall, Derbyshire.

For helping me find some of the gardens used in the book and the series, my thanks to Pat Taylor and Clive Lane of the Cottage Garden Society and particular thanks too, to Anne Jennings of the Museum of Garden History who went to a great deal of trouble on my behalf

My thanks also to my son Stephen who has surprised me again with his terrific photography, and to Nicky Copeland, Ruth Baldwin and Sarah Amit from BBC Books. I always expect a superb job and they always surpass expectations.

Finally, though they're nothing to do with the book, I'm not going to let this opportunity pass without thanking the crew who made the television series (my baby) come alive. To cameraman John Couzins, sound men John Gilbert and Andrew Chorlton, production manager Sarah Greene and our brilliant director Andrew Gosling, my admiration and gratitude. I don't care what anyone says - they still do it best at the BBC.

❁

PRECEDING PAGES *The cottage garden 'style' was not invented; it simply evolved. So you can just step into that process of evolution to make a traditional, romantic cottage garden − wherever you live.*

❁

Published by BBC Books, a division of BBC Enterprises Limited,
Woodlands, 80 Wood Lane, London W12 OTT

First published in 1995

© Geoff Hamilton 1995

ISBN 0 563 36985 X

Illustrations by Gill Tomblin
Diagrams by Hilary Coulthard

Set in Caslon
Printed and Bound in Great Britain by
Butler Tanner Ltd, Frome.
Colour separations by Radstock Reproductions, Midsomer Norton
Jacket printed by Lawrence Allen Ltd, Weston-super-Mare.

Contents

Introduction

The cottage garden style has endured in one form or another in England since the Middle Ages. Even before then, of course, country cottages had gardens, but they were very different from the romantic image conjured up in our minds today. That was to come much later.

What all cottage gardens have in common is that they were there to be *used* – a need which, I think, still exists.

In times gone by, that precious plot of land was home to the pig and a few chickens and also had to raise enough food to feed them, plus something left over for the kitchen. And it was used to raise herbs, mainly for the country medicine chest and to mask much stronger household odours than we're used to today. An aesthetic design was simply not considered at first; but later, when the style was adopted and adapted by wealthier craftsmen and the gentry, the simpler cottage gardeners must have been influenced. They too will have aspired to growing flowers to lift the spirits and to decorate their houses. Nonetheless, inevitably, their designs were very simple.

Well, these days there's no need for medicinal herbs (though many country gardeners do still use them), and a pig or two would drive the neighbours into fits of apoplexy! But gardens are just as necessary now as ever they were.

We live in stressful times and the medical profession is quite clear that stress is a major cause of modern health problems. You only have to spend half an hour in the garden after a day battling with the telephone, the word processor and the rush-hour traffic to appreciate its value as a calming influence.

I suppose there's no real need these days to grow your own vegetables and fruit. It's much more convenient to buy them ready-washed and neatly shrink-wrapped in plastic, even ready-cooked. But just grow one row of fresh lettuce in your own garden and the difference in the quality of your life will shoot through the ceiling, while the cost of it plummets.

Just as important, the garden allows you to use your skill, your artistry and your creative talents to make a thing of beauty. I'm convinced that we all need that. The reasons may be different, but gardens are just as important to a fulfilled life as ever they were.

You may feel that the cottage garden style, with roses round the door and tall hollyhocks lording it over marigolds and violets, is old hat. Yet the style perfectly fits modern gardens and lifestyles. Just ask yourself how and why the cottage tradition arose. Country cottagers long ago had three restrictions: they had little space, less time and no money. And those are precisely the restrictions that many of us face today.

These days, however, we can make much *better* cottage gardens than ever before. With improved varieties of flowers, fruit and vegetables, better materials and techniques and, let's be honest, a bit more time and a lot more money to spend, we can *all* bring a breath of fresh country air into our gardens wherever they are. And that's what this book is all about.

Many old cottages have now been refurbished and brought up to twentieth-century standards. However, where conversions and improvements have been done sensitively, using traditional materials and techniques, they retain their rural charm.

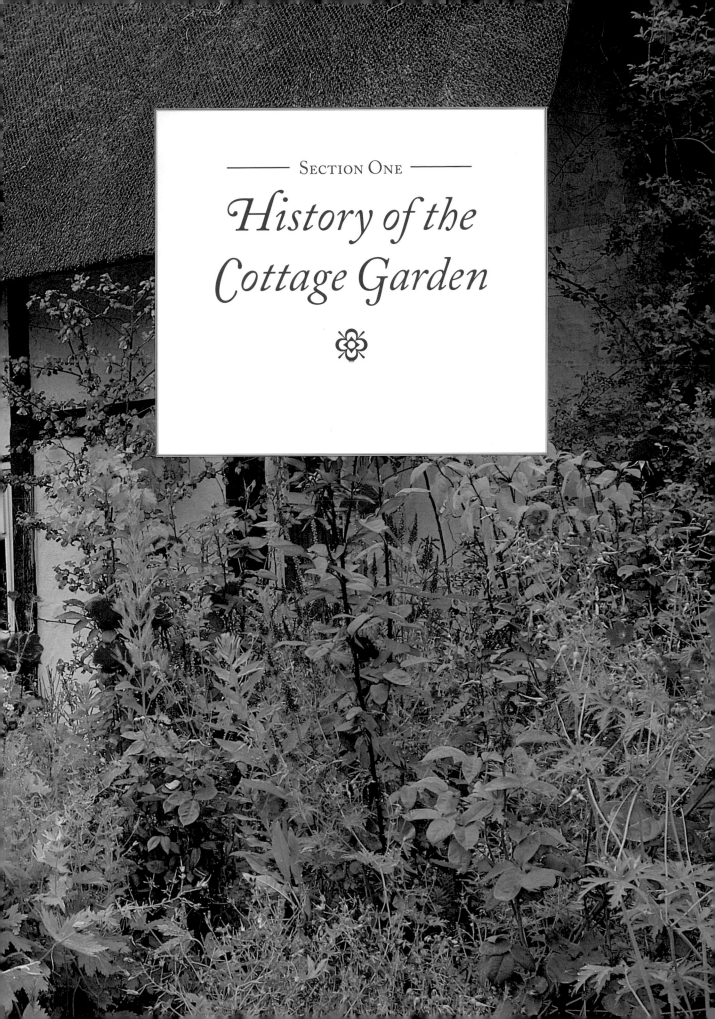

SECTION ONE

History of the Cottage Garden

*T*HE COTTAGE GARDEN style was never deliberately devised. It has grown over the years from medieval times to the present day, evolving and developing according to need and changing fashion. Though billions of chocolate-box tops have tended to give the impression of a romantic, rural idyll, it certainly didn't start out that way.

The Middle Ages

In the Middle Ages (500–1400) the labouring classes, who made up the vast majority of the population of the countryside, lived in relative

ABOVE *The pig was the mainstay of the medieval cottager's diet and shared the family's facilities.*

PAGES 8–9 *Thatched cottages with wattle-and-daub walls remain, but modern materials and techniques have made them far more comfortable than the originals.*

OPPOSITE *A fine stand of fennel (*Foeniculum vulgare*), backed by the purple spikes of* Agastache foeniculum *with roses in the background, illustrates how plants can be mixed in true cottage garden fashion to produce dramatic effects.*

squalor. Their primitive hovels were made mainly of timber faced with wattle and daub, with leaky thatched roofs, damp walls and wet floors. If they owned animals, these would have shared the space *en famille*, with all the muck and smells, noise and 'wildlife' associated with livestock. At least they provided a primitive sort of central heating.

In such conditions the 'art' of the garden and the thought of improving living conditions with things like flowers in the living room simply weren't considered. Survival was the name of the game.

A bit further up the social strata came the rural craftsmen like the blacksmith and wheelwright and the small farmers. They were important people in the village economy and their comparative wealth and social status reflected that position. They would have lived in slightly more substantial houses, still thatched in the main, but probably drier, warmer and with a separate barn for the animals. Even at this elevated level, however, gardening as we know it hardly existed.

Vegetables certainly were grown, but many of these were used to feed a pig and a few chickens. However, the really poor existed on a diet of cabbages, kale, leeks, onions, turnips and perhaps a few peas and beans plus whatever game they could trap. Meat and cheese were looked upon as luxuries, and a 'pottage' – a sort of thick soup – of dried peas and beans, with the addition of whatever fresh vegetables were available at the time, was much more common.

The wealthier English, on the other hand, have always been great meat eaters. If people could get beef, bacon, mutton or game, they scorned vegetables completely. Indeed, the theory that King Henry VIII (1491–1547) died of malnutrition as a result of an exclusively carnivorous diet does seem to carry some weight. Even as late as the nineteenth century William Cobbett (1763–1835) was proudly proclaiming his good fortune in never having to eat potatoes.

Fruit was quite widely grown, mostly apples, pears, plums, damsons and cherries, with a few wild strawberries dug from the hedgerows, but storage through the winter would have been a problem. No doubt a few morsels were dried and, since bee-keeping was also common, some kind of preserving, making use of the honey, probably existed, but the winter months in particular must have been pretty bleak.

Medieval Medicine

Before the dissolution of the monasteries by Henry VIII in 1536, religious orders were largely responsible for dispensing herbal medicines. And, when villagers visited them for help, they would very likely have gleaned information on cultivation techniques and the uses of herbal remedies.

When the monasteries disappeared, however, this early form of healthcare went with them. The cottagers then had to rely on what they had

Medieval cottages were spartan in the extreme. The walls may have been made of wattle and daub or, if stone was locally available, it would have been used instead. Windows had wooden shutters instead of glass panes and there would have been a fire in the centre of the single living room. Without a chimney the smoke circulated before escaping through a hole in the gable end. With none of today's creature comforts, it's easy to understand why life was lived mostly outside.

been taught by the monks and nuns and grow their own. Almost certainly they would have raided the abandoned monastery gardens for herbs, fruit and decorative plants for their own gardens too.

Inevitably, without the learning and religious discipline of the monks, a generous degree of folklore, superstition and witchcraft crept in.

Some of the properties bestowed upon herbs beggar belief. But perhaps belief was what it was all about – a kind of psychosomatic faith healing process. Valerian is a good case in point: according to Thomas Hill, writing in 1577, it 'provoketh sweat and urine, amendeth stitches, killeth mice, moveth the termes, prevaileth against the plague, helpeth the straightness of breath, the headache, fluxes and Shingles, procureth clearness of sight and healeth the piles'.

Astrology was, in those days, a well respected science and was the basis of what now seems to us the incredible theory behind the 'Doctrine of Signatures'. It was thought that the shape, colour

The small area of land around the cottage was used to house a pig or two and a few chickens and perhaps ducks. The garden grew mainly herbs for medicines and for flavouring stews and soups, plus a few vegetables to feed the livestock and the family. Wheat and more vegetables were grown in strips of land outside the cottage and some wild plants and game would have been hunted in the woods. There would also have been common grazing rights in surrounding woods and on grassland on the common.

and markings of plants indicated their usefulness. Pulmonaria, for example, with its heart-shaped leaves spotted with silver, resembled a diseased lung and was therefore considered to be useful as a cure for consumption; hence its common name of lungwort. Red roses cured nose-bleeding and the fine hairs on the quince made it a sure-fire cure for baldness! My favourite example of early lateral thinking, though, is Thomas Hill's assertion that lentils, famed for causing flatulence, should therefore be sown in exposed gardens to reduce damage from wind!

Primitive Pleasure Gardens

There's a possibility that, even in the deprived conditions under which many of them existed, a small desire for beauty continued to beat in the hearts of some of the less brutalized country folk. Plants would have been collected from the wild and it's quite likely that some small corner of the garden was home to a few violets, primroses and cowslips, perhaps a dog rose and a wild honeysuckle. It's good to think that we still grow all these plants in our gardens today.

Cultivation techniques were primitive but in principle not a million miles from modern methods. The vegetable patch was no doubt rotated: the animals would be penned in with willow or hazel hurdles to muck a piece of land and then moved on, after which the manured area would be used for vegetables and herbs. Fertility came from the proceeds of the privy too. Four centuries ago Thomas Tusser (*c.* 1520–80) in his *Five Hundred Points of Good Husbandry*, an extraordinary instruction manual for small farmers and cottagers, written in doggerel, has this advice for what to do in November:

Foule privies are now to be cleansed and fide [purified],
Let night be appointed such baggage to hide:
Which buried in gardens in trenches alowe,
shall make very many things better to growe.

In fact, of course, this method of fertilizing the soil persisted up to about fifty years ago. In some more remote areas I'm sure it still does.

My own garden is no more than a hundred and fifty years old, yet it's easy to see even now the effect of what was, from the very beginning of man's cultivation of the soil right up to the Victorian age, the *only* method of fertilizing the land. In most of the garden, the soil is light brown in colour and quite heavy clay, except in what was known as the 'crew yard'. Here the pigs and chickens roamed free and I have no doubt that there were a few privy-loads buried there too. The soil is jet-black and it still grows wonderful crops!

In this enlightened age we couldn't contemplate such heathen practices, so we pollute the sea instead. Our plant food is, in the main, put on out of a bag, but the principle is just the same.

Wherever possible, the modern cottage gardener would do well to adopt the traditional methods of manuring and fertilizing with animal wastes just as our ancestors have always done.

The Elizabethan Age

The enlightened era of Queen Elizabeth I (1533-1603) saw the first real improvement in the lot of the peasant. For the times, these were comparatively settled years, with relatively stable government, success in battle and a great surge of exploration. Wealth rolled into England and, because everything relied on manpower, it 'trickled down' even to the labouring classes. There was a marked improvement in working conditions, housing and diet, and even a little spare time to enjoy leisure. This was a golden age for England when even a small farmer, by dint of hard work and a little luck with the weather, could better his standard of living beyond the wildest dreams of his precedessors.

There was no sentiment about preserving history in those days. Here, at last, was a chance for the peasant to improve his living conditions and the energetic Elizabethans seized it with both hands. Whole villages were torn down, probably 'disinfected' with fire and rebuilt. All society, both rich and poor, began to take a pride in its appearance.

The gentry and the richer farmers were now being influenced greatly by the outside world. Many a gentle household would employ a cook from France, Belgium or Italy, so the cuisine became much more varied. At last vegetables and herbs began to assume a more important part in the daily diet.

Revolutionary garden styles and new plants were also imported from the Continent and even from the New World across the Atlantic. It might not be strictly true to say that gardening started in this period, because there were certainly gardens here in Roman times, but a horticultural renaissance had definitely begun. Naturally the innovative styles that became fashionable with the wealthier classes were copied by the peasantry too and cottage gardens began to have a designed shape and form. Most plants would still have been collected from the wild, but it's likely that seeds and cuttings from wealthier gardens found their way into cottages too.

In 1557 Thomas Tusser gives us a good insight into the way in which various plants were spread among the people in the villages:

The Elizabethan era saw major progress in living conditions. Building methods improved and many new plants were imported from abroad.

New garden styles were imported from the Continent to the big houses of the gentry and would certainly have been copied on a much smaller scale by cottage gardeners. This knot garden at Hatfield House is much as it was in the sixteenth century.

Good huswifes in sommer will save their owne seedes
against the next yeere, as occasion needes.
One seede for another to make an exchange,
with fellowlie neighbourhood seemeth not strange.

That's still pretty good advice and widely prac-tised today among gardening friends.

Tusser also provides a quite comprehensive list of herbs and flowers, many of which survive in cottage gardens to this day. Corn marigold, eglantine (sweet briar), campion and heartsease (viola) would probably have been collected from the wild, but clove carnations, lavender and love-lies-bleeding must have come from cultivation.

Vegetables included the protein-rich 'runcivall' peas (to our everlasting shame we seem to have lost this wonderful name and now call them 'marrowfat' or, worse still, 'mushy' peas!) and beans, though he doesn't specify what type the latter were. There were plenty of root vegetables, of course, like carrots and turnips, and even artichokes and pumpkins as well as many kinds of salad crops including endive.

Fruit-growing also expanded greatly. Some gardens now included vines, probably taken from the abandoned monasteries and used to make wine, as well as gooseberries, strawberries and even peaches to add to the apples, pears, plums and cherries.

Apart from the vines to produce wine, Tusser implies that cottage gardeners, or at least small farmers, also grew hops on quite a scale. Certainly we know that ale was consumed in quantity at the time.

In larger gardens, designs from the Continent became fashionable and it's certain that some elements of them were taken and used in humbler gardens too. Formal patterns were all the rage, so the cottager's 'huswife' would have grown vegetables, herbs and flowers in rectangular beds and would probably have planted roses and honeysuckle to grow over a simple form of rustic arch. The cottage garden as we know it was beginning to emerge.

The First Gardening Book

Twenty years after Tusser's rustic doggerel came Thomas Hill's book *The Gardener's Labyrinth*. This was no doubt written with the educated upper classes in mind and the advice is a little more sophisticated. The plans for gardens and parts of gardens are on the grand scale too, but he gives us a very good idea of what was grown.

Comparing Hill's list with Tusser's shows that cottage gardeners grew much the same plants.

Vegetables included 'parsnep, radish, pease, scallions [shallots], lettice, turneps, beanes, cabbage, leekes and onyons' as well as the less usual 'garlike, cucumber, mellion and artechoke'. There's also mention of some vegetables, like 'skerrot' (skirret), that are no longer commonly grown. Among the flowers Hill recommends are marigolds, 'dazie', columbine, sweet John (like sweet Williams), carnations, 'pincks' and, of course, roses. Many of the plants he lists still bring joy to modern cottage gardeners.

In Hill's book, designs are also very formal and, interestingly, there seems to be no distinction made between types of plants. So lettices grow among the gillieflowers, 'parcely' with the 'lupines' and 'ruberb' with the 'musk mellions' – just as in cottage gardens through the ages.

Hill's designs for knot gardens (formal plantings generally of box set out in symmetrical patterns) are fantastically complicated. In fact they're very reminiscent of Moorish designs that can be seen today on the walls of the Alhambra in Granada in Spain, a clear indication of the

The Elizabethans were fond of the formal style and much of their gardening was done in rectangular beds, mixing flowers with vegetables and herbs.

Continental influence on English gardening. The Elizabethans were also great ornamenters, so their garden buildings, arches and even plant supports were elaborately carved and painted, and this could well have also been due to foreign influences.

It's evident that many plants were grown in pots and large containers. Flowers like carnations, which need very good drainage, were suited to this kind of cultivation where the soil would have been lightened with grit and animal manure. Pots were used to grow such fruit as peaches, oranges and lemons too. They were put into a frost-free building in cold weather and brought out again when the danger of frost had passed.

These then, were comparatively comfortable times for cottage gardeners, but they were not destined to continue forever.

Enthusiasms

Inside every gardener there beats the heart and soul of a craftsman. We all know the great personal satisfaction to be had from growing a fine border, a good crop of vegetables or even a superb specimen of a single plant. Cottage gardeners through the centuries have been no exception.

Gardening was a relatively cheap pastime so, from as early as the sixteenth century, the growing of 'special' plants was an occupation keenly espoused by artisans and cottagers.

Gardening has always been enriched by people with special enthusiasms. Nowadays there's enormous competition to see who can grow the biggest pot leek or the heaviest onion. There are coveted prizes for specialist plants like chrysanthemums and dahlias and every village has its annual show where local gardeners vie with each other in friendly competition. It's a tradition that has been handed down through centuries.

It's generally thought that when, towards the

end of the sixteenth century, Huguenot weavers arrived in England from France, they brought with them the auricula, a member of the *Primula* family with flowers so perfect in geometry and delicacy of markings that they could almost be hand-painted. This was a plant well suited to the cottage artisan's life: it needed a great deal of minute attention but was hardy, asking only protection from rain, wind and snow. Since the weavers and lace-makers worked at home, their precious plants could be put outside within easy reach in case of a sudden rainstorm.

The cultivation and breeding of auriculas was therefore centred round weaving towns, but elsewhere other plants were enthusiastically bred with the aim of producing perfect flowers. By the eighteenth century eight species were predominant: anemone, auricula, carnation, hyacinth, pinks, polyanthus, ranunculus and tulip. The art of growing and breeding them became known as 'floristry' (nothing to do with the modern usage of the word for the selling of flowers). And, as

The aim of amateur auricula breeders was to grow a perfectly round, almost geometric flower with unusual and delicate markings. It became the speciality of cottage weavers.

plants were exchanged and ideas passed from one enthusiast to another, the logical progression was the formation of florist's societies. They were the forerunners of our modern specialist societies and the grandfathers of today's horticultural societies and garden clubs. Later they also attracted the attention of the gentry, and great feasts were held before each show, with the accent more on food and drink than on plants. Indeed, some of today's enthusiasts blame the eventual demise of most of the societies on this over-indulgence.

Why it is that some plants should have fired the imagination of generations of gardeners is hard to say. The gooseberry, for example, may seem to the gardening philistine a rather mundane sort of a plant. Yet its history is as intriguing as the development of the most exotic orchid.

The gooseberry was adopted by cottage gardeners in the industrial Midlands and the North. Though first recorded in England in 1275, it seems to have been hardly grown until the sixteenth century. But by the nineteenth century there were over 2000 varieties available.

ABOVE *Florist's tulips were highly bred with the aim of producing perfect stripes in unusual colours, again with the rounded shape.*
BELOW *When wealthier plant-lovers took over the florist's movement, they turned their meetings into important social occasions and much food and wine was consumed.*

It was a good plant for cottagers because it could be raised from seed without difficulty, it was small, hardy and easy to grow. Again, competition was the spur to the breeding of such variety. Clubs were formed and, in late July and August, members would bring along their prize berries to be weighed. The 'weigh-ins' were occasions of great jollity and friendship and fierce and serious rivalry. It's a tribute to the humble gooseberry that those very societies still exist today and the friendly rivalry continues.

Topiary

Another abiding passion of the cottage gardener was topiary. The art of clipping plants into various shapes has been practised since Roman times and it became very popular in England in the sixteenth century. Box, yew, rosemary, hyssop, myrtle and holly were among many plants used to

Topiary was in high fashion in the sixteenth century and many examples can still be seen in the gardens of large, old houses.

form living sculptures. The same plants were also planted to make dwarf hedges around flower and vegetable beds and elaborate knots and parterres in larger gardens.

Often there was a strong religious message expressed in 'foot-mazes' which were planted with low-growing box. They were intended to symbolize man's tortuous passage through life.

The style was eagerly hijacked by cottage gardeners, who often used the faster-growing privet to make all kinds of shapes and figures. Even today it's possible to find cottage entrances dominated by peacocks, chickens, aeroplanes, railway engines and all kinds of human figures.

However, just like the much-maligned leylandii today, topiary was considered in Victorian times to be 'vulgar', and gardens containing it to be over-planted, and many fine specimens were pulled out or cut down in the name of fashion. Fortunately some survived to become an inspiration for the modern renaissance of the art.

Cottage gardeners enthusiastically copied the trend for topiary, often with great art and a fine sense of humour. The tradition still exists, as is shown by this locomotive in yew outside a Leicestershire cottage.

Social Division

The eighteenth century and the beginning of the nineteenth were very difficult times for working people. Power was vested solely in the upper classes where corruption was rife. Intent on maintaining the established order, they used their power mercilessly.

First came Enclosure which took away the peasant's right to put his animals on common land. It had been going on continuously since the seventeenth century, and in the eighteenth it gathered pace with 1631 Acts enclosing nearly three and a half million acres.

Without their traditional communal grazing and strips of land outside their gardens, many peasants were unable to feed their stock and were forced to live on home-grown vegetables and whatever their meagre wages could provide. It wasn't much.

Model Villages

The power of the upper classes over the poor was nothing short of savage and I'm afraid that the passion for gardening had a marked effect. Much common land was enclosed simply to provide parks and gardens for the gentry, regardless of the effect it had on their tenants.

The fashion of the day, influenced by designers like 'Capability' Brown (1716-83) and Humphry Repton (1725-1818), was to turn cultivated gardens into agricultural 'parks'. In grand houses, the paved terrace was divided from the park with a stone balustrade and from then on looked out on to rolling pastures. They even went as far as to import cattle, not for any economic reason but purely to provided a 'living landscape'.

Many of their ideas designed for the distraction of the gentry seem outrageous today. Repton, for example, suggested that, at a suitable distance only, the peasantry should be allowed to enter the park for their Sunday stroll, to provide entertainment for the gentry who would be viewing them from the comfort of their opulent salons.

At this time whole villages considered to be 'eyesores' were removed and their tenants thrown out to fend for themselves as best they could. Often they were reduced to roaming the countryside or were sent to the dreaded workhouse. In some cases, though, houses were rebuilt to form 'model' villages. The motive was often less than philanthropic – simply a desire to improve the landscape with a contrived 'rural idyll'. Many were placed where visitors would pass by on their way to the big house to be impressed by the philanthropy of the landlord.

Whatever the reasons behind the construction of model villages, the housing was generally better and the tenants far happier. Naturally this had an effect on their gardens and was later to 'gentrify' the cottage style. Many such villages remain today, though others have almost disappeared in a welter of modern development. In examples like Harlaxton near Grantham in Lincolnshire, stylized thatched country cottages stand cheek by jowl with dwellings built throughout this century. But in Blaize Hamlet near Bristol, they remain unadulterated.

Blaize Hamlet was built in 1810 by a Bristol tycoon, J. S. Harford, to house old retainers. Harford's estate had been designed by Repton in about 1797 and included such indulgences as a vernacular woodman's cottage and a Marie Antoinette-like dairy attached to the house. Later Harford's enthusiasm for the 'traditional' style prompted him to commission John Nash to design Blaize Hamlet. It consisted of a group of cottages built around the village green opposite the estate entrance. There were ten of them, all different and all incredibly ornate. Some had thatched roofs, some slated, some were given

dovecote fascias at the front and all had fantastic Elizabethan chimneys. Today it looks like a Disney theme-park, but then it was much admired and set the pattern for other model villages all over the country.

Developments like this no doubt contributed to the popular view that the peasants were the ones living the good, simple, country life, which was later to encourage the wealthy to follow their 'example'. Meanwhile for the real cottagers life continued to deteriorate.

Despair and Revolt

In 1804 the Corn Laws were introduced. They forbade the import of cheap foreign grain so that British farmers could keep prices high. Larger farmers benefited greatly, but labourers and

ABOVE *When their cottages were demolished to 'improve the view', families were often simply thrown out to tramp the roads in search of work and shelter.*
LEFT *One of ten cottages designed by John Nash for J. S. Harford at Blaize Hamlet near Bristol to house his old retainers. All were self-consciously different and incredibly ornate. They are now owned by the National Trust.*

artisans could no longer afford to buy bread and starvation was common. The effect this had on gardens was not, in fact, to encourage harder work and greater productivity. So miserable were the conditions of the labouring classes that they simply became discouraged and took to crime and the demon drink. It seems hard to believe today that men should be transported and even hanged for the crime of poaching a rabbit or two to feed their starving families. It's even more incredible that their desperation was such that they were driven to take that risk.

Such was the gulf between rich and poor that many of the gentry had no conception of the privations of rural life. From the safe distance of the road they saw the countryman's thatched cottage with neat rows of vegetables and flowers, the housewife contentedly working at her tub while half a dozen grubby children romped around her feet. In reality the thatch leaked, the vegetables were all that made up the family's meagre diet, the far-from-contented housewife took in washing to earn a crust and the 'grubby' children were ragged and ingrained with filth almost from birth.

Yet, despite all the evidence, there was a craving among the upper classes for the simplicity of rural life. Many of them, often recently 'impoverished' (though by no means really poor), built 'cottages' far bigger and more luxurious than the average peasant would dare to dream of and surrounded them with a romantic interpretation of a cottage garden. It was now that the 'chocolate-box' style began to evolve. However, far from being content with the plants the true cottagers grew, mostly collected from the wild, they filled their plots with many of the same plants that were becoming fashionable in the huge houses of the country estates. There were dahlias from Mexico, tulips from eastern Europe and the most sought-after roses from China.

Reform

The end of the eighteenth century saw the birth of a philanthropic movement, strongly resisted by the 'establishment', whose aim was to improve the lot of the rural poor. Men of influence like William Cobbett and John Claudius Loudon (1783–1843) took up their cause. Loudon was a professional gardening journalist and writer and an architect to boot and, perhaps because he seems to have been more tactful and diplomatic than Cobbett, had a great though undramatic influence on political thinking. His influence on horticulture, however, was immense.

Loudon wrote books on every conceivable horticultural subject from hothouses to cemeteries and churchyards, including advice for cottage gardeners. And he still found time to edit the most influential gardening magazine of its time, *The Gardener's Magazine*.

Cobbett, on the other hand, was a man of overweening self-confidence and astonishing lack of tact. He said what he meant and he said it loud and clear in a succession of pamphlets and his own publication, the *Political Register*. By the standards of the day he achieved enormous publicity for his reformist views – so much so that he spent two years in Newgate Prison and two periods of self-imposed exile in America to avoid trouble at home. He eventually became MP for Oldham in the first Reform Parliament.

By the middle of the nineteenth century, reform was irresistible. The Corn Laws were repealed in 1846 and there was a generally more tolerant attitude towards the poor. But the beginnings of the Victorian era brought a morality which we would see today as patronizing and sickly, and even that showed in the gardens of the day.

For some 'philanthropists' the provision of picturesque cottages set around a green, with neat gardens enclosed by hedges and stuffed with flowers, was enough. Surround the poor with the

The romantic, 'chocolate-box' style of cottage gardening really began in the nineteenth century. Malt Cottage in Essex is a weatherboard house typical of the area.

beauty of nature and they would automatically become civilized and educated. Fortunately others, like Cobbett and Loudon, were more realistic. They realized that the single most important factor for a stable life was security of tenure. So they suggested that rural workers should aspire to the freehold of their houses, or at least an absolute guarantee that they would no longer risk being thrown out at a moment's notice at the whim of their landlords – a great idea, but one that has only recently been achieved.

Many of the reformers devised plans for self-sufficiency. Some believed that the cottager should have up to an acre of land, but Loudon felt that an eighth of an acre was all that was needed. Rather optimistically he suggested that this would support a family of four or five. It would house a pig, chickens, rabbits and ducks plus all-year-round vegetables and soft fruit, with apples and pears trained against the house. And he still found space for an enclosing hedge of quickthorn or, better still, varieties of apple to be grafted on wild crab apple roots dug from the woods, and cherries, plums and pears similarly grafted on to their wild counterparts. (This was, of course, before the days of modern rootstocks.) The cultivated food would be supplemented by whatever could be culled from the wild.

Loudon knew that self-sufficiency in home-grown food was vital for many poor country dwellers, but he was essentially an artistic gardener, so no cottage garden, however small it was, should be without its flowers. Few of us today could disagree with his sentiment that 'a few Brompton or ten-week stocks, carnations, picotees, pinks and other flowers ought never to be omitted: they are the means of pure and constant gratification which Providence has afforded alike to the rich and the poor'. Through his writing, Loudon did much to encourage cottagers to take pride in their gardens again.

Evolution of the Typcal Cottage Garden

All this encouragement naturally resulted in a general quickening of enthusiasm for gardening and, gradually, what you and I see as a 'typical' cottage garden began to evolve.

Gardening, as you will know if you're a gardener, is a great leveller. A consuming passion for growing plants transcends social differences, and it did so even in those divided days. Then, as now, gardeners began to exchange ideas and, of course, plants. In this way many cottage gardens owned by farmworkers, too poor even to think of spending money on luxuries like plants, became stocked with exotica previously reserved only for the 'big house'. I'm quite sure that many plants were also distributed throughout the village by gardeners to the rich in the form of collected seeds and cuttings snipped off when no one was looking.

Now many cottage gardeners were able to grow dahlias, improved hollyhocks, large-flowered delphiniums, and new, larger-flowered sweet peas. There would have been many more roses available, including the newly introduced hybrid teas and a much wider variety of pinks and border carnations.

Wild clematis had probably always been grown in gardens, but now new, far superior varieties, like 'Jackmanii', were beginning to appear. Crown imperial fritillaries and the cottage lily (*Lilium candidum*) were introduced way back in the mists of time and were grown widely. By the end of the nineteenth century, however, a much wider range of species and varieties started to become available.

Geraniums were among the most popular bedding and windowsill plants, and every Victorian cottage garden would certainly have

In the late eighteenth century the encouragement of writers and artists filtered down to working cottagers who began to take great pride in their gardens. Apart from the addition of a few modern annuals, this row of cottages has changed little and looks today much as it would have done then.

been perfumed by mignonette, which was another well established favourite.

It's hard to say exactly what made a 'cottage garden' plant. There seems little doubt that genuine cottage gardeners would grow almost anything they could get their hands on provided it was easy to grow and propagate, and not so big or rampant that it would overwhelm the plot. Personally I'd go along with the description used by the great Victorian garden writer William Robinson (of whom more later), who suggested that they should be 'unpretentious'.

The Victorians and Beyond

For me there's something rather odious about the Victorian era. All that preaching of morality while sending starving kids up chimneys does not sit easily. But this book is not about politics and I mention it only to put the evolution of the cottage garden into perspective, because the maudlin romanticism of the period did have a bearing on the development of gardens.

In an age where every chimney in every industrial town belched black smoke and covered gardens in soot and sulphur, the cottage garden was an escape to the simple life. Now, more than ever, the rural worker was looked upon as a model of simple happiness. Ignorance was bliss and the blind eye was almost universal.

The change from the worship of wealth and opulence to the idealization of the simple life was largely brought about by artists. Bear in mind that painting, drawing and wood engraving, as well as writing, formed the Victorian equivalent of watching television. Magazines, newspapers and pamphlets gained huge readerships and had enormous power to influence contemporary thinking.

Painters like Myles Birket Foster (1825-99) and Helen Allingham (1848-1926) interpreted cottage life to make it appear ever idyllic. The sun always shone, the flowers never stopped blooming, the housewife was rosy-cheeked and smiling and the children spotless and well-fed. The typhoid, cholera, tuberculosis and diphtheria brought about by insanitary living conditions and appalling diet were rarely, if ever, depicted. With a few honourable exceptions, writers too 'bent' realism somewhat allowing wealthy consciences to be salved. Many gardens painted in the Birket Foster and an Allingham style were recreated by the wealthy, the middle classes, and even by artisans and labourers

But gardening in the mid-nineteenth century was strangely polarized. On the one hand there were the old romantic cottage gardens; on the other there was the new fashion for carpet bedding. Bright annuals were raised every year in the huge, cheaply heated glasshouses of the wealthy and planted out by an army of cheap labour. And, just as plants and ideas from the big house had filtered through to the cottager, so did carpet bedding. Somehow greenhouses and frames must have been afforded, country cottage borders were ripped out and replanted with the bright colours of annuals. In those days, of course, there were no F1 hybrids, so seed could be collected from one year to another and the costs would not therefore have been too hard to bear. The style persisted in many cottage gardens and indeed is still popular today – but only over the dead body of a most influential gardener and garden writer.

A school of romantic artists portrayed the cottager's life as idyllic. They influenced many of the wealthier classes to try to capture the rural dream in the form of flowery cottage gardens.

William Robinson

William Robinson (1838-1935) was a practical gardener first in his native Ireland and then in England, where he was herbaceous foreman at Regent's Park. He later became a prolific journalist, writing for *The Times*, among other publications. In 1871 he founded a magazine, *The Garden*, but his most enduring work was undoubtedly his book *The English Flower Garden*, published in 1883.

Robinson was first and foremost a plantsman

RIGHT AND BELOW *William Robinson was one of the most influential gardeners of his time. His own house at Gravetye Manor, in West Sussex, is now a hotel, but the garden faithfully reflects his love of cottage garden planting.*

and he was much disturbed by what he considered to be the artificial and pretentious fashion that persisted at the time. He disliked carpet bedding and railed against it. He abhorred topiary and all kinds of formal garden design, and he said so loud and clear. For him it was plants that made a garden and he loved the simplicity of real, 'pre-bedding' cottage gardening. To my mind his explanation of the 'secret' of cottage gardening – not an easy thing to define – was perfect.

*Cottage gardeners are good to their plots,
and in the course of years they make them fertile,
and the shelter of the little house and hedge favours
the flowers. But there is something more and it is
the absence of any pretentious 'plan', which lets the
flowers tell their story to the heart.*

Robinson brought Gravetye Manor, a large house with 200 acres near East Grinstead in Sussex, and, during the fifty years he lived there, made his ideal garden. The house is how a hotel, but fortunately the owner is also a keen gardener and has restored the garden to its former splendour.

Because of the influence of artists and plantsmen like Robinson, the cottage garden had become something of an art form. And in the 'genuine' cottages of country workers, another important development was to affect the style of the nineteenth century.

Allotments

Agricultural workers were still very badly paid and lived constantly on the edge of starvation, but now they perceived a way out. Many of them,

George Flatt, a retired Suffolk farmworker, now has running water in his cottage, but he remembers tougher times when he had to draw his supplies from the well. Working as a farm horseman in the early part of this century meant that growing his own vegetables, fruit and herbs was an absolute necessity. And, because the hours were long, he often had to dig his half-acre of vegetable garden by the light of the 'parish lantern' – the moon!

fed up and disillusioned with the grinding poverty, poor housing conditions and constant toil of rural life, opted to seek work in the new industrial towns and cities. Farmworkers left the land in droves and, partly to help to retain the remainder and – let's be generous – partly because of an increasing feeling of unease among the wealthier classes about their dire conditions, the allotment movement was conceived.

It started slowly at the beginning of the nine-teenth century, but by the end there were many pieces of land rented to agricultural workers to grow vegetables and fruit and to keep a few animals. Vegetables were still grown at home, but now the housewife, who rarely worked on the allotment, had a little more room for her herbs and flowers.

Into the Twentieth Century

A contemporary of Robinson was the great Gertrude Jekyll (1843-1932) who was to have a profound effect on garden design that's still apparent. She too was fascinated by the cottage garden style, but here I tend to disagree with the experts. Her influence, and that of other great gardeners of her time and a little later, while masquerading as 'cottage gardening', in my view missed the essence.

She was, of course, a great gardener with a sensitive and artistic eye. Indeed she started out as a painter, but was forced to give that up because of failing eyesight. She turned instead to gardening and used her undoubted sense of colour to create stunning and original schemes in herbaceous and mixed borders. Her renowned collaboration with the architect Edwin Lutyens (1869-1944) resulted in a number of quite superb gardens that are still an education in the art of colour combination.

Miss Jekyll was followed by other wonderful

gardeners of much the same style who must have been inspired by her. Vita Sackville-West (1892-1962), for example, created the amazing garden at Sissinghurst in Kent, complete with a 'white border' that is the model for many imitations.

Great gardeners, talented artists and original plantswomen they certainly were, but were they really cottage gardeners? For me the answer has to be no – the cottage garden is an *artisan's* creation, not an artist's. I agree with William Robinson that simplicity is at its very heart. As soon as the style begins to take on a degree of sophistication, the essence of it is lost. The charm of cottage gardening is its naivety, its honesty if you like. No fancy designs, no coordinated colour schemes, no elaborate statues: just the heart and soul of a simple creator working with nature.

Gertrude Jekyll's garden at Munstead Wood in Surrey shows a strong cottage garden influence. But her interpretation displayed an artistry of planting that would not have existed in genuine cottage gardens.

The cottage garden at Sissinghurst in Kent has also been 'artistically' planted with great thought and care and is the inspiration for countless others.

In the last fifty years society has changed more dramatically than in the previous four hundred. Farmworkers are few and far between now and those that are left often live in their own houses or at least with full security of tenure. And they have a standard of living that would have been inconceivable only a century ago. In fact most of us, wherever we work, whether we're in the town or the country, live in 'cottages' – smallish houses with gardens which may be tiny but which still, albeit for different reasons, are an essential part of our lives. In a frenetic, stressful world we *need* our 'rural idyll' more than ever. We need to surround ourselves with the calming influence and the inspiration of flowers and to indulge our senses in the simple pleasure of growing plants. Cottage gardening is due for another, gentle change in its evolution.

With diligence and application, patience and, yes, a little cash, we can *all* do it and we can make just as good a job of it as our country ancestors.

Of course, that doesn't mean that you should

avoid equipping yourself with as much knowledge as possible about plants and gardening. Certainly we should draw from the experience that has been accumulated over the five centuries that cottage gardening has been around – then we can avoid repeating mistakes that have been made along the way. But it's real folly to allow the ideas of other gardeners, however great, however successful, to submerge your own flair and imagination. Gather together the basic precepts, learn as much as you can about the plants in particular, and then do your own thing.

You'll find that you make mistakes. You'll put sun-lovers in the shade, you'll plant some things too close together and you'll create colour clashes you can't live with. No problem. Provided you realize your errors before too many seasons have passed by, you can do what the old cottagers did. Simply pour a bucket of water over a wrongly positioned plant, lift it, replant it and give it another good drink. Most will never look back.

Remember above all that the great rule in cottage gardening is to avoid the pretentious. Bear in mind the advice of William Robinson and 'Just be good to your plot, make it fertile and let the flowers tell their story to the heart'.

The romantic style suits modern 'cottages' perfectly, as this house in Norfolk shows. You don't need a thatched roof to create a traditional 'rural idyll'.

SECTION TWO

Creating a
Cottage Garden

*M*Y BRIEF GLANCE through cottage history indicates that there were really two distinct types of cottage garden. The original was definitely a work place, used to feed the cottager's family and, though it gradually evolved to include many ornamental features, it remained a working garden.

Then there was the stylized cottage garden which developed from the enthusiastic espousal of the rustic ideal by more comfortably-off gentlemen and women. There may have been some attempt to grow a few vegetables but it wasn't strictly necessary as it was for the real cottagers. Cottage flowers evoking the romantic rural idyll were the thing.

And, if you detect a note of criticism there, it certainly isn't intended. My own view is that gardens are just as important to refresh and sustain the spirit as they are to feed the body. So a concentration on flowers in Victorian times, for example, when half the country was covered in the soot and grime of the Industrial Revolution, was understandable.

These days, most of us who own or rent a garden can afford to feed our families without the absolute necessity of growing our own. Admittedly there are many allotment gardeners who grow prodigious amounts of food but, unlike the cottagers of old, there aren't many who'd actually starve if they didn't. Having said that, more and more young people in particular, are growing their own, purely because they feel they can produce healthier food, untainted by pesticides. The need is still there.

But the most important function of a garden these days is for relaxation and the restorative value of getting close to the soil and the natural world. Some gardeners, of course, will be able to afford simply to buy their gardens complete. These days, many house owners bring in a designer and a landscaper and have the job done for them. I think they miss a lot.

Others will be able to afford expensive materials that they'll install themselves. But most of us will have to do it ourselves and buy materials as the budget allows. That's *real* cottage gardening and I believe that the creative enjoyment it produces is of the greatest benefit.

But while a young family may not be able to afford all they'd like immediately, things nearly always improve. The kids grow up and leave home, a job promotion generally means more money and, some fine day, most of us actually pay off the mortgage. Then we may want to improve the garden and have the money to do so.

So, I've designed and built two gardens: the first I call the *Artisan's Garden* and it's unashamedly a poor man's garden, just like the originals. Everything is home-made or bought second-hand, and all at low cost.

The second is the *Gentleman's Garden* which has been built with no regard for budget at all. It felt rather grand to be able to order exactly what I liked, regardless of cost. I even began to develop a bit of a swagger! But the funny thing is that I enjoyed doing-it-myself in the poor man's garden much, much more.

I hope that you'll be able to mix and match, with a bit from this garden and a bit from that. Perhaps starting out with beaten earth and gravel paths until brick paving becomes affordable. Or knocking up a coldframe when you start as the teaboy and then buying a greenhouse when you become managing director.

I do urge you, however, to do as much as you can, even if you don't actually have to. You'll have much more fun if you do.

PAGES 34–5 Even mundane artifacts like the water butt become beautiful when they're surrounded by plants.
OPPOSITE These days, when the pace of life is hectic, the garden earns its keep as a place of relaxation and restoration.

The Artisan's Garden

HERE AND THERE, all over the British Isles, there are old country cottages. Most of them have been got at.

In these days of relative affluence few of us want to live like medieval peasants, so it's hard now to find a cottage with no running water, with damp walls and leaky thatch and tiny windows designed to let in a little light but to retain as much warmth as possible. Nowadays you have to visit a rural museum to see the real thing.

Many old country cottages have had the roof stripped of thatch and replaced with tiles or slates. Most have central heating and nearly always a television aerial or even, horror of horrors, a *dish* on the roof. We mustn't turn up our noses at such improvements. All the owners have done is what the Elizabethans did, for example, during their period of affluence. We are, after all, as much a part of history as they are.

Nonetheless there are quite a few cottages that have retained the *spirit* of their origins. The history of these places is unmistakably impregnated into the walls and in the soil outside. That may sound a little romantic and fanciful but it's not quite so far-fetched as it seems. Most people who buy a country cottage do so because they have an interest in and an empathy with the way of life it's bound to entail. Bear in mind that there will often be much time and expense necessary to 'do it up' and you simply don't buy an old place unless you're interested in doing the job sympathetically.

The modern artisan's cottage garden, like this one built at Barnsdale, suits present-day architecture and building materials but captures all the rural spirit of the old days, and at surprisingly little cost.

Most people, then, would set about discovering the history of their 'dream cottage'. And, because the house is old, it'll be on your side and give you a helping hand. In other words, luck will nearly always be with you, because anyone who has ever lived in the house will inevitably have left bits and pieces lying around waiting to be discovered.

My own house, for example, though only about 170 years old and extensively changed throughout the years, has yielded quite a few clues to the previous inhabitants. In one corner of the garden is the old privy. It's built of brick with a slate roof, which was in a very bad state of repair. To put it right I had to take the roof off, replace the timbers and then put back the slates. In doing so, I made a discovery. Lodged inside, between the top of the wall and the slope of the roof, was an old clay pipe. It had obviously been there since at least the turn of the century, because pipes like that have not been made since then. I like to imagine the old farm labourer creeping in there for a quiet sit-down and a smoke while he rested his weary back in a snatched moment of peace and quiet.

The soil, too, has been a treasure trove. I've dug up horseshoes by the dozen, some of them obviously cart-horse size, bits of old tools and machinery and even the end board of a cart, complete with Victorian sign-writing. All are now carefully preserved.

Plants, of course, are a bit more perishable, but old gardens will often be graced by an ancient gnarled apple tree, a pear or a plum of some unknown variety now rarely grown.

Cottage gardens bought by gardeners are often lovingly re-created in the style that fits the age of the building. Many of these works of art are open to the public and collectively form a superb museum of ancient gardening practice. They can certainly provide enormous inspiration for new cottage gardeners. So, if you can bear the suspense, before you do anything to your own plot, get out and about to have a look at as many good cottage garden re-creations as you can. Quite a few sell plants too which, since they'll have been propagated from the garden, will naturally suit you own new cottage garden.

The Principles

Gathering inspiration from old cottage gardens will improve your knowledge and enthusiasm and greatly benefit your own garden. But to imitate them exactly could be disastrous: it depends on the setting. Naturally, if you're the lucky owner of an old thatched cottage in the country, you couldn't do better than to get hold of a chocolate box or two for your research. But for a brand-new cottage you'd finish up with something twee and pretentious and William Robinson would do another turn in his grave. Let the old chap rest in peace.

I think it's exciting to realize that we're involving ourselves in the next step in the evolution of the cottage garden style. It's been developing for centuries and there's no reason why we should stop now.

You can create a wonderful cottage garden for today's equivalent house. A brand-new semi on an estate may not, at first sight, look like a rural idyll, but by the time your planting has grown a little, you'll swear you can hear the clip-clop of the ploughman's horse as he slowly wends his way! Your cottage doesn't even have to be in the country. Remember the weavers and the spinners, many of whom, in days gone by, lived and worked in the towns. They produced cottage

The inspired gardeners at this cottage in Leicestershire have created a cottage garden that's perfectly in tune with the modern style of their house.

gardens every bit as attractive as their country cousins, albeit with some differences in design. You can do it too, wherever you live. The thing to avoid is pretension.

If your house is modern, don't fill the garden with old cartwheels painted white and pseudo plastic carriage-lamps. Modern materials are often just as attractive in the right setting as older ones, and sometimes quite a lot better.

The Layout

Landscape architects and historians, far cleverer than me, can dissect, analyse and explain classic garden design from the Greeks to Geoffrey

TOP AND ABOVE *The design of the demonstration artisan's garden couldn't be simpler: just four main beds and a straight border round the edges. Yet, in its first summer, it really begins to look the part.*

Jellicoe. But the trouble with cottage garden design is that it simply doesn't exist. At most, cottagers of old would have copied the stark, businesslike layouts of the monastery gardens and divided their gardens into rectangles.

Country front gardens are a perfect example of unpretentious simplicity that really *works*. Nearly always the front path runs straight from the gate to the door, but that's no artistic design principle: it's very simply the shortest distance between two points.

That also tells you that the layout can be infinitely variable. If you have, say, an existing tree between gate and door, the path will have to bend round it or, if you simply *prefer* a curve, then that's what you make.

Mind you, I appreciate that, if you're torturing your brain with your first garden design, all this airy-fairy stuff is not a lot of use to you. It's all very well letting your imagination run riot, but where do you start?

Well, you start by firmly establishing that the garden is there to be *used* and that the most important feature has to be the plants.

Then it helps – though it's not entirely necessary – to draw a plan of the garden. The drawing needn't be anything fancy, but you'll find that it has the effect of crystallizing your ideas and reminding you where your imagination has brought you. That's important because, by the time you've drawn and rubbed out your twentieth idea, you'll need a break and you don't want to have to start again because you can't remember what went before.

Above all, keep reminding yourself that this is nothing more or less than a rough, working plan. You're making an artisan's garden, not an artist's, so you'll no doubt change things here and there on the ground once you start work outside. That's how it was always done and no cottager ever got paranoid about 'line, balance or impact'. That stuff's strictly for the birds.

It also helps to make a list of what you need. You may have more special requirements if, for example, you have children or grandchildren who visit, but here's a typical list:

Sitting-out area
Path to gate
Table and bench
Shady arbour
Space for dustbins
Washing line
Compost bins
Somewhere to store tools
Coldframe
Plants, plants, plants and more plants

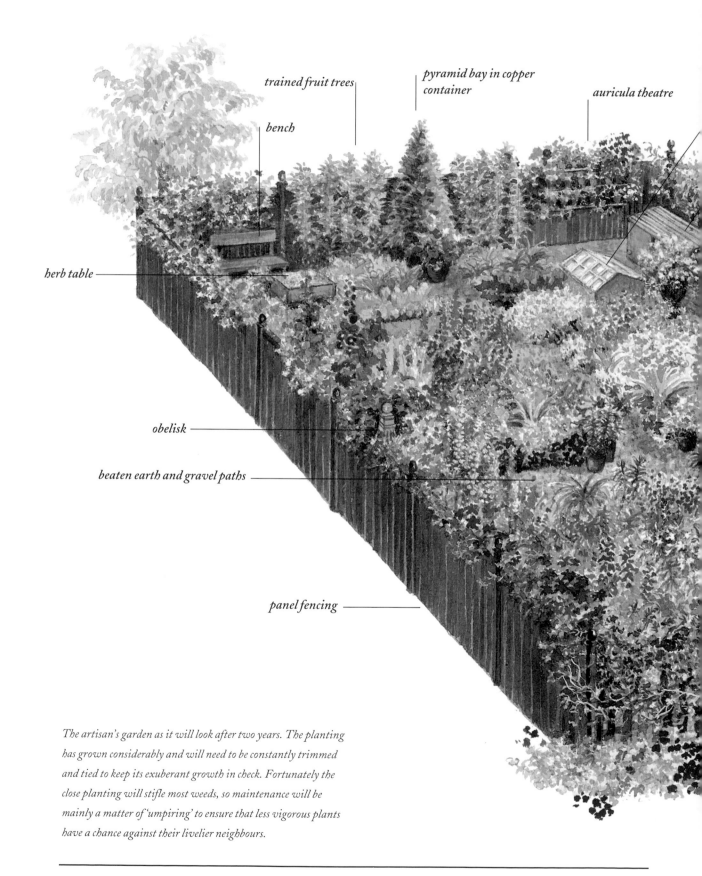

trained fruit trees

pyramid bay in copper
container

auricula theatre

bench

herb table

obelisk

beaten earth and gravel paths

panel fencing

*The artisan's garden as it will look after two years. The planting
has grown considerably and will need to be constantly trimmed
and tied to keep its exuberant growth in check. Fortunately the
close planting will stifle most weeds, so maintenance will be
mainly a matter of 'umpiring' to ensure that less vigorous plants
have a chance against their livelier neighbours.*

coldframe

tool box

beehive compost bins

arbour

mixed planting of shrubs and
herbaceous perennials throughout garden

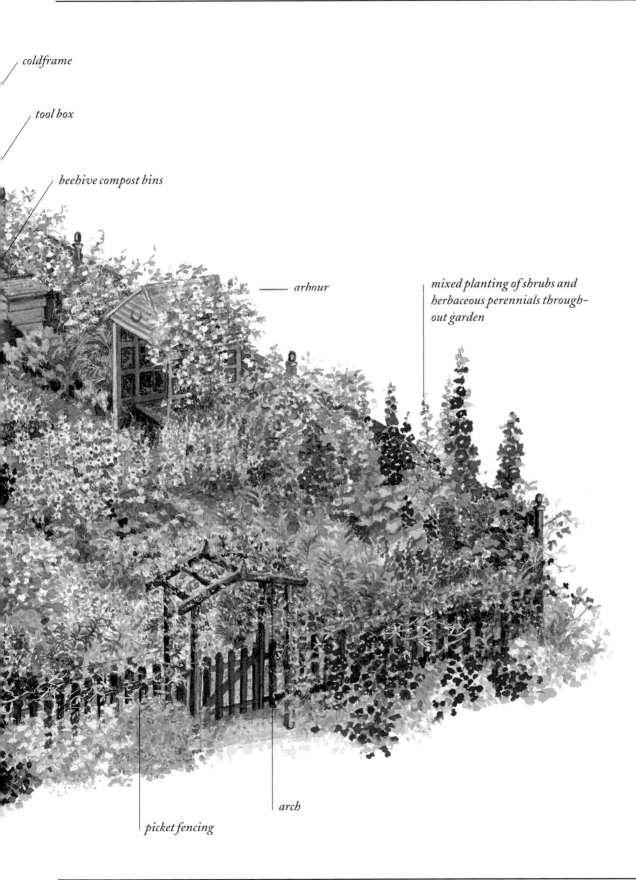

arch

picket fencing

The final item is undoubtedly the most important, so put it right to the front of your mind all the time. Apart from the obvious fact that plants are really what the garden's all about, they have the great advantage of being able to hide the unsavoury things you might not want to see. However, I believe that *everything* in the garden should be made to be attractive – yes, even the compost bins – but more of that later.

Designing Step-by-step

First of all decide where you want your main essentials. If you take the illustrated garden as an example, you would first ascertain the position of the path. That has to go from one end to the other, and in this case it seems sensible to make it straight. Don't ever worry that straight lines are boring, because the plants will quickly spill over the edges and remove all signs of rigidity.

For maximum convenience the sitting-out and eating area should go near the house, so that can be roughly positioned. I know I want a utility area somewhere near the house too, because it's where the dustbins will be, so that can be roughly drawn in too.

I would dearly love a west-facing seat to catch the evening sun and that should naturally be surrounded by fragrant plants. There's really only one place to put it and there must be a path to get to it too.

I don't want a lawn, so the rest of the garden simply consists of spaces for plants. Suddenly it all begins to take shape.

I obviously need beds along the fences, because those are valuable vertical growing areas for climbing plants, wall shrubs and trained fruit, and I intend to pinch a little extra growing space outside my paling fence too. Those beds will also need narrow access paths to them.

All in all, with only the simple addition of

1 Start by putting in the necessary path (A) from the gate to the house door.

2 The sitting-out area (B) and the utility area (C) should be positioned near the house.

3 There's only one logical place for the west-facing seat (D) and that too needs an access path.

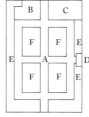

4 With beds at the sides (E) and in the centres (F), plus their access paths, the garden has effectively designed itself.

rectangular flower beds, the garden has virtually designed itself. True, it looks blindingly simple and that's exactly what cottage gardens should be. But don't judge it by the straight lines on paper. Just wait till you see it planted.

Different Shapes

If your garden is exactly the same size and shape as mine, you're in luck and you can skip the next few pages. But the chances are it won't be, so you'll have to fiddle the design around a bit. It's really quite easy if you stick to the idea of modules.

For example, if your garden's wider than it is long, it's easy to create exactly the same garden by simply moving everything around. The only other factor you really must take into consideration is the position of the sun. If your house faces north, say, you won't want to put the eating-out area near the door where you'll never see the sunshine. But – in small gardens especially – there's no reason why it shouldn't be at the other end of the garden in the warm.

It goes without saying that the sun's position is also going to affect which plants go where. At this stage, however, there's no need to worry about that.

Not every garden is as conveniently shaped as my example, and thank goodness for it. I get as excited about gardens with odd shapes and levels as I do about old houses with nooks and crannies. A bit of individuality gives a lot of scope for ideas. Obviously the permutations of shapes and sizes are endless, but with the module method of design, it's easy to work round each and every devious alternative. What could differ more is

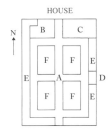

1 In the original design, the house is situated at the end of a rectangular, south-facing garden.

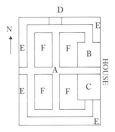

2 If the house is on the east side, the garden is short and wide, so simply move the components about.

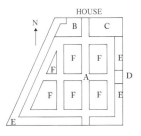

3 A couple of extra beds and access paths cope with an irregularly shaped plot.

Of course, paths need not be straight. At Eastgrove Cottage in Worcestershire irregular brick paths make an attractive foil for the plants spilling over the edges.

your own personal taste. Again, thank goodness for that. You may want curves, you may decide that grass is essential, you perhaps need more space for vegetables: use the modular idea, but simply change the shapes. Circles, semi-circles and ovals fit the modular scheme well too, but keep the shapes simple, strong and not too fiddly.

But, please, treat my examples purely as a basis for your own imagination. Go outside, walk around viewing the garden from every possible angle and imagine yourself sitting on your bench in the sunshine or in the perfumed arbour on a still summer evening. Imagine what you'd like to see around you as you sit there and make sure you realize that absolutely nothing is impossible given a bit of time and patience.

If the garden's small, 'borrow' from next door by hiding your fences with plants so that all you see are the neighbour's trees. They'll look for all the world as if they're in your garden.

If you budget's tight, don't worry. The great beauty of cottage gardening is that it's designed to be painless. All the plants are easily propagated from seed or cuttings which you can collect from friends' plants or buy cheaply and gradually. And provided you're prepared to put in a little effort, the construction materials are not expensive. Looking out for second-hand materials is also great fun and could save you a considerable amount of money.

Don't even worry about the effort. In the artisan's cottage garden you can do a small amount at a time, and I'll give you a cast-iron guarantee that, come rain, shine, snow or heat-wave, you'll *love* every minute.

RIGHT *A mixed hedge with clematis and roses growing through it makes an impenetrable barrier and a superb show of colour throughout the spring and summer.*
OPPOSITE *A rose-covered arch set into a cottage hedge makes a fine welcome for visitors.*

Building the Garden
❀

Hedges

'The most commendable inclosure for every Garden plot is a quick-set hedge, made with brambles and white thorn.' Thomas Hill's advice of 1577 still holds good today, but only if you have the space. A country hedge made with quickthorn (*Crataegus monogyna*) set 30 cm (1 ft) apart in a well-prepared trench will grow fast, can be closely clipped and looks superb. What's more, if it's well looked after to keep it tight and well-furnished at the bottom, it makes an impenetrable barrier against animal and human intruders. It's regarded mostly as a field hedge, but close and regular trimming turns it into a wonderful green wall, ideal for gardens.

If you have enough room to let it grow in a slightly more unkempt way, you could grow wild and eglantine roses through it, planting one at every 6 m (20 ft) or so, to transform it into high

If you have the space, an informal hedge of shrubs makes an excellent boundary and a fine background for the borders. This hedge of Berberis darwinii *produces bright orange flowers over a long period in spring.*

romance. And you'll find that it'll become home to thousands of insects and dozens of birds.

There are other plants you could use, like holly, some of the berberis varieties (such as *Berberis darwinii, B. stenophylla* and *B. thunbergii*) and perhaps beech or hornbeam, but avoid the much-too-hungry privet and most conifers except, of course, for yew. This most perfect of hedges can be clipped to form a green, living wall but it's expensive and more suited to the gentleman's garden. In some gardens I'm not at all averse to the ubiquitous leylandii which, with regular attention, can form an excellent, close-clipped hedge. But for our simpler, rural artisan's garden, hawthorn is definitely the thing.

Another alternative is to grow a mixed hedge, often seen in the countryside where plants that happen to have been growing there have been trimmed to form the hedge. Plants like blackthorn or sloe (*Prunus spinosa*), guelder rose (*Viburnum opulus*), damson (*Prunus institia*), elderberry (*Sambucus nigra*) and hazel (*Corylus avellana*) can be brightened up with the dog rose (*Rosa canina*), the blackberry (*Rubus fruticosus*) and the eglantine rose (*Rosa eglanteria*).

If you plant something like holly here and there along the hedge, you could let it grow above the hedge line and involve yourself in the cottage art of topiary (see page 203).

When you plant a hedge, you'll want to achieve fast growth, so make sure that the soil is really well prepared beforehand. Dig a strip at least 1 m (3 ft) wide and preferably two spades deep, and use plenty of bulky organic matter plus about a handful of organic fertilizer per plant or, if you're planting in winter, bonemeal only.

To achieve a really dense hedge right from the base, some plants need to be cut back hard after planting. Hawthorn, privet, sloe and hazel should all be pruned to within about 15 cm (6 in) of the ground. But don't prune beech, hornbeam or any conifer until it has exceeded the required height by 15 cm (6 in).

Then mulch around the plants with a thick layer of manure, compost or bark to deter weeds and retain moisture. The following year the hedge should again be trimmed quite hard, but allow a little more growth this time.

This is one job where you need a lot of patience to achieve the desired result. Take advice from Thomas Bernhard who, in 1797, published a pamphlet describing in glowing terms the cottage garden of a farmworker, one Britton Abbott, who lived near Tadcaster in Yorkshire. He remarks that the fine quickthorn hedge surrounding his garden was cut down *six years running* after

*Hawthorn (*Crataegus monogyna*) is the traditional hedging plant of cottage gardens. It produces white flowers in spring – the well-known 'May blossom' – followed by red berries, and it has good thorns too.*

planting to produce a very fine, dense hedge.

Unfortunately, you'll need to allow a width of at least 1 m (3 ft) for most hedges to grow to maturity and, in a tiny garden, that's just too much. In any garden under about 10 m (33 ft) wide, you'll have to settle for a solid barrier which takes up less space.

If you happen to have existing walls in stone or brick, praise the Lord and get planting. The extra heat retained by a wall that faces any direction but north will enable you to grow a wonderful range of plants you would never have been able to otherwise.

If you don't have one, forget it. Building walled gardens is now, alas, the prerogative of the very rich and not for the likes of us poor artisans! Fencing is the next best thing.

Panel Fencing

The intricacies of putting up fences are dealt with in other books, but there are a few main points that bear repeating.

The first concerns your choice of timber. Cottage gardeners of old would have had one great advantage over us. Because timber was cheap and plentiful, they would have used solid, seasoned English oak for their posts. Today it not only costs too much to be an economic proposition, but is also normally kiln-dried, which means that it'll warp and twist all over the place as it ages. I've seen oak posts with a knot half-way up, which have bent at 45 degrees. And that, of course, both looks bad and destroys the connecting panels.

I would therefore always recommend softwood posts, though here we can get our own back. The old cottagers could never have heard of 'tanalizing'. In this process the timber is treated under pressure with preservative, which is forced into the pores of the wood, right the way through, guaranteeing it more or less for life. If you want to take advantage of this bit of technology (and in my opinion it's crazy not to), give the timber merchant a few days to get it done and expect to pay a little more. It's well worth it.

For me concrete is the only really permanent way to secure posts, but it has one big disadvantage. Unless they're properly pressure treated beforehand (and I have to say that most fencing posts aren't), they'll fairly quickly rot at ground level. You can buy metal sockets that are driven into the ground to take the posts and keep them above the soil, but it's virtually impossible to get them in exactly straight and square, especially in stony ground, and they always finish up wobbling. The good old English compromise gives the best of both worlds: you can also buy metal sockets that concrete into the ground, and

If you have no space for a hedge, at least you can make the fence hedge-coloured by painting it with matt-finish, dark green wood preservative.

these are much the best bet. Fix them to the posts before you concrete them in and they'll last more or less forever.

One other aspect of modern fencing worries me too. Nearly all panel fences are sold in a ghastly orange colour. In small gardens especially they stand out like a sore thumb and make you feel as though you're living in a matchbox. My solution is to paint them green. You can actually buy green panels now, but the preservative used is too pale for my taste, so I use it as an undercoat and paint on top with a dark green matt finish. They look great, but I have to admit that painting does put the price up quite a bit.

Finally, and most important, when you're putting up panel fencing, it's *essential* to build the whole thing, posts and panels, as you go along. Never be tempted to put the posts in first and hope to fit the panels later because they have a nasty habit of shrinking or stretching just enough not to fit! Put in the first post, then measure and dig the hole for the second. Nail the panel to the first and then nail the other end of it to the second before you concrete it in.

Plant Supports

All the fences will be used to grow fruiting plants and climbers, so some means of support is necessary. At all costs avoid plastic trellis which is expensive and looks forever like plastic trellis. Much cheaper and a million times better is galvanized wire stretched between the posts and simply nailed to each with staples. Space the wires about 30 cm (1 ft) apart. To wire walls, use vine-eyes, which are galvanized steel tags you simply hammer in, or drill holes and plug them.

For fruit trees, briar fruits or roses, that's all you need, but if you want to grow twining plants like clematis, you'll have to make a mesh with some vertical wires too. Use thin-gauge wire and simply twist it round the horizontals.

Paling Fences

Look at any Victorian painting of a cottage garden and it's obvious that a paling fence in the front garden was more or less obligatory. Right in the middle was the mandatory wicket gate, often slightly cock-eyed on its rusting hinges and the sort of nuisance no cottager worth his salt would have tolerated for long, although visually it added greatly to the charm of the scene.

There's no doubt that a paling fence does characterize the cottage garden and it certainly looks lovely. If you can arrange to plant cottage flowers either side of the fence, it makes a wonderful welcome to the garden. In small gardens a paling fence defines the boundary without completely cutting off the view, so there's no claustrophobic effect. That's perfect for the front garden but, because of the lack of privacy, often not ideal for the back.

It's possible to buy paling fences in ready-to-erect sections, and they're very easy to put up. It's also not difficult and very much cheaper to make your own. If you do decide to do it yourself, the

Picket fencing can be bought as 1.8 m (6 ft) panels, but it's also very easy to make yourself. The effect is greatly enhanced by growing plants through it. In fact, if you pinch a little border outside your fence, the local authority will rarely object since the effect is so attractive.

posts can be set in first, though it's wise to measure them fairly accurately and, again, put them into metal sockets before concreting them in. They need to be about 2.4 m (8 ft) apart. Leave the concrete to harden for a few days before fixing the horizontal bars and the palings.

The horizontals are made from 75 x 25 mm (3 x 1 in) timber and the palings from 75 x 20 mm (3 x ¾ in). Make sure that it's all pressure-treated with preservative before you start. Then it's just a case of drilling the horizontals and fixing them to the posts with coach screws and nailing on the palings with about 5 cm (2 in) between them.

Gates

You can buy gates ready-made and, unless you're pretty proficient with saw and hammer, that's the best way. However, it is possible to make your own.

The one piece of equipment you might not have is a bevel square. It's an invaluable tool for quite a few jobs where it's necessary to cut angles. If you're going to build, say, a porch, an arbour or compost bins, you'll need one for those too, so it's worth the investment.

A paling gate obviously sets off a similar fence best of all, but if your garden is bounded by a hedge or another type of fence, you may prefer a

A paling or 'wicket' gate is the traditional entrance to old cottage gardens. It's easy to make your own from the same materials used for the fence, or of course you can buy one ready-made.

different type of gate. There are lots of designs and materials that could be suitable, depending on the existing boundary, varying from rustic through to solid, close-board gates, though the more sophisticated they are, the more skilled you'll have to be to make one. The one gate I think I would draw the line at for a cottage garden would be modern wrought iron, but if you could pick up an old iron farm wicket gate, that would be just the job.

Arches

It's likely that the cottage garden arch was an imitation of the common church lychgate where the coffin stood to await the attention of the clergyman. There are no such macabre connections with cottage gardens, though! It's almost obligatory to have an arch spanning the front gate at least, and arches can also be used to good effect in the garden. Covered with roses or honeysuckle, they add instant height and a waft of perfume every time you walk through.

You can buy all kinds of arches from those made of willow withies to plastic-covered metal, and your choice will depend on the garden and, to a large extent, the budget. In one of the cottage gardens I built I used ready-made willow arches down the middle of the garden and these were joined together with a cross-bar of willow too. The cross-bar was made by binding willow shoots around a metal rod normally used for reinforcing concrete (available from builders' merchants).

Roses were planted at the base to train over the arch and along the cross-bar to make a very attractive effect. Ramblers rather than climbing roses are probably the best bet here, since they're more vigorous. They do have the disadvantage of flowering only once with perhaps a smaller second flush later, so a late-summer-flowering

Paths

It isn't absolutely necessary to edge the paths in the cottage garden, but it'll certainly make them look a lot neater and it has one other great advantage. When you move into a new house, there's rarely much money left over for the garden. Certainly the modern artisan won't be able to afford thousands. So you need to look for ways of offsetting the costs by making do early on with a view to improving things at a later date. Paths are a perfect example of how this can be done.

Your ideal may be to lay attractive paving slabs or, better still, brick paviors as I've done in the much more expensive gentleman's garden. You may not be able to run to it straight away, but once you've got over buying the curtains and the new cooker and the carpets and the cat flap, you may decide to upgrade the garden.

In the meantime create a hard, dry surface with gravel. It makes an excellent path and it's certainly the most sympathetic material for the artisan's garden. In the old days they would probably have put up with plain beaten earth, and from Victorian times right up to now many gardeners simply spread the ashes from the fire to make a good, dry surface. I wouldn't mind betting that you grow to love your gravel, so you never do actually change, but just to be on the safe side it's a good idea to edge the borders.

If you make the top of the edging boards finish 7.5 cm (3 in) above the level of the path, you'll have space later on to lay the bricks or paving in the easiest possible way. When you decide to do this, all you need do is just work a little dry cement powder into the gravel with a shovel or two of sharp sand and you'll have a ready-made, hard base for the bricks which can be placed straight on top with the minimum of fuss and bother.

Several materials can be used to edge the

Bricks and cobbles make an attractive and durable path, but they may be too expensive to start with.

borders and, over the years, many different types have been employed. If you have, for example, a source of old bricks, they could be sunk about a third into the ground either upright or at an angle of about 45 degrees for a more decorative effect. Only harder stock or engineering bricks which will withstand frost are suitable in this situation. Fletton or common bricks will flake when they freeze, and they'll look very tatty indeed.

The Victorians made special edging tiles with scrolled or scalloped tops and they're still available today. Realistically, however, both bricks and tiles, even second-hand, are too expensive for this garden, though I've used them in the gentleman's garden.

Timber edging 75 mm (3 in) wide and 25 mm (1 in) thick is much cheaper. It looks good; if it's tanalized it lasts a long time; and it's very easy to install. You may wish to stain the timber, which should naturally be done before fixing. I stained mine dark green to match the fencing.

Start by setting out the garden with string lines. If the site's level, there's no need to dig out because the boards should be installed on top of

ABOVE *Gravel laid straight on to consolidated soil is certainly the cheapest way to make a very attractive, traditional, cottage garden path. The plants can spill over on to it and many will seed into the gravel too, to create a very informal effect.*

the soil. In practice this generally means a certain amount of scraping and filling to ensure that they lie straight.

If the garden slopes slightly, the paths can follow the slope, reducing the amount of soil that has to be re-graded. Simply set the line for the first edging board in the correct place and put a house brick on edge under the line, one at each end. This will raise the line 7.5 cm (3 in) above the ground and all you have to do is to ensure that the tops of the boards comply with the line.

Fix them in position by nailing them to pegs made with the same 75 x 25 mm (3 x 1 in) timber banged in about 30 cm (1 ft) so that they finish just below the top of the board and are effectively hidden. Naturally the pegs should go on the bed side of the edging rather than on the path side. When nailing, put a sledge hammer behind the

Victorian edging tiles make an attractive and authentic edging for paths. They're still available and are even sometimes made in the identical moulds used since the end of the last century. They can also be bought second-hand, though not necessarily at lower cost.

In this old garden there's a grass path, so the plants have to be restrained from growing over it with low hazel hurdles. Hazel has been widely used since medieval times for making similar hurdles to pen animals and for wind-breaks. They're still available.

peg and use nails slightly longer than the width of the peg and board together so that they turn over against the sledge hammer when driven fully home. With two nails to each peg, the boards will never move. (See the photographs on page 58.)

When the first board is in position, set the line up on the other side of the path for the second one, and when you're installing it, check with a spirit level from time to time to ensure that it's going in level with the first one.

In the artisan's garden I made an octagon at the intersection of the two main paths. This was just to add a bit of interest and to create space for a few decorative pots. I made it the final job, after setting the edgings of all four beds. Then I simply marked a circle on the ground and cut the boards *in situ*. It looks complicated but it really is quite difficult to go wrong.

With the edgings in, it's easy to see any high or low spots in the path and these should be levelled off. Generally, since there will be no vehicular traffic on the paths, all that's necessary is to tread the soil down firmly with your weight on your

heels, paying special attention to the edges. If the soil is particularly light or it's an organic soil like peat, it's a wise precaution to cultivate the top 5 cm (2 in) and to rake in some cement powder. Once trodden firm, it'll harden off perfectly. After firming, all that's necessary is to spread small gravel (pea-shingle) over the top for a very attractive effect.

There are three problems with gravel. First, weeds seed in it and must be controlled by hand weeding. You could, of course, use a path weed-killer, but that's hardly in the spirit of the cottage garden and you'll also kill everything – which would be a shame because many flowers will seed in the gravel too. You'll find things like small violas and erigerons coming up in places where you don't walk and adding greatly to the natural, cottage effect.

Hand weeding won't take long and will have to be done only about twice a year. A much bigger problem is cats. If you're plagued with them in the neighbourhood, they're likely to home in on your gravel as the easiest thing to scratch aside

If you use hard materials for the path, the edges tend to look rigid and formal, so plant low-growing subjects like this lavender to soften them.

before performing their ablutions. You can solve this problem completely by using larger gravel.

Stones about 13 mm (½ in) in diameter will generally deter them.

Finally, you'll find that the gravel sinks into the soil to some degree and also works its way into the borders as you tidy up any soil that may have fallen on to the path. You'll therefore have to put

1 The wooden edgings for a gravel path are held by pegs driven about 30 cm (1 ft) into the ground. Put them on the border side of the edging to hide them.

2 Put a sledge hammer behind the peg and nail the edging to it, checking with a spirit level at the same time. The nails should go right through and bend over.

3 To make the octagon where the paths cross, mark out a circle using a loop of string on a peg in the centre, fix the edging and cut off the excess.

down an extra barrowload of gravel about once a year or so, but the overall effect make it well worth the effort.

The Borders

The paths will look fine now, but the borders will be about 7.5 cm (3 in) below the level of the edging boards. That's good because it allows you to cultivate deeply and to work in some organic matter, which will raise the soil quite a bit more than the 7.5 cm (3 in). Remember Robinson's advice to 'look after the plot and make it fertile'.

If you can manage to double dig, then so much the better. It's hard work, but you'll have to do it only once and it's much the best thing for a new plot. But if you can't manage it, single digging will do.

To double dig, you take out a trench about 60 cm (2 ft) wide, putting the soil temporarily on to one of the adjacent beds. Break up the bottom of the trench with a fork and put in some manure, garden compost or one of the alternatives like composted straw or spent mushroom compost (but *not* peat), that you can buy in the garden centre. Then half-refill the trench with soil dug from the next one and thrown forward. Put in another layer of organic matter and completely refill, afterwards putting more organic matter on the top. The final trench is filled with the soil you dug out of the first one. Yes, it's hard work, but old William Robinson will be proud of you.

To single dig, you simply dig one spade deep, throwing the soil forward as you go to make a narrow, V-shaped trench. Put the organic matter in this trench and fill by digging out the next one and throwing the soil forward as before.

After all this exertion you'll find that not only will you feel *terrific*, but your soil will also have risen slightly above the edging boards and looks ready to welcome its first plants: exciting times.

Working with Wood

❀

The first Elizabethan cottage gardeners would not have had our resources. Garden centres were, to say the least, thin on the ground and even nurseries were very few and far between. Even in the Victorian era, cottage gardeners would have had very little money to spare for their gardens, though really keen plantsmen certainly spent quite large sums and travelled long distances to satisfy their irresistible urge for plants. We all know *that* feeling.

Artifacts and ornaments, however, would have largely been home-made. From necessity, most cottagers would have been quite handy with tools and there was always a certain amount of bartering of skills. The carpenter provided the bench for the blacksmith in return for a bit of

The initial digging is hard work, but you'll only have to do it once. Remember that the initial creation of fertility is the key to ultimate success. After that, the plants very nearly grow themselves.

decorative wrought iron and I can imagine the weaver exchanging a length of cloth with the farmer's load of manure for his precious auriculas.

In the main, though, cottage garden furniture was simple and home-made. These days most of us are immeasurably better off than our gardening predecessors and, perhaps after a little saving, we could no doubt buy most of our needs ready-made. If you do, believe me, you'll miss out on one of the most satisfying and creative aspects of the garden.

Even if you have no problem finding the ready cash for all your gardening needs, the pleasure of making your own artifacts far outweighs the convenience of buying them. What's more, you can very often, with a little patience and ingenuity, design and build something far more suited to your special requirements and of far better quality than is available in the garden centre.

In the following pages I have suggested a few projects for the cottage garden. They were all made for the artisan's garden and none is difficult. They have all been designed for gardeners with minimum woodworking skills, and the only tools you'll need are a saw, a hammer, a drill, a spanner

If you can use a hammer and a saw, with a little ingenuity you could make a rustic bench like this. Probably the hardest part is finding suitable timber. Bear in mind that, without treatment, it'll be prone to rotting, so treat it annually with a colourless, matt-finish preservative.

to tighten coach screws and a screwdriver. Simply follow the drawings.

As a general rule, make sure that every bit of wood you use has been pressure-treated with preservative to ensure that it lasts.

Bench

One of the great pleasures in life is to sit in the sunshine on a summer's afternoon, listening to the buzz of the bees and the song of the birds and smelling the perfume of the plants while you shell the home-grown peas. So a bench is mantory.

Like everything else, it's made of pressure-treated softwood which has been planed all round and finished with a wood stain. I used a blue/grey finish but, of course, you'll want to choose the colour to suit your own taste.

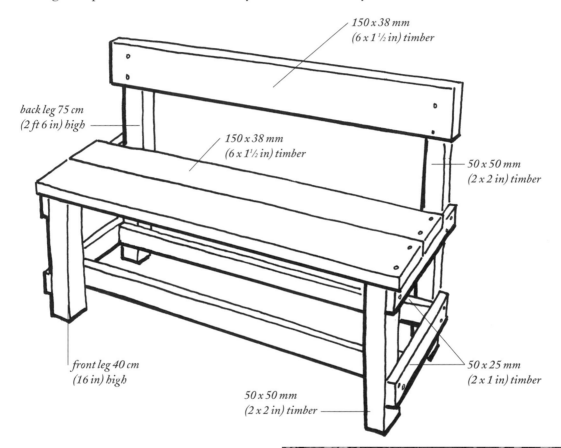

150 x 38 mm
(6 x 1½ in) timber

back leg 75 cm
(2 ft 6 in) high

150 x 38 mm
(6 x 1½ in) timber

50 x 50 mm
(2 x 2 in) timber

front leg 40 cm
(16 in) high

50 x 25 mm
(2 x 1 in) timber

50 x 50 mm
(2 x 2 in) timber

All the timber measurements for the bench in the drawing above are 'nominal' – in other words, for rough timber before planing, so they finish slightly smaller.

Naturally the width is optional and should be made to fit your own garden. This one fitted exactly into the small sitting area in the artisan's garden and measures 1.2 m (4 ft) long. If you want to make a much longer bench, you may have to use thicker timber for the seat.

Facing south to catch the sun and surrounded by perfumed roses and with the small, aromatic herb border on one side, it makes a very pleasant place to sit.

Herb Table

The herb table was an idea I pinched from my friend the designer Dan Pearson. I've never seen it done before, but it's such a great idea for a cottage garden that I couldn't resist it. It's proof, if proof were needed, that the cottage garden style is, after at least four centuries, still evolving.

Don't skimp on the thickness of the timber: the table has to carry quite a lot of weight. Fill the central part of the table with a specially well-drained compost consisting of equal parts of good soil, coarse grit and either garden compost or fine bark. Then set a few slates or tiles into the compost. I found a few old thin stone roofing slates kicking around my garden and they're ideal. Try to find natural stone if you can. They should also be flat and set as level in the compost as you can make them, because it's here that you'll place your cup of tea or your plate when you're eating out.

Plant common thyme (*Thymus serpyllum*)

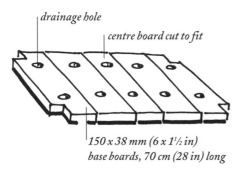

drainage hole

centre board cut to fit

150 x 38 mm (6 x 1½ in) base boards, 70 cm (28 in) long

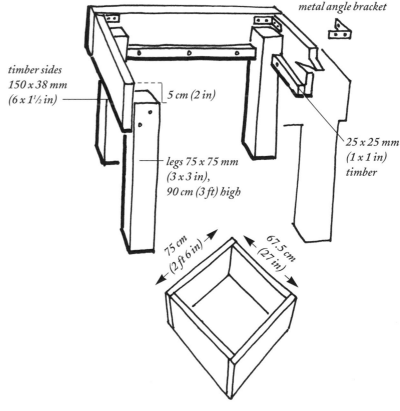

timber sides 150 x 38 mm (6 x 1½ in)

metal angle bracket

5 cm (2 in)

legs 75 x 75 mm (3 x 3 in), 90 cm (3 ft) high

25 x 25 mm (1 x 1 in) timber

75 cm (2 ft 6 in)

67.5 cm (27 in)

The herb table measurements are again nominal since it's best to make it in planed timber. It's also, of course, essential to have it pressure-treated with preservative because the wood will be constantly moist since the box is filled with compost. Again, the corners are held with metal angle brackets, but use ones at least 5 cm (2 in) long. If the wood twists, as it's likely to do, the brackets will be under considerable strain.

The finished table looks and smells wonderful. You'll have to water it from time to time in very hot weather, but don't overdo it; remember that these are Mediterranean plants and are quite happy in fairly dry conditions. The thymes can be clipped back after flowering to keep them compact and in check. They'll need little feeding but, if they look as if they're not growing well, give them a little organic fertilizer in the spring.

around the slates. Eventually this will spread out and merge together to form a complete, sweet-smelling mat which will release its delicious aroma every time you bruise a leaf or two. Romance? You can't go wrong.

Arbour and Love Seat

In the cottage garden the sun shines nearly all the time – at least, because of the bright borders, the strong fragrances and the constant bird song, it certainly *seems* to. So, as well as the bench and table in the sun, it's good to provide a quieter, shadier bower where you can relax in the late afternoon after a day's gardening, book in hand, cool drink at your side, and just dream.

I'm sure that the shady, perfumed arbour was an idea the cottagers copied from the gentry. Somehow it seems much more to suit the languid, pale-skinned maiden rather than the red-faced, buxom and probably slightly grubbly village lad and lass. Wherever it originated, it's become a traditional part of the cottage garden.

You can build an arbour from all kinds of materials. In older gardens the use of 'rustic' poles is quite common and they make attractive structures. But you'll need to be very careful about the wood you use. I learnt my lesson many years ago when I built one of pine poles which lasted no more than about three seasons before they rotted off. Oak, ash, hazel or chestnut seem to last longer but are pretty hard to come by. My recommendation would be to use sawn timber, again tanalized to prevent rotting.

Put the corner posts into metal sockets and concrete them in first, and then fit the timbers to them and hold them in place with coach screws. Naturally, you'll have to drill the wood beforehand, so you'll need a brace and bit or an electric drill for this job.

My last task was to nail to the front, one of the horseshoes I dug up when I was digging the garden. It was pretty rusty, but still perfect after its hundred years or so underground. Before putting it up I wire-brushed all the rust off and painted it with clear matt varnish to prevent further rusting and to stop it transferring brown rust marks on to the woodwork. But make sure that you put the horseshoe with the open end upwards because that's more or less guaranteed to bring you good fortune.

When the structure's finished, prepare the soil at either side with manure or compost and plant perfumed climbing roses and a clematis or two to add the final dimension.

To keep costs down, you can use all kinds of materials that would be considered junk by some. Here, two old tin baths have been painted and fitted with a seat. Bolt them to the wall and surround them with plants and you have an instant flowery bower for two.

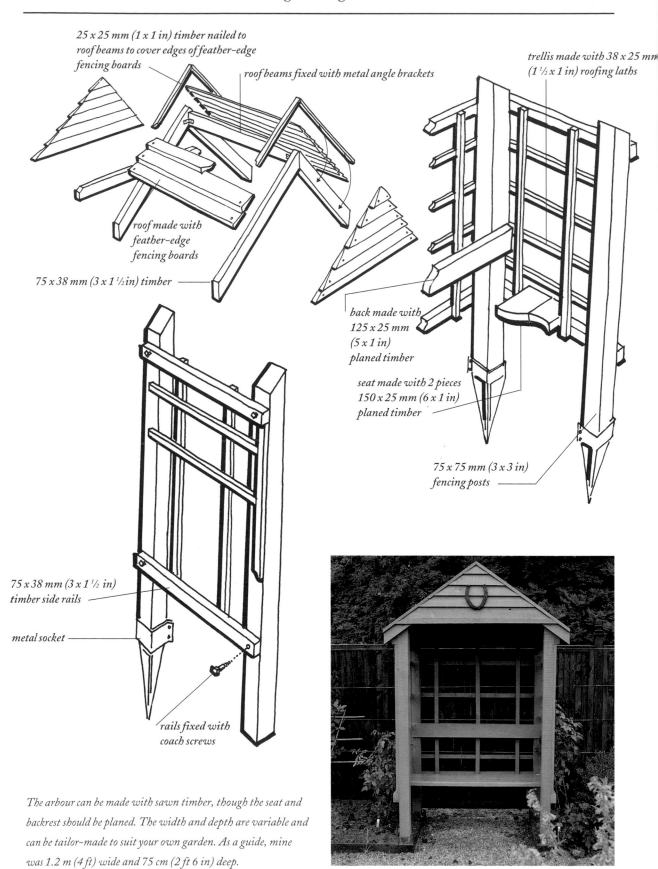

25 x 25 mm (1 x 1 in) timber nailed to
roof beams to cover edges of feather-edge
fencing boards

roof beams fixed with metal angle brackets

trellis made with 38 x 25 mm
(1 ½ x 1 in) roofing laths

roof made with
feather-edge
fencing boards

75 x 38 mm (3 x 1 ½ in) timber

back made with
125 x 25 mm
(5 x 1 in)
planed timber

seat made with 2 pieces
150 x 25 mm (6 x 1 in)
planed timber

75 x 75 mm (3 x 3 in)
fencing posts

75 x 38 mm (3 x 1 ½ in)
timber side rails

metal socket

rails fixed with
coach screws

*The arbour can be made with sawn timber, though the seat and
backrest should be planed. The width and depth are variable and
can be tailor-made to suit your own garden. As a guide, mine
was 1.2 m (4 ft) wide and 75 cm (2 ft 6 in) deep.*

Rustic poles are readily available at garden centres and can be used to make all kinds of garden furniture. It's important to choose wood that will last a while: some types will rot after only a few seasons. You need minimal carpentry skills for this kind of work – well-fitting joints are just not necessary. The poles are nailed or screwed together, but drill them first to prevent splitting. If you surround the seat with roses like this one, make sure that you have plenty of room to avoid getting scratched.

Obelisk

Opposite the arbour, at the far end of the path, I wanted a focal point to catch the eye and, in doing so, to make the path appear longer. It's a landscape trick that really does work. You can use anything eye-catching, like a statue, for example, or a bird bath. But both are really a bit too upmarket for this garden and in any case, in a space this small, I greatly begrudge the 'loss' of any land that could be used for plants.

My solution was again to grow climbers, but this time I fancied old-fashioned sweet peas – another group of plants capable of filling the whole garden with perfume and making a very good source of cut flowers for the house too.

The original cottagers would no doubt have simply banged a tall post into the ground and tied in the climbers to that, and it's a perfectly good way to grow them today. But the obelisk looks good even in winter when there are no plants on it, and it's very cheap to make.

It could quite easily be made from four lengths of 50 x 50 mm (2 x 2 in) timber for the uprights with thinner struts nailed across. I used 38 x 25 mm (1 ½ x 1 in) roofing lathes because you can buy them in bundles very cheaply from builders' merchants and they're already tanalized. I use them a lot around the garden and they also come in handy if you're making the trellis and love seat.

The ball on top of the obelisk is the plastic float from a modern lavatory cistern and you can buy those from builders' merchants too. Unfortunately the only one I could find was brilliant dayglo orange, so obviously it had to be painted.

Shortly after I'd made my obelisk I was very pleased to see an almost identical model in an up-market garden centre. It was priced at just under *ten times* the cost of my home-made effort.

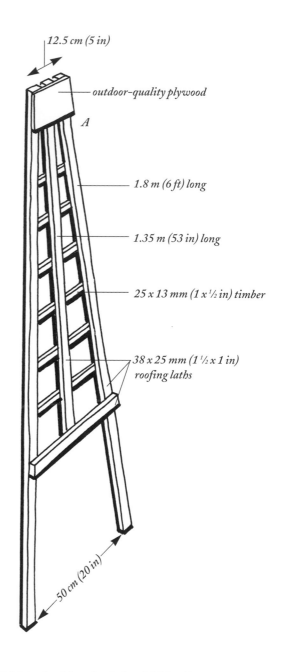

12.5 cm (5 in)

outdoor-quality plywood

A

1.8 m (6 ft) long

1.35 m (53 in) long

25 x 13 mm (1 x ½ in) timber

38 x 25 mm (1 ½ x 1 in) roofing laths

50 cm (20 in)

The obelisk is made with roofing laths with 25 x 13 mm (1 x ½ in) timber cross-pieces. It is, I confess, a bit of a fiddle to make and you'll need patience. The best way is to cut the roofing lath uprights to size, lay them on the floor and then fix the cross-pieces so that they overlap the uprights. When they're all fixed, cut off the excess later. It's also important to fix the thinner cross-pieces before you put the whole thing together.

It can be covered with sweet peas, clematis or climbing(but not the more vigorous rambler) roses.

cistern ball

150 x 150 x 25 mm
(6 x 6 x 1 in) timber

25 x 25 mm (1 x 1 in) timber

trim to fit

A

Compost Containers

Cottage gardeners have always been thrifty. They've had to be. And even today, though we may not need to skimp and scrape like our less fortunate predecessors, it's pretty dumb to throw away resources and then have to buy them again.

Garden compost is an invaluable way to 'be good to your plot and make it fertile'. It avoids your having to buy expensive organic matter, or at least reduces the amount, and it gets waste out of sight quickly and conveniently. Returned to the soil, it does wonders.

It's possible to compost organic material by simply piling it into a heap and waiting. But if you can retain the heat generated by the working of bacteria, the rotting process will be speeded up considerably. Some form of container is therefore advisable.

Ideally, every garden should have at least two compost containers, so that the contents of one can rot down while the other is being filled up. If you have a small garden the containers don't need to be large, but even so, the problem is that they'll be constantly on view. You simply can't hide things away, and whatever you can see has to be easy on the eye – even compost containers. There are all kinds available at garden centres, but not one of them is good to look at, so you'll have to make your own. You can do it easily for half the cost of buying them.

My design is, of course, a copy of a traditional beehive, so it fits the cottage garden set-up very well. Note that there are no holes in the sides, because plenty of air will be able to get in between the boards, while high temperatures are still maintained. Here it's absolutely essential to use tanalized timber or, filled with rotting vegetation,. the containers won't last five minutes. So that they fit in with the rest of the garden furniture, I've painted mine blue/grey, but you may prefer to

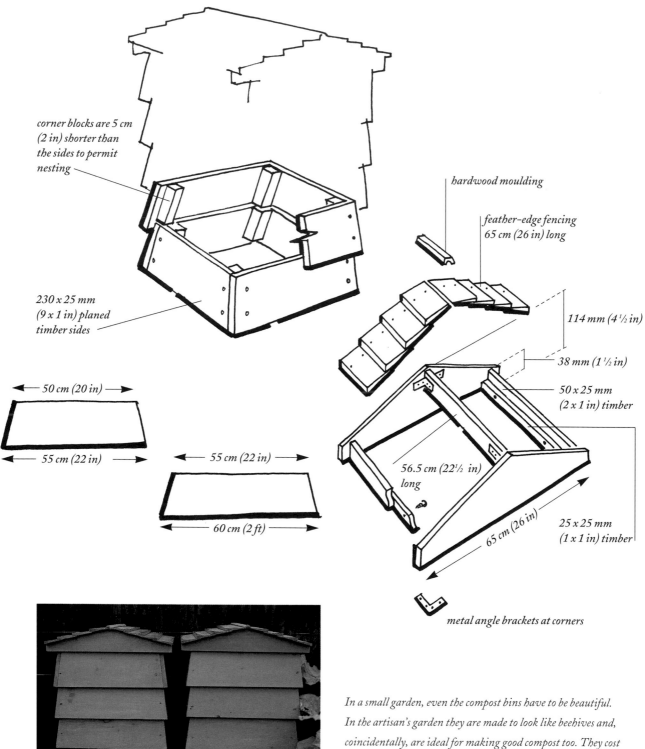

corner blocks are 5 cm
(2 in) shorter than
the sides to permit
nesting

hardwood moulding

feather-edge fencing
65 cm (26 in) long

114 mm (4 ½ in)

38 mm (1 ½ in)

230 x 25 mm
(9 x 1 in) planed
timber sides

50 x 25 mm
(2 x 1 in) timber

50 cm (20 in)

55 cm (22 in)

55 cm (22 in)

56.5 cm (22½ in)
long

60 cm (2 ft)

65 cm (26 in)

25 x 25 mm
(1 x 1 in) timber

metal angle brackets at corners

*In a small garden, even the compost bins have to be beautiful.
In the artisan's garden they are made to look like beehives and,
coincidentally, are ideal for making good compost too. They cost
about half the price of similar-sized containers bought from the
garden centre.*

*You'll need to set the bevel square first and then it's best to
cut all the sides before assembling them.*

make them more like proper beehives by painting them white. It's all a matter of personal preference, though I think that too bright a colour tends to detract from the plants, so I prefer to tone it down a bit.

ing them on a little earlier and greatly improving the quality.

Again, there are plenty of different designs available and a very few of them will fit in with this garden design – at a price. You can make your own for about a quarter of the cost of buying one

Coldframe

A coldframe is not an essential piece of equipment but will save you pounds at the end of the day and will greatly increase the interest of your gardening. You can use it to raise many ornamental plants and vegetables from seed and it's perfect for further increasing your stock of plants from cuttings. In the winter it comes in handy again to protect over-wintered vegetables, bring-

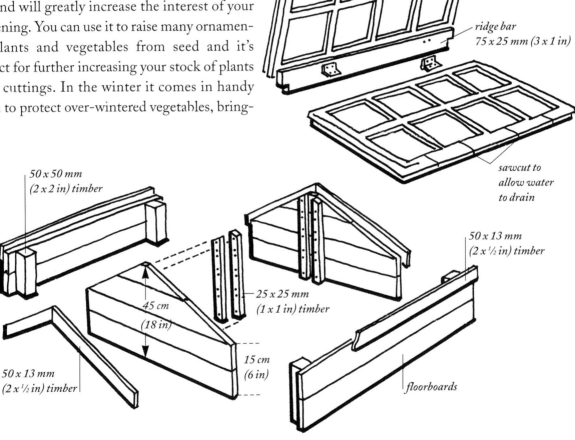

ridge bar
75 x 25 mm (3 x 1 in)

sawcut to allow water to drain

50 x 50 mm (2 x 2 in) timber

45 cm (18 in)

25 x 25 mm (1 x 1 in) timber

50 x 13 mm (2 x ½ in) timber

15 cm (6 in)

50 x 13 mm (2 x ½ in) timber

floorboards

The dimensions of the coldframe will depend on the window frames you use. As a guide, mine worked out to 90 cm (3 ft) wide and 107 cm (42 in) long. Note that the ridge bar is notched at the ends and drops between the two upright struts in the centre. Then screw it through both struts to hold it firm. In my prototype, rainwater collected in the window frames. I solved the problem with a sawcut through each frame to let the water drain away.

Enhanced by flowers in the borders and on the bare fence, even the working area can be made to look beautiful.

and it should be possible, with a little patience, to create a nice, old-fashioned look.

You need patience because I suggest that you make the glass top with two old window sashes, and you may have to wait a while before the ones you want turn up. Pay a visit to the local double-glazing or window-fitting firm. There is one in my local town from which I was able to get a couple of the wooden windows, removed when new aluminium jobs were being fitted. I wanted Georgian-style sashes with small, square panes, so I had to bide my time. Eventually they did appear and they cost me nothing.

Then, of course, you have to fit the body of the frame to the two sashes, so you may not be able to follow my measurements exactly. They refer only to my own two windows, but they give you the proportions at least, and the accurate measurements are easy to work out by measuring the sashes.

The body is made with floorboards, which

again I asked to be tanalized. Bear in mind, though, that if you buy your timber second-hand from a demolition contractor, you'll get it a lot cheaper, but you won't be able to have it preserved. So make sure that you give it a few coats of paint and that you keep the painted surface up to scratch to stop the timber rotting.

Tool Chest

If you have a shed or a garage, you won't need this. But many small gardens don't have storage space attached and I've even heard of gardeners with a garage who keep their car in it!

The chest is big enough to take all the tools you'll need, including even the mower if you decide to have a lawn too. Note that the top can be set level by engaging the flap along the front, so you can also use the top as a work-bench for potting and so on. I keep a sheet of outdoor-quality plywood in the chest to make a level surface.

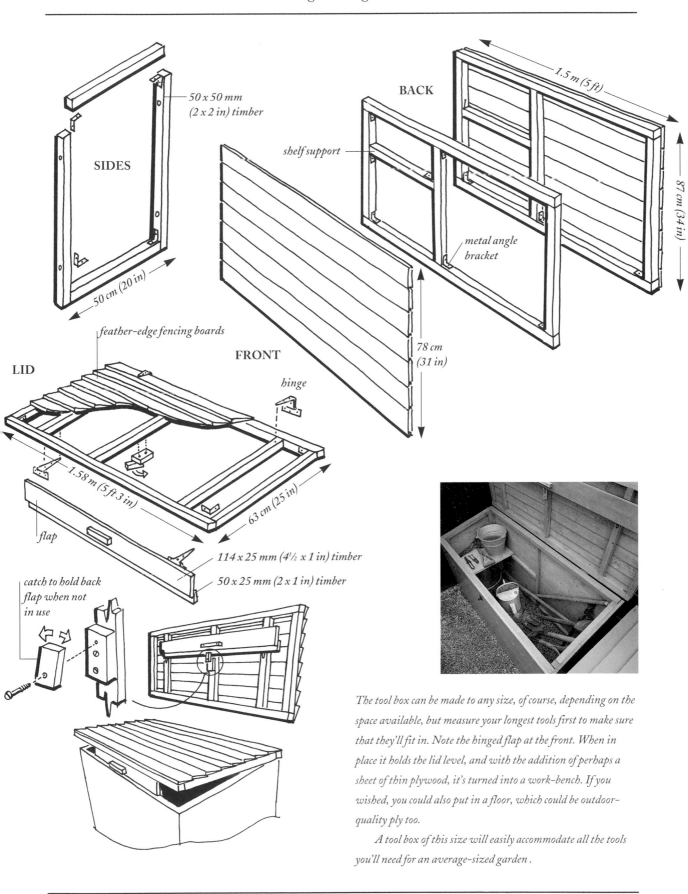

SIDES

50 x 50 mm
(2 x 2 in) timber

BACK

1.5 m (5 ft)

shelf support

87 cm (34 in)

metal angle
bracket

50 cm (20 in)

78 cm
(31 in)

feather-edge fencing boards

FRONT

LID

hinge

1.58 m (5 ft 3 in)

63 cm (25 in)

flap

114 x 25 mm (4½ x 1 in) timber

50 x 25 mm (2 x 1 in) timber

catch to hold back
flap when not
in use

The tool box can be made to any size, of course, depending on the
space available, but measure your longest tools first to make sure
that they'll fit in. Note the hinged flap at the front. When in
place it holds the lid level, and with the addition of perhaps a
sheet of thin plywood, it's turned into a work-bench. If you
wished, you could also put in a floor, which could be outdoor-
quality ply too.

A tool box of this size will easily accommodate all the tools
you'll need for an average-sized garden .

Auricula Theatre

So obsessed were the old cottage 'florists' with their precious plants that they would build special 'theatres' in which to display them. These were often quite elaborate affairs with a proscenium, raked shelving and curtains and, as the gentry took up the challenge, they spent more and more on them and, in true Victorian fashion, produced some really rococo designs reminiscent of the Royal Opera House in London.

The 'theatres' were mostly used to display auriculas and, where there is in your own garden an area of wall or fence that perhaps has concrete or paving underneath, preventing you growing plants there, it might be a good idea to copy them. I wouldn't suggest that you go to quite the extremes that the Victorians did, and you won't want to restrict yourself to auriculas.

My 'theatre' is really no more than a set of shelves fixed to the fence, but it makes the perfect place to display windowsill plants like geraniums, calceolarias and fuchsias during the summer. The structure is simply fixed to the fence posts. There's also no reason why it shouldn't be fixed to the wall of the house by drilling the back supports and screwing them into pre-set wall plugs. Bear in mind that some water will always run through the pots so don't hang it over a border full of drought-loving plants.

SHELVES

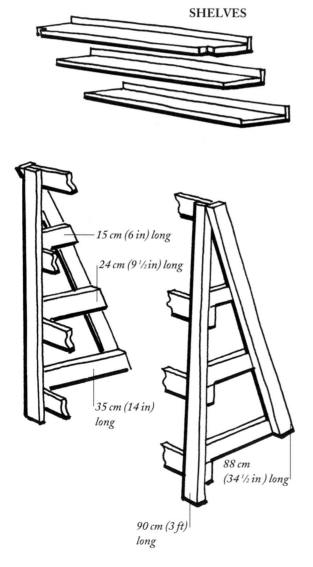

— 15 cm (6 in) long

24 cm (9 ½ in) long

35 cm (14 in) long

88 cm (34 ½ in) long

90 cm (3 ft) long

The 'auricula theatre' is really just a set of shelves. The uprights are made from 38 x 25 mm (1 ½ x 1 in) roofing laths with shelves of 125 x 25 mm (5 x 1 in) timber. It can be any length you like, though it's easiest to make it 1.8 m (6 ft) long, so that it can be screwed to the fence posts. Mine was a little shorter; I therefore fixed some metal hooks on the top and simply hung it on a fence panel.

LEFT *When it's filled with flowering pot plants, the 'auricula theatre' makes a fine feature.*

Containers

The old cottage gardeners would have had a wonderful choice of plant containers for which we'd give our eye teeth today. Terracotta was, until around the 1950s, a common and cheap material used widely for all kinds of containers. The hand-made ones are still as beautiful but relatively expensive, though well worth saving for. More on those in the gentleman's cottage garden.

Artisan gardeners would also have had attractive containers made of wood, clay and other natural materials that were originally intended for something else. I managed, for example, to pick up a couple of potters' saggars – coarse clay pots that were used to protect china when it was put into the old bottle kilns.

Cottage gardeners would use just about any container for plants. Even this old washing-up bowl looks attractive. As ever, it's the plants that make it.

Potters were just as much cottage gardeners as weavers and spinners, even though they often lived in towns. They used old, damaged saggars as plant containers once they had been discarded. Cottage potters would sometimes even stack them one on top of the other to make walls between their back-to-back houses.

Modern saggars are still available, even though the bottle kilns are seen these days only in pottery museums. Now they're used in the production of colour pigments, but they're no longer hand-made, so they lack that attractive, craftsman finish. However, here and there you might find a modern reproduction as I did or, if you're ever in an area where pottery is made, you may even be lucky enough to find an original. They make marvellous plant pots with a good bit of history attached.

My own dissatisfaction with the modern saggars was really because of the colour – a very light biscuit brown. However, I found that a coat of ordinary matt paint completely transformed them. So again I used the blue/grey paint left over from the woodwork and the result was very acceptable.

A very appealing couple of pots can be made from an old copper water cylinder. You should be able to get one from your local plumber, though these days you'll have to pay for even an old, leaking cylinder, because the copper's worth quite a bit. But it should cost no more than a few pounds and you'll get two good containers from it. Of course, if you have your own water cylinder replaced, you'll already have the raw material – remember to ask the plumber to leave the old cylinder on site.

The first job is to remove the foam insulation which is sprayed on these days. It comes off easily with an old screwdriver. Before cutting the cylinder in half, mark a line all round by stretching a strap round, levelling it carefully and marking with a felt-tipped pen. Then you can cut through the thin copper with a hacksaw, a jigsaw with a metal-cutting blade or a small angle grinder. Remove the piping from inside, file down any rough edges and the job's done.

You'll need to support the domed part of the cylinder by putting it on perhaps a clay pot, while the tub made from the other, flat end is self-supporting.

Wooden containers are also quite easy to make in the style of the decidedly up-market Versailles tubs. Use tanalized timber throughout. The sides are made with tongued-and-grooved 'matching' and the decorative balls at the top are available at most good DIY stores.

Saggars were made of coarse clay and not really designed for use as plant pots. If you can find one, you'll need to drill drainage holes in the bottom, which is easily done with a masonry bit in an electric drill. If you don't like the colour, they can be painted with emulsion paint.

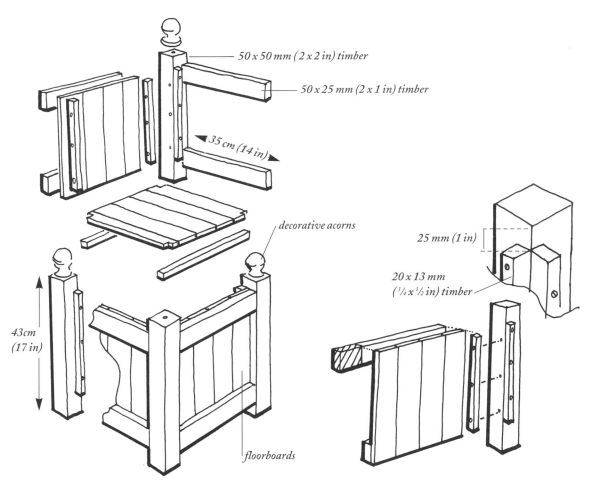

50 x 50 mm (2 x 2 in) timber

50 x 25 mm (2 x 1 in) timber

35 cm (14 in)

decorative acorns

25 mm (1 in)

20 x 13 mm
(³/₄ x ¹/₂ in) timber

43cm
(17 in)

floorboards

A wooden plant box is easy to make, requiring no complicated
joints and costing a fraction of the shop price.

Basketwork Supports

The first Elizabethans grew all kinds of plants in pots, sometimes because they were tender and needed to be brought inside for frost-protection in winter and also when soil conditions in the borders were unsatisfactory. Of course, we do exactly the same thing today. Pinks and carnations were particularly prized in those days, but they do need good drainage, so where gardens were made on, for example, heavy clay these plants were grown in pots. They and many other similar plants have a lax habit of growth though, so some kind of support is always necessary. Naturally the supports themselves have to be decorative.

Four centuries ago all country people were adept at working with their hands and they had all the necessary materials for this sort of job growing on their doorstep. It was no problem to make plant supports much like the lobster pots and fishing traps, the baskets and containers that were a daily part of their lives.

We may have more difficulty finding the materials. You need flexible, straight, thin twigs, the ideal being willow. If you have a willow growing in your garden, you too will have to hand all the material you need. If not, you should be able to buy willow withies from a wattle fencing maker or perhaps cadge some from a friend at pruning time. If the worst comes to the worst, you can buy basket-making material from the craft shop.

Mine came from a golden willow (*Salix vitellina*) in my garden. It's pruned hard every year to keep it small and to encourage the new wood, which has much brighter bark. If you have room, it's a very worthwhile plant to brighten up the winter scene. There are other plants that could be used including the coloured-bark dogwoods which also need to be pruned hard in spring to encourage better colour.

Use the thinnest shoots, cut them to length and make them up in the pot you're going to use. If you fill it with garden soil first, the shoots are held firm while you tie and the job's much easier. Where the shoots cross, they're tied with florist's wire to make a really firm support.

'Lobster-pot' plant supports can be made from willow shoots or from the coloured-barked dogwoods. Use the thinner shoots and, if they're inflexible, soak them in water for a few days. Skilled basket-makers will experience no difficulties, but if you're a novice fix the withies where they cross with thin florist's wire.

Galvanized containers look very attractive filled with flowers, especially if you can find some with an unusual shape. I used an oval mop bucket and these florist's buckets normally used to hold cut flowers. They're still available.

The Gentleman's Garden

ᴇarlier in this book I railed against preten-sion. The cottage garden is very much an artisan's garden and should be 'hand-made' with love and patience. Yet my gentleman's garden is expensive and elaborate.

Well, I justify the building of it because I feel it's necessary to give all the options. I do firmly believe that there is far more enjoyment to be had from the garden if the plants are home-raised and if you make the artifacts yourself. It's not a matter of saving money (though that's not to be sniffed at!), but of sheer creative pleasure. However, today we can go out and buy beautiful things ready-made for the garden, and I suppose some

ᴀʙᴏᴠᴇ ᴀɴᴅ ʙᴇʟᴏᴡ *The design divides the short, wide plot into five distinct areas: a herb garden (A), a 'secret' garden (B), a vegetable plot (C), and a fruit and greenhouse area (D), plus, of course, the main central part which is the ornamental garden you'd see from the kitchen window (E).*

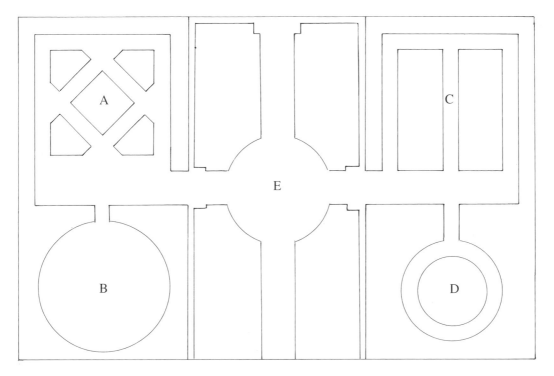

ᴏᴘᴘᴏsɪᴛᴇ *The gentleman's garden spares no expense. The paths, for example, are made with hand-made brick paviors which are far from cheap. I have tried to present something to aspire to and to suggest some more expensive ideas that could be used in either this or the artisan's garden depending on your budget. Hopefully you'll be able to take ideas from both gardens.*

people may prefer to do that. What I hope is that you'll be able to pick some ideas from each garden to use in your own – to mix and match as appropriate for your individual situation. Naturally the plants I suggest in the next chapter will be suitable for both gardens.

The Design

As builders cram more and more houses together into smaller and smaller spaces, so the shapes and dimensions of the plots have to adjust. Not only are gardens shrinking, they're changing shape too. One result is the short, wide garden, which is difficult to plan and rarely catered for in design books.

I've therefore planned the gentleman's garden to suit that particular shape, but it's also done in modular fashion. With five separate gardens in one, you should be able to juggle around the component parts more or less to fit your own plot.

I confess that no expense has been spared. The bricks for the paving are hand-made and not cheap, the trelliswork and arches are built with expensive hardwood, the building was made by a well-paid craftsman and the whole plot is surrounded by slow-growing and therefore pricey yew hedging. Even the pots and containers are top-of-the-range.

No, I couldn't afford it all at once either! This is the kind of garden most of us will have to build slowly over several years, replacing, say, gravel with bricks later, upgrading the arbour from perhaps a rustic home-made job when the finances allow and even changing plants from cheap 'fillers' to more expensive specimens as we go along. Actually it's quite fun to make the dream come true gradually, and it's a very rewarding and creative exercise.

The principles of designing the garden are exactly the same as for the artisan's garden.

Decide first of all that the garden is there to be used and not just looked at, and then make a list of what you want to include.

Here there's space for a small vegetable plot and even a greenhouse, so the scope will be greater and the season of practical enjoyment longer. Again, there's a place to sit and enjoy the sunshine and there's space for a separate herb garden.

The 'secret' garden is simply a small area filled with attractive plants, perhaps in greens and pastel shades and certainly fragrant, where you can 'get away from it all' and simply sit.

I well remember, in my youth, my friend Harry, who was a real, genuine old cottage gardener. He must have been one of the last of the generation that worked on the farm with horses when he was a lad and he had his priorities right. Unnoticed, I watched him one summer's day for perhaps half an hour as he sat on his old bench outside his back door, gazing into space. When I asked him what he was doing, he replied, 'I were just cogitatin' my lawn, old 'un.' (He called everybody 'old 'un', though he was eighty-eight – I was nineteen at the time.) Somehow country folk know that's an important part of life and I look forward to doing it myself in my own secret garden.

Though planting schemes of the gentry's cottage gardens from the eighteenth century onwards were much more sophisticated, planned affairs, I have resisted the temptation to follow the Gertrude Jekyll example and make the planting 'blended and coordinated'. As I've already pointed out, that conflicts, in my view, so violently with the very idea of a cottage garden that it would turn it into something else. I've therefore used the same plants as in the artisan's garden. Some have been grown in cottage gardens for centuries and others are the improved versions of them that are available now.

One feature the artisan's garden would not have included is the small knot garden. Though later cottage gardeners did use clipped box to edge paths, there's no evidence I can find that they followed their wealthier neighbours by building knots and parterres. Still, well grown these do look wonderful, even on a very small scale, so there's no reason at all why you shouldn't include one, even if your garden's tiny.

Mind you, even a knot of this size uses plenty of plants which are by no means cheap. You may find that you have to buy only a few to start with and then to propagate your own from cuttings. Box is very easy to increase in this way and not nearly as slow as you might imagine.

Alternatively, you may wish to use other plants, which are cheaper and quicker to grow. Lavender, cotton lavender and rosemary all make superb dwarf hedges that can be clipped in the same way.

Building the Garden

Boundaries

I surrounded my gentleman's garden with a yew hedge. If you have the room, I would recommend that you do the same, because there's no doubt that it's the finest boundary of all. It can be close-clipped to form a perfect green wall and it makes a much better windbreak than a solid barrier. Unfortunately yew is expensive and has a reputation for slow growth. It's certainly not as fast as other conifers like leylandii or Lawson's cypress, but if you prepare well (see page 48), it'll put on at least 20–25 cm (8–10 in) a year. It's well worth waiting for.

Plant about 1 m (3 ft) apart and, if the site is exposed to cold winds, erect some form of windbreak to protect the young plants until they get established. I used willow hurdles wired to strong posts. This puts the cost up, of course, but provides a temporary boundary (lasting about ten years) while the hedge is growing and it speeds up growth considerably. Alternatively plastic windbreak material is available, though it's not in the least attractive.

If you're in a desperate hurry, you can use either *Thuja plicata*, which makes a looser hedge but with fine, glossy, green foliage and grows about 60 cm (2 ft) a year, or *Cupressocyparis leylandii*

Yew, certainly the queen of hedging plants, will make a perfect green wall that can be clipped to form very straight, formal lines. It's evergreen, of course, and not as slow-growing as is generally believed. It has the extra advantage that it will grow out of old wood, so if it gets browned by freak cold winds, or if it becomes neglected and therefore scruffy, it can be cut hard back right to the main trunk and it'll regenerate in quite a short time.

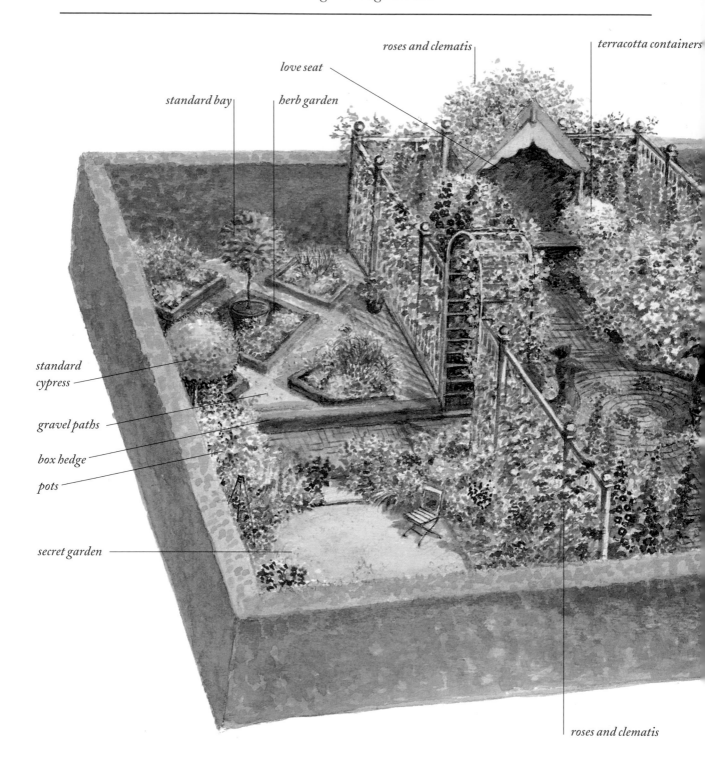

standard bay

herb garden

love seat

roses and clematis

terracotta containers

standard cypress

gravel paths

box hedge

pots

secret garden

roses and clematis

which will easily win any growth race at the remarkable speed of 1 m (3 ft) a year.

Prepare and plant as recommended for other types of hedging (see page 48), setting the plants 1 m (3 ft) apart. Don't prune the tops until they've reached 30 cm (1 ft) above the required height and then cut them back to 15 cm (6 in) below the finished height. That allows for

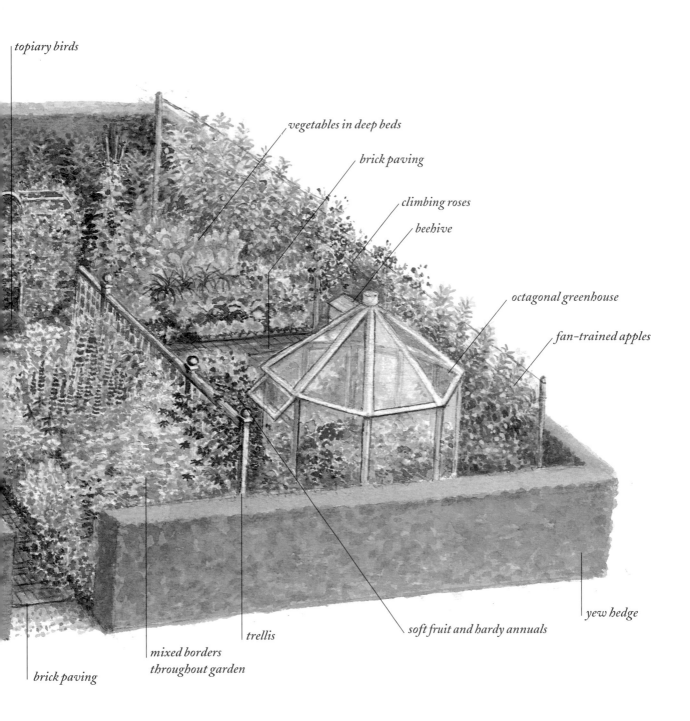

topiary birds

vegetables in deep beds

brick paving

climbing roses

beehive

octagonal greenhouse

fan-trained apples

yew hedge

soft fruit and hardy annuals

trellis

mixed borders
throughout garden

brick paving

re-growth to form a good, bushy top. The sides of
the hedge should be trimmed as soon as they
exceed the required width.

The one snag with coniferous hedges is that

*When it's fully matured, the gentleman's garden should look like
this. It'll be quite labour-saving, the main work being trimming
and tying, though, because of the close planting, that's certainly a
job you'll need to keep on top of.*

they're not really suitable for growing climbers, except perhaps for the scarlet Scotch flame flower (*Tropaeolum speciosum*) – if you have acid soil – and a few of the less vigorous clematis.

Another good, close, formal hedge to consider planting is *Lonicera nitida,* but it can really be grown satisfactorily only up to about 1.5 m (5 ft) before it becomes floppy. It makes a perfect, low hedge, though, and is ideal for dividing the garden. Plant 30 cm (1 ft) apart and don't cut it back but clip it regularly when it reaches the required size.

Brick Paving

The brick paving in this garden is a real indulgence. It's possible to buy concrete brick paviors but they do tend to look a bit municipal and are not ideal in this situation. There's no doubt in my mind that hand-made bricks are the very best but, as you would expect, they're also the most expensive.

It's sometimes possible to buy second-hand bricks that are suitable, but it's essential to make sure that they're hard enough to withstand frost. Most bricks are intended for walling, where rain

is quickly shed. If it stays on a horizontal brick, soaks in and then freezes, the surface will flake and look very messy indeed. It's best to buy special paviors intended for the job.

The edging bricks I used for the paths are moulded with an attractive Tudor rose design and are, alas, even more expensive. They're not absolutely necessary, of course.

The bricks are set on a sand base which has to be retained to stop it drifting out from underneath. You can set the edge rows of bricks on a mortar base and then lay the centre of the path, as I did when I used the special, decorated, edging bricks. Or you can take a cheaper route and make the edging with wood. I used 75 x 25 mm (3 x 1 in) pressure-preserved timber fixed with pegs exactly as recommended for the artisan's garden paths (see page 55).

Before fixing the bricks, lay them out on the ground in the pattern you're going to use, and

OPPOSITE *Sometimes you can find second-hand stock bricks that will do the job, but it's essential to ensure that they're hard enough to withstand freezing without flaking. Plants tumbling over the edges will soften hard lines and blend the path into the rest of the garden.*

1 To lay brick paving, put in the edging as recommended for the artisan's garden path (see page 55). Level it both sides, dig out and put in a layer of dry concrete.

2 Cover this with a layer of sand, consolidate it by treading it down hard and level it with a notched board to make a hard, level surface.

3 Lay out the bricks in the required pattern. Then brush in kiln-dried sand and consolidate the bricks by hand or, preferably, with a vibrator.

This larger area of brick paving has been softened by planting prostrate and low-growing herbs in a formal pattern to form a symbolic foot-maze.

measure the exact width. That'll save a lot of cutting later.

After setting the edging, dig out the soil between the boards and lay down a base of lean concrete. Use an 8:1 mix of ballast and cement mixed dry and just rake it out to make a 5 cm (2 in) bed. Tread it down, rake it again to level it roughly and cover with about 5 cm (2 in) of builder's sand.

Tread this layer down firmly and then make a notched board which will fit across the edging boards to level the sand accurately all over. Lay the bricks on the sand in the required pattern and brush fine sand all over it to fill in any spaces.

You can consolidate the bricks by putting a thick board across the path and bashing it down with a fence post. Alternatively you can hire a vibrating pad which does a much better job much more quickly.

The paved circle takes a lot more work because many of the bricks have to be cut. Hire an angle grinder for the job and it'll not prove too arduous. In the centre of the circle all the bricks have to be cut to a wedge shape to fit. Later, as the diameter increases, a wedge-shaped brick is needed only now and then.

Make sure that you leave a few bricks out here and there in strategic places to provide planting pockets.

In the very centre of the circle I used an idea I borrowed from Gertrude Jekyll's working partner, Edwin Lutyens. The concentric circles are made by sinking a series of terracotta flower pots inside each other, adjusting the heights with sand. The small pot in the middle is inverted to complete the pattern.

When the brick paving is complete, you'll need to knock out the concrete at the bottom of the planting holes, fill with a gritty, soil-based compost and plant with low-growing, aromatic plants like thyme.

If I can refer back to the artisan's garden at this point, I should say that, if you started with gravel paths and have after a year or two decided to relay with bricks, the soil should be consolidated enough to do without the concrete base. Just rake a little cement powder into the top 5 cm (2 in) of the gravel and continue from there.

Slab Paving

I wanted to find space for a tiny greenhouse in this garden so, since there's not much room, I decided on an octagonal shape, 1.8 m (6 ft) across. This is erected on a paving base, using random-sized slabs.

After marking out the area, set a series of pegs over it, with their tops corresponding to the finished level of the paving. Level them carefully with a spirit level.

Then prepare a base exactly as recommended for brick paving but excluding the final layer of

Old, natural stone lifted from pavements is sometimes available. It makes a wonderful finish, but it's very expensive.

A small, octagonal greenhouse was erected on a paved base. Making a circle of rectangular paving presented some problems but, of course, a square base would do as well.

sand (see page 84). Lay the slabs on five points of mortar, one at each corner and one in the middle. Tap them down with the handle of a club hammer so that the top surface is exactly level with the pegs.

For my octagonal greenhouse I decided on a circular base, which does present some problems. I found that the best way round them was to lay the slabs out on the ground first and then to draw a circle on the slabs using a piece of string fixed to a cane at the centre. Then I cut the slabs where they were, again using the angle grinder. With the circle all laid out, it was a simple matter to transfer the cut slabs to their proper positions.

Naturally, to allow the concrete to harden, you shouldn't walk on the slabs for a couple of days after laying.

Trellis

The open nature of trelliswork allows you to divide the garden into separate 'rooms' without creating a claustrophobic effect. Because you can always see through the trellis in places, even when it's clothed with plants, you retain the feeling of the whole space of the garden and so get the best of both worlds.

This type of hardwood trellis is definitely not a do-it-yourself job. Each piece is jointed, a task that would take hours and quite a lot of skill to do

Trellis like this is really high-quality garden furniture and making it should not be attempted by the average do-it-yourselfer. When the weather tones it down to a light grey, it looks superb and it makes a light, airy division for the garden without giving a 'shut-in' feeling. As you would expect, it's expensive, but because it's made of hardwood it has a long life.

by hand, and the finish is superb. If you want something this stylish, I'm afraid you just have to pay for it.

Fortunately it's not difficult to erect. Because the posts are made of hardwood (naturally I checked that it came from sustainable plantations and is not contributing to the destruction of the rainforest), there's no problem of rotting in the soil, so they can be concreted straight in.

Check and measure very carefully to ensure that each post is at exactly the right height and, just as for panel fencing, put in a post, then a panel and then fit the second post to the panel. Never put in all the posts first. All the panels are pre-drilled when they arrive and brass screws are supplied.

The very attractive arches came as part of the trellis system and are also very easy to erect. In fact, because the arches are fixed by the position of the path underneath them, that's the place to start. If, when you fit the trellis, it finishes a few centimetres short of the yew hedging, it doesn't matter, but it certainly would if it didn't fit exactly over the path.

In larger gardens grass is the perfect foil for the borders, but in cottage gardens it's best not to treat it like a bowling green. Leave it to grow a bit longer.

Grass

I've included a small area of grass as a restful foil to the borders in the 'secret' garden and as a place to lie and dream in the summer sun. Grass was a very common component of older cottage gardens, but it was there for a very different purpose. There would probably have been quite an area used to feed perhaps a cow, a sheep or a goat or two, and the hens and ducks would have scratched around on it too. Today it would be used for relaxation which is, of course, also a very important function.

However, I just can't see the bowling-green type of lawn in a rural cottage garden. In my view the grass should be kept quite a bit longer than that and the modern cottage gardener should not get worked up over the sight of a daisy or a dandelion. Indeed I think that, in moderation, they're to be positively encouraged.

The grass can be raised from seed or turf and the basic preparation is the same for both. Dig the soil over, incorporating coarse grit if it's very heavy. Rake it down roughly with the back of a fork and then, when the soil's dry enough not to stick to your boots, tread all over it with your weight on your heels to consolidate it thoroughly. Finally rake it level.

The difference between seed and turf is largely an economic one. Seed is much cheaper than the best turf but, of course, you'll have to wait longer to achieve results.

If you decide on seed, my recommendation would be for one of the new rye-grasses which make a tough, drought-resistant yet fine lawn. You'll need to sow at about 50 g per sq. m (1½ oz per sq. yd). On a small area it's not difficult to sow by hand. For a bigger lawn put two large plastic flower pots one inside the other and turn them so that the holes in the bottom don't coincide. Fill with seed and you'll find that you can shake it out very evenly. After sowing, rake it in with a wire lawn rake, aiming to cover about half the seed.

If you prefer turf, it pays hands down to choose a special, cultivated turf that has itself been raised from seed. There should be no weeds in it, it'll be evenly cut and will consist of good, fine grasses.

Lay out the edges first and then, working from the longest straight side, lay out the first row. When you get to the end of the row, lay the end of the last turf over the edging turf and cut off the excess with an old knife. Tap the turves in with the back of a rake.

Subsequent rows are laid in the same way working off wide boards laid on the turf to protect it from footmarks. When you've finished, make sure that the grass never goes short of water until it's rooted or the turves will shrink.

When you first mow either a seed or a turf lawn, raise the cutters as high as they'll go and lower them over the next two cuts until they're cutting the grass to a length of about 2.5 cm (1 in). That's plenty short enough for a cottage garden and will provide a good home for insects.

Wildflowers

In true cottage tradition you could turn your grass into a wildflower meadow. Even if it's quite a small area, it'll still attract millions of insects, birds and butterflies.

Instead of using straight grass seed, you could

start off with a grass and wildflower mixture. If you do, never fertilize the soil either before or after sowing. Wildflowers are used to poor conditions and they wouldn't thank you. Alternatively, if you use turf or already have established grass, the easiest way is to raise the plants by sowing into modules just as for hardy annuals (see page 198). The plants can then be planted into the turf, where they should thrive.

Bear in mind that wildflower lawns should be cut only a couple of times a year, once after flowering and again, if necessary, in the early spring. It's essential to allow the plants to seed into the grass to maintain the population. And note that

A cottage lawn sown with wildflowers looks great and attracts many insects. But you should cut it only twice a year to allow the flowers to seed, and the grass must then be raked off to avoid overfeeding.

this will change over the years as the species that are really happy thrive, while other species less content with their conditions will die out.

Knots and Parterres

Formal knot gardens and the French equivalent, parterres, were very popular with the gentry in their romanticized gardens and completely shunned by cottagers. They were often to be found in monasteries in medieval times, when they were sometimes fashioned into foot mazes representing man's journey through life. The idea was gradually adopted in grand gardens across Europe and reached a peak of popularity in the sixteenth century. Today knots and parterres are benefiting from a great revival of interest, perhaps because the formality of the design is ideally suited to small spaces.

You'll need to decide, first of all, whether you want a pure knot garden, which consists of dwarf hedging and nothing else, or if you want the hedges to retain flower borders. For borders, the scheme will need more room and have to be much more open and expansive in design.

Box is the favourite plant to use for the hedging, either the vigorous common box (*Buxus sempervirens*) or the dwarfer edging box (*Buxus suffruticosa*). You could also incorporate other plants like dwarf lavender (*Lavandula* 'Hidcote') or cotton lavender (*Santolina chamaecyparissus*). Both need clipping regularly to stop them sprawling. I've

This tiny knot in a small cottage garden measures only 1.5 m (5 ft) square, but it makes an attractive formal feature in what is an otherwise very informal garden. As a contrast to the dwarf box hedging, it's planted inside with a golden-foliage thuja and lavenders.

also used dwarf barberry (*Berberis thunbergii* 'Atropurpurea'), which adds a fine, red leaf colour to the scheme. Wall germander (*Teucrium chamaedrys*) is another traditional plant to provide a contrast of colour and texture, as is rosemary (*Rosmarinus officinalis* 'Miss Jessopp's Upright') or rue (*Ruta graveolens*).

Patterns can be quite complicated, though you should again bear in mind that, if you want to grow flowers or herbs inside the hedging, you'll need fairly wide areas to do so. Mark out the shape on the ground using sand poured from a wine bottle and plant about 15–23 cm (6–9 in) apart.

Always remember that it's essential to clip the hedges at least every autumn or spring, and some gardeners like to tidy them up in summer too.

The Vegetable Plot

Over my years of gardening I've come to the conclusion that the most effective way to grow vegetables in a small space is to put them into 1.2-m- (4-ft)-wide beds. The method of cultivation is covered fully later, but a word here about how they were made. It's essential, of course, for them to be decorative as well as productive.

The beds were edged with tiles of a Victorian design which are still available new, made with exactly the same materials and, indeed, in the very brickworks which produced many of those used by Victorian gardeners. They're set on a bed of mortar for extra rigidity, since constant cultivation is likely to move them if they're simply sunk into the soil. Set a tile at each end first and then

There's not much room for vegetables in the gentleman's garden, so they're grown in narrow beds with all the work being done from the paths. It's certainly the most productive way and it can be made very decorative too.

run a tight line along the top. This will mark both the lines and the level and make the rest of the laying quick and easy.

The paths were simply made with gravel on beaten soil like those in the artisan's garden (see page 55).

The Fruit Garden

The area housing the greenhouse was planted with fruit trees and bushes surrounded by flowering plants. Again, cultivation methods are covered in the next section, but this garden presents one problem. To maximize the small space avail-able, I wanted to use fan-trained and espalier trees. But in the absence of a fence or wall, a post-and-wire structure had to be erected. The 2.4-m (8-ft) tanalized posts were set in concrete with 2 m (6 ft 6 in) above the ground. Three straining bolts were fixed at the end of each row to take wires at the top, 30 cm (1 ft) up from the bottom and one in the middle. To hide the posts, roses can be planted at the base and trained tightly to them.

The remainder of the garden round the green-house was planted with redcurrants and black-currants, raspberries in a column (see page 245), standard gooseberries and strawberries.

Fan-trained fruit trees look very attractive even in winter when the branches are bare. Contrary to popular opinion, they're extremely easy to prune and they certainly produce bumper crops. Train them on wires fixed to posts or to the wall or fence.

The Plants

COTTAGE GARDENERS, like any others, grew whatever plants they could get their hands on. We all know that, once enthusiasm takes a hold, there are no limits to your interest in trying something new. Even the old cottage gardeners would have felt the same way. So how do you define 'cottage garden plants'?

They started out, undoubtedly, as plants with a purpose. Primarily there would have been subsistence plants: the fruit trees and bushes and the vegetables to provide food for both the cottager's family and the livestock. Later, after the dissolution of the monasteries in the sixteenth century, there would have been medicinal herbs and some for the pot too. They've changed very little over the centuries and, of course, the modern cottage gardener will want to grow them as well. But what of the ornamental plants? They have been described as 'simple' or 'unpretentious' flowers, even as 'old-fashioned', but those descriptions don't really get to the nub of it.

I feel sure that cottage gardeners years ago would have given their eye teeth for some of the plants we grow today and would certainly not have turned up their noses because they were 'sophisticated', whatever that means. Yet look at any cottage garden and it's true that the charm does come from a simplicity in both the planting scheme and in the actual plants themselves. There's a decidedly *rural* feel about a real cottage garden, even if it's in the city.

Well, my own definition is perhaps more objective. I think that the old cottage gardeners would have grown whatever they could get their hands on. But they had to do so with very slim resources indeed. They would therefore have taken plants from the wild and later would have 'liberated' them from the gardens of the gentry where they worked. Then these would have been spread around other cottage gardens. So my own theory is that cottage garden plants are those that are essentially easy to grow and to propagate.

---

1 *Campanula persicifolia*

2 *Papaver rhoeas* 'Mother of Pearl'

3 *Paeonia lactiflora*

4 *Linaria purpurea* 'Canon Went'

5 *Rosa* 'Mischief'

6 *Rosa* 'Conrad Ferdinand Meyer'

7 *Linaria purpurea*

Typical cottage garden borders lack uniformity. There's a real charm in a glorious 'jumble' of colour like this.

Keys are provided to identify the main flowering plants in the photographs.

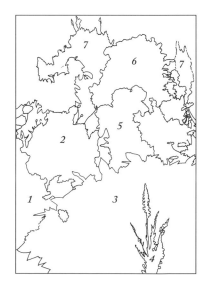

And that's exactly what modern gardeners want too. I don't think I could be accused of being patronizing when I say that most of us, certainly for the first several years of our gardening lives, find that the biggest restriction to developing our plots exactly as we want them is money. So we too will be looking for ways to reduce our expenditure on plants.

We'll want to grow them from seed, or from cuttings given to us by friends. We'll want to grow plants to swap too, just as our ancestors did in Thomas Hill's time, and we won't be able to spend a lot on the facilities to do it either: no expensive greenhouses with mist propagation and computerized heating and ventilation; no light-rooms and fogging machines; just the same simple equipment our predecessors have been using for centuries.

All the plants I've described here, then, the old favourites and a few newer ones too, can be grown with the simplest of equipment and, provided you can find a source of material, for a minimum of expense. Gardeners are generally delighted to swap plants and to give away cuttings and home-collected seed if you ask. So ask! The best bet is to join the local garden club or society, where you'll meet like-minded people, make a lot of friends and find that you can fill your garden for next to nothing. Even better, join a national society too, like the Cottage Garden Society, which distributes seeds to members each year and is generally eager to give away and exchange plants.

Of course, there's no sense in restricting ourselves to the old cottage plants for purely sentimental reasons. There are lots of excellent new ones that measure up to our criteria of simplicity of cultivation and propagation and would also fit our cottage scheme very well.

Indeed, there are examples of great improvements in the vigour and disease-resistance of some modern varieties. Roses, for example, are bred these days with an eye very much on disease resistance. Modern gardeners don't want to spend their lives spraying noxious chemicals, so if new varieties are prone to blackspot and mildew, they just don't get on the market. None are completely immune but many are now resistant.

Old-fashioned pinks have excellent flowers and superb perfume, but they only flower once. Many new varieties have been bred for the size of flower and repeat flowering, but in doing so have lost the delicacy of the old ones and much of their perfume too. Now a new race is being developed with the old-fashioned look plus the perfume and the long-flowering of modern varieties. That doesn't mean that we must abandon the old ones – heaven forbid! But we should certainly not turn up our noses at the new ones just because they are new. You can be sure that William Robinson wouldn't have done.

Planting

The old cottage gardeners would have done much by trial and error and would have learnt by observation. Being country people in the main and working with plants and animals every day, they couldn't have failed to glean much knowledge of the natural world. So if they dug a plant from, say, a shady woodland edge, they'd know to plant it in a similar position in the garden. Just like us, I daresay, they went wrong quite often too. But generally, if they did, they could go out and dig up another plant. These days, especially if we have to buy our plants, we won't be able to afford the luxury of getting it wrong too often. Even if you're raising your own plants from seed and cuttings, you'll lose heart if you fail more than is necessary.

It's important, therefore, to get to know your plants. Find out how tall they grow and how much they spread, when they flower and also their preferences as to soil and position. The list of plants here includes all those details.

However much you research, you'll nonetheless still go wrong from time to time. In my travels I have met several very experienced cottage gardeners who have been growing plants all their lives. They *all* admitted that they still made mistakes now and then. That's the bad news.

The good news is that, to a man (and woman), they all said the same thing. If you go wrong, don't worry. As soon as you realize that you've planted this plant too close to that one, or that you simply can't live with the colours of those two adjacent flowers, change them. All you need do is to pour a bucket of water over the plant to be moved, dig it up with as much soil as possible and plant it somewhere else. Then give it another good drink and it'll never know it's been disturbed. It's very comforting to know that, provided you move trees and shrubs within a season or two of their original planting, they'll be quite happy. And, of course, most herbaceous plants will love being shifted at any age.

As for positioning plants, remind yourself again that you're involved in an *artisan's* craft. I have to say that, in my own gardening, I have *never* been worried by clashing colours. That doesn't mean I've got it right every time – far from it. It's perhaps testament to my philistinism that the lovely jumble of colour I achieve more by luck than judgment looks spot-on to my eye. And in my garden that, of course, is what matters.

So, in the first instance at least, concentrate on finding the right soil and aspect for each plant and, as a general rule, putting the tallest at the back and the shortest at the front. Even that rule should not be hard and fast, because a change of height will add a lot more interest than a uniformly graded border.

In my view, one of the great interests of garden-ing lies in the critical appraisal of the borders you've planted and the re-arrangement of any-thing you feel could be improved. You might decide that two colours live uneasily with each other or that the addition of another one would add to the appeal of the grouping. You may feel that the delicate flowers of one plant would be better appreciated against a background of dull green, or it might be that one plant has grown more than you thought it would and so hides another. The fascination of gardening is that it never seems to stop. You'll *always* be adding, changing and improving.

Whatever you do, you *will* succeed. The fact is that nature's *really* in charge here and there's no more creative artist in this world or the next.

Many of the plants in this wonderful garden on the Isle of Wight were grown from seed from the Cottage Garden Society, while others were raised from cuttings given or more often exchanged through gardening friendships.

Trees

Trees were of much greater importance to the old cottage gardeners than they are to us today, because they were used for food, for fuel and to make most of what the cottager needed for his livelihood from buckets to hay forks, carts to thatching pegs. Thomas Tusser gives us an insight into the various uses of different timbers in the sixteenth century, in some more of his charming doggerel:

Save elme, ash and crabtree, for cart and for plough,
save step for stile, of the crotch of the bough.
Save hazel for forks, save sallow [willow] for rake,
save hulver [holly] and thorne,
thereof flaile for to make.

Naturally these were woodland trees, though some of them found their way into gardens for purely decorative reasons.

Trees are the only plants that don't fit the general specification I've laid down for cottage garden plants because, with a very few exceptions, they simply aren't subjects for home propa-gation. Some, like willows, alders and poplars, are pretty easy to raise from cuttings, but most of these are big, vigorous trees and not really suitable for our purpose. Others, like hawthorns, wild plums and cherries, can be raised from seed, but take so long that it's always best to buy them as young trees from a nursery. Many varieties are budded or grafted on to special rootstocks, so this really is a job for the grower.

It's likely that you'll want only one or at most two trees, so it's best to choose those that give you two or more displays through the year; perhaps flowers followed by berries or good autumn foliage colour, or even attractive winter bark.

All the trees listed below will grow in virtually any soil and position unless otherwise stated, but for the sake of the rest of the garden be careful with the siting. Trees will naturally cast shade and, though this can often produce another welcome type of habitat, in very small spaces it can shed so much gloom that you're stuck with growing shade-loving plants whether you like it or not.

When you buy a tree from the garden centre, you may find the suggested height misleading. To avoid putting customers off, they often state the

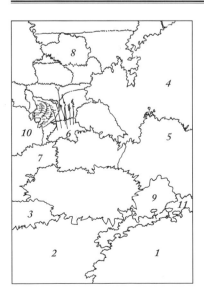

1 *Anthemis punctata cupaniana*

2 *Viola labradorica*

3 *Epimedium rubrum*

4 *Cotinus coggygria* 'Royal Purple'

5 *Geranium phaeum* 'Album'

6 *Thalictrum aquilegifolium*

7 *Pulmonaria officinalis* 'Sissinghurst White'

8 *Rosa* 'Canary Bird'

9 *Polemonium caeruleum*

10 *Osmanthus delavayi*

11 *Pelargonium* hybrid

Trees and shrubs form the basic bones of this border and act as a background to herbaceous plants.

height the tree will reach in ten years, but if you intend to stay in your garden for longer, expect a bigger tree. However, don't be alarmed at the eventual heights stated in the following list. Though a 10-m (33-ft) tree sounds huge, when you see it growing, it's really relatively small. What's more, the heights I've given are the eventual tallest expected. The trees would, in most cases, take many years to get there. I suppose, as a rule of thumb, that they would grow about a third of the stated height in ten years.

Planting

Bare-rooted trees should be planted in the dormant season between late autumn and early spring. Container-grown stock can go in at any time if you're prepared to water.

It's most important, first of all, to prepare a big area for a new tree. If you simply dig a hole in otherwise uncultivated soil, it'll drain all the surrounding water and become a sump.

Dig the hole and break up the bottom, checking that it's deep enough to allow you to plant at *exactly* the level the tree grew on the nursery. Before planting, bang in a short stake, which should come no more than a third of the way up the trunk. Next sprinkle fertilizer on the heap of soil you've dug out, using bonemeal in winter and a balanced organic feed in the growing season. Put the tree in the hole, refill with a little soil and shake the plant up and down a few times to settle the soil around the roots. Then completely refill, firming gently with your boot.

Fix the tree with a proper plastic tree tie which is held firmly to the stake with a nail. Then mulch round the plant with manure or compost to eliminate weed growth and retain moisture.

Most trees that fail do so because of lack of water, so check the soil for at least a year and water if necessary.

Make sure that trees and shrubs are planted at the depth they grew on the nursery. Even on heavy soil it's a mistake to use peat, which holds too much water. If any addition is necessary, use rotted manure or compost.

Choosing trees

If you have space for only a single tree, I'd have to say that I would go along with the old cottagers and state a preference for an apple. Here's a tree with stunning blossom in spring, followed by huge, attractive fruits in late summer that you can actually eat too. No other tree offers so much. But in small spaces, there are other ways to grow them that take up less room. All that's covered later.

Amelanchier lamarckii Juneberry, serviceberry or snowy mespilus
Height: 12 m (40 ft). Spread: 9 m (30 ft).
The small, black berries produced by the Juneberry were once used as a substitute for

raisins, but the value of this tree is really in its three shows of colour. It has white flowers in spring, set off by lovely bronze young foliage. The leaves turn green through the year and then finally bright yellow if it's growing in shade or brilliant red in sunshine. It's not at all happy on very chalky soils, but I've found it fine on slightly alkaline land.

Arbutus unedo STRAWBERRY TREE
Height: 9 m (30 ft). Spread: 9 m (30 ft).
A native of Ireland, the strawberry tree makes a small, gnarled tree with reddish, shredding bark. It always looks good, summer and winter. It bears small, white flowers in drooping clusters in autumn, followed by red fruits. Often both are there at the same time. Its close relative *A. andrachnoides* is even lovelier, with cinnamon-red bark. These are slow-growing trees that won't take over, despite their eventual height. They do best on acid soil, but will tolerate some lime.

Betula spp. SILVER BIRCH
Height: 30 m (100 ft). Spread: 7.5 m (25 ft).
The native birch (*Betula pendula*) is a well-known woodland tree noted for its white bark, its delicate tracery of bare branches in winter and yellow catkins in spring. It would certainly have found a home in many old cottage gardens, but it's a bit large for most modern plots. The Himalayan birch (*Betula utilis* 'Jaquemontii') is a little smaller and has brilliant white, peeling bark.

Corylus spp. HAZEL
Height: 7 m (23 ft). Spread: 5 m (16 ft).
The native hazel (*Corylus avellana*) has always been valued for its timber, used for jobs like thatching pegs and in hedge laying, and for its crop of cob nuts.

Some varieties are valuable as ornamental trees and can be grown to produce a crop of nuts too,

The beautiful red fruits of the strawberry tree are often accompanied by white flowers in autumn, but it's well worth its place in the garden just for its fine reddish bark and gnarled shape.

provided you grow two varieties for pollination and can keep the squirrels at bay. They can also be used in a mixed hedge for a very traditional cottage effect. The varieties of *C. avellana* and *C. maxima* are the ones to grow.

'Kentish Cob', 'Butler' and 'Longue d'Espagne' are all good nut-producing varieties with excellent, long, yellow catkins in spring.

If you're determined to defeat the squirrels, you'll have to grow the trees with a stem at least 1.8 m (6 ft) high before the branches start. Plant them about 3.6 m (12 ft) from any other trees in the garden so that the squirrels can't jump from tree to tree and then, well before harvest time, wire a sheet of rigid plastic around each trunk.

The squirrels won't be able to get a grip on it and they'll be forced to leave the nuts for you.

The purple-leaf filbert (*C. maxima* 'Purpurea') makes an excellant large shrub or a small tree with superb, intense purple foliage, but it is not really a fruiting type.

Crataegus spp. Flowering thorn
Height: 10 m (33 ft). Spread: 10 m (33 ft).
A small tree, making a rounded head in the early years and eventually spreading. The common hawthorn (*Crataegus monogyna*) is the one the old cottagers would have grown. In spring this has large, fragrant clusters of white blossom known as 'May blossom', which is the subject of many old country sayings and superstitions. 'Ne'er cast a clout till May be out' is one of the more sensible. The blossom is followed by red berries in autumn. It's a fine tree and a really authentic cottage garden plant.

The 'Glastonbury thorn' (*C.m.* 'Biflora') was, according to legend, planted by Joseph of Arimathaea who brought it from the Holy Land. It can produce flushes of white flower during winter, but it's for sheltered gardens only.

There are various varieties of the Midland hawthorn (*C. laevigata*) available, like the double red 'Paul's Scarlet' and 'Masekii' which has double pink flowers. All bear red berries. These are perhaps the most suitable for small gardens. The species is a native, but the varieties are hybrids.

C. prunifolia has fine, shiny foliage and white flowers followed by large, red fruits, but its most notable feature is its superb autumn leaf colour. Its origin is unknown.

Euonymus europaeus Spindle
Height: 6 m (20 ft). Spread: 5 m (16 ft).
A native shrub or small tree, the spindle was often used in mixed hedgerows. It got its name from the fact that the hard wood was used to make spindles. It bears small, greenish white flowers in spring followed by scarlet capsules which open to reveal orange seeds. The leaves also turn bright red in autumn. The variety 'Aucubifolius' has foliage which turns pinkish, mottled yellow and white in autumn.

Ilex aquifolium Holly
Height: 20 m (65 ft). Spread: 6 m (20 ft).
Another native, the holly is a plant with many religious and magical connections. Common holly (*Ilex aquifolium*) has been grown in gardens for centuries as a shrub or small tree, as hedging and as a subject for topiary. It has evergreen, glossy leaves and, if you have a male and a female plant or the self-fertile variety 'J. C. van Tol' or 'Pyramidalis', bright red berries too. The variety 'Bacciflava' bears handsome yellow berries.

All the hollies can be controlled by judicious pruning or by clipping to a formal shape.

Laburnum spp. Golden rain
Height: 7 m (23 ft). Spread: 7 m (23 ft).
The laburnum has been grown in this country since about 1560. The variety originally grown would have been the common laburnum (*L. anagyroides*), but the best for modern gardens is certainly *L. watereri* 'Vossii', which carries long, pendulous racemes of yellow flowers in late spring to early summer. All parts of this plant are poisonous, but this variety sets very few seeds so it's an obvious choice where children live.

Malus spp. Crab apples
Height: 6–8 m (20–26 ft). Height: 5–6 m (16–18 ft).
The native crab apple (*Malus sylvestris*) bears white flowers followed by yellow fruits flushed with red and was possibly taken from the woods and grown by cottage gardeners. However, the

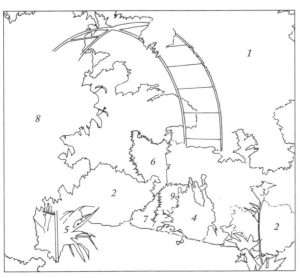

1 *Gleditsia triacanthos* 'Sunburst'

2 *Alchemilla mollis*

3 *Filipendula rubra*

4 *Sisyrinchium striatum*

5 *Phormium cookianum* 'Cream Delight'

6 *Daphne mezereum*

7 *Helichrysum petiolare*

8 *Cornus* 'Eddie's White Wonder'

9 *Campanula persicifolia*

Even before the climbers have grown over this metal arch, the plants in the mixed borders have begun to take away its formality and blend it in with the rest of the garden.

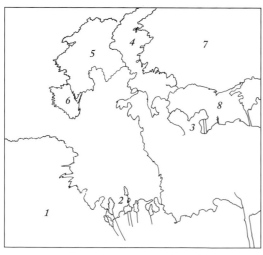

1 *Myosotis* 'Royal Blue'

2 *Tiarella cordifolia*

3 *Tulipa* 'Princess Margaret Rose'

4 *Prunus* 'Pink Perfection'

5 *Acer pseudoplatanus* 'Brilliantissimum'

6 *Cytisus praecox* 'Allgold'

7 *Camellia japonica*

8 *Hesperis matronalis*

This spring border is brightened by the young, pinkish foliage of an acer and the display of cherry flowers.

apple (*M. domestica*) has been here so long that it was more likely, because of its usefulness, that they grew some form of that in preference to the crab apple.

With the exception of the variety 'John Downie', which has long been used to make jam and jelly and is covered in the fruit section (see page 239), the newer hybrids are much more suitable for modern gardens if you're looking purely for ornament.

'Evereste' is one of the smaller ones and is covered with red buds opening to white flowers in spring followed by orange/yellow fruits.

'Golden Hornet' has pink buds which open to pinkish white followed by bright yellow berries. This is one of the best varieties for pollinating apples.

'Liset' has bronze/purple leaves and deep red flowers followed by small red fruits.

'Lemoinei' has the same colouring as 'Liset', but the flowers and fruits are larger.

There are many others with slightly different flowers and fruits, all worth growing.

Prunus spp. FLOWERING CHERRY
Height: 6–10 m (20–33 ft). Spread: 6–10 m (20–33 ft).
Many of the flowering cherries available today originated in Japan and can, by no stretch of the imagination, be called original cottage plants. But old cottage gardens certainly grew the sweet cherry and the 'gean' or 'mazzard' (*Prunus avium*).

These are big trees and, though superb if you have the space, are not appropriate for a small garden. The Japanese types will provide the same stunning spring blossom but on a smaller scale.

In my opinion the spring cherry (*Prunus subhirtella* 'Autumnalis') should be made obligatory in every garden. The white flowers appear on naked stems at intervals right through the winter

and then have a final, superb fling in early spring. Even better is the pink variety 'Autumnalis Rosea'. Both make small trees.

One of the earliest of the Japanese hybrids is 'Accolade', which forms a small, spreading tree and is unfailingly covered in deep pink blossom even on young plants. It's one of the earliest to flower in spring.

'Mount Fuji' is a real spring tonic. Again, it's a small, spreading tree but this time with fragrant flowers of snow white, set off by the freshest of spring-green foliage.

P. sargentii is a little gem. A small, round-headed tree, it has single, pale pink flowers in spring and is one of the first to colour fiery red in autumn.

The cherry plum (*Prunus cerasifera*) is not known in the wild, but was certainly cultivated in gardens in the sixteenth century. Its plentiful white flowers open before the leaves, which are very dark green. Better for modern gardens is the variety 'Nigra', which has deep red leaves and

The Japanese flowering cherries make superb substitutes for the much larger native species early cottage gardeners would have grown. This one, 'Accolade', is one of the first to flower and is totally reliable.

Robinia pseudoacacia *'Frisia' is a recent introduction but well worthwhile for a small cottage garden. It doesn't move well, so always buy it in a container.*

pink flowers: a very striking tree indeed and easy to grow almost anywhere.

The one native that was pretty certainly grown in cottage gardens from earliest times, and which would fit even a small space, is the bird cherry (*P. padus*). The flowers, hanging in long, pendulous racemes of almond-scented white, are quite different from those of most other cherries. Look out too for the variety 'Colorata', which has coppery foliage and pink flowers.

If you wonder why I have not included the superb flowering peaches and almonds with the cherries, it's because of the debilitating disease peach-leaf curl to which they are prone. This fungus causes characteristic red blisters on the leaves and can be controlled only with constant spraying – which simply doesn't fit in with the cottage philosophy.

Rhus typhina STAG'S HORN SUMACH
Height: 6 m (20 ft). Spread: 5 m (16 ft).
Originally from North America, the stag's horn sumach was often grown in cottage gardens. It has superb, deeply cut foliage which turns fiery red in autumn. The fruits consist of large, brownish cones at the ends of the branches and the bark is an attractive, furry brown. It has the big disadvantage that it suckers badly, sending up shoots a good distance from the parent. You can easily control these by pulling them out, provided they don't appear in a lawn. The variety 'Dissecta' has very attractive, finely cut leaflets. Both trees will grow on quite dry soil in sun or shade.

Robinia pseudoacacia BLACK LOCUST
Height: 25 m (80 ft). Spread: 6 m (20 ft).
The black locust or common acacia was introduced to France from North America in 1601 and soon found its way to Britain, where it quickly became naturalized. It has attractive foliage and pendulous, white, pea-like flowers in mid to late summer. It's a bit big for most gardens, so the smaller variety 'Frisia' is to be preferred. This has bright golden foliage, which makes it an attractive tree, and though it dates from only 1935, you can bet that the old cottagers would have fought over it.

Sorbus aria WHITEBEAM
Height: 15 m (50 ft). Spread: 6 m (20 ft).
The native whitebeam (*Sorbus aria*) is a fine sight in spring. The new leaves are silvery grey, sparkling in the early sunshine. The tree has small, white flowers in spring, followed by red berries, but these are relatively insignificant.

The old cottagers would therefore have much preferred *Sorbus thibetica* 'John Mitchell', a Chinese species. It's much the same tree except that the silver-grey leaves are very much bigger and more dramatic.

Sorbus aucuparia ROWAN or MOUNTAIN ASH
Height: 8–15 m (26–50 ft). Spread: 6–8 m (18–26 ft).
A native and therefore certain to have been grown in original cottage gardens. The real rowan (*Sorbus aucuparia*) makes quite a large, conical tree with lots of white blossom in spring followed by clusters of red berries in late summer. Like most rowans it keeps its fruits until the birds decide to have a go. Then they disappear rapidly. So they're a very useful food source in early winter.

The modern cottager would be well advised to grow one of the varieties like 'Autumn Glow' which has fiery red foliage in autumn, contrasting well with pinkish yellow fruits.

S. cashmiriana makes a small tree with large, pink flowers in spring followed by pendulous clusters of large, white berries, while the variety 'Joseph Rock' has bright yellow berries.

Sorbus domestica SERVICE TREE
Height: 20 m (65 ft). Spread: 6 m (20 ft).
The service tree has been cultivated in this country for centuries. It has typical rowan leaves and slightly off-white flowers in spring, followed by greenish yellow fruits which can be eaten when bletted (partly rotted). Another genuine early cottage garden tree.

Taxus baccata COMMON YEW
Height: 20 m (65 ft). Spread: 10 m (30 ft).
One of the only three native conifers, the yew is part of the British heritage and has been grown for centuries. It was an important tree since it was used to make arrows; and, being poisonous to livestock, it was often planted in churchyards where it was presumed cattle wouldn't stray.

It's doubtful that a small cottage garden would be able to afford the space for a fully mature yew that has been allowed to grow unchecked. It can

be a dull plant unless it's clipped to a formal shape: then it becomes a focal point and an exciting sculpture (see page 203). It's also the best possible hedging plant (see pages 81 and 132).

Climbers

Climbers add instant height to the garden and should be used to cover the fences and walls more or less completely. In a small garden the more leaf cover you can get on the fences, the less claustrophobic they'll look. Of course, you should leave space for productive plants like trained fruit trees, but allow room to grow a climber of some sort

Use all vertical structures in the garden – walls, fences, trellis and so on – to add almost instant height by planting them with climbers. This bare trellis in the gentleman's garden will be transformed when it carries a mixture of climbing roses and clematis.

between them to add colour and interest.

Climbers can also be used to add height to the borders: simply grow them over free-standing supports. An obelisk is ideal (see page 66) or even just a post driven into the ground.

Where you're growing climbers over an arbour or round a seat, they should naturally be scented and, where they cover an arch, it's often better to avoid thorny roses to avoid scratching your unwary visitors.

Planting

By their nature climbers generally prefer a deep, rich, moisture-retentive soil, so take special care to prepare the planting holes well.

Remember that the soil at the base of the house wall is often the driest in the garden: it's therefore best to plant about 30 cm (1 ft) away from it and simply to point the climber where you want it to grow. It will eventually get there. You should also keep a special eye on it and water when it dries out – for at least the first season until it can fend for itself.

Most plants should be planted at the depth at which they grew on the nursery. Since you'll buy most in pots, that's easy to see. But there are   exceptions. It's best to put roses about 5 cm (2 in) below soil level to encourage growth right from the base of the plant. That goes for bush roses too.

Clematis should also be planted deeply, but for a different reason. They're subject to the fungus disease clematis wilt, which makes the plants wilt from the top and die. Since the fungus affects only parts above ground level, deep-planted plants will have plenty of buds left to regrow if the plant does succumb and has to be cut back.

After planting always give the plants a good handful of organic fertilizer, water them well, and mulch round them with compost.

Self-clinging plants can't be induced to stick to the wall or fence. It's only the new growth of ivy, Virginia creeper, climbing hydrangea and so on that will stick, so you have to leave it to them. Just point them at the wall. They'll be frustratingly slow until they do stick, but then they'll get away like a race-horse.

Some plants, like clematis and honeysuckle, climb by twining. They may need a little help to get started, but after that they'll roar away under their own steam. Others, like roses, will need to be tied in to wires and their shoots pulled horizontal to restrict sap flow and so encourage flowering.

Chaenomeles japonica FLOWERING QUINCE
This wall shrub came to Britain from Japan in about 1869 and is quite different from the quince grown to eat, which was known in this country certainly in the seventeenth century, if not before (see page 240). The flowering quince is grown for its decorative value and was a popular Victorian cottage garden plant. It has bright orange flowers in spring, followed by large, yellow, pear-shaped fruits.

Chaenomeles speciosa arrived in Britain at about the same time and there are several more modern seedlings in a range of colours, but with the authentic cottage feel. 'Apple Blossom' is white, tinged pink; 'Brilliant' is scarlet; 'Rosea Plena' is a double with pink flowers; and 'Nivalis' is pure white.

Quinces are very hardy and will grow on a fence or wall, where they will need tying in and training. Propagate by softwood cuttings in June in the coldframe (see page 200).

Clematis spp.
Old man's beard or traveller's joy was grown in gardens of old, but it's much too rampant for modern gardens. Its small, white flowers and

Two varieties of Clematis viticella *climb happily through shrubs in late summer, providing another season of flower. After flowering they can be cut back hard to give the shrubs light and air and both will give a repeat performance the next season.*

hairy seed heads are not that exciting in any case. Some other species and varieties have also been grown for centuries and no cottage garden should be without these attractive twining plants. The new cottager has a wealth of wonderful clematis to choose from.

The main point to bear in mind is that the small-flowered species are generally much more vigorous than the large-flowered hybrids, so choose carefully. While a species like *C. montana* can be used to cover a building or a large pergola, it's not suitable for an obelisk and certainly not for growing through another plant as some of the less vigorous types are.

Pruning sometimes baffles gardeners, so remember the simple rule of thumb. If it flowers before the end of June, prune it after flowering by cutting side shoots back to within a bud or two of the main branches. If it blooms later, cut it hard back to within 15 cm (6 in) of the ground in February. Propagate by cuttings in June (see page 200).

Clematis alpina, introduced in 1792, is not too vigorous for small gardens. It has smallish, blue flowers with a white central tuft and flowers in April and May. Its varieties 'Frances Rivis' with larger blue flowers, 'Ruby' with red flowers and 'White Moth' are also worth growing.

The hybrid 'Bill Mackenzie' is a vigorous variety with thick petals of bright yellow. It flowers from July to October and the flowers are followed by fluffy white seed heads.

C. flammula was certainly grown in the sixteenth century. It's quite vigorous and covered in tiny, white, sweetly scented flowers from August to October, followed by silky seed heads.

C. macropetala is a lovely early-flowering species, producing violet-blue flowers paling towards the centre and again followed by attractive seed heads. 'Lagoon', with blue flowers, 'Markham's Pink' and 'White Swan' are also good.

C. montana is vigorous to rampant and bears small, white flowers in profusion in May. Its varieties, the pink 'Elizabeth' and 'Tetrarose', have much the same habit.

C. viticella has been cultivated in cottage gardens since the sixteenth century and is useful for growing through other plants to give a late show. After flowering it should be cut right down and the old growth removed to give its host plant a free run. The flowers are red/violet or blue. Much later varieties offer the modern gardener a wider range. Look for the wine-red 'Madame Julia Correvon', the deep pink 'Margot Koster' and the violet 'Etoile Violette' especially.

The large-flowered hybrids date from the late nineteenth century onwards, but are wonderful cottage plants. There's a huge choice, so visit a nursery before buying. Popular varieties include:

'Comtesse de Bouchaud' – pink flowers with yellow stamens from June to August.

'Ernest Markham' – petunia-red flowers from June to September.

'General Sikorski' – blue flowers, red at the base, in June and July.

'Gravetye Beauty' – bell-shaped, cherry-red flowers from July to September.

'Hagley Hybrid' – shell pink flowers with brown anthers from June to September.

'Jackmanii Superba' – violet-purple flowers from July to September.

'Lasurstern' – deep lavender-blue flowers with golden stamens in May and June and again in autumn.

'Mrs Cholmondeley' – pale blue flowers from May to August.

The large-flowered clematis hybrid 'Hagley Hybrid' is a very free-flowering variety introduced in 1956. Prune it hard in early spring.

'Perle d'Azur' is a vigorous variety introduced in 1885. Try growing it through dark foliage plants like yew which will display the pale-coloured flowers to their best advantage.

'Nelly Moser' – mauve/pink flowers with a central carmine bar on each petal in May and June and again in late summer.

'Niobe' – deep red flowers with yellow anthers from July to October.

'Perle d'Azur' – light blue flowers from June to August.

'The President' – purple-blue flowers with a silver reverse from June to September.

'Ville de Lyon' – carmine-red flowers with golden stamens from June to October.

'Vyvyan Pennell' – double, blue/purple flowers with a carmine centre from May to July.

Hedera spp. Ivy

The common ivy (*Hedera helix*) is a native and was certainly grown in cottage gardens since the Middle Ages and before. It has numerous folk-lore connections and has been used since before early Christian times at Christmas.

Ivy is particularly useful for growing on north-facing walls and in soils where nothing else will do. It will cling to both walls and fences and can also be used as a scrambling plant to cover difficult areas of soil. The flowers are insignificant, but the evergreen leaves are most attractive. It's an excellent wildlife attractor, providing a home for many insects and a favourite nesting site for several species of birds.

In 1577 Thomas Hill suggested that garlands of ivy be tied around trees to attract ants, where they could then be killed.

There are several new varieties of ivy which you may like to grow, but for a genuine cottage garden avoid the more contrived forms like the bright yellow 'Buttercup' and the green-and-yellow 'Goldheart'. 'Green Ripple' is an interesting variation, bearing leaves with wavy edges, while the other native, the Irish ivy (*H. hibernica*), is noted for larger leaves than the English form. Well worth growing. Propagate by layering.

Humulus lupulus Hop

Hops have been grown by cottagers for centuries and were used to make ale which was consumed in much greater quantities than today. Indeed, even quite small children were weaned on the stuff!

These days, gardeners rarely have the space to grow hops for brewing, but they make decorative (if very rampant) plants. The young shoots can also be eaten like asparagus.

For the small garden it's advisable to stick to the slightly less vigorous golden hop, the variety 'Aureus'. It has soft yellow leaves and is best grown up a free-standing post or an obelisk, where it will twine happily. But make sure that you control the running roots by digging them out where they're not wanted.

If you want to grow hops really well and you have access to pigeon manure, take Thomas Tusser's sixteenth-century advice: 'For hop ground cold,/Dove doong woorth gold.' Otherwise farmyard manure is the next best thing. Propagate by division.

Jasminum spp. Jasmine or jessamine

The common white or poet's jasmine has been seen in cottage gardens since 1548. This twining plant is still a great favourite and it's not hard to see why. It produces numerous small, white and very fragrant flowers and, if you grow it on your own cottage wall, it'll perfume your days all summer. In colder districts it needs a south wall and some shelter. Thomas Hill recommends growing it over a willow arbour, where it 'not only defendeth the heat of the sun but yieldeth a delectable smel much refreshing the sitters under it'.

The winter jasmine (*Jasminum nudiflorum*) can be grown as a wall shrub. It bears bright yellow flowers from November to February and soon covers a wall, though it needs tying in initially.

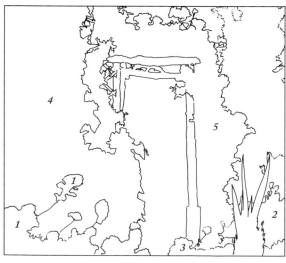

1 *Centranthus ruber*

2 *Campanula persicifolia*

3 *Alchemilla mollis*

4 *Hedera canariensis* 'Gloire de Marengo'

5 *Rosa* 'Albertine'

The large, evergreen leaves of ivy make it an excellent climber, especially where the soil or conditions are not ideal. It's a plant that will grow almost anywhere.

J. stephanense is much more modern, but worth growing for its variegated creamy yellow, young leaves and fragrant, pink flowers in summer.

Propagate jasmines by layering or hardwood cuttings in autumn.

Lathyrus odoratus SWEET PEA

The sweet pea is a twining, summer-flowering annual which first came to Britain from Sicily in 1697. By 1754 there were three colours, but in 1870 Henry Eckford began a very successful breeding programme and by 1900 there were 264 varieties. The flowers were smaller than modern varieties and mostly had frilled edges, but the perfume was always mentioned as sweet and strong. They were great favourites with cottage gardeners.

Modern varieties were bred for size and began to lose their frilled edges and their fragrance. Now perfume has largely been bred back in, using varieties found in old cottage gardens where seed had been collected for generations. When selecting new varieties always ensure that perfume is mentioned in the description. There's no point in growing sweet peas that don't smell.

They come in a vast range of pastel colours and are very easy to raise each year from seed sown in February in special sweet-pea tubes (or rolled-up newspapers or even old toilet-roll centres) in a coldframe. Grow them in full sun.

Lathyrus latifolius PERENNIAL SWEET PEA

This perennial sweet pea is a European native, first mentioned in 1596, and was enthusiastically grown by the earliest cottagers. The species has rose-pink flowers, but there are good white, pink and red forms too. Propagate by seed sown in spring, and once the plants are established, don't move them. Grow in full sun. They look especially good when they are allowed to scramble through a shrub.

Lathyrus nervosus LORD ANSON'S BLUE PEA

Brought from Patagonia in 1744, this perennial has clear blue, perfumed flowers. It's very rare, but if you can find it, grow it.

Lonicera periclymenum HONEYSUCKLE or WOODBINE

A British native and an absolute must. I say that not purely sentimentally, but because the common honeysuckle is, in my opinion, still the very best. In summer it has gloriously scented, creamy white flowers which are purple or yellow on the outside. The flowers darken with age in a most attractive way and they're followed by bright red berries.

Honeysuckle is a twining plant that will grow in sunshine or shade, flowering slightly better in sun, but less prone to attack from greenfly in shade. Propagate by layering.

Other good varieties include the early Dutch honeysuckle, called 'Belgica', with red/purple

The perennial sweet pea is an old cottage plant and invaluable for growing through shrubs and over herbaceous plants to give another season of flower.

flowers fading to yellow; its similar, later cousin 'Serotina'; and the wonderful *L. tellmanniana* with large, red buds opening to coppery yellow flowers.

Parthenocissus quinquefolia Virginia creeper

A very popular, rampant, self-clinging climber introduced to Britain in 1629. The leaves are glossy and attractively shaped and turn brilliant red in autumn.

The later introduction *P. henryana* has leaves beautifully veined with white. It's especially good on a shaded north wall. It grows in any fertile soil and can be propagated by layering or hardwood cuttings.

Passiflora caerulea Passion flower

Perhaps surprisingly the passion flower has been a favourite cottage garden climber in warmer counties since 1609. Given a south-facing wall, it makes a very vigorous twining plant and should produce many flowers during the summer. They're undoubtedly one of the most complex, interesting and beautiful of all flowers and folklore has it that they represent the instruments of Christ's Passion – the nails, the crown of thorns, the wounds and the halo. Plants may get cut down by frost during the winter but, if the base is protected, they generally re-appear the following spring. Propagate by cuttings in late summer in the coldframe.

Ribes speciosum Fuchsia-flowered gooseberry

Grown in Britain since 1828, this spiny wall shrub bears superb, pendulous, red flowers in late spring. The foliage is glossy and semi-evergreen. In colder districts it needs a south-facing wall (where it requires tying in), but will thrive in any reasonably fertile soil. Propagate by hardwood cuttings in autumn.

Rosa spp. and varieties

Climbing and rambling roses are obviously such a traditional part of the cottage garden that there's simply no question of excluding them. Older varieties have such superb shape and perfume that they're irresistible, even though some of them flower for only a short period.

Many of the newer climbers in particular flower repeatedly and lots of them produce the most exquisite perfume. There's absolutely no point and no need either to buy roses that have had the perfume bred out.

The big difference between ramblers and climbers is this. Ramblers are more vigorous and will give a superb show of flower but generally only in one fine flush. The flowers are smaller and borne in large clusters. Climbers are less vigorous but flower continually, on and off, during the summer or have one good flush and another later but with fewer flowers, which are generally larger but sparser. Prune ramblers after flowering by

'Bobbie James' is a vigorous rambler rose ideal for growing through quite large trees.

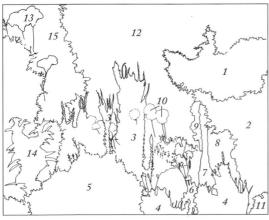

1 *Rosa glauca*

2 *Cotinus coggygria* 'Royal Purple'

3 *Linaria purpurea*

4 *Eschscholzia californica* 'Alba'

5 *Cistus hybridus*

6 *Lychnis coronaria*

7 *Atriplex hortensis rubra*

8 *Astrantia major* 'Rubra'

9 *Campanula persicifolia*

10 *Allium aflatunense*

11 *Lotus hirsutus*

12 *Rosa* 'New Dawn'

13 *Rosa* 'Pink Peace'

14 *Lilium* 'Corsage'

15 *Buddleia davidii*

The climbing rose 'New Dawn' dominates this border with its large, white flowers which are touched with a soft pink flush.

removing old wood and shortening side shoots. Climbers are pruned in early spring in much the same way.

Climbers and ramblers can be grown against a wall or fence or they can be trained up pergolas, arches, obelisks and arbours. Both need tying in. When training, always try to pull branches downwards to restrict growth and encourage flowering. The majority prefer a south- or west-facing wall, but there are one or two that are successful facing north or east. Propagate by hardwood cuttings in autumn.

As with clematis, there are hundreds of varieties to choose from and it's impossible to describe them all here. This list includes many that were grown in old cottage gardens and those which have, in my view, an old cottage garden appeal. Still, you'd be well advised to visit a specialist nursery or to get hold of a catalogue. If you do visit, do so when you want your roses to flower, see them blooming and order for later delivery or, if they're pot-grown, take them away with you.

That roses were appreciated for their ornamental quality in the sixteenth century is confirmed by Thomas Tusser, who recommends that they should be grown as decoration in the fruit plot:

The Goosebery, Respis [raspberry],
and Roses, al three,
with strawberies under them trimly agree.

Most of the 'old-fashioned' climbers we associate with cottage gardens were raised in France from the nineteenth century, but long before that a few varieties were dug up from the wild and were certainly grown by cottagers.

The dog rose (*Rosa canina*) entwined itself through their hedges to provide flowers in summer and could still be used in the same way today. Its simple, single, pink, perfumed flowers are a real delight and they're followed by bright red hips in autumn. The hips are used to make rose-hip syrup as they have been by generations of country folk.

If you've ever allowed one of your budded modern roses to be overcome by suckers, you could well have discovered some beautiful pink blooms and prolific hips. That's because the rootstock on which it has been budded is a close relation of the old dog rose.

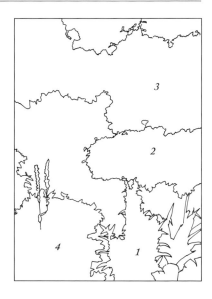

This is an imaginative planting of roses,
using relatively modern varieties.
'American Pillar' was introduced from
the USA in 1909 and 'Eye Paint' came
from New Zealand in 1975.

1 *Penstemon* 'John Nash'
2 *Rosa* 'Eye Paint'
3 *Rosa* 'American Pillar'
4 *Anemone magellanica*

Climbing or rambler roses are the ideal plants to clothe a garden arch. In a small garden it's probably best to choose varieties that flower on and off all summer, but the once-flowering old-fashioned varieties are very hard to resist.

The sweet briar or eglantine rose (*R. eglanteria*) is another native that's been grown for centuries in gardens. It should certainly grace some part of your cottage garden and is also at its best growing through a hedge. It has soft pink, single flowers followed by good, red hips. But its real charm lies in the fragrance of apples given off by the leaves, especially after rain. Trim the plants back each year to encourage fresh, young growth, because the tips give off the strongest perfume.

All old-fashioned roses are susceptible to disease, so may need spraying.

Old Climbers

'Aimée Vibert'. A Noisette rose bearing clusters of small, double, pure white flowers with yellow stamens and a fine perfume. Good, glossy foliage. Repeat flowers. Introduced in 1828.

'Blairii No. 2'. This Bourbon rose has pale pink outer petals, deeper pink inside and with a superb perfume. It flowers once and is recommended for a north wall. Raised in 1845.

'Blush Noisette'. Small, semi-double flowers, pink fading to white throughout the summer. Good perfume. Raised in 1816.

'Gloire de Dijon'. A Bourbon rose with pendulous flowers of buff-yellow tinted with pink and superbly perfumed. Flowers continuously and is good on a north wall. Raised in 1853.

'Guinée'. A Hybrid, the deepest crimson of them all. The flowers are large and very well scented. Flowers once with a few blooms later. Raised in 1938.

'Lady Hillingdon'. A Tea rose whose warm apricot-yellow flowers look marvellous against its bronze foliage and whose perfume is magnificent. Flowers through the summer. Raised in 1917. Not to be missed

'Madame Alfred Carrière'. This Noisette rose bears large blooms of white with a tinge of pink and a lovely perfume. Flowers all summer and is ideal for a north wall. Introduced in 1879.

Rosa banksiae normalis. A vigorous Banksian rose with perfumed, single, white flowers and thornless stems. Introduced in 1877.

Rosa banksiae alba plena. As above but with double flowers. Introduced in 1807.

Rosa banksiae lutea. The yellow Banksian rose. Produces large trusses of small, double, yellow flowers in late spring. Slightly scented. Introduced in 1825.

'Zéphirine Drouhin'. A Bourbon rose bearing semi-double, deep pink flowers with a strong perfume which are produced all summer. Thornless and good on a north-facing wall. Introduced in 1868.

The very old variety 'Rambling Rector', which produces large trusses of white flowers with yellow stamens, is ideal for growing through trees.

Ramblers

'Albéric Barbier'. A Wichuriana rose whose yellow buds open to large, creamy yellow flowers with an excellent perfume. A very reliable flowerer with one large flush followed by a few flowers later. Recommended for a north-facing wall. Introduced in 1900.

'Albertine'. This Wichuriana is one of the most popular. It has large, copper-pink flowers and an excellent perfume. Introduced in 1921. Flowers once.

'Félicité et Perpétue'. A much-branched Sempervirens variety with creamy white flowers and a delicate fragrance. Flowers once in late summer. Introduced in 1827.

'Léontine Gervaise'. A Wichuriana with fragrant double flowers of clear pink tinged with orange. Shiny foliage. Once-flowering. Introduced in 1903.

'May Queen'. A Wichuriana bearing large, deep pink, scented flowers in a single, magnificent flush. Introduced in 1898.

'Rambling Rector'. This Moschata hybrid is worth growing just for the name! Large clusters of small, creamy white, semi-double flowers with a fine perfume. Probably introduced in Tudor times.

'Veilchenblau'. A Multiflora bearing large clusters of flowers of magenta fading to blue, purple and then lavender with a fine fragrance. Introduced in 1909.

Newer Climbers

'Anne Dakin'. An attractive variety with flowers of the 'old-fashioned' shape. Coral pink fading to creamy pink in summer. Introduced in 1974.

'Breath of Life'. Apricot-pink, Hybrid Tea flowers with a pleasant fragrance. Repeat flowering and not too vigorous. Introduced in 1981.

'Compassion'. Salmon-pink, Hybrid Tea flowers suffused with orange and a superb fragrance. Its repeat flowering and fine, glossy foliage make it one of the best. Introduced in 1973.

'Climbing Crimson Glory'. A sport of the favourite bush rose, it produces masses of deep crimson blooms in early summer and a few later too. Excellent perfume. Introduced in 1935.

'Dreamgirl'. Delicate coral-pink flowers with the 'old-fashioned' shape and an excellent fragrance. Introduced in 1944.

'Climbing Ena Harkness'. 'Ena Harkness' is a favourite bush rose with crimson/scarlet flowers with a fine perfume. The heads tend to droop, so it's better as a climber. One flush in summer and a few flowers later. Introduced in 1954.

'Golden Showers'. Masses of golden-yellow, semi-double flowers throughout the summer. Excellent fragrance and good for a north wall. Introduced in 1956.

'Highfield'. A fine yellow sport of 'Compassion' and just as good. Introduced in 1980.

'Kathleen Harrop'. A sport of 'Zéphirine Drouhin' but with soft pink, very fragrant flowers which repeat. Introduced in 1919.

'Lady Sylvia'. A lovely deep pink suffused with apricot, and with a wonderful fragrance. Repeat flowers. Introduced in 1933.

'Lawrence Johnston'. A strong grower with large, double yellow flowers with a strong

Old cottage gardeners grew wild roses through their hedges and there's no better way to brighten up an otherwise dull boundary. Even better, grow roses and clematis together, like this rose 'New Dawn' with the clematis 'Perle d'Azur'.

fragrance. Once-flowering. Introduced in 1923.

'Madame Grégoire Staechelin'. Huge, deep pink flowers in clusters and with an exquisite fragrance. Once-flowering. Introduced in 1927.

'Maigold'. Bronze/yellow, semi-double flowers with golden stamens and a strong perfume. Flowers once with a few blooms later. Introduced in 1953.

'Mrs Herbert Stevens'. A Tea rose with white flowers tinged with green and a delicate yet strong perfume. Flowers once. Introduced in 1922.

'New Dawn'. Large clusters of silvery pink flowers with a fruity fragrance and glossy foliage. Introduced in 1930.

'Paul Lede'. A Tea rose which has a lovely old-fashioned look. Buff-yellow flowers with a superb perfume and very free, repeat flowering. Introduced in 1913.

'Pink Perpétue'. Large clusters of deep pink, almost red flowers throughout the summer. An excellent rose, but only a slight fragrance. Good on a north wall. Introduced in 1965.

'Souvenir de Claudius Denoyel'. Strongly perfumed, bright crimson flowers in June and again later. Vigorous. Introduced in 1920.

Tropaeolum majus NASTURTIUM

A rampant hardy annual introduced to Britain from Peru in 1684, this easy-to-grow, twining plant has been a favourite cottage plant ever since. In Elizabethan times it was called 'yellow larkes heels'. It has highly attractive, shield-shaped leaves and masses of lovely trumpet flowers in bright yellow, red, orange, crimson and pink. It's available with single, semi-double and double flowers too. The seeds can be pickled to use as a substitute for capers. It will flower from early summer to the first frosts and does best in poor soil. Sow it in spring where it's to flower and stand back!

There's surely no easier climber to grow than the nasturtium. It can be sown direct in the soil without any preparation whatever and it will often resow itself the following year. It's an ideal first plant for children to sow too.

Canary creeper (*Tropaeolum peregrinum*) came to Britain in 1810 and this has small, yellow flowers. It's best sown inside and grown on in the frame. Otherwise grow it in the same way as nasturtium.

Look out too for the tuberous-rooted perennial *T. tuberosum* 'Ken Aslet', with typical nasturtium flowers in yellow and scarlet. In colder areas it's worth covering the tubers with a thick mulch in winter. Propagate by division.

Vitis vinifera GRAPE VINE
Grapes were grown widely in England in the monasteries and, after the dissolution, they were to be found in cottage gardens. Their cultivation for wine is covered on page 246.

For purely decorative purposes, choose varieties with large leaves turning red and purple in autumn. They'll also produce fruit, of course, but if they're allowed to ramble freely, it'll be small.

The variety 'Brandt' is a vigorous variety often used for wine. The leaves turn purple in autumn and the fruits are numerous and deep red.

The most spectacular of all vines is *V. coignetiae* which has huge leaves turning crimson-scarlet in autumn, but it needs a lot of space.

Generally vines, which are twining plants, like a sunny position. The best autumn leaf colours come from plants growing in poor soil. Propagate by layering or hardwood cuttings in the coldframe in autumn.

Border Plants

Of course, there are hundreds of plants that will fit well into a cottage garden. I've restricted myself mainly to those that are old or derived from 'old-fashioned' plants that were grown in the earlier cottage gardens. In a new garden there's no reason at all to stick to the list, but if you want to keep the genuine 'feel' of a country cottage, you'll need to choose carefully.

I think it's vital, especially if your budget's tight, to make sure that your plants can be grown and propagated easily in the way they have been for centuries by gardeners with limited facilities. You'll note that even when you choose older plants, better, newer varieties of them are often available.

I've classified the plants in the following lists according to height. Obviously you'll want to place the tallest plants at the back and the shortest at the front of the border – usually. A little variation of this rule adds interest and avoids the 'serried ranks' look.

In fact I have included some slightly taller plants among those suggested for the front of the border, but they're ones that will flop slightly to break up the hard line of the path edging.

Cottage gardens have always relied mainly on herbaceous plants, but you'll need at least a framework of shrubs and especially evergreens that will give you something to look at in winter.

Bulbs should not be forgotten: they really take up no space at all and many will provide a welcome show of colour when there's little else about.

All types of plant will be grown in the same mixed borders of course, so my lists include every one you'll be likely to grow – shrubs, herbaceous plants, roses and bulbs – simply classified by size. Only the food plants (which start on page 211) have been deliberately excluded. But don't discount the possibility of raising vegetables and fruit in the borders too. They can look very attractive grown that way and you'll be carrying on a tradition that began when our ancestors started gardening. Earlier gardeners did not categorize their plants as we do today, so it was quite common to find patches of vegetables and herbs growing amonst the flowers

Planting

Bare-rooted shrubs should be planted from autumn to spring exactly as for trees (see page 100), except that no stake is necessary.

Herbaceous perennials can go in during spring or autumn unless they're pot-grown, in which case any time will do. They're generally planted in prepared soil, using a trowel and firming with your fingers (see below). A dressing of organic fertilizer and a good watering in afterwards are essential.

Bulbs that flower in spring are planted in late summer and autumn, summer flowerers in spring and autumn flowerers in summer. There are exceptions, but normally it's best to plant in groups either with a trowel or, if in heavy soil, by taking out a hole, putting in a layer of grit and covering. The grit simply protects the vulnerable base-plate.

Before planting it's always a good idea to spend a bit of time improving the soil with garden compost, manure or one of the alternatives. For plants requiring free drainage, include an equal quantity of coarse grit.

Scatter a little organic fertilizer and then plant with a trowel, making sure that the plant is at the level it grew in the nursery. Firm down well with your fingers and always water in well afterwards.

Plants for the Back of the Border

Plants that are suitable for the back of the border will be mostly shrubs and herbaceous plants. There are, of course, some bulbs that are tall enough, but my own view is that they're much better used among lower-growing plants to rise above them and add another level of interest.

In island beds like those in the artisan's garden, these taller plants will go in the middle rather than at the back.

Shrubs

Berberis vulgaris BARBERRY
Height: 1.8–2.7 m (6–9 ft). Spread: 1.5–1.8 m (5–6 ft). Flowers: Late spring to early summer.
Grown since the sixteenth century, the berries of the barberry were pickled, or candied and used to decorate meat. The native species is no longer grown because it harbours wheat rust. There are better decorative varieties, many of which also make superb, impenetrable hedges. They grow well in shade and in poor soils. Propagate deciduous species by half-ripe cuttings in late summer and evergreens by hardwood cutting in autumn.

B. julianae. A dense evergreen, especially good for hedging. Flowers are yellow followed by shiny, black fruits.

B. lologensis. Evergreen with an upright habit and bright orange flowers.

B. ottawensis 'Superba'. A fine variety with purple leaves.

B. stenophylla. A superb, graceful shrub with arching branches swathed with yellow flowers in spring. There are also some orange varieties.

B. thunbergii. A useful shrub with green leaves and excellent for its superb autumn colour and bright red berries. The variety 'Atropurpurea' has red/purple leaves. Dwarf varieties are suitable for the middle of the border (see page 142).

Buddleia davidii BUTTERFLY BUSH
Height: 2.4 m (8 ft). Spread: 1.5 m (5 ft).
Flowers: Late summer.
Not introduced until 1890, but well known to cottagers from the late Victorian era onwards, buddleia is especially prized as an attractor of butterflies in their hundreds. It produces long, cylindrical clusters of florets in several colours from white, through pink and blue to deepest purple. Grow in sunshine in any soil. Prune last year's growth back hard in early spring. Propagate by hardwood cuttings in autumn.

Chaenomeles speciosa FLOWERING QUINCE
Height: 1.2 m (4 ft). Spread: 1.5–1.8 m (5–6 ft).
Flowers: Late winter to mid-spring.
Can be grown as a free-standing shrub. See under 'Climbers', on page 108, for a full description.

Cytisus scoparius COMMON BROOM
Height: 1.5 m (5 ft). Spread: 1.2 m (4 ft).
Flowers: Late spring.
A native British shrub, well-known to the gardeners of the Middle Ages, common broom bears butter-yellow flowers in profusion, rather like gorse but without the spines. It grows well in full sun and will flower best in poor soil. Prune carefully after flowering, avoiding cutting into old wood. Propagate by half-ripe cuttings in summer. There are several named varieties, the best being:

'Andreanus' – yellow marked brown and crimson.

'Cornish Cream' – creamy white.

'Firefly' – deep yellow and crimson.

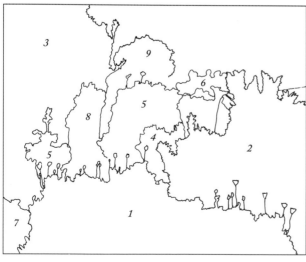

1 *Osteospermum* 'Lady Leitrim'
2 *Lonicera nitida* 'Baggesen's Gold'
3 *Rosa* 'Canary Bird'
4 *Lavandula stoechas pedunculata*
5 *Lunaria annua*
6 *Tulipa* 'Black Swan'
7 *Alchemilla mollis*
8 *Aquilegia* 'Hensol Harebell'
9 *Cytisus praecox* 'Allgold'

Shrubs provide both flower and foliage colour in this spring border.

'Fulgens' – orange and crimson.

The Warminster broom (*Cytisus praecox*), which is slightly more compact, and has masses of cream flowers, arose in 1867. There are a few good varieties:

'Albus' – white.

'Allgold' – yellow.

'Gold Spear' – deep yellow.

Deutzia hybrida

Height: 1.5–2.4 m (5–8 ft). Spread: 1.2–1.5 m (4–5 ft). Flowers: Early summer.

Deutzias have been grown in cottage gardens since the nineteenth century, with many new hybrids becoming available from France in the early twentieth century. Look for 'Magicien', with purple buds opening to reveal pink, white-edged flowers. 'Mont Rose' is smaller with pink flowers and yellow stamens, while 'Pink Pompom' is larger with arching branches hung with double pink flowers fading to white.

D. scabra is an older species and more vigorous, growing to 1.8 m (6 ft). 'Pride of Rochester' is double-flowered with white inside and pink outside, while 'Candidissima' is double white.

Deutzias are easy to grow in any well-drained soil in sun or part-shade. Propagate by hardwood cuttings in autumn or softwood cuttings in summer.

Forsythia spectabilis

Height: 1.8 m (6 ft). Spread: 1.5 m (5 ft). Flowers: Spring.

One of the best-known shrubs of all and deservedly popular. Its arching branches are massed with yellow flowers and it's very easy to grow. There are now several named varieties, but this older one remains one of the best.

Look out too for 'Lynwood', 'Beatrix Farrand' and 'Karl Sax', which tend to have larger flowers. Forsythia can be grown successfully in any reasonable soil in either full sun or part-shade. Propagate by hardwood cuttings in autumn.

Garrya elliptica SILK TASSEL BUSH

Height: 4 m (13 ft). Spread: 3 m (10 ft). Flowers: Early winter to late winter.

Introduced in 1828, this elegant evergreen became a cottage favourite. It produces long, silvery tassels when there's little else in flower. Look for the variety 'James Roof', which has the longest tassels of all. It's especially good on a north-facing wall, thriving on most soils, but dislikes cold winds. Propagate by hardwood cuttings in autumn.

Garrya elliptica *'James Roof' is a vigorous male variety with catkins that can be as long as 20 cm (8 in). It's not an old variety, having been raised in California in about 1950, but old cottage gardeners would have gladly grown it.*

The shrub in the front of this border, Berberis thunbergii *'Rose Glow', is a modern introduction and probably got its variegation from a virus.*

Kerria japonica 'Pleniflora' JEW'S MALLOW
Height: 1.8–2.4 m (6–8 ft). Spread: 1.8 m (6 ft).
Flowers: Spring.
A vigorous, suckering shrub that needs regular pruning to keep it in control. It may also need to be restrained with a spade at the roots from time to time to stop it spreading, so it's not for the tiny garden. Well-grown, the green, cane-like shoots hung with yellow balls are most attractive. It'll grow in almost any soil but prefers a little shade to prevent the flowers fading. Propagate by detaching a shoot or two with a piece of root.

Leycesteria formosa HIMALAYAN HONEYSUCKLE or NUTMEG TREE
Height: 1.8–2.4 m (6–8 ft). Spread: 1.5 m (5 ft).
Flowers: Late summer/autumn.
This is a vigorous shrub introduced in 1824. It produces a clump of tall, hollow, green stems, topped by white flowers with conspicuous red bracts, followed by purple fruits in warmer areas. It needs a retentive soil in sun or part-shade.

Prune it hard to the ground every few years, or even every year, to keep it in check and growing tidily. Propagate by seed or hardwood cuttings in spring. The fruits are very attractive to pheasants so they were planted as cover on estates and the berries were much sought after by poachers!

Myrtus communis MYRTLE
Height: 3 m (10 ft). Spread: 2 m (6 ft 6 in).
Flowers: Late summer.
The aromatic, evergreen common myrtle has been grown in England since the sixteenth century, when it was valued for its aromatic properties and recommended for planting round arbours. Its white flowers are followed by purple/black berries. Unfortunately it's not reliably hardy; it needs full sun and preferably a south-facing wall. Myrtle grows on any soil and is especially recommended for seaside areas. Propagate by half-ripe cuttings in late autumn.

Philadelphus spp. MOCK ORANGE .
Height: 1–2.4 m (3–8 ft). Spread: 1–1.8 m (3–6 ft). Flowers: Early to mid-summer.
A relatively recent introduction at the end of the nineteenth century. Many hybrids have been raised since, a number of which have the true cottage garden qualities. Most produce white flowers, some with attractive markings and excellent perfume. They thrive in almost any soil in sunshine and flower in summer. Propagate by hardwood cuttings in autumn.

'Belle Etoile' is one of the best, with single, creamy white flowers splashed purple at the base and an excellent perfume.

'Manteau d'Hermine' is much more compact and could do for the middle of the border too. It has superb, creamy white, double flowers and is also very fragrant.

'Beauclerk' has large, single, creamy white flowers with a band of cerise towards the centre.

Ribes sanguineum FLOWERING CURRANT
Height: 1.8 m (6 ft). Spread: 1.5 m (5 ft).
Flowers: Spring.
A popular and easy-flowering shrub introduced from the USA in 1826. The flowers are deep pink with white petals and hang down from leafless branches at first, but are soon complemented by fresh, green, young leaves. The whole bush has a pungent smell of blackcurrants.

There are several varieties: 'Tydeman's White' has white flowers, 'King Edward VII' is deep crimson, while 'Pulborough Scarlet' has red flowers. Look out too for the strongly clove-scented *Ribes odoratum*, which bears attractive yellow flowers. They'll grow in any soil in sun or light shade. Prune annually, removing old wood to the base. Propagate by hardwood cuttings in autumn.

Rosa spp. and varieties
There are, of course, hundreds of rose varieties to choose from, so I've listed only those I think most suited to the cottage garden. This, you'll notice,

The pure white flowers of the mock orange produce the sweetest perfume that pervades the whole garden. It's one of the easiest shrubs of all to grow and definitely not to be missed.

doesn't include many modern Hybrid Teas or floribundas. Somehow they don't seem quite to match the rather looser, informal nature of growth of older varieties, and the more stylized shape of the blooms and the vivid colours tend to jar. You may agree. Obviously what you need before you buy is a specialist's catalogue or, better still, to visit a nursery at flowering time and make a choice based on first-hand knowledge.

However, my list would not exclude modern roses entirely. There are some excellent modern shrub roses, and the range of 'English' roses has great advantages. The latter combine the old-fashioned cabbage shape with the modern rose's ability to repeat flower, so they're a great improvement for the new cottage garden.

A few words of warning: the breeders of some of the newer roses have concentrated on other factors and ignored the plant's ability to resist disease. So a few are prone to attack from rust, blackspot and mildew. If you don't want to spray regularly, they're to be avoided. However, disease resistance is a top priority with breeders, so in the main modern varieties tend to be more disease resistant than older ones.

Since I would rarely contemplate a rose without perfume, all my selection can be considered to be scented unless otherwise stated.

'Abraham Darby'. Height: 1.5 m (5 ft). Spread: 1.5 m (5 ft). An English rose bearing deeply cupped blooms of apricot-yellow from early summer to autumn.

'Ballerina'. Height: 1.2 m (4 ft). Spread: 1.2 m (4 ft). A modern shrub rose with large, hydrangea-like heads of small, single, pink flowers. One of the most continuous and free-flowering of all, but with only a slight scent.

'Baroness Rothschild'. Height: 1.8 m (6 ft). Spread: 1.2 m (4 ft). A very large-flowered, pink Hybrid Perpetual rose, freely flowering in summer and again in the autumn.

'Belle Amour'. Height: 1.5 m (5 ft). Spread: 1.8 m (6 ft). A strong-growing moss rose with dusky purple flowers and a good perfume. Flowers once in the summer.

'Belle de Crécy'. Height: 1.2 m (4 ft). Spread: 1 m (3 ft). A Gallica rose, which is the parent and forerunner of all the cottage roses. It opens rich pink and fades to purple. Flowers once in the summer.

'Blanc Double de Coubert'. Height: 1.5 m (5 ft). Spread: 1.8 m (6 ft). A Rugosa rose with semi-double, ivory-white blooms throughout the summer.

'Boule de Neige'. Height: 1.5 m (5 ft). Spread:

That I suggest growing a rose with only a little perfume is a recommendation for its other qualities. 'Ballerina' is not to be missed because it flowers reliably right through the summer, looking superb when the flowers are young and even when they begin to fade.

1 m (3 ft). Small, white, ball-shaped flowers with a fine perfume.

'Buff Beauty'. Height: 1.5 m (5 ft). Spread: 1.2 m (4 ft). A fine modern shrub rose with buds opening deep apricot and maturing to buff-yellow throughout the summer.

'Cardinal de Richelieu'. Height: 1.2 m (4 ft). Spread: 1 m (3 ft). A rich, dark purple Gallica. Flowers once in summer.

'Centifolia'. Height: 1.8 m (6 ft). Spread: 1.5 m (5 ft). Grown in the sixteenth century, a superb pink and very heavily perfumed.

'Comte de Chambord'. Height: 1 m (3ft). Spread: 60 cm (2 ft). A superb Damask rose which repeat flowers through the summer. The flowers are strong pink with lovely, ruffled petals and a fine fragrance.

'Fru Dagmar Hastrup'. Height: 1.5 m (5 ft). Spread: 1.5 m (5 ft). A fine Rugosa with very attractive, single, pink flowers throughout the summer and a stunning display of large, orange hips in autumn.

'Frühlingsgold'. Height: 2.1 m (7 ft). Spread: 2.1 m (7 ft). A large, arching, modern shrub rose with richly fragrant, creamy yellow flowers in early summer.

'Général Kléber'. Height: 1.2 m (4 ft). Spread: 1 m (3 ft). One of the best Moss roses. Soft pink with a superb perfume. Flowers once in summer.

'Gertrude Jekyll'. Height: 1.2 m (4 ft). Spread: 1 m (3 ft). A deep, rich pink English rose with large, rosette-shaped flowers. The scent was selected for making real rose perfume for the first time in 250 years. Flowers all summer.

'Golden Wings'. Height: 1.2 m (4 ft). Spread: 1.2 m (4 ft). A modern shrub rose with large, single, yellow flowers all summer.

'Graham Thomas'. Height: 1.2 m (4 ft).

'Graham Thomas' is a fine English rose with a long flowering habit and the typical 'cabbage' blooms of the older roses. In my garden the glossy foliage has proved to be fairly resistant to disease.

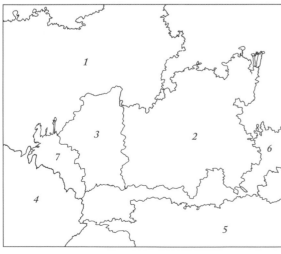

1 *Rosa* 'Canary Bird'

2 *Lunaria annua*

3 *Aquilegia* 'Hensol Harebell'

4 *Lotus hirsutus*

5 *Sedum* 'Ruby Glow'

6 *Myosotis scorpioides*

7 *Lavandula stoechas*
pedunculata

Here a standard rose provides
height in the border above a
colourful display of herbaceous
perennials and biennials.

Spread: 1.2 m (4 ft). An English rose with cup-shaped flowers in rich yellow all summer.

'Heritage'. Height: 1.2 m (4 ft). Spread: 1.2 m (4 ft). An English rose with very fine, cup-shaped, pink flowers all summer.

'La Reine Victoria'. Height: 1.5 m (5 ft). Spread: 1.2 m (4 ft). Bourbon rose with delicate pink, cup-shaped flowers all summer.

'Nevada'. Height: 2.1 m (7 ft). Spread: 2.4 m (8 ft). One of the most striking modern shrubs with large, semi-double, creamy white flowers in early summer. Not scented.

'Queen of Denmark'. Height: 1.5 m (5 ft). Spread: 1.2 m (4 ft). One of the best Albas with strong pink flowers, paler on the margins. Flowers once in summer.

Rosa gallica officinalis. Height: 1.2 m (4 ft). Spread: 1.2 m (4 ft). The 'apothecary's rose' with bright crimson flowers and golden stamens.

Rosa moyesii 'Geranium'. Height 2.4 m (8 ft). Spread: 2.1 m (7 ft). A large shrub rose with great arching branches with single, bright red flowers followed by lovely, orange, flagon-shaped hips. Flowers once in summer.

Rosa mundi. Height: 1.2 m (4 ft). Spread: 1.2 m (4 ft). The oldest striped rose from the sixteenth century. Pink with pink/purple stripes. Flowers once in summer.

Rosa mutabilis. Height: 1.8 m (6 ft). Spread: 1.2 m (4 ft). A China rose with copper-coloured buds opening to yellow and fading to pink. Flowers once in summer.

Rosa xanthina 'Canary Bird'. Height: 2.4 m (8 ft). Spread: 1.8 m (6 ft). Masses of single yellow flowers borne on ferny foliage in early spring. Unfortunately it has no scent. One of the earliest roses to flower and often grown as a standard.

'William Lobb'. Height: 1.8 m (6 ft). Spread: 1.5 m (5 ft). Dusky purple and prolific. Flowers once in summer.

Sambucus nigra ELDER
Height: 3 m (10 ft). Spread: 2.4 m (8 ft).
Flowers: Summer.
A native shrub or small tree, long cultivated and still well known for its aromatic white flowers and black berries used for cordial and wine-making. Elder is ideal as a hedge plant, but in the small garden and for purely decorative purposes it's best to grow one of the varieties with decorative leaves.

'Laciniata' has deeply cut, green leaves, but the brightest is 'Aurea' with golden leaves. Cut back to two buds each spring to keep the plant to size and to generate the brightest colouring. It grows absolutely anywhere. Propagate by hardwood cuttings in autumn.

Syringa vulgaris LILAC
Height: 2.4–3 m (8–10 ft). Spread: 1.5–1.8 m (5–6 ft). Flowers: Mid-summer.
Introduced to England in the sixteenth century, lilac has naturalized itself in many parts of the

The wonderful, large flowers of lilacs will perfume the whole garden. They come in many colours and this one, 'Congo', is among the best lilac reds. Look for micropropagated plants to avoid suckering.

country. The common variety has lilac flowers, of course, with a superb perfume and is still one of the best. It does, however, have a nasty habit of suckering, but modern propagation methods have solved the problem. It's now possible to buy plants that have been raised by micropropagation and these don't sucker. They'll grow in any soil and are especially useful in lime. They'll flower best in a sunny spot. Propagate by layering. Look out also for some of the many varieties – there are over 500, but here are a few:

'Congo' – lilac/red.

'Hugo Koster' – purple/crimson.

'Madame Charles Souchet' – soft lilac/blue.

'Mont Blanc' – green in bud, opening white.

'Souvenir de Louis Späth' – wine-red.

'Belle de Nancy' – red in bud, opening lilac/pink; double.

'Charles Joly' – dark purple-red; double.

'Katherine Havemeyer' – purple/lavender.

'Madame Lemoine' – pure white; double.

'Président Grévy' – lilac; very large, double flowers.

For small gardens it's also worth searching out *Syringa meyeri* 'Palibin', which has violet-purple flowers on a small-to-medium-sized shrub.

Viburnum opulus GUELDER ROSE

Height: 1.5–1.8 m (5–6 ft). Spread: 1.2–1.5 m (4–5 ft). Flowers: Early to mid-summer.

A large, vigorous native, grown in gardens since the sixteenth century, the guelder rose bears showy white flowers like those of lacecap hydrangeas, followed by glistening red berries and superb autumn foliage colour. It thrives in wet conditions.

An excellent and popular variety is the snowball tree (*Viburnum opulus* 'Roseum' or 'Sterile'). This produces white globes of flowers but no berries. Propagate by hardwood cuttings in autumn or half-ripe cuttings in late summer.

Viburnum tinus LAURUSTINUS

Height: 1.2–1.5 m (4–5 ft). Spread: 1.2–1.5 m (4–5 ft). Flowers: Winter to mid-spring.

A popular evergreen grown since the sixteenth century. The bushy habit and dark, glossy leaves make a superb background and the white, pink-budded flowers, which appear from autumn to early spring, are especially welcome. Propagate by softwood cuttings in summer or half-ripe cuttings in late summer.

The old favourite laurustinus is one of the best winter-flowering evergreens of all and deservedly popular. It will spread to form quite a large bush, but can be kept in control easily by judicious pruning. Especially recommended is the variety 'Eve Price', which is more compact with pink-tinged flowers.

Taxus baccata COMMON YEW

Height: 20 m (65 ft). Spread: 10 m (30 ft).

Obviously yew is far too big to grow unfettered as a tree (see page 107), but it was and still is widely used to make probably the best hedge of all and for topiary. Trimmed regularly, it makes a splendid specimen. It's not at all fussy as to soil, will tolerate quite heavy shade and can be cut hard back, even if quite old, when it will always re-grow. Propagate by seed sown in a coldframe in autumn or by stem cuttings also in a coldframe at the same time.

The Irish yew (*Taxus baccata* 'Fastigiata') was found in Ireland in 1780. It forms a green column and retains its shape well. There's also an attractive golden form, 'Fastigiata Aureomarginata'.

Herbaceous Plants

Acanthus mollis BEAR'S BREECHES
Height: 1.5 m (5 ft). Spread: 1 m (3 ft). Flowers: Late summer.
Grown since medieval times when it was known to herbalists as 'brank-ursine'. It has long, shiny, green leaves and produces tall spikes of foxglove-like mauve/pink flowers. It grows well in sun or shade. Propagate by seed sown in late spring or division in late winter.

Acanthus spinosus. Similar but with more divided, spiny leaves and it flowers more freely.

Achillea filipendulina YARROW
Height: 1.2 m (4 ft). Spread: 45 cm (1½ ft). Flowers: Late summer.
A well-known plant introduced in 1803. It has attractive, feathery leaves and plates of golden flowers. 'Gold Plate' is the best-known variety. It requires good drainage and a sunny spot. Propagate by seed, division or basal cuttings, all in spring.

Aconitum carmichaelii MONKSHOOD or WOLF'S BANE
Height: 1.2 m (4 ft). Spread: 30 cm (1 ft). Flowers: Autumn.
Introduced in 1886, though the original native monkshood was mentioned in the tenth century. This one is far better than the native species, having rich green foliage and Wedgwood-blue flowers, hooded on top. Note that all parts of the plant are poisonous. In medieval times the poison extracted from the plants was used to kill wolves when it was put on to arrow tips and on meat used as bait.

Monkshood likes full sun or part-shade and a retentive soil. Propagate by division in autumn.

Aconitum napellus is a native but has been cultivated in gardens since the sixteenth century. The flowers are indigo-blue and there are white and pink forms.

Alstroemeria PERUVIAN LILY
Height: 1–1.2 m (3–4 ft). Spread: 45 cm (1½ ft). Flowers: Early summer.
Introduced to Britain in the nineteenth century, the original species have been superseded by modern hybrids. Called 'princess lilies', they have small, lily-like flowers, beautifully marked and in various colours from yellow through orange and

The 'princess lilies' are modern hybrids of the traditional cottage alstroemeria and are particularly valuable for their long flowering period from early summer to the autumn.

pink to deep red. Give them full sun and good drainage. On heavy soils dig in some grit and compost and plant the roots deeply. Propagate by division.

Althaea spp. HOLLYHOCK
Height: 2.7 m (9 ft). Spread: 1 m (3 ft). Flowers: Summer/autumn.
Hollyhocks are synonymous with cottage gardens, where they've been grown since the sixteenth century. They're quite short-lived perennials, so need to be replaced frequently. They're easily raised from seed sown in spring, then should be potted up and over-wintered in a frame, and planted out the following spring. The plants must be staked. They're excellent bee plants.
Althaea rosea. Height: 2.4 m (8 ft). Spread: 1 m (3 ft). Flowers: Summer. The cup-shaped flowers are borne up the tall stem and can be white, yellow, cream, pink, red or deep crimson. Look out for the double-flowered 'Chater's Double'.
A. ficifolia. The 'Antwerp hollyhock' is another popular form, with yellow or orange flowers.

Anemone hybrida JAPANESE ANEMONE
Height: 1.5 m (5 ft). Spread: 60 cm (2 ft). Flowers: Autumn.
Introduced in 1848, this wonderful autumn flowerer produces heads of striking, rounded, pink blooms with golden stamens. There's also a stunning white, 'Honorine Jobert'. They'll grow in almost any soil in sun or part-shade and can become mildly invasive, though never a problem. Propagate by division or root cuttings in autumn.

Campanula spp. BELLFLOWER
All the tall bellflowers prefer sun and must be staked. They can be propagated by seed sown outside in late spring, by division in autumn or spring and by basal cuttings in early spring.

Campanula lactiflora. Height: 1.8 m (6 ft). Spread: 60 cm (2 ft). Flowers: All summer. A fine perennial, grown in cottage gardens since the early nineteenth century. It produces tall spikes topped by branching heads of lilac bellflowers.
C. latifolia. Height: 1.2 m (4 ft). Spread: 60 cm (2 ft). Flowers: Summer. This native of Britain makes a fine spire of violet, blue or white flowers. It seeds itself freely, so it may be necessary to cut down the spikes after flowering.
C. pyramidalis. Height: 1.5 m (5 ft). Spread: 60 cm (2 ft). Flowers: Summer. The 'chimney bellflower' has been grown since 1596 and is still one of the most attractive. It's a short-lived plant best treated as a biennial, but worth the extra trouble for its huge spikes of cup-shaped flowers in pale blue or white. Propagate by seed sown in late spring.

Delphinium spp.
Height: 1.2–2.4 m (4–8 ft). Spread: 1 m (3 ft). Flowers: Summer.
Among the classic cottage garden plants, the delphinium hybrids produce tall flower spires in all shades of blue, white and pink. Hybrids have been produced since 1875 and specialists are still breeding named varieties. They also produce selected seed, which is excellent value, but only if you're prepared to coddle the plants a little. Otherwise grow Pacific hybrids or Belladonna hybrids.
To produce the best spikes, they need a rich, well-fed soil, sun and shelter. It's essential to stake the tall flowering spikes as they grow. They can be raised from seed sown in May outside, but will not come true, so if you get a good one, propagate it by root cuttings in late winter.

Echinacea purpurea CONEFLOWER
Height: 1.2 m (4 ft). Spread: 45 cm (1½ ft). Flowers: Mid- to late summer.

The tall spires of delphiniums are an absolute 'must' for any cottage garden. They're easy to grow provided you can keep them free from the attentions of slugs. They're most vulnerable in the early spring when the soft, young shoots are just coming through.

Wonderful, large heads of daisy flowers in shades of purplish pink, rose-pink or white with a striking central boss of deep brown. It likes a sunny spot and well-drained, retentive soil.

The species came to England from the USA in 1699 and was widely grown in cottage gardens as it can be raised from seed. It has more or less disappeared now, to be replaced by even better hybrids like the rich mauve/crimson 'Robert Bloom' and a new variety, 'Magnus', with huge, rose-pink flowers. The hybids can be propagated by division but with some difficulty because in my experience they don't transplant well, so take root cuttings in late winter or collect and sow seed as soon as it's ripe.

Echinops ritro GLOBE THISTLE
Height: 1.2 m (4 ft). Spread: 60 cm (2 ft).
Flowers: Late summer.
Grown in gardens since 1570, this striking plant has jagged, thistle-like foliage and steely blue balls of flower on strong spikes. However, a much better plant is *Echinops ruthenicus*, which has more attractive foliage of shining green with a silvery sheen beneath and flowers of strong, bright blue. It will grow in most soils in full sun. Propagate by division or, for *E. ritro*, by seed.

Eremurus stenophyllus FOXTAIL LILY
Height: 1.5 m (5 ft). Spread: 60 cm (2 ft).
Flowers: Summer.
A majestic plant grown since 1885. It produces slender spikes of clear yellow flowers, fading to orange so that the two colours are on the plant together making a very attractive sight.

The delicate pink flowers of gypsophila in the front spill over the path and make a fine contrast to the bolder blooms of the ornamental onion. This excellent cottage plant is easy to grow and to raise from seed.

Perhaps even better is *Eremurus robustus*, introduced in 1874. It's a towering plant with 1.2-m (4-ft) flower spikes laden with pink flowers with a brown basal blotch and a green keel: very striking. It needs good drainage and full sun. New crowns should be planted just below the soil's surface and care must be taken not to damage them. Protect them with straw, compost or leaf litter in the first winter. New crowns tend to work upwards and these should be lifted and split off for re-planting after the leaves have died down in late summer. They're well worth the extra trouble.

Euphorbia characias SPURGE
Height: 1.2 m (4 ft). Spread: 1 m (3 ft). Flowers: Early spring.
A striking evergreen plant producing great towering spikes of green. Look out for the variety *Euphorbia characias wulfenii* with wider spikes forming large cylinders of greenish yellow. The varieties 'Lambrook Gold' and 'John Tomlinson' have improved yellow flowers.

They'll grow in most well-drained soils and in sun or shade. Propagate by seed or basal cuttings in spring, but avoid getting the irritant sap on your hands and particularly in your eyes.

Gypsophila paniculata BABY'S BREATH or CHALK PLANT
Height: 1–1.2 m (3–4 ft). Spread: 1.2 m (4 ft). Flowers: Summer.
Introduced in 1759, this plant produces a great cloud of white stars on a mass of delicate foliage. Grow 'Bristol Fairy' which is double white, and 'Flamingo' which is double pink. It's particularly valuable to contrast with bolder foliage plants like hostas and is much sought after by flower arrangers. It likes full sun and poor, dry soil. Propagate by seed (though the resulting plants can be variable) or cuttings in July.

1 *Eschscholzia californica*
'Alba'
2 *Lychnis coronaria*
3 *Campanula persicifolia*
4 *Nigella damascena*
5 *Atriplex hortensis rubra*
6 *Santolina pinnata*
neopolitana 'Sulphurea'
7 *Allium aflatunense*
8 *Linaria purpurea*
9 *Rosa* 'New Dawn'

Even with a whole range of different colours, there's perfect harmony in this border.

Helenium autumnale SNEEZEWEED
Height: 1.5 m (5 ft). Spread: 45 cm (1½ ft).
Flowers: Early autumn.
Brought to Britain in 1729, this bears vivid yellow, sunflower-like flowers. But there are better hybrids now, like 'Bressingham Gold'; 'Bruno', which has crimson/brown blooms; and 'Coppelia', whose flowers are coppery orange.

They like a retentive soil in full sun. Lift and divide every couple of years to prevent deterioration. Propagate by division.

Helianthus decapetalus SUNFLOWER
Height: 1.5 m (5 ft). Spread: 60 cm (2 ft).
Flowers: Summer.
The sunflower has been with us since 1596 and is a great favourite with record-breakers. It's a somewhat coarse flower, but fun to grow. The best hybrid is 'Loddon Gold', which grows tall and has huge, bright yellow, double, daisy-like blooms which don't need supporting.

The sunflower likes sun and heavy soil. Propagate by division. The annual sunflower, of course, is raised by direct-sown seed.

Hemerocallis fulva DAY LILY
Height: 1.2 m (4 ft). Spread: 1 m (3 ft). Flowers: Summer.
The old day lily dates from 1576. It has bright orange flowers with a brown marking on the throat and an apricot line on the petals. It likes a sunny spot and a retentive soil. Propagate by division in autumn. The variety 'Maculata' is particularly choice, with copper flowers with a darker centre. Other varieties are shorter (see page 154).

Hesperis matronalis SWEET ROCKET or DAME'S VIOLET
Height: 1.2 m (4 ft). Spread: 60 cm (2 ft).
Flowers: Summer.

A cottage garden favourite since the fourteenth century, this is a 'must'. It produces tall, branching stems decked with white or lilac flowers rather like those of a stock in appearance and with a superb perfume.

It'll grow in any soil in sun or part-shade, but it's a short-lived plant. However, if you stick to the single-flowered varieties (much better in any case), they'll seed themselves freely. Either collect the seedlings or the seed and raise it yourself or, better still, allow it to find its own home.

Kniphofia spp. and hybrids RED HOT POKER
The red hot pokers, which make a brilliant show of spiky blooms in the border, have been grown since the eighteenth century. Unfortunately they have untidy foliage that looks a bit messy for a small garden. However, with judicious planting around them to hide the leaves, they're a valuable addition to the mixed border.

Kniphofia uvaria. Height: 1.5 m (5 ft). Spread: 60 cm (2 ft). Flowers: Autumn. Grown since 1707, this striking plant produces pokers of coral pink, changing to red, orange and then greeny yellow. It's not entirely hardy.

'Royal Standard', one of the best of the tall hybrids, is just a little shorter than the above. It has scarlet buds which open to reveal yellow flowers.

'Wrexham Buttercup' is clear yellow. There are several other good hybrids, but watch out if you live in a cold area because not all will survive. Give them a sunny spot and propagate by division in spring.

Lavatera olbia TREE MALLOW
Height: 1.8 m (6 ft). Spread: 1.2 m (4 ft).
Flowers: Summer to autumn.
This large, vigorous, shrubby mallow has been grown since 1570 in cottage gardens, where its masses of pink flowers make a brilliant display.

The hybrid lavateras are showy and easy to grow but it must be borne in mind that they're short-lived plants. Just in case, take cuttings in summer.

The variety 'Rosea' is generally grown. However, it is a plant that needs quite a lot of space, so for smaller gardens it's probably best to stick to the varieties of *Lavatera thuringiaca*, which is slightly shorter and more open. The variety 'Barnsley', which has light pink flowers, is very popular, as is the crimson-flowered 'Burgundy Wine' . They need a sunny spot and will grow in most reasonable soil. Prune them back quite hard in early spring when they start to shoot. Propagate by cuttings in late summer.

Lythrum salicaria PURPLE LOOSESTRIFE
Height: 1.2 m (4 ft). Spread: 45 cm (1½ ft).
Flowers: Summer.
This British native must have been grown in the earliest cottage gardens. It produces slender flower spikes of pink or red. The variety 'Robert' has clear pink flowers, while 'Firecandle' and 'The Beacon' are deep red. They prefer wet, even boggy soil but are very adaptable, also flowering well in dry conditions. Either way, they like sunshine. Propagate by division.

Malva alcea MALLOW
Height: 1.2 m (4 ft). Spread: 60 cm (2 ft).
Flowers: Summer.
Introduced in 1797, mallow produces large, cup-shaped, mauve/pink flowers. It'll do well in poor soil in sun and is a very reliable flowerer. Propagate by seed.

Polygonum amplexicaule KNOTWEED
Height: 1.2 m (4 ft). Spread: 1.2 m (4 ft).
Flowers: Summer/autumn.
Makes big clumps which slowly increase and produce large spikes of crimson flowers. There's also a bright red, 'Firetail', and a white with a pink tinge. They like a moist, retentive soil and sun or part-shade. Propagate by division.

Cottage garden planting doesn't have to be entirely random. In this border mainly purples have been grouped together to give a very pleasing effect with purple hebe in front, lupins and the bright, round blooms of ornamental onions behind and, right at the back, the blue spires of camassias.

more common *Rudbeckia fulgida* (see page 162). It has large yellow daisy flowers with drooping petals and a central boss of deep brown. Give it a sunny spot in ordinary soil and it should do well. Propagate by division.

Rudbeckia maxima CONEFLOWER
Height: 1.2 m (4 ft). Spread: 60 cm (2 ft).
Flowers: Summer.
Introduced in 1818, this is the big brother of the

Sidalcea malviflora WILD HOLLYHOCK
Height: 1–1.2 m (3–4 ft). Spread: 45 cm (1½ ft).
Flowers: Summer.
Introduced in 1838 and popular in cottage

gardens ever since. It produces branching spikes of small, silky, hollyhock-like flowers in various shades of pink. Look for 'Sussex Beauty' and 'The Reverend Page Roberts'. Slightly shorter are 'Loveliness', 'Oberon' and 'Puck'.

They grow well in sun or part-shade in any reasonable soil. Propagate by seed, root cuttings or division and bear in mind that seed-raised plants don't come true to type and are rarely as good as the named varieties. Still, if you have the space they're worth growing because some of the seedlings could produce even better flowers. This, after all, was the way that existing named varieties arose.

Solidago canadensis GOLDEN ROD
Height: 1.2 m (4 ft). Spread: 60 cm (2 ft).
Flowers: Late summer/autumn.
This is a rather rank plant now replaced by the variety 'Mimosa', which is definitely an improvement. It produces tall stems topped by spikes of bright yellow flowers. It's easy to grow in sun or part-shade in any soil. Propagate by division. There are also shorter varieties (see page 181).

Thalictrum delavayi MEADOW RUE
Height: 1.5 m (5 ft). Spread: 60 cm (2 ft).
Flowers: Summer.
A tall, stately plant with delicate, divided foliage and great, airy sprays of flowers. Look closely at the individual flowers for the creamy white stamens hanging from the crown of lilac petals. It likes a rich, retentive soil in part-shade, though it will thrive in sun if the soil doesn't dry out. Propagate by seed.

Verbascum spp. and hybrids MULLEIN
Height: 1–1.2 m (3–4 ft). Spread: 45 cm (1½ ft).
Flowers: Summer.
Some of the mulleins are biennials, but there are several perennials you should never be without. They form tall spires with delicate pastel flowers all the way up. One of the most commonly grown is *Verbascum chaixii*, which has small, yellow flowers with a purple centre, and there's a good white form too.

Never be without the purple mullein (*V. phoeniceum*), which flowers in several fine pastel shades. It's a short-lived plant, often lasting only one season, but it has the happy knack of seeding itself around, so my own borders have never been without it. Of course, they seed where *they* want to be, but in a cottage garden, that's just as it should be. This was one of the most prolific seeders in the gravel paths in my artisan's garden. Any seedlings growing where they were not wanted were easy to transplant.

There are several good hybrids too, like the light brown 'Helen Johnson', the apricot-yellow 'Royal Highland', the superb 'Cotswold Queen' (buff-orange with a touch of purple) and the white 'Mont Blanc'.

All like well-drained soil and full sun. Species can be propagated by seed, but the hybrids must be done by root cuttings.

Bulbs

Allium spp. ORNAMENTAL ONION
The onions have been grown for centuries in gardens and there are two that are especially good for the back of the border. Both require full sun and may need staking.
Allium aflatunense. Height: 1.2 m (4 ft). Spread: 30 cm (1 ft). Flowers: Late spring. This produces large, round heads of tiny, lilac flowers, and there is a white variety 'Album'. Plant the bulbs in early autumn 12.5 cm (5 in) deep. Propagate by division in autumn or by seed.
Allium giganteum. Much the same as the above but with larger heads in summer.

Plants for the Middle of the Border

Shrubs

Artemisia 'Powis Castle' LAD'S LOVE or
SOUTHERNWOOD
Height: 75 cm (2½ ft). Spread: 75 cm (2½ ft).
One of the best of all the artemisias, this
produces a mound of silver, finely cut foliage and
is a great improvement on the larger *Artemisia
abrotanum*, grown since at least the tenth century.
Look out also for wormwood (*A. absinthium*),
which is much the same. The variety 'Lambrook
Silver' is the best. They absolutely *must* have a
well-drained soil, so work in plenty of coarse grit
before planting and give them a sunny spot.
Propagate by softwood cuttings in summer.

Berberis thunbergii 'Atropurpurea Nana'
BARBERRY
Height: 60 cm (2 ft). Spread: 60 cm (2 ft).
Flowers: Spring.
A small, rounded bush with fine, red foliage
turning orange in autumn. Also recommended is
the variety 'Aurea' with golden foliage. Propagate
by half-ripe cuttings in autumn.

Cistus purpureus ROCK ROSE or SUN ROSE
Height: 1.2 m (4 ft). Spread: 1 m (3 ft).
Flowers: Summer.
Grown since 1790, this sun-lover has crimson
flowers with chocolate-brown centres, rather like
a single rose, and is very free-flowering. If it's a
bit too large for the centre of your border, grow
one of the smaller named varieties. 'Grayswood
Pink' grows to about 1 m (3 ft) and 'Warley Rose'

to about 60 cm (2 ft). Give them a dry soil and
a sunny spot and propagate by half-ripe cuttings
in autumn. They're not long-lived plants, so
propagate every three or four years.

Cytisus purpureus BROOM
Height: 45 cm (1½ ft). Spread: 60 cm (2 ft).
Flowers: Early summer.
A low-growing plant with arching branches
covered in lilac flowers. There's also a white
variety, 'Albus'. 'Atropurpueus' has deeper-purple
flowers. Give them a sunny spot and well-
drained soil and propagate by half-ripe cuttings
in summer.

Daphne mezereum MEZEREON
Height: 1 m (3 ft). Spread: 60 cm (2 ft).
Flowers: Late winter/early spring.
Introduced in 1561, it was doubtless not long
before a few cuttings of this little gem reached
cottage gardens. It bears pink/lilac flowers all
the way up naked stems and fills the garden
with sweet perfume. The variety 'Alba' has white
flowers; 'Rubra' has deep red ones. It can be
subject to virus attack and is not generally a
long-lived shrub, but well worthwhile none
the less. Grow it in well-drained soil in sun or
part-shade. It thrives in chalky soils.

The British native spurge laurel (*D. laureola*) is
about the same size but it's evergreen, with good,
shiny foliage. It bears slightly scented, yellow
flowers in early spring. It prefers a retentive soil
in full or partial shade. Propagate by seed.

Deutzia 'Nikko'
Height: 60 cm (2 ft). Spread: 1 m (3 ft).
Flowers: Early summer.
A fairly recent introduction, this delightful shrub
forms a compact mound of fresh green foliage
covered with small, white flowers. It grows in any
well-drained soil and prefers full sun. Propagate

by hardwood cuttings in early autumn or softwood throughout the summer.

Fuchsia hybrids
Height: 30 cm–1.2 m (1–4 ft). Spread: 30 cm–1.2 m (1–4 ft). Flowers: All summer/autumn.
Invaluable plants for the middle of the border. Some do grow a bit tall, but can be pruned hard in winter so that they don't become an embarrassment. They're quite hardy and produce lovely, skirted flowers, often in two colours. Look for 'Mrs Popple', a taller one with deep red and violet blooms; 'Tom Thumb', one of the smallest with flowers of the same colour; and 'Eva Boerg' with two-tone pink flowers. They like a sunny spot and a well-drained soil is essential. In colder areas cut back the shoots in winter and cover the root with leaf litter or straw; otherwise prune hard in spring before the new shoots start to grow. Propagate by softwood cuttings in summer.

The hardy fuchsias, like 'Mrs Popple' here, never fail to fill with bloom in late summer.

Genista tinctoria DYER'S GREENWEED
Height: 45 cm (1½ ft). Spread: 1 m (3 ft).
Flowers: Late spring/early summer.
Grown since 1570, the species is not really worthwhile as an ornamental plant, having not very conspicuous, yellow flowers. But two more recent varieties cover themselves in bright yellow, double blooms. Look for 'Golden Plate' and 'Plena'. 'Royal Gold' is more upright, growing to about 1 m (3 ft).

Hydrangea macrophylla
Height: 1–1.5 m (3–5 ft). Spread: 1–1.5 m (3–5ft). Flowers: Summer.
Most cottage gardens would have a hydrangea or two. The mophead varieties, or 'hortensias', bear large, round heads of pink or blue florets, though even blue varieties will show their true blue colours only on acid soils. Otherwise they stay pink unless treated with 'blueing agent', available at garden centres. There are many named varieties, like the deep rose-pink 'Altona'; 'Blue Prince'; the large-flowered pink or deep blue 'Goliath'; the dwarfer, deep red 'Souvenir du Président Paul Doumer'; and more.

Then there are the lacecaps, which bear large, flat flowers, surrounded by a ring of florets. They have a more delicate, airy look and are ideal for the cottage effect. 'Blue Wave' has blue flowers surrounded by pink florets; 'Lanarth White' is blue or pink surrounded by white; and 'Tricolor', has flowers varying from pink to white and leaves variegated green, grey and yellow.

All prefer to be in a semi-shaded place and a free-draining but retentive soil. Prune shoots that have flowered in the following spring and propagate by softwood cuttings in late summer.

Hypericum androsaemum TUTSAN
Height: 1 m (3 ft). Spread: 1 m (3 ft).
Flowers: Summer.

Grown since 1370, the hypericums, with their bright yellow flowers and long flowering period, became popular cottage garden subjects. The fresh green leaves are almost hidden by masses of yellow, saucer-shaped flowers most of the summer and these are followed by attractive, shining, red fruits which later turn black. Unfortunately the plants are somewhat prone to rust disease these days, but it won't strike every year. When it does, I cut the stems right down to ground level and burn them: the plants re-grow happily the following season.

Also popular is the variety 'Hidcote', with similar flowers but without the fruits. It doesn't seem nearly so prone to rust. Grow hypericums in a sunny spot in reasonable soil and propagate by dividing the roots or by softwood cuttings.

Potentilla hybrids Cinquefoil
Height: 1.2 m (4 ft). Spread: 1.2 m (4 ft).
Flowers: All summer.
A very adaptable and tough shrub, popular because of its long flowering period and range of flower colours. They include the superb, pure white 'Abbotswood'; the peachy cream 'Daydawn'; the canary yellow 'Elizabeth'; the rich gold, dwarfer 'Goldfinger'; the vermilion 'Red Ace'; and the orange 'Hopley's Orange', a good, recent introduction.

They prefer full sun, but some of the newer hybrids tend to fade, so a little shade is probably better. They'll grow in almost any well-drained soil. Prune them after flowering by clipping with shears and propagate by softwood cuttings in summer.

Rosa varieties
'Brother Cadfael'. Height: 1 m (3 ft). Spread: 1 m (3 ft). An English rose with very large, peony-like, soft pink flowers.

'Cottage Rose'. Height: 1 m (3 ft). Spread: 75

The lacecap hydrangeas bear large blooms with a central boss of flowers surrounded by a ring of florets, sometimes of matching colours, sometimes different, depending on variety.

cm (2½ ft). An English rose producing cupped flowers of real old-fashioned shape in warm pink. Repeat flowers well.

'Duchesse de Buccleugh'. Height: 1 m (3 ft). Spread: 1 m (3 ft). A Gallica rose with large, quartered flowers of lilac-pink.

'Evelyn'. Height: 1 m (3 ft). Spread: 1 m (3 ft). A delightful English rose with shallow, cup-shaped blooms of apricot and yellow.

'Félicité Parmentier'. Height: 1 m (3 ft). Spread: 1 m (3 ft). A lovely Alba rose with delicate, pale pink flowers, deeper-coloured in the centre and turning to pale pink as the flower opens.

'Glamis Castle'. Height: 1 m (3 ft). Spread: 75 cm (2½ ft). A pure white English rose with cupped flowers and a fragrance of myrrh.

'Gloire de France'. Height: 1 m (3 ft). Spread:

1 m (3 ft). A Gallica rose with cupped flowers of pink with a deeper pink centre.

'Hermosa'. Height: 1 m (3 ft). Spread: 1 m (3 ft). A lovely China rose with cupped flowers of mid-pink. It hangs its head slightly to give a delicate appearance and flowers all summer.

'Jayne Austin'. Height: 1 m (3 ft). Spread: 75 cm (2½ ft). An English rose with rosette blooms of soft yellow with a hint of apricot.

'Pompon de Bourgogne'. Height: 1 m (3 ft). Spread: 60 cm (2 ft). Introduced in 1664, this bears the smallest flowers of all the old roses. It has tiny, dark green leaves and small, deep red flowers. Often used to make hedges in parterres.

'Rose de Rescht'. Height: 1 m (3 ft). Spread: 75 cm (2½ ft). A compact Portland rose with crimson flowers. Flowers throughout summer.

'Sharifa Asma'. An English rose with flowers of blush pink fading to white on the outer petals.

'Soupert et Notting'. Height: 1 m (3 ft). Spread: 75 cm (2½ ft). Full flowers of strong lilac-pink.

'Souvenir de la Malmaison'. Height: 1 m (3 ft). Spread: 75 cm (2½ ft). A lovely Bourbon rose with large, pink flowers touched with light brown which repeat throughout the summer.

'The Countryman'. Height: 1 m (3 ft). Spread: 1 m (3 ft). An English rose forming flat, many-petalled rosettes of clear pink. Two flowerings a year with some in between.

'The Dark Lady'. Height: 1 m (3 ft). Spread: 1 m (3 ft). A deep red English rose producing large blooms like those of a tree peony.

Rosmarinus officinalis ROSEMARY
A fine decorative shrub for the middle or front of the border, covered under 'Herbs' on page 231.

Senecio 'Sunshine'
Height: 1 m (3 ft). Spread: 1.8 m (6 ft).
Flowers: Summer

A lax, spreading shrub which forms a mat of felty grey leaves topped by yellow daisies. It needs a well-drained soil and sun. Prune lightly after flowering and cut old, straggly plants back hard to the ground every so often to rejuvenate them. Propagate by softwood cuttings in summer.

Herbaceous Plants

Achillea hybrids
Height: 60 cm (2 ft). Spread: 38 cm (15 in).
Flowers: Throughout summer.
The native British yarrow was no doubt dug up and planted in early cottage gardens, but is certainly not worth growing now, having been replaced by much better species and hybrids. They all like a retentive, well-drained soil in full sun and can be propagated by division, seed or basal cuttings, all in spring.

'Moonshine' is an excellent modern hybrid with sulphur-yellow flowers. From Germany come several others certainly worth a place: 'Cerise Queen' has cherry red flowers; 'Apple Blossom' is lilac-pink; 'Great Expectations' is buff-primrose; and 'Salmon Beauty' is salmon-pink.

Alchemilla mollis LADY'S MANTLE
Height: 45 cm (1½ ft). Spread: 60 cm (2 ft).
Flowers: Early summer.
Introduced in 1874, this is a plant that will grow almost anywhere, in sun or deep shade, though it looks best in shade. Its delightful, rounded, fresh green leaves catch droplets of rain which sparkle in the sun and they're topped by yellow flowers on delicate stems. It will seed itself readily, so it may be best to remove the flower heads when they fade. Propagate by seed or division.

Anthemis tinctoria 'Grallach Gold'
Height: 1 m (3 ft). Spread: 1 m (3 ft).
Flowers: Summer.

A striking plant producing masses of stunning, acid-yellow daisies over a long period. Propagate by basal cuttings or division. (See also page 172.)

Anthemis sancti-johannis. Height: 60 cm (2 ft). Spread: 60 cm (2 ft). Flowers: Summer. Like the above but with bright orange flowers and somewhat shorter petals. A short-lived plant but easily raised from seed or cuttings.

Aquilegia spp. and hybrids Columbine
These are real cottage garden plants dating from about the thirteenth century. They've been grown in cottage gardens since the earliest times. I've included them in the middle of the border, but some should certainly drift towards the front where their delicate flowers and foliage can be best seen.

Aquilegia canadensis. Height: 60 cm (2 ft). Spread: 30 cm (1 ft). Flowers: Early summer. This graceful plant has delightful red-and-yellow flowers and typical dark green divided foliage. It prefers well-drained soil and sun. Propagate by seed.

Long-spurred hybrids. Height: 60–90 cm (2–3 ft). Spread: 45 cm (1½ ft). Flowers: Early summer. These are the really well-known 'granny's bonnets' that are as much part of cottage gardens as hollyhocks. They have beautifully shaped blooms with a long spur on the back, in various shades of yellow, pink, red, purple and mauve: not to be missed. They also like good drainage and a sunny spot. Propagate by seed sown in pots in the coldframe in late summer. Some will also seed themselves.

A mass of lady's mantle at the front of this border lights up an otherwise shady spot with a foam of yellow flowers. After rain, the drops will be caught in the cupped leaves and will sparkle like jewels.

Arum maculatum LORDS-AND-LADIES or
JACK-BY-THE-HEDGE

A British native that must have been dug up in
early times by cottagers to grow in their gardens.
That's illegal now, of course, but there's a much
better garden variety anyway.

Arum italicum 'Pictum'. Height: 45 cm (1½ ft).
Spread: 30 cm (1 ft). Flowers: Spring. This variety has large, sword-shaped leaves of glossy green
marbled with cream and grey, making a fine show
in winter. The flowers are greenish white spathes
with purple staining at the base and a creamy
central spadix. Give it a moisture-retentive soil
and a sunny position, though it will take some
shade. Propagate by division in spring.

Astrantia major MASTERWORT

Height: 60 cm (2 ft). Spread: 45 cm (1½ ft).
Flowers: Summer/autumn.

Introduced in 1597, this fine old cottage
favourite forms branched heads of interesting
flowers with their central florets surrounded by a
ruff of bracts. The flowers are greenish white
with a pale green collar. Look for the variety
'Shaggy', which is particularly good. 'Rubra'
has beautiful red flowers and a new variety,
'Sunningdale Variegated', has leaves striped with
yellow. They like a well-drained soil in sun or
partial shade and can be propagated by division
or seed.

Catananche caerulea BLUE CUPIDONE

Height: 60 cm (2 ft). Spread: 30 cm (1 ft).
Flowers: Summer.

Introduced in 1596, this was one of the plants
grown by the herbalist John Gerard (1545-1612)
in his own garden. It makes a clump of grassy
leaves and numerous wiry flower stems with
small, deep blue flowers surrounded by a papery
'everlasting flower' calyx: most attractive. There
are some good named varieties like 'Perry's

White', the lavender-blue 'Major', and 'Bicolor'
which is white with a dark blue centre. Give them
a sunny but sheltered position and propagate by
seed or, in the case of the named varieties, by root
cuttings in early spring.

Centaurea montana MOUNTAIN KNAPWEED

Height: 45 cm (1½ ft). Spread: 60 cm (2 ft).
Flowers: Early summer.

Gerard called this the 'Great Blew-Bottle or
Corne-Floure' and it has been grown in cottage
gardens since 1596. It produces large, cornflower
blooms of deep blue with a red centre. There are
also white and pink varieties. It grows in almost
any soil and is most at home in sun. Propagate by
division in autumn or spring.

Centranthus ruber VALERIAN

Height: 60–90 cm (2–3 ft). Spread: 45 cm
(1½ ft). Flowers: Summer.

A popular cottage plant often to be found growing on walls. It loves chalky soil and a sunny spot
and, given the right conditions, it'll seed itself
freely. The seedlings should be controlled where
they're not wanted. It has large, elongated heads
of small pink flowers. Best of all are the white
form 'Albus' and the deep red 'Atrococcineus'.
Propagate by seed sown outside in early summer.

Chrysanthemum maximum or correctly
Leucanthemum superbum SHASTA DAISY

Height: 1 m (3 ft). Spread: 45 cm (1½ ft).
Flowers: Summer.

A wonderful, easy, strong grower that has been in
cottage gardens since 1816. It produces masses of
white daisies over a long period. There are also
some selected forms, like the well-known 'Esther
Read', that are very worthwhile. It'll grow almost
anywhere in any soil but prefers sun or part-shade
and a retentive soil. Propagate by division in
autumn. It does best when divided regularly.

The shasta daisy is the easiest of plants to grow, simple to propagate and one of the most reliable flowerers: a perfect cottage garden plant.

Dendranthema hybrids
HYBRID CHRYSANTHEMUMS
Height: 45 cm–1 m (1½–3 ft). Spread: 30 cm (1 ft). Flowers: Late summer.
There are hundreds of florist's chrysanthemums that are too tender for our purposes, but also several hardy varieties. Get hold of a specialist catalogue, but don't miss 'Anastasia', which has small pink 'buttons', and 'Emperor of China', known as the 'old cottage pink', with pink flowers with a crimson centre right through to the first frosts. 'Innocence' is a single pink well worth growing. They like a sunny position and may be propagated by cuttings in spring.

Coreopsis verticillata TICK SEED
Height: 60 cm (2 ft). Spread: 45 cm (1½ ft). Flowers: Summer/autumn.
Brought to Britain from the USA in 1759, this must have been readily accepted by cottage gardeners. It has bright green, narrow foliage and brilliant yellow, daisy-like blooms over a long period. Look for the variety 'Grandiflora', sometimes called 'Golden Shower', which has a richer yellow colour, and 'Moonbeam' which is primrose-yellow. It'll grow in any soil in sunshine. It's a short-lived plant, but can easily be raised from seed sown in spring outside.

Dianthus hybrids CLOVE CARNATION
Height: 45 cm (1½ ft). Spread: 30 cm (1 ft). Flowers: Summer.
Carnations or 'gillyflowers', like the old crimson clove, have been grown since the sixteenth century. It's dark red and has a very strong perfume. 'Lord Chatham' bears bright pink, perfumed flowers. Grow plants in full sun and well-drained soil and stake them early to prevent the flowers flopping. Propagate by cuttings in early summer.

Diascia rigescens
Height: 45 cm (1½ ft). Spread: 45 cm (1½ ft). Flowers: Summer.

Not exactly a traditional cottage garden plant, but one I'm quite sure the old cottage gardeners would have loved. It has masses of deep pink flowers that cover the stems over a long period. It could be tender in colder areas and must have full sun and excellent drainage everywhere. Prop-agate by cuttings in mid-summer.

Dicentra spectabilis BLEEDING HEART or DUTCHMAN'S BREECHES
Height: 60 cm (2 ft). Spread: 45 cm (1½ ft). Flowers: Late spring.
Introduced in 1810, this plant has the distinction of more common names than any other, I'm sure. It produces beautiful, white-tipped, red, pendulous, locket-shaped flowers which dangle from arching stems. And it's worth growing just for its attractive much-divided foliage. It needs a shady spot and retentive soil. Propagate by division.

Dicentra formosa was introduced from the USA in 1796. It also makes tussocks of lovely, ferny foliage and has pendulous flowers. They're red/purple and there are a few varieties like the dark pink 'Luxuriant' and the soft pink 'Boothman's Variety' that are worth hunting out. Grow them like *D. spectabilis*.

Doronicum plantagineum LEOPARD'S BANE
Height: 75 cm (2½ft). Spread: 30 cm (1 ft). Flowers: Early spring.
An easily grown plant introduced about 1570 that forms large clumps of attractive, fresh green foliage from which arise masses of bright yellow daisies. It likes retentive soil and some shade, though it will put up with sun if the soil is moist. Propagate by division in autumn.

Erigeron hybrids FLEABANE
Height: 45–60 cm (1½–2 ft). Spread: 45 cm (1½ ft). Flowers: Summer.
Grown in cottage gardens since the nineteenth

century, but the older species have now been replaced by better hybrids. They produce masses of daisy flowers rather like Michaelmas daisies, only on shorter plants. Look out for the single, pink 'Amity' and 'Charity'; the violet-blue 'Dignity'; and the red 'Rotes Meer'. All like a sunny site and well-drained soil. Propagate by division.

Eryngium maritimum SEA HOLLY
Height: 30 cm (1 ft). Spread: 30 cm (1 ft). Flowers: Summer.
The British native sea holly must have been grown in coastal cottage gardens by the earliest gardeners, but is now quite rare. Like all the sea hollies, it has attractive, thistle-like foliage and very blue flowers. Two other sea hollies are worth considering:
Eryngium alpinum. Height: 75 cm (2½ ft). Spread: 45 cm (1½ ft). Flowers: Summer. Introduced in 1597, this striking plant has the largest, blue, conical flowers of all. Look out for the improved variety 'Donard'.
E. bourgatii. Height: 60 cm (2 ft). Spread: 30 cm (1 ft). Flowers: Summer. Striking, deeply cut foliage with white veins is one of the features of this species. The flowers are green.
All need a very well-drained, dry soil in full sun. Propagate by carefully lifting self-sown seedlings or by root cuttings in autumn.

Erysimum hybrids PERENNIAL WALLFLOWER
Height: 30–60 cm (1–2 ft). Spread: 30 cm (1 ft). Flowers: Spring/summer.
Wallflowers were great favourites in cottage gardens and still should be. However, they're biennials, so they take a lot of room to grow each year. The perennial wallflowers are there-fore especially useful where space to grow the biennials is not available. There are several good varieties, but they're all fairly short-lived, so it's

advisable to take cuttings every couple or three years as an insurance. They all like a sunny spot or part-shade and retentive but well-drained soil. Look out for the yellow 'Harpur Crewe'; the purple 'Bowles' Mauve'; 'Chelsea Jacket', which is orange and pale mauve; and the shorter 'Jacob's Jacket', whose flowers change from bronze to orange and then to lilac.

Euphorbia spp. SPURGE or MILKWEED

Some of the spurges are native to Britain and, even though treated as weeds in many gardens, are actually quite attractive, so they will have been nurtured in early cottage gardens. There are several great improvements to be found in the plants available today.

Euphorbia palustris. Height: 1 m (3 ft). Spread: 1 m (3 ft). Flowers: Late spring. Grown in the sixteenth century, this species makes a spectacular splash of yellow in spring followed by green plumes all summer which turn orange and yellow in autumn.

E. polychroma. Height: 45 cm (1½ ft). Spread: 45 cm (1½ ft). Flowers: Late spring. This type of spurge forms well-rounded clumps of fresh green with masses of yellow flowers over a long period.

Euphorbia polychroma *produces a rounded bush covered in spring flowers of bright greenish yellow. Be careful of the irritant, milky-white sap.*

It's best to plant them alone or you lose the beauty of their rounded shape.

Euphorbias will grow in sun or partial shade. Propagate by softwood cuttings in summer – and wear gloves as protection against the sap, which can be irritant.

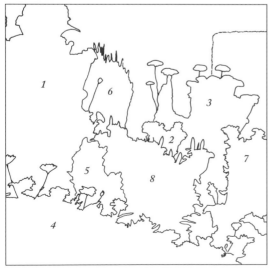

1 *Helianthus* 'Loddon Gold'
2 *Erigeron* 'Serenity'
3 *Achillea filipendulina* 'Gold Plate'
4 *Argyranthemum* 'Jamaica Primrose'
5 *Phlox paniculata* 'Brigadier'
6 *Linaria purpurea*
7 *Astrantia major*
8 *Lilium* hybrid

A summer border full of bright yellow really catches the eye and lifts the spirits.

Gaillardia grandiflora BLANKET FLOWER
Height: 60 cm–1 m (2–3 ft). Spread: 45 cm
(1½ ft). Flowers: Summer.
An easily grown, striking plant existing in various
forms in cottage gardens since the eighteenth
century. The clumps of foliage produce spikes of
daisy-like flowers in yellow to deep maroon with
a brown centre. They'll grow almost anywhere
and are easily raised from seed.

Geranium pratense CRANESBILL
Height: 60 cm (2 ft). Spread: 60 cm (2 ft).
Flowers: Summer.
This British native was grown by the very earliest
cottagers and is still a superb plant, making
mounds of violet flowers. However, it tends to
seed rather too freely so, unless you have a wild
garden, it's perhaps best to stick to the double
forms like 'Mrs Kendall Clarke' with greyish pink
flowers and 'Plenum Violaceum' which produces
tight rosettes of deep blue. There are dozens
more species and varieties, so it's worthwhile

*Geranium oxonianum 'Claridge Druce' is a vigorous grower
producing masses of flowers over a long period in summer.
It will need to be controlled.*

getting hold of a specialist's catalogue, especially
as some will thrive in the difficult area of dry
shade. I list only a few.

Geranium endressii. Height: 45 cm (1½ ft).
Spread: 60 cm (2 ft). Flowers: Summer to
autumn. Introduced in 1812, this low-growing
spreader has chalky pink flowers.

G. 'Johnson's Blue'. Height: 30 cm (1 ft).
Spread: 60 cm (2 ft). Flowers: Early summer.
Good, divided leaves and blue flowers with dark
blue veins.

G. macrorrhizum. Height: 30 cm (1 ft). Spread:
60 cm (2 ft). Flowers: Late spring. A vigorous
grower, even in dry shade. It produces pink
flowers in profusion and the leaves turn bronze in
autumn and generally stay on the plant all winter.

G. maculatum. Height: 60 cm (2 ft). Spread:
45 cm (1½ ft). Flowers: Spring. Introduced from
the USA in 1732, this is a superb plant with
excellent, soft-looking foliage topped by masses
of lilac-pink flowers. Not to be missed.

G. riversleaianum 'Russell Prichard'. Height:
23 cm (9 in). Spread: 1 m (3 ft). Flowers:
Summer to autumn. A fine plant that seems to
produce its chalky pink flowers right through the
summer. It should also be considered for the front
of the border for edging a path.

G. sanguineum. Height: 30 cm (1 ft). Spread:
45 cm (1½ ft). Flowers: Early summer. Known as
the bloody cranesbill, this has deep magenta
flowers, while its better form, *G. s. lancastriense*,
bears light pink flowers with deep crimson veins.

Geraniums will grow in almost any soil except
bog and will thrive in sun or shade. Propagate by
seed or division.

Helleborus corsicus HELLEBORE
Height: 60 cm (2 ft). Spread: 1 m (3 ft). Flowers:
Winter to spring.
A spreading, bushy plant with fine, leathery,
green foliage. The thick stems produce clusters of

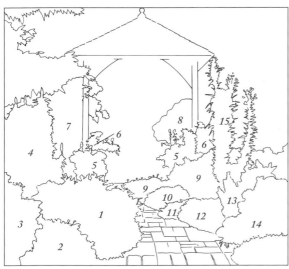

1 *Hebe* 'Primley Gem'

2 *Geranium sanguineum* 'Shepherd's Warning'

3 *Ruta graveolens*

4 *Agastache foeniculum*

5 *Petunia* hybrids

6 *Rosa* 'Margaret Merril'

7 *Rosa* 'Bantry Bay'

8 *Rosa* 'Pink Perpétue'

9 *Geranium riversleaianum* 'Russell Prichard'

10 *Artemisia schmidtiana*

11 *Phlox douglasii*

12 *Aubrieta gloriosa*

13 *Nepeta faassenii*

14 *Rosa* 'The Countryman'

15 *Lilium* 'Connecticut King'

A brick and paving path is softened with plants sprawling over the edges. Maintenance is needed from time to time to keep everything in check.

green bells that hang down from the ends of the branches. It grows in shade or sun on almost any soil, but does need support if it's not to flop. Cut off old, flowered stems after flowering when the new leaves start to show. Propagate by division.

Helleborus orientalis. Height: 45 cm (1½ ft). Spread: 60 cm (2 ft). Flowers: Early spring. Known as the Lenten rose, this wonderful plant is one of the great joys of spring. It has cup-shaped flowers varying from pure white to deep maroon, many with intricate spotting. It's a promiscuous plant, so it'll cross with its fellows, producing lots of seedlings around the plants in spring. They're worth searching out and trans-planting to a nursery bed to grow on. All of them will be worth keeping. The Lenten rose likes a retentive soil and will revel in shade, but will grow in sun too. Cut off the old leaves in spring to display the flowers better: a new crop will soon grow. It resents disturbance, so try to leave clumps alone.

Hemerocallis hybrids DAY LILY
Height: 38 cm–1 m (15 in–3 ft). Spread: 60 cm (2 ft). Flowers: Summer.

There are numerous new hybrids that are a great improvement on most of the older ones. 'Anzac' has red flowers; 'Canary Glow' is yellow; 'Hyperion' is scented yellow; 'Stella D'Oro' is gold; 'Pink Damask' and 'Varsity' are pink. They all like sun or partial shade in most soils and are propagated by division.

Iris spp.
The irises have been grown in cottage gardens since earliest times. They're all easy to cultivate and will increase quite fast.

Iris florentina. Height: 60 cm (2 ft). Spread: 30 cm (1 ft). Flowers: Early summer. The ground, dried rhizomes of this plant, which was known as orris, were used in ancient times to make toiletries and pot-pourri. The leaves are typical, sword-shaped iris leaves and the flowers are greyish white and sweetly scented.

I. foetidissima. Height: 45 cm (1½ ft). Spread: 60 cm (2 ft). Flowers: Early summer. A British native grown in the earliest cottage gardens, the gladdon or stinking gladwyn, as it is known, produces a fine sheaf of leaves which are supposed to smell of roast beef when crushed. The greenish flowers are not striking, but in autumn the pods burst to show bright orange seeds. It's well worth growing and seems to sur-vive almost anywhere.

I. sibirica. Height: 1 m (3 ft). Spread: 25 cm (10 in). Flowers: Summer. Grown since the six-teenth century, this clump-forming plant pro-duces grassy leaves and masses of flower spikes. There are several good named varieties of which I grow 'White Swirl', the violet 'Tycoon' and light blue 'Papillon'. They grow almost anywhere, but prefer a moist soil in sun and are ideal bog plants.

Hemerocallis 'Stella D'Oro' produces a succession of gold flowers over a long period in summer. Ideally day lilies should be grown in sun where they'll clump up quickly. Divide them every three or four years.

The bearded irises like this one, 'Helga', are easy to grow and to propagate. Give them a sunny spot and make sure that the fleshy rhizomes are planted at soil level.

I. germanica. Height: 60 cm–1 m (2–3 ft). Spread: 45 cm (1½ ft). Flowers: Early summer. Known as the bearded iris, this is the most common cottage iris, still seen in many gardens. The flowers are purple with darker 'falls'. There are hundreds of varieties available in many colours, so get hold of a specialist catalogue. I like the brown-and-white 'Kent Pride'; 'Shampoo', which is brown and green; and the yellow 'Berkeley Gold'.

All the irises do best in full sun and the rhizomatous kinds should be planted with the rhizomes exposed. Divide them every three or four years by splitting off young rhizomes with a fan of leaves. Cut the leaves back by half before replanting.

Clump-forming types are propagated by simple division and can be raised from seed.

Kniphofia dwarf hybrids RED HOT POKER
Height: 1 m (3 ft). Spread: 45 cm (1½ ft).
Flowers: Summer.
Ideal for making a strong contrast in mixed borders, there are several good colours. 'Canary Bird' is dark yellow; 'Little Maid' is the palest ivory; and 'Firefly' is orange-red. There are many others. They like full sun and a retentive soil. Propagate by division in spring.

Linum narbonense FLAX
Height: 60 cm (2 ft). Spread: 45 cm (1½ ft).
Flowers: Summer.
Introduced in 1759, flax is used to make linen and now to produce oil for the linoleum industry. It produces many silky, open flowers of the loveliest azure-blue. Look out for the variety 'Six Hills' and the white 'Saphyr'. It likes full sun and a well-drained soil. Propagate by cuttings.

Lupinus polyphyllus LUPIN
Height: 1.2 m (4 ft). Spread: 60 cm (2 ft).
Flowers: Early summer.
Introduced from North America in 1826, this bright flower is a great cottage garden favourite. From a clump of attractive, divided foliage come tall spikes of blooms, and there are many colours.

The most famous hybrids, the Russell lupins, were bred and selected by nurseryman George Russell in the 1930s and were widely grown. However, in recent years they deteriorated, mainly as a result of virus diseases. They have, however, been re-selected to form the 'New Generation' hybrids, which are even better than the originals.

Lupins like a sunny spot and a retentive soil and can be raised from seed to produce mixed colours. After flowering, cut them back and they should flower again later.

To propagate a particularly good colour, increase by basal cuttings in early spring.

No cottage garden would be complete without lupins, seen here in the artisan's garden at Barnsdale. They're very easy to grow and can be raised cheaply from seed, though it's worth seeking out the re-selected hybrids. After flowering, be sure to remove the flower spikes or the plant will be short-lived: this may also encourage the bonus of another, sparser flowering later in the year.

Lychnis chalcedonica MALTESE CROSS or JERUSALEM CROSS
Height: 1 m (3 ft). Spread: 30 cm (1 ft).
Flowers: Summer.
Supposedly brought to Britain by the Crusaders, this plant has been grown since 1593. It produces brilliant red flowers over a long period. There's also a rare, double-flowered variety and a white. Give it a sunny but sheltered spot and propagate by seed or division.

Lychnis coronaria ROSE CAMPION or DUSTY MILLER
Height: 1 m (3ft). Spread: 45 cm (1½ ft).
Flowers: Summer.
From clumps of grey, felted leaves arise magenta flower heads. Some gardeners feel that the colour is impossible to use in gardens, since it's so bright, but in a cottage garden it fits perfectly. The plant

likes full sun and a well-drained soil and can be propagated by seed or division.

Malva moschata MUSK MALLOW
Height: 1 m (3 ft). Spread: 60 cm (2 ft).
Flowers: Summer.
This British native has attractive, finely cut foliage and large, cup-shaped flowers of pink or white. It flowers over a very long period. Grow it in any soil in sunshine and propagate by seed.

Monarda didyma BEE BALM or BERGAMOT
Height: 1 m (3 ft). Spread: 45 cm (1½ ft).
Flowers: Summer.
Introduced from the USA in 1744, this plant quickly found favour in cottage gardens because it was used to make a soothing tea and it's also a very good bee plant. The flowers are hooded and rather like those of sage. The best varieties to

grow are *Monarda* 'Adam', which is rich red, and the pale pink 'Beauty of Cobham'. It needs sun and a moist, retentive soil. Propagate by division.

Monarda fistulosa is much the same plant but about 30 cm (1 ft) taller. Look for the varieties 'Croftway Pink'; 'Cambridge Scarlet'; and the dark purple 'Prairie Night'. This species will grow happily in dry soil and is also propagated by division.

Nepeta gigantea GIANT CATMINT
Height: 1 m (3 ft). Spread: 1 m (3 ft).
Flowers: Summer.
A tall version of catmint, this has spikes of lavender flowers over greyish foliage. It tends to be hardier than catmint and is, of course, twice as big. Give it a sunny spot and well-drained soil and propagate by division.

Paeonia spp. PEONY
Peonies have been grown in British cottage gardens since the tenth century and they're highly valued for foliage and flowers. The early leaves are often deep red or pinkish and deeply cut, and the flowers, though not long-lasting as a rule, are one of the garden's most sumptuous.

Paeonia officinalis. Height: 60 cm (2 ft). Spread: 60 cm (2 ft). Flowers: Late spring to early summer depending on variety. Attractive green foliage sets off sometimes single flowers, sometimes doubles. Look out particularly for 'Anemoniflora Rosea', a deep pink with a tufted centre of stamens that are crimson edged with yellow. 'China Rose' bears an excellent salmon-pink, single flower with orange stamens. Also recommended are the double crimson 'Rubra Plena', the pink 'Rosea Superba Plena' and the white 'Alba Plena'.

P. lactiflora. Height: 1 m (3 ft). Spread: 60 cm (2 ft). Flowers: Early summer. A superb, large, single, white flower with yellow stamens and red foliage. Much appreciated also as the likely beginning of a race of Chinese hybrids that have really taken over now. There are dozens of them in all colours and most, if not all, are worth growing. These are the ones normally offered in garden centres.

P. mlokosewitschii. Height: 60 cm (2 ft). Spread: 60 cm (2 ft). Flowers: Spring. Nicknamed 'Molly-the-Witch' for obvious reasons, this most attractive of spring flowerers has soft, grey/green foliage with large, primrose-yellow blooms and golden anthers.

Peonies like full sunshine and a retentive soil and they hate being moved. They do often take a year or two to settle down before flowering, but don't be tempted to dig up the crown and move it or you'll be back where you started. Enjoy the foliage for a while instead. They're propagated by division, but it's best to delay that for as long as possible because it means doing without flowers for a couple of years again. When planting the crowns, don't plant them too deeply: covering with 2.5 cm (1 in) of soil is enough.

Papaver orientale ORIENTAL POPPY
Height: 60 cm–1.2 m (2–4 ft). Spread: 60 cm (2 ft). Flowers: Early summer.
Introduced to Britain in 1714, this is one of the most striking plants in the garden. It has its snags, in that it tends to flop, especially after rain, so it needs support and, after flowering, it must be cut back to induce new foliage, thus leaving a space in the border. But it's so striking that it's worthwhile growing a pot or two of something else to fill the space while the leaves are growing.

'Beauty of Livermere' is a strong, single red; 'Harvest Moon' is orange and semi-double; 'Cedric Morris' is greyish pink with deep red, almost black blotches; 'Turkish Delight' is clear pink; and 'Perry's White', you will not be surprised to hear, is white.

Penstemon spp. BEARD TONGUE

Often slightly tender plants, the first of which came to Britain from the Americas in the eighteenth century, these are not suitable for cold gardens, though one or two have proved quite hardy in my own, far-from-Mediterranean plot.

To give penstemons the best chance of survival, make sure that you grow them in a sunny, sheltered position and improve the soil drainage with coarse grit.

Penstemon barbatus. Height: 1 m (3 ft). Spread: 30 cm (1 ft). Flowers: Summer. From a tuft of leaves grow branching stems with rose-red, tubular flowers touched with pink in the hairy throat.

P. venustus. Height: 45 cm (1½ ft). Spread: 60 cm (2 ft). Flowers: Summer. Mauve flowers in profusion over a long period. This one is perfectly hardy in my own garden.

Hybrids. Height: 45–60 cm (1½–2 ft). Spread: 60 cm (2 ft). Flowers: Early summer to autumn. There is a wide variety of hybrids in a full range of colours. 'Blackbird' is purple; 'Charles Rudd' has pink flowers with a white throat; 'Cherry Ripe' is red; 'Drinkstone' is deep pink; 'King George' is crimson with a white throat; 'Osprey'

Penstemon *'Alice Hindley' flowers over a very long period in summer and is easy to propagate.*

is creamy white and pink. There are many others to choose from, all worth growing.

Don't be put off by the fact that they may not be hardy, because all are very easy to propagate by soft cuttings in August. They'll over-winter happily in the coldframe provided you cover up on very cold nights.

A bright cottage border that might have existed centuries ago since all the plants have ancient uses.

1 *Monarda* 'Vintage Wine'

2 *Tanacetum parthenium*

3 *Helichrysum angustifolium*

4 *Artemisia abrotanum*

5 *Dianthus plumarius*

6 *Filipendula ulmaria*

7 *Nepeta melissifolia*

8 *Agastache foeniculum*

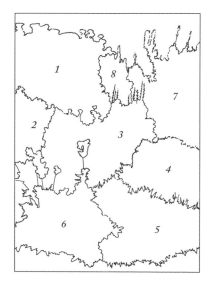

Phlox maculata has been overshadowed by its showier cousin P. paniculata, *but is an excellent cottage plant none the less. It may need staking, but it's much less prone to eelworm attack.*

Phlox spp.

Phlox maculata

Height: 1 m (3 ft). Spread: 45 cm (1½ ft). Flowers: Summer.

An elegant plant introduced in 1740 and not so flamboyant as its cousin, *Phlox paniculata*. It produces cylinders of small flowers on strong stems that don't need staking. The species is lavender-pink and fragrant, while 'Omega' is white with a red eye and 'Alpha' is pink. They like a light soil and a sunny or partially shaded spot. They're much less prone to eelworm attack than *P. paniculata*, but should still be propagated by root cuttings.

P. paniculata. Height: 1.2 m (4 ft). Spread: 60 cm (2 ft). Flowers: Late summer. Introduced to Britain in 1730, this is a showy perennial that grows well on light soil with a little shade. It's very subject to eelworm attack, which causes twisting and swelling of the stems, so buy plants propagated by root cuttings from clean soil.

Look out for the varieties 'Eva Callum' (pink); 'Blue Ice' (white with a blue tint); 'Red Indian' (deep red); 'Mary Fox' (salmon pink with a red eye); and 'Marlborough' (violet-purple).

Remove weak shoots in spring, to concentrate the plant's energies on the remaining flowers. Some shoots can be shortened before flowering to produce branching shoots which will flower later than the main batch. It's best to stake plants, though in dry areas with little wind it's not always necessary. I grow mine through a 'lobster-pot' support made with prunings from my coloured-bark dogwoods.

Physalis franchetii CHINESE LANTERN
Height: 60 cm (2 ft). Spread: 1 m (3 ft). Flowers: Summer/autumn.

The Jacob's ladder is an ancient cottage garden plant, well worth growing for its superb flowers which vary in shade from white to deepest blue. It'll hybridize freely, so it's worth saving seedlings.

A better plant than the ancient bladder cherry (*Physalis alkekengi*), grown since 1549 for its red lanterns and edible fruit. This one has larger lanterns in autumn and more flowers in summer. It has running roots, so needs control and will grow almost anywhere. Propagate by division.

Physostegia virginiana OBEDIENT PLANT
Height: 1 m (3 ft). Spread: 60 cm (2 ft).
Flowers: Late summer.
The running roots of this plant, introduced in 1683, produce a dense clump of shoots with small flowers of pink, white or mauve. If moved from one side to another, the flowers stay where they're put – hence the name. It grows in any reasonable soil and prefers shade. Propagate by division.

Polemonium caeruleum JACOB'S LADDER
Height: 60 cm (2 ft). Spread: 60 cm (2 ft).
Flowers: Early summer.
This ancient plant was grown by the Romans and has been present in cottage gardens ever since. It has attractive, green foliage topped by clear blue bells with orange stamens.

There are several forms to look out for, among them the pinkish white 'Dawn Flight' and the rich blue 'Richardsonii'. They grow in any soil in sun or partial shade and will seed themselves readily, sometimes producing varying colours. Propagate by seed.

Polygonatum hybridum SOLOMON'S SEAL
Height: 1 m (3 ft). Spread: 30 cm (1 ft).
Flowers: Late spring.
An ancient plant, introduced into Britain in 1265. It produces arching stems hung with greenish white bells. There's also a double form, 'Flore Pleno'.

Polygonatum grows well in retentive soils in shade and can be propagated by division of the fleshy rhizomes when the leaves die down.

Ranunculus aconitifolius
BACHELOR'S BUTTONS, FAIR MAIDS OF FRANCE
OR FAIR MAIDS OF KENT
Height: 1 m (3 ft). Spread: 1 m (3 ft).
Flowers: Spring.
Introduced in 1579, this is a strong, vigorous plant and was a great favourite with cottage gardeners of old. It bears single, white buttercups on branching stems. The variety 'Flore Pleno' is supposed to be connected with Huguenot refugees, hence the name 'fair maids of France'. It has double, white flowers. Another variety, 'Grandiflorus', bears larger, white flowers.

Ranunculus likes to be planted in a moist soil and in sun or part-shade. They can be propagated by seed or division.

Rudbeckia fulgida Coneflower
Height: 60 cm (2 ft). Spread: 30 cm (1 ft).
Flowers: Summer/autumn.
Introduced in 1760, this easy plant produces masses of vivid yellow daisies with drooping, yellow petals round a striking, dark brown centre. Look out for the variety 'Goldsturm'. It grows happily in almost any soil in full sun. Propagate by division.

Rudbeckia fulgida *'Goldsturm' is one of the best of the coneflowers. It increases freely, forming large clumps quite quickly, so it's easy to propagate by division.*

Saponaria officinalis Soapwort
Height: 1 m (3 ft). Spread: 1 m (3 ft).
Flowers: Summer.
A native of Europe and naturalized in Britain, this was once used to make soap and is still used for cleaning very fine materials like old tapestries.

It's a coarse, untidy plant for the larger garden and has campion-like single or double flowers of white, pink or crimson. It grows in almost any soil and prefers full sun. Propagate by division or seed.

Scabiosa caucasica Scabious
Height: 60 cm (2 ft). Spread: 60 cm (2 ft).
Flowers: All summer.
Lovely, long-stemmed pincushion flowers surrounded by a ring of petals in white, blue or lavender. Look for 'Clive Greaves' (lavender), 'Moerheim Blue' and 'Loddon White'.

There are also two good new varieties, 'Butterfly Blue' and 'Butterfly Pink', which are more compact. Give them a sunny position and divide the plants every two years and re-plant.

Stachys byzantina Lamb's ears
Height: 45 cm (1½ ft). Spread: 30 cm (1 ft).
Flowers: Summer.
This well-known plant was introduced in 1782 and makes a fine, grey carpet of woolly leaves. It produces magenta-coloured flowers on woolly stems, but after flowering looks rather unkempt. So a few non-flowering varieties have been selected and these are generally to be preferred. The variety 'Silver Carpet' is the best and looks wonderful under roses. It needs a free-draining soil in sunshine and should be propagated by division.

Thalictrum aquilegifolium Meadow rue
Height: 1 m (3 ft). Spread: 60 cm (2 ft). Flowers: Early summer.
Introduced in the early eighteenth century, this stately plant is noted for its delicate foliage (hence the Latin name, which indicates that it has leaves like those of a columbine). It produces mauve/purple flowers and there's also a good white. It likes retentive soil and a sunny spot.

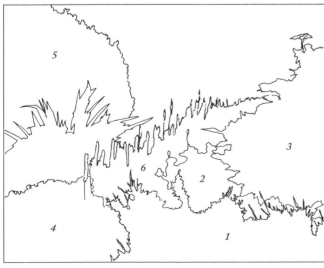

1 *Fabiana imbricata*

2 *Meconopsis cambrica*

3 *Anemone hybrida*

4 *Geranium himalayense*

5 *Clematis* 'Alba Luxurians'

6 *Salvia nemorosa*

In mid-summer the mixed planting in this border looks wonderful: lots of colours but not a jarring note.

Propagate by seed or division. There are taller kinds too (see page 141).

Veronica gentianoides SPEEDWELL
Height: 45 cm (1½ ft). Spread: 45 cm (1½ ft).
Flowers: Early summer.
Introduced in 1784, this is a mat-forming plant which produces spikes of pale blue flowers.

Veronica spicata grows to about the same size, but forms clumps. There are several named varieties worth growing, like 'Heidekind' with rosy red flowers; 'Icicle' (white); 'Romiley' (dark violet); and 'Pink Damask' (dusky pink).

All are easy to grow in well-drained soil in sun. Propagate by division.

Bulbs

Allium spp. ORNAMENTAL ONION
The onions have been grown in cottage gardens since earliest times. Even edible onions produce grey, spiky foliage that looks good among flowers. Try planting a few leeks in the flower border after you've finished digging the crop for the table. The following summer they'll produce fine, large, rounded heads of blue/grey flowers.

However, it's the cultivated ornamentals that really steal the show. Some are quite tall, but they belong in the middle of the border where they'll rise above other plants.

Allium cernuum. Height: 45 cm (1½ ft). Spread: 23 cm (9 in). Flowers: Summer. A smaller, clump-forming plant, valued for its pretty onion foliage and lilac flowers which hang down on small stalks.

A. christophii. Height: 60 cm (2 ft). Spread: 45 cm (1½ ft). Flowers: Summer. This produces fine, rounded heads about 25 cm (10 in) across in a rich violet colour.

A. schubertii. Height: 60 cm (2 ft). Spread: 45cm (1½ ft). Flowers: Summer. Carries large, loose globes of lilac-pink flowers at varying heights. Later, the seed heads are most attractive.

A. tuberosum, known as garlic chives, has starry white flowers and leaves that have a mild taste of garlic. It is also often grown in the herb garden and used in the kitchen.

All the alliums like full sun and a well-drained soil. Propagate by seed or division.

Fritillaria imperialis CROWN IMPERIAL
Height: 1 m (3 ft). Spread: 45 cm (1½ ft).
Flowers: Spring.
One of the good old cottage garden standbys this has been grown since before 1590. It produces large heads of big, bell-shaped flowers at the top of stout stems, topped by a tuft of green leaves. Most are yellow, but the orange variety 'Aurora' makes a fine contrast. There are two with variegated leaves, 'Aureo-marginata' and 'Argentea Variegata', and both are well worth-while growing.

They like a rich soil and do well in limy conditions in sun or shade. Make sure that you plant them deeply or they won't flower. They can be propagated by seed.

Lilium spp. LILY
Some of the lilies have been grown for centuries, and there's a new race of hybrids available that could well be used in modern cottage gardens. They tend to be shorter and to present their blooms upwards, creating quite a show. However, for the aficionado it's the few older species that give the real cottage garden feel.

Lilium candidum. Height: 1–1.5 m (3–5 ft). Spread: 30 cm (1 ft). Flowers: Summer. Known as the madonna lily, this is probably the oldest recorded of them all, and it was certainly grown as far back as the tenth century. It produces wonderful, scented, pure white flowers and is known as the symbol of purity. It's a bit of an odd

The newer hybrid lilies have been bred so that the flowers present themselves upwards, creating a more striking, perhaps somewhat brash effect. Nonetheless some, like 'Enchantment', are well suited to the modern cottage garden.

man out because it *must* be planted in autumn in a sunny spot and it should be covered with no more than about 2.5 cm (1 in) of soil.

L. martagon. Height: 1.2 m (4 ft). Spread: 23 cm (9 in). Flowers: Summer. Another old plant, the Turk's-cap or martagon lily has been cultivated since at least 1596. It has up to about twenty pink flowers per stem, each with reflexing petals like a turban – hence the name. There's a white form, 'Album', and a superb, almost black one, 'Dalmaticum'.

L. lancifolium or *L. tigrinum.* Height: 1.8 m (6 ft). Spread: 30 cm (1 ft). Flowers: Late in summer. A splendid plant, the tiger lily produces black-spotted, orange flowers. Unfortunately it's very prone to virus diseases.

L. pyrenaicum. Height: 60 cm–1.2 m (2–4 ft). Spread: 30 cm (1 ft). Flowers: Summer. Another old variety cultivated since the sixteenth century, the Pyrenean lily produces spikes with ten or more small, greenish yellow, Turk's-cap flowers with spots and lines. There's also an orange variety.

L. regale. Height: 1–1.8 m (3–6 ft). Spread: 30 cm (1 ft). Flowers: Summer. The regal lily is one of the best whites with a strong perfume. Each stem has up to twenty trumpets with white on the inside and purple staining on the outside. There's also a pure white variety, 'Album'.

L. auratum. Height: 2.4 m (8 ft). Spread: 30 cm (1 ft). Flowers: Late summer. Introduced from Japan in 1862, the popular golden-rayed lily produces about twenty scented flowers of ivory with a central band of yellow and purple spotting.

Most lilies should be planted in autumn or spring among herbaceous plants or shrubs where the roots will be shaded but the heads in the sun. Prepare the soil first by digging in organic matter, and on heavy soil rest the bulbs on a good layer of grit. Generally plant so that the tops of the bulbs are covered with 10–15 cm (4–6 in) of soil. They can be propagated by removing and planting 'scales' taken from the bulbs.

Ornithogalum nutans BATH ASPARAGUS
Height: 45 cm (1½ ft). Spread: 15 cm (6 in).
Flowers: Early summer.
A British native, rare in the wild but widely cultivated. It was popular in the earliest cottage gardens for its panicles of green-and-white flowers and for its edible shoots. It prefers some shade and an open, well-drained soil. Propagate by division immediately after flowering.

Ornithogalum thyrsoides. Height: 45 cm (1½ ft). Spread: 15 cm (6 in). Flowers: Early summer. Known as the chincherinchee, this was introduced to Britain from South Africa in 1757. It produces attractive, creamy white flowers over a long period. Unlike the British native, this needs a sunny spot. Propagate by division after flowering.

Scilla peruviana
Height: 45 cm (1½ ft). Spread: 30 cm (1 ft).
Flowers: Early summer.
Produces large heads of white or violet, star-shaped flowers. Needs a retentive soil and a sunny spot. Propagate by division.

Tulipa spp. and hybrids TULIP
Of course, there are hundreds of tulips that admirably suit the cottage garden and they're far too numerous to list here. I suggest you get hold of a specialist catalogue to choose. But bear in mind that tulips need to be baked in the sun to thrive and produce new bulbs. In a cottage garden that's not easy, because the bulbs are swamped with the foliage of surrounding plants and in almost total shade. You may therefore need to replace them every year or two.

My own experience has been that, happily, the one type to survive for a long time is the cottage tulip. So that would be my own priority, and it certainly looks best in cottage gardens. There are many varieties in all colours. Lily tulips and parrot tulips also fit in well, as does the species *Tulipa sprengeri* which has lovely, orange-red flowers and seems to seed itself around. Plant the bulbs in the autumn or early winter.

Plants for the Front of the Border

❀

Shrubs

Cytisus kewensis BROOM
Height: 30 cm (1 ft). Spread: 60 cm (2 ft).
Flowers: Early summer.
A prostrate broom raised at Kew in 1891, this has delightful, creamy white flowers. Look out also for the variety 'Nikki' which bears yellow flowers. *Cytisus prostratus* 'Golden Carpet' is about the same size and has brilliant yellow flowers. Grow them in a sunny spot in well-drained soil and propagate by half-ripe cuttings in summer.

Genista pilosa BROOM
Height: 30 cm (1 ft). Spread: 1 m (3 ft). Flowers: Late spring/early summer.
This British native is closely related to *Cytisus* and confusingly also called broom. It forms a prostrate mat of yellow pea-like flowers. Look for the variety 'Lemon Spreader' or the slightly taller 'Goldilocks'. Grow them in any well-drained soil in full sun and propagate by softwood cuttings in summer.

Lavandula angustifolia OLD ENGLISH LAVENDER
Height: 60 cm (2 ft). Spread: 60 cm (2 ft).
Flowers: Summer.
Old English lavender has been around since 1265, but actually it's not English at all, having been brought to Britain from the Mediterranean. Of course, it's quite indispensable in the cottage

The French lavender at the front of this border displays its peculiar flowers with two 'rabbit's ears' petals protruding from the top. It goes well with a fine clump of honesty at the back.

garden. Its grey foliage and copious blue flowers are superbly perfumed and a magnet for bees. It has been used as a scent for centuries and is still one of the best air fresheners available.

There are now many different named varieties, like the white 'Alba' and the vigorous lavender-blue 'Grappenhall'. If you want to mix colours, there are also several pink varieties, such as 'Loddon Pink' and 'Hidcote Pink'. None, in my view, is as satisfactory as the traditional lavender-blue varieties.

If you want a dwarf hedge, go for 'Munstead' or the white 'Nana Alba'. The variety 'Vera' is Dutch and has large, grey leaves. French lavender (*Lavandula stoechas pedunculata*) is also worth searching out; it has strangely shaped flowers with petals protruding from the top like rabbit's ears and is very attractive, though it's for warm gardens only.

Clip over plants in the spring, removing all flower heads and cutting down to within a few centimetres of the old wood but not into it. Regular attention will ensure that the plants remain compact and bushy. Give them a sunny spot and very good drainage, and propagate by softwood cuttings in summer.

Rosa spp. and varieties

'Cécile Brunner'. Height: 75 cm (2½ ft). Spread: 60 cm (2 ft). A delicate little Polyantha rose, producing perfectly shaped, pink blooms from pointed buds.

'Emily'. Height: 75 cm (2 ½ ft). Spread: 60 cm (2 ft). An English rose with soft pink, cupped flowers and a strong fragrance.

'Kathryn Morley'. Height: 75 cm (2½ ft). Spread: 60 cm (2 ft). An appealing little English rose with numerous soft pink flowers.

'Little White Pet'. Height: 75 cm (2½ ft). Spread: 60 cm (2 ft). A cottage favourite, producing a cushion of delicate, creamy white blooms.

'Nathalie Nypels'. Height: 75 cm (2½ ft). Spread: 60 cm (2 ft). An attractive Polyantha rose with semi-double flowers of strong pink. Very free-flowering.

'Pretty Jessica'. Height: 75 cm (2½ ft). Spread: 60 cm (2 ft). A good, repeat-flowering English rose with cupped flowers of strong, deep pink.

---

1 *Tanacetum haradjanii*

2 *Arabis alpina* 'Flore Pleno'

3 *Ajuga reptans*

4 *Aurinia saxatilis* 'Dudley Nevill Variegated'

5 *Thymus vulgaris* 'Silver Posie'

6 *Anthemis punctata cupaniana*

7 *Myosotis*

8 *Armeria welwitschii*

9 *Phlox douglasii*

10 *Erysimum torulosum*

11 *Osteospermum* 'Langtrees'

12 *Teucrium polium*

13 *Alchemilla mollis*

14 *Lunaria annua*

15 *Lonicera nitida* 'Baggesen's Gold'

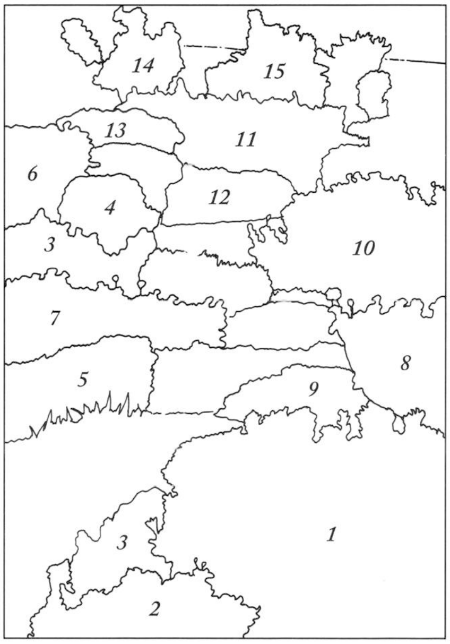

A superb cottage border in early summer, filled with low-growing plants.

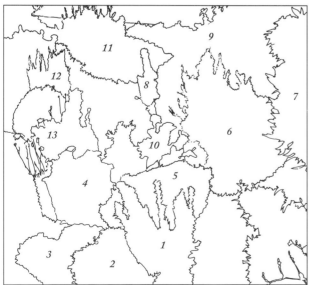

1 *Sisyrinchium californicum*

2 *Eschscholzia californica*

3 *Nemophila menziesii*

4 *Anthemis punctata cupaniana*

5 *Santolina chamaecyparissus* 'Lemon Queen'

6 *Lonicera nitida* 'Baggesen's Gold'

7 *Weigela* 'Florida Variegata'

8 *Delphinium* 'Blue Tit'

9 *Philadelphus* 'Boule d'Argent'

10 *Rosa* 'Pink Peace'

11 *Lavatera olbia*

12 *Berberis thunbergii* 'Red Pillar'

13 *Campanula persicifolia* 'Alba'

However little you may feel you know about the artistry of planting, remember that nature will always give you a helping hand. Here a little natural backlighting creates a magical effect.

Another English rose, 'The Prince', produced the longest flowering season of all in my artisan's garden.

'Pretty Jessica' is an English rose ideal for near the front of the border. It retains the lovely 'quartered' shape of the old roses while flowering continuously.*

Rosa richardii. Height: 1 m (3 ft). Spread: 1.2 m (4 ft). Probably the oldest rose in cultivation. It forms a sprawling shrub with clear pink, single flowers followed by black hips. Leave unpruned.

'The Prince'. Height: 75 cm (2½ ft). Spread: 60 cm (2 ft). A superb English rose with deep crimson flowers turning deep purple. An excellent colour and free-flowering habit.

Santolina chamaecyparissus 'Nana' COTTON LAVENDER
Height: 30 cm (1 ft). Spread: 45 cm (1½ ft).
Flowers: Summer.
Grown in cottage gardens since the sixteenth century, this is really a foliage plant with bright, silvery leaves which are finely divided and very delicate. The bright yellow flowers are a bonus.

It must have a sunny and very well-drained position, so add plenty of coarse grit if your soil is very heavy. Propagate by taking cuttings in late summer.

Santolina virens is about the same size, but has green leaves which contrast well with the vivid yellow flowers.

Teucrium fruticans SHRUBBY GERMANDER
Height: 30–60 cm (1–2 ft). Spread: 60 cm (2 ft).
Flowers: Summer.
A lovely, grey-leaved, evergreen shrub grown in cottage gardens since 1714. All summer long it's clothed in delicate blue flowers which contrast well with the foliage. It's considered to be tender, but I've grown it in my cold garden for years with no problems. Still, it's best to give it the protection of a south wall if you can. It must have full sun and excellent drainage. Propagate by softwood cuttings in summer.

Wall germander (*Teucrium chamaedrys*) is smaller and has a creeping rootstock, so it could need controlling. It has attractive, toothed leaves and pink flowers. Give it similar conditions as shrubby germander, or plant it in a wall pocket. Propagate by dividing the root.

Herbaceous Plants

Anemone nemorosa WOOD ANEMONE or
WINDFLOWER
Height: 15 cm (6 in). Spread: 30 cm (1 ft).
Flowers: Spring.
A British native that grows in shady woodland
and is ideal under shrubs. It produces dainty
flowers in white or sometimes pale pink or even
blue. There are several named forms in pink, lilac
and blue. It runs easily, but is never intrusive.
Propagate by division.

Anthemis punctata cupaniana
Height: 30 cm (1 ft). Spread: 1 m (3 ft).
Flowers: Early summer.
A lovely edging plant for a sunny spot, this
produces silvery mats of foliage topped by
chalk-white daisies. Propagate by division.

I would also recommend golden marguerite
(Anthemis tinctoria) for the front of the border
even though its flower heads reach 1 m (3 ft),
because it will flop over the paths and make an
excellent edging plant. The mats of green foliage
are a fine foil to masses of brilliant yellow daisies
in summer. Look out especially for the variety
'E.C. Buxton', which is lemon-yellow, and the
creamy yellow 'Wargrave'.

Arabis caucasica ROCK CRESS
Height: 23 cm (9 in). Spread: 60 cm (2 ft).
Flowers: Early spring to early summer.
Introduced in 1798, this well-known and popular
cottage plant is widely grown to tumble down
walls and to edge paths. It forms a mat of
grey/green foliage covered in snow-white flowers. There are a few pink varieties too. It must
have good drainage, so work in some coarse grit
before planting. Propagate by seed sown in spring
in the coldframe.

Armeria maritima THRIFT or SEA PINK
Height: 10 cm (4 in). Spread: 20 cm (8 in).
Flowers: Summer.
A British native and grown in cottage gardens as
edgings to paths since the sixteenth century. It
makes hummocks of spiky, green foliage covered
with deep pink flowers. There are also a few
varieties of *Armeria juniperifolia* (or *caespitosa*)
worth growing. 'Bevan's Variety' is bright pink
and 'Alba' is white.

Aubrieta hybrids
Height: 15 cm (6 in). Spread: 45 cm (1½ ft).
Flowers: Spring
Introduced in the late seventeenth century, this
delightful little edging or rock plant has been a
favourite ever since. There are several good
modern hybrids which are far superior to the old
cottage plants. Look for the carmine 'Alix Brett'
and the red double 'Bob Saunders'. 'Maurice
Prichard' is pink and 'Red Carpet' is, of course,
red. They must have a well-drained soil and sun.
After flowering, cut them over with shears to
keep them bushy and perhaps to restrict their
spread. They can be increased by cuttings in
spring in the coldframe.

Campanula carpatica BELLFLOWER
Height: 10 cm (4 in). Spread: 20 cm (8 in).
Flowers: Summer
Introduced in 1774, this is another invaluable
edging plant, making mats of green foliage
covered in upward-facing bells of white or blue.
There are several good named varieties, all of
which need a well-drained soil and a sunny spot.
They love to warm themselves on path edges.
Propagate by division in autumn or spring.

Cerastium tomentosum SNOW-IN-SUMMER
Height: 5 cm (2 in). Spread: 1 m (3 ft).
Flowers: Early summer.

The pinks in the front of this border flower for a long time and stand out well against the dark foliage of Berberis thunbergii *'Atropurpurea Nana' and the purple sage on the left of the picture. The planting is dominated by a hybrid lily in the centre.*

Grown since 1648, but too invasive for small gardens. For preference grow *Cerastium tomentosum columnae*, which is better behaved. It makes mats of silvery foliage topped by masses of white flowers. Grow it in sun in poorish soil and propagate by division.

Convallaria majalis LILY-OF-THE-VALLEY
Height: 23 cm (9 in). Spread: 30–60 cm (1–2 ft).
Flowers: Late spring.
Grown in gardens since the earliest times, but not without its problems. It's a rapid and rampant colonizer, so it needs regular control. However, it produces lovely, sweet-smelling white flowers in profusion. It'll grow almost anywhere in sun or shade and in any soil. A much better form is the large-flowered 'Fortin's Giant', and there's a pink one too: 'Rosea'. If you can find it (and afford it!), there's an extraordinary variety with green-and-

yellow-striped leaves called 'Vic Pawlowski's Gold'. It's superb, but expensive. Propagate by either digging up a chunk and transplanting it, or setting out individual roots in autumn or early spring.

Dianthus hybrids GARDEN PINKS
Height: 25 cm (10 in). Spread: 30 cm (1 ft).
Flowers: Summer.
Grown in cottage gardens certainly since the seventeenth century, the old pinks are not to be missed. They have delightful flowers in many shades of pink, white and red, often with wonderful markings and the finest perfume in the garden. Alas, the old pinks flower, in the main, only once, but modern hybrids are perpetual. However, some have lost the old-fashioned look in the breeding and a few have even lost some of their perfume. The best bet is to grow modern

hybrids that combine the old-fashioned look and perfume with perpetual flowering. Varieties like 'Gran's Favourite', white with purple lacing; 'Becky Robinson', pink laced with red; 'Devon Cream', an unusual variety with a yellow background streaked with pink; and, of course, 'Doris' with shrimp-pink flowers with a carmine ring and a very strong perfume.

Don't miss out on the older varieties, though, such as 'Mrs Sinkins', raised in 1868 by the master of Slough workhouse and named after his wife; it has fringed white flowers and a powerful perfume. 'Bridal Veil' was raised in the seventeenth century and bears very double flowers with fringed petals and a red central zone; while 'Nonsuch', from the same period, is single and pink with red markings.

Above all, pinks must have good drainage, so on heavy soil use lots of coarse grit and give them a sunny position. Propagate by cuttings in the coldframe in mid- to late summer. They can also be grown in gritty, soil-based compost in pots.

Dodecatheon meadia SHOOTING STAR
Height: 50 cm (20 in). Spread: 23 cm (9 in).
Flowers: Early summer.

A delightful little plant which came from the USA in 1774. It produces clumps of fresh green foliage and pink, cyclamen-like flowers. It needs moist soil and semi-shade and resents disturbance. Propagate by division or seed.

Erigeron karvinskianus or *E. mucronatus*
Height: 15 cm (6 in). Spread: 15 cm (6 in).
Flowers: Summer.

A marvellous small daisy that starts white and changes to pink and then red before fading; it continues flowering all summer. It likes a sunny spot, but will also grow in shade and even seeds itself in walls. Propagate by seed sown in the coldframe in spring. Though it's a perennial, it's probably best grown as an annual.

Euphorbia myrsinites SPURGE
Height: 15 cm (6 in). Spread: 30 cm (1 ft).
Flowers: Early summer.

Introduced in 1570, this unusual plant produces straggling, prostrate stems with rosettes of evergreen, blue-tinged leaves and flowers of greenish yellow. This type of spurge likes to be grown in a sunny spot at the front of the border. It can be propagated by division.

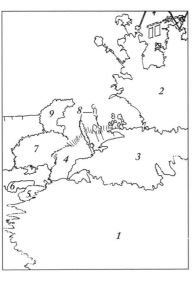

1 *Nepeta faassenii*
2 *Rosa* 'Chapeau de Napoléon'
3 *Acanthus mollis*
4 *Stipa arundinacea*
5 *Dianthus deltoides*
6 *Viola* 'Bowles' Black'
7 *Paeonia lactiflora*
8 *Aconitum* 'Bicolor'
9 *Lavatera olbia*

William Robinson's garden at Gravetye has been restored to its original splendour.

Geranium himalayense *is ideal for the front of the border. Its leaves often produce brilliant autumn colours, but it runs underground so it could need restraining. Still not to be missed.*

Geranium spp. Cranesbill

Many of the cranesbills are suitable for the front of the border, especially those that spread. See page 152.

Geum rivale Avens

Height: 30 cm (1 ft). Spread: 30 cm (1 ft).
Flowers: Early summer.
A British native for cool places. Look out for 'Leonard's Variety' with bell-shaped flowers of coppery pink flushed with orange, and 'Lionel Cox' with similar flowers in primrose-yellow.

Geum borisii is a hybrid with large, warm orange flowers, well worth growing in sun or part-shade.

G. chiloense. Height: 60 cm (2 ft). Spread: 45 cm (1½ ft). Flowers: Early summer. Taller plants with the flowering heads on longer stems and also sun-lovers. Two popular varieties are 'Mrs Bradshaw' which is bright, deep red and 'Lady Stratheden' which is deep yellow. Both can be raised from seed and are well worthwhile. Otherwise propagate by division.

The strong orange flowers of Geum borisii *are considered by some to be difficult to place. Try using them as contrast in a blue border and they really come into their own.*

Helleborus niger Christmas rose

Height: 30 cm (1 ft). Spread: 45 cm (1½ ft).
Flowers: Winter.
Pure white flowers are produced generally after Christmas, though a lot depends on the particular plant. Some will make it, most won't. If you must have them for the festive season, put a cloche over them. For cultivation details see under 'Lenten rose' on page 154.

Heuchera spp.
Heuchera americana Alum root or coral flower

Height: 45 cm (1½ ft). Spread: 30 cm (1 ft).
Flowers: Early summer.
Introduced to Britain from the USA in 1656, this species is really grown for its foliage. Its rounded

leaves are mottled green and coppery brown, and the dainty spikes of green flowers are a bonus.

H. sanguinea is the same-sized plant as the above species, but with green leaves marbled with white. It produces tall spires of bright red flowers. It has, however, been superseded by several hybrids like 'Red Spangles', the pink 'Charles Bloom' and crimson 'Gloriana'. They make excellent edging plants or ground cover and are happy in most well-drained soils in sun or part-shade. It's important to divide them every two or three years and this should be done in late summer/early autumn.

Iris chrysographes
Height: 45 cm (1½ ft). Spread: 30 cm (1 ft).
Flowers: Early summer.
Makes a clump of grassy leaves with several spikes of almost black flowers. Look for the variety 'Black Knight'. It will grow in sun or part-shade. Propagate by seed or division.

Limonium latifolium SEA LAVENDER or STATICE
Height: 30 cm (1 ft). Spread: 45 cm (1½ ft).
Flowers: Late summer.
Grown since 1791, this attractive plant produces clouds of tiny lavender-coloured flowers which are often dried for winter decoration. It likes full sun and a well-drained soil. Propagate by seed, division or root cuttings in early spring.

Liriope muscari LILYTURF
Height: 30 cm (1 ft). Spread: 45 cm (1½ ft).
Flowers: Autumn.
This old plant has long been used to edge borders in cottage gardens. It makes tufts of grassy leaves from which arise spikes of small, violet flowers. It likes sun and a well-drained soil. If, as sometimes happens, it refuses to flower, shift it to another place, at the same time dividing it. Propagate by division.

Lychnis flos-jovis FLOWER OF JOVE
Height: 45 cm (1½ ft). Spread: 45 cm (1½ ft).
Flowers: Early summer.
A close relative of the British native campion, this has been grown since 1726. From clumps of greyish, woolly foliage arise heads of typical campion-red or deep pink flowers. The variety 'Hort's Variety' is clear pink. Grow them in sunshine and ordinary soil and propagate by division.

Nepeta faassenii CATMINT
Height: 45 cm (1½ ft). Spread: 45 cm (1½ ft).
Flowers: Summer.
Introduced in 1784, this lovely plant has graced cottage gardens ever since. Its blue, lavender-like flowers are borne above attractive, greyish foliage. It's beloved of cats, which like to find a plant in the sun and lie in it, but they can be deterred by a sprig or two of holly or berberis placed in the middle of the clump. It prefers a sunny spot and well-drained soil. Propagate by division. See also *N. gigantea* on page 157.

Omphalodes cappadocica BLUE-EYED MARY
or NAVELWORT
Height: 23 cm (9 in). Spread: 23 cm (9 in).
Flowers: Summer.
A delightful small plant for a shady spot. It has simple, blue flowers throughout the summer and requires retentive soil and some shade. Look out too for the 'Irish Form', whose flowers form a five-pointed cross of dark blue on a very pale blue background.

Omphalodes verna has been grown since 1633. It's slightly smaller and differs in its cobalt-blue flowers which appear in spring. Treat it in the same way. Propagate both by division in spring.

Polygonum affine (correctly now *Persicaria affinis*)
KNOTWEED
Height: 23 cm (9 in). Spread: 30 cm (12 in).

Flowers: Summer/autumn.

A slowly spreading, carpeting plant that can become invasive if not controlled with a spade in spring. The variety 'Superba' is the one to grow, with pinkish white flowers turning crimson. It likes retentive soil in sun or part-shade.

Persicaria amplexicaulis grows to 1.2 m (4 ft), but the variety 'Arun Gem' will reach only 60 cm (2 ft) and is well worthwhile for its bright pink flower spikes. The variety 'Inverleith' is crimson.

All like a reasonably retentive soil and some shade.

Potentilla hybrids Cinquefoil
Height: 45 cm (1½ ft). Spread: 60 cm (2 ft).
Flowers: Summer.

Most of the hybrid potentillas have strong-coloured flowers which will last for a long period during summer and are ideal for the front of the border. They tend to spread and sprawl across the surface. Look out particularly for the bright red 'Gibson's Scarlet', the mahogany-and-red 'Gloire de Nancy' and the orange 'William Rollison'.

Potentilla nepalensis has much the same habit and some very good varieties too. 'Roxana' is rosy orange; 'Miss Willmott' is a good pink; while 'Master Floris' is yellow and deep pink.

All prefer good drainage and full sun and are propagated by division.

Primula spp.
Members of this large genus have been grown in cottage gardens since the earliest times. Then they would have been collected from the wild but now, of course, that's illegal. Fortunately the natives are generally not difficult to raise from seed.

Primula veris. Height 20 cm (8 in). Spread: 23 cm (9 in). Flowers: Spring. The cowslip is a well-known British native with spires of scented, yellow flowers. It prefers full sun and a limy soil.

There are many named varieties of Primula vulgaris, *our native primrose, including this one called 'Quaker's Bonnet' (now correctly called* P. vulgaris *'Lilacina Plena'. They quickly form a good clump and are best divided every other year.*

Propagate by seed sown in trays or modules in the coldframe. It can be grown in grass but is best established by growing in pots or modules and planting rather than by direct sowing.

P. vulgaris. Height: 15 cm (6 in). Spread: 15 cm (6 in). Flowers: Spring. The primrose bears characteristic, flat, yellow flowers and prefers shade and a retentive soil. Propagate by seed as for cowslips or by division. There are also many named varieties, both singles and doubles, in a wide range of colours. Look out for the superb, double pink 'Quaker's Bonnet'; the double purple, edged white 'Miss Indigo'; the deep crimson 'Roy Cope'; and the yellow 'Sunshine Suzie'. There are many, many more excellent varieties. For best results they should be divided regularly, preferably annually.

P. polyanthus. A cross between primrose and cowslip, the polyanthus forms a large group with many varieties in a huge range of colours from blue to yellow, orange, red and white. The most popular are perhaps the Pacific hybrids, but the Barnhaven strain is quite superior.

P. elatior. Height: 25 cm (10 in). Spread: 23 cm (9 in). Flowers: Spring. Another British native carrying tall stems of scented yellow flowers, the oxlip prefers a sunny spot and ordinary soil. Propagate by seed or division.

P. denticulata. Height: 30 cm (1 ft). Spread: 30 cm (1 ft). Flowers: Spring. Known as a reliable plant, the drumstick primula, introduced in 1842, produces tall stems on top of which are large, spherical flowers like drumsticks. Hybrids are available in shades of lavender, purple, pink, crimson and white. It prefers a moist soil and some shade. Propagate by seed or division.

Candelabra primroses. Height: 50 cm (20 in). Spread: 30 cm (1 ft). Flowers: Summer. Tall stems carry loose heads of flowers in shades of yellow, orange, pink, cream, red and purple. The plants prefer moist soil and some shade and should be propagated by division. Look out especially for *P. beesiana* with yellow-centred, pink flowers; *P. bulleesiana*, which has flowers in a wide range of colours; the salmon/orange 'Inverewe'; 'Miller's Crimson', with flowers of red/pink with a black eye; and 'Postford White'.

P. florindae. Height: 60 cm (2 ft). Spread: 60 cm (2 ft). Flowers: Summer. A vigorous, spreading plant producing tall stems with loose heads of yellow, drooping flowers. It prefers moisture and sun or partial shade. Propagate by seed or division.

Pulmonaria officinalis LUNGWORT
Height: 25 cm (10 in). Spread: 45 cm (1½ ft). Flowers: Spring.
Grown since before 1597 and thought to be a cure for diseases of the lungs because the spotted leaves were said to resemble a diseased lung. Actually they're quite attractive. The plant bears pretty pink-and-blue flowers too. There are also some lungworts without spotted leaves, among which is the superb 'Sissinghurst White'.

P. angustifolia. Height: 23 cm (9 in). Spread: 45 cm (1½ ft). Flowers: Spring. Introduced in 1731, this lower-growing plant produces pink buds which open to blue, so there are always the two colours on the plant at once.

P. saccharata. Height: 30 cm (1 ft). Spread: 60 cm (2 ft). Flowers: Spring. Introduced before 1683, this handsome plant has long leaves which are spotted or completely silver/grey. The flowers are pink in bud, opening to blue.

All lungworts like a shady spot and a retentive soil, though they'll grow well under trees. Propagate by division or seed, or collect the numerous self-sown seedlings.

Pulsatilla vulgaris PASQUE FLOWER
Height: 30 cm (1 ft). Spread: 30 cm (1 ft). Flowers: Spring.
A now rare native, this beautiful flower was certainly dug up and grown in cottage gardens. It's not difficult to raise from seed, so it's still readily available. It produces wonderful pink, purple or white flowers from a clump of silky, finely divided foliage. It prefers well-drained soil in full sun. It was once used to dye eggs green at Easter.

Saponaria ocymoides BOUNCING BET
Height: 15 cm (6 in). Spread: 30 cm (1 ft). Flowers: Summer/autumn.
A fine plant for the front of the border, this will form spreading hummocks covered in pink flowers over a long period. It prefers sun and a well-drained soil. Propagate by seed.

Sedum spectabile ICE PLANT
Height: 45 cm (1½ ft). Spread: 45 cm (1½ ft). Flowers: Late summer and autumn.
A clump of thick, fleshy leaves produces large,

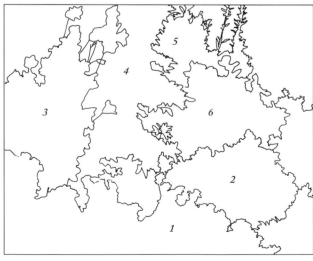

1 *Alchemilla mollis*
2 *Viola cornuta* 'Belmont
Blue'
3 *Campanula persicifolia*
4 *Choisya ternata*
'Sundance'
5 *Brachyglottis greyi*   *A yellow and blue summer*
6 *Clematis viticella* 'Etoile   *border with real,*
Violette'   *old-fashioned charm.*

flat heads of deep pink. Look for the varieties 'Brilliant', 'Autumn Joy' and 'September Glow', which are darker and more intense. They prefer a well-drained soil and full sun. The plants must be divided at least every two years or the stems flop away to leave a bare centre.

Silene dioica CAMPION
Height: 30 cm (1 ft). Spread: 30 cm (1 ft).
Flowers: Spring and early summer.
The taller red and white campions are common hedgerow weeds, but still lovely plants. I don't deliberately grow them, but if they happen to land in the border, I let them live until after flowering, when they look tatty. But I do grow the dwarf variety 'Minikin'. This forms a neat hummock of downy foliage covered with deep pink, campion flowers: well worth growing in any soil in a sunny spot. Propagate by division.

Solidago 'Golden Thumb' GOLDEN ROD
Height: 25 cm (10 in). Spread: 25 cm (10 in).
Flowers: Late summer.
A dwarfer version of golden rod (see page 141), forming a neat clump topped by bright yellow flowers. It prefers a sunny position and grows in almost any soil. Propagate by division.

Viola spp. VIOLET and PANSY
The sweet violet was first mentioned in the tenth century, so it's clear that violets have been grown in cottage gardens for many years. Indeed no cottage garden could be called genuine without them. There are many species and hybrids, most not difficult to grow. The larger-flowered pansies are very popular in modern gardens but are better grown fresh each year since they're never as good after the first season.
Viola odorata. Height: 15 cm (6 in). Spread: 15 cm (6 in). Flowers: Spring. This is the sweet violet of nosegays and a delightful little plant

producing, naturally, violet flowers with a delightful and typical perfume. There are now several named varieties worth looking out for, so get hold of a specialist catalogue. They need a shady spot in summer, and are therefore ideal under shrubs or in shade. Divide them annually if you can.
V. cornuta. Height: 30 cm (1 ft). Spread: 60 cm (2 ft). Flowers: Summer. A plant that produces masses of leaves and masses of flowers too. They're deep violet and there's a paler one, 'Lilacina', and a good white, 'Alba'. After flowering, cut the plants back with shears and water them and they'll flower again. They like a fertile soil and sun or part-shade.
V. labradorica. Height: 7.5 cm (3 in). Spread: 30 cm (1 ft). Flowers: Late spring. A rampant ground coverer, but not a problem because it's easy to pull out, and the purple leaves make it much to be desired. The flowers are light purple. It grows in any soil in sun or shade. Propagate by division.
V. tricolor. Height: 15 cm (6 in). Spread: 15 cm (6 in). Flowers: All summer. A lovely, unassuming little native with a delightful 'face' of yellow, purple, blue, cream or white, the heartsease is short-lived but will seed itself around and is always welcome. It'll grow almost anywhere, but after the first year it'll choose its own spot. Propagate by seed.
V. wittrockiana. Height: 15 cm (6 in). Spread: 15 cm (6 in). Flowers: Most of the year, depending on variety. A short-lived perennial, generally grown as a biennial.
There are hundreds of pansy varieties in every colour imaginable and there are hundreds more coming off the breeding production line every year. Sow in pots or trays in early summer for the following year. Bear in mind when germinating pansy seed that they need to be dark and not too hot, so the coldframe will be ideal.

Bulbs

Anemone blanda WINDFLOWER
Height: 15 cm (6 in). Spread: 15 cm (6 in).
Flowers: Spring.
Introduced in 1898, this easy and reliable plant produces lovely blue, white or pink flowers early in the year. Plant in large drifts in sun in rich soil. Propagate by division. There are named varieties available and recommended are 'White Splendour', the soft pink 'Charmer' and the magenta 'Radar'.

Anemone blanda *likes good drainage and sun, so it's a popular plant for the rock garden but equally at home in the front of a border. Improve heavy soil with coarse grit before planting.*

Anemone coronaria
Height: 15–30 cm (6 in–1 ft). Spread: 30 cm (1 ft). Flowers: Early spring.
Introduced in 1596, this tuberous plant produces white, red or blue flowers. It prefers good, retentive soil and semi-shade.

Crocus spp.
Height: 10–15 cm (4–6 in). Spread: 7.5 cm (3 in). Flowers: Early spring.
The Dutch yellow crocus (*Crocus aureus*) has been grown since before 1597. The Scotch crocus (*C. biflorus*) is another old one, with white flowers

flushed silvery blue. They like an open, sunny situation but, because they flower early, are fine under deciduous shrubs. Propagate by division in late summer.

Cyclamen hederifolium
Height: 15 cm (6 in). Spread: 23 cm (9 in).
Flowers: Autumn.
This delightful little plant unfailingly produces pink flowers over lovely marbled leaves in green and grey. It's perfect under trees in semi-shade, where it thrives. Very similar is *Cyclamen coum*, which flowers in the early spring. Propagate both by collected seed sown as soon as it's ripe.

Cyclamen coum *flowers in the early spring and makes a very welcome splash of colour. Always buy plants and not dry corms which are rarely successful.*

Erythronium dens-canis DOG'S-TOOTH VIOLET
Height: 15 cm (6 in). Spread: 23 cm (9 in).
Flowers: Spring.
Grown since at least 1596, this has lance-shaped, spotted leaves and attractive, purple-pink flowers with reflex petals. It likes a moist, retentive soil and some shade. The name refers to the shape of the bulb, which resembles a dog's tooth. There

are also excellent species available from the USA now, where the spotted leaves have won the plant the name of toad lily. *Erythronium revolutum* has taller, brighter pink flowers with a yellow centre. Look out too for the variety 'Pagoda', which can reach up to 30 cm (1 ft) and produces delightful, yellow bells.

Fritillaria meleagris SNAKE'S-HEAD FRITILLARY
Height: 38 cm (15 in). Spread: 15 cm (6 in).
Flowers: Spring.
This delightful, delicate plant produces hanging bells of chequered flowers in shades of maroon, purple, pink, grey and white. It grows well in the shade of shrubs or trees, or in grass in sun. Plant in the autumn and don't disturb the clumps. Fritillaria will spread quite encouragingly, though not rapidly.

Galanthus nivalis SNOWDROP
Height: 20 cm (8 in). Spread: 15 cm (6 in).
Flowers: Late winter.
One of the first bulbs to flower and a cheering sight. The small, white, green-tipped bells are well known and there are very attractive doubles too. Don't buy dry bulbs, which have a low chance of survival: it's better to look for plants lifted fresh after flowering. Plant them straight away in retentive soil beneath trees or shrubs where they won't be disturbed. They'll seed themselves freely and can be propagated by division.

Iris danfordiae
Height: 30 cm (1 ft). Spread: 10 cm (4 in).
Flowers: Late winter.
A delightful little bulbous iris which produces its yellow flowers before the leaves: a cheerful sight in winter. It needs a sunny spot and good drainage. Plant 10 cm (4 in) deep in an attempt to prevent the bulbs splitting up after flowering,

which will mean that there are no blooms in the following year. Otherwise, plant every year.

Iris reticulata
Height: 15 cm (6 in). Spread: 10 cm (4 in).
Flowers: Early spring.
Following on from the above is this small, blue-flowered bulb. It needs the same conditions and is available in a few interesting varieties.

Leucojum spp. SNOWFLAKE
The snowflakes have been grown in cottage gardens since the sixteenth century. They're somewhat like larger snowdrops and will grow in moist soil in shade, except for the autumn snowflake which likes sun and good drainage.
Leucojum aestivum. Height: 45 cm (1½ ft). Spread: 30 cm (1 ft). Flowers: Late spring/early summer. This, the summer snowflake, produces pendulous bells of white, prettily marked with green.
L. autumnale. Height: 25 cm (10 in). Spread: 15 cm (6 in). Flowers: Late summer/autumn. The autumn snowflake bears similar flowers to those of its summer cousin but pale pink.
L. vernum. Height: 20 cm (8 in). Spread: 15 cm (6 in). Flowers: Late winter/early spring. The spring snowflake has white flowers marked with green.
Like snowdrops, snowflakes are best planted freshly lifted while the leaves are still green. Propagate by division.

Muscari botryoides GRAPE HYACINTH
Height: 30 cm (1 ft). Spread: 15 cm (6 in).
Flowers: Spring.
The Elizabethans grew grape hyacinths, but this particular one was introduced in 1896 and supersedes others. It produces prolific blue or white flowers over a long period, but the foliage persists for some time, so plant later-leafing

Crocus and anemones produce a fine show in the early spring underneath deciduous trees which will not, of course, shade them from the spring sunshine.

herbaceous plants to cover the fading leaves. Plant in autumn. It likes sun and well-drained soil. Propagate by division, lifting the clump straight after the leaves have faded, and re-plant the divisions immediately to prevent drying out.

Narcissus spp. DAFFODIL

A tremendously varied plant, producing well-known and favourite flowers in spring. Taller varieties are not too happy in small cottage gardens since the leaves are very messy after flowering has finished. It is possible, of course, to plant to cover them, but my own preference would be to stick mainly with the smaller types at the front of the border. The flowers vary from pure white

Snowdrops (Galanthus nivalis) *are often the first flowers to appear in the new year and are a welcome reminder that spring is just around the corner. They were widely grown in monastery gardens. On 2 February, Candlemas Day, statues of the Virgin Mary were removed from altars and replaced with snowdrops for the Feast of the Purification of the Virgin.*

to orange and even pale pink. All grow well in well-drained soil in sunshine. Plant in late summer or early autumn, covering the bulbs with twice their own depth of soil: shallow planting leads to non-flowering. After flowering, allow the foliage to die down naturally so that it has time to build up the bulbs for flowers for the following year. For a wide choice of varieties, get hold of a specialist's catalogue.

Annuals and Biennials

Hardy annuals were a mainstay of old cottage gardens. The seed could be collected from year to year and, indeed, many of them will seed themselves with no encouragement whatever. Once you sow the poached egg plant (*Limnanthes*) or a few marigolds, you've got them forever. Don't be alarmed by the prospect, though, because they're very easy to pull out if they're growing in the wrong place.

They can be sown where they're to flower and they're best grown in patches between other plants. So just scratch some shallow furrows with a stick and sow into those in early spring. When they appear, they can be thinned out to the required distance. Alternatively they can be raised in plastic modules and planted out (see page 198).

Few half-hardy annuals are really cottage flowers, though I can't imagine the modern cottager being able to resist putting in a few. The best way with these is to buy plants after all danger of frost has gone and plant them, as for hardy annuals, in patches. Alternatively they can be raised on the windowsill and put out into the coldframe when the weather warms up a little.

Biennials were also very popular and no cottage garden was without its wallflowers and forget-me-nots. They're a bit more of a problem because they need to be sown in a seed bed in early

There can be few plants quite so typical of the traditional cottage garden as the English marigold. It was widely grown in pots on windowsills and was a more or less obligatory tenant of the borders outside. It was also popular in herb gardens where it was used both medicinally and in cooking. The seed is very easy to collect and sow, but it'll happily sow itself too. Not to be missed.

summer and transplanted to a nursery bed about 15 cm (6 in) apart to grow into bushy plants before being put into their flowering positions in autumn. If you have the space to do it, you'll always grow much better plants than you can buy.

Hardy Annuals

Alyssum
Height: 15 cm (6 in).
White flowers. There is a pink too, but it's not a good cottage garden plant and should be strenuously avoided.

Anchusa
Height: 23 cm (9 in).
Star-like flowers of deep blue. Good insect attractor.

Antirrhinum SNAPDRAGON
Height: 15–60 cm (6 in–2 ft).
Well-known annuals in a mixture of colours and heights. Some older varieties were subject to a rust disease but there are now resistant ones.

Bartonia
Height: 45–60 cm (1½–2 ft).
Produces large, glistening, golden flowers.

Calendula ENGLISH MARIGOLD
Height: 30–60 cm (1–2 ft).
Well-known flowers in orange and yellow shades.

Centaurea CORNFLOWER
Height: 75 cm (2½ ft).
This bears very double flowers in deep blue. There are other colours, but not as good.

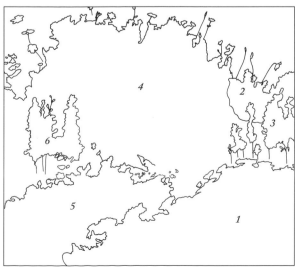

1 *Calendula* 'Fiesta Gitana'

2 *Papaver commutatum* 'Ladybird'

3 *Antirrhinum* 'Dwarf Mixed'

4 *Agrostemma* 'Milas'

5 *Gypsophila* 'Elegans'

6 *Delphinium* 'Dwarf Hyacinth-Flowered'

Hardy annuals make a brilliant border for just a few pounds and many will reappear the next year.

Clarkia
Height: 30–45 cm (1–1½ ft).
A great cottage favourite with semi-double flowers in pink, purple and white.

Convolvulus minor
Height: 30 cm (1 ft).
An eye-catching plant with bells of pink, blue and white with contrasting centres. A good insect attractor.

Delphinium LARKSPUR
Height: 1–1.2 m (3–4 ft).
Produces stunning tall spikes of pink, lavender, violet and white.

Dimorphotheca
Height: 30 cm (1 ft).
White, yellow and orange daisies. A good cut flower.

Echium
Height: 30 cm (1 ft).
Blue, pink and white flowers over a long period.

Eschscholzia CALIFORNIAN POPPY
Height: 30 cm (1 ft).
Produces silky flowers in shades of red, pink, orange and white.

Godetia
Height: 15–45 cm (6 in–1½ ft).
Another cottage favourite with azalea-like blooms of pink, lavender, lilac and white.

Gypsophila
Height: 45 cm (1½ ft).
Produces clouds of dainty, white flowers often used to mix with cut flowers. Unfortunately, it's often called 'Baby's Breath', but the flowers are none the worse for that.

Helianthus SUNFLOWER
Height: 2–3 m (6–10 ft).
A fun plant to grow, with huge, yellow flowers, but not beautiful.

Helichrysum STRAWFLOWER
Height: 30 cm–1.2 m (1–4 ft).
Bears mainly yellow and orange blooms which are often used for drying.

A packet of mixed seeds of Helichrysum bracteatum *will provide dried flowers for winter decoration. Pick them as they're just opening.*

Iberis CANDYTUFT
Height: 23 cm (9 in).
An edging plant in shades of pink, lavender and white.

Lathyrus SWEET PEA
Height: 30 cm (1 ft).
Apart from the climbing varieties (see page 113), there are a few low-growing ones that are excellent towards the front of the border. They come in the normal range of colours.

Lavatera ANNUAL MALLOW
Height: 60 cm–1.2 m (2–4 ft).
Similar flowers to its perennial cousin, in glowing pink and white.

Leptosiphon
Height: 12–15 cm (4–6 in).
A dainty edging plant producing masses of small, star-shaped flowers in many colours.

Limnanthes POACHED EGG PLANT
Height: 15 cm (6 in)
Produces masses of yellow flowers edged with white: a real eye catcher and an excellent insect attractor.

The poached egg plant, Limnanthes douglasii, *will unfailingly reseed itself each year. It's one of the best attractors of the greenfly-eating hoverfly which feeds on its pollen before laying eggs.*

Linum SCARLET FLAX
Height: 30–45 cm (1–1½ ft).
Bears silky, open flowers of brilliant red.

Nigella LOVE-IN-A-MIST
Height: 45 cm (1½ ft).
Pretty, rounded flowers in shades of pink, blue and white.

Papaver POPPY
Height: 30 cm (1 ft).
There are some superb hardy annual poppies now. Look out for the orange, yellow and white mixture 'Summer Breeze' and especially the bright-red-and-black 'Ladybird'.

Phacelia
Height: 23 cm (9 in).
An excellent plant for edging, it has bell-shaped flowers in the deepest gentian blue.

Reseda odorata MIGNONETTE
Height: 30 cm (1 ft).
No Victorian cottage garden was ever without this. The greenish flowers are not striking, but the perfume is sweet and very strong in the evening.

Tropaeolum NASTURTIUM
Height: 23 cm (9 in).
Brilliant, trumpet-shaped flowers in red, orange, yellow and pink. It will grow in the poorest soil and flower its heart out. There are also trailing and climbing varieties.

Half-hardy Annuals

Amaranthus LOVE-LIES-BLEEDING
Height: 75 cm (2½ ft).
Mentioned by Thomas Tusser in the sixteenth century and described as a 'countrywoman's

flower', this has been grown as a windowsill plant and in cottage borders ever since. It produces drooping tassels of deep crimson. It looks best as a single specimen.

Aster
Height: 60–75 cm (2–2½ ft).
Valuable because it flowers in late summer and autumn, producing large, daisy flowers in a range of blues, pinks, yellows and white.

Centaurea
Height: 1 m (3 ft).
The annual centaurea has thistle-like flowers of lilac-pink all summer.

Cosmos COSMEA
Height: 1 m (3 ft).
Indispensable cottage garden flowers. The ferny foliage sets off large daisies like single dahlias, in pink, red and white.

Dianthus ANNUAL PINKS
Height: 30 cm (1 ft).
These have much of the charm of the you get with perennials without the difficulties. They produce typical flowers in scarlet, white, crimson and pink.

Heliotropium HELIOTROPE or CHERRY PIE
Height: 38 cm (15 in).
A well-known plant in cottage gardens for generations. It forms compact cushions of deep purple flowers.

Nicotiana FLOWERING TOBACCO
Nicotiana sylvestris grows to 1.5 m (5 ft) with large, shining, green leaves and great sprays of scented, tubular, white flowers: not to be missed. *N. langsdorffii* is a little shorter with smaller leaves and delicate green flowers.

Biennials

Bellis ENGLISH DAISY
Height: 15 cm (6 in).
Cheerful little double daisy in pink or white. It makes an excellent companion for the smaller forget-me-not.

Campanula grandiflora CANTERBURY BELL
Height: 45–75 cm (1½–2½ ft).
Produces upright spikes clothed with semi-double, cup-and-saucer-shaped flowers in pink, lavender, blue and white.

Cheiranthus WALLFLOWER
Height: 30–45 cm (1–1½ ft).
A very showy, old-fashioned plant available in all the colours of the rainbow. Shorter varieties are especially good for spring containers. Always raise them yourself from seed sown outside. Bought plants are nearly always thin and weedy and those now offered in trays at garden centres are definitely to be avoided. Remember that after planting in autumn they'll make only a small amount of growth before flowering, so strong, bushy plants are essential.

Dianthus barbatus SWEET WILLIAM
Height: 15–60 cm (6 in–2 ft).
Lovely, old-fashioned flower making a large head filled with individual florets like auriculas. However, flowering in mid-summer makes it an awkward customer, so it's now rarely grown, with the preference being for longer-flowering half-hardy bedding. If you can find room for at least a few, they're well worthwhile.

Digitalis FOXGLOVE
Height: 1–1.5 m (3–5 ft).
Grown in cottage gardens since the earliest times, this plant, bearing tall, majestic spikes of

bell-shaped flowers, is indispensable. It's available in maroon, yellow, pink, purple and white, many of the colours with attractively spotted throats. It'll grow happily in shade, and seed itself.

Lunaria HONESTY
Height: 60 cm (2 ft).
Produces strong, branching stems with spikes of pretty purple or white flowers followed by attractive seed heads suitable for drying.

Matthiola incana BROMPTON STOCK
Height: 45 cm (1 ½ ft).

Wonderfully fragrant spring bedding plant with single or double flowers in pink, crimson, lavender and mauve.

Matthiola tricuspidata EAST LOTHIAN STOCK
Height: 30 cm (1 ft).
A bushier plant than the Brompton stock but otherwise much the same. It flowers late, in early summer, so, like sweet Williams, it can be a bit difficult to fit into the scheme of things.

Myosotis FORGET-ME-NOT
Height: 15–38 cm (6–15 in).
Wonderful blue flowers in spring, the smaller

A typical cottage combination for the spring is the small English daisy or bellis planted with forget-me-nots. When they've finished, the border could be filled with hardy or half-hardy annuals.

varieties mixing well with bellis and the taller ones with tulips. It'll naturally seed itself, but when you pull out plants, shake them over areas where you want them next year, just to make sure.

Viola PANSY
Often grown as a biennial (see page 181).

Tender Perennials

Never be put off growing tender perennials because they're a bit more trouble than hardy plants. That they certainly are, but most have so many good attributes that they're well worth a little extra effort. They're very easily propagated from cuttings in late summer and over-wintered on a sunny windowsill in a cold but frost-free room. They'll grow so little during the winter that they need only low levels of light, and when they get going again in spring they can be put out into the frame. Just make sure that you keep an eye on the weather forecast and cover with a thick blanket or sacking if hard frost is forecast.

They can be planted out in late spring or early summer, generally before the half-hardy annuals but after danger of hard frost has passed. Many will flower right through the summer, especially if you dead-head the blooms that have faded.

Argyranthemum spp. MARGUERITE
Height: 45–60 cm (1½–2 ft).
This easy-to-grow plant produces large daisy flowers in the genuine cottage tradition. It's available with single or double flowers in white, yellow, pink and apricot, and is very easy to propagate from cuttings.

Dahlia varieties
Height: 45 cm–1 m (1½–3 ft).
Another plant with hundreds of varieties, so get hold of a specialist's catalogue. There are two varieties which are generally recommended for cottage gardens and both are excellent, though I would suggest that you should not let your interest remain there.

The airy, lilac-flowered *Dahlia merckii* is a graceful plant for the middle to the back of the border. There's a similar white variety too, called 'Hadspen Snowflake', which is well worthwhile.

For a really dramatic display grow the large-flowered scarlet 'Bishop of Llandaff', which has superb bronze foliage and so stands out in any

Tender perennials make a colourful show in late summer. Don't be put off growing them, because they're all easy to over-winter as cuttings on the windowsill of the spare bedroom or, with care, even in a coldframe.

1 *Osteospermum* 'Lady Leitrim'
2 *Argyranthemum* 'Jamaica Primrose'
3 *Salvia microphylla neurepia*

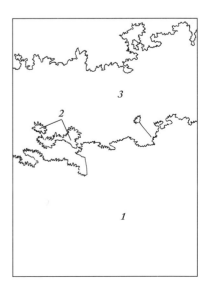

The marguerites, like this Argyranthemum *'Jamaica Primrose', are among the best of the tender perennials, producing a mass of superb daisy flowers right through the summer. Dead-head them regularly.*

border. It's rather subject to virus disease, though, so you might prefer 'Bednall Beauty', which is very similar.

The plants should be set out after all danger of frost has passed and supported with strong stakes. After the autumn frost has touched the foliage, dig up the tubers and box them up in garden compost with the tops just showing. In spring put them on a sunny, warm windowsill and water them, when they will produce shoots that can be used as cuttings.

Fuchsia varieties
Height: 45 cm–1 m (1½ –3 ft).
The hardy fuchsias are covered on page 143. Their half-hardy cousins are more flamboyant and will flower throughout the season. They come in a complete range of reds, pinks, blues, purples and whites, generally with two-coloured flowers. They can be grown as bushes, or single stems can be grown on over a few seasons to produce standards. This is done simply by removing all side shoots but leaving the leaves all the way up the stem. When the plant reaches the required height, the top is pinched out and the side shoots allowed to grow. They're pinched back subsequently to make a bushy head. Fuchsias are very easily propagated by cuttings taken in late summer and over-wintered on a cool windowsill or in a frost-free greenhouse. The parent plants can be lifted and kept in a just-frost-free place for the winter.

Pelargonium varieties GERANIUM
Height: 30–45 cm (1–1½ ft).
The favourite windowsill plant of cottage gardens and grown widely in all gardens in summer. It's so well known that it's hardly necessary to describe the large, ball-shaped heads of florets in a range of whites, pinks and reds, some with attractive markings on the petals. Many have two-colour zoning on the leaves too and there are also variegated varieties.

Like fuchsias, geraniums can be grown as

The perennial salvias, such as Salvia patens, *are not at all like their rather regimental-looking annual cousins. They produce a succession of intensely coloured flowers throughout late summer.*

Osteospermum varieties
Height: 23–60 cm (9 in–2 ft).
An attractive and showy plant from South Africa, but very much in the cottage tradition. It produces dazzling, large daisies in shades of blue, pink, purple, yellow or white. Given a sheltered, sunny spot and very good drainage, some have proved quite hardy in my cold garden, but it's still wise to take cuttings in late summer as an insurance. Again, over-winter the young plants on a cool windowsill and put them in the coldframe as soon as the danger of hard frost has passed.

Penstemon varieties
Height: 23–75 cm (9 in–2½ ft).
The hardy types are covered on page 159, but there are several that are on the borderline. Give them similar conditions to osteospermums (see above) and take cuttings in late summer.

Salvia spp.
Height: 23 cm–1.2 m (9 in–4 ft).
There are several varieties of the perennial salvia that are hardy only in the warmest gardens and many that won't even survive there. Give them sun, shelter and excellent drainage and they may last the winter. *Salvia uliginosa*, for example, has stood several very cold winters in my garden and its airy stems of blue flowers make it perfect for cottage gardens. But I always take cuttings just in case.

S. patens has never survived and doesn't come easily from cuttings. Fortunately it produces abundant seed which is collected in late summer and stored over winter in envelopes in a dry cool place. Sow in spring in a gentle heat. It has flowers of the most vivid gentian-blue and there's also a light blue and a white.

Look out too for the red-flowered *S. involucrata* 'Bethellii' with large crimson flowers. It's not difficult to propagate from cuttings.

bushes or standards. They're easily propagated by cuttings in late summer and I take cuttings from the cuttings too once they start to grow in spring, to double or quadruple the stock. The parent plants can also be lifted and stored in boxes of garden compost in a frost-free shed or garage during the winter. Keep them cold and very dry. The best way, though, is to grow young plants taken from cuttings and kept on the windowsill as described for fuchsias (see page 194). They can also be raised from seed, but this is not for us: they need to be sown in winter in a heated greenhouse and thus are very expensive to grow.

The only problem with over-wintering is a disease called black-leg. Avoid it by keeping plants very dry and airy.

Propagation

❀

Growing new plants from those in your garden or that of a friend is one of the most satisfying of gardening pursuits. It's also, of course, by far the cheapest way to fill your garden and it takes less time than many new gardeners might imagine.

In days gone by, nurseries were very few and far between and geared only to supplying the gentry. Cottage gardeners could ill afford to buy plants, though the real enthusiasts, and particularly those growing florist's plants, would not only walk miles to find new specimens, but would also spend much more than was wise. Of course, some of us still do that today!

On the whole, though, plants were propagated by the cottagers themselves, mainly by division – they would simply dig them from the wild or beg a piece from a friend. Many plants were distributed by monks and nuns too, and I'm sure that they would also have given seeds and cuttings to working people to take home and grow on.

Equipment was necessarily simple and techniques were sometimes quite outlandish. There are many suggestions in the first gardening manuals of, for example, practices like grafting apples on to elm or oak to change their characteristics: techniques which today we know to be biologically impossible.

In the main, rural cottage gardeners would have had no truck with such methods in any case. They were well used to the ways of nature and were no doubt expert at handling seeds and cuttings. We can learn a lot from those simple, old-fashioned techniques, all of which are just as valid today. But, of course, with modern matrials they're much easier and more successful.

PERENNIALS WITH SEEDS SUITABLE FOR COLLECTION

Acanthus	*Dierama*	*Kniphofia*	*Primula*
Achillea (but not hybrids)	*Digitalis*	*Lathyrus*	*Prunella*
Agapanthus	*Echinacea*	*Liatris*	*Rodgersia*
Alchemilla	*Echinops*	*Limonium*	*Rudbeckia*
Alstroemeria	*Erigeron*	*Linaria*	*Salvia*
Anaphalis	*Euphorbia*	*Liriope*	*Sidalcea*
Anchusa	*Festuca*	*Lychnis*	*Sisyrinchium*
Aquilegia	*Filipendula*	*Malva*	*Stipa*
Astrantia	*Gaillardia*	*Meconopsis*	*Tellima*
Campanula	*Gentiana* (some)	*Oenothera*	*Teucrium*
Catananche	*Geranium*	*Omphalodes*	*Thalictrum*
Centaurea	*Geum*	*Paeonia*	*Tiarella*
Cimicifuga	*Helleborus*	*Papaver*	*Trollius*
Coreopsis	*Hesperis*	*Phlomis*	*Veratrum*
Delphinium	*Heuchera*	*Physalis*	*Viola*
Dictamnus	*Incarvillea*	*Polemonium*	

Raising Plants from Seed

Since it's always best to use fresh seed, collect your own if you can, though bought-in seed will normally have been properly stored and will give results almost as good.

Try to collect seeds just before the plant sheds them naturally. That often means daily trips to check progress, the alternative being to wait until the seed heads turn brown and then to put a paper bag over them, tied to the stem.

It's slightly different with berries, which have to be collected before the birds strip them. However, sowing them slightly before they're ripe does no harm. Before sowing, squeeze them out of their fleshy coating.

Bring the seed heads into a dry place to clean them. It's always best to separate the seeds from the chaff, since it's there that fungus diseases lurk. I find that the best way is to separate them with the end of a knife, but if you can master the cottage skill of winnowing, so much the better. That involves tossing them up in a shallow dish to allow the breeze to blow the lighter chaff away before the seeds fall back. It takes skill and practice, which I confess I've never managed to master.

Hardy herbaceous plants, shrubs, trees and alpines should be sown straight away. Use a compost consisting of equal parts of good sieved soil, coarse grit and coir (coconut-fibre) compost in a clay pot. Water the compost and sow the seeds on top. Cover with a shallow layer of coarse grit and put the pot into the coldframe.

The seeds of herbaceous plants will be collected throughout the growing season as they mature,

If you're collecting seed, choosing the right time is probably the most difficult part of the operation. You can be sure that it's ripe if you wait until the first seed pod has released its contents naturally. Then collect the whole head into a paper bag and detach it from the plant for further drying.

and some of the earlier collections could be sown direct in shallow drills in the soil of a nursery bed. Sowing in pots, though, does give more control over conditions. It's certainly the best bet for later-maturing seeds.

They, together with the seeds of trees, shrubs and alpines, can stay in the coldframe over winter without protection from frost. The frame serves simply to keep them from becoming water-logged. The natural cold spell will trigger germination and they'll normally start to grow in the spring.

Tender perennials and annuals are somewhat different. A genuine cottage garden will contain few modern F1 hybrids, but it's worth remembering that there's no point in collecting the seeds from these since the new plants won't resemble the parent. The chances of them being worth having are remote in the extreme.

All hardy annuals and the non-F1 hybrid half-hardies are worth collecting. Take them from the plants and clean them (see page 197), but this time store them over winter and sow them in spring. They must be stored in airtight containers (film canisters are ideal) in a dry, cold place.

Sowing Hardy Annuals

Hardy annuals can be sown direct in the soil outside in early spring, in shallow drills in well-prepared but unfertilized soil. They need little in the way of nutrients and will flower better if they're a bit hungry.

Even though you'll almost certainly want to grow them in an informal drift, it's still best to sow them in rows within the required area. Weeds will also germinate at the same time as the annuals, and it's much easier to differentiate the latter if they're in straight lines. Later they can be thinned out to the required distances and transplanted if required.

Many plants can be easily raised from seed sown direct into plastic modules, though avoid the type with very small cells that growers use. Sow a tiny pinch of seed per cell, then cover with a little silver sand.

To get an earlier show, or if your soil is cold and wet, you can also sow in modules. These are plastic trays divided into many separate cells and I'd bet that the old cottagers would have killed for them.

In late winter fill them with coir compost and sow a tiny pinch of seed to each cell. Put them in the coldframe if you have room, but if not they'll germinate perfectly well outside. I grow mine on a paved area, but first I put down a piece of old sacking or felt carpet underlay to act as an absorbent base. This is kept wet so that the plants can draw up water as and when needed. Plant out as soon as the plants have formed enough roots to hold the root ball together. This is also a good way to raise hardy herbaceous plants.

Sowing Half-hardy Annuals

Half-hardy annuals need heat to germinate, so they'll have to be raised inside. Germination is

*Half-hardy annuals like these tobacco plants will have to be
raised inside. In the gentleman's greenhouse there's no problem,
but artisans can also succeed growing them on the windowsill.*

easy either over a radiator or, much better, in a
small electric propagator.

There are actually very few seeds that need
darkness to germinate, so I have a rule-of-thumb
method for all except those that the seed packet
tells me need to be kept dark. I sow on the surface
of moist coir compost and cover with vermiculite.
Then I cover the seed trays or pots with clear
plastic and place them over the heat source. If,

like pansies, for example, they must have darkness, I cover them with black polythene.

It's when they germinate that the problems
begin, because there's simply not enough light,
even on a bright windowsill, to produce strong,
bushy seedlings. One solution is to make a light
box by cutting the front out of a strong cardboard
box and painting the inside with white gloss to
reflect all available light round the seedlings.

A better answer is to make a portable coldframe
by again painting a strong box gloss white inside
and outside. Cover the top with a piece of rigid
polythene and fix some string handles to the

sides. Then, whenever the temperature is high enough, the seedlings can be conveniently taken outside in the morning and brought back in when it gets colder in the late afternoon. It works very well, provided sowing is delayed until early spring. That's plenty early enough anyway.

Sowing Herbaceous Perennials and Biennials

The easiest way to raise new herbaceous perennials and biennials from seed is to sow outside and the method is the same for both kinds of plants. Sow in late May or early June in shallow drills in a seed bed outside. Cover the seeds and tamp down with the back of a rake. When the seedlings germinate and have grown big enough to handle, transplant them about 15 cm (6 in) apart in a nursery bed to grow on. Plant them in their final positions in the early autumn and they'll flower fully the following year.

Taking Cuttings

Softwood Cuttings

Softwood cuttings of shrubs and herbaceous perennials can be taken at any time between early and late summer. Look for soft shoot tips that have grown in the current year and cut them off about 7.5 cm (3 in) long. Put them into a polythene bag straight away and keep them out of the sun.

As soon as you get them back to your work bench, trim the cuttings below a leaf joint and remove the lower leaves with a sharp knife. It's hard to be precise about exactly how many leaves to leave on, but generally two would suffice. In fact, if the remaining leaves are very big, there's no reason why they shouldn't be cut in half to reduce moisture loss from the cutting.

Dip the whole cutting into a fungicide solution

In the artisan's garden I use a portable potting bench on the tool-box-cum-workbench to take the cuttings which are put into pots, covered with polythene and then put straight in the coldframe.

like copper fungicide (old cottage gardeners would probably have called it Bordeaux mixture) to ensure complete protection and then dip the end into hormone rooting powder or liquid. Dibble the cuttings into a pot of compost consisting of equal parts of coir seed-and-cuttings compost and vermiculite. Then water in with the fungicide solution. Cover the cuttings with a very thin, clear polythene sheet so that it's actually touching the leaves and tuck it in underneath or secure it with an elastic band. The aim is to make an airtight seal to eliminate moisture loss.

The pots can then go into the coldframe, which should be kept shaded with netting. If you have the time to put two layers of netting over the frame on very bright days, one layer on fairly bright days and none at all on dull days, you'll have even greater success, though it's not absolutely necessary. The cuttings should root in six to twelve weeks.

Tender perennials like argyranthemums and geraniums are treated in the same way except that the cuttings should be taken in late summer and there's no need for the polythene cover. Put them on a dull windowsill, out of direct sunlight.

Half-ripe Cuttings
If you fail with shrubs from softwood cuttings, you get another chance in late summer with half-ripe cuttings. Look for shoots about 7.5 cm (3 in) long that have grown in the current year. Instead of cutting them, pull them off the main stem, taking a little sliver of bark with the shoot. Again, put them in a polythene bag until you get to your work bench.

Then trim the sliver of bark to leave a very short stub and remove the lower leaves. Dip the cuttings into fungicide and rooting powder or liquid as for softwood cuttings and put them into pots of the same 50/50 compost, but this time dispense with the polythene. Place them in the coldframe and close it up. They should take about eight to twelve weeks to root.

If you want to take a lot of cuttings, as you would, for example, when you're building up enough box plants to plant a knot garden, you can dispense with the pots and put the cuttings straight into a bed of compost in the coldframe. Here the compost consists of equal parts of coir and sharp sand. Never use builder's sand.

Hardwood Cuttings
Hardwood cuttings are the easiest type to use for propagation and no doubt were the most common among the earlier cottagers. Many shrubs and roses and a few trees will respond well.

The best time to take hardwood cuttings is autumn, when the soil is still warm from the summer sun. Look for shoots about 23 cm (9 in) long that have grown during the current year and take them preferably from near the base of the plant. Cut them off as close to the main stem as possible. Trim off the soft top just above a leaf joint and trim the bottom just below one.

Dip the cuttings into hormone rooting powder or, better still, liquid and then cut a trench in a corner of the garden by pushing in the spade and pulling it backwards and forwards. Line the bottom with sharp sand and put in the cuttings 7.5 cm (3 in) apart so that only the top 7.5 cm (3 in) is above ground. Push the soil back into the trench and firm with your boot.

The cuttings will take all year to root, so simply leave them there, weed from time to time and lift them the following autumn for planting in their permanent positions.

Division

The simplest and most commonly practised way of increasing your stock of herbaceous perennials is to divide the roots in autumn or spring. In fact, division can start late in summer and continue through until early winter when the soil will still be warm, but after that, if the plant is anything but completely hardy, vigorous and reliable, it's best to wait until spring.

Then simply lift the whole plant and remove the stronger, younger outside pieces, either by pulling them off or cutting with a sharp knife. In the case of tough roots like those of hostas, it's easiest to use an old bread knife to saw them into pieces.

Most herbaceous perennials respond well to this treatment and prefer to be divided and re-planted in this way every three to five years. In the process you can make many more plants. If you decide to re-plant in the same place, make sure that you dig out all the old root and revitalize the soil with plenty of organic matter.

In autumn or spring most herbaceous perennials can be lifted and divided. It should be possible to split them by pulling the root system apart with your fingers. Wash off excess soil first.

Sometimes the roots are too tough for this and you'll have to attack them with a knife. That's no problem as long as you can see that you're taking a bud or some leaves with each piece.

Topiary

As well as clipping and training shrubs and trees growing in the garden into pleasing shapes, you can use topiary to great effect on container-grown plants to make architectural features that are interesting and attractive all year round. Box, bay and holly are suitable subjects.

Training simple shapes, like cones, cubes or balls, is largely a matter of clipping slowly with secateurs, simply by eye. This can be a daunting task, since one slip can take some time to grow back again. The secret is to trim the plants little but often, perhaps even as frequently as every

Crowded cottage garden borders have immense charm and are not difficult to achieve. Of course, you'll make mistakes, but if you master the skills of propagating your own plants, it doesn't really matter a lot if you lose the odd one or two.

three to four weeks. And you have the consolation of knowing that, if you do make a mistake, it will eventually grow back again.

With some shapes, like cones and pyramids, for example, you can make up a template with canes to act as a guide.

The attractive spirals cut into cylindrical box and yew plants are first lined out with a piece of rope twisted round the plant. A shallow cut is then made into the foliage, the rope removed and the cut deepened to the main stem. Then the foliage is carefully trimmed to round the edges of the corkscrew shape.

Creating elaborate sculptures is more complicated. Here it's best to make up a design first of all, using thick wire. The shape is placed over the young plant and supple young growths are tied into it at regular intervals. The design is finished off by clipping. Again, do it little but often.

SECTION THREE

A Cottage Economy

*T*HE ORIGINAL COTTAGE GARDENS were there for only one purpose. They were essential to feed the working man's family. Until the Black Death in 1348, labourers worked for their masters on a feudal basis, exchanging their labour for the rent of their cottages and perhaps some food. Mostly they had to be self-sufficient, growing what they could, keeping livestock, and hunting and gathering from the wild. Anything they 'bought' was obtained by the age-old barter system.

However, the scourge of bubonic plague wiped out about a third of the population, so suddenly labour was hard to come by and the serfs found themselves in a seller's market. Many of them were able to negotiate wages to buy some of their essentials. Still, it wasn't much, and the cottage garden and surrounding common land were always vital to their existence.

Conditions for the modern cottage gardener are, thankfully, very different. But while there's no physical need to grow your own, there are still enormous advantages. As ever, raising the food to feed your family will improve the quality of your life greatly.

First there's the fact that you'll be confident that you know exactly what chemicals did or did not go on to your crops. Of course, it may be that there's absolutely nothing to worry about, but I'd just like to know why the tractor driver has to get himself all dressed up like a spaceman before he sprays my lettuces. No thanks. Growing plants organically is the natural way in a cottage garden and it's much cheaper too.

There's also a tremendous difference in the quality of good, home-grown fruit and vegetables. I'm not convinced that organic gardening improves flavour and I'm not at all sure that, asked to taste the difference, I'd be able to pick out the chemically grown produce from the real McCoy. But the difference in home-grown flavour because of its *freshness* is very easy to detect. Just try it with early potatoes or peas and I know you'll agree.

Above all, there's a primeval satisfaction in growing your own produce. I suppose it's those hunter-gatherer genes talking to us, but I know that I get a very warm feeling when the shed's full to overflowing with winter roots and I know my family will eat this winter. Yes, I *know* I could go to the supermarket and buy all I wanted, but the satisfaction's still there.

PAGES 204-5 *Don't let anyone ever tell you that fruit and vegetables have no aesthetic value. In a cottage garden they look very beautiful.*

OPPOSITE *Even the artifacts used in the vegetable plot have a country appeal.*

RIGHT *Growing food was the original reason for the cottage garden and is just as important today.*

Vegetables

❈

Cultivation Methods

After Enclosure gathered pace, cottage gardeners had to make use of every bit of space that was left to them and, for different reasons, we need to do the same. Most modern gardens are small and our priorities are different. Without the absolute necessity of growing our own food, most of us prefer to devote the lion's share of the space to ornamental plants. These days they're just as important to our mental well-being as food was to the early cottagers' physical health. Whatever space is left over must therefore be used to maximum effect. There are two approaches.

The Bed System

After all my years of gardening, I've come to the conclusion that there's no better way to make use of small spaces than to grow vegetables on 1.2 m (4 ft) wide beds.

The idea is to raise the fertility to a very high level with annual applications of good compost or manure. That, coupled with the fact that all the work is done from the side paths and the soil is trodden on only once a year when it's dug, makes the best possible environment for rapid growth and massive crops.

The organic matter supplies plant nutrients, improves drainage and water-holding capacity and also provides a home for billions of beneficial bacteria. The raising of the soil resulting from its addition improves drainage and makes the bed much warmer. The fact that the bed is never

I decided to grow my vegetables in small beds in both the gentleman's and the artisan's garden. Here in the gentleman's I edged the beds with Victorian tiles to add a decorative touch.

In the artisan's garden I used tanalized timber for the edgings, then double-dug and planted up a tiny salad area. There's very little space, but enough for at least a few really fresh veg.

walked on increases the air space between soil particles and prevents compaction, giving the roots a free run and increasing the area from which they can draw food.

Ideally the beds should initially be dug two spades deep, but that's not essential. After the first year, single digging is all that's needed.

When sowing or planting, do so in blocks rather than in rows. In other words you many plant, say, six rows of lettuce 15 cm (6 in) apart each way to form a large block, without any need for access paths in between. So, by growing on the space that would, under the conventional system, be used for access paths, you straight away double productivity. Add to that the well-known fact that high fertility equals bigger yields and you can expect bumper harvests every year.

Growing in the Borders

Some gardens, of course, don't have room for even the smallest vegetable bed, but that needn't stop you growing vegetables. The answer is to grow them, just like the old cottagers did, in among the flowers in the borders.

This is another method I investigated thoroughly for my book *The Ornamental Kitchen Garden*, but I can claim no credit for the idea. That goes to an unknown cottager some time back in the Dark Ages.

The fact is that vegetables were *always* grown in patches among flowers and herbs. It was only when Turnip Townsend invented the horse-drawn seed drill that we began to grow in rows. Up to that time even the farmer broadcast seed by hand in random fashion. When the drill and the horse-hoe were invented, they were, of course, of immense value to farmers, so gardeners copied the trick of growing in long, straight rows in the mistaken idea that it must be good for them too. Nothing could be further from the truth.

First, growing vegetables in patches among flowers dispenses at a stroke with the farmer's biggest problem – monoculture. If we can hide our vegetables away, they're much less likely to be attacked by pests or diseases. And if pests do seek them out, the balanced environment of the flower borders will have attracted a colony of other wildlife that includes the enemies of those pests. Nature will do the job for us.

There's also something very enjoyable about growing in small patches, because it's much less daunting. You can come home from work and, before you sit down to eat, you can have dug over a small patch and sown it with the next crop of fresh veg.

The technique is very simple. Leave a few patches in the front of the border where you can get at them. They can be almost any size, because you can grow two or three patches of one vegetable if you need more. To keep the fertility high put on a 5 cm (2 in) layer of compost every time you sow or plant, add a little organic fertilizer and fork it all in with a small border fork. Deep digging is unnecessary and will disturb the roots of neighbouring plants. Then firm the soil a little by tamping it down with the back of the fork.

If you're sowing, simply scratch shallow furrows in the soil at the required distances apart, sow thinly into them, cover by scuffling some soil over the drills with your hand and pat them down.

For bigger seed like broad beans, sow individually in a circle. When the beans come up, they make an attractive column and can be supported by a single cane in the middle.

It's a very simple, very productive method and, most importantly, the vegetables and flowers mix quite happily together. They look good and produce high yields which don't need any spraying, and the tool kit needed is a fork, bucket and a stick. This is *real* cottage gardening.

The Victorian gentry came up with the peculiar idea that vegetables were ugly and should therefore be hidden away in a separate vegetable plot lest delicate young 'gels', setting eyes upon them, should have an attack of the vapours. Cottage gardeners at the time fortunately never experienced the dubious advantage of such high-born nonsense and continued to grow their vegetables in among the flowers. Few could deny that, grown this way as a part of the whole garden, they add a great deal and will certainly improve the lot of the gardener in every way.

Old Methods

Vegetable-growing techniques for gardeners have hardly changed since those early days when cottagers *had* to produce most of their food from their gardens. It's still sensible to add manure to the soil if possible, or to substitute compost where it's difficult to obtain. The soil still needs fertilizer and, though we would rarely think of using the contents of the privy and there's often not room for even a few chickens, we can certainly put on much the same kind of plant food in the form of organic fertilizer bought by the bag. We still hoe and plant, harvest and sow in much the same way. Indeed the best cultivator of all, the spade, was brought here by the Romans and has hardly changed in design since.

But there are many ways in which we can improve on the results of the cottagers of old. While old vegetable varieties have a certain charm, there's no doubt that, if you're after flavour, quality and disease resistance, the newer ones are far better. So it would be folly to become stuck in the past for purely romantic reasons. Get a modern seed catalogue and grow the new varieties that the old cottage gardeners would have loved to have planted.

Globe artichoke

This delicious vegetable flower has been grown in Britain since the middle of the sixteenth century, but I can't imagine early cottage gardeners eating it. It was certainly grown by Victorian cottagers, though, and is a valuable ornamental plant, so I include it here.

It can be raised from seed sown in early spring inside and planted out in late spring 45 cm (1½ ft) square. If you have the space, you can prolong the season by leaving in every other plant to crop again much earlier the next year while another planting of seed-raised plants produces a later harvest.

Jerusalem artichoke

The root vegetable equivalent of the globe artichoke was certainly grown by cottage gardeners and was recommended by Thomas Tusser in 1557. It's a permanent crop which takes up quite a lot of space and is not very decorative, so you'll need a big vegetable plot. Plant the tubers 30 cm (1 ft) apart in early spring and dig them the following winter. Those you leave in the soil will re-appear, so further planting is unnecessary.

The globe artichoke is something of an acquired taste but generally considered a delicacy by more sophisticated and better-travelled modern cottage gardeners. It's easily raised from seed.

BROAD BEAN

An extremely ancient plant, almost certainly eaten by Neolithic man and always one of the staples of the cottager's diet. It's a valuable source of protein, and the roots of the plant enrich the soil with nitrogen.

Sow outside in early spring in double rows, setting two seeds together 15 cm (6 in) apart in 10-cm- (4-in)-deep drills set 30 cm (1 ft) apart. If both seeds germinate, pull out the weaker seedling. They can also be grown in a circle in the borders.

FRENCH BEAN

Cultivated in North America as early as 5000 BC, this bean arrived in Europe in the sixteenth century. At first cottage gardeners seem to have cultivated only the climbing varieties, which are grown just like runner beans.

Bush types were here by the early eighteenth century and Cobbett suggests that they could be had in flower only ten days after germination. That must have been under glass and even then a pretty prodigious feat of horticulture.

Sow them outside, two seeds together, in late spring, setting them 30 cm (1 ft) square. Again, if both germinate, remove the weaker seedling. At the end of the season it's a good idea to leave some pods to go brown so that the beans can be dried and stored in airtight jars for use in winter.

RUNNER BEAN

Thought to have been introduced by John Tradescant in 1633, the runner bean was first grown as a purely decorative plant, trained over arbours and pergolas where the red or white flowers were much admired. It was not until the eighteenth century that the beans themselves were eaten. From then, of course, they became more or less obligatory in cottage gardens and allotments everywhere. In small gardens in particular they're a real asset, producing huge crops from a quite small area, as well as being of tremendous decorative value. Set up a row or wigwam of 2.4-m (8-ft) canes 30 cm (1 ft) apart and sow two seeds at the base of each in late spring. When they emerge, thin to one seedling.

They may need some help to start up the right cane, but after that they should look after themselves. Pick the beans regularly to ensure that you have a continuous supply.

Runner beans take up little space for the huge crops they produce.
I like to grow mine up hazel rods rather than canes to create
a more rural effect – they're still available from coppiced
woodland, but you'll need to search out a supply.

BEETROOT

It's likely that the beets mentioned by writers like Thomas Tusser in the sixteenth century were either swedes or turnips or both, because he mentions in his list 'Bleets or beets, white or yellow'. Red beet was certainly cultivated by the Romans in England, but many of the Roman vegetables went out of favour after the occupation. However, there is mention of 'Roman Beet' in 1557, so I'm not sure. Certainly they were grown by later cottage gardeners and were valued not only for their roots but for the leaves too. If you haven't tried the leaves, cook and serve them like spinach.

Sow beetroot in succession from mid-spring until mid-summer, setting the seed clusters 5 cm (2 in) apart. If more than one seedling appears, thin to leave the strongest. Beetroot can be stored through the winter in boxes of garden compost or sand in a frost-free place.

Beetroot can be grown in succession all summer and will store well over the winter. One variety will serve both purposes.

BROCCOLI

Introduced into England during the sixteenth century, this was one of the cottage gardeners' 'worts' that were so important to them. It produces delicious, flowering heads in late winter, and I have no doubt that the leaves were boiled, and boiled and boiled and eaten: they're not recommended now, though. Sow in a seed bed in mid-spring and transplant 60 cm (2 ft) apart each way when the seedlings are big enough to handle. Harvest the young shoots regularly.

BRUSSELS SPROUTS

Very popular with Victorian cottage gardeners and up to this day, but not introduced into Britain until the nineteenth century. They had been grown in Europe since about 1750. Cobbett suggests that 'the large leaves are broken down in the month of August to give the little cabbages room to grow' – advice to be studiously ignored.

This is one crop where it is probably best to choose the old-fashioned varieties. The F1 hybrids now produced for farmers and sold to gardeners are bred to crop all at once for machine harvesting: just the opposite of what we want. The old ones have a stronger flavour too.

Sow in a seed bed in mid-spring and plant out 60 cm (2 ft) apart when the plants are large enough to handle comfortably. Ideally intercrop a fast vegetable like lettuce in between.

CABBAGE

Certainly one of the most important of all cottage vegetables. John Claudius Loudon, for example, suggested that the cottager with a family of five needed a 20 rod or 505 sq. m (605 sq. yd) garden and that he should devote 3 rods or 76 sq. m (90 sq. yd) to cabbages producing, he reckoned, 525 cabbages annually. That's 100 cabbages a year *each*, which I'm sure most of us would now consider a bit of an overdose!

Spring cabbage is always one of the most welcome of vegetables early in the year. It can be eaten as 'greens' or left to heart up later – or both.

Cabbage was probably a native plant and so has been eaten in Britain since pre-history. Even the red cabbage was here in the fourteenth century, and Gerard grew Savoys in 1597. Modern varieties are generally a great advance on the old ones.

Start summer cabbage in the coldframe in late winter and plant out in early spring 23 cm (9 in) square. Follow this by sowing in early spring and transplanting to the same distances.

Sow autumn and winter cabbages in a seed bed in mid-spring and transplant them 60 cm (2 ft) apart, just as Thomas Hill recommended in the sixteenth century: 'cabbadges may be removed when they are a handfull high'. It's still good advice.

Sow spring cabbages in a seed bed in late summer and, again, transplant them when they're large enough to handle. Set them about 15 cm (6 in) apart with a view to removing every other one for spring greens and leaving the others to heart up later.

CARROT

Carrots were on Thomas Tusser's list of pot herbs and were grown in medieval times, but they were very different from the roots we know today. Pretty certainly they were much-branched and yellow, orange or, the most popular, purple. Red carrots came in during the eighteenth century and ousted all the rest.

The seeds were used medicinally and Thomas Hill claims that they 'removeth the venereall act, procureth Urine and asswageth the Chollerick, sendeth down the termes in Women and profiteth the Melanchollicke'. He also suggests that 'the wearing of this root is profitable', though he doesn't explain how or why.

Mostly the roots were used as pot herbs in the ubiquitous soups that poorer cottagers seemed to live on.

Early sowings of a quick-maturing variety can be grown in the soil of a coldframe in late winter, and the first sowings outside can be made in early spring in rows 15 cm (6 in) apart. The seedlings should be thinned to the same distance.

Continue sowing one of the later varieties until mid-summer, though these larger roots will need more room and should be sown 23 cm (9 in) apart and thinned to 15 cm (6 in). Late sowings will store in slightly moist compost or sand throughout the winter.

CAULIFLOWER

The cauliflower was not really an early cottage garden vegetable. Though probably introduced in the sixteenth century, it didn't achieve popularity here until the seventeenth. Gerard called it 'Cole flowery' and was very enthusiastic. It's probably the most demanding and difficult of our

OPPOSITE *Even on the allotment it's a good idea to allow a few flowers to creep in. They help to attract beneficial insects and to lift the spirits.*

Cauliflowers are certainly the most challenging of vegetables to grow. The secret is to get them started and to keep them growing steadily with never a check.

Some of the newer varieties of self-blanching celery, like 'Celebrity', have very white stems and are much less stringy than the older ones.

vegetables to grow, but has been enthusiastically produced in cottage gardens certainly since the eighteenth century.

Start early varieties in seed trays in the cold-frame in early spring and plant out 23 cm (9 in) square in mid-spring. Continue successional sowings of the same varieties outside in a seed bed until late spring.

Sow autumn and winter varieties outside in a seed bed in mid-spring and plant them out 60 cm (2 ft) apart. Never let the seedlings get too big before transplanting and don't let them dry out or they'll produce tiny, premature curds.

Celery and smallage

Celery is a native and has been eaten since the earliest times, but probably only the leaves were used. It's likely that the early plants grown were like the wild celery, or smallage, which has feathery leaves with a celery flavour and is used to flavour food and in soups. The plant with the fleshy stem we all know was introduced from Italy in the seventeenth century.

New self-blanching types are easy to grow and, provided they have sufficient water, produce good, succulent stems. Sow in trays or modules in the coldframe in early spring and plant out 23 cm (9 in) square in late spring.

Courgette and marrow

The vegetable marrow came from the Americas to Europe probably in the sixteenth century, but didn't reach Britain until the eighteenth century. Loudon thought it came from Persia, but it's likely that, by that time, it was fairly widely distributed anyway. Later cottagers enthusiastically adopted it, not just to eat but again, to show off their gardening skills by growing huge specimens, though these were, of course, eaten too.

The courgette is a very recent introduction and

is simply a small marrow. Start seeds off in the coldframe in late spring in individual pots, setting two seeds per pot and removing the weaker seedlings. Plant out bush varieties about 60 cm (2 ft) square only after all danger of frost has passed. Trailing types are too vigorous for small gardens unless you grow them over an archway, pergola or even an arbour. The large fruits will need support, with a string around the neck, but they make quite a talking point.

Cut courgettes regularly to encourage further production, but leave a few marrows to harden in the sun in late summer and store them in nets in a cool place until the end of the year.

CUCUMBER

Grown and introduced by the Romans, the cucumber was such a favourite of the Emperor Tiberius that he ordered that he should have one every day. Thomas Hill, in the sixteenth century, waxed lyrical about 'Cowcumbers', suggesting that they should be covered with sheets during thunderstorms because they 'much feare the thunder and lightning' and that bowls of water under the fruits would stretch and straighten them as they reached for the moisture.

They were always grown outside by cottagers, mostly too poor to own greenhouses, and these would have been trailing types, allowed to wander over the ground. There are still many good trailing varieties of what we now call 'ridge' cucumbers and they can be grown up a wigwam of canes or hazel poles to save space. Alternatively there are now bush varieties which produce excellent crops and take up much less room.

Cultivate them as for courgettes and marrows.

KALE

Grown since at least the sixteenth century, kale was considered very much a working man's vegetable, if not fit only for cattle. Cottage gardeners also grew perennial kinds which could be easily propagated by cuttings. Modern varieties are tasty and certainly not to be scoffed at. Being very hardy, they're particularly useful in colder areas. Sow in a seed bed in mid-spring and transplant 60 cm (2 ft) apart each way.

LAMB'S LETTUCE

A native used widely by cottage gardeners as a winter salad, lamb's lettuce fell from favour in the eighteenth century to be replaced by lettuce. Cobbett reviled it as a common weed and it's rarely offered in seed catalogues now. I think Cobbett was right.

Lettuce, an extremely valuable garden crop, is much better when picked fresh and eaten straight away. By using cloches and some hardier varieties in winter, it's possible to get a long succession for harvesting.

LEEK

The leek is a native of Europe and mentioned by Chaucer, so is certainly very old. The cultivated form was possibly brought to Britain by the Romans and its adoption by the Welsh as the national emblem may be connected with a victory over the Saxons in the sixth century. Thomas Hill suggested that leeks stuffed into mole tunnels would drive them away or even kill them. Thomas Tusser gives us an idea of how cottagers in the sixteenth century relied on them:

Now leekes are in season for pottage full good,
and spareth the milchcow and purgeth the blood.
These having, with peason for pottage in Lent,
thou sparest both otemell and bread to be spent.

Sow them in a seed bed in mid-spring and, when they're large enough to handle comfortably, transplant by making holes with a dibber 15 cm (6 in) apart and 15 cm (6 in) deep and dropping them in. Don't refill the hole, but water them in.

Lettuce

Cos lettuce is a very ancient vegetable and was brought to Britain by the Romans, but cabbage types seem to be a sixteenth-century introduction. Certainly they have been grown in cottage gardens since then and have long been the most important salad vegetable. As with many other vegetables, their flavour can be improved, according to sixteenth-century advice, by steeping the seeds in rose water. Modern varieties need no such treatment.

Sow quick-maturing varieties in trays on the windowsill in late winter and transfer to the coldframe or under cloches three weeks to a month later. Start the main sowing in early spring outside, thinning seedlings to 20 cm (8 in) square. Some of the row can also be transplanted to give a later crop. Continue sowing once a fortnight until late summer. Winter-hardy varieties can be sown in late summer to mature in spring, but the quality will be much improved if they can be covered with cloches.

Onion

Though introduced by the Romans and used by wealthier gardeners, the onion doesn't seem to have found favour with cottage gardeners until quite late, probably the late eighteenth or early nineteenth century. They used to grow scallions or shallots (or perhaps Welsh onions) and garlic. Later the onion became a mainstay of the cottager's diet and it's still one of the most useful vegetables in the kitchen.

Onions can be raised from seed sown thinly in early spring outside in rows 23 cm (9 in) apart and thinned to 7.5 cm (3 in) between plants. Alternatively use sets (small bulbs), planted at the same spacings in late winter. Sets are particularly useful if you're gardening on very heavy soil and it's now possible to buy a good range of varieties, some of which will mature very early in the season. Put them in shallow drills so that the top of each set is just covered. Lift them in late summer and ripen them in the sun, then store in ropes or nets.

Shallots are grown like onion sets except that they're put in with 15 cm (6 in) between the sets. While the onion set simply grows to form a single, much larger bulb, the shallot will produce a clump of bulbs from each set and should be harvested in June or July. Save some of the sets for re-planting.

Orage or orach

This was the name given to the plant *Atriplex hortensis*, which was grown before the advent of spinach (or spinedge) in the mid-sixteenth century. The name was also given to the weed fat hen, and the leaves of both were boiled and used in pottage. I've never seen the seeds offered in today's vegetable lists, but the purple type is available as an ornamental and worth growing in the border for both decorative and culinary purposes. Sow in early spring.

This cottage garden in Suffolk grows a large crop of onions every year. After harvesting they're laid out on the soil to dry for a few days, then cleaned up and stored in strings hung in the shed. They last all winter. Each year a few are transplanted into a corner of the garden, together with a few leeks, and these are left to produce seed. In late summer it's collected and stored ready to be sown in spring. The onions, and many other vegetables too in this garden, cost nothing to grow.

Parsnip

The parsnip is woody and almost inedible in its wild form, but better types were bred as early as the Middle Ages. It was a staple of cottage gardens and used to make beer, wine and even bread and cakes. Strangely Thomas Hill recommends that 'The gardener which would posess faire and big roots ought to pluck away the leaves often times and to cover light earth on the heads ...'

My own advice would be to sow in early spring in rows 23 cm (9 in) apart, setting two seeds at stations 10 cm (4 in) apart. They take some time to germinate, so sow a few radish seeds in the same drill to mark the row. Thin to one seedling and harvest after they've had a frosting. They can be left in all winter, though harvesting and storing in moist sand or compost is preferred. Grow Hamburg parsley in exactly the same way.

Purple orach is grown as an ornamental. It's a hardy annual but seeds itself about freely. Well worth growing in the borders.

PEAS

Introduced by the Romans, 'peason' were one of the great mainstays of the cottager's diet and a valuable source of protein. They were originally mostly of the round type and eaten dried in soups. By the eighteenth century many varieties existed and work began on breeding the sweeter, wrinkled peas.

Nowadays many of the varieties that are being offered to gardeners have been bred for farmers and designed to mature together for combine-harvesting, so you'll have to be careful to pick varieties that will mature over a longer period.

Sow them in broad drills about 5 cm (2 in) deep made with a spade. Start in early spring, setting the seeds about 5 cm (2 in) apart in the drill to make a double row. Continue at about three-weekly intervals until mid-summer. You'll need to provide support with twiggy pea sticks or with netting, which will soon be hidden by the plants. Pick regularly, and after harvesting cut down the haulm and compost it but leave the roots in the ground to release their nitrogen for other crops.

Later cottage gardeners also used to grow asparagus peas, which are eaten complete with pod. They have the disadvantage that they soon go stringy, so it's best to stick to modern sugar-pod varieties. If you want the old-fashioned dried 'peason', allow some pods to go brown in the sun and store in airtight jars.

POTATO

Though this most valuable of all root crops arrived in Europe in the sixteenth century or perhaps even before, it was not enthusiastically espoused by cottage gardeners until the eighteenth century. It's not really clear why, because it *was* grown earlier in Ireland, where over-planting was later to result in the disaster of potato blight and a mass exodus.

It was also grown keenly in Lancashire in the seventeenth century, but it's not really clear why it became regionalized. When it was finally universally accepted, it rapidly became essential to the poor cottage gardener's diet. Even so, in the nineteenth century, William Cobbett

Potatoes have become a real staple in the modern cottager's diet and you'd have to go a long way to find a more nutritious, healthy food. They have the advantage that they can be stored right through the winter, and maincrop varieties will last until the next crop is ready – just. Lift them, dry them on the soil for an hour or two and store in a frost-free shed in paper (not polythene) bags.

claimed never to eat it, preferring bread.

In small gardens, maincrop varieties take up too much room to make them a realistic crop. However, every garden should try to grow a few early varieties for their exquisite flavour. Buy the seed tubers in late winter and set them up in a box in the light and in a cool but frost-free place to 'sprout'. This will greatly increase the yield. Plant them in early spring about 15 cm (6 in) deep and 30 cm (1 ft) apart in rows 60 cm (2 ft) apart. If you have no room for that, plant single tubers with a trowel in the borders. They'll make an attractive mound of foliage and produce heavy crops. If you have room for maincrop varieties, plant in early to mid-spring, setting them 38 cm (15 in) apart in rows 75 cm (2½ ft) apart.

Protect the haulm from threatened frost by drawing up soil over the leaves if necessary. Dig early varieties in early summer and the late crop in late summer or early autumn.

Radish

A very ancient root vegetable, probably developed by selection from the wild radish. Before the sixteenth century there seem to have been many different varieties ranging from small, as we know them today, to very large indeed. The illustrations in Gerard's *Herball* of 1597 show very large roots more like beetroot, some long and others round. The larger-rooted types appear to have died out after the sixteenth century and are only now coming back into fashion. Today it's possible to get varieties as big as a cricket ball and with a fine, nutty flavour.

The more common, smaller varieties are the quickest of all vegetables to mature and should be sown in short rows regularly. Start in early spring and continue at fortnightly intervals until autumn. Sow in wide drills, scattering the seed thinly and, instead of thinning out, harvest selectively to give the remaining plants more room.

Seakale

A European native, often seen growing near the sea, seakale was eaten by cottage gardeners, though until the late eighteenth century it seems to have been gathered from the wild rather than cultivated. Being a maritime plant, it needs a well-drained, sandy soil. It's now generally bought as crowns which are planted about 45 cm (1½ft) apart each way in spring.

Seakale is at its best when forced: put a special terracotta forcer (or a bucket) over the top in early spring. For the earliest crop the forcers are put on in late winter and covered with fresh manure to warm them up.

Seakale has attractive, grey foliage and can be used to advantage in the borders. I edged my gentleman's garden herb plot with it, interspersed with flowering plants, and it looked very handsome indeed. The forced young shoots are a real delicacy.

SHALLOT
See under 'Onion' (page 218).

SPINACH
An important leaf crop for cottage gardeners, spinach was introduced in the mid-sixteenth century. It's in Tusser's list and Hill mentions it for both culinary and medicinal purposes. He also suggests that the older the seed, the faster will be the germination, but I'd take that with a pinch of salt.

The first crops can be raised in pots or modules in the coldframe from an early spring sowing and planted out in mid-spring. Also sow direct in mid-spring, sowing thinly in rows 30 cm (1 ft) apart. Thin to leave single plants 15 cm (6 in) apart.

A newer introduction is Swiss chard, which is like spinach but with a fleshy mid-rib, much sought after by gourmet cooks. Indeed it's often suggested that the leaves should be removed and only the mid-rib eaten. In true, thrifty, cottager fashion I eat both and find them delicious. They're grown just like spinach, though they're hardier, so a winter crop can also be sown.

SWEDE
The swede was introduced from Sweden in the late eighteenth century and used by cottage gardeners both for their beasts and themselves. In those days there was no distinction between varieties and they must have made a pretty uninteresting dish. Modern varieties are far, far better and, after being touched by frost, have a sweetness that makes them highly desirable. Delay sowing until early summer to avoid the risk of mildew, and then scatter the seed thinly down drills 23 cm (9 in) apart. Thin to 23 cm (9 in) apart. Swedes can be left in the ground all winter or, better, lifted after a week of frost and stored in damp compost or sand.

TOMATO
Introduced to Europe from the Americas in the sixteenth century, the tomato was at first grown only decoratively. It was thought to have aphrodisiac properties, hence its common name of 'love-apple'. It wasn't until the nineteenth century that it became universally accepted as a food crop and was then taken up by cottage gardeners in a big way. Today there are few gardens that don't grow a few and any gardener with a small greenhouse always seems to produce enough to feed a large extended family. Tomatoes are a very satisfying crop to grow.

The plants can be raised on a windowsill, but a better bet is to buy them from a nursery since they require good light conditions to make them short and bushy. They can be planted out 60 cm (2 ft) square in late spring under cloches or in the open in early summer when all danger of frost has passed.

Older cottage gardeners would have grown only upright varieties which have to be staked, tied and side-shooted throughout the season. Newer bush types can be planted and, apart from watering, forgotten until harvest time.

TURNIP
The turnip was a real cottage garden staple. It's an ancient native plant, used to feed beasts and man alike. Some types were grown for their roots and others for their tops. Today the same type is used for both purposes, and the tops are delicious provided they are picked quite young. In the eighteenth century turnips were used a lot on an agricultural scale for grazing sheep and cattle in winter and the practice remains today.

The first crop can be raised in the coldframe: select an early variety and sow in late winter. Sow direct outside in early spring in rows 23 cm (9 in) apart. Thin to 15 cm (6 in) and harvest when the roots are quite young and tender.

Herbs

Herbs were the early cottage gardener's medicine chest and were very important to all families both for healing and in the kitchen. Modern cottagers may not know much about the medicinal properties of herbs, but they are quite knowledgeable about their culinary uses. The increase in travel has broadened our experience of foreign cooking, for which a wider range of herbs is essential, so a well-stocked herb garden is still important.

Herbs are also desirable as decorative plants, of course, and can be used to freshen the air far more effectively and pleasantly than those ghastly chemical aerosols which smell worse than the odours you want to banish. Strewing herbs were used to take away the much stronger smells that no doubt pervaded early cottages and to deter lice and all kinds of other creepy-crawlies. Again, that's hardly necessary today, but a bowl of pot-pourri made from herbs and flowers collected from the garden will certainly fill your rooms with the fresh smell of the countryside.

Cultivation

Most herbs need a sunny spot and a well-drained soil. So, if yours is heavy, prepare the area with plenty of coarse grit and add as much compost or manure as you can. If you can raise the soil in this way, it'll improve the drainage and warm the soil too.

You could make a special place for herbs and I've allowed for a small herb garden in both the artisan's and the gentleman's gardens. If you can make the garden near the back door, where the cook won't have to brave the elements for a sprig of parsley, so much the better.

Both my herb gardens are small, and it's therefore vital to choose the plants very carefully. Some, like lovage and angelica, make huge plants up to 3 m (10 ft) tall and are obviously not to be grown in a small plot. Many others, like mint, will run through the soil or spread to cover and choke out other herbs. The way to control the growth of those that are only a bit too exuberant is to harvest them regularly. Pinching out the growing tips provides fresh herbs and prunes the plants too. However, at times when you don't need the herbs you'll still have to do the pinching job or the more vigorous will take over.

Other than that, once they're planted, there's very little cultivation to do. Obviously keep the garden weed-free and feed only if the plants look as though they're suffering.

A small herb garden is essential for the modern cottager, so I planted one in both gardens. Here in the artisan's garden, it was sited outside the 'back door' where it would be convenient for the cook and next to the sitting area to take advantage of the pleasant aromas.

If space is limited, you can grow herbs in pots where they look very decorative indeed. Choose terracotta pots if you can and fill with a compost consisting of equal parts of good garden soil, coir compost or really good garden compost, and coarse grit. Add a handful of pelleted chicken manure fertilizer or some other organic feed to each bucketful of compost.

Allium sativum GARLIC
Height: 30 cm (1 ft).

A venerable herb that has been cultivated in Britain since Roman times and probably naturalized itself too. It has been credited with many remarkable medicinal properties, including increasing energy, protecting against plague and deterring vampires. Even today it's still widely

ABOVE *Garlic has become one of the most sought-after herbs for the modern cottager's kitchen. I've found it best to stick to English varieties, having had little success growing from bulbs brought back from France.*

OPPOSITE *It's important to find out about the plants before planning a small herb garden. Taller species like fennel, lovage and angelica will have to be grown in the borders where they'll look very decorative.*

used as a general tonic and, of course, to discourage greenfly, though regrettably that has never worked for me.

In the kitchen garlic is widely used to flavour meat dishes, salads, vegetables – in fact almost any savoury dish.

It needs a sunny and well-drained spot. Plant the separate cloves in late autumn or in early spring, though autumn planting produces much better results. Lift in late summer, dry the bulbs in the sun and store in boxes.

Allium schoenoprasum CHIVES
Height: 20 cm (8 in).

This mildly flavoured onion was first recorded in Britain in 1375, but was probably collected from the wild before that. Its leaves were widely used in soups and salads and mixed with cheeses as they are today.

It wants a sunny spot and a rich, moist soil for the best leaves, though it flowers better on poorer soil. It makes a very fine border plant with its ball-shaped, deep pink flowers and was widely used in cottage gardens to edge vegetable beds. Chives can be propagated by dividing the bulbs in spring or autumn.

Anethum graveolens DILL
Height: 60 cm–1.5 m (2–5 ft).

During the Middle Ages dill was prescribed as a protection against witchcraft and as an aid to digestion. It's still used for the latter purpose for young children.

It has a subtle flavour of caraway with a refreshing sharpness and the leaves are used in pickling. The seeds are also useful in soups and fish and vegetable dishes as well as in cakes and bread.

It needs a sunny, protected position and a rich soil. Sow it where it's to grow from mid-spring to mid-summer. Keep it away from fennel, with which it cross-pollinates.

Anthriscus cerefolium CHERVIL
Height: 38 cm (15 in).
Grown in Britain since Roman times, chervil has a refined, parsley-like flavour. It was traditionally eaten on Maundy Thursday as a restorative and the roots were eaten with vinaigrette. It's used – generously because of its mildness – in salads and many other dishes, including those containing chicken and fish. The sprays of white flowers are very dainty and beautiful in the borders.

Chervil is an annual and will run to seed in dry soil, so add plenty of compost or manure before planting and grow it in semi-shade. Sow outside where it's to grow in early spring, and, because of its habit of running to seed, again in mid- and late summer. Cover with cloches if you want a supply during winter.

Armoracia rusticana HORSERADISH
Height: 60 cm (2 ft).
Another plant that was probably introduced to Britain by the Romans and used originally mainly as medicine. It served in the prevention of scurvy and to relieve rheumatism and chilblains. In the sixteenth century it was used to make the sauce we know today, but it was generally eaten with fish rather than meat.

Horseradish is not an easy plant to grow – or rather it's *too* easy. If you plant a tiny piece of root in a border, it'll soon take hold and then you'll never eradicate it. I think it's best grown in a bed of soil on a concrete path where it can be lifted and re-planted each year. Better still, collect it from the hedgerows like the old cottagers did.

Artemisia dracunculus TARRAGON
Height: 60 cm (2 ft).
There are two types of tarragon – the French and the Russian. The latter, however, is a rank-flavoured herb, so the French type is much to be preferred. It seems to have arrived in Britain in the late sixteenth century, when it soon became used to flavour vinegars, salads and roast meat in particular. It's still used for the same purposes.

It prefers a sunny spot and must have a well-drained soil. It's best to buy a plant to start with, or take a half-ripe cutting in autumn. In winter it's safest to protect the plants with a cloche. Lift and divide the plants every four or five years, but take care when untangling the tortuous roots.

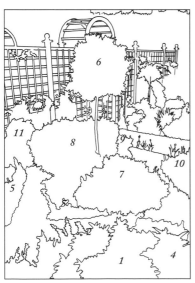

1 *Salvia officinalis* (sage)
2 *Salvia officinalis* 'Icterina'
(gold variegated sage)
3 *Salvia officinalis* 'Purpurascens Variegata'
(purple variegated sage)
4 *Salvia officinalis* 'Purpurascens' (purple sage)
5 *Buxus sempervirens* (box)
6 *Laurus nobilis* (bay)
7 *Artemisia dracunculus* (French tarragon)
8 *Monarda didyma* 'Croftway Pink'
(bergamot)
9 *Borago pygmaea* (creeping borage)
10 *Petroselinum crispum* (parsley)
11 *Mentha piperita*

The herb plot in the gentleman's garden was planted in formal fashion in the form of a knot garden or parterre with beds surrounded by low box hedging.

Borago officinalis BORAGE
Height: 30–60 cm (1–2 ft).
Grown in Britain since the thirteenth century, borage is undoubtedly the best herb for lifting the spirits. Gerard recommended that it be drunk with wine, when 'it makes men and women glad and merry, driving away all sadness and dullness' (though this could *just* have been the effect of the wine!).

The leaf can be cooked like spinach, but its main use is as an addition to summer drinks. It was widely used in cordials until about the early twentieth century and was generally stocked by chemists. Now, of course, the flowers and leaves are used to garnish the drink Pimm's, but that's hardly a cottage garden tradition! You can preserve the herb by freezing it into ice cubes.

Borage is an easy and decorative plant which greatly brightens up the borders even if you don't use it. Give it a sunny spot, since it won't do at all well in shade. Sow it where it's to grow in mid-spring. Ever after it'll seed itself where it wants to grow, but it's easy to remove.

Campanula rapunculus RAMPION
Height: 60 cm–1 m (2–3 ft).
This biennial salad herb was a commonly grown plant in cottage gardens in the sixteenth century, but is now almost unavailable. I have found it in only one specialist seedsman's catalogue. It was grown for its leaves and roots, both of which were cooked in soups and also used in winter salads. It's a decorative plant too, with small blue or white, bell-shaped flowers.

Mix the fine seed with sand and sow in shallow drills in early summer. Thin to 10 cm (4 in) apart.

Claytonia perfoliata and *Portulaca oleracea*
PURSLANE
Height: 15–23 cm (6–9 in).
Claytonia, called both 'winter purslane' and 'min-er's lettuce', is a hardy annual; portulaca or 'summer purslane' is half-hardy. Both were cultivated widely in cottage gardens during the sixteenth century for their succulent leaves, which were eaten raw in salads. William Cobbett thought little of purslane, writing that it was 'eaten by Frenchmen and pigs when they can get nothing else'. But then he didn't rate potatoes very highly either, so try it yourself. I like it.

Sow winter purslane in late summer and protect it in winter with a cloche, if you can, to produce a much better quality crop. Summer purslane should be sown in well-drained soil in sun about every month during the season.

Coriandrum sativum CORIANDER
Height: 60 cm (2 ft).
Probably introduced to Britain by the Romans, this hardy annual was used during the Middle Ages as an aphrodisiac and against scrofula. It also found a use in the kitchen to flavour roast meat in particular and is used today in curries and stews.

It needs a sunny spot and a deep, rich soil. Sow it in mid-spring where it's to grow.

Eruca vesicaria ROCKET
Height: 23 cm (9 in).
Another salad herb grown widely in old cottage gardens, rocket was probably introduced by the Romans who used it medicinally as well as in the salad bowl, where a few leaves will give a refreshing tang. The leaves can also be cooked like spinach. The boiled root was thought to draw out bone splinters from wounds.

Sow in a sunny spot in mid-spring and thin to 15 cm (6 in) apart. Repeat the sowings monthly.

Foeniculum vulgare FENNEL
Height: 2.1 m (7 ft).
An ancient perennial herb, probably native to

A fine herb bed dominated by the vivid scarlet of bergamot (see page 156). This is used in the kitchen to flavour salads, jams, jellies and even milk. It's also used to make a soothing herb tea.

Britain, and a favourite of the Romans who ate it to keep in good health and prevent obesity. It was considered by the Anglo-Saxons to be protective against evil, to increase the flow of mothers' milk and to 'make the fat grow gaunt and lank'. It was used in the kitchen by cottagers in medieval times in much the same way as today, to flavour fish in particular and their all too common soups.

In small gardens fennel's much too big for the herb garden, but it makes a very attractive plant in the border. It's probably best to buy a plant or to beg a division from a friend, but it can also be raised from seed sown in mid-spring.

Hyssopus officinalis HYSSOP
Height: 45 cm–1 m (1½–3 ft).
This hardy shrub was recorded in Britain in the thirteenth century and possibly brought here by Benedictine monks who used it to flavour liqueurs. It was popular with cottage gardeners

because it's attractive, a good bee plant and useful against ailments of the mouth and throat. Now it's used in salads and particularly with fatty foods. The flowers and leaves are added to pot-pourri.

Give it a well-drained, sunny spot and buy a plant or obtain a softwood cutting from a friend in mid-summer.

Laurus nobilis BAY
Height: Depends on pruning.

Bay was used extensively in cottage gardens and often made into topiary, though it was more popular for this purpose in the grander gardens. Though a mediterranean plant, it was grown in England in the eleventh century.

It's a tender plant, so only to be grown outside all year round in the warmest areas. Elsewhere it

Bay is widely used in the kitchen and makes an attractive feature plant in the herb garden. In colder areas it must be grown in a pot.

must be grown in a pot and brought inside in winter: a porch or a cold room will do.

Bay is used to flavour lots of different cooked dishes, especially soups, stews and casseroles. The leaf is removed before serving. Bay leaves can be dried and stored in airtight jars.

You'd need to buy a plant to start with, or take a cutting from a friend's plant. Softwood cuttings root quite easily in summer. Pot into the equal-parts mixture and bring inside in late autumn. Naturally container-grown bay will need watering and feeding during the growing season.

Melissa officinalis BALM
Height: 1 m (3 ft).

Cottagers used the lemon-flavoured leaves as a nerve tonic and a heart stimulant. In the kitchen it was added to salads, to fruit and vegetables before cooking and as an infusion especially to reduce temperatures.

It also found a use as an excellent bee plant and the leaves were rubbed on hives to encourage the bees to stay. It was thought to be effective against bee stings too.

Balm prefers semi-shade and a moist soil, so it's probably best to select a spot in the border. Keep harvesting regularly and cut the whole plant back hard in autumn to retain its bushy habit. Propagate by division or seed sown in mid-spring outside.

Mentha spp. MINT, PEPPERMINT and PENNYROYAL
Height: 60 cm–1 m (2–3 ft).

Many different types of mint have been grown in Britain since at least the ninth century. They were used widely to purify water and air and to rid a room of fleas and lice, to cure headaches and mad dog bites and as strewing herbs.

In the kitchen mint was used, just as it is today, to flavour lamb in particular, with vegetables, in pea soup and to make a pleasant infusion.

In the garden the problem is its running roots. It cannot be grown in the herb garden or the borders or it'll take over. If you have a small bed surrounded by lawn, you can control it by cutting off the new young shoots when you mow the grass, but the easiest way to grow it is in a pot. Use an equal-parts mixture of soil, compost and coarse grit and take the plant out of its pot each autumn, split it up and re-plant a few roots in fresh compost.

Ocimum basilicum BASIL
Height: 45 cm (1½ ft).
This invaluable herb was used to settle the stomach, especially after excess alcohol, and was thought to relieve snake bites. It has a pungent flavour, is sprinkled on many dishes as a garnish, and is used in tomato dishes, egg dishes, soups and pesto sauce. The dried leaves are used in pot-pourri.

Basil is a tender herb, so it needs full sun and shelter from wind. Sow it on a windowsill in early spring and transfer the pots to the coldframe in mid-spring. Don't set it outside until all danger of frost has gone. Pinch off the flower buds as they appear and, in autumn, lift a few plants, pot them and cut them back. If you put them on the windowsill inside, they'll produce another crop of leaves. The leaves can be frozen or dried.

Origanum onites, Origanum majorana and *Origanum vulgare* MARJORAM and OREGANO
Height: 15–60 cm (6 in–2 ft).
First recorded in Britain in the tenth century, this ancient herb had many medicinal purposes from curing dropsy to toothache, rheumatism to hayfever. It was also used as a strewing herb, especially to spread on the floor of the bridal chamber. Elizabethan cottagers used it to flavour meat dishes, in salads and as an infusion just as

we do today. Oregano has a somewhat stronger, peppery flavour than the two marjorams.

All do best on a sunny site, though the golden marjoram (*Origanum vulgare* 'Aureum') can scorch in strong sunshine so may need a little shade. All can be sown in mid-spring, but germination is slow and erratic. A better method of propagation is by stem cuttings or simple division. Note that sweet marjoram (*O. majorana*) is half-hardy, so will need replacing each year in cold areas.

Petroselinum crispum PARSLEY
Height: 15 cm (6 in).
This has been the most popular herb in Britain since the seventeenth century, but before then it was considered poisonous and a probable cause of epilepsy. None the less, it was used in the sixteenth century to 'cast forth strong venome or poyson', so it seems that opinions were divided. Today, of course, it's used as a garnish, in salads and sandwiches, in a superb fish sauce and, chopped with shallots, as persillade.

It's said to be difficult to germinate, but the foolproof method is to raise it on the windowsill in plastic modules in early spring. Alternatively wait until mid-spring and pour boiling water down the seed drill before sowing.

Rosmarinus officinalis ROSEMARY
Height: 1–2 m (3–6 ft).
A Mediterranean shrub, first recorded in Britain in 1340, though probably introduced by the Romans and long used by cottagers to add flavour to meats, especially lamb, rabbit and poultry. There are many folklore stories attached to rosemary. It improves the memory and is good for the head generally. Made into 'rosset sweetcakes', it makes the heart merry, it's an effective hair restorer and cures bubonic plague and bad eyesight. It's still looked upon today as a plant of

Parsley is often difficult to germinate. The seed responds to sharp changes in temperature, so the secret is to pour boiling water down the drills before sowing.

remembrance, so it's often planted on graves and in gardens in memory of the dead.

It's best to start off by buying a plant or taking a softwood or a half-ripe cutting from a friend either in early summer or autumn. It's essential to give it a well-drained, sunny spot in the garden and, because it grows tall, to harvest it regularly to keep it in shape. It will produce attractive, mauve or blue flowers if allowed to, but it's very important to trim it back in the spring after it's finished flowering to keep it neat.

Rumex acetosa SORREL

Height: 23 cm (9 in).

A native to Britain and used widely for medicinal purposes and in the kitchen, sorrel was prescribed for ulcers, as a laxative, to fix teeth in the gums, for the liver and even to restore the lost voices of singing birds. In the kitchen it was, and still is, boiled or steamed like spinach, used in the famous sorrel soup and added, in moderation, to salads.

It needs a rich, well-drained soil and will grow in sun or part-shade. Sow in mid-spring in patches with about 23 cm (9 in) between plants – you won't need a lot. It tends to run to seed in summer, when it should be cut right down to the ground, after which it'll soon produce another crop of leaves. For a winter supply of sorrel, cover the plants with cloches.

Salvia officinalis SAGE
Height: 30–60 cm (1–2 ft).

A native of southern Europe, sage was first recorded in Britain in the tenth century and was probably used before then. It was credited with the power of longevity and, even to this day, country people insist on their daily intake of sage to prolong their lives. It's still recommended to relieve indigestion, but it should be taken for this purpose only after professional advice. In the kitchen it's now used to flavour fatty meat and, of course, to make the famous sage and onion stuffing.

There are several varieties of sage with different and very attractive leaf colours including purple, variegated purple and cream, and a slightly less hardy variety with leaves splashed green, pink and white. All the coloured varieties are as useful in the kitchen as the green ones. A hardy shrub, it has purple/blue flowers and there is also a white variety.

Grow it in well-drained soil in full sun and cut it back quite hard after flowering to encourage new young shoots. Propagate by taking softwood cuttings in early summer or half-ripe cuttings in autumn.

Satureja montana WINTER SAVORY
Height: 38 cm (15 in).

This hardy shrub was first recorded in Britain in the tenth century, but was eaten well before. It was used medicinally to ease flatulence, so it was often included in dishes containing quantities of beans and peas. It's still used today for gastric complaints.

It has a peppery taste and its main use in the kitchen is still to flavour pea and bean dishes.

Herbs, like the purple sage growing here, can be used for purely decorative purposes in the borders. Because most revel in good drainage and poorish soil, they thrive in the competitive environment.

It has quite attractive small, pink flowers in summer.

It prefers full sun and a well-drained soil and can be raised from seed sown in autumn or, much better, from softwood cuttings in early summer.

Thymus spp. THYME
Height: 7.5–38 cm (3–15 in).

Thyme was almost certainly introduced by the Romans and quickly naturalized itself here. It was thought, in the Middle Ages, to enable the partaker to see fairies, and it was used to relieve the 'meloncholicke and troubled in spirit and mind'. It induced sleep and today is still incorporated in the stuffing of herb pillows.

In the kitchen thyme is used in stuffings and soups and with fatty meat. It's also made into an infusion to relieve headaches and hangovers. Common thyme (*Thymus vulgaris*) is generally best in the kitchen, though lemon thyme (*T. citriodorus*) is also used in chicken, fish and vegetable dishes, while the prostrate caraway thyme (*T. herba-barona*) is used with beef.

It must have full sun and good drainage. In the artisan's garden it grows well in the herb table, and in the gentleman's garden in planting holes in the brick paving where it spreads to form an attractive mat. Cut back any straggling plants to encourage them to form bushy growth. Propagate by half-ripe cuttings in autumn.

Tropaeolum majus NASTURTIUM
Height: 30 cm (1 ft).
Brought to Britain from the Americas, this hardy annual was grown mainly for its flowers which it produces in a range of reds, yellows and oranges throughout the spring and summer. The leaves were used to add a pleasant tang to salads, and the seeds can be chopped and used like horseradish or pickled as a substitute for capers.

Nasturtiums are very easy to grow in a sunny spot in poor soil. Sow in early spring and thin to about 20 cm (8 in) apart.

Tree Fruit

❀

If you have the room for an orchard of big, bush or standard fruit trees, or even for two or three in your garden, praise the Lord and plant them. Nothing invokes the rural idyll more than gnarled old apple trees, bearing full pink-and-white blossom in spring or groaning under a crop of red, yellow or orange fruit in late summer and autumn. Under-sow with grass and wildflowers, add a few sheep, a duck and a goose or two and you won't be far from heaven.

It's still possible to buy old varieties too, and to get them grafted on replicas of the old-fashioned rootstocks to give large trees.

If you fancy apples like 'Broad Eyed Pippin' from about 1650, 'Catshead' from 1600, 'Old Pearmain' produced as far back as 1200, or the 'Bloody Ploughman' from 1883, they're still all available. And remember that, according to sixteenth-century writers, if the grafting wood is

You can grow plenty of fruit even in a tiny garden. This 'step-over' apple is no more than 30 cm (1 ft) high, yet it produces a fine crop of 'Bountiful' cooking apples without fail every year while taking up no more than 15 cm (6 in) of space along the edge of the path.

Apples are among the most decorative of trees with fresh pink-and-white blossom in spring, followed by bright red, yellow or green fruits in autumn.

soaked in pike's blood before being grafted on to the rootstock, the apples will always be red.

Alas, few of us new cottage gardeners have room for that kind of luxury, but we can still grow plenty of tree fruit, even in the smallest plot. The answer is to grow trained trees against the house wall or the fence. And if you have a hedge round the plot, grow them trained to canes fixed to a post-and-wire support.

Tree Shapes and Training

The best shapes to grow in small cottage gardens are fans, where the branches radiate out like the ribs of a fan: this method is suitable for apples, pears, plums, peaches, nectarines, apricots and cherries. Espaliers, where the branches run horizontally and then rise in tiers of probably four, five or six branches, are an alternative way of growing apples and pears. Step-over trees are also a good idea to edge paths: these are simply single-tier espaliers.

Initial training is not difficult, but it's far better to leave that to the nurseryman and buy the trees ready-trained. Then the pruning is very simple indeed.

Apples and pears are pruned in late summer or early autumn. You simply look for shoots that arise directly from the main stems and cut them back to 7.5 cm (3 in), cutting back to just above a bud. Then look for side shoots that have come from these shoots during the year and cut them back to 2.5 cm (1 in). And that's it.

Cherries, plums and apricots are pruned in spring just as they start to grow. Simply reduce to two or three buds any shoots that are growing out from the wall, are overcrowded or not needed to increase the size of the tree. Figs can be pruned in the same way.

Fan-trained fruit trees are tied in to canes fixed to horizontal wires. This is a method that can be used for all trees you're likely to want to grow, and all will look very decorative as well as producing good crops in virtually no garden space at all.

Peaches and nectarines are a little more difficult, but not if you remember that the fruit is borne on wood made the year before. So, in the winter, cut out shoots that bore fruit the previous season and tie in a replacement shoot below, made last season. That shoot is pinched back when it has made five leaves and will bear fruit. Pinch out any other shoots that grow, except one, which you allow to grow as your replacement shoot for the next year.

Medlars and mulberries need no pruning except to remove old and overcrowded wood in winter. Try to keep the head open and well shaped because both these trees are attractive ornamentals too. Most of the fruit of medlars will be borne on two-year-old wood while mulberries fruit on new wood too.

Pollination and Harvesting

Most fruit trees need to be pollinated to produce a full crop. Where this is not so, you can get away with one, self-fertile variety, but normally you need at least two trees of different varieties. The important point to note is that they must both flower at the same time.

Usually that's enough, but there is one small complication. Some trees are triploids, which means that they won't pollinate anything else. The 'Bramley's Seedling' apple is a good example, and if you grew that you'd need at least three trees: one to pollinate the 'Bramley' and another to pollinate the pollinator.

However, though trees flower at the same time, they don't necessarily fruit at the same time, so it's

While apples can be grown against more or less any wall or fence, it's best to reserve a south- or west-facing position for the fussier pears, especially if your garden is in an exposed situation. Against a south fence they produce superb crops of high quality and flavour.

possible to choose varieties to give you a longer period of harvesting.

With apples, for instance, you could start in late summer, taking and eating apples from early varieties (which don't store well), and go right through to those harvested in early winter (which can be eaten from the tree and also stored). So it's actually possible to be eating home-grown apples in Britain from late summer through to early spring the following year.

And the beauty with space-saving, trained trees is that you can grow several even in a small garden. There's another, more fascinating advance too, but let me explain about restricting and encouraging growth first.

If a branch is growing vertically, it tends to put all its energies into making strong growth, without really bothering to produce fruit. But if you pull the branch down to the horizontal or near to it, growth is restricted and fruit formation is encouraged.

In the early years of training fans and espaliers, therefore, when you want rapid growth, you tie the branches in about 45 degrees to the vertical. Later on you pull all espalier branches down to the horizontal and some of the fan's branches too.

Now for the new development. As far as I can see, the early French fruit growers, who were the undisputed masters of grafting and training trees, never thought of this and I wonder why. I bet cottage gardeners of old would have been ecstatic at the prospect.

Modern growers are now producing 'family fans'. This means that there are three different varieties grafted on to the one rootstock. So the pollination problem and the extended period of harvesting are all achieved at a stroke and on the same tree.

The big disadvantage with family trees, however, is that it's virtually impossible exactly to match the vigour of varieties, so the strongest variety eventually takes over. Yet, with a cunning the French would be proud of, British fruit tree growers graft the strongest varieties on the bottom of the fan where they'll be pulled down and restricted, leaving the more vertical, weaker ones to grow away happily. In fact, it should be possible to match the vigour of all the branches exactly just by moving them up or down.

Rootstocks

All fruit trees are grafted or budded on to a special rootstock that determines their eventual size and how quickly in their lives they produce a full crop of fruit. The rule of thumb is that the more the rootstock reduces the size of the tree, the sooner in its life it will produce a full crop. With apples, for example, the most dwarfing rootstock will produce a good crop in two years. Much development has gone on in this field, so we are no longer stuck with the large trees that old cottage gardeners would have had to grow.

With apples, for example, you can now buy trees grafted on to dwarfing, semi-dwarfing or vigorous rootstocks. And the more the stock dwarfs the tree, the quicker it'll come into bearing a full crop.

When you buy trees, therefore, ask for varieties on dwarfing stocks. This is not so important with apples and pears, because most are usually done that way these days, but with plums and cherries it's essential.

Apples

Rootstock M27 is very dwarfing and used for trees in containers; M9 is a little bigger for small trees on good soil; both need staking all their lives. MM106 is bigger and recommended for most situations. M111 is vigorous and only for large bush or standard trees.

A very decorative way of growing apples and pears is the 'double U', but trees like this are a bit hard to find and relatively expensive.

Espaliers are easier to locate and make attractive trees which crop well. They can be bought ready-trained, and developing extra tiers is not difficult.

Pears

All today are on EMLA Quince A and generally certified virus-free.

Plums

St Julien A is the most vigorous used today and produces big trees. Pixy is dwarfing.

Cherries

Most trees are budded on to Colt, which is semi-dwarfing. There is no really satisfactory dwarfing stock at present.

Peaches, Nectarines and Apricots

Generally St Julien A is used since Pixy is not satisfactory. St Julien is fine for fan-trained trees.

Recommended Varieties

Apples
Modern varieties

Variety	Harvest	Introduced
'Discovery'	Aug.	1955
'Katy'	Sept.	1947
'Fiesta'	Oct.	1972
'Sunset'	Nov.–Dec.	1933
'Rubinette'	Oct.–Jan.	1966
'Bountiful' (cooker)	Oct.–Feb.	1984

All the above varieties will pollinate each other.

Old varieties easily available

Variety	Harvest	Introduced
'Early Victoria' or 'Emneth Early' (cooker)	Jul.	1899
'Beauty of Bath'	Aug.	1864
'Charles Ross'	Sept.	1890
'Blenheim Orange'	Oct.–Nov.	1740
'Golden Delicious'	Nov.–Feb.	1890
'Sturmer Pippin'	Nov.–Apr.	1831

All the above varieties will pollinate each other.

Very old varieties obtainable from a specialist

Variety	Harvest	Introduced	Remarks
'Court Pendu Plat'	Dec.	1200	Flowers very late, so needs another late flowerer
'Ashmead's Kernel'	Dec.	1700	Flowers late
'Ribston Pippin'	Nov.	1700	Flowers early
'D'Arcy Spice'	Dec.	1785	Flowers late
'Egremont Russet'	Oct.	1872	Flowers early
'Orleans Reinette'	Dec.	1776	Flowers late
'Bramley's Seedling' (cooker)	Nov.	1813	Triploid

Crab apples

The only variety suitable for jams and jellies is 'John Downie'. For ornamental varieties see page 105. Grow them like apples.

Pears

Modern varieties

Variety	Harvest	Introduced	Remarks
'Beth'	Aug.–Sept.	1938	Flowers mid-season
'Concorde'	Oct.–Nov.	1985	Flowers mid-season

Old varieties easily available

Variety	Harvest	Introduced	Remarks
'Conference'	Oct.–Nov.	1885	Flowers mid-season
'Doyenné du Comice'	Nov.–Dec.	1849	Flowers late
'Williams' Bon Chrétien'	Sept.	1770	Flowers mid-season
'Beurre Hardy'	Oct.	1830	Flowers mid-season
'Fertility'	Sept.	1875	Flowers mid-season
'Gorham'	Aug.–Sept.	1910	Flowers mid-season
'Louis Bonne de Jersey'	Oct.	1780	Flowers early
'Pitmaston Duchess'	Sept.–Oct.	1841	Flowers late
'Old Warden'	Feb.	1575	Flowers mid-season

Probably the most popular variety of pear is 'Conference', which is one of the easiest to grow. It's also partially self-fertile, though without a pollinator yields are slightly less and the fruit tends to be elongated.

Quinces

Variety	Harvest	Introduced	Remarks
'Vranja'	Oct.	*c*.1920	Self-fertile
'Meech's Prolific'	Sept.	1850	Self-fertile

Grow quinces like pears.

Plums

Modern varieties

Variety	Harvest	Introduced	Remarks
'Avalon'	Aug.	1985	Partly self-fertile
'Cambridge Gage'	Aug.–Sept.	1927	Partly self-fertile
'Opal'	Jul.–Aug.	1925	Self-fertile

All the above varieties will pollinate each other. If you have room for only one, choose a self-fertile variety.

Old varieties

Variety	Harvest	Introduced	Remarks
'Denniston's Superb'	Aug.	1790	
'Marjorie's Seedling'	Sept.–Oct.	1912	
'Victoria'	Aug.–Sept.	1840	
'Czar'	Jul.–Aug.	1871	All self-fertile
'Giant Prune'	Sept.	1893	
'Oullin's Gage'	Aug.	1856	
'Purple Pershore'	Aug.	1877	
'Transparent Gage'	Sept.–Oct.	1838	
'Shropshire Damson'	Sept.–Oct.	16th cent.	

Peaches

Variety	Harvest	Introduced	Remarks
'Duke of York'	Jul.	1902	
'Peregrine'	Aug.	1906	All self-fertile
'Rochester'	Aug.	1900	
'Amsden June'	Jul.	1865	
'Bellegarde'	Sept.	1732	

Nectarines

Variety	Harvest	Introduced	Remarks
'Lord Napier'	Aug.	1869	Self-fertile
'Early Rivers'	Jul.	1893	Self-fertile

Figs

Variety	Harvest	Introduced	Remarks
'Brown Turkey'	Aug. onwards		Both self-fertile and grown on their own roots
'Brunswick'	Aug. onwards		

Figs were brought to this country by the Romans and have been grown here ever since. While wealthier gardeners force huge crops in greenhouses, it's not difficult to grow varieties like 'Brown Turkey' outside.

Medlar

Variety	Harvest	Introduced	Remarks
'Nottingham'	Oct.–Nov.	995	Self-fertile and grown on its own roots as a standard tree

Mulberry

Variety	Harvest	Introduced	Remarks
'Black Mulberry'	Aug.	About 1150, but possibly introduced to Britain by the Romans	Self-fertile and grown on its own roots as a standard tree

Grown in the open, figs take two seasons to ripen. Fruits that are formed at the end of the year are subject to frost damage and only the very small ones will escape. Larger figs will often remain on the tree only to fall off the following spring.

However, in my own quite cold garden I still manage to produce an excellent crop from a tree trained against a west-facing wall. But even without fruit, the superb foliage makes it well worthwhile.

Soft Fruit

❁

Soft fruit formed an important part of the diet of the cottager and was certainly grown in gardens by the sixteenth century as well as being collected from the wild. People have been blackberrying since Neolithic times and we probably still collect fruit from descendants of the same plants. Many fruits were used medicinally and to make wine, as well as being eaten fresh and cooked. They were, and indeed still are, a rich and important source of vitamins.

In old gardens, soft fruit bushes would often form part of the hedge, which would contain plants like elder for their berries, and brambles, blackcurrants and gooseberries, valued for their prickles. As well as the favourites we know and still value today, old cottage gardeners ate many fruits which we would now shun, like barberries from the berberis plant and the small berries from the amelanchier tree, which were used like raisins. It's hardly worthwhile growing them for their fruit now, except out of interest, but many ancient fruits still survive and have been much improved by breeding.

All bush fruits do best in a sunny position. They can be grown in shade, though this will reduce the crop slightly and make it a week or two later.

Blackberry

A native of Britain and grown in hedgerows everywhere. There are several cultivated varieties, but few taste as good as the wild one and all take up too much room to be worthwhile growing in small gardens. However, if you're lucky enough to have a quickthorn or a mixed hedge that you can allow to over-grow a bit during the summer, it's ideal as a support for a blackberry.

If you want to do the job properly, layer the tip of a wild plant by digging a shallow hole, putting in the growing point of a briar and covering with soil. It'll soon root and produce a new plant. Otherwise grow the variety 'Ashton Cross', a new one that gets nearest to the real flavour.

If you have room, grow blackberries up a post-and-wire structure 1.8 m (6 ft) high. Plant in autumn and cut the plant right down. The following season, shoots will grow and should be trained in a half-fan shape to one side of the plant. The following year they'll fruit while new shoots are growing. The new shoots are trained into the other side of the fan and the fruited shoots are cut out. Repeat the process annually.

You might like to try an ancient cottage garden recipe that involved peeling young shoots and putting them in salads.

Blackberries really taste best when they're picked from the wild, but some cultivated varieties are quite acceptable. This new one, 'Loch Ness', has the great advantage of being thornless, so is very easy to handle when you're tying it in.

Loganberry

This is a modern plant introduced from the USA. It's a cross between a blackberry and a raspberry and has the characteristics of both parents. It produces large succulent fruits ideal for eating raw or for cooking. The only worthwhile variety is called 'L654' and has never been named. Grow it just like a blackberry.

Blackcurrant

The blackcurrant is another native that must have been collected from the wild in ancient times. It seems to have been grown in cottage gardens since about the fifteenth or sixteenth century.

It has the disadvantage in small gardens that it's quite vigorous, needing at least 1.5 m (5 ft) between plants. I have seen them trained on a wall as fans, but the plants were straggly and not very successful. There is, however, a new variety available called 'Ben Sarek' which is more compact and can be planted about 1–1.2 m (3–4 ft) apart. Blackcurrants can be grown as individual bushes in the border too. I can find no varieties

for sale older than twentieth-century ones.

After planting, cut the shoots down to the ground. The following year there's no pruning to do, but subsequently cut all fruited branches right out each autumn. Propagate by hardwood cuttings in autumn.

Redcurrant and whitecurrant

Also natives of Britain and collected from the wild from the earliest times. They were grown in gardens a little in the sixteenth century, but did not become very popular until the seventeenth, when many new varieties were introduced. Few remain today.

'Laxton's No. 1', introduced in 1925, is the most common redcurrant now available. For a whitecurrant look for 'White Versailles', which dates from 1843.

They can both be grown as cordons against a fence or wall. Buy trained trees or prune a bush to have three shoots in a trident shape. Set three

Blackcurrants are a bit space-consuming for small gardens, but are nonetheless among the best of the soft fruits. They produce heavy crops of delicious fruits packed with vitamin C and they bottle well and can be frozen.

The whitecurrant is not as widely grown now, but it has a very pleasant flavour, especially when cooked, so you may consider it worthwhile. 'White Versailles' is the most popular variety.

canes 30 cm (1 ft) apart on wires on the fence and plant the bush at the centre cane. Then train the shoots up the three canes by tying them in regularly. In late summer, prune all the side shoots to about three buds and any shoots that come from those side shoots to one bud, just as for trained apples and pears.

If you want to grow free-standing bushes, plant them 1.2 m (4 ft) apart and prune back the tips of the new shoots to leave five buds in winter, removing crossing or crowded branches and any that are growing towards the centre of the bush. Propagate by hardwood cuttings in autumn.

GOOSEBERRY

The gooseberry was a great cottage garden plant and hundreds of varieties were bred for competition, possibly springing from French ones brought to England in 1276. Gooseberry clubs were numerous in the nineteenth century, especially in the industrial centres of the North, and some of them still flourish and hold annual competitions. Varieties like 'Crown Bob', 'Wonderful', 'London' and 'Garibaldi' appear time and again in winners' lists and you might still be able to beg a cutting or two from a gooseberry enthusiast. Old varieties available now from nurseries include 'Leveller' from 1885, 'Careless' from 1860 and 'Whitesmith' from the early 1800s.

All the old varieties are, unfortunately, a bit prone to mildew attack, so new cottage gardeners would be well advised to stick with the resistant 'Invicta' or 'Jubilee'.

As well as in free-standing bush form, gooseberries can be grown as cordons like redcurrants.

The recent gooseberry variety 'Invicta' produces huge crops of tasty berries and is resistant to gooseberry mildew. This one is grown as a standard on a tall stem, so it can be under-planted, therefore taking up no garden space at all.

There's also another advance that doesn't seem to have been available to cottage gardeners of old: you can now buy plants on standard stems about 1.2 m (4 ft) tall. The latter are ideal for small gardens since you can grow other plants underneath. However, as gooseberries hate root disturbance, it's best to under-plant with permanent plants such as low-growing shrubs. Prune standards like bush redcurrants and propagate by hardwood cuttings in early autumn.

RASPBERRY

The raspberry is native to Europe and was mentioned by Roman writers in the fourth century. It seems likely that its domestication didn't occur in Britain on a wide scale until the latter part of the sixteenth century. By the seventeenth century there were many different types, including some with white and yellow fruits, and breeding has continued until this day. Modern varieties are a great improvement, and newly bought canes will also be free from virus disease, so older ones have all but disappeared.

The new varieties of raspberry now available are far better than the old ones and new cottage gardeners should certainly take advantage of them. 'Glen Prosen' is a heavy-cropping late variety with a fine flavour.

My recommendations now would be for 'Glen Moy' for an early variety, followed by 'Glen Prosen'. They'll give you picking from early to late summer.

Autumn-fruiting varieties have been known since the seventeenth century, but it wasn't until the twentieth that breeders achieved real improvements. By far the best variety is 'Autumn Bliss'.

One of the problems with growing summer-fruiting raspberries in a small garden is that a row takes up a lot of space. If you have room, grow them on a 1.8-m (6-ft) post-and-wire structure, planting in autumn and cutting them down to the ground afterwards. New shoots will grow during the following season and these should be tied in at 10 cm (4 in) spacings on the wires. In the following year the tied-in canes will fruit, while new ones grow from the bottom. After fruiting, remove the old canes and tie in the strongest of the new ones to replace them.

If you have no room for a row, grow them in a column. Fix two cross-pieces of wood to a tall stake and run wires round them to take the canes. Plant one plant either side of the stake and, when the new shoots grow, tie them into the canes to form a pillar. They crop very well and look attractive too.

Autumn-fruiting varieties also take up quite a lot of space, but they need no support. Plant in autumn and cut the plants to the ground. They'll produce new shoots and fruit the following autumn. Subsequently prune down to ground level every spring.

Propagate in winter by digging up canes that have strayed into paths.

Grapes

The grape vine is, of course, a very old plant, grown by the ancients and is still an important crop today. In Britain vineyards were common in medieval times and, indeed, before the dissolution the monasteries made vast quantities of wine and even exported it to Europe.

Wine-growing is not really successful in colder areas where, in bad years, no harvestable crop is produced at all, so it's worth attempting only in warmer parts. However, grape vines are widely grown as decorative climbers and will sometimes produce small bunches of wine grapes when they're grown in that way. If yours do, it's important to prune them back during the season to limit the size of the plant or the grapes will be too small to use.

Grapes can be grown in Britain to produce, in good years, excellent crops and very drinkable wine. However, it's not always possible to guarantee a crop every year, so if space is limited it's probably better to stick to growing them as ornamentals.

For wine grapes, choose the varieties 'Madeleine Angevine' (introduced in 1863) or 'Seyve Villard' (introduced in 1930) to produce white and 'Triomphe d'Alsace', a more modern variety, to make red. For a crop of wine grapes, with perhaps a few for eating in a good year, plant vines 1.5 m (5 ft) apart on a post-and-wire structure 1.2 m (4 ft) high. Prune back to leave three strong buds. In the first year allow three shoots to grow and take them up a central cane.

In the following spring pull two of the branches down horizontally and tie them to the bottom wire. Prune the third to three buds to provide the three shoots for the following year. They are again grown up the central cane.

The two fruiting shoots will produce side shoots which should be grown vertically and tied in to the wires. When they reach the top wire, pinch out the tops.

The fruit will be borne on these side shoots, after which they're cut right out and two of those growing up the cane are brought down and tied in their place. Once again, the third shoot is pruned back to three buds.

Propagate by hardwood cuttings in autumn.

Strawberry

The verdant fields and woodlands of Britain would have yielded many wild strawberries for early cottagers to gather, including the small-fruited alpine strawberries, which were first mentioned in the tenth century. The woodland varieties were reputed to have the finest flavour.

These relatively small-fruited varieties were, however, replaced by the larger types from America by the sixteenth century and were widely grown in the seventeenth. The biggest breeding programme was carried out by the British breeder T. A. Knight, who produced hundreds of new varieties in the nineteenth century.

Unfortunately many of those old varieties were

Strawberries produce fine crops even in colder areas and no cottage garden should be without them. The maincrop variety 'Elsanta' gives heavy yields of good-quality fruit.

plagued by virus diseases and even the favourite British strawberry, 'Royal Sovereign', introduced in 1892, was almost lost, one lone survivor, free from virus, being found on an Irish bog to save the variety for modern gardeners. Now cleaned of virus, but still susceptible, it's again available.

It's best, though, to stick to modern varieties. For a succession of harvesting I'd recommend 'Honeoye', 'Elsanta' and the autumn-fruiting

Since strawberries are so decorative, with white flowers in spring followed by the attractive red berries and good foliage too, they can be planted in the borders. In the gentleman's garden they edge the vegetable plot.

In the artisan's garden rhubarb is forced under a (second-hand) terracotta forcer to produce blanched shoots of excellent flavour and greatly reduced acidity. The harvest is also earlier and, for the first fruit of the year, that's very welcome.

'Aromel'. Plant them in late summer 60 cm (2 ft) apart each way. When the fruit starts to colour, mulch with straw underneath to keep it clean and away from slugs. After harvesting, cut back the foliage to just above the crown of new leaves in the centre of the plant and remove them together with the straw.

To propagate strawberries, root a few of the small plants that grow on the ends of runners, either fixing them to the soil with a wire staple or in pots of compost. When they've rooted, detach them from the parent, dig them up and re-plant.

Strawberries are sometimes affected by virus diseases which are spread by greenfly. So, though it may go against the cottage garden ethos, it's worthwhile buying new plants when the time comes to replace the old. Commercial strawberry growers take great pains to ensure that their plants are free from insect attack and should be able to guarantee their plants. For this reason, it's also wise to buy from a specialist grower.

However, in the gentleman's garden which has the facility of a greenhouse, there's another very good reason to propagate each year. The young plants can be rooted into 7.5 cm (3 in) pots and later repotted into 12.5 cm (5 in) pots for forcing in the late winter.

Keep the pots outside until they have been subjected to a spell of frosty weather. They can then be brought into the greenhouse and grown in gentle heat to produce the earliest crop of the season. After forcing the plants will be exhausted so it's best to throw them away.

Rhubarb

In the sixteenth century rhubarb was used only medicinally and it was not until the eighteenth that it was eaten.

'Timperley Early' and 'Hawke's Champagne' are both old, early varieties suitable for forcing. The best main-crop variety is 'Cawood Delight'; if you have room for only one root, choose this and force it too. It's possible to buy container-grown plants now, so planting can be done at any time. The plants are very decorative and would look good planted in the border. If you grow more than one plant, set them 1 m (3 ft) apart.

In late winter cover a root with a terracotta forcer or a large bucket and harvest in early spring. The shoots will be paler, but much less acid and with a delicious flavour. Propagate by division in early spring, splitting the crowns with a sharp spade.

Garden Plants Recommended by Thomas Tusser in his* Five Hundred Points of Good Husbandry *in 1573*

Seeds and Herbes for the Kitchen

Avens, beet, betony, bloodwort, borage, bugloss, burnet, cabbage, clary, colewort, cress, endive, English saffron, fennel, French mallow, French saffron, leeks, lettuce, liverwort, lungwort, marigold, mercury, mint, onion, orach, parsley, patience, pennyroyal, primrose, rosemary, sage, sorrel, spinach, succory, summer savory, tansy, thyme, violet, winter savoury.

Herbes and Rootes for Sallets and Sauce

Alexanders, artichoke, asparagus, blessed thistle, cress, cucumber, endive, mint, musk mullion, mustard, purslane, radish, rampions, rocket, sage, sea-holly, skirrets, sorrel, spinach, succory, tarragon, violet. (He also suggested that the housewife should buy: capers, lemons, olives, oranges, rice and samphire.)

Herbes and Rootes to Boile or to Butter

Beans, cabbage, carrot, gourd, parsnip, pumpkin, rape, rouncival peas, swede, turnip.

Strowing Herbes of All Sortes

Balm, basil, camomile, costmary, cowslips, daisies, germander, hop, lavender, marjoram, maudlin, pennyroyal, red mint, rose, sage, santolina, sweet fennel, tansy, violet, winter savory.

Herbes, Branches and Flowers for Windowes and Pots

Bachelor's buttons, bay, campion, carnations, columbine, cowslips, daffodils, eglantine, feverfew, French marigold, hollyhocks, iris, larkspur, lavender, lily, love-lies-bleeding, marigold, nigella, ornithogalum, pansy, pinks, rosemary, roses, snapdragons, stock, sweet rocket, sweet Williams, violet, wallflower, white narcissus.

Herbes to Still in Sommer

Betony, blessed thistle, dill, endive, eyebright, fennel, fumitory, hop, mint, plantain, raspberry, roses, saxifrage, sorrel, strawberry, succory, woodruff.

Necessary Herbes to Growe in the Garden for Physick, not Rehearsed Before

Anise, archangel, betony, celery, chervil, cinque-foil, cumin, dittander, gromwell, hartstongue, honeysuckle, horehound, liquorice, lovage, mandrake, mugwort, plantain, poppy, rhubarb, rue, saxifrage, stitchwort, valerian.

Thus ends in breefe,
Of herbes the cheefe,
To get more skill,
Read whom ye will,
Such mo to have,
Of field go crave.

*I have modernized some of the names a little for today's readers: for example, 'peneriall' becomes 'pennyroyal'

Picture Credits

BBC Books would like to thank the following for providing photographs and for permission to reproduce copyright material. While every effort has been made to trace and acknowledge all copyright holders, we would like to apologize should there have been any errors or omissions.

Page 17 British Museum; 18 Victoria and Albert Museum/ET Archive; 19 *top* ET Archive, *bottom* frontispiece from *The Florist, Fruitist and Garden Miscellany* 1851; 24 Manchester City Art Gallery/Bridgeman Art Library; 28 courtesy Christopher Wood Gallery; 29 *top* Royal Horticultural Society, Lindley Library; 31 David Secombe/Garden Picture Library; 32 Henk Dijkman/Garden Picture Library; 48, 49 & 54 *top* Photos Horticultural; 56 *top* Elizabeth Whiting & Assoc.; 81 John Glover/Garden Picture Library; 90 Jerry Harpur; 101 Harry Smith Horticultural Photos; 110 John Glover/Garden Picture Library; 121 Linda Burgess/Garden Picture Library; 125 Brian Carter/Garden Picture Library; 132 Brigitte Thomas/Garden Picture Library; 143 Harry Smith Horticultural Photos; 161 & 169 Photos Horticultural; 171 John Glover/Garden Picture Library; 176, 184, 185, 189, 193, 195 & 219 Photos Horticultural; 242 *left* John Glover/Garden Picture Library, *right* Michael Howes/Garden Picture Library; 245 Photos Horticultural.

All remaining photographs are by Stephen Hamilton.

Useful Addresses

COTTAGE GARDEN SOCIETY
c/o Clive Lane
Brandon
Ravenshall
Betley
Cheshire CW3 9BH

MUSEUM OF GARDEN HISTORY
The Tradescant Trust
Lambeth Palace Road
London SE1 7LB

BRICK PAVIORS
The York Handmade Brick Company Ltd
Forest Lane
Alne
Yorks YO6 2LU

VICTORIAN EDGING TILES
The Bulmer Brick and Tile Co. Ltd
Bulmer
Nr Sudbury
Suffolk CO10 7EF

PAVING
Bradstone Garden Products
Okus
Swindon
Wilts SN1 4JJ

TRELLIS
Stuart Garden Architecture
Burrow Hill Farm
Wiveliscombe
Somerset TA4 2RN

OCTAGONAL GREENHOUSE
Parklines
Gala House
3 Raglan Rd
Edgebaston
Birmingham B5 7RA

LOVE SEAT
Woodworks
7 North Street West
Uppingham
Rutland
LE15 9SF

WILLOW OBELISK AND WATTLE FENCING
English Basket and Hurdle Centre
Curload,
Stoke St Gregory
Taunton
Somerset TA3 6SR

WOOD STAIN
Sadolin (UK) Ltd
Sadolin House

Meadow Lane
St Ives
Cambs PE17 4UY

CHICKEN COOP
George Carter
Silverstone Farm
North Elmham
Norfolk NR2 5EX

GALVANIZED FLOWER BUCKETS
Terrace and Garden
Orchard House
Patmore End
Ugley
Bishops Stortford
Herts CM22 6JA

LARGE CLAY POTS
Whichford Pottery
Whichford
Shipston-on-Stour
Warks CV36 5PG

SMALL CLAY POTS
The Potting Shed
Lee Valley Forge
Wharf Road
Wormley
Herts EN10 6HF

Index

83146

AUTHORS
James Curtis
Jane Simms
Jennifer Small

MANAGING EDITOR
Angela Pumphrey

PICTURE EDITOR
Emma Selwyn

BRAND LIAISON DIRECTORS
Simon Muldowney
Claire Pollock

DESIGNER
Pete Usher

LOEWY

Special thanks goes to **Mintel** for providing a considerable amount of market research material.

Other publications from Superbrands in the UK:
Consumer Superbrands Volume VI ISBN: 0-9547510-0-0
Cool BrandLeaders Volume III ISBN: 0-9547510-1-9
Sport BrandLeaders Volume I ISBN: 0-9547510-4-3

For more information, or to order these books directly from the publisher, email brands@superbrands.org or call 01825 723398.

For Superbrands international publications email: brands@superbrands.org or telephone 020 7379 8884.

© 2005 Superbrands Ltd

Published by Superbrands Ltd
19 Garrick Street
London
WC2E 9AX

www.superbrands.org/uk

All rights reserved.

No part of this publication may be reproduced or transmitted in any form by any means, electronic, digital or mechanical, including scanring, photocopying, recording or any information storage ard retrieval system relating to all or part of the text, photographs, logotypes without first obtaining permission in writing from the publisher of the book together with the copyright owners as featured.

All of the companies who own the brands featured in this publication have given consert for the brand name, logotype and photographs to be shown. Any enquiry regarding a specific brand should be made to the relevant company as listed in the Directory at the end of this book.

Printed in Hong Kong.

ISBN: 0-9547510-6-X

The Library
University College for the Creative Arts
at Epsom and Farnham

658.
804
094
1
CUR

Contents

JOHN NOBLE

Director
British Brands Group

The case studies in this book are a celebration of the versatility and relevance of branding. Here are companies of all sizes, from the global to the local, with pedigrees ranging from the established to the recently acquired. Most striking of all is the staggering array of sectors represented.

These companies are intent on setting themselves apart, recognising that superior performance must be sought not only in what they do but how they do it, and are prepared to invest for the long term.

Their ceaseless efforts to understand the businesses and people they serve, to deliver consistently and to communicate with clarity has created trust, reassurance, loyalty and ultimately competitive edge.

For the Business Superbrand it has also created a reputation that stretches far beyond their customers.

PAUL GOSTICK

International Chairman
The Chartered Institute of Marketing (CIM)

The Chartered Institute of Marketing

The Chartered Institute of Marketing (CIM) is pleased to endorse publications that promote best practice in branding, and CIM has endorsed the Superbrands' publications over a number of years. We are now delighted that the independent Council have included CIM this year as a Business Superbrand.

CIM works tirelessly to raise awareness and understanding of marketing within business – specifically the value that marketing creates, and the impact that

it has on the bottom line. Including CIM in the list of Business Superbrands is clear recognition of marketing's place at the heart of business and CIM's leadership role in representing the marketing profession.

Branding is not just for consumer goods, it has an important part to play for business and service brands too. Most business to business and services relationships are built on trust – and in reading this book, you will gain insight into how the featured companies build trust into their brands.

JANET HULL

Head of Marketing
Institute of Practitioners in Advertising (IPA)

What value can you put on relationships? Above all, these Business Superbrand case studies demonstrate the importance of collaboration between client and customer in delivering the brand promise. Winning customers is the first stage in a process. Keeping customers is as, if not more, important to long term success. Fulfillment is as important as trial: sustained marketing effort as important as novelty. In today's fast-moving business and communications

environment it is easy to be bamboozled by change and lose sight of first principles. This new selection of best practice examples helps ground our thinking.

Angela Pumphrey

Managing Editor
Business Superbrands

In this, Superbrands' tenth anniversary year, we are proud to present the fourth edition of Business Superbrands. The first Business Superbrands book was launched in 2000, following four previous editions of the business to consumer version, Superbrands. These editions established our tradition of celebrating achievement and exceptional practice in branding. It was, at this time, becoming apparent that branding excellence was just as important in the business to business market. Concurrently, the business world was changing to embrace the growth of the internet and ecommerce. Other key issues that have increased in stature over this period include the role of Corporate Social Responsibility and work/life balance policies.

The importance of business to business branding has become increasingly recognised. This is reflected by the fact that the Business Superbrands book has expanded to incorporate a wider range of businesses, all of which are closely aware of and concerned about the strength of their own brand and reputation.

The brands you will find on the pages that follow have been highly rated by the independent and voluntary Business Superbrands Council, which is made up of eminent figures from the world of branding. All its members have a deep understanding of what makes an exceptional brand. Using a shortlist of just over 1,000 brands, the Council was tasked with identifying the strongest based on their personal perceptions of the brands strength and quality in the market. When scoring, they keep the following definition in mind: "A Business Superbrand has established the finest reputation in its field and offers customers emotional and/or tangible advantages over competitors, which (consciously or sub-consciously) customers want, recognise, and are confident about investing in. Business Superbrands are targeted at businesses and organisations (although not exclusively so)."

We have found that the aggregate perceptions of experienced market professionals is as valuable a guide to brand excellence as any other apparently more scientific processes. It enables the brands to be judged against their peers across a diverse range of sector.

We hope that the following best practice examples help to further understanding of branding and the work and investment needed to become one of the UK's finest in a business to business environment.

Miles Templeman

Director General
IoD

In recent years, business and service industry brands have learned many lessons from the business to consumer market as the importance of branding in the business to business sector has grown. Many operate in a more volatile and changeable market and have had to deal, for example, with competition from the online sector. They have in turn learned lessons, which the consumer brands now appreciate. Superbrands and Business Superbrands recognise the great achievement of creating a brand in highly competitive markets and the often greater attainment of maintaining the status of the brand.

All business brands face a very tough challenge. In many cases the brand is not simply the product but is the whole service provided by the business. A product can be judged alone whereas a service brand, which many of these are, is built by all the employees that have contact with or can influence the customer; every employee can influence the reputation of the brand.

The IoD has a wide membership and many of them have a great interest in the success of branded products and services. Not many of them, however, have as yet achieved the success of the Superbrands and Business Superbrands. I am very happy for the IoD to introduce and to be associated with the fourth edition of Business Superbrands.

What are the key challenges facing business to business brands?

STEPHEN CHELIOTIS
Chairman
Business Superbrands Council

GILL ALLEN
Head of Marketing
CNBC Europe

Accountability is one of the key challenges that a brand and its owners face on a number of levels.

Technological advances and the breakdown of geographical boundaries are levelling the competitive playing field for brands. Accountability to the customer is becoming increasingly vital. The fulfilment of the brand promise and, more importantly, the brand experience are becoming key as brands fight to establish differentiation in the face of ever-more broad service offerings.

Customers are now looking for assurances that the brand has substance, integrity and longevity. Accountability on social and environmental issues is paramount and business brands will need to seek to adopt values that promote a human focus, communicating corporate ethics and social responsibility alongside the more traditional price, function and advantage messages.

For marketers, accountability is a hot topic in the boardroom and measuring bottom line impact of communications is not a task to be taken lightly. While great brands generally equal great businesses, for marketers leveraging brand equity to maximise marketing return on investment will remain the key challenge.

JONATHAN CUMMINGS
Marketing Director
IoD

The major challenge facing all brands, business to consumer or business to business in 2005 will be to consistently and significantly exceed the expectations of customers. Any organisation worth its salt will be working to harness the power of data-driven marketing strategies, using direct and interactive channels to reach and keep customers; building revenues whilst continuing to drive down costs. Technology, if well utilised is making it easier for smaller organisations to compete, creating a more competitive environment, building customer awareness of a greater level of choice and making it easier to switch. So for all brands, and even more so for Business Superbrands, where customer expectations are typically that much higher, the key challenge is to make their company easy to do business with – and to meet that challenge at a justifiable cost.

MIKE HEWITT
Publishing Director
Management Today

For all of us in business to business communications, the biggest challenge is salience. When a corporate executive in Coventry has access to the pick of the world's suppliers from his or her PC screen, how do we make our offering stand out from the rest?

The answer, of course, is just the same for business today as it has been for more than 100 years in consumer goods: *branding*.

As business products and services become commoditised, deciding between rival suppliers is as much about intangibles such as quality of service and commitment to the customer as it is about the inherent features of the product.

These are benefits that are hard to convey unless they are *experienced*, and still harder to repeat unless they are *remembered*. And that, ultimately, is why the company that can wrap up all the emotional attachments we form to suppliers we trust into a truly memorable brand is the one that will win against all comers, local and global. More than ever before, today is the age of the Business Superbrand.

DAVID MITCHELL
Head of Advertising – EMEA
Intel

Business Superbrands face many challenges when establishing a perception in the mind of their customer. A Business Superbrand should be based on fundamental truths about the business; these could be that of reputation, quality of service, quality of product, ability to innovate or any number of factors that defines that business.

In a business market where products can be commoditised and are technically very similar, taking that fundamental truth and translating it into something that will differentiate your company from the competition can be tough. It requires total honesty about your strengths and weaknesses as a business, combined with exquisite understanding of your customers, their requirements and their attitudes towards you and your competition.

Successful Business Superbrands recognise that the key challenge is knowledge and understanding – of yourself as a business and of your customers. Once you have cracked that, the other challenges you face will seem small in comparison.

SIMON BOLTON
CEO UK & Ireland
JWT

It is only thirteen years old, younger than the youngest brand in this book, younger than my favourite t-shirt. In its short life the internet has driven change of an unprecedented scale and pace. In 'The Experience Economy' Pine and Gilmore state "the internet is the greatest source of commoditization ever known to man", yet for many brands, old marketing and organisational habits, (like my t-shirt) die hard. It is simply no longer enough to provide excellent products, prices, logos or even service offers anymore. They are both comparable and replicable in an instant. Instead we have to deliver a total experience that is perfectly aligned both internally and externally. Let's be rigorous, even ruthless about this. And then we must deploy our most powerful weapon against commoditization: – imagination. Let's apply it to create far more compelling and original brand communications that, guess what, customers actually want to spend time with. And if we gain their time, we are winning the battle against commoditization.

ANTHONY CARLISLE
Executive Director
Incepta Group & Citigate Dewe Rogerson

Conviction, not confection. Brands start with a clear, unswerving vision of corporate purpose and intent. This vision 'thinks through the customer's mind' i.e. not what is best and easiest for me; but what is best and easiest for you, my customer. This vision comes not from focus groups, but from the conviction there is a better way and we will provide it. The success of this vision depends upon execution, upon the customer experience of service, services and value, i.e. a friendly call; helpful information; delivery beyond expectation; not gripping me warmly by the throat and trying to ram unwanted goods through my wallet. Branding and communication capture the spirit of business purpose, vision and delivery, and magnify it by bringing it to life through the line. Great brands understand this. Too many do not. Lip service; values that are wish lists; brand manuals that are just rules; mantra, not reality.... Stop it. Conviction, not confection.

MICHAEL DENT
General Manager Marketing
DHL Express (UK)

A business to business brand is generally in far closer direct contact with its' customers than a business to consumer brand. This strength also brings with it two associated problems. The first is the speed at which an organisational change (merger, acquisition or take-over) can shake the brand credentials. Although these are (hopefully) rare events clear thinking in advance is essential and will pay dividends. The second relates to the nature of the customer relationship. In this respect the motivation and enthusiasm of the employees is absolutely key. This is even more true for business to business service organisations.

The direct link between the company culture and the essence of the brand is therefore something which needs to be guarded and nurtured extremely jealously.

JON GELDART
Marketing Director
PricewaterhouseCoopers LLP

This is a world of increased regulation and legislation, harsher competition and unrelenting pressure on recruiting and retaining the best people. There remains a never-ending struggle to innovate quicker and manage risk better. However, many business brands continue to assume customers buy only with their heads and not their hearts. We have the same issue as consumer brands; dealing with emotionally complex human beings who have just bought The Times, had a cup of Costa and have a daughter running up a big bill on her mobile. Both as individuals and as groups. where team dynamics add complexity to purchase decisions, our buyers don't leave their emotions at the doors of their businesses. Our challenge is to make the offer clear and the benefits *emotionally* as well as cerebrally compelling. Simple really.

JOANNA MANNING-COOPER
Director of Communications
FT

The past few years have seen all brands – both business to business and consumer – fighting to be heard against a background of increasing noise, with potential customers constantly surrounded by different marketing messages, all claiming to offer improved business performance.

The key challenge facing business to business brands is threefold: one, to ensure that their brand proposition credibly meets and exceeds the needs and expectations of business customers, two, to creatively distinguish themselves from the competition enough to attract customer attention, and three, to establish a reputation as a brand which cherishes its customers and deserves their loyalty. Ideally, your customers should become your greatest ambassadors – the unsolicited endorsement of a respected business leader is surely the best kind of viral marketing available for a business brand.

To some extent, the first element is the most crucial – the brand itself needs to create a sense of dependency in the consumer: if they feel their business performance is tangibly enhanced by a business brand, that brand will, in time, become an integral part of their daily business routine. If you know your customers are hooked, you're more than half way there.

JOHN MATHERS
CEO
Enterprise IG, UK

Brands today must be compelling to get noticed. But they must also be truthful to survive. One without the other breeds cynicism. The key to success, to longer lasting relationships with customers, to a better reputation in the marketplace, and to an improved bottom line, lies in striking the right balance between the two qualities.

This 'Compelling Truth' is the touchstone of authenticity. The business to business brand that bores will never become a market leader, simply because it will be ignored. The brand that tells a compelling story but provides an inconsistent experience will never be trusted. The point at which a business proposition meets a belief system is where great brands are created. Get this balance wrong and customers will not forgive you, and the market may never forget.

Great brands are compelling because they cut through the communications chatter with a clear, relevant message. And they are true because they consistently deliver on an enduring promise.

MARK QUARTERMAINE
Director of Marketing
Cable & Wireless, UK

Rising above the pack.

Never has the power of a brand been so important in today's marketing saturated world. We are all bombarded everyday with literally thousands of marketing messages not only as a consumer but more and more so in the business to business environment. It comes in so many different forms – TV, radio, internet, papers magazines, e-mails, direct mail, telemarketing, sponsorships etc etc. Businesses are under information overload – so how do we assimilate all of this, how do we differentiate between all the marketing messages, how do we make our decisions on what we buy and from whom.

As such never has the brand been more important. If we truly attribute value, quality, customer service or innovation to a brand then it stands a chance of lifting itself above the masses and being successful. So how do *you* rise above the pack – that's the key challenge.

JOHN WEEKS
Executive Chairman
Mintel

Mimicking the consumer economy, the explosion in products and services in business markets is putting greater pressure on brands. Success will be measured not by whether a brand is 'front of mind today' – (front of mind presence without reputation, consistency and experience can be easily confused with brand attributes in the short term) but whether it was here 20 years ago, and whether it will be here in 20 years time. And the hallmarks of this success will be delivering great value for money, huge repeat business, and yes, delivering profits with no surprises. Now that is a true Brand. The owners of true brands have to act as long term custodians, not short term gamblers. Their goal is not transient or fleeting, nor is it their fifteen minutes of fame...

So the biggest challenge must be the continual re-investment and development of the brand. This means being better at foretelling what customers will want tomorrow, whilst still maintaining the brand's core values and its raison d'etre – all the while delivering a return on investment to the brand owners. The ever-changing methods used to measure brand equity over time may yield illusionary blips and virtual changes to the order of things. But astute brand owners will not be diverted by this from their true goal.

3M

Market

3M's business is innovation. From small beginnings making sandpaper, 3M is now a US$20 billion global diversified technology company with leading edge solutions in, for example, biometrics, fibre optics, supply chain software and touch screen computers. Through its commitment to innovation, 3M has continually developed its offering. Its business now spans markets covering: consumer and office; display and graphics; electro and communications; health care; industrial; safety, security and protection services; and transportation. One of the world's most diverse organisations with some 50,000 different lines, 3M products touch people in all walks of life – in the home, in schools, in the work place and in the street. Today, 3M has principal operations across 63 countries and products available in more than 200.

Achievements

3M's stated vision is to be the most innovative enterprise and the preferred supplier. Not only does 3M strive to achieve this year-on-year, achieving accolades both for its management of innovation and for specific new products, but it continues to deliver impressive profits, regularly earning itself a mention amongst the world's most respected companies. 3M has built a reputation not just for its great products and solutions but also for how it conducts its operation.

The company has developed an ongoing commitment to the management of innovation that it justifiably claims to be unrivalled. Boosting growth, improving productivity and reducing costs without limiting creativity is a huge challenge, which 3M has overcome through its strong entrepreneurial culture. 3M involves people at every level in innovation – in technology, process, product and environmental progress. This delivers not only a constant stream of new ideas and opportunities, but is also a supreme motivator and a source of challenge for its employees. More than 67,000 people contribute to its success worldwide but 3M is unusual in that it employs mostly local nationals. Today, fewer than 300 3M employees worldwide are expatriates not residing in their home countries.

Examples of national and international awards in the last four years include: UK Business in the Community for Innovation in the Environment; Best New Bodyshop Product or Service (Europe) AutoTrade magazine;

US R & D magazine for 3M™ Composite Conductors as one of the power industry's most technologically advanced products in a century; and Post-it® Notes as one of the top inventions of the 20th century by Fortune magazine. In addition, 3M's CEO James McNerney was last year cited as one of the world's top business leaders – as CEO of the Year (Industry Week) and featured in the Best Manager list (Business Week). 3M's reputation for managing innovation and the way it conducts its business (which it claims are inextricably linked) mean it is frequently referred to in case study material by educational institutions such as Harvard, INSEAD and the London Business School.

History

3M's history reads as a roll call of breakthroughs over more than a century. Founded in 1902 as the Minnesota Mining and Manufacturing Company, the first breakthrough came with WetorDry™ Sandpaper in the 1920s. Many more followed with the burgeoning car industry, including Scotch® masking tape, new adhesives to replace tacks in bonding upholstery, and sound-deadening materials for the new metal-framed cars. In the early 1940s, 3M was diverted into defence materials for World War II, which was followed by new ventures, such as Scotchlite™ Reflective Sheeting for road markings, magnetic sound recording tape, filament adhesive tape and the start of 3M's involvement in the graphic arts field with offset printing plates. In the 1950s, 3M introduced the Thermo-Fax™ copying process, Scotchgard™ Fabric Protector, videotape, Scotch-Brite™ Cleaning Pads and several new electro-mechanical products. Dry-silver microfilm was introduced in the 1960s, along with photographic products, carbonless papers, overhead projection systems, and a rapidly growing healthcare business of medical and dental products. Markets further

expanded in the 1970s and 1980s into pharmaceuticals, radiology and energy control. In 1980, 3M introduced Post-it® Notes, which created a whole new category in the marketplace, changing people's communication and organisation behaviour forever. An array of innovative products continued, including brightness enhancement films for electronic displays and flexible circuits used in inkjet printers, mobile phones and other electronic devices. Today, innovation is taking the business into whole new areas such as security and personal identification systems incorporating biometric data and cancer treatment pharmaceuticals.

Product

In countless different combinations, 3M brings together its technologies as the base for innovative new products. More than 30 technology platforms underpin 3M solutions – ranging from the earliest platforms such as abrasives and adhesives through to more recent breakthroughs such as light management and microreplication. As a global enterprise, 3M is characterised by substantial inter-company co-operation in the sharing of these technologies through research, manufacturing and marketing of its products. It also partners with leading organisations in the search for the best solution for the customer.

Some 90% of 3M's products are for commercial or industrial use. 3M works closely with these customers to understand their needs. It claims no boundaries to the breadth of its people's imagination or the lengths they will go to deliver a result – and boasts many anecdotal stories such as the development of its award winning Paint Preparation System through observation in car repair bodyshops. Teams work across the organisation focused on ideas and converting these to viable commercial opportunities. For example, the vision for the Eden Project was to create a tropical environment in a huge greenhouse. This required the world's largest self-supporting roof construction made from lightweight transparent material which would enable the tropical plants to thrive. Working with the architects, transparent membrane cushions made with a triple layer of 3M™ Dyneon™ ETFE film were developed as the solution.

Protection of a priceless book collection was another problem solved by 3M. For the first time, the public has access to one of the world's most famous reading rooms, the magnificently restored British Museum Reading Room. 3M™ Tattle-Tape™ Security System was developed to safeguard the books and 3M library specialists worked alongside architects and library staff to ensure that the installation of two security exit gates complemented the historic setting.

3M's consumer products span iconic brands such as Scotch®, Post-it®, Scotchgard®, Thinsulate™, Scotch-Brite™, Filtrete™ and Command®. It is nearly 25 years since Post-it® Notes were first invented and through continuous innovation the brand now represents a range of communication products for the 21st century which includes: Post-it® Super Sticky Notes and Post-it® Software Notes, part of the Microsoft® Partner Pack for Windows®.

Recent Developments

The 3M name goes from strength to strength with greater international market penetration outside the US. The company is expanding significantly in Asia, particularly in China and South Korea.

Healthcare represents a major opportunity and already represents 21% of annual turnover. 3M has invented a new class of drugs, immune response modifiers (IRMs) and in 2003 the first approved IRM, Aldara, was recognised for use in the treatment of superficial basal cell carcinoma, a common form of non-melanoma skin cancer. The 3M name is highly respected and trusted in the field of healthcare and in addition to a range of pharmaceutical products and drug delivery systems (including CFC-free asthma inhalers) the company is forging ahead with innovations in dressings, surgical equipment and digital stethoscopes.

Another major growth area for the company is in the field of electronics and interconnections. OEMS (original equipment manufacturers) – such as Fujitsu, Siemens and Nokia – turn to 3M for bespoke solutions. The pace of competition in this field means 3M is often involved in ground breaking technology in strictest confidence with customers. For instance, 3M microinterconnect solutions are currently enabling a range of leading edge devices: fibreoptic cameras that go inside a patient, high speed broadband solutions and rear-view mirrors that dip automatically. Working in increasingly competitive markets, 3M has recognised that its strengths lie not just in its ability to innovate but its ability to be first into the market. Numerous processes and programmes have been implemented to ensure it identifies new products with significant potential and allocates resources to commercialise them even faster.

Promotion

The diversity of 3M's offering means it comes to market through many channels and distributors. The company promotes its range of technologies, solutions capability and products through its sales teams to channel partners as well as marketing direct to end users. Indeed, its relationship with end users and customers is integral to 3M's continued success. The company helps them to understand the breadth of its technologies and how these can be combined to solve their problems.

Worldwide, 3M houses Innovation Centres at many of its offices, such as the one at its UK headquarters in Bracknell, where its technology and solution capabilities are cleverly portrayed.

The distinctive but simple 3M brand is used consistently on websites, packaging and advertising worldwide. The short memorable '3M' could have been designed for the rapid 21st century global market, though in fact the short form name has

been in use almost since the company first started. The original Minnesota Mining and Manufacturing Company was first depicted as '3M Co' in 1906 in a diamond shape. However, for many years different logos were in use. The consistent, familiar, and internationally recognisable red 3M logo was introduced in the 1970s and is now a highly prized asset. It is not just a symbol of corporate identity, it is also a trademark and a brand.

Brand Values

The 3M brand needs no translation. It is viewed by people worldwide – customers and end users – as an authority brand. It says: 'reputation, quality, value and service'. Research shows that customers see 3M as a problem solver; they know the 3M brand will deliver practical, skilful, systematic and simple solutions that work reliably and consistently. The brand stands for 'ingenuity' – practical and ingenious solutions that help customers succeed. 3M employees tend to stay with the company, as they claim it offers a breadth of opportunities, and are proud to be ambassadors for one of the world's leading brands

www.3m.com/uk

THINGS YOU DIDN'T KNOW ABOUT

3M

❯ Authors Jim Collins and Jerry Porras named 3M as the only company 'built to last' in their book Built to Last: Successful Habits of Visionary Companies.

❯ 3M has paid a quarterly shareholder dividend without interruption since 1916.

❯ 3M is one of only 3% of US companies that have harnessed innovation in order to survive for more than 100 years.

❯ 3M has been part of many world achievements – from Neil Armstrong's 'one small step' on the moon (his space suit's soles were made from 3M material) to Michael Johnson's record breaking golden shoes (made with Scotchlite™ Reflective Fabric) at the 2000 Olympics in Sydney.

❯ 3M started out as the Minnesota Mining and Manufacturing Company and would have failed had it not been for the persistence of its founders.

recruitment **solutions**

Market

The UK recruitment market is big business. The companies that match employers and workers, not only keep the economy ticking over, but also generated some £24.5 billion in revenue in 2003/04 (Source: Annual Recruitment Industry Survey). This was a 6.6% increase on the year before. Although the sector experienced a slow period between 2002 and 2003, the industry has grown an astonishing 40% since 1999.

The market for temporary and contract recruitment services is the biggest in terms of turnover, generating 87% of the industry's total income. Permanent recruitment turnover was £1.58 billion in 2003/04, but grew faster than the temporary sector, up by 7.6%.

The UK recruitment market is often over looked as an important contributor to the labour market and is closely linked to the health of the national economy.

The industry is highly fragmented, containing a wide variety of large and small firms. Alongside Adecco, which is a leading brand in the UK and international recruitment market, other major players include Hays Personnel Services, Manpower, Reed Executive and Select Appointments.

With a network of 5,800 offices in more than 71 territories and 350 branches in the UK, Adecco is a formidable force in this extremely competitive market, helping three million people work every year.

The company is market leader in the global market for general staffing, the third biggest player in the professional staffing and services sector and second biggest in providing career development consultancy.

As a result of the increasingly globalised economy, labour has become internationally mobile, requiring recruitment specialists with global capacity and knowledge.

Globally, the recruitment industry generates around US$400 billion in revenues. Temporary staffing accounts for US$140 billion of this with independent contractors generating over US$200 billion in revenue.

Around 1.5% of the European Union's working population – a daily average of around 2.2 million workers – are employed through staffing companies, largely on short-term contracts ranging from a day to a year (Source: International Confederation of Private Employment Agencies -CIETT in 2000).

In the US, the recruitment industry provides around 2.16% of the workforce, equating to nearly three million workers per day (Source: American Staffing Association May 2002).

Achievements

Despite uncertain economic conditions over the past few years, Adecco has performed strongly, reporting a 20% increase in profits in the third quarter of 2004.

The company has built an enviable position of strength, now ranking first or second in eleven of the world's top thirteen staffing markets, which account for 95% of total industry revenue.

Thanks to the strength of its service and brand, Adecco has the highest market share, revenue, cash flow and market capitalisation in the industry.

Worldwide, Adecco generates revenues of some £11 billion. This is enough to put it among the world's business superstars, ranking 150th in the Forbes International list.

The scale and impact of the company is impressive. On any given day, Adecco serves some 130,000 clients, and over 250,000 per year. Helping millions of people find work, Adecco payrolls 650,000 people daily. Around the world, Adecco employs some 312 people every minute.

The company takes its role as a good corporate citizen very seriously, with membership to Business in the Community, Investors in People, a Member of Employers Forum on Disability, Race for Opportunity and the Third Age Employment Network.

The world's largest recruitment specialist is creating unique service commitments within the recruitment industry. The introduction of our 12 commitments will answer the concerns of every professional company and candidate.

Committed?... we are

Whether you are a large or small company, a candidate looking for temporary work, or a career professional looking for your next move, our commitments will give you peace of mind.

Committed to you.

recruitment **solutions**

To find out more about our commitments, call us on **0800 4580577**, go to **www.adecco.co.uk** or contact your local Adecco branch.

History

Despite its position as the worldwide and UK industry leader in recruitment services, the Adecco name is a relative newcomer. The name only appeared on the UK high street in January 1997, following the merger of ADIA and ECCO Employment. In fact, the company's original trading name was Alfred Marks, the first recruitment agency to be formed in the UK, in 1919.

In 1977 Alfred Marks joined the ADIA group (founded in 1957) and ECCO was founded in 1964. The wealth of knowledge and experience that comes from this background, supported by the resources of an international company, means Adecco is well placed to provide a service, which meets the needs of the constantly changing world of work.

Product

Adecco's services encompass staffing, career services, executive search and e-recruitment. Adecco is the trading name for the Group's world-leading Staffing Services Division, providing administrative, technical and industrial staff to clients all over the world. Adecco specialises in offering clients flexible staffing solutions that help them operate more efficiently and productively, providing the people it places with rewarding temporary assignments or careers.

Adecco UK serves clients in office, financial, industrial, retail, education, catering & hospitality, health & social care and contact centre sectors, as well as local customers of all sizes and sectors looking for flexible staffing solutions.

Specialising in temporary recruitment, temporary to permanent recruitment, permanent recruitment and staff-related services, the Staffing Services Division provides a fast response to clients' business fluctuations or skill shortages. This may require servicing their needs across multiple sites around the globe.

Adecco have onsite offices at over 80 major blue chip organisations across the UK. Adecco's Managed service area of the business can provide clients with a one-stop shop for all their HR requirements.

Recent Developments

Adecco has invested heavily in e-commerce solutions over the past five years, and is in the process of transforming its entire global back-office operation to a web-based platform. This will allow Adecco to fully reap the benefits of a number of web-based solutions which have been developed to help interface directly with clients and candidates.

This e-commerce solution will help Adecco keep pace with its clients fast changing demands. Whether it is an international corporate client who wants a recruitment company to help move its workforce across the world at the press of a button, or a local employer who wants a more simple service, Adecco is equipped to meet the challenge.

The company understands that not all customers want to deal with them over the internet, and so it continues to offer a face to face as well as an online service. Adecco calls this its 'clicks and bricks' strategy.

Adecco also recently launched 'Adecco Plus', a dedicated programme focused on integrating potentially disadvantaged groups into the job market. This will involve the development of specific services addressing the ageing population, diversity and disability within the workplace.

Another new initiative from Adecco in 2004 is a global 'Commitments' programme.

This is an innovative new scheme incorporating six commitments to clients and to six candidates designed to redress some of the negative perceptions of the recruitment industry. By making its service as 'transparent' as possible, Adecco hopes to highlight the quality of innovative services and products to both clients and candidates.

The programme also offers very clear compensation should these Commitments ever be broken. For example, Adecco commit to provide clients with 100% satisfaction on all Adecco candidates or a replacement will be offered within half a day.

Promotion

Adecco is well known for its association with high profile international sporting events. Adecco showcased its unique ability to manage large-scale workforces at Euro 2000 (Belgium & Holland), the Sydney 2000 Olympic Games and also the Davis Cup tennis competition. As official sponsor of the Volunteer programme at the Manchester Commonwealth Games Adecco provided a management team tasked with co-ordinating the recruitment and training of more than 10,000 volunteers across fifteen venues.

More recently, Adecco has become a Business Club member of the Global Challenge world yacht race supporting the Save the Children boat. Adecco views this link as an ideal way to demonstrate the shared qualities of the workplace and crewing a racing yacht, such as leadership, dedication, teamwork and competition.

Brand Values

Adecco's mission is to match companies that need workers with qualified people to perform the work.

Work can give people dignity and a sense of community and belonging. Helping people find meaningful work is what Adecco is all about.

www.adecco.co.uk

THINGS YOU DIDN'T KNOW ABOUT

Adecco

❯ Around the world, Adecco employs some 312 people every minute.

❯ The company's roots lie with the original trading name of Alfred Marks, the first ever recruitment agency in the UK that was formed in 1919.

❯ Adecco co-ordinated the recruitment, training and management of 10,000 volunteers for the 2002 Commonwealth Games in Manchester which was the largest volunteer force assembled since World War II.

❯ Over 650,000 associates are paid on any given day with approximately three million having worked during the year.

Allied Irish Bank (GB)

Our business is business banking.

Market

Allied Irish Bank (GB) is a specialist business bank offering a full range of products and services, including personal and private banking for its business and professional customers. The Bank's primary target market is medium corporate companies with a minimum turnover of £1 million.

With a market share of around 2% of the business market, Allied Irish Bank (GB) has a strong credit culture and has created a quality franchise, building a strong reputation as a focused bank within its target markets.

In the future, Allied Irish Bank (GB) intends to continue on this path in establishing itself as the bank of choice for growing businesses and professionals and as a serious alternative to the traditional British banks.

The Bank is in an excellent position to achieve these goals through a personalised service that large banks with centralised operations cannot match and a continued commitment to its five key business cornerstones, which are:

Developing long-term relationships with customers; Providing local bankers who are knowledgeable, experienced and fully involved with all decisions; Maintaining short lines of communication and speedy decision-making; Having a management team that works closely with centralised specialists; Upholding a high level of organisational efficiency.

Achievements

The core achievement at Allied Irish Bank (GB) is its relationship-led approach to business banking that it believes delivers the finest customer service available. Allied Irish Bank (GB) prides itself on listening and reacting to its customers, allowing them to focus on their own business.

This quality of service has been publicly acknowledged by the biennial Forum of Private Business survey, which has identified Allied Irish Bank (GB) as 'Britain's Best Business Bank' on six consecutive occasions since 1994. The survey quantifies the relationship between businesses and their banks, in particular the quality of its people and its operational efficiency.

Evidence of these relationships is that the Bank gains most of its new business through recommendations from existing customers. In fact, 81% of Allied Irish Bank (GB)'s customers have recommended the service they have received at least once to a colleague.

Allied Irish Bank (GB) has always recognised the needs of its business customers and, as a result, has seen the demand for its services grow. The Bank currently has 47 offices throughout Britain, and plans are in place to continue expanding the network, where appropriate, at a time when many competitors are closing branches.

Allied Irish Bank (GB) is committed to delivering customer service excellence. On an annual basis, the Bank is in touch with its customers' views using a detailed customer satisfaction survey. Results completed in 2004 showed that – for the sixth year running – satisfaction levels had increased, reaching an outstanding 84.2%.

Customers remain fiercely loyal, with more than 50% of customers who completed the survey being with the Bank for six years or more. In the six years the Bank has been surveying its customers, satisfaction ratings have consistently risen.

Further to this, 87.6% of its customers said that they are likely to be banking with Allied Irish Bank (GB) in two years' time. The Bank also showed an ability to attract new business with 13% of customers surveyed being new clients that have been with the Bank for less than one year.

Another serious achievement is the reputation that Allied Irish Bank (GB) has developed within the professional sector, housing associations, charities and educational institutions – with one in eight higher education institutions in Britain choosing to bank there.

It is testament to the Bank's longstanding commitment to staff development that Allied Irish Bank (GB) has achieved the recognition of the 'Investors in People' standard across its office network since 1995. Allied Irish Bank (GB) was amongst the first banks to be awarded corporate recognition through the scheme, preceding many of the big clearing banks. It believes that its continuing investment in staff development has been the key to its success in not only retaining employees, but also in providing the exceptional service that its customers receive.

History

Allied Irish Bank (GB) is part of Allied Irish Banks, plc (AIB Group), Ireland's leading banking and financial services organisation and a major player in the financial sector worldwide. Operating principally in Ireland, Britain, Poland and the US, AIB Group has shares listed on the London, New York and Irish Stock Exchanges.

Since its formation more than three decades ago, AIB Group has become a dynamic and successful organisation. In 1966, AIB Group aggregate assets were €323.8 million – the June 2004 figure was in excess of €95 billion.

Allied Irish Banks, plc is the parent company of AIB Group (UK) plc, which trades in Northern Ireland under the name First Trust Bank and in Britain under the name Allied Irish Bank (GB). AIB Group (UK) plc is authorised and regulated by the Financial Services Authority.

The Bank has had a presence in London since 1825 and over the years has developed a reputation for offering tailored banking services through a relationship

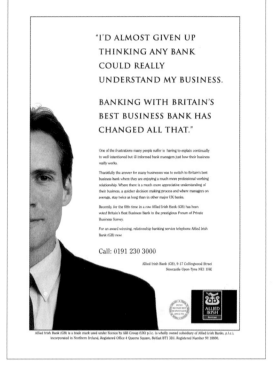

"I'D ALMOST GIVEN UP THINKING ANY BANK COULD REALLY UNDERSTAND MY BUSINESS.

BANKING WITH BRITAIN'S BEST BUSINESS BANK HAS CHANGED ALL THAT."

One of the frustrations many people suffer is having to explain continually to well intentioned but ill informed bank managers just how their business really works.

Thankfully the answer for many businesses was to switch to Britain's best business bank where they are enjoying a much more professional working relationship. Where there is a much more appreciative understanding of their business, a quicker decision making process and where managers on average, stay twice as long than in other major UK banks.

Recently, for the fifth time in a row Allied Irish Bank (GB) has been voted Britain's Best Business Bank in the prestigious Forum of Private Business Survey.

For an award winning, relationship banking service telephone Allied Irish Bank (GB) now.

Call: 0191 230 3000

Allied Irish Bank (GB), 9-17 Collingwood Street Newcastle-Upon-Tyne NE1 1HE

Allied Irish Bank (GB) is a trade mark used under licence by AIB Group (UK) p.l.c. (a wholly owned subsidiary of Allied Irish Banks, p.l.c.), incorporated in Northern Ireland, Registered Office 4 Queens Square, Belfast BT1 3DJ. Registered Number NI 18800.

banking approach. The Bank offers a full range of banking services to business and professionals and has a network of 47 business offices covering all of the major population centres across Britain. It also has an established Private Banking offering.

Product

Allied Irish Bank (GB) is committed to tailoring products and services to meet clients' specific needs and adapting them as clients' requirements change.

The Bank strives hard to understand the workings of every business it deals with, providing closer working relationships and quick decision making through direct lines of communication. Another plus is that personal banking is also offered as an extension of the service the Bank provides to business customers.

While many key competitors are stepping up the provision of their online services and focusing on extending call centres and automated banking, Allied Irish Bank (GB) provides a comprehensive online service that complements rather than replaces its personal relationship approach. The Bank takes the view that internet banking will never replace human interaction and provides the online service as a convenience to its customers only.

Sixth Sense.

A real feel for business banking. Allied Irish Bank (GB) has been voted 'Britain's Best Business Bank' 6 times in a row.

Allied Irish Bank (GB)
Our business is business banking.

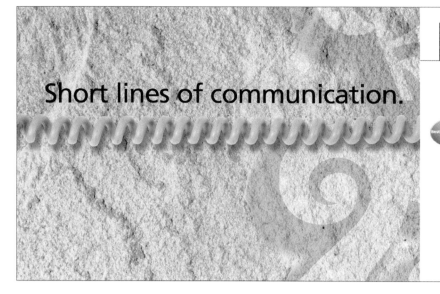

Short lines of communication.

Voted Britain's Best Business Bank for the 6th time.

Long lines of awards.

When it comes to awards for service, no other business bank comes close. But what makes us truly different? Why exactly have we won the coveted title of 'Britain's Best Business Bank' for an unprecedented six times in a row?

We believe that it's because our services stem from a single-minded business banking philosophy, that your interests are best served by a dedicated, partnership approach. It is this focus that will achieve the quality of relationship that will drive your business forward.

When independently assessed in the Forum of Private Business survey, we demonstrated high levels of performance, as judged by our customers – Allied Irish Bank (GB) was also judged to have consistently outperformed its competitors, improving standards that were already at significantly high levels.

So, as well as winning awards for service, Allied Irish Bank (GB) is also winning the hearts and minds of our business customers.

Its four key areas of business are: Business Banking, Corporate Banking, Public Sector & Charities and Private Banking.

The Bank provides a professional Business Banking service by tailoring financial packages and solutions to the individual needs of business customers. All managers are decision-makers and develop long-term relationships with their customers as they provide day-to-day banking services and are closely involved with their local business community.

Allied Irish Bank (GB) has the knowledge and experience necessary to excel in Corporate Banking, coupled with a real understanding of the complexities of corporate and institutional business. The Bank's strategy is to deliver a first-class service by ensuring fast turnaround of credit decisions due to its flat structure, knowledgeable people and short lines of communication. It can provide all the essential facilities to meet a company's financing requirements, including Acquisition Finance and Working Capital Finance. The Corporate Banking teams work closely with each branch in ensuring that customers receive seamless service.

The dedicated Public Sector and Charities Team at Allied Irish Bank (GB) focuses solely on non-profit seeking enterprises. This can be broken down into three sub-sectors; Education, Charities and Registered Social

Landlords. The team's continuing interaction and experience with not-for-profit organisations gives excellent insight and knowledge of current developments within the sector. Its bespoke funding packages ensure that all customers get financing solutions and day-to-day banking matched to their needs.

Traditional banking continues to be at the core of Allied Irish Bank (GB)'s Private Banking, with personal contact and close customer relationships being central to the service. The Private Banking service provides comprehensive wealth-management including in-house investment, advice and access to investment, stock-broking and taxation specialists. Personal managers identify the options that best suit customer requirements, enabling them to enjoy more financial control and flexibility with support and guidance when needed.

Recent Developments

In 2004, for the sixth time in succession, Allied Irish Bank (GB) was voted 'Britain's Best Business Bank' by the Forum of Private Business. Also in 2004, Standard & Poor's rating services assigned its 'A/A-1' long- and short-term counterparty credit and certificate of deposit ratings to the AIB Group (UK) plc. Standard & Poor's stated: "The ratings reflect the Bank's sound financial profile and consistent strategy."

The same year saw the continuance of branch redesign for Allied Irish Bank (GB). Branches have been restyled away from the traditional British bank style of rows of tellers, to something much more suitable to the needs of Allied Irish Bank (GB)'s corporate customers.

Natural materials such as marble and steel have been used in the refined and uncluttered interior design. Meeting rooms and open space create branches that are in keeping with a business lounge rather than a bank and provide an atmosphere conducive to doing business.

Promotion

Allied Irish Bank (GB) recognises the need to continue raising its profile, with an objective of achieving growth. Through an integrated approach, the Bank's focus is on decision-makers and owners within the business, professional and public sector.

This approach is underpinned by the recently launched 'Sixth Sense' national, regional and specialist advertising and direct mail campaign. The campaign objectives are to reinforce the Allied Irish Bank (GB)'s key messages; short lines of communication that lead to quick decisions, long-term relationship building with customers and in-depth knowledge and commitment. An additional objective was to raise awareness of the outcome of the Forum of Private Business survey – which voted

Allied Irish Bank (GB) 'Britain's Best Business Bank' for the sixth consecutive year – to customers and the wider business market.

The 'Sixth Sense' campaign was supported by PR with press releases sent to all key business media. This resulted in national and local coverage of the campaign and reinforced the key messages. Allied Irish Bank (GB) engages with the media on a daily basis and has strong relationships with targeted publications, providing opinions on key business topics. Business sponsorship is a key part of the Banks' promotional activity and it actively seeks opportunities to work with business organisations and professional bodies.

Brand Values

At Allied Irish Bank (GB), the brand values centre around one main aim: to deliver superb service. Teams aim to act in the best interest of the customer to deliver best value and to deliver on customer expectations.

They are encouraged to take personal ownership for ensuring customers receive the best service possible, to clearly understand the client's particular needs, circumstances and preferences and to seek to create value that is shared fairly and openly between the Bank and its customers. The Bank strives to demonstrate determination to progress, to be distinctive and to compete vigorously with competitors to win new business.

The AIB Group's Code of Business Ethics for all employees of the Group reaffirms the general principles that govern how AIB Group conducts its affairs. It recognises that maintaining the trust and confidence of customers, staff, shareholders and other stakeholders by acting with integrity and professionalism, as well as behaving with prudence and skill, is crucial to the continued growth and success of the AIB Group.

www.aibgb.co.uk

THINGS YOU DIDN'T KNOW ABOUT

Allied Irish Bank (GB)

❯ AIB Group was formed in 1966, bringing together three distinctive Irish banking traditions. The Provincial Bank, founded in 1825, the Royal Bank established in 1836 and the Munster and Leinster, formed in 1885.

❯ In 2004, 34 of the Bank's staff celebrated 25 years of employment.

❯ The first London office of the Bank opened in 1825 in Throgmorton Avenue.

❯ Allied Irish Bank (GB) was one of the first business banks to obtain the Investors In People standard and has held it since 1995.

Less staff turnover.

Build up a long term relationship with our service managers.

More customer continuity.

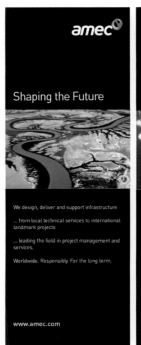

Shaping the Future

We design, deliver and support infrastructure

... from local technical services to international landmark projects

... leading the field in project management and services.

Worldwide. Responsibly. For the long term.

www.amec.com

World skills on your doorstep

We are 45,000 people in over 40 countries - focused on you.

We find solutions in sensitive and challenging environments.

We provide local access to skills across the world.

www.amec.com

Safe delivery

Delivering reliably, every time.

Working safely.

Managing risk and reputation with confidence.

www.amec.com

Today through tomorrow

We design, deliver and support for best lifetime value.

We look to the long-term - with all our stakeholders.

Working in a sustainable way.

www.amec.com

Market

AMEC is active in a broad range of sectors, working for an equally broad range of clients. In general terms, AMEC designs, delivers and supports infrastructure assets – such as huge oil and gas installations, local hospitals, railways, roads, airports, wind farms, defence installations and office buildings.

In all, AMEC competes in eighteen main market sectors. In transportation, which accounts for 18% of the group's turnover, AMEC has decades of experience in the construction of the world's busiest airports and roads and is Europe's second largest provider of railway services.

In the chemicals, industrial and pharmaceuticals sectors, it serves the majority of the top pharmaceutical, biotechnology and fine chemicals companies and supports plants for bulk chemicals and food as well as general manufacturing. AMEC is a European market leader in electronics and telecommunications, and has global expertise in pulp and paper facilities for the forest industry. It also has multi-disciplinary expertise in the mining and metals sector.

For the energy, oil and gas and power markets, (27% of AMEC's revenue is from oil and gas-related work) AMEC's expertise spans complex installations, gas processing, operations and maintenance. The company is a leading global contractor for large diameter pipelines, and its power generation and transmission services include wind and nuclear energy. Wind energy is becoming a key sector for AMEC. Its portfolio of wind farms makes it a major player in a market which, thanks to recent Government policy supporting wind farm development, is growing rapidly.

Finally, in the infrastructure, commercial and public sector, AMEC provides facilities and infrastructure for public and private sector clients in the defence, detention, education, financial, healthcare, retail, sports and leisure sector. It also works with local authorities in urban renewal.

In 2003, this broad range of activities saw AMEC record £112.5 million in pre-tax profits – up 7% on the previous year.

Achievements

With 45,000 people in 40 countries, AMEC is one of the world's leading project management and services companies, often operating in extreme conditions and

fragile environments that require special and expert care. Few other companies can match AMEC's experience in designing, delivering and supporting infrastructure. Furthermore, its powerful global network means AMEC can bring its world skills to the doorstep of local clients, wherever they are.

AMEC's outstanding performance has helped it win The Queen's Award for International Trade, and the company's chief executive, Sir Peter Mason, was knighted in 2002 for his services to British industry.

The company's long experience and expertise means it is trusted to work on prestigious landmark projects including Heathrow's new Terminal 5, the illumination of the Eiffel Tower, some of the largest wind farms yet seen in the UK, giant oil and gas contracts, reconstruction work in Iraq, and high profile regeneration work across the UK.

In France, where AMEC recently designed a customised, underground-powered tram system for Bordeaux, AMEC has participated in most of the local rail and tram systems built over the last decade.

In 2003, the company won numerous industry awards in the UK, including five Gold Awards and an Order of Distinction from the Royal Society for the Prevention of Accidents and a Safe Contractor of the Year Award from ExxonMobil. It also won the Vision in Business for Environment Scotland award for its approach to integrating environmental management.

History

The AMEC name and brand was introduced in 1982, but the foundations of the companies that eventually became part of the AMEC group go back much further. The Continental European business dates back to France in 1846, with a company founded to manufacture locomotives, and which built the first boring machine to attempt to dig a tunnel under the English Channel in 1882.

The beginnings of the UK business go back to 1848, with the Americas business dating back to 1907, when Monenco (the Montreal Engineering Company) was founded.

AMEC was formed with the merger of the Fairclough and William Press groups in 1982. In 1996, AMEC bought 41.6% of SPIE, which is now its Continental European business. In 2000 it gained a major foothold in the Americas with the acquisition of AGRA in North America. Its stake in SPIE was increased to 46%

in 2001, with the acquisition of the balance of the company taking place in 2003, when it was rebranded AMEC SPIE.

Product

Project management is AMEC's core skill, and to add value for its clients, AMEC has thousands of specialists in disciplines ranging from thermo-dynamics and geology, through to environmental chemistry and risk assessment.

AMEC divides its business into three main segments: Engineering and Technical Services, Oil and Gas, and Project Solutions.

The Engineering and Technical Services division provides a wide range of specialist engineering services, from design and environmental consultancy to mechanical, electrical, and voice and data communications services. Examples of the division's work include a customised local tram system for the city of Bordeaux, and the creation of a solution for a local landslide problem in Lethbridge, Canada. Other specialist services include monitoring environmental conditions like surface water or pollution at airports or on defence sites.

The Oil and Gas business provides a wide range of services, including the design, support and enhancement of floating oil facilities, pipelines and refineries. AMEC looks after these facilities in the long term, providing services such as environmental consultancy, audits and operator training. For example, for BP, AMEC conducted a major project to renovate 60 offshore platforms in Indonesia and for Shell it has a six-year contract to support the company's Malampaya deepwater gas-to-energy production facilities in the Philippines.

The Project Solutions part of the business delivers large public sector or public-private sector projects of particular kinds, including wind farms and urban regeneration projects. Often, AMEC takes equity in these projects and follows them through the planning process and development to sale. In other cases,

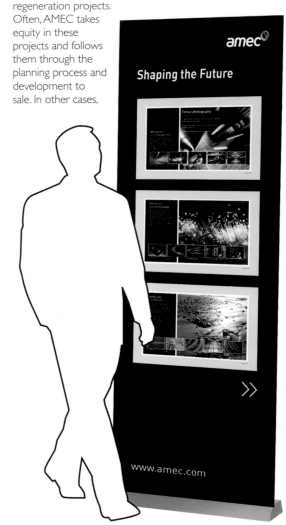

AMEC doesn't take equity, but manages the whole project including the actual delivery or construction. Examples of this include the Docklands Light Railway and the Channel Tunnel Rail Link.

AMEC's design, deliver and support value chain means it can plan its customers' projects from feasibility and financing to design; it can project manage construction and offer engineering services; and look after the finished asset, including facilities management. Finally, it can undertake decommissioning at the end of the asset's life.

All in all, AMEC can offer an A to Z of services, comprising: architecture, commissioning, communications systems, concept development, construction services, consultancy, decommissioning, engineering services, environmental services, facilities management, feasibility, front-end design, installation, maintenance services, master planning, mechanical and electrical, operational support, private finance, procurement, programme and project management, technical services, and training and development.

Recent Developments
AMEC is engaging in major new projects all the time, but recent highlights include the 2003 completion of the first section of the £1.9 billion Channel Tunnel Rail Link and work with the British Airports Authority to create a taxiway for the new 'Super Jumbo' at Heathrow Airport.

Internationally, AMEC delivered Bonga, one of the world's largest floating oil and gas facilities, for Shell.

In 2003, it also won two further contracts to aid in the reconstruction efforts in Iraq. The contracts, worth up to US$1.1 billion, are to restore public works and water infrastructure and form part of the major round of contracts currently being awarded by the Coalition Provisional Authority, the US-led body in charge of Iraq reconstruction.

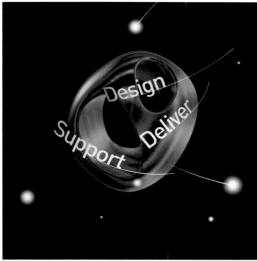

Over the last few years, AMEC has also been busy in its marketing activities. A new AMEC logo was launched in 2000 and is now well established around the world. To take this to the next level, new brand messages, accompanied by distinctive brand visuals – including a new dynamic version of AMEC's touchstone logo – were launched in 2004.

This latest phase was undertaken as AMEC completed a seven-year-long transformation from a UK construction company to an international project management and services group.

Steady progress has been made in shifting the balance of AMEC's activities further towards services, with the most recent figures showing the proportion of total operating profit accounted for by services work now amounting to 69%.

The change in the company's business mix was reflected in its relisting on the London Stock Exchange from the construction to the support services sector in November 2004.

The new brand was rolled out in 2004, to be supported by a culture change programme, called

'Shaping AMEC', in 2005. The new brand for the first time unites AMEC behind one vision, one description and three sales propositions, and transforms its visual style from old-style industrial company to new-style professional services company.

Promotion
Helping to communicate this new positioning, AMEC has launched a range of new internal and external promotional materials. These include a new video/CD, which provides an overview of the company's brand values and a cross section of its services. The company has also developed a corporate brochure to accompany the CD. This is a big step forward in the way AMEC is marketed and offers opportunities to present the strengths of the group and for cross-selling.

AMEC has also launched a magazine, In Touch, which sets a new standard for the company.

Rather than undertaking any global or national advertising, AMEC relies on its reputation, which is built on its expertise in the industries in which it operates, as its most powerful form of marketing. Most important is the strength of the relationships it builds with customers – the company has built long relationships with major global companies and much of its work is repeat business.

Sustainability is a natural

extension of AMEC's long-term approach in working with customers and its desire to offer them lifetime value. AMEC introduced a formal sustainability programme in 2001, when it also published its first sustainability report.

An improvement in AMEC's corporate responsibility rating from 70% to 80% in 2003 placed the company 56th in the Business in the Community survey in the UK and AMEC topped its sector in the Dow Jones Sustainability Indexes at the first attempt in 2004.

Brand Values
The diverse company that is the modern AMEC is encapsulated in its three brand messages: world skills on your doorstep, safe delivery and today through tomorrow.

The first reflects the company's scale and experience. Its extensive network – AMEC operates in over 700 locations from the Australian outback to the Arctic – means that, while it can service global companies, it can also deliver local solutions to companies that work in regional or local markets.

Safe delivery is central to the AMEC promise. A health and safety discipline is fundamental to the company's culture and runs through everything it does. But safe delivery goes beyond health and safety concerns. Working on customers' valuable assets, AMEC takes responsibility for their investment, treating its customers' risk and reputation as its own.

Investing in capital assets is a major decision – and getting the most from them over time is important, which requires planning for the future from the very beginning of a contract. This is reflected in the 'today through tomorrow' message, which also refers to the company's commitment to sustainability – considering the long-term impact on the community and environment.

These three brand messages are summarised in AMEC's vision – Shaping the Future – which reflects the impact that the company's projects around the world will have now and in years to come.

www.amec.com

THINGS YOU DIDN'T KNOW ABOUT

AMEC
> AMEC has a new technology called GeoMelt that uses high voltage electricity to turn toxic and nuclear contaminated ground into a harmless glassy, rock-like mass.

> The Eiffel Tower now lights up the night sky in Paris thanks to AMEC, which was responsible for installing 20,000 bulbs and 78km of cabling.

> AMEC assisted with the post-September 11th recovery work at both the World Trade Center and the Pentagon, with its round-the-clock emergency cleanup work beginning just hours after the attacks.

> AMEC is developing the next generation of theme park rides, with its RoboCoaster technology on which riders sit in giant robotic arms while travelling through interactive theme zones.

ARRIVA

Market

Arriva is one of the largest transport services organisations in Europe. A FTSE 200 company, it employs over 30,000 people and operates in eight European countries: the UK, the Netherlands, Germany, Denmark, Sweden, Portugal, Spain and Italy.

Arriva runs an extensive range of services, including buses, trains, commuter coaches, taxis and water buses. It provides over one billion passenger journeys every year, and over the past five years has invested around €1 billion in improving services for its customers.

Arriva has first mover advantage among its UK peer group: only one other company, France's Connex, is building a pan-European position in the bus and rail markets. Arriva's UK competitors have instead targeted North America or Australasia.

The European Union has estimated that the bus and rail markets are worth around €100 billion (Source: EU statistics 2000), however this figure doesn't take into account the ten countries that joined the EU in 2004.

Achievements

Arriva's most significant achievement is recognised as its fundamental repositioning over the past eight years.

In 1998 Arriva was substantially composed of major motor retailing and finance businesses. A strategic review by chief executive Bob Davies, who joined the board in 1998, led to the decision in 1999 to focus management and financial resources on the significant opportunities in passenger transportation in the UK and mainland Europe.

By the summer of 2003 the Group had completed the disposal of its major motor retailing and finance businesses and had established itself as one of the leading transport services organisations in Europe.

In 1997 Arriva provided passenger transport services in the UK and Denmark, by 2004 its business had grown significantly in both of those countries and had extended to Sweden, the Netherlands, Spain, Portugal, Italy and Germany.

Arriva's expertise in delivering effective and efficient transport services is founded on the strong partnerships it forges with a wide range of customers, including local, regional and national authorities.

History

Arriva's predecessor, Cowie, began as a family business based in Sunderland selling second-hand motorcycles. As the business extended into new market sectors through acquisition and organic growth, it amassed a raft of different names and identities. Arriva came into being in 1997 and replaced a complex and confusing brand structure comprising no fewer than 140 separate brands and sub-brands.

The name Arriva was derived from the verb 'to arrive' – the ultimate deliverable of any transport service provider. The acceptability of the name to other cultures has assisted Arriva's international growth. The new name was accompanied by a distinctive 'wheels within wheels' symbol, which sought to combine visually the key elements of a transport services operator.

Born in the north east of England, and the company still has its head office in Sunderland, the Arriva brand is now visible across Europe from Malmo to Mallorca, Manchester to Milan. It is a pan-European brand.

Product

Arriva is one of the largest bus operators in the UK. It is also the biggest bus operator serving London, the largest provider of bus services in Denmark, the largest private sector bus operator in Italy and the provider of around one-fifth of regional bus services in the Netherlands.

It is the major operator of scheduled bus and coach services to the south of Lisbon in Portugal and operates inter-urban bus services in the north west of the country. It provides bus services in Germany, the Spanish province of Galicia, the island of Mallorca, and the south of Sweden.

Arriva also operates passenger rail services in the UK as a result of winning a fifteen-year franchise. Arriva Trains Wales delivers services throughout Wales and the English border counties.

Arriva was also the first private company to win passenger rail franchises in Denmark, serving mid and north Jutland. It operates NoordNed, a rail and bus operator in the north of the Netherlands, and provides passenger rail services in seven of Germany's federal states.

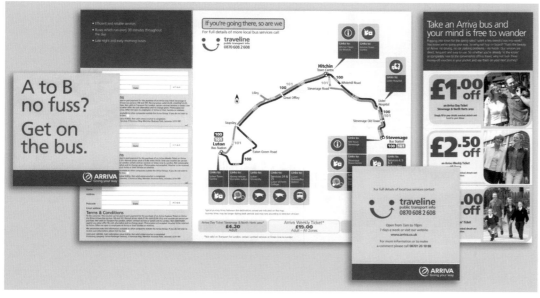

Arriva also operates one of the UK's leading vehicle rental businesses, Arriva Vehicle Rental, which provides around 12,000 cars and light commercial vehicles for public sector and corporate clients.

Arriva is also London's premier sightseeing bus tour operator, providing over one million 'The Original Tour' journeys every year. And finally, with its Arriva Bus & Coach business, it is a bus and coach distributor too.

Recent Developments

In April 2004 Arriva made its first foray into the German passenger transport market, the biggest in Europe, with its acquisition of German rail company Prignitzer Eisenbahn Gruppe. Later in the year it acquired Regentalbahn AG, a rail operator in Bavaria. It now operates passenger rail franchises in seven of Germany's federal states.

During 2004 Arriva consolidated its position in two other important passenger transport markets with significant bus acquisitions in Denmark and Italy.

In early 2005 it entered the German bus market with the acquisition of Sippel, one of the country's largest privately owned bus operators, based in the Rhine-Main area.

With both bus and rail markets moving rapidly to a competitive tendering environment, Arriva is well placed to develop its German business.

In the UK passenger rail sector Arriva has pioneered the concept of 'Adopt a Station'. The scheme involves local people and customers carrying out regular spot checks at stations, in addition to those conducted by Arriva employees, to ensure they are tidy and clean and that issues that arise are addressed promptly. Other passenger rail operators in the UK have since emulated the scheme.

Arriva is leading the industry with a number of initiatives designed to protect the safety of customers and employees. It has introduced CCTV cameras onto bus and train services, as well as at stations, and has pioneered technology on buses that records critical information about incidents involving customers, employees and vehicles. It is increasingly using Global Positioning Systems to improve service delivery.

Arriva invests in its people through a range of training initiatives, including online programmes, designed to enhance their skills and increase their focus on customer service, and it has recently widened its innovative approach to technology-led training. For example, its award-winning bus simulator assists driver selection, assessment and training.

It is also focused on creating a working environment that values difference and maximises the potential of both current and future employees.

Promotion

From its inception, the Arriva brand has been used as an umbrella brand and employed extensively across all of the company's operations.

The Arriva brand vision is 'to be recognised as the leading transport services organisation in Europe.' When the company acquires businesses it incorporates them into the branding architecture as soon as they share the continuously reinforced Arriva brand values.

The benefits of this umbrella branding approach are manifested in Arriva's UK bus business, the first division in Arriva to adopt a disciplined brand identity. Arriva is the primary brand on buses, with the route number as the product descriptor.

While the livery applied to all the Arriva buses in the UK is a particularly powerful and tangible expression of the brand, the brand identity is also expressed in areas from timetables, through publicity and marketing, to recruitment materials.

Where Arriva lacks marketing freedom it applies the spirit of its brand values in working closely with its partners to promote passenger transport. For example, it is the biggest bus operator in London, but its customer Transport for London determines the level of branding, not least the colour of the buses – they have to be red.

Outside London, across England, Wales and Scotland, Arriva is not just a business to business brand but a consumer brand too. This allows much greater marketing freedom, which is manifested in campaigns such as the award winning 'Going Your Way' which was launched in 2002 to encourage more people to use buses. The campaign uses direct marketing to deliver key

information to everyone who lives within ten minutes of a bus route, and has been supplemented by radio, press and cinema advertisements, along with extensive PR, designed to revitalise the image of bus travel.

Arriva also embraces new channels of communication and produces all its timetables on the web.

Always looking for new ways to make buying tickets easier, Arriva already sells student tickets over the internet and is rolling out ticket sales through local shops in conjunction with PayPoint.

Arriva prides itself on the level of customer research it carries out, and on its response to customer feedback. It has an industry-leading customer comments process, and conducts extensive customer satisfaction research, which informs ongoing improvements to its services.

In 2004, working with the local authority, it piloted a 'big bang' approach to market development with a re-launch of bus services in Medway. In addition to new and refurbished buses, the programme included an upgrading of driver training. Based on the success of the re-launch, the company is planning to roll out similar programmes across other UK regions.

As a public transport operator that plays a vital role in the social and economic lives of the communities it serves, Arriva takes its social responsibilities seriously. In addition to a strong employee diversity policy, it works closely with Business in the Community on social and economic regeneration, supports Age Concern and Changing Faces, the charity for people with facial disfigurements, is engaged with a number of education initiatives and has established a partnership with the Leicester Racial Equality Council.

Brand Values

Arriva's vision is to be recognised as the leading transport services organisation in Europe. To this end it works tirelessly to deliver better service, innovation and marketing designed to help it both win and retain contracts and to continue to grow organically and through targeted acquisitions.

Arriva's values and ethics support its vision. They include putting the safety of employees and customers first; respecting individuals and the diverse communities it serves, supported by a culture of integrity and honesty; managing the environmental impact of its operations and encouraging the sustainable development of public transport; recognising that working together and maintaining strong local relationships are essential to delivering high quality services; anticipating change and identifying better ways to meet customers' needs; and maintaining a strong commercial focus that delivers long-term value for all stakeholders.

www.arriva.co.uk

THINGS YOU DIDN'T KNOW ABOUT

Arriva

> Arriva hosts over 20 million journeys every week across Europe.

> The trains operated by Arriva Trains Wales travel 16.5 million miles every year – the equivalent of travelling 660 times around the world.

> The army of people who clean Arriva's UK Bus division fleet of over 6,000 vehicles use 13,000 litres of disinfectant, 32,000 mop heads and enough cleaning cloths to stretch from Lands End to John O'Groats and back again, every year.

> If all of Arriva's employees across the UK and mainland Europe met up they could fill the Albert Hall over six times.

> Arriva has around 24,500 vehicles ranging from buses and trains to cars, vans and water buses.

BARCLAYS

Market

Barclays is one of the largest financial services groups in the UK and competes in the banking, investment banking, investment management sectors, insurance and stockbroking businesses.

In terms of market capitalisation, Barclays is the third largest bank in the UK and ninth in the world. With 8.6 million current account holders and 3.7 million online banking customers, Barclays is a major player in the retail banking market, but it is also a strong force in the business sector, servicing almost a quarter of the UK business banking market and working for more than half of Britain's top 100 companies. It is also a major player in the small and medium sized business banking market, supporting over half a million SMEs in the UK. Barclays is also a leading provider of co-ordinated global services to multinational corporations and financial institutions worldwide; operating in over 60 countries with over 70,000 employees.

Barclays is a leader in several other banking sectors. For example, it is the UK's number one stockbroker and Barclays Global Investors is the world's biggest institutional asset manager. It is one of the world's top five internet banks and, with Barclaycard, it has the leading credit card operation in Europe. It also has an increasingly strong presence in the global investment banking sector with Barclays Capital.

Achievements

Over its history, Barclays has developed a breadth and depth of expertise across the world that few other financial organisations can claim. In the process, it has built one of the strongest and most recognised brands in global finance.

Barclays has grown from a group of English partnerships to a global bank represented in Europe, the US, Latin America, Africa, the Caribbean, Asia, the Middle East and Australasia.

With a strong track record of innovation, Barclays has scored numerous firsts in the UK banking sector. It was the first to introduce a credit card in 1966, offer the first ATM machine in the world in 1967, the first telephone banking service, Barclaycall, in 1994 and the first to introduce PC-banking, in 1997. It has also launched a raft of customised services, such as Barclays Private Bank and Barclays Premier.

Its growth into a force in the international banking market is reflected by its many global achievements. For example, in 1981, Barclays became the first foreign bank to file with the US Securities and Exchange Commission and raise long-term capital on the New York market. In 1986, it became the first British bank to have its shares listed on the Tokyo and New York stock exchanges. In

2003 Barclays acquired the Banco Zaragozano, increasing its presence in the Spanish market.

Barclays investment banking division, Barclays Capital, has been a particular success. Since its inception in 1997, Barclays Capital has focused on its key businesses in bonds, loans and risk management products such as convertible bonds, derivatives and commodities trading. The expertise it has developed has been recognised by the broadest spectrum of clients, including governments, multinationals, financial institutions and corporate borrowers.

The company has won numerous awards in acknowledgement of its many achievements in all areas of its business activities, including being named 'Best Stockbroker' by Proshare in 2004, and 'Best Online Broker' in the Signet Investor Awards. Other recent awards include Barclaycard being named Best Commercial Card Provider of 2004 by Business Britain Magazine and Global Pensions magazine awarding

Barclays with 'Corporate Pension Fund of the Year' for 2004. Barclays was the only UK pension team nominated for this global award.

In 2003 Barclays marketing and communications attracted numerous plaudits, with the 'Fluent in Finance' campaign winning the Gold Film Award at the 50th International Advertising Festival in Cannes. 'Fluent in Finance' has also been nominated for 'Most innovative Marketing or Advertising Campaign' at the IFS Financial Innovations Awards.

The company has also been recognised for its substantial corporate citizenship work, winning the Corporate Social Responsibility Award 2004 at the National Business Awards in London.

History

Barclays origins can be traced back to 1690 when John Freame and Thomas Gould set up business in Lombard Street, in the heart of London's financial district. The name Barclay became associated with the company in 1736, when James Barclay – who had married John Freame's daughter – became a partner.

Private banking businesses were commonplace in the 18th century, keeping their clients' gold deposits secure and lending to credit-worthy merchants. The leading partners of this bank, which was named Barclay and Company, were connected by a web of family, business and religious relationships. This led it to become known as the Quaker Bank, because this was the tradition of the founding families. The development of today's global business began in earnest in 1925, with the merger of three banks – the Colonial Bank, the Anglo Egyptian Bank and the National Bank of South Africa to form Barclays' international operations.

In 1969, Barclays acquired Martins Bank, the largest UK bank to have its head office outside London. And in 2000 it took over The Woolwich, a leading mortgage bank and former building society.

Barclays' global expansion was given added impetus in 1986 with the creation of an investment banking operation which has since developed into Barclays Capital. In 1995 Barclays purchased the fund manager Wells Fargo Nikko Investment Advisers. The business was integrated with BZW Investment Management to form Barclays Global Investors.

In January 2003 Barclays also acquired the retail stock broking business Charles Schwab Europe.

Barclays most recent acquisition, announced in October 2003, was the purchase of Gerrard Management Services Limited. This acquisition brought together one of the UK's leading private client wealth managers with Barclays Private Clients.

Generally speaking, it's better not to.

At Barclays, instead of generalising, our relationship directors are focused on specific industries. They know what they're talking about, but more importantly, they know what you're talking about. Which would explain why Barclays are rated number one for understanding customers' businesses.

business.barclays.co.uk

Tough summer?
A six month loan break will help you plough on.

With over 300 years experience in the farming industry, we know when times are hard. That's why we're offering you a six month capital repayment holiday, in case you need some time to get back on track. For more details, call Daniela Roberts on 020 7699 2609.

BARCLAYS
FLUENT IN FINANCE

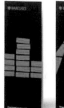

Product

Barclays divides its business into four core areas: Private Clients and International; Wholesale and Institutional (including Barclays Global Investors and Barclays Capital) UK Banking and Barclaycard.

Private Clients and International brings together Barclays' wealth management operations and the group's non-domestic retail and commercial banking activities. Private Clients serves affluent and high net worth clients while International provides banking services to personal and corporate customers internationally.

Barclays Global Investors (BGI) is one of the world's largest asset managers and a leading global provider of investment management products and services.

BGI offers structured investment strategies and related investment services such as securities lending, cash management and portfolio transition services. In addition, BGI is the product leader in Exchange Traded Funds (iShares), with over 100 funds for institutions and individuals trading in ten global markets.

Barclays Capital is the investment banking division of Barclays, providing large corporate, institutional and Government clients with solutions to their financing and risk management needs.

The Barclays Capital business model focuses on a broad span of financing and risk management services in the interest rate, foreign exchange, commodities and credit markets as well as equities. Activities are divided between two areas: Rates, which includes fixed income, foreign exchange, commodities, emerging markets, money markets sales, trading and research, prime brokerage and equity related activities; and Credit, which includes origination, sales, trading and research relating to loans, debt capital markets, structured capital markets, commercial mortgage backed securities, private equity and large asset leasing.

Barclays UK Banking division delivers banking solutions to retail and business banking customers. It offers a range of integrated products and services and serves its customers through a variety of channels, including its UK network of branches, cash machines, telephone banking, online banking and relationship managers. UK Banking is managed through four divisions – Larger Business, Medium Business and Agriculture, Small Business and Home finance.

Barclaycard is one of the leading credit card businesses in Europe and now incorporates all of the group's UK unsecured and card lending products and expertise. In August 2004 Barclaycard announced the acquisition of Juniper Financial Corporation. The transaction will enable Barclaycard to enter the US credit card market by purchasing one of North America's fastest growing issuers.

Recent Developments

Barclays has a strong Corporate Social Responsibility agenda. Some of the highlights from this agenda are: Upgrading a further 312 branches to meet the needs of customers with disabilities; providing financial inclusion through Barclays' Cash Card account for 55,500 new customers; co-developing and adopting the Equator Principles to support the brand's commitment to socially and environmentally responsible lending; achieving an Excellent Environmental Assessment (BREEAM) rating for the new HQ building at 1 Churchill Place, Canary Wharf, London and introducing an innovative new pension scheme, called 'afterwork', for Barclays' UK employees designed to provide them with more certainty at retirement.

In 2004, Barclays launched a campaign to encourage employees to take part in Make a Difference Day, the single biggest day of volunteering action in the UK.

By sponsoring the campaign, Barclays actively encouraged its employees, customers and the wider public to make a real and lasting difference to the areas in which they live and work.

In 2004, over 7,500 Barclays employees volunteered for Make a Difference Day and nearly double that number took part.

Another important development in 2004 was the introduction of a new visual identity for Barclays, making the famous Barclays eagle more striking, simple, contemporary and modern.

Promotion

To communicate its position as 'The Money Experts', Barclays has created a multi-layered communications programme, called 'Fluent in Finance'.

The most visible aspect of this is the Fluent in Finance advertising campaign introduced by Barclays in 2002, starring Samuel L Jackson. Now in its third phase, the 2004 campaign saw Barclays continue to demonstrate how it uses its financial expertise to create superior value for its customers. In these latest advertisements, Donald Sutherland and Gary Oldman build on the success of the previous campaigns where it was revealed that people talk about money in many different ways and that Barclays understands them all because it is 'Fluent in Finance'.

Sponsorship is also extremely important to Barclays, which is now the title sponsor for the FA Premier League. It invested £57 million to secure the global title sponsorship rights from 2004/05 through to the 2006/07 season, during which time the competition will be known as the Barclays Premiership.

The deal underlines the group's long-term commitment to football in the UK and fits Barclays international presence and brand visibility in the many markets around the world in which it operates.

The deal includes exclusive worldwide marketing rights, UK and international TV programme credits and branding in 170 countries, an extensive advertising package which covers perimeter boards, interview backdrops, exclusive awards and match programmes and a significant amount of tickets and hospitality.

During its three-year sponsorship of the Premier League, Barclaycard injected £4 million into grassroots football through its Free Kicks programme. The sponsorship attracted 250,000 customers to the Premiership Barclaycard, making it the UK's biggest sports affinity card.

Under Barclays sponsorship, even more will be invested in community programmes, with a new £30 million community initiative to create sustainable sports facilities across the UK. The scheme, called Barclays Spaces for Sports, will also provide kit and equipment. This investment is the single largest injection of cash into grassroots sport ever committed by a corporate company in the UK.

Barclays also sponsored The Global Challenge Yacht Race 2004/05 as well as other important sporting events, such as the Barclays Scottish Open golf tournament. All these sponsorships aim to build and develop existing and new relationships with high value and loyal clients by offering unique and world-class hospitality.

Brand Values

While many financial providers try to attract customers by appearing increasingly friendly, Barclays believes it is more important to tell people about the expertise that runs throughout the whole group. 'Money Expertise' is the single main thought underpinning the Barclays brand – achieved while delivering skilful customer service.

This expertise runs through the whole group, with every employee – from a personal banker recommending the right product to a customer, to a service manager ensuring the technology behind the ATM network runs smoothly.

Three values underpin Barclays position as money experts: knowledge to do its job expertly; understanding of customers' needs and being easy to do business with in an empathetic way. The way Barclays expresses these values to its customers is through the 'Fluent in Finance' concept.

www.barclays.co.uk

THINGS YOU DIDN'T KNOW ABOUT

Barclays

❯ Barclays has 20 million customers worldwide.

❯ In 1959, Barclays was the first UK bank to order a computer.

❯ Barclays manages over US$1 trillion of assets.

❯ In 1982 Barclays became the first UK bank to open on Saturdays.

◻◾ BASF

The Chemical Company

Market

BASF, the world's leading chemical company, is a major supplier to the chemical, automotive, energy and construction industries worldwide. Its most important customers also include the agricultural, health and nutrition sectors as well as electrical/electronics, textile, packaging and paper companies.

With a portfolio ranging from chemicals, plastics, performance products, agricultural products and fine chemicals to crude oil and natural gas, BASF is one of the few corporations with processes and products along the entire chemical value-adding chain. The extremely broad product range, and the extraordinary number of different industries supplied, makes the company relatively resilient to factors affecting individual industries.

BASF, which has its global headquarters in Germany, posted sales of £33.4 billion in 2003. It has production sites in 41 countries, customers in 170, and employs 87,000 people around the world.

Most BASF products are sold in the UK, where BASF has plants producing fibre intermediates, polyurethane raw materials, and vitamins and mineral premixes for animal feed.

Achievements

When Friedrich Engelhorn founded the company back in 1865, he had a vision – to bring dye research and production under one roof. Each production facility would be linked to other plants so that the products and leftover material from one plant could serve as raw materials in the next.

The original site in Ludwigshafen, Germany, is today the world's largest chemical complex. All 350 plants are connected to others by at least one product or process stage.

BASF uses raw materials, energy and intermediates efficiently and also re-uses by-products and residual materials. This reduces the impact on the environment and saves money.

BASF takes a few raw materials and uses them to manufacture several dozen basic materials, which in turn are used to produce several hundred intermediates. After passing through a network of value-added production chains, these intermediates give rise to approximately 8,000 different products.

The company has a history of scientific innovation. It produced the first synthetic dyes, including the indigo used to colour jeans, the first polystyrene and the first magnetic recording tape. A BASF employee won a Nobel Prize for helping to develop the process for synthesising ammonia, which led to synthetic production of nitrogen fertilisers. Today BASF is a world leader in new fields of development such as biotechnology and nanotechnology.

The company is quick to act on market impulses, thanks to its strong network of employees collaborating with research and industry partners to develop solutions tailored to customer requirements.

BASF shares are traded on the stock exchanges in Frankfurt, London, New York, Paris and Zurich. Over the past ten years they have performed considerably better than the DAX 30 and the EURO STOXX 50 indexes. The holding has increased in value by close to 2,813% since 1993, which corresponds to an average annual return of 14.5%.

History

BASF, originally known as Badische Anilin & Soda-Fabrik, was founded in Germany in 1865 to produce coal tar dyes and precursors.

Soaring population growth led to strong demand for dyes, and within a few decades BASF had gained a leading position in the world dye market. It produced the first synthetic indigo in 1897, and in 1901 came another pioneering development, the exceptionally lightfast and wash fast indanthrene dyes which soon took over the supremacy of indigo in dyeing and printing.

The development of the Haber-Bosch process between 1908-12, ushered in a new phase in the history of the chemical industry. This process for producing ammonia paved the way to the synthetic production of nitrogen fertilisers and opened up new opportunities in process engineering.

Following the success of the motorcar in the 1920s, BASF invested heavily in the development of fuels, synthetic rubber, surface coatings, and other products for the automotive industry.

In the 1930s BASF produced the first polystyrene and created a sensation with another pioneering invention: the Magnetophon, developed in co-operation with AEG. This led to a 60-year period of manufacturing magnetic

tape – the company's most famous consumer product. BASF stopped maufacturing tapes when it sold the business in 1997.

The 1950s saw nylon become a bestseller and in 1951 BASF developed Styropor, a lightweight foam ideal for insulation and packaging fragile goods.

In the 1960s, BASF began building or acquiring production sites around the world, including several in the UK. Acquisitions included the pharmaceutical business of Boots, the polypropylene business of ICI, the textile dyes business of Zeneca, and the crop protection business of American Home Products.

In recent years portfolio rationalisation and a strategy of concentrating on core businesses has resulted in a number of divestitures, including the sale of the tapes business in 1997, the pharmaceutical business in 2000, and the Printing Systems business in 2004.

Product

BASF uses its integrated approach to produce a full range of chemicals. The products are organised in five segments – Chemicals, Plastics, Performance Products, Agricultural Products & Nutrition, and Oil & Gas.

BASF is one of the leading global producers of styrenics, engineering plastics and polyurethanes. Its broad range of Performance Products includes high-value performance chemicals, coatings and functional polymers for the automotive, oil, paper, packaging, textile, sanitary care, construction, coatings, printing and leather industries.

In addition, BASF is a major supplier of agricultural products as well as fine chemicals for the farming, food processing, animal and human nutrition and personal care industries. In plant biotechnology, the company is

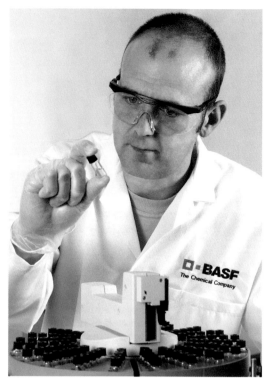

developing plants that are less sensitive to drought or are more nutritious.

A BASF subsidiary explores and produces crude oil and natural gas. Together with a Russian partner it markets, distributes and trades natural gas in Europe.

Recent Developments

BASF 2015, a new strategy described by chairman Jürgen Hambrecht as BASF's 'route to the future', was launched in 2004. With it came a new brand positioning and a new corporate design.

BASF's future strategy is a coherent combination of proven strengths and new elements – it is an evolution, not a revolution. The four guidelines are: earn a premium on cost of capital; help customers to be more successful; form the best team in the industry; and ensure sustainable development.

BASF believes that growth alone is not sufficient in the international competition for capital. Companies need to grow profitably. That is why they intend to concentrate funds on those business areas that are attractive and in which they perform well.

BASF is focusing even more closely on the needs of its customers. The company is increasingly developing new products and services in close collaboration with key customers and entering into research and development partnerships with customers to find tailormade solutions that ensure their mutual success.

Innovations are a decisive tool for BASF when it comes to shaping a promising and profitable future. More than £1 billion is invested annually in research and development, and BASF is among the top five companies in Europe for patent applications.

Committed and qualified employees and an excellent management team ensure BASF's success. The company aims to broaden further the international nature of its management team, increase the number of women in management, and enhance employees' opportunities for self-learning and learning on the job.

For BASF, sustainable enterprise means contributing to a future worth living, for coming generations by combining economic success with environmental protection and social responsibility. Management systems and tools for sustainability create value for BASF and, at the same time, fulfil the needs of customers and consumers. For example, BASF's eco-efficiency analysis can show customers which products and processes are superior for their specific applications from both economic and environmental viewpoints.

Promotion

BASF's new brand positioning provides concrete support to the company's communications with investors and analysts as well as its other target groups.

BASF concurrently introduced a new corporate design and a new logo based on the letters 'BASF', which stand for tradition and the continuation of a clear strategy. Two matching squares have been added to represent partnership and collaboration to ensure mutual success, and an essential new element is the claim. By adding 'The Chemical Company', BASF has clearly stated what it is and what it wants to remain – the world's leading chemical company.

Like the seven previous versions in the company's 138-year history, the new logo is not in colour, but the new corporate design does feature six corporate colours which are used to express BASF's diversity and dynamism.

The branding process has given a new and brighter look to BASF's literature and advertising. In Europe, where the company has been running corporate advertising since 2001, a new campaign was launched using the new corporate design and a new slogan – Invisible contribution. Visible success.

BASF is presenting itself to a larger target group as an important part of society and a responsible partner. The campaign focuses on customer needs and on the benefits provided by the company's products and services.

Ads in 2004 have featured special concrete additives used in bridge construction, UV absorbers for sunscreens, and plastics for leisure equipment such as surfboards. These ads have appeared frequently in the national press in the UK and also on posters on the London Underground.

In addition to advertising in trade magazines, BASF produces a number of publications for customers,

including plastics and coatings magazines as well as a long running magazine for farmers.

BASF has been involved in a number of sponsorships over the years in education, the arts and the industries it supplies. For more than 30 years the company has been a sponsor of Manchester's Hallé Orchestra. BASF also sponsors the BASF/Daily Telegraph Young Science Writer competition, the energy gallery at the Science Museum and an award for environmental initiatives in the plastics industry.

Brand Values

BASF's mission is to be of value to people – to create value for the company, its customers, shareholders, employees, and the countries in which it operates.

BASF develops and maintains partnerships characterised by mutual trust and respect. BASF helps shape the future successfully and sustainably by means of intelligent solutions. BASF's corporate philosophy is based on the principle of sustainable development. Key to this approach is taking accountability for balancing business development with environmental protection and social responsibility.

By subscribing to the 'Responsible Care' initiative launched by the chemical industry, BASF has committed itself to steadfastly pursuing improvements in the realms of environmental protection, health and safety as well as customer satisfaction. Economic considerations do not take priority over safety and health issues and environmental protection.

As a founding member of the United Nations' Global Compact initiative, BASF is committed to promoting and implementing the Compact's nine principles concerning the safeguarding of human rights, labour and environmental standards. BASF carries out partnership projects with public sector organisations and Non Government Organisations.

www.basf.com

THINGS YOU DIDN'T KNOW ABOUT

BASF

> BASF coatings make it possible for Rolls-Royce to offer their customers cars in bespoke shades. BASF Coatings is the sole supplier of automotive OEM coatings for the new Rolls-Royce factory at Goodwood. Rolls-Royce Motor Cars Limited has also contracted BASF Coatings to supply automotive refinish products worldwide.

> BASF subsidiary Wintershall and Russian gas producer Gazprom have a joint venture producing natural gas in Siberia. WINGAS has a 2,000 km pipeline network and Europe's largest underground natural gas storage facility. HydroWingas, a joint venture with Norsk Hydro is now targeting the UK gas market.

> It is now possible to produce MDF with colour all the way through, thanks to pigment preparations developed by BASF. This technique has opened up new market opportunities for manufacturers of wood composites.

> BASF scientists have developed nanocubes – metal-organic materials with extremely high storage capacity – which can be used as hydrogen reservoirs for fuel cells. Applications include portable electronic devices like mobile phones, laptop computers and PDAs.

Invisible Contribution. Visible Success.

Invisible Contribution – BASF is an essential partner in many industries, working with customers to develop and optimise solutions. Throughout the world we meet the most diverse challenges, mainly from behind the scenes.
Visible Success – The results of our partnerships are worth seeing. Additives to strengthen load-bearing building materials and to protect valuable structures are one example of the way in which we improve processes, increase quality and lower costs – contributing to the success of our customers and a better quality of life for us all.
www.basf.com/more

◻ ▪ **BASF**
The Chemical Company

CHEMICALS   PLASTICS   PERFORMANCE PRODUCTS   AGRICULTURAL PRODUCTS & NUTRITION   OIL & GAS

BDO

BDO Stoy Hayward

Market

The international accountancy market is going through major change. The image of big accountancy firms has been dented following high profile corporate financial scandals, most notably Enron and WorldCom in the US. Meanwhile, accounting legislation, such as Sarbanes-Oxley, is demanding more expertise from accountancy. Despite these issues, or perhaps because of them, it is estimated that the UK accountancy market is growing at a compound annual growth rate of 7.7% (Source: Accountancy 2003 – Key Note report). Key Note also estimated that the total fee income from accountancy and related services in 2003 was around £14.44 billion.

As a result of these changes in the market, clients are looking beyond the Big Four. This represents a great opportunity for mid-tier firms, as the Big Four – PricewaterhouseCoopers LLP, Deloitte, KPMG and Ernst & Young – currently audit all of the top 100 UK public companies, as well as the overwhelming majority of the top 350. Firms outside the Big Four have far greater opportunity to target larger, higher value mid-corporates. As the UK member firm of BDO International, a worldwide network of public accounting firms, BDO Stoy Hayward is already benefiting.

Achievements

With more than 600 offices across 100 countries, no other firm outside the Big Four has the asset of an international network with the scale and depth accessed by BDO Stoy Hayward.

The brand is challenging many of the prevailing assumptions about the accountancy market, especially opinions that the Big Four's size is a promise of quality service, or that only they can service larger companies. With strong client satisfaction ratings and a client list that includes multinationals, BDO Stoy Hayward is winning business traditionally viewed as the preserve of the Big Four.

With strong experience in retail, property and advertising, media and communications, and also considered experts in specialist tax, the firm has proven that it has a full-service offering and that accountants can innovate.

Despite difficult market conditions, these strengths on many levels helped BDO Stoy Hayward achieve extremely strong results in 2004. During the year, the firm handled 150 deals, 20 takeover disputes, an EU anti-competition suit and was appointed to over 200 new forensic accounting cases. Fee income from specialist services rose from £83.6 million to £99.2 million – the forensic accounting unit being the fastest growing business line within the firm in 2004. The firm's full service offering was reflected in 2004 by the fact that 10% of its clients bought three or more services. Its international strength is evident in that over

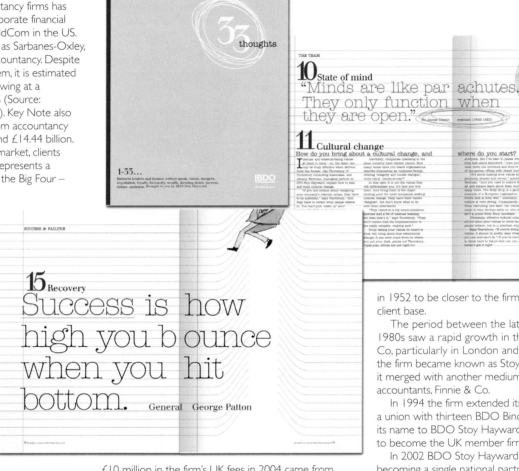

£10 million in the firm's UK fees in 2004 came from referrals from the BDO International network – a rise of 21%. Overall, the firm's fees rose in 2004 by 11%.

BDO Stoy Hayward is also achieving much as an employer: the firm was recently named one of the UK's greatest employers in the prestigious The Sunday Times '100 Best Companies to Work For' survey – the only accountancy firm to be included on the list. It was awarded the title of Employer of the Year in the 2004 Accountancy Age awards and gained a place amongst the Times Top 100 Graduate Employers for the second year running. This survey sampled the views of over 15,000 university students on who provides the best opportunities and the brightest prospects for future careers. The firm can claim to have written the book on flexible working (The ICAEW Guide to Flexible Working Practices) and its internal staff survey – 'The Pulse of BDO Stoy Hayward' – conducted by ISR consistently rates the firm well above high performance norms.

History

A F (Fred) Stoy founded the firm in 1903 as Stoy & Co and was joined in 1919 by R J (Jack) Hayward. In the late 1940s the firm developed a client base drawn from a number of emerging post-war industries, most notably retail and property. Originally based in the City, the move to the West End was made

in 1952 to be closer to the firm's new entrepreneurial client base.

The period between the late 1970s and the late 1980s saw a rapid growth in the size of Stoy Hayward & Co, particularly in London and the South East. In 1988, the firm became known as Stoy Hayward and in July 1992 it merged with another medium-sized firm of chartered accountants, Finnie & Co.

In 1994 the firm extended its national network through a union with thirteen BDO Binder Hamlyn offices, changed its name to BDO Stoy Hayward and applied successfully to become the UK member firm of BDO International.

In 2002 BDO Stoy Hayward achieved its goal of becoming a single national partnership with an associated office in Belfast.

The firm converted to LLP status with effect from January 1st 2004. This has provided protection for the business and greater transparency to clients.

Today, BDO Stoy Hayward operates across the UK with some 2,000 partners and staff operating from fifteen integrated business centres, each offering a full range of services.

Product

BDO Stoy Hayward prides itself on its fresh thinking and practical understanding of the key issues its clients face. It lays an emphasis on developing strong, personal relationships with its clients, sharing their entrepreneurial spirit and growth aspirations and working hard to help them achieve their full potential.

The firm's principal lines of service include:

Business assurance – working with clients to ensure they are compliant with all current rules and regulations and that every part of their organisation is fine-tuned to achieve their business objectives.

Tax – servicing all tax needs, providing tax advice that is practical, to the point and commercial.

Corporate finance – providing specialist advice on flotations, mergers and acquisitions, private finance initiatives, raising private equity and public company transactions.

Forensic accounting – providing specialist guidance on claim assessment, dispute resolution services, investigations, litigation services, risk advisory services and tax investigations.

Business recovery services – helping clients get their businesses out of trouble or, in the worst-case scenario, returning whatever value can be achieved back to creditors and shareholders.

BDO Stoy Hayward can also provide expert advice on business services and outsourcing, business systems, corporate pensions, investment management and risk management.

BDO Stoy Hayward has dedicated teams of partners and professional staff nationwide who focus on developing strong industry insight enabling them to tailor business solutions for their clients. Key sectors include:

Advertising, media and communications – working for many of the leading players in the media business, offering a number of services including tax compliance, strategic planning, tax planning schemes and dealing with international growth.

Property – offering a multi-disciplinary tax and accounting team recognised for its commercial and pragmatic approach to solving problems and close links with property specialists nationwide.

Retail – expertise ranging across a number of retail sub sectors including fashion and footware, pharmacy and personal care, grocery, household goods and textiles, and restaurants.

Other sectors that the firm regularly operates in include financial services, business services, professional practices, manufacturing, charity, education, family business and leisure and hospitality.

Recent Developments

BDO Stoy Hayward has made significant investments in all its offices to extend its range of local expertise. In 2003 BDO Stoy Hayward moved to new premises in the heart of Birmingham's square mile and, in 2004, its Leeds office acquired another large and highly respected local firm, more than doubling its presence in the region. The firm now operates from fifteen full service business centres in the UK.

The firm's stability has been underpinned by its conversion to LLP status in 2004. All partners are now equity partners, underlining their commitment to the future performance of the firm.

BDO Stoy Hayward was instrumental in convincing the Government to reject the concept of an absolute cap on audit liability, which would limit the liability of larger firms yet provide little, if any, benefit to clients whose exposure on any individual audit was less than the absolute amount. In rejecting this, the Government has shown it is listening to the firm's opinions.

Internally, BDO Stoy Hayward continues to work to its recently developed 'values at work' – honesty and integrity, personal responsibility, mutual support and strong and personal client relationships. The values ensure the firm continues to deliver benefits to clients and make it distinctive in the market.

Other important developments include; the expansion of the BDO International network – an additional 50 offices opened worldwide giving the network 621 in total and a staff of over 25,000; the new Private Finance Initiative (PFI) team – a national team providing services such as financial modelling, project finance and refinancing advice; and the launch of the weekly sales index for high-profile retailers – enabling them to track and benchmark their results and form a close group of contacts from the industry.

Promotion

Creative communication plays an important role in building the BDO Stoy Hayward brand, with the firm using all communication media, including events and seminars, direct mail, PR, the web (www.bdo.co.uk) and advertising in newspapers and business publications.

The firm recently launched its high-profile magazine, '33 thoughts' – an inspiring and accessible notebook style magazine, offering ideas, observations, advice and comments. The magazine is designed for

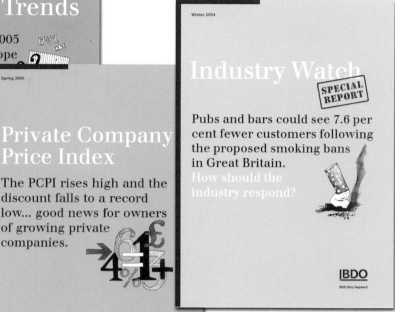

people who are busy leading companies and is filled with the thoughts of business leaders, top business writers and from unexpected sources, simply because what they had to say was relevant, clever, intriguing, challenging… and brief.

The firm also gains valuable brand awareness from its specialist reports. Its quarterly Industry Watch study, the first to make projections of total business failures in Great Britain by sector, analyses the issues and challenges faced by different industry sectors and provides insights and tips for businesses to approach them. The study always attracts extensive media coverage, with statistics released prior to publication date.

The Private Company Price Index (PCPI), Business Trends and FraudTrack reports, also attract widespread interest, are regarded as highly authoritative and are avidly read by business leaders, media analysts and influential decision-makers. The PCPI provides a value benchmark for private companies, Business Trends provides a comprehensive indicator of turning points in the economy, growth and inflation for the UK and Europe respectively, and FraudTrack is an annual study conducted into the trends and activities of fraud in the UK. BDO Stoy Hayward also runs numerous high profile events and seminars

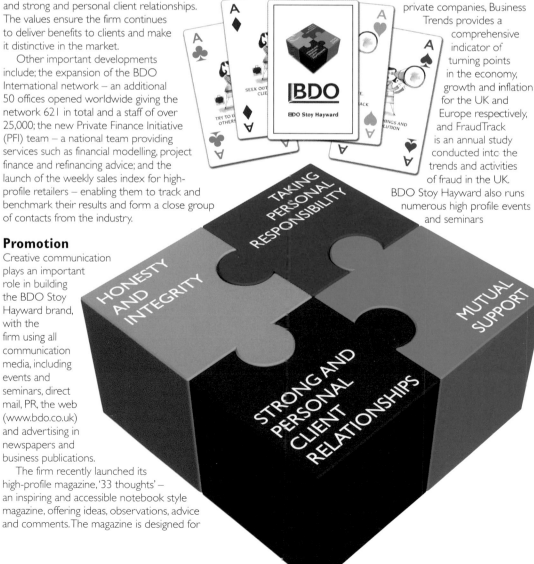

throughout the year. Recent events include the Property Accounts Awards in November 2004. The awards, hosted by BDO Stoy Hayward and co-sponsored by Estates Gazette, recognise high levels of transparency and clarity in annual reporting and aim to raise the level of information available to shareholders year-on-year.

The firm's ongoing media seminars provide a platform for debating key issues facing the media industry, and provide a good opportunity to demonstrate the expertise and industry connections of BDO Stoy Hayward's Advertising, Media and Communications team.

Other key events include regular economic briefings, technical updates and sector specific networking events.

In addition to this, the firm's website continues to be a highly effective communication tool with all the latest news posted on a regular basis with email updates sent direct to clients and contacts.

Brand Values

BDO Stoy Hayward offers breadth and depth of technical expertise. An increasing number of experienced hires, from junior managers to partners, have joined BDO Stoy Hayward from the Big Four firms in the last three years.

People want to join BDO Stoy Hayward because it has a different outlook on life from the accounting giants. It is successfully different because of its attitude towards people – people are at the heart of how the business thinks and acts. This commitment liberates talent and creates motivated, loyal employees who are passionate about their clients' success.

BDO Stoy Hayward's people are professional, passionate, and personable. For clients this translates into responsive, efficient delivery of the right accountancy services.

www.bdo.co.uk

THINGS YOU DIDN'T KNOW ABOUT

BDO Stoy Hayward

❯ BDO Stoy Hayward's Corporate Finance team concluded a deal virtually every other day during the year ending June 2004.

❯ BDO Stoy Hayward claimed the top slot as most active reporting accountant on AIM with 36 admissions in 2004.

❯ The restraint and confiscation unit has advised the Hong Kong, Singaporean and South African governments and its staff are members of the United Nations Working Party on Effective Asset Forfeiture.

❯ The BDO Stoy Hayward Investment Management team has the number one managed fund in the UK over the past one, three and five years.

❯ BDO Stoy Hayward's people are among the best in the profession, achieving a 100% pass rate in the Advanced Stage ACA papers and topping all the Financial Training Company (FTC) league tables in 2004.

BG GROUP

Market

The world's need for energy is growing fast and natural gas is increasingly regarded as the fuel of choice. It is the cleanest of the fossil fuels and least harmful to the environment. Natural gas is plentiful and, compared to other fuels, is competitive on price. As such, there is an increasing demand for gas around the world as energy consumption increases, particularly in developing economies in Asia and Latin America. The US-based

Energy Information Administration expects a growth rate of 2.2% in gas consumption per annum between 2000 and 2025 – substantially more than other competing fuels.

Demand for natural gas in energy policies around the world is also being driven by the need to address climate change. Because gas has the lowest CO_2 content of all hydrocarbon fuels, demand is stronger wherever the battle against global warming is a priority. Growth is also being fuelled by newly liberalised economies, where gas is being put forward as the fuel of choice. All of this means there has never been a better time to be in the gas business and BG Group is well placed to take advantage of the opportunities available by drawing on its considerable experience and skills in the industry.

Within the highly competitive energy sector, BG Group's competitors – such as BP, Royal Dutch Shell and ExxonMobil – can also be its co-venturers. Due to the sheer size and scale of the industry, projects tend to be entered into as joint-ventures. For example, BG Group's operation of the Armada gas field in the North Sea is comprised of BP (18.2%), Total (12.53%), ConocoPhilips

(11.45%) and Centrica (11.05%) with BG Group taking the remaining 46.77%.

Another example of this industry partnership can be found in Kazakhstan where BG Group have a 32.5% share of the giant Karachaganak gas condensate field with Eni, who are joint operators, taking 32.5%, ChevronTexaco with 20% and LUKoil with the final 15%.

Achievements

With a market capitalisation of over £12 billion as at December 2004, BG Group has a proud history of achievement in the energy sector, particularly natural gas, where it has experience across the entire gas chain – from the exploration and production of natural gas to the delivery to the consumer and power generation. It has built a formidable business, being active in all parts of the natural gas business with operations in some 20 countries over five continents.

Seizing the growth opportunity of natural gas around the world, BG Group increased its turnover by 44% from 2001 to 2003, and over the same period, boosted its earnings (excluding exceptional items) from £465 million to £683 million – an increase of 47%.

Fulfilling its aim to be a good corporate citizen, BG Group contributed some £3 million to social projects in 2003 – 30% more than the year before.

The company is building an ever-stronger position on the world energy market, delivering 1.1% of the US daily gas requirement and around 53% of LNG imported into the US in 2003. Given the US's vast energy consumption, this is a significant proportion.

BG Group is one of the industry's strongest performers in terms of its exploration and production, with production volumes growing at a compound average rate of 15% between 2000 and 2003.

History

Although BG Group is a relatively youthful brand, it draws on a heritage of over 100 years experience in natural gas. In February 1997 the shareholders of the former utilities company, British Gas plc, approved the

Il BG Group: leader globale nel settore del GNL

demerger of Centrica plc with British Gas plc being renamed BG plc. In December 1999, BG plc completed a financial restructuring which resulted in the creation of a new parent company, BG Group plc. In October 2000, BG Group plc completed the demerger of Lattice Group plc (now part of National Grid Transco) creating two separate companies.

Product
BG Group has four core business areas: Exploration and Production (E&P); Liquefied Natural Gas (LNG); Transmission and Distribution (T&D) and Power.

The high-performing E&P division remains the centre of gravity for BG Group which is recognised as one of the top E&P businesses in the world due to its success in finding and commercialising natural gas reserves quickly and efficiently.

BG Group's aim to maintain a balance of circa 70% gas and 30% oil, differentiates it from many of its competitors in the energy industry, which have more of an oil focus in their business.

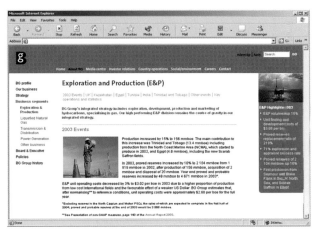

In the LNG division, BG Group combines its export and import facilities with the purchase, shipping and marketing of LNG. In 2003, BG Group made great progress building its LNG activities in the Atlantic Basin and, during the year, processed 2.8 million tonnes of LNG – an increase of 155% on the year before.

Expertise in T&D is an important feature of BG Group's integrated gas strategy, helping to develop markets (or demand) for natural gas. BG Group's principal T&D operations are currently in the UK, Argentina, Brazil and India – all markets that may offer strong growth potential for market participants.

Power will continue to be a strong driver

of long term gas demand and for BG Group is a significant and consistent contributor to profit. BG Group has a portfolio of modern, highly efficient combined cycle gas turbine (CCGT) power stations in the UK, Italy and South East Asia.

Recent Developments
In February 2004, BG Group moved towards a more powerful brand by launching a new visual identity to communicate the Group's key qualities. The move was important in the evolution of the business, reflecting the qualities and success of the BG Group, while differentiating it from its competitors. The new brand identity clearly displays the robust nature of the company, leaving it well placed to deliver its business targets in the future.

Promotion
As a predominantly business to business brand, BG Group's promotional focus is on communicating with key known stakeholders. Marketing supports this activity through a range of functions including an active presence at industry exhibitions and events, bespoke sponsorship projects and targeted advertising in appropriate industry journals.

Sponsorship initiatives include BG Group's sponsorship of BG SPIRIT which is competing in the 2004/05 Global Challenge round-the-world yacht race. This is widely regarded as the world's toughest yacht race as it requires teams to sail 'the wrong way' around the world. The crew includes BG Group employees along with other non-professionals.

BG Group also supports the 'Energy Challenge' which is run in the UK, Egypt, Trinidad and Tobago as well as South America. It is a physical challenge and aims to bring together companies that work in the energy sector while raising money for a number of worthwhile charities.

Under the new brand, all advertisements aim to convey the global BG Group story and position BG Group as part of a solution or the partner of choice for stakeholders around the globe.

Brand Values
BG Group's new brand identity is based on four key brand values: Confidence; Closeness; Agility and Solutions.

'Confidence' is based on BG Group's expertise and ability, and its pride in its heritage.

BG Group
Natural gas is clean, abundant and competitively priced. That's why it is increasingly becoming the fuel of choice around the world. BG Group has an outstanding record for finding, developing, and delivering gas to markets. Throughout Asia, we see tremendous growth potential and are working with industry partners, governments and other stakeholders to help meet the region's growing energy needs.

Natural gas. It's our business

Powering Asia's growth.

'Closeness' conveys the company's ability to get close to its markets and understand the needs of its partners and customers. It is easy to get close to; its senior decision-makers are accessible and it is a reliable partner of choice.

'Agility' describes a company that is dynamic and fleet of foot, able to react swiftly, see opportunities and move on them faster than its larger competitors. It has intuition based on experience.

'Solutions' communicates BG Group's focus on the needs of its stakeholders, finding solutions and making things happen. It is a company which keeps its promises.

These four values have been distilled into a single core statement: 'BG Group is a global natural gas business that, because of its innovative use of technology, flexibility of approach and the abilities of its people, is a partner of choice all over the world.'

www.bg-group.com

THINGS YOU DIDN'T KNOW ABOUT

BG Group

> BG Group produced an average of 428,000 barrels of oil equivalent a day in 2003.

> BG Group was the largest importer of LNG to the US in 2003.

> The Armada gas field in the North Sea (of which BG Group holds a 46.77% majority stake) covers 390km² which is more than 55 football pitches.

> BG Group is the largest producer of gas in Tunisia, supplying more than 50% of the domestic gas demand from its Miskar field.

> The giant Karachaganak field in North West Kazakhstan, where BG Group is joint operator, is estimated to hold over sixteen trillion cubic feet of gas and 2.4 billion barrels of condensate, potentially recoverable over the 40 year licence period. The gas alone would be enough to supply London's domestic and commercial gas requirements for the next 42 years (Source: www.citylimitslondon.com).

> The largest BG Group transmission pipeline in 2003 was from Bolivia to Brazil which stretched over 3,150km.

Blue Circle™

Market

Lafarge Cement UK, owner of the Blue Circle brand, is the leading player in the cement market in the UK. Through its eight Works around the UK, the company has the capacity to manufacture more than six million tonnes of cement a year, supplying approximately 50% of the UK cement market.

Demand for cement is closely linked to a country's overall economic activity. For example, according to the Brussels-based Cembureau, consumption in the industrialised countries multiplied six to eight times following World War II. Over the last 25 years, some European countries have doubled or even tripled their consumption with countries such as Greece, Portugal, Spain and Turkey – all of which have experienced significant growth over the last ten years – among the highest users.

In the UK over recent years, the construction market has remained in good health. According to the research firm MBD, total construction output in the UK is estimated to have increased by 63% between 2000 and 2004, reaching a total output of £98.3 billion. This growth, according to the report, is largely due to relatively low interest rates, good employment levels and affordability and is a trend which looks set to continue.

Achievements

Lafarge Cement UK's market-leading position is reflected in it winning numerous industry awards and accolades. For example, in 2004 it was re-accredited the prestigious Investors In People (IIP) standard for all its UK sites, recognising the company's commitment to the training and development of its 1,500-plus employees.

The company's strong contribution to society and the environment was also evident in its being ranked second in the Construction and Building Materials Sector in Business in the Community's (BITC) Corporate Responsibility Index 2004. Lafarge Cement UK achieved a 100% score on environmental management and was ranked 41st out of 139 companies assessed in total for all-round performance.

The company has a strong commitment to minimising its environmental impact and, in 2004, reached a major environmental improvement target seven years ahead of time. This involved Lafarge Cement UK recording a reduction in emissions of dust per tonne to less than 30% of the levels in 1990. The company invested more than £20 million in new filtering systems to achieve this.

Blue Circle's pre-eminent position as one of the best-known brands in the UK construction industry is also reflected in its involvement in many of the country's most famous and important construction projects, including The Channel Tunnel, the Canary Wharf Development and The Millennium Stadium in Cardiff.

History

Lafarge Cement UK has a history stretching back to 1900 when 27 small, mainly Kent-based cement manufacturers and their subsidiaries merged to form the Associated Portland Cement Manufacturers (1900) Ltd. These companies had produced cement using bottle, beehive and chamber kilns over the previous 40-50 years. With the introduction of the rotary kiln, production methods became far more efficient, making consolidation and mergers inevitable.

In 1919, the company began a process of establishing interests overseas, initially in Mexico, Canada and South Africa and the famous Blue Circle brand was introduced in 1928.

Throughout the first half of the 20th century, further operations were established in New Zealand, Australia, Nigeria, Chile, Indonesia, Malaysia, Spain, Rhodesia (Zimbabwe), Kenya, Tanzania and Brazil.

As the company entered the second half of the 20th century, it became one of the first to make up the FT30 Index, being listed on the London Stock Exchange on November 3rd 1953.

The famous brand name was adopted as the company name – Blue Circle Industries plc – in the late 1970s. The 1980s and 1990s saw development of further worldwide interests, most notably in the US.

In 2001, Blue Circle Industries was taken over by the Lafarge Group to become part of the world's leading

MAKING THE FUTURE TAKE SHAPE.

Few products are helping to shape the future of Britain more so than those from Lafarge Cement UK. Think of some of the highest profile civil projects in the UK and you'll find that our bulk supplied cement has turned them into stunning reality – the Falkirk Wheel, as seen in the image, the Canary Wharf development, the Channel Tunnel, the Tay Bridge and Cardiff's Millennium Stadium. Our most powerful ingredient is 100 years of leadership in cement technology. Rely on our dedicated technical sales team and world-beating products to help shape your ideas for the next century.

Need technical advice?
Call 0870 609 0011

www.lafargecement.co.uk

The cement technology leaders

producer of cement and building materials. Lafarge holds market leading positions worldwide in each of its four business divisions, Cement, Aggregates and Concrete, Roofing, and Gypsum.

The UK cement making operation changed its company name to Lafarge Cement in early 2002, but retains the famous Blue Circle brand of cement which it makes and markets nationwide.

Product

Lafarge Cement UK produces a range of cement products throughout its nationwide network of plants located at: Aberthaw, South Glamorgan; Barnstone, Nottinghamshire; Cauldon, Staffordshire; Cookstown, County Tyrone; Dunbar, East Lothian; Hope, Derbyshire; Northfleet, Kent and Westbury, Wiltshire.

The full Blue Circle product range is divided into four key areas:

Standard Cement, or Blue Circle Ordinary Portland Cement (OPC), is a general purpose cement suitable for all types of concrete, including structural concrete, mortars, renders and screeds. Blue Circle OPC is available in bags and bulk.

The Enhanced Cement range mixes traditional cement with extra ingredients for specialist uses, such as use in very low or high temperatures. Products include: Blue Circle Ferrocrete; Blue Circle Snowcrete; Blue Circle Sulfacrete; Blue Circle Phoenix; Blue Circle Lightning; Blue Circle Extra Rapid and Blue Circle Mastercrete Original.

Blue Circle Ready-To-Use is an innovative range of products specifically designed to meet the requirements of builders and DIY enthusiasts by ensuring straightforward application, no mixing, and an excellent finish. Products in the Blue Circle Ready-To-Use range include Blue Circle Slablayer; Blue Circle Postcrete; and Blue Circle Quality Assured Mortar Mix. All of the Ready-to-Use range is packed in Lafarge Cement UK's innovative plastic packaging, which means that the products can be stored outside in all weathers. The advantage this provides to customers is a good example of how the Blue Circle brand continues to maintain its edge over the competition.

Blue Circle also supplies a full range of Renders, such as Blue Circle Colourtex S; Blue Circle Rendadash Backing Coat; Blue Circle Fibrocem GRC; Blue Circle Rendaplus; and Blue Circle Rendadash.

Recent Developments

During 2004, Lafarge Cement UK introduced a number of new initiatives to improve its service to its customers. Among these was a focus on the Ready to Use range. This was supported by a proactive marketing drive to demonstrate to customers the benefits of using Ready-to-Use products that require no mixing and ensure consistently excellent results.

During 2004, Lafarge also began an information campaign to inform Blue Circle cement stockists of the value to both the customer and the stockist of selling customers Ready-to-Use products over separate ingredients.

The company has also recently focused on improving the efficiencies of its supply chain with the opening of its sixth new distribution depot in four years. The new depot, in Carlisle, was designed to improve Lafarge Cement's service to customers in the north west of the UK. With the capacity to store over 2,000 tonnes of cement, the new depot provides security of supply to customers in the region and allows Lafarge Cement to offer the 'just in time' delivery service that many customers now demand.

The innovative design of the depot allows trains to run directly into the warehouse, which also helps Lafarge reduce dust emissions, which may harm the environment. Each weekly train delivery is equivalent to 40 lorry loads of cement, cutting the number of lorry journeys to the depot by 2,000 trips a year. The company is opening a similar new £3.5 million depot at Theale, near Reading.

Continuing with its aim to protect the environment, Lafarge has unveiled a number of new initiatives designed to reduce the carbon dioxide emissions and waste from its works. These include testing the use of paper ash – a derivative of the paper industry – to fuel its Cauldon Works in Staffordshire and introducing meat and bone meal (MBM) to replace the use of fossil fuels at its Aberthaw Works.

Lafarge is also committed to training its staff in effective waste management practises with the result that, in the past two years,

on-site waste generation at its works has been cut by more than 60%.

Promotion

Lafarge Cement UK supports its product range with ongoing promotional activity, which in turn helps merchants drive Blue Circle cement products through their stores and keeps end-users up to date with the latest industry news.

Typically, the company uses a full range of media, including advertising in the trade press, direct mail, PR, in-store marketing, internet and sampling.

Exhibitions are another important means of promotion for Lafarge Cement UK's products and during 2004 the company participated in a number of the most popular shows, including Housebuilding 2004; the National Homebuilding and Renovating Show 2004; Plan Expo; and the BBC DIY Show. To support its other marketing activities, the company used the exhibitions to highlight its range of Ready-to-Use products and gave live demonstrations to visitors to the stand.

Lafarge Cement UK also used some of these exhibitions as an opportunity to team up with the other companies in the Lafarge UK Group – for the first time in the company's history – to demonstrate to customers the wide range of products available from the Lafarge stable. It was an effective means for the companies to cross-sell their products and services and, as a result, emphasise the combined strength of their brands.

Complementing this UK-wide marketing activity, Lafarge Cement UK also markets its products on a more local level and, in 2004, ran two bespoke campaigns to promote its products in Wales and Scotland.

For example, the 'Made in Wales' campaign was designed to encourage Welsh builders and DIY enthusiasts to support their local economy by buying cement manufactured in Wales. Lafarge's Works at Aberthaw in the Vale of Glamorgan employs more than 110 people and makes a vital contribution to the area's

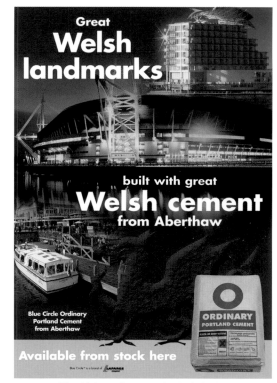

economy. The high-profile campaign included poster advertisements throughout Wales, 'admobiles' touring Welsh towns, promotional material in Welsh stockists and direct mail items sent to end users.

The highly-visual campaign appealed to Welsh pride by using images of famous Welsh landmarks which had been built using Blue Circle cement, such as The Millennium Stadium and the regenerated Cardiff Bay.

Following the success of the 'Made in Wales' campaign, Lafarge Cement UK launched a similar exercise in Scotland later in the year. The campaign was designed to appeal to a wider audience than 'Made in Wales', including civil engineers as well as professional builders and DIYers.

Lafarge's Blue Circle branded cement has been used in some of Scotland's most recognisable landmarks, including the Falkirk Wheel; the Royal Scottish Museum, Edinburgh; the Kylesku Bridge; and the Carnoustie Club House and hotel complex adjoining the world-famous Carnoustie Championship Golf Course.

The campaign also made use of visually-striking posters, direct mail items, 'admobiles' and in-store merchandise to encourage end user interest and drive sales through stockists.

Brand Values

Lafarge Cement UK's Blue Circle brand stands for a number of values, most typically encapsulated by the words: quality; trust and durability. All of which can be summed up by regarding Blue Circle as 'the cement experts'.

www.lafargecement.co.uk

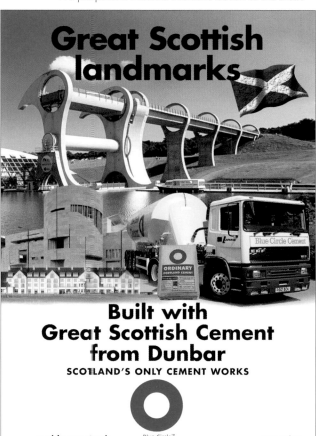

THINGS YOU DIDN'T KNOW ABOUT

Blue Circle

❯ Lafarge Cement UK uses scrap tyres to fuel cement making at some of its plants. They have the same high energy value as coal and save fossil fuels.

❯ Blue Circle Extra Rapid Cement sets within four hours – the fastest time yet achieved for a cement.

❯ Lafarge Cement UK is the only cement manufacturer in Scotland. Its Dunbar Works in East Lothian contributes over £10 million a year to the local economy, making it an important industry for the Dunbar area and Scotland as a whole.

Market

It is often said that 'Knowledge is Power'. But to be effective, that knowledge must be reliable, accurate and timely – and independent market research aims to deliver exactly that. The better informed we are about our markets, our customers, our staff and our competitors, the better the decisions we are likely to make.

Market research has seen a huge growth in demand in a number of key areas. Businesses are increasingly looking to research for consumer insight. Research has an important and growing role in forming Government social policy. Businesses and organisations want to know what drives employee loyalty and commitment. In increasingly fragmented media markets, against a background of proliferating communication channels, the media industry needs fast and accurate audience measurement. Organisations want to make greater use of the data they have by using increasingly sophisticated analysis of customer transaction information.

BMRB has the expertise and resources to meet these demands – without compromising on the need to deliver research that is both accurate and reliable.

The size of the UK research market has more than doubled in the last ten years, according to British Market Research Association (BMRA) figures and was worth an estimated £1.22 billion in 2003. As one of the largest market research agencies in the UK, BMRB has been at the forefront of this growth.

Achievements

BMRB's achievements run across all areas of the business, and its commitment to quality, its staff, and its customers.

BMRB Social Research won the 'Best Application of Research' award from the MRS in 2001 for a survey conducted for the NSPCC into 'The Prevalence of Child Maltreatment in the UK'.

BMRB Media managed the 'Urban Life' online readers' panel on behalf of Metro Newspapers. In 2003 the research won Media Week's 'Media Owner Research Project of the Year' and Campaign's 'Research Project of the Year'.

In 2002, Compass Group (the world's largest global food services and vending company, and 10th largest employer in the world) decided to embark on a global programme of employee loyalty. BMRB were chosen to carry out the programme across 53 countries. The research helped Compass Group win Personnel Today's 2004 Award for 'Global HR Strategy'.

BMRB has become one of the largest commercial suppliers of public policy research in the UK. It is highly respected for conducting large-scale complex projects such as the British Crime Survey from which the Government takes its official crime statistics.

BMRB was one of the first market research companies to have professionally recognised training programmes for both research and operations executives.

BMRB's commitment to best practice and high quality was rewarded when it became amongst the first research agency to achieve BSI 7911 and ISO 9001 quality accreditation. In further recognition of its approach to quality it was a finalist for the British Market Research Association's 2004 research effectiveness awards.

Very high standards of client satisfaction are consistently achieved. In 2004, 96% of clients gave the company an overall performance rating of 'excellent', 'very good' or 'good'.

History

Originally the research department of JWT, its first reported survey was 'Report of Investigation on Pears Soap Consumers, United Kingdom' in 1925. However it wasn't until 1933 that the British Market Research Bureau was set up – making it the longest established research agency in Britain.

The company carried out one of the earliest and largest studies on newspaper readership for the Daily Herald in 1934. Five years later, BMRB became one of the first agencies to conduct major surveys for Government, including a survey for the Ministry of Food to monitor war-time rationing and the Board of Trade to investigate clothing coupons.

Now try interviewing them...

Designing research to be conducted among children and young people involves a unique set of challenges. A career with BMRB Social Research will embrace these and many other research-related issues.

We are one of the UK's leading suppliers of social policy research, with a strong reputation for thoughtful and creative design, rigorous methodology and perceptive interpretation of findings. Our work covers a wide range of social policy areas, including children and young people, crime and policing, government advertising campaigns and adult literacy.

We have a vacancy for an **Associate Director** and **experienced researchers** within our specialist unit of over 70 social research staff. You will need a good degree, at least 2 years' experience of carrying out quantitative social surveys, excellent business development, client handling and communication skills, and experience of managing and motivating junior research staff. Knowledge of social policy areas will be an advantage.

If you have the experience, enthusiasm and commitment, we can provide the opportunities. To find out more about these jobs and how to apply, please download the application pack at www.bmrb.co.uk/careers.

bmrb

Sue Brooker
BMRB Social Research
Hadley House
79-81 Uxbridge Road
Ealing, London W5 5SU
Telephone
020 8433 4405
Email
sue.brooker@bmrb.co.uk
Web
www.bmrb.co.uk

BMRB developed the Target Group Index (TGI) in 1969 – since then it has become a standard trading currency for the UK media sector. TGI has rapidly expanded its coverage in the last ten years and has become the world's leading single-source measurement of consumers' product and brand usage, media consumption and attitudes. The global TGI network now operates in over 50 countries worldwide.

A significant point in the company's development came in 1987, when it became part of WPP Group plc.

In 1997 BMRB became the first to conduct multi-media CAPI interviewing nationally. In the same year, its first web-based research project was conducted; a readership survey for The Lancet.

The following year BMRB formed the KMR Group to create an international platform for integrated research, information and software provision.

Product

BMRB has established specific areas of considerable expertise by concentrating on key sectors within market research. The company offers market-leading research services in: Social and public policy research; Media research; Stakeholder relationship measurement; Omnibus surveys; Syndicated market and media studies – the TGI (Target Group Index) and Consultancy services.

BMRB also has extensive experience of conducting complex, large-scale

Tap into our Expertise
Centre for Excellence seminar programme

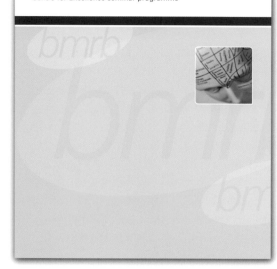

surveys. Its comprehensive resources enable the company to provide high quality tailored solutions – maximising the value that clients achieve from their research investment.

BMRB Social Research is one of the largest providers of public policy research in the UK with a team of around 60 dedicated social researchers. Its reputation for quality, technical excellence and creative solutions is second to none. It regularly conducts prestigious national projects such as the British Crime Survey.

BMRB Media is a specialist unit of researchers who work with the leading media owners and advertising agencies. It offers research expertise across the media of cinema, internet, outdoor and ambient, press, radio and television; and regularly provides insight into work relating to mixed media. The media team provides excellent client service and creative solutions for media buyers, sellers, advertisers and regulators alike.

BMRB Stakeholder Solutions helps businesses measure and manage the needs of their customers, employees and other key stakeholders to improve business performance. BMRB is a founding member of the Walker Information Global Network, the leading provider of stakeholder relationship measurement.

Fast, accurate and cost effective, Access Omnibus is a leader in face-to-face, telephone, online and global omnibus surveys. Its broad portfolio of services offers flexible schedules and methodologies to suit client's research requirements.

TGI marketing and media surveys are the world's leading single-source measurement of consumers' product and brand usage, media consumption and attitudes. Originally developed in Britain by BMRB, TGI now operates in over 50 countries and is used by advertisers, media owners and agencies to provide worldwide consumer insight.

Enlightenment is a new brand consultancy service drawing on the expertise and resources of BMRB in partnership with Millward Brown. The Enlightenment service recognises the need for fast turnaround, whilst maintaining integrity of results. By harnessing the power of in-house and other data sources and applying these to a range of applications, the service provides answers to all types of marketing questions, quickly and flexibly.

Recent Developments
In 2004 BMRB launched Enlightenment, the consultancy service for brand-owners, and early clients included consultancy services for Egg and Masterfoods. Other product launches in 2004 included Compose, a media planning facility which shows how different media can work together and complement each other to deliver campaign objectives more efficiently.

BMRB's Scottish office opened in Edinburgh in 2004 and conducts work for a range of clients in the social research and media sectors.

Kantar, the information, insight and consultancy division of WPP set up The Operations Centre in 2004. This allows Kantar companies' clients (including BMRB's) to benefit from operational excellence across all methodologies, whether face-to-face, telephone, postal or online.

BMRB moved into new state-of-the-art premises in April 2005 and is launching a new identity. The new logo provides a more contemporary, forward looking and dynamic design in keeping with BMRB's new modern surroundings, and in harmony with its international partner networks.

Promotion
BMRB uses a wide range of marketing communications tools to raise awareness and develop business for the products and services it specialises in.

BMRB's integrated marketing approach utilises advertising, PR, direct mail, website, email, delivering conference papers and sponsoring industry events. In addition, it regularly publishes a wide range of paper-based and online newsletters which focus on Social, TGI, Media and Stakeholder research issues.

BMRB's findings and thinking are regularly published in the research and marketing trade press and beyond and has achieved coverage in publications such as Research Magazine, SRA News, Marketing, Campaign, the FT, The Times, Guardian, BBC Online and The Business.

Its Stakeholder Solutions division annually conducts the National Employee Benchmark Survey which provides an insight into the attitudes and loyalty of Britain's workforce. Findings have been given coverage in the FT Personnel Today and BBC Breakfast News.

Its Centre for Excellence seminar programme plays an active role in helping clients better understand all aspects of the research process. BMRB runs over 100 seminars and workshops a year for clients.

All BMRB materials, case studies, newsletters and application for seminars are available through its website www.bmrb.co.uk.

Brand Values
The BMRB name has been synonymous with quality, reliability and integrity in market research for over 70 years. By providing unimpeachable information, BMRB empowers clients to make better business decisions. An important contributory factor in maintaining BMRB's high standards is the quality of the company's staff training programmes – regarded as the best in the industry.

BMRB consciously avoids being a 'jack of all trades'. The company's established excellence in specific research sectors, reinforced by its comprehensive operational resources, enable it to be flexible and creative in meeting client needs. BMRB's core values are encapsulated in the words 'high quality tailored research solutions'.

www.bmrb.co.uk

THINGS YOU DIDN'T KNOW ABOUT

BMRB

> When BMRB launched TGI in 1969 it researched 25,000 respondents. By 2005 TGI had grown to over 700,000 respondents annually worldwide.

> Over the last five years BMRB has conducted over 150,000 interviews for the British Crime Survey.

> From 1969 to 1983 BMRB, backed by the music industry and the BBC, produced the Record Charts (the 'Top 20').

> Jay K, lead singer from the band Jamiroquai, once worked as a research interviewer in BMRB's telephone unit in Ealing.

BOSCH
Invented for life

Market

Bosch is a global manufacturing and service company with numerous subsidiaries, affiliates and overseas representatives.

The group's activities focus on three strategic business sectors – consumer goods and building technologies, automotive and industrial technology. The consumer goods and building technology division includes power tools and accessories, garden products, the Bosch thermotechnology division and household appliances. Bosch household appliances is a joint venture between Bosch and Siemens and had sales of €9.5 billion in 2004. Automotive technology is the largest business sector and accounted for €25.3 billion in sales in 2004. This sector comprises six divisions which develop and manufacture equipment for the world's automotive industry and a separate division responsible for sales of products to the automotive aftermarket. With the acquisition of Buderus AG in 2004, the industrial technology business sector is split between automation, metals and packaging technologies and sales in this area reached €5.2 billion in 2004. The company's total turnover in 2004 was €40 billion.

Achievements

Bosch is a world leader in many of its markets. It is one of the world's largest independent manufacturers of automotive parts and systems. In 2003 alone, Bosch applied for 2,750 patents on new inventions, most of which were in automotive technology, making Bosch the most innovative company in this field.

Bosch is also one of the world's leading manufacturers of power tools and accessories. Its UK subsidiary Worcester Heat Systems, is the market leader in both gas-fired combination boilers and oil-fired boilers. It introduced the first combi boiler in 1971; until then hot water was typically stored in a copper storage tank. The acquisition of Buderus in 2003 meant that Bosch could add floor-standing gas and oil-fired boilers to its activities.

BSH, the Bosch/Siemens household appliances joint venture, is one of the world's top producers of domestic appliances.

Bosch is also one of the world's leading suppliers of packaging technology, with customers in the food, confectionery, pharmaceuticals, chemicals and cosmetics industries. In 2004 the division acquired SIG Pack which will further strengthen its competence in packaging technology. Bosch is already a market leader in capsule filling and closing machines. These lines fill powders, pellets and various types of tablets into capsules.

Bosch's considerable research and development budget – over 7% of turnover – ensures that the company remains at the forefront of innovation. In 2004 Bosch posted sales of around €40 billion and spent €2.7 billion on research and development.

In the UK Bosch employs over 4,000 people, and has an annual turnover of more than €1.8 billion.

History

In 1886, Robert Bosch opened a Workshop for Precision Mechanics and Electrical Engineering in Stuttgart. The following year, Bosch developed the first low voltage 'magneto' ignition system for use in a gas engine. This was used in Gottlieb Daimler's 'internal combustion engine' for stationary machines. In 1898, this was the first system to be used in a car, an event which marked Bosch's first step into the automotive components industry. In the same year Bosch opened its first overseas subsidiary in the UK. Nine years later the Bosch Magneto Company Limited was founded just off London's Oxford Street; shortly after, manufacturing began in the UK.

These beginnings laid the foundations for the company's long-term business strategy in the UK, resulting in Bosch's position as one of the UK's largest European investors, as well as being a significant manufacturer and exporter. The UK headquarters is based in Denham, Buckinghamshire and houses the majority of Bosch's sales and distribution activities in the UK. There are other major sites at St Neots, Worcester, Stowmarket and Milton Keynes.

At its plant in Miskin, South Wales, Bosch manufactures high quality alternators and has invested €240 million since its inception in 1991. In 2003, there was a new investment of €115 million to produce the new LI-X alternator. Over 4.2 million alternators are manufactured every year and over 80% of the plant's output is exported to automotive manufacturers all over the world.

The history of Bosch is a history of innovation. During the early part of the 20th century, Bosch continued to strengthen its business through the development of new products. In 1927 the first automobile diesel injection pump was launched and in 1928 the first power tool, an electric hair clipper called the Forfex, went on the market.

The following year Blaupunkt, a subsidiary of Bosch, launched the world's first stereo car radio. This was the foundation for Blaupunkt's growth towards market leadership in navigation systems and in-car entertainment.

In 1933 Bosch began production of household appliances by launching the first domestic refrigerator. In 1958 Bosch launched its first washing machine, followed in 1964 by its first dishwasher.

The company has always had a sense of social responsibility. Known as 'Red Bosch' for his concern for welfare, Robert Bosch introduced the eight-hour working day well in advance of legislation. The Robert Bosch Foundation, established in 1964, is now one of Germany's largest corporate foundations. The statutes of the foundation are based on Robert Bosch's last will and testament and stipulate that the company's assets should be administered for the benefit of the public. The foundation owns approximately 92% of the capital stock of Bosch. Up to the end of 2003 it had made some €630 million available for charitable purposes, primarily in the areas of public health, social work, international understanding, education, arts and culture, humanities, as well as social and natural sciences.

During the 1970s the company continued to innovate and, in 1974, the first maintenance-free car ignition system entered production. The world's first swivel-arm robot followed in 1976. The 'SCARA', as it was known, was able to perform a number of functions from simple pick-and-place tasks through to more complex assembly processes.

In 1978 Bosch introduced an antilock braking system, (ABS) which has now become a standard component, allowing drivers to steer while braking heavily. Bosch traction control (ASR) was launched in 1987. This inhibits wheel spin when pulling away and during acceleration on slippery roads. Since 2000 Bosch has enhanced its reputation in this area even further with Adaptive Cruise Control (ACC) which, with the help of a radar sensor, recognises and calculates the speed of the vehicles in front and maintains an appropriate distance by acting on the brakes and engine. Ten million ESP (electronic stability programme) braking systems have been supplied since its introduction in 1995. Bosch is working towards the production of 'the sensitive car' by networking ESP with passive safety systems to help warn the driver of potentially dangerous situations.

Bosch's high-pressure fuel injection systems have made diesel engines more efficient, quieter and cleaner. 2003 saw the start of the series production of third-generation common-rail technology, using piezo inline injectors helping to secure Bosch's technological leadership in this area.

Blaupunkt, the car multimedia supplier, has launched the TravelPilot E1 which is an affordable navigation system and was the first manufacturer to launch an in car digital radio with integrated MP3 player. In 2003, Bosch was the first manufacturer to introduce lithium-ion technology for cordless power tools.

12 patents a day
keeps competitors away.

In 2003 Bosch applied for 2,750 patents.
Our inventions in automotive technology focus
on increasing active and passive safety as well
as reducing emission and fuel consumption.
And this brings benefits for every road user.

BOSCH
Invented for life

The Bosch Group is now one of Germany's largest industrial enterprises and has subsidiaries and associated companies in nearly 50 countries, over 193 manufacturing sites, 37 joint ventures worldwide and has over 232,000 employees worldwide.

Product
Bosch automotive products and technology can be found on virtually every make of car throughout the world. More than 25 years ago, Bosch introduced its 3S programme (in German) – sicher (safe) sauber (clean) sparsam (economical) and continues to develop systems under this umbrella. The four largest areas of automotive business are fuel injection technology for petrol and diesel engines; vehicle safety systems such as ABS and ESP (electronic stability program); electrical machines such as starters, alternators, and small-power motors; and under the Blaupunkt brand, car multimedia products such as satellite navigation systems, CD players, MP3 technology and accessories.

Bosch engine management systems already enable compliance to the requirements of Euro IV emissions standards, effective in 2005, which stipulate a further 50% reduction in harmful emissions. Demand for diesel engines is growing and Bosch is contributing to this

success with its modern high pressure diesel injection systems. Mini cars to luxury limousines can be equipped with these systems which are characterised by high performance, smooth operation and superlative torque at all speeds yet, at the same time, significantly reduced fuel consumption and emissions.

Bosch also produces one of the most comprehensive ranges of automotive aftermarket products available – from spark plugs to filters. As Europe's largest manufacturer of vehicle diagnostic equipment, it offers a comprehensive range of test equipment, including micro-processor controlled units.

Aimed at both the consumer and professional markets, Bosch produces power tools suitable for many tasks including drilling, sanding, sawing and grinding. Bosch also markets Skil and Dremel branded power tools in addition to Atco and Qualcast garden tools. The Qualcast product range also includes hedge cutters, shredders, garden vacuums, chainsaws and tree pruners.

The thermotechnology division sells gas-fired hot water heating systems and combi boilers under the Junkers, Vulcano, Worcester and Radson brand names as well as under Bosch and Buderus.

The Bosch/Siemens joint venture, sells washing machines, dishwashers, ovens, and microwaves under the Bosch, Siemens, Constructa, Gaggenau and Thermador brands for the consumer market.

Bosch Rexroth, the automation technology division is the only global machine supplier offering industrial hydraulics, electric drives and controls, linear motion and assembly technologies, pneumatics, service automation and mobile hydraulics.

Bosch's range of security equipment includes CCTV, intruder and fire detection through to public address, voice evacuation and congress systems. Bosch Security Systems can provide solutions ranging from small residential systems up to complete integrated business management systems.

Recent Developments
In July 2004, Bosch's packaging technology division acquired SIG Pack which will enable it to become a total solutions provider in the packaging machinery market Also in 2004 a new corporate design was launched for the Bosch Group with new logo and slogan; Invented for life. The Bosch brand already stands for quality, reliability

and durability and the new and improved corporate design will place a greater emphasis on the modern, dynamic and innovative aspects of Bosch's image. The aim of the new corporate design is to maximise the potential of Bosch's powerful brand and keep consistency across all of its products.

Promotion
On the automotive side, the focus in 2004 has been on promoting ESP (electronic stability programme). An advertorial campaign was run in the national press to promote the benefits of ESP to consumers. In addition to this there was a driving day at Brands Hatch to demonstrate Bosch's braking systems ABS and ESP on the tracks to members of the press.

Power Tools ran a primetime TV advertising campaign on ITV, Channel 4 and Sky channels after launching the Dremel Cordless Lithium Ion using Lithium-Ion technology. Bosch is the first manufacturer to use this technology in cordless tools.

Worcester Heat Systems which is part of the Bosch Buderus Technology (BBT) division has run a widespread national advertising campaign with ads placed in the trade and consumer magazines. There have also been advertisements on internet search engines and national radio stations.

Brand Values
The Bosch brand is synonymous with engineering excellence, quality and innovation and the products are designed with the end-user in mind. The new slogan 'Invented for life' is relevant to all Bosch products. In the words of the founder; "The best that can be produced by applying good will, mature consideration and comprehensive testing and by using the most sophisticated technical aids available together with the best possible materials only just qualifies to bear the name 'Bosch'". Bosch lives by its core values which are future and results focus, responsibility, initiative and determination, openness and trust, fairness, reliability, credibility and legality and cultural diversity.

www.bosch.co.uk

THINGS YOU DIDN'T KNOW ABOUT
Bosch
> Bosch registers over 2,750 patents every year with the emphasis on automotive technology.
> Bosch Rexroth was heavily involved in the construction of the London Eye. It supplied the drive system, the electronic controls and the anchorage and stabilising system for the landmark structure.
> Robert Bosch introduced the eight-hour working day in 1906.
> Bosch power tools are used to mark the ski runs for Alpine World Cup races.

Market

Founded in 1901, the BSI Group is a leading global provider of professional services to organisations worldwide. The Group's services include independent certification of management systems and products, commodity inspection, product testing, development of private, national and international standards, management systems training and delivery of information on standards and international trade.

The Group has over 5,400 employees in 110 countries and in 2003 its turnover was £237.3 million.

Businesses all over the world rely on BSI's integrity, authority and independence: 25% of companies listed on the FTSE 100 index and one sixth of Fortune 500 businesses utilise BSI's services. Customers range from global companies to small local businesses. The collective range of their products and services encompasses virtually every field of human endeavour including communications, banking, oil, engineering, electronics, food and drink, agriculture and consumer goods.

Achievements

The BSI Group has at its core the world's first National Standards Body – producing an average of 2,000 new standards annually. BSI British Standards provided the model for other countries to follow and instigated the formation of the International Organization for Standardization (ISO) in 1946.

BSI remains one of the world's leading providers of standardisation documents covering every aspect of the modern economy from protection of intellectual property and knowledge management to electromagnetic compatibility specifications; from guidelines on managing risk for corporate governance and standards on project management, to specifications on flood protection products, biometrics and nanotechnology.

BSI British Standards is active on the international arena, being one of the five leading members of ISO and one of the three main National Standards Bodies in Europe. British Standards is also increasingly building bi-lateral relations with other National Standards Bodies, and in 2004 developed closer relations with the National Standards Bodies of China and Japan through joint co-operation agreements.

British Standards is also a major provider of technical assistance to countries around the world and has undertaken projects in Russia, Turkey and Albania, assisting these countries in developing and improving their standardisation infrastructures.

In addition, BSI is one of the world's largest independent certifiers of management systems, with 45,000 clients across the globe. Moreover the internationally accepted concept of management systems standards was pioneered by the BSI Group. The ISO 9000 quality series – adopted, to date, by around 500,000 organisations in 150 countries worldwide – was also developed from British Standard BS 5750, first published in 1979. The most widely accepted environmental management system, ISO 14001, was derived from BS 7750 – established by BSI in 1992.

The BSI Group continues to innovate. In 2004 it became accredited to verify greenhouse gas emissions under the EU Emissions Trading Scheme and developed a unique proprietary tool called BSI BenchMark, which enables companies to understand and compare the performance of their management system relative to their peers and industry norms. Also in 2004, BSI led the international standards community's work on nanotechnology.

History

The BSI Group was founded as the Engineering Standards Committee (ESC) in 1901. Among the first standards published was one which reduced the number of sizes of tramway rails from 75 to five, resulting in an estimated saving of £1 million a year. Standardisation was on its way.

In 1903, the British Standard Mark, now known as the Kitemark, was registered as a trademark and standardisation work gathered momentum: by 1918, 300 committees were in place with 31,000 standards being sold that year.

In 1929, what had been the Engineering Standards Committee was awarded a Royal Charter and in 1931, the name British Standards Institution was adopted.

World War II brought accelerated standards

production, including over 400 wartime emergency standards. In the post-war era, the slow shift towards an affluent society created more demand for consumer standardisation work, characterised by the 1953 introduction of the Kitemark's application to domestic products. By the 1960s, Government regulations were mandating compulsory Kitemarking of car seat belts and motorcycle helmets.

The next major development was the introduction of a standard for the quality of company management systems. BS 5750 was introduced to help companies build quality and safety into the way they work to meet the needs of their customers. In 1979 the Registered

Firm mark was introduced to indicate that a company had been audited and registered to BS 5750 standard.

From 1994, BS 5750 became known as BS EN ISO 9000. From this point on a major part of BSI's work became registering companies to the world's most popular management systems standard, now known as ISO 9001:2000.

In 1991, BSI Inc was established in Reston, Virginia in the US. The following year, BSI published the world's first environmental management standard, BS 7750. In due course, this was adopted internationally and in 1996 ISO 14001 was published.

In 1998 the BSI Group acquired Inspectorate – a global commodity testing business. This gave the group a foothold in around 100 countries, running over 170 facilities. With this acquisition, BSI virtually doubled its sales to around £170 million a year. Its total worldwide workforce grew to around 3,400, with a highly effective global reach, extending into emerging markets such as China, Eastern Europe and South America.

The BSI Group subsequently acquired CEEM, a leading American management systems training and publication services provider in 1998, and in 1999, Rocky Mountain Geochemical, one of America's leading precious metals testing companies and Mertcontrol, among Hungary's leading inspection, testing and certification companies. It also acquired International Standards Certification Pte Ltd, a Singapore based certification organisation.

In January 2002, KPMG's ISO registration business in North America was bought, making BSI Group the largest standards body in the world and the largest registration body in North America.

In 2003, BSI acquired 100% of BSI Pacific Ltd, in order to consolidate the Group's penetration of the immense Greater China certification market. BSI also acquired a 49% shareholding in British Standards Publishing Limited (BSPL) realising a new sales, distribution and licensing agreement to expand the Group's ability to deliver standards worldwide.

In 2004, the Group acquired Swedish inspection and testing company, LW Cargo Survey AB, enhancing the company's services to clients involved in commodity trading and shipping in the Scandinavian region and KPMG's certification business in the Netherlands – KPMG Certification B.V. – to provide an enhanced range of services to businesses across the Benelux region and the rest of continental Europe.

As a result of these strategic acquisitions, and through more than a century of growth, the BSI Group can now provide a comprehensive service to its clients, helping them raise their performance and enhance their competitiveness worldwide.

Product
The BSI Group is made up of five key business units:

BSI British Standards is the world's leading provider of standards, covering every aspect of the modern economy from protection of intellectual property to technical specifications for personal protective equipment. As part of British Standards, BSI Business Information exists to raise awareness and understanding of new standards and regulations through publications and training. It provides a comprehensive range of books, manuals, CD Roms and online services.

BSI Management Systems provides independent certification of management systems, including ISO 9001:2000 (Quality Management), ISO 14001 (Environmental Management), Greenhouse Gas Emissions Verification, OHSAS 18001 (Health and Safety) and BS 7799 (Information Security Management).

BSI Product Services tests products against standards, helps firms with new product development and provides third party certification. Product Services is the owner of the Kitemark brand, which was first registered as the British Standards mark in 1903.

Finally, BSI Inspectorate is a global commodity inspection and analysis company that joined the BSI Group in 1998. The core objective of BSI Inspectorate's global business is to minimise risk through independent inspection, analysis and testing of commodities.

Recent Developments
BSI is now a truly global brand. Since July 2002 when BSI first consolidated its fifteen distinct brand identities into the current monolithic BSI brand, the organisation has leveraged the power that a single brand identity can bring. The brand now enjoys a consistent and clear visual identity across the Group's global operations, while retaining the brand's strong heritage. In addition, all BSI staff across the Group's divisions understand the importance and power of the brand and aim to deliver it consistently.

The strength of the BSI brand is a key strategic asset which is invaluable when expanding its global reach. In the previous twelve months, BSI has expanded its services, plant or facilities across the globe, including in China, Brazil, Peru, Vietnam, Romania, Russia, Dubai and the Netherlands to name a few.

In addition to strengthening the global brand, BSI also embarked upon a major research and communications programme to engage senior business leaders across the UK to workshop the major strategic advantages that standardisation offers their companies. Such companies have the opportunity to shape the future of their industry sectors and markets by participating in standardisation at a strategic level.

Promotion
Subsequent to the development of one unified brand, BSI's marketing communications continue to focus on achieving the long-term goal of a coherent global brand identity. Three key creative challenges continue to be of prime importance. Firstly, communicating BSI's global focus as well as positioning the Group as an independent commercial enterprise, as opposed to a Government institution. Secondly, continuing the internal branding communications strategy to bring about understanding and buy-in of the BSI brand for all staff around the world. Finally, developing international promotional strategies addressing varying and diverse cultures.

To meet the first objective, BSI sought to raise brand awareness with external senior decision-makers by emphasising the brand's benefits and values and featuring carefully selected imagery. The key channels for engagement were through media and public relations and the publication of a business magazine, Business Standards (www.businessstandards.com).

Sponsorship was another brand communication vehicle utilised by the BSI Group to meet the first objective. The BSI Environmental Design Award scheme,

shape the future

run in conjunction with London's Royal College of Art (RCA), has evolved with the brand, from an award for standards in design into an environmental design award that aligns the BSI Group with the best in contemporary design and positions BSI as a leading player in sustainability issues.

To reinforce the brand internally, BSI continues to internally market its brand identity website which makes the corporate guidelines and the various brand elements easily accessible to all staff and key suppliers around the world. In addition, the website provides a means of engaging BSI staff in a conversation on what the brand stands for and where it is going – a dialogue which is critical to maintaining the fierce commitment that staff have to the brand.

Although the Group follows a carefully defined brand strategy, the business units tailor their marketing campaigns to meet the specific requirements of their individual customers across varying regions. BSI has developed expertise in understanding how its brand translates into local business cultures and local languages. Subsequently, the majority of BSI communications are now regionally focused, instead of being UK-centric. They utilise key elements of the marketing mix including print advertisements in key industry publications, posters, direct mail and exhibitions. Significant innovations have also taken place within e-marketing, with BSI's web presence now representing a major channel for communications and marketing, supplemented with email marketing.

Brand Values
BSI Group's brand values are integrity, innovation and independence. They are the foundation of the BSI brand, supporting the organisation as it strives towards its vision of being a world leader in advancing industry and business for a better quality of life. For over a century these brand values have been at the heart of the organisation, defining and driving the Group's operations.

BSI continually strives to deliver its brand values, with the aim of building a powerful, globally recognised brand, ultimately satisfying the needs of clients, staff, members and other key stakeholders.

www.bsi-global.com

THINGS YOU DIDN'T KNOW ABOUT

BSI

❯ BSI Inspectorate first went into business as an assayer of gold in 1855 during the Australian and US gold rushes.

❯ BSI was founded by Sir John Wolfe Barry, who also engineered Tower Bridge – his father designed the Houses of Parliament.

❯ The original BSI committee met for the first time on the day Queen Victoria died – January 22nd 1901.

❯ BSI has developed approximately 1,400 standards based on food or food preparation, aiming to ensure that we can eat safely.

❯ BSI's Kitemark is currently recognised by more than 80% of the UK adult population.

Market

Information, communications and networking technologies are converging; so too are the companies that deliver them. In the past, businesses have viewed IT services, telephony, communications and networking technology as different areas, often managed by diverse departments, and have worked with various suppliers to provide each. BT describes this new IT- and communications-driven marketplace as 'the digital networked economy' and is marketing a portfolio to cover the range of converged services.

BT is one of the UK's best-known companies, providing services to more than 20 million business and residential customers around the globe. Businesses look to BT for everything from basic telephony to managed call centres; workforce mobility solutions to sophisticated network management and IT systems to broadcast services. BT is well positioned to become the UK's first truly converged provider of information, communications and networking services.

Every business market in which BT competes is characterised by stiff competition. The telecoms sector is acknowledged by industry analysts to be a shrinking one with tough competition on margins. IT and networking services companies are still struggling to recover from the downturn of the early 2000s, aggressively stretching into new markets in an attempt to find the double-digit growth that characterised their industries five years ago. BT must fight to win and maintain business; a well-trusted and successful brand plays a vital role.

Achievements

More than 80% of the FTSE 100 and 60% of the largest Fortune 500 companies rely on BT for networking, applications and system integration. Organisations as diverse as the National Health Service, Unilever, the Bavarian National Government and ebookers.com are working with BT to exploit the power of networked IT and communications services.

BT claims the world's most extensive MPLS (multi-protocol layer switching) network, allowing global movement of voice and data at high speed and quality of service. Business customers can exploit this to drive their own success, whether through providing better customer sales and services or improving 'back office' functions like the mobility of the workforce or establishing connections between partners and suppliers. BT has an order intake for IT and networking services business with major corporate customers of more than £7.5 billion.

A third of the world's financial traders rely on networked IT services from BT. BT runs the National Rail Enquiries line, Britain's busiest telephone number, with an average of 150,000 calls a day. In the UK, eighteen out of the top 20 high street financial organisations depend on BT's network. BT enables more than five million citizens to interact with their local councils through a variety of media. BT's networks process 80% of all UK credit card transactions (more than 400,000 per hour) and has ATM capabilities in 22 countries.

BT has been a driving force behind the success of 'Broadband Britain'. The company has rolled out services across the UK, spent millions on marketing campaigns and developed a portfolio of consumer and business products. These have led to the UK enjoying great success with broadband. More than four million broadband users use a service provided over BT's network and the UK has the widest availability of DSL services in the G7 as a result of BT's investment in the technology.

Industry praise includes Frost & Sullivan's choice of BT as winner of the 2004 award for Business Development Strategy Leadership and the 2004 European Data Communication Service Provider of the Year. Government computing analyst Kable lists BT as the number two supplier of outsourcing and IT to the Government market. Computer Business Review listed BT as the third most successful IT services vendor in the UK, ahead of Accenture and IBM, and Retail Week listed BT as the number five supplier of IT services in their marketplace.

History

BT was privatised in 1984, making it the only state-owned telecommunications company to be privatised in Europe. In 1991, British Telecom was restructured and re-launched as BT.

In May 2001, as a part of a restructuring and debt reduction programme, BT announced a '3 for 10' rights

issue to raise £5.9 billion – the UK's largest ever rights issue – and the sale of Yell for £2.14 billion.

In November that year, BT Wireless – BT's mobile business, re-branded as mmO2 – was demerged from BT.

The new BT is structured so that BT Group plc provides a holding company for the separately managed businesses that make up the group. These are BT Retail, BT Wholesale and BT Global Services, each of which has the freedom to focus on its own markets and customers.

The company has recently announced group turnover up 2.1%, and profit before tax up 4% – the company's best quarter for revenues for three years – while debt sits at a manageable £8.3 billon and continues to fall.

Product

In the business market, BT provides IT, communications and networking services to help enterprises achieve five things; establish the right infrastructure for their needs; serve their customers and citizens better; enable their workforce to work in ways when, how and best for the company, customer and individual; extend their organisation seamlessly through networks of partners and suppliers; and ensure security and manage risk related to IT and networks.

BT's core portfolio covers traditional telephony products such as calls, analogue/digital lines and private circuits. To meet the customer needs above, BT combines these traditional products with products and services such as networking and network management, broadband, mobility, CRM, applications management and hosting as well as desktop services.

It is also pioneering the take-up of public wireless broadband in the UK through BT Openzone. BT customers on the move can now surf the web, check emails and download documents at broadband speeds at over 20,000 BT Openzone hotspots across eleven countries following new roaming agreements with four major international wireless operators. It is critical, for the future of Wi-Fi, that major operators join forces to promote and drive awareness of the benefits of using hotspots.

BT's vision is to ultimately provide customers with access to all their applications and information, wherever they are, on their choice of device, whilst utilising the best network available.

Recent Developments

The last year has seen BT at the forefront of technological innovation. The company has been spearheading the UK's success with broadband, it has been developing its world-leading plans for a 21st century network and it has advanced plans that will see fixed and mobile services converge in the future.

Broadband is an area of particular importance to both BT and the UK economy. BT has invested huge sums to date to ensure that the whole of the UK has access to the technology and this has led to the UK having wider availability of DSL broadband than any other G7 country despite the challenging geography of the UK.

As well as having almost universal availability of DSL broadband, the UK is also climbing the league tables for adoption of broadband. BT passed the four million wholesale connection milestone in December 2004 and the company is on course to hit its challenging five million target a full year ahead of schedule. The rapid adoption of broadband by SMEs will ensure that businesses in the UK have the ability to compete in the increasingly competitive global market.

BT's investment does not stop at broadband however. The company has ambitious plans to create a '21st century network' based solely on Internet Protocol (IP) technology. This network will be one of the most advanced in the world and will deliver increasingly converged services to both residential and business customers in years to come. BT has plans to invest more than £10 billion over the next few years.

BT is pioneering an innovative project whereby fixed and mobile services will converge with 'smart' phones able to identify the best network over which to function. Effectively, mobiles will use BT's fixed network wherever possible and customers will only need one number for all their needs. BT is working with telcos and suppliers across the world as well as being a founder member of the Fixed Mobile Convergence Alliance.

BT's continued growth in the IT and networking services market has been characterised by a string of major new contracts. These include BA, McDonald's,

Astra Zeneca, Nato and Hilton Hotels. One of the company's highest profile contracts is its work with the UK National Health Service to deliver real and tangible benefits to staff and patients alike. The BT supplied infrastructure will deliver vital NHS Care Records Service to clinicians and medical practitioners, connecting the Local Service Provider (LSP) regional IT networks into one standardised system, which will benefit both patients and medical staff.

Promotion

In bringing its view of the digital networked economy to life, BT has created new and innovative communications vehicles to reach that illusive audience – senior business people.

Advertising provides strong air cover to establish the digital networked economy and build BT's credibility. Below-the-line media delivers evidence of BT's capability, but not the traditional below-the-line mix, because traditional ways of contacting customers – direct mail and face-to-face events – have been replaced by online activities.

Interactive media has created more than 800 sales days of virtual face-to-face time with customers, in a way that's measurable and accountable. Web seminars are replacing expensive conferences, virtual tours online mean that people don't have to spend hours travelling and on demand presentations inform and engage in a way that enables customers to gain knowledge without feeling 'sold to'.

These activities have been brought together under the umbrella of The Insights Programme, where individuals can pick and choose to suit their personal interest and learning needs. More than 20% of web seminar attendees have received an invitation forwarded on by a colleague.

Brand Values

The nature of BT's business has evolved and will continue to do so. What was once a provider of voice telephony is now a global IT, communications and networking services company. New technologies such as broadband, IP networks and CRM are at the heart of its business strategy. The company structure and culture of distinct lines of business with their own brand identities is migrating to a single company, with a single-minded brand promise.

This does not mean discarding a heritage of years of trust and reliability. It means taking these strengths and building a more dynamic and progressive brand image in order to meet the brand's strategic business goals and deliver what its customers want from BT.

Today, BT's brand has five key attributes that unify its employees and define the company's approach to its customers: Trustworthy, Helpful, Straightforward, Inspiring and Heart.

This focus has helped to drive a greater integration of BT's businesses, structure and processes. In short, the re-statement of 'one BT' that will enable the company to counter any residual negative perceptions and build its business and its brand.

www.bt.com

THINGS YOU DIDN'T KNOW ABOUT

BT

❯ BT processes 320 million transactions per day with sub one second response speeds.

❯ BT has more than 34,000 people working on IT networking services – that's 36% of the workforce.

❯ BT is the second largest outsourcing company in the Government market, relied upon by organisations like the NHS, the MOD and councils such as Liverpool City Council.

❯ BT manages 800 call centres globally.

❯ BT manages over 450 network firewalls for customers, has defended more than fourteen million unauthorised attempts to access BT's infrastructure and blocks 40,000 viruses per month.

CABLE & WIRELESS

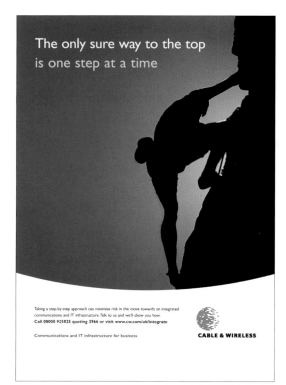

The only sure way to the top is one step at a time

Taking a step-by-step approach can minimise risk in the move towards an integrated communications and IT infrastructure. Talk to us and we'll show you how.
Call 08000 925825 quoting 2966 or visit www.cw.com/uk/integrate

Communications and IT infrastructure for business

CABLE & WIRELESS

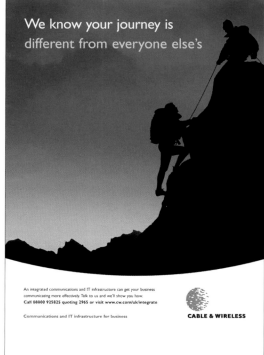

We know your journey is different from everyone else's

An integrated communications and IT infrastructure can get your business communicating more effectively. Talk to us and we'll show you how.
Call 08000 925825 quoting 2965 or visit www.cw.com/uk/integrate

Communications and IT infrastructure for business

CABLE & WIRELESS

Sometimes you need simple, practical help more than theory

An integrated communications and IT infrastructure increases business agility, drives innovation and cuts cost and complexity. Talk to us and we'll show you how.
Call 08000 925825 quoting 2967 or visit www.cw.com/uk/integrate

Communications and IT infrastructure for business

CABLE & WIRELESS

Market

In today's international business marketplace, companies have never been more reliant on communications and IT to compete. The communications and IT infrastructure that underpins companies are as important as the bricks and steel backbone of their buildings – they probably could not survive without it. Cable & Wireless is a leader in communications and IT infrastructure. Tesco, Heinz Shell, O₂ and The Post Office are just some of the brands that use Cable & Wireless to help make them Superbrands. It commands an overall 14% share of the market, making it as big as Energis and MCI combined. And in many niche sectors, such as providing the underlying communications technology for advanced customer call centres, it has the largest market share.

This is a complicated and fragmented sector, characterised by fast-changing technology, downward price pressure, and ever-higher performance demands. The biggest category by value is the 'every day business telephone calls' market, which is worth £3.7 billion in the UK. However, although this is a massive sector, many in the industry wonder how long the 'traditional' telephone network has left. The internet – or more specifically, voice over internet protocol (VoIP) – is the voice network of the future. Using the internet, business telephone calls could certainly be substantially cheaper than they are now, or even free – which spells big challenges ahead for companies like Cable & Wireless.

Although the numbers are small in comparison, the value of the VoIP market in the UK is expected to grow from £170 million in 2005 to £555 million by 2007/08. Over the same period, the value of traditional voice traffic will fall 8% to £3.4 billion.

However, there are many many more areas of the telecommunications business to consider, such as broadband, local area network (LAN) solutions for business, hosting, security, mobile working and call centre solutions – all of which are growing rapidly.

Achievements

From its beginning in the 1860s, Cable & Wireless has played a major part in the establishment and development of telecommunications around the world. The company's forefather was scotsman John Pender, an ambitious entrepreneur whose company and partnerships led to the manufacture and laying of the first copper telecommunication cable across the Atlantic, in 1866. This historic project has been described by the writer Arthur C Clarke as the Victorian equivalent of the Apollo initiative.

Today the company's strengths are acknowledged by customers and recognised by many independent groups. For example, at the Internet Service Providers Association Awards Cable & Wireless has won 'Best Carrier' for the quality, breadth and depth of its internet transit backbone and supporting services. In the Communications Managers Association (CMA) Survey 2005, Cable & Wireless were named the Best Value for Money Operator.

It was also won accolades as the 'Worlds Leading Provider of Communications Solutions' and the 'Worlds Leading Provider of High Speed Internet Access' at the World Travel Awards 2004. Over 150,000 frontline travel agents and over 80,000 travel agencies worldwide voted online for their choices, which resulted in Cable & Wireless beating rivals including BT, Deutsche Telecom and AT&T.

History

Cable & Wireless can trace its history back to the 1860s as Victorian entrepreneurs began to connect parts of the British Empire with London via a series of undersea telegraph cables. In 1934 after a series of mergers and acquisitions of around 40 companies bearing names such as The London-Platino Brazilian Telegraph Company and The African Direct Telegraph Company, Cable & Wireless emerged. The name was designed to more clearly reflect the combined radio and cable services it offered. At this stage, Cable & Wireless was really an overseas arm of the UK Government, with a principal role in providing the communications to link the sprawling British Empire. However, following the deregulation of the market in the early 1980s Cable & Wireless became a Public Limited Company and joined the FTSE 100.

Cable & Wireless has a history of strong local market brands – after de-regulation, it launched Mercury in the UK and also had on its portfolio HongKong Telecom and Telecommunications of Jamaica.

However, this meant that by 1996 the company had over 70 brand names, with seven of its ten largest operations not branded with the Cable & Wireless name.

During 1996 this was addressed by moving to a single global brand. This was designed to help the group compete more forcefully in the global communications marketplace, to strengthen the local company offerings and also to bring the scale of the group's operations and capabilities to the attention of potential partners, governments, regulators and international companies.

In the UK Cable & Wireless decided to concentrate on the business to business market in 1999, resulting in the sale of its residential interests. In many of its overseas markets, however, Cable & Wireless continues to offer the whole range of telecommunications services to both the business and consumer sectors.

Product

Today Cable & Wireless is a leader in communications and IT infrastructure. Cable & Wireless offers its clients an integrated communications solution. One designed to seamlessly link organisations to their customers, partners and suppliers and also to allow them to consolidate their data, voice and video networks in one infrastructure.

Branded Cable & Wireless Integrate, this solution can help companies provide staff, suppliers or partners with access to information and online services, whenever and wherever they need them. It also helps them roll out new IT applications more smoothly, by giving them a solid, consistent and easily adaptable foundation to build on. Wherever a company is on the journey towards unified communications and IT, Cable & Wireless can help them go forward with confidence. By creating infrastructures which increase agility, enable innovation and cut costs and complexity, while making the most of current systems, Cable & Wireless Integrate solutions transform business effectiveness.

Nowadays, companies want to be able to adapt to many new ways of working, such as employees spending more time away from the office, and the need to offer customers multiple contact options – all of which Cable & Wireless can help with. Companies can choose from a wide range of Cable & Wireless Integrate solutions that cover all aspects of their communication needs, such as secure data, mobile working, voice and customer interaction. Norwich Union is one of many UK clients to have benefited from the Cable & Wireless Integrate offering, allowing it to converge seven different data and voice networks onto one integrated infrastructure.

Recent Developments

Cable & Wireless is constantly working with big-name clients to improve their competitiveness with innovative solutions. A recent example is Volkswagen UK which, in December 2004, signed a three-year contract with Cable & Wireless to provide a new wide area network (WAN) to support its 500 UK car and commercial vehicle dealers. The Internet Protocol Virtual Private Network (IP-VPN) delivers 25% savings on data costs and allows the company to deliver an enhanced level of service to its retailers and customers across the

country. For example, 'Audi TV' provides dealers with information about the latest models or details on new car launches. Dealers can also use the network to participate in live video auctions, which help to increase productivity by eliminating travelling time.

Demonstrating its breadth of offering, Cable & Wireless also recently won a contract with Tesco to provide its new online music download service. The new Tesco.com digital download music store provides customers with access to more than half a million tracks, via a secure Cable & Wireless platform.

Promotion

A major part of Cable & Wireless' promotional strategy over the last decade has been its move to being a single global brand. This had a dramatic effect.

Between 1997 and 1999 more than 30 of the group's major operations around the world were re-named Cable & Wireless, including HongKong Telecom, at that

time the group's largest single operation, and IDC in Japan. A new corporate identity and branding structure was developed to aid this programme, covering online, advertising, marketing collateral, promotional and partnership activities.

The number of people exposed to the brand increased from 1.3 million at the start of the programme to over 140 million by 1999.

The adoption of the new identity was supported by a major global sponsorship programme, including the successful round-the-world powerboat attempt in 1998 and the less successful round-the-world balloon attempt the following year. Despite its failure, the latter endeavour created media coverage valued at over US$30 million.

The success of the re-brand was reflected by research by PricewaterhouseCoopers in 1998, which valued the Cable & Wireless brand at 2-6% of total Group turnover.

In 2004, Cable & Wireless embarked on another major business to business promotional programme, linking up with Times Newspapers Limited (TNL) to create a new raft of advertising, sponsored supplements, online activity and events.

As part of the deal, Cable & Wireless initiated its first UK advertising campaign in four years. The ads introduce the idea that, wherever customers are on their journey towards integrated communications and IT, Cable & Wireless can help them go forward with confidence. As such, it clearly states the company's position as the leader in integrated communications and IT infrastructure solutions for business. This thought is brought together with the creative idea that Cable & Wireless will take the customer on a pragmatic, step-by-step journey, whereas others will depict an idealistic nirvana.

To access the widest possible business audience, the advertising is carried in major regional titles, including The Scotsman and The Western Mail, as well as The Times and The Sunday Times.

Cable & Wireless also sponsored The Times Power 100 – the definitive list of leading executives, announced annually in November – and The Sunday Times FastTrack 100. In addition, it is holding a series of sports events in partnership with The Sunday Times.

Brand Values

Cable & Wireless has a strong reputation in the telecommunications industry, offering experience and expertise in delivering communications infrastructure solutions for business customers internationally.

Cable & Wireless is universally recognised by its core brand values of being expert, dependable and collaborative.

It is also renowned for recognising its responsibility as a good corporate citizen and for understanding that sound relationships with colleagues, customers, suppliers, shareholders and other stakeholders are important to its success.

www.cw.com/uk

THINGS YOU DIDN'T KNOW ABOUT

Cable & Wireless

❯ Over two-thirds of companies in the Fortune 500 use Cable & Wireless.

❯ In 1872 the cost of sending a message to India was £4.

❯ In 1873, the Eastern Telegraph Company transmitted 225 thousand words. 100 years later, Cable & Wireless was transmitting nearly 225 million words.

CASIO®

Market

Famous around the world for its consumer electronics products such as digital cameras, digital pianos and watches, CASIO also has a strong business to business heritage. It has sold EPOS, cash registers and hand-held data capture terminals for more than fifteen years, and more recently has added products such as projectors and mobile hand-held technology devices for blue- and grey-collar workers to its range. As well as producing its own products for businesses, it also provides components such as liquid crystal display (LCD) units to other manufacturers.

While times remain hard for the electronics industry as a whole, with stagnation in the world's industrialised economies depressing consumer spending, CASIO continues to buck the market trend. It has renewed its focus on brand development as a key plank of growth, and is now concentrating on three key areas – Digital Imaging (Cameras and Projectors), Mobile Network Solutions and Timepieces. It is also redefining its business globally into 'traditional' products, such as calculators and cash tills, as well as 'growth' products, including projectors, digital cameras and hand-held devices.

This strategy helped CASIO grow annual UK sales by 15.3% in 2003 and by a further 12.5% in 2004. Its UK success is replicated on a global scale, based on strong sales of its digital cameras and mobile phones in Japan, and sales of components to other manufacturers – 50% of all branded digital cameras contain CASIO LCDs.

The brand ascribes its ability to lead the consumer electronics market to its aim of surpassing users' highest expectations, rather than simply incorporating new technologies into yesterday's products. Yet it abhors technology for technology's sake. "CASIO helps people do important things better and more easily," says Tomoki Sato, Director of Corporate Strategy.

What's more, it never wavers from its determination to offer its customers products, services and solutions that combine high quality and value for money.

Achievements

As the creator of products such as the famously 'indestructible' G-Shock wristwatch in 1983, and the QV10 – the first digital camera with an LCD viewing screen – in 1995, CASIO enjoys a well-deserved reputation as a revolutionary electronics manufacturer.

Since its birth in 1957, the company's mission has been to use ingenious concepts and state-of-the-art technology to create products and services that will make people's lives more enjoyable, comfortable and efficient.

Among its constellation of pioneering products, CASIO counts the first all-electronic compact calculator in 1956; the first inkjet printer in 1971; the first hand-held PC (Cassiopeia with Windows CE) in 1996; the first CD titlers for office and home use; and, in 2003, the world's first dual-band atomic timepiece – Wave Ceptor, the most accurate watch on the market.

But while its historic achievements remain important to a company with such a strong heritage, CASIO is keen not to rest on its laurels.

For example, it has worked hard to revitalise the CASIO brand in the UK, through a combination of communication and rapid-fire product development in both the consumer and business to business sectors. Among its recent product stars is the Exilim P600 digital camera, which has picked up more than ten camera awards in the UK and won the European Imaging and Sound Association award for the best compact camera.

EISA AWARDS
DIGITAL COMPACT CAMERA 2004-2005
Casio Exilim Pro EX-P600

History

CASIO was founded by Tadao Kashio, who grew up in a farming family in Nangoku City in Japan. Tadao loved creating things and was eager to start his own business, and in 1946 he set up a firm making aeroplane parts. At a trade exhibition in 1949 he saw an electric motorised calculator the size of an office desk. It was operated by gears and was extremely noisy. Tadao was convinced he could do better and started to develop his own calculating machine. In 1954, he created an electric calculator that weighed 30kg and was about the size of a backpack.

Tadao's three brothers then joined the firm and set about creating a better version. But it wasn't all plain sailing. On one occasion the brothers were due to unveil their new device to a prospective buyer but it wouldn't fit on the plane to make the journey to his offices. They took it to pieces, but when they reassembled it at the other end, it wouldn't work. However, the 'Model 124-A' calculator subsequently proved a major sales hit with manufacturers from Japan and overseas and the CASIO Computer Company went from strength to strength.

Rival manufacturers began to create their own calculators, which were smaller and easier to use. CASIO responded in 1965 with the first electronic calculator, and began to expand its market from businesses to well-to-do consumers who could afford to pay around £80 for one of its products. In 1972 the CASIO Mini was an immediate success, and from then on CASIO focused on miniaturisation.

In 1975 CASIO launched a digital watch called the Casiotron, which is now highly collectable. January 1980 saw the release of the company's first electronic musical

instrument, the Casiotone 201. CASIO then applied its world-leading LCD and power management technology to developing pocket TVs and word processors for the Japanese market.

Among its more recent innovations are the world's first mass-market digital camera and the Cassiopeia, a hand-held PC. CASIO's mantra is 'if it's not totally original, it's not CASIO' and this spirit drives its relentless quest for innovation.

Product

CASIO's product range is vast, but whatever the product or the market, the CASIO hallmarks of technological innovation, value and miniaturisation are constant.

The brand has also brought together some of its business products, such as EPOS, cash registers and hand-held data capture terminals, to provide innovative solutions for customers. For example, the London Eye and WH Smith have taken advantage of CASIO's 'queue busting' solution, while Britannia Airline aircrew and bar and restaurant staff use CASIO's 'wireless waitressing' solution to take and process orders, process bills and accept payments. Such applications use CASIO touch screens, tills and hand-held PCs, which are connected together so that information is always up to date.

All CASIO products have a technological fingerprint. For example, they invariably have an LCD. CASIO also shrinks the technology so that people can wear the product or carry it with them. For example, the new Exilim S100 camera has a ceramic lens in order to fit a 2.8x optical zoom into the small housing.

Provide an environment for creativity.

2x zoom: adapts to fit any room.

Smaller than A4: fits any briefcase.

Ultra-light: take it anywhere!

Autofocus and automatic keystone correction: the right setting at all times.

Up to 2,800 ANSI lumens: high brightness in any lighting.

We've reinvented the art of presentation.

The new, ultra-portable generation of CASIO projectors and the accompanying multi-functional camera system offer unlimited opportunities for your ideas.

Arrive fully relaxed and make a big impression: the new generation of CASIO projectors sets new standards in integrating high-end technology within the smallest confines, thus providing perfect mobility and the maximum variety of applications. Despite the extremely light weight and small size – the XJ-350 is smaller than a sheet of B5 paper – you can use it to present your ideas brilliantly and in large format even in the brightest surroundings, thanks to up to 2,800 ANSI lumens. And the integrated double zoom lens means that you can convince your audience in small rooms just as well as in a spacious conference setting. As if that wasn't enough, CASIO brings you another small revolution in the shape of an optionally available multi-functional camera system. Combined with our high-performance projectors, the camera system lets you do things while you're actually giving a presentation that you have never even dreamt of before. You can incorporate up-to-date photos, newspaper clippings and handwritten notes into your presentation, or you can use this set as a documentation tool. Everything in top visual quality, for a perfect presentation that's sure to be a success! For more information, go to www.casio.co.uk.

NEW: YC-400
- 4 million pixels
- 3x zoom
- Document camera
- Whiteboard camera
- Digital camera
- Scanner
- Folds up to B5 size
- Weighs only 1.8 kg

NEW: XJ-350 *2x zoom*
- 2,200 ANSI lumens
- 2x optical wide-angle zoom lens
- DLP™ technology
- Size (W x H x D): 230 x 55 x 171 mm
- Automatic vertical keystone correction
- XGA resolution (1,024 x 768 pixels)
- Weighs only 1.8 kg

NEW: XJ-450
- 2,800 ANSI lumens
- 2x optical wide-angle zoom lens
- DLP™ technology
- Size (W x H x D): 278 x 64 x 197 mm
- Automatic horizontal and vertical keystone correction
- Autofocus
- XGA resolution (1,024 x 768 pixels)
- Weighs only 2.4 kg

PICTURE BY DLP
A TEXAS INSTRUMENTS TECHNOLOGY

CASIO Electronics Co. Ltd., Unit 6, 1000 North Circular Road, London NW2 7JD
Tel: 0208 450 9131   Fax: 0208 452 6323
The DLP™ logo and the DLP™ medallion are registered trademarks of Texas Instruments.

CASIO.
www.casio.co.uk

Recent Developments

The convergence of digital technologies means that CASIO's traditional organisational structure continues to change to reflect the increasing crossover between different types of products. Business to business products now includes handheld PCs containing a bar code scanner, digital camera and wireless communications. This technology has proved highly successful at the London Eye, which uses a CASIO IT-700 wireless pocket PC as a 'queue busting' device to enable staff to sell souvenirs, drinks and disposable cameras to people waiting to board the giant wheel.

CASIO is also looking at ways to extend its products into new markets. For example, a major UK telecom company chose CASIO FX7400, a graphic calculator used mainly in education, as an effective 'productivity solution' for its 15,000 mobile engineers.

Among the company's newest business to business products are the QT-6000 EPOS systems, designed for the hospitality sector, featuring a three-colour back-lit remote display, user-friendly touch screen and wireless network, as well as a new range of ultra-light and bright projectors which incorporate a revolutionary document and camera system.

On the pure business to business side, CASIO runs a series of dealership conferences. It has developed a programme called CASIO Mobility Partners, which aims to formalise its relationship with systems integrators to ensure that CASIO products are a key ingredient in any solution. The company also produces case studies to demonstrate its business solutions to its target business sectors.

In addition, CASIO is boosting and publicising its corporate social responsibility activities in the UK, with particular focus on education. For example, it teaches maths teachers how to use digital technology in class, as a way of improving performance, especially among under-achieving boys. Research relating to this project, which CASIO carried out in 2004, showing that children want to learn more about maths and science, received wide press coverage.

The products also have excellent power management – the 'Super Life' batteries last longer than those of competitors, and the company is even developing fuel cell technology in Tokyo for hand-held devices and laptops. The new Cassiopeia IT-10 rugged PDA can run continuously for up to 27 hours while the tough, ergonomic industrial device, the DT-X5, can operate for over 200 hours from a single charge.

CASIO products are also simple to operate. For example, the 'best shot' mode helps camera users improve their photographs, while key lighting keyboards allow people to play a tune. Products are also reliable and rugged, built to withstand all kinds of environments. The G-Shock watch is famously 'indestructible', while the rugged and splash-proof qualities of the Cassiopeia IT-10 and DT-X5 make them ideal for industrial use.

As a part of CSR activities, CASIO is designing its products to be increasingly environmentally friendly, with the introduction of products such as solar-powered and radio-controlled watches. In addition, new inventions are lightweight, compact, energy-efficient and easy to 'reuse, reduce and recycle'.

Promotion

While its traditional emphasis on PR to build product awareness will continue, CASIO is now seeking to build a more consistent brand message with an integrated approach to advertising, brochures and point-of-sale material, rather than focusing on individual products. Its challenge is to revive products it is known for, such as digital watches, calculators and keyboards, while increasing awareness of its new growth products, such as digital cameras, projectors and hand-held devices.

Its new approach is designed to increase desire for the CASIO brand by creating more of an emotional bond between consumers and the brand. CASIO is working with Blueprint magazine to run a six-month photo portrait exhibition at NPG, which showcases 21 designers whose designs are part of our lives.

CASIO is also boosting its visibility at shows, such as 2005's Focus on Imaging, the Outdoors Show and Music Live at the NEC, and is investing heavily in its website in order to convey the brand's dynamism and diversity.

Brand Values

From the original company credo of 'creativity and contribution', the UK company has developed a unique brand story and positioning definitions that will strengthen its future development.

The driving thought for CASIO is that it creates personal possibilities. At the heart of this is the idea of 'discovery' – people can see how the brand's expertise in personal technology can truly make a difference to their personal and professional lives.

The brand is, by nature, vibrant, energetic and daring. CASIO wants to remain one of the few brands that stimulate people, by constantly finding new and better ways of doing things.

CASIO also recognises and creates desire – in its people, through it products, in its attitude. When you look at what the brand achieves every day, you understand its real influence on the world.

www.casio.co.uk

THINGS YOU DIDN'T KNOW ABOUT

CASIO

❯ The CASIO QV-10 digital camera was voted as one of the top ten 'Greatest Gadgets', by the US Mobile PC magazine in 2005.

❯ CASIO's 'handheld terminals' are used on board London double deckers and National Railway Services (Virgin Trains etc).

❯ CASIO becomes the official watch licensor for the World Cup in Germany in 2006.

❯ CASIO's Wave Ceptor watches check themselves for accuracy: the National Atomic Clock in Teddington updates the time, through the Rugby transmitter.

❯ CASIO's original hand-held terminals were developed in the early 1980s to allow insurance companies to collect their premiums door to door. This was the precursor of the hand-held PC.

❯ CASIO LCDs are used in the instrumentation panels in the new range of Airbus.

CATERPILLAR®

Market

With a history stretching back 100 years, Caterpillar is a powerhouse of industry, with products and services helping to build the world's infrastructure. Caterpillar is a leading player in the diesel engine and power generation markets, with engine sales accounting for approximately one third of the company's total sales and revenues.

The company is also the world's leading manufacturer of construction and mining equipment, and industrial gas turbines. Its diverse activities mean Caterpillar is involved in and leads numerous industrial sectors, spanning construction, transportation, mining, forestry, energy, logistics, electronics, financing and electric power generation.

With more than 75,000 employees, 90,000 dealer employees, and thousands of suppliers doing business on six continents, Caterpillar has nearly 280 operations in 40 countries. Approximately half of its sales are to customers outside the US, solidifying its position as a global supplier and leading US exporter.

In 2004, Caterpillar posted sales and revenues of US$30.25 billion and a record profit of US$2.03 billion. The company manufactures its products and components in 50 US facilities and in 65 other locations in 23 countries around the globe.

Achievements

Over the last 75 years, Caterpillar has built a position of enviable strength in many of its business sectors. For example, oil and gas producers have relied on Caterpillar since the industry's earliest days, with Cat engines at work in more petroleum applications than any other brand. The brand is similarly dominant in the large marine engine market, selling more marine diesel engines over 250 bhp (186 bkW) than any other manufacturer in the world. In mining equipment, Caterpillar is the standard-setting brand.

Caterpillar is a remarkable American business success story, with the company sustaining an annual compounded growth rate of 7.65% each year since 1929. If an investor bought just one share of Caterpillar Tractor Company at US$56.25 in 1929, by today that investment would be worth US$14,173.20.

The company's success across its wide range of activities has been recognised with a clutch of high-profile awards. For example, its financial services arm, Caterpillar Financial Services Corporation, was recently awarded The

Malcolm Baldrige National Quality Award. This is America's top award for performance excellence and quality achievement. US President George Bush presided over a ceremony honouring recipients of the 2003 award ceremony, with Caterpillar financial president Jim Beard and Caterpillar Inc chairman and CEO Jim Owens accepting the award on the company's behalf.

Caterpillar is regularly recognised for its leadership in corporate responsibility. Caterpillar has been named on the Dow Jones Sustainability World Index for four years in a row and was one of just 317 companies from 24 countries on the prestigious list in 2004. An example of Caterpillar's award-winning CSR work is in South America, where in 2003 Caterpillar Brazil earned its fifth Brazilian Public Affairs award for development of the 'Whispers in the Forest' project – a recreation of the Brazilian rain forest which has been visited by over 80,000 Brazilian students.

Caterpillar has also won plaudits for its achievements in providing education. The Caterpillar University, an internal organisation responsible for developing learning initiatives at the company, recently took first place at the third annual Corporate University Best in Class (CUBIC) awards. Additionally, David Vance, president of Caterpillar University, was honoured with the Corporate University Leader of the Year Award.

Caterpillar has built a reputation for its efforts to protect the environment and launched the Caterpillar Environmental Excellence Awards to honour Cat facilities that are succeeding in becoming more environmentally friendly. To date, these awards have recognised projects which have resulted in significant reductions of landfill waste, hazardous waste, and wastewater discharge.

Caterpillar has been able to reduce direct greenhouse gas emissions from its facilities by 35% since 1990 in the US alone. Several of the company's largest facilities are in the process of converting from coal-based power to alternative energy sources.

History

The story of Caterpillar began over one hundred years ago, in Stockton, California. This is when Benjamin Holt first demonstrated his innovative design for a new type of tractor, moving on self-laying tracks, on Thanksgiving Day, November 24th 1904. The machine was revolutionary and ultimately lead to the formation of Caterpillar Tractor Co, the predecessor of Caterpillar Inc.

Regarded as one of the 20th century's greatest inventions, track-type tractors have cemented their place in history by being at the forefront of massive and majestic projects such as the Hoover Dam, the US Interstate Highway System, the Golden Gate Bridge, the Trans Alaska Pipeline System, the Saint Lawrence Seaway, the Channel Tunnel and the Three Gorges Dam in China.

In 1931, the company created a separate engine sales group to market diesel engines to other original equipment manufacturers. This group was replaced in 1953 with a sales and marketing division to better serve the needs of a broad range of engine customers.

In 1963, Caterpillar and Mitsubishi Heavy Industries Ltd formed one of the first joint ventures in Japan to include US ownership. Caterpillar Mitsubishi Ltd started production in 1965 in a new facility at Sagamihara, 28 miles south west of Tokyo. Renamed Shin Caterpillar Mitsubishi Ltd in 1987 to reflect an expansion of the original agreement, the joint venture today is the second largest maker of construction and mining equipment in Japan.

Following a boom period in the 1970s, the worldwide recession of the early 1980s forced Caterpillar to look at long-term changes to lessen the adverse impact of future economic downturns. Among the changes was a US$1.8 billion modernisation programme, launched in 1987 to streamline the manufacturing process. Caterpillar also diversified its product line to meet a greater variety of customer needs and to reduce sensitivity to economic cycles.

Over the course of time the company has grown and diversified to incorporate many other areas, including Caterpillar Financial Services Corporation and Caterpillar Insurance, both established for the benefit of Cat dealers and end users. Meanwhile, Caterpillar Service Technology Group provides Cat dealers with a single source for tools, supplies and shop equipment.

Product

Caterpillar's product line comprises more than 300 different models of earthmoving machines, diesel engines, and gas turbines. Caterpillar engines power everything from trucks, buses, ships, pleasure boats and locomotives to earthmoving, construction and material-handling equipment. Caterpillar is the world's largest manufacturer of medium speed engines, as well as one of the world's largest manufacturers of high speed diesel engines, with ratings available from 54 to 13,600 hp (40 to 10,000 kW).

Through generating systems, Cat engines supply power to areas inaccessible to utility power grids, including off-shore oil drilling rigs, remote mines and isolated communities. Cat generator sets provide emergency power to hospitals, schools, factories, office buildings and airports. Caterpillar is also the leading supplier of industrial gas turbines through its subsidiary Solar Turbines Incorporated, purchased in 1981.

Caterpillar's global dealer network is an important aspect of its product offering, providing a key competitive edge. Cat dealers serve equipment, service and financing needs for customers in more than 200 countries. Rental services are offered through more than 1,400 outlets worldwide. Almost all dealerships are independent and locally owned, with many having long-standing relationships with their customers.

Caterpillar is also one of the world's largest re-manufacturers, re-manufacturing more than two million units annually, and recycling tonnes of used products in the process. Caterpillar Remanufacturing Services allow clients to leverage Caterpillar's technology, scale and global reach while at the same time lowering its warranty costs.

Caterpillar is a major provider of logistics, with its Logistics Services division providing world-class supply chain solutions and services to its parent company, Caterpillar Inc, and more than 50 other leading corporations throughout the world. Headquartered in Morton, Illinois, Caterpillar Logistics operates more than 100 offices and facilities in 25 countries on six continents and serves companies in diverse market sectors, including automotive service parts, industrial service parts, consumer durables, technology and electronics manufacturing logistics, and aerospace service parts.

Recent Developments

In 2003, Caterpillar became the first engine manufacturer to offer a complete line of diesel engines fully compliant and certified by the US Environmental Protection Agency (EPA). Caterpillar's breakthrough emissions control technology is designed to comply with EPA standards without sacrificing performance, reliability or fuel efficiency. The company used its proprietary ACERT® Technology to achieve this. ACERT Technology is an innovative performance-enhancement and emissions-reduction solution for diesel engines which Caterpillar developed as part of a long-term effort to create cleaner-running engines that maintain performance, efficiency, and service life.

ACERT Technology is advanced combustion technology that provides a higher degree of control over a larger number of combustion variables than ever possible before. This, combined with advances in air management and electronic control improves the overall performance of diesel engines while reducing harmful emissions.

Along with enhancing overall engine performance, ACERT Technology enables Caterpillar to produce engines that meet increasingly stringent worldwide emissions standards, such as new regulations for diesel engines in the US and European Union, plus standards for marine engines set by the International Maritime Organisation.

Cat engines with elements of ACERT Technology for road vehicles were first introduced in October of 2002. That same year, Caterpillar became one of North America's largest suppliers of school bus engines with the signing of a long-term engine supply agreement with Blue Bird Corporation, North America's leading school bus manufacturer. ACERT Technology is now being introduced in off-road applications. By meeting Environmental Protection Agency Tier 3 emissions standards, Caterpillar has reduced emissions in off-road machines by 70% since 1990. By 2014, Caterpillar plans to reduce emissions by an additional 90%.

Promotion

Caterpillar's use of trademark-licensed merchandise has historically played, and continues to play, a very important role working with Caterpillar business units and dealers to support marketing efforts, special events, and promotions.

Scale models of Caterpillar are an important part of this licensing programme, and have been in existence for more than 35 years, servicing Caterpillar business units, dealers, and the general public. With over 100 models in the range, they help broaden awareness of the types of real equipment Caterpillar manufactures and markets, ranging from Track-Type Tractors to Landfill Compactors.

In the early 1990s, Caterpillar expanded this merchandise strategy to embrace consumer-oriented branded products. Rugged work boots have become a particularly successful line, with obvious relevance to the core brand. The strategy has paid dividends, with over 56 million pairs of Cat Footwear sold through 2004, providing the company with the opportunity to positively influence new consumers who may or may not have direct experience of Caterpillar products. Most recently, Caterpillar is using its association with construction to develop construction-themed toys, such as bulldozers, big trucks, loaders, and excavators, and a new range under the brand of Equipped to PLAY™.

Another opportunity for brand awareness is through sponsorship. 2005 is Caterpillar's 12th year as sponsor in the NACSCAR racing venue in the US and in Australia, Caterpillar has teamed up with Ford Performance Racing to field a team on the V8 Supercar Circuit – the CAT FPR Race Team. With three-time series winning Craig Lowndes at the wheel, the CAT FPR Race Team is becoming a regular winner on the circuit.

Brand Values

For more than 75 years, Caterpillar Inc has been building the world's infrastructure, and in partnership with Caterpillar dealers, is driving positive and sustainable change on every continent. Caterpillar has a vision to be the global leader in customer value and has created a brand for which the watchwords are ruggedness, durability and reliability.

www.cat.com

THINGS YOU DIDN'T KNOW ABOUT

Caterpillar

> Caterpillar invested nearly US$670 million in research and technology in 2003.

> Worldwide, Caterpillar's employees have earned more than 3,700 patents since 1997.

> Caterpillar participated in the first crossing of North Atlantic in an open inflatable boat powered by a Cat Marine engine.

> A Taurus Sports racing car – powered by an advanced engine using Perkins Technology and Cat electronics – was debuted at the 2004 LeMans 24 hour race, becoming the first diesel-powered entry in 50 years.

The Chartered Institute of Marketing

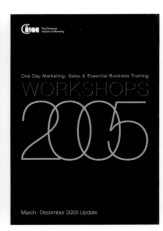

Market

The Chartered Institute of Marketing (CIM) is a leading player among the raft of membership and training organisations set up over the past century to support the UK's growing sales and marketing industry. CIM campaigns to ensure that sales and marketing work closely with other areas of the business to enhance shareholder value, and that business leaders recognise the contribution that marketing makes to the bottom line. CIM's qualifications and training represent the quality standard in marketing, and are recognised as such by major corporates around the world.

CIM has over 50,000 members worldwide, with 72% of members in the UK and 28% of members overseas in more than 130 countries. Around half of them are aged between 30 and 45, and the majority work at middle manager level and above, with over a quarter of them operating at Director level.

CIM leads the development of professional marketing standards and practice, and champions big issues and new ideas in the marketing world. This pivotal position means that it can help marketers do a better job, building their credibility, knowledge and contacts, as well as their professionalism.

Achievements

CIM was the first institute in the field of marketing to publish professional standards. Furthermore, it became the only professional marketing organisation to hold a Royal Charter, when this status was granted in 1989. The number of Chartered Marketers now stands at 4,500.

All members receive CIM's membership magazine, the marketer. This publication has seen success in its own right, having won Business to Business Front Cover of the Year at the 2004 Magazine Design Awards.

History

On May 16th 1911 twelve sales managers met at the Inns of Court Hotel in London to form the Sales Managers Association (SMA), with the aim of improving sales techniques and putting their role on a more professional footing. The SMA held regular dinner meetings addressed by prominent businessmen and public figures.

Ten years later the association was incorporated and changed its name to the Incorporated Sales Managers' Association, or ISMA. The organisation continued to grow and in 1925 ISMA held its first national conference and launched its magazine. Three years later it held its first annual 'Certificate' examinations. In 1929 the second national conference inaugurated the annual conference programme, which has attracted delegates and influential speakers from across the country, and, more recently, the world, ever since. In 1931 the ISMA magazine was renamed Marketing.

In 1934 the association revised its examination syllabus and set up an annual system of intermediate and final exams. The first finals were taken a year later, with successful candidates becoming eligible for 'Associateship'. The association published its first paper, on market research.

In 1940 the association contributed to the war effort with the first correspondence courses for service personnel. Captain Guy Ward, a prisoner of war in Germany, won the Pickup Medal for the most successful student. In 1943, the Sales Managers' Association of Philadelphia in the US presented ISMA with its Howard J Ford Award in recognition of its wartime efforts, as a tribute to 'courage and enterprise in carrying on the essential functions of distribution while meeting the demands of a nation at war.'

In 1946 ISMA expanded its definition of sales management to include 'distribution', and by 1960 its membership had grown to 8,000, and it changed its name to the Institute of Marketing and Sales Management. It reintroduced its examination the following year as the Diploma, with successful candidates eligible to use the letters 'DipM' after their names.

In 1965 it established the first chair in Marketing, at the University of Lancaster, an innovation adopted so enthusiastically by others that by 2000 there were 38 marketing professors across the UK. The same year it founded the College of Marketing – a permanent residential faculty providing seminars and short, intensive courses.

By 1968 annual student registrations had grown to around 2,500 and the number of technical colleges offering the Diploma to 108, and the institute changed its name again to the Institute of Marketing.

In 1971 the institute launched new marketing groups for specific industries, including construction, travel, hotels, agriculture, transport and distribution, and moved from Marketing House in Holborn to Moor Hall, a nine-acre site in Cookham, Berkshire. The following year it launched residential courses for all levels of marketers, and within twelve months was running over 80 courses a year, becoming Europe's largest examining,

training and servicing body in marketing by the end of the decade.

In 1975 the Royal College of Arms authorised the institute's use of the motto 'The world is our market' and in 1980 it took the bold decision that future Fellowship and full membership would be by qualification.

In 1984 the institute redefined its strategic objectives and in 1985 it launched a new logo and strapline, 'Marketing means business'.

In 1989 the institute became chartered, and in 1998 the concept of 'Individual Chartered Marketer', which recognises personal achievement in theory, practical experience and expertise, was launched. Only full members and Fellows of CIM committed to Continuing Professional Development (CPD) can hold chartered status.

In 2003 CIM announced its vision to become the world's leading professional body for marketing by 2010, and during the next two years it launched a new range of benefits for members.

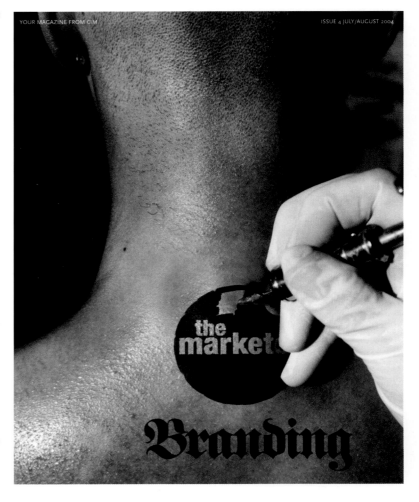

Professional Marketing
Qualifications

Professional
Sales Qualifications

How to Join

Professional Marketing
Communications Qualifications

Product

CIM offers a range of internationally recognised qualifications for both new and experienced marketers. These include a Professional Postgraduate Diploma in Marketing, a Professional Diploma in Marketing, a Professional Certificate in Marketing and an Introductory Certificate in Marketing. Diplomates can put the letters FCIM (Fellow), MCIM (Member) or ACIM (Associate) after their names, and FCIMs and MCIMs may go on to earn the prestigious Chartered Marketer status by completing the required CPD.

The qualifications are based on CIM's newly launched Professional Marketing Standards, which can be used to assess marketing competencies, and to set, plan and develop marketing skills improvement. The Professional Marketing Standards at www.cim.co.uk/standards outline six key marketing competencies at four levels of seniority. The marketing roles established through research are: research and analysis, planning, managing brands, implementing marketing programmes, measuring marketing effectiveness and managing marketing people.

As well as gaining a globally recognised qualification, studying members have access to a huge range of high-quality study support and resources. In addition to a unique and extensive marketing Information and Library Service, CIM offers the 'Learning Zone' at www.cim.co.uk/learningzone, a website containing 'how to' guides, online jobs, a case study archive and access to past papers, which is accessible 24-hours a day, seven days a week.

'Cutting Edge' at www.cim.co.uk/cuttingedge, a weekly e-news round-up from the leading marketing and business press, allows members and students to stay up-to-date, while the monthly magazine the marketer (www.cim.co.uk/themarketer) contains contemporary and inspiring international views on current issues, together with in-depth case studies and expert opinion.

CIM students and qualified members are entitled to a raft of member benefits. For example,

www.cim.co.uk/knowledgehub, the web's leading source of marketing intelligence, offers free online access to business and marketing journals and a database of global company profiles. Meanwhile, www.shapetheagenda.com presents the best new ideas from academics and practitioners from around the world, along with links to a wealth of resources to help marketers respond to new challenges.

Around the world, regional CIM branches offer regular opportunities to meet other marketers, hear inspirational speakers and share marketing best practice. Moor Hall, the institute's headquarters in Cookham, Berkshire, offers training rooms, meeting rooms, state-of-the-art conference facilities, accommodation and leisure activities, that can be used to hold business meetings, launch products or host social events, with special rates for members.

In total CIM offers over 135 marketing and sales courses for people wanting to learn more about the discipline. These include intensive residential courses, one-day workshops, part-time study, e-learning and blended learning, which comprises a combination of distance learning, online learning and face to face delivery. Training is conducted either at one of CIM's dedicated training centres or in-company.

CIM Academy (www.cimacademy.com) affords an additional study route for sales and marketing professionals serious about gaining internationally recognised qualifications to accelerate their career. Courses are tailored according to experience and study needs, and include online and traditional classroom solutions.

Recent Developments

In 2003 and 2004 it launched an impressive list of new and enhanced training and member benefits. It rationalised the training portfolio to give more emphasis to board-level training needs; it introduced a new portfolio of professional qualifications in marketing, communications and sales, including a new postgraduate diploma; and introduced a new company membership programme, Company Connect, an exclusive package of benefits for senior marketers in the UK's leading companies. In 2004 it launched a brand new membership magazine, the marketer. The website was developed significantly with facilities such as the 'Knowledge Hub', the launch of quarterly agendas focusing on topical issues and new ideas, and the 'Learning Zone' to give students and tutors a complete range of online study resources.

Promotion

CIM undertakes extensive PR activities to raise the status of marketers and marketing within business. The website, email and direct marketing campaigns all ensure that training products, marketing and promotion reflect CIM's ability to help organisations put marketing at the heart of their business. Each year the institute holds a well-attended conference, and its magazine, the marketer, helps reinforce its values and positioning as the leading professional marketing organisation.

CIM has a strong moral code, supporting local and national charities with key input from staff. CIM has a long-established Benevolent Fund, which supports members in financial difficulties.

Brand Values

CIM's core values were established in 1911 and have been developed over almost 100 years. The institute is recognised around the world as a trusted professional body, whose purpose is to lead the marketing industry forwards. Through the high calibre and heritage of its qualifications and training, CIM defines UK marketing standards and champions best practice globally, enabling its members to deliver exceptional results for their organisations. CIM's vision is to be the world's leading professional marketing body, and its business purpose is to help all marketers do a better job.

www.cim.co.uk

THINGS YOU DIDN'T KNOW ABOUT

CIM

> HRH Prince Philip is the patron of CIM.

> CIM's current President is Lord Heseltine. Former CIM Presidents include Lord Leverhulme and Lord Colin Marshall of Knightsbridge. Past 'Marketers of the Year' have included Dame Margaret Thatcher and Princess Anne.

> Moor Hall, CIM headquarters, was once a film studio, designed to rival Walt Disney. Staff included some of the cartoon and film industry's brightest newcomers, such as a young Bob Monkhouse.

> CIM has 50,000 members in 130 countries.

> CIM Information and Library Service is the largest specialist marketing library in Europe, with over 120 journal titles, 21,500 market research reports, 6,400 reference books and more than 4,000 general marketing titles.

Market

CIMA (The Chartered Institute of Management Accountants) is the largest professional body in the world whose sole focus is the qualification and support of accountants in business.

CIMA's members work in all sectors of industry, commerce, not-for-profit and public sector organisations and small and medium sized enterprises (SMEs).

CIMA supports some of the world's leading employers and course providers around the globe to educate, train and qualify first-class financial managers and strategists. CIMA prides itself on the commercial relevance of its syllabus which is regularly updated to reflect the latest business developments and employer needs. According to an independent survey by Robert Half in 2004, CIMA remains the most popular choice of accountancy qualifications.

Achievements

From its ten international divisions/branches and headquarters in London, CIMA supports over 65,000 members and 85,000 students in 156 countries. In the year to October 1st 2004, CIMA experienced a 15% growth in new membership and a 29% growth in student recruitment.

CIMA members work throughout the commercial world with over half working for an organisation with an annual turnover of £50 million or more. Some 15% of working members are finance directors (including chief financial officers) and 14% are financial controllers, while 7% are chief executive officers, managing directors or other board directors. The CIMA qualification is regarded as a leading global professional business qualification as its scope extends far beyond accountancy.

CIMA seeks leading industry partners and has developed partnerships with companies such as

Rolls-Royce, Shell and Marks & Spencer. CIMA recognises the importance of input from and requirements of multi-national business.

CIMA Training provides a ready-made package for employers to ensure that the training of Chartered Management Accountants is delivered everywhere to the same consistently high standard.

CIMA made a considerable investment in developing products and services before launching its new generation qualification in 2004. Developed with the University of Bath School of Management, the professional chartered management accounting qualification takes CIMA into a league of its own, especially when it comes to supporting members' ongoing professional development.

A significant development on CIMA's lifelong learning agenda occurred when CIMA entered in to partnership with the Henley Management College to provide a fast track through the college's prestigious MBA programme. Additionally CIMA secured access for all its members to Harvard Business School Publishing's Harvard ManageMentorPlus e-learning package.

CIMA has entered the corporate governance debate wholeheartedly and has contributed to the evolution of boardroom behaviour and corporate culture. CIMA's report 'Performance Reporting to Boards' was sent to the UK's top 250 finance directors and audit committee members. The report sets out principles for reporting both financial and non-financial information, the systems that need to be in place for it, and crucially, the culture that supports it.

Following a series of high profile failures over the past few years, it has never been more important for accountants to uphold the highest standards and show integrity. Ethics play an increasing role in business, and CIMA's qualification reflects that.

History

In 1919 the 'Institute of Cost and Works Accountants' was founded, its objective being to provide the range of information needed to plan and manage modern business. In 1975 the Institute was granted the Royal Charter.

The Institute changed its name to 'The Chartered Institute of Management Accountants' in 1986, recognising the importance and commercial relevance of management accounting and in 1995 CIMA's members were given the right to use the title 'Chartered Management Accountant'.

The CIMA network has now grown to include divisions in Australia, Hong Kong, Ireland, India, Malaysia, Singapore, South Africa, Sri Lanka and Zambia.

Product

It has never been more important for accountants to demonstrate integrity and ethical standards. CIMA plays an essential role in protecting the public interest by regulating its members and contributing to the ongoing development of the profession through technical research and development.

Today's marketplace demands a qualification that is desirable to employers. CIMA qualified people bring more than basic accounting skills to the table. They take a strategic view of the future; what it will look like; the demands it will present; and what it will take to achieve success. CIMA has a total business focus with 99% of CIMA members and students working in business.

Overall, CIMA provides more management, more management accounting, more project management and more strategy than any other UK accounting qualification. CIMA's unique blend of academic training and practical experience continues to provide employers with what they want, which is known to be 'Chartered Management Accountants who have leading edge skills to drive business growth'.

Unlike other accountancy qualifications, TOPCIMA (the case study and final test of professional competence) tests for business awareness and the higher level cognitive skills of analysis, synthesis and evaluation. This requires students to take account of business, financial, ethical and human resource strategy issues which are all part of the syllabus.

There are other unique elements of the syllabus that aim to ensure that the CIMA Professional Qualification stands out from its competitors as the chartered qualification of choice for business.

CIMA is the first UK professional accounting body to give its commitment to promoting the lifelong employability of its members as part of a lifelong learning philosophy. CIMA's Lifelong Employability Framework is relevant to all individuals within and beyond the finance community who wish to develop competence and knowledge in financial management. This framework supports individual requirements for continuing professional development at all levels: knowledge development in key specialist areas; CIMA Certificate

SUCCESS *m*

the power of financial management in business

in Business Accounting; CIMA Advanced Diploma in Management Accounting; CIMA Professional Qualification; and Director level training appropriate for Fellowship of CIMA.

CIMA offers support benefits to members specifically designed to help them progress and develop their career. The aim is to provide benefits that help secure greater employability for its members. They are grouped into three areas: CIMA provides a high-quality range of tools, planners and extensive learning resources to assist in Professional Development and specific CPD activity; CIMA also provides benefits designed to support members in their careers and general working lives. These include guidance on professional standards, networking facilities and access to career progression opportunities. In addition, CIMA offers a range of specially negotiated, work related offers with reputable third parties. These 'best of breed' opportunities can be requested online and provide value to members.

Supporting CIMA's qualification is a range of complementary and dynamic products and services. CIMA Publishing and CIMA Mastercourses keep students and members fully updated on commercial issues, and its research team takes a proactive look at the shape of business to come.

CIMA Publishing is the specialist publisher in management accounting, producing a comprehensive and informative range of books, guides and CD Roms.

CIMA Mastercourses offer an extensive programme of financial and business management seminars held throughout the UK. These courses can be tailored to individual company needs.

CIMA's technical activities cover three key areas, namely the Technical Information Service, which aims to help members with work-related queries; the Research Foundation, which funds an ongoing programme of academic research in the field of management accountancy; and a range of technical products and services on topics of interest to management accountants.

The CIMA Training programme sets out quality standards with significant benefits to both employers and students: increasing the ability to attract and retain the brightest students and results in greatly improved motivation and examination pass rates.

Recent Developments
CIMA Professional Development is a key focus for 2005. CIMA has been working closely with its membership to develop a Professional Development Policy and framework that fully supports them, contributes towards CIMA's purpose – the ever greater employability of its

members – and satisfies revised requirements of IFAC (International Federation of Accountants). CIMA's policy is driven by the outcomes of members' development activity, and not by the hours spent undertaking it. This will mean new levels of support and new products to enhance members' professional development, as well as providing ethical and accountability assurances to the public.

Computer based assessment (CBA) revolutionised examination assessment in August 2001 in the UK. This service has now recently been made available to all CIMA students globally. CBA is available for the five Certificate level subjects. This means that students can sit the relevant subject exams at any time during the year and progress to the subsequent Managerial level papers.

There has been a great deal of change in the corporate world in recent years which prompted CIMA to undertake extensive international research into the CIMA syllabus, ensuring the ever increasing employability of members and students, and maintaining and enhancing the CIMA brand. CIMA has introduced new structure, new content and new assessment for its new Professional Qualification.

Promotion
CIMA instigated a number of brand initiatives in 2004 in order to reflect the current organisation and its aspirations. These initiatives included CIMA's Annual Conference in November 2004 which was followed by the Annual CIMA and 'Financial Management' Awards. The awards attracted a large number of submissions from organisations including HSBC, AMEX, Procter & Gamble, Morgan Stanley and the Metropolitan Police.

The CIMA Conference attracted some 250 delegates from its membership around the world. Key note speakers included Roger Bootle – one of the City of London's best-known economists, Marta Andreasen – whistleblower and former Chief Accounting Officer and Budget Execution Director for the European Commission and Ken Farrow – Head of the City of London Police Economic Crime Department.

Aside from the conference and awards, CIMA organises its CIMA Training Annual Conference for employers. This event enables companies to learn about best practice for training their in-house finance managers, how to implement training schemes for employees and how to get the best out of their graduates. In addition CIMA visited some of the larger organisations individually in a series of employer roadshows.

In 2004 CIMA underwent a re-branding exercise to reflect the changes in the syllabus and to differentiate itself from other accounting bodies. The updated brand identity is dynamic and inventive, and challenges assumptions about the stereotype of accountants. This re-branding was furthered when, CIMA co-sponsored with CODA, a software company, an initiative called 'Extreme Accounting'. The Extreme Accounting website takes a light-hearted look at accounting (www.extreme-accounting.com).

CIMA's press office provides opinion to the business world via the media and representatives are regularly interviewed by national and trade publications and make regular contributions through articles and comment.

CIMA also promotes itself internally and has an internal branding programme, engaging staff with the brand through the CIMA Values project.

the power of financial management in business

In 2003, CIMA successfully met the criteria to continue to be recognised as an Investor in People. CIMA constantly monitors itself ensuring that managers within the Institute own these standards and that staff understand CIMA's commitment to upholding them. In late 2004 CIMA conducted an internal staff survey which effectively acted as a 'health check' ensuring CIMA meets its obligations to staff.

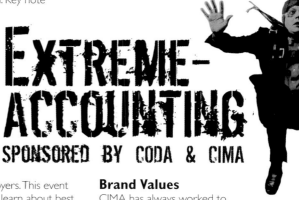

Brand Values
CIMA has always worked to maintain the highest standards in serving its students, members and business partners.

Everything CIMA does reflects five core values that drive its relationships with its students and members, ensuring a consistent internal company culture and one that is understood, supported and lived by all CIMA employees. These values are: Customer focused, Professional, Open, Accountable and Innovative.

CIMA's purpose, vision and mission also give it a very definite sense of direction: Purpose – the ever greater employability of CIMA members; Vision – CIMA members driving the world's successful organisations; and Mission – to be the first choice for employers in the qualification and development of professional accountants in business.

www.cimaglobal.com

YOU^m

the power of financial management in business

THINGS YOU DIDN'T KNOW ABOUT

CIMA

> CIMA supports leading academic research into management accounting and related business issues.

> 35% of members earn between £50,000–£90,000, whilst 6% earn in excess of £100,000.

> One fifth of CIMA's members are employed in the public sector.

> CIMA closely aligns itself with higher education establishments including the Harvard Business School, INSEAD and the Henley Management College.

CNBC EUROPE

Market

In today's economy, businesses and investors operate across borders and time zones in a 24-hour world. In this environment, the demand for up to the minute news has never been greater, especially in business where having the right information at the right time, can help you stay one step ahead. Demand for real-time TV coverage of international business affairs is also driven by greater integration of financial markets, as well as political issues, such as the recent expansion of the European Union and increased pan-European regulation.

The pan-European TV market attracts US$200 million every year in advertising revenue (Source: PETV Group) and the market is expected to grow by 5% per year. Pan-European TV viewing has increased every year since 1997, with news and business channels growing particularly fast. TV has overtaken print as the most important source of information for affluent Europeans.

CNBC Europe is a key player in this ultra-competitive market, where news providers such as BBC World, CNN and Bloomberg vie to provide exclusive news, around the clock.

According to audience research conducted in 2004 by EMS, which measures the media habits of Europe's top 20% income earners, CNBC Europe increased its daily and weekly viewing figures in 2003-2004. The results show that CNBC Europe is the most watched business and financial news channel in Europe, outreaching Bloomberg on a weekly basis by 13% and on a monthly basis by 27%.

EMS audience data also shows that the channel attracts more elite international viewers than any of its rivals, being the most-watched business news channel among groups earning over €150,000. It is also the most popular channel amongst CEOs, doubling its daily audience between 2003 and 2004.

Furthermore, CNBC Europe's own research shows a particularly strong performance in the UK and Germany with year on year audience growth of 47% and 74% respectively.

Achievements

Since its launch in 1998, CNBC Europe has become synonymous with business broadcasting in Europe. It has quickly established itself as the only pan-European real-time financial and business channel dedicated to European CEOs, senior executives, the European financial services industry and European investors. It has built a strong distribution, available in 85 million homes, 1,400 banks and financial institutions and 340,000 four and five-star hotel rooms throughout Europe.

With recent research by GfK Media showing it has an average audience of 2.6 million viewers every week in the UK, CNBC Europe is able to reach its valuable and influential audience better than any of its rivals, many of which have been established longer.

Its team of expert business journalists and presenters help CNBC Europe break the major financial stories of the day and provide up-to-the-minute market information and detailed analysis and interviews with business leaders.

The quality of its product has helped CNBC Europe win numerous awards. For example, its best-known show, 'Squawk Box Europe', which provides commentary and analysis of the business issues of the day from leading business figures making the news, was voted Most Influential TV Brand by Campaign magazine in 2003. Another of its shows, 'Advantage Technology', sponsored by Sun Microsystems, won Best Corporate Campaign, at the M&M Awards 2004. The campaign consisted of twelve half-hour weekly programmes bringing together high-profile CEOs to discuss their experience in addressing business issues through technology.

History

CNBC was first launched by the National Broadcasting Company (NBC) in the US in 1989. NBC has been a pioneer in the television industry for more than 70 years and has a strong heritage of innovative television programming and technology. CNBC quickly led the market in television business news and broke new ground as the first television company to broadcast directly from the floor of the New York Stock Exchange.

In December 1997, NBC and Dow Jones & Company entered into a global business television alliance, bringing together the most recognised business-news brands in the world – the Wall Street Journal, CNBC and Dow Jones. Together, NBC and Dow Jones strengthened their international operations, drawing on Dow Jones' editorial resources including Dow Jones Newswires, and NBC properties such as NBC News and MSNBC.

CNBC Europe was established in 1998 as Europe's dedicated financial and business TV news network, catering for people who need to be informed about the latest business developments, with real time, up-to-the-minute data they can act and trade upon.

In May 2004, CNBC Europe's parent, NBC, merged with Vivendi Universal Entertainment to create a new world-leading media and entertainment company, NBC Universal. The new company's revenues in 2005 are expected to be in the region of US$15 billion. The deal puts CNBC Europe at the heart of a family of world-famous media brands, including Telemundo, Sci-Fi Channel, Bravo, Universal Pictures and Universal Studios.

Product

CNBC Europe is the leading pan-European real-time business and financial TV channel, providing live market information and analysis. The channel broadcasts 24-hours a day directly from the major financial centres in Europe, the US and Asia and also has bases in Paris,

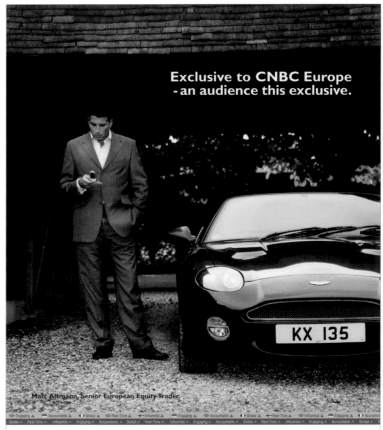

Exclusive to CNBC Europe - an audience this exclusive.

Marc Altmann, Senior European Equity Trader.

Marc Altmann is not a typical TV viewer. But he is a typical CNBC Europe viewer. A Senior European Equity Trader in the city, he drives an Aston Martin, has a house in the country, and has the means to enjoy the best things in life.

Marc is part of an extremely affluent European demographic that would be difficult to reach without CNBC Europe. He says "I very, very rarely watch television", yet watches CNBC Europe in the office, in the gym, and at home in the evening. That's because to Marc and other viewers like him, CNBC Europe is not a TV channel; it's a business tool that offers valuable, real-time information.

If you'd like to reach our exclusive and elusive audience, call Liz Jones on +44 (0)20 7653 9421.

CNBC EUROPE
a service of NBC Universal and Dow Jones

Get a briefing from the CEO every morning

Squawk Box Europe, CNBC Europe's signature show, provides commentary and analysis of the day's big business stories in the run-up to the opening bell across Europe.

Every day, presenter Geoff Cutmore invites a leading executive such as Kevin Roberts, CEO, Saatchi & Saatchi (pictured) to be guest host, and to answer questions about their own business and other burning issues of the day. So if you want to stay in the know, stay tuned to CNBC Europe – the channel that sets the agenda for the European business day.

today's business	squawk box)))	morning exchange ▶⊐	▶ power lunch	closing bell ◉	europe tonight ◉
06.00 - 0.700 CET	07.00 - 10.00 CET	10.00 - 12.00 CET	12.00 - 13.00 CET	17.00 - 19.00 CET	20.00 - 20.30 CET

For information on how to recieve CNBC Europe please go to www.cnbceurope.com/receiving

www.cnbceurope.com

Frankfurt and Brussels, providing up to the minute news on the financial markets.

CNBC Europe's programming sets it apart from the competition. One of its key visual cues is the CNBC Europe real-time share ticker. It is specific to the channel and is a powerful trading tool, combining live data from all the leading Europe stock exchanges and giving immediate, real-time data on buying and selling activity.

CNBC Europe also displays a 'stack' on the right side of the screen which shows the main blue chip indices of the major markets and currency rates against the euro. These indices automatically update and rotate with the euro and are all live.

The company also has a 21-screen video wall which can display graphics and data from the European markets and industry sectors. It can be used as a large screen for interviewing guests across Europe and displays a map of Europe showing all the exchanges and real time price changes, shown in green and red to represent positive or negative positions.

CNBC Europe has five key programme brands. Viewers can wake up to a summary of the day's events on 'Today's Business', followed by the lively and topical financial market pre-opening show, 'Squawk Box Europe'. This award-winning programme attracts some of the most influential figures in global business, with WPP chairman Sir Martin Sorrell and Saatchi & Saatchi CEO Kevin Roberts making regular appearances.

The morning schedule also includes 'Morning Exchange', which gives an assessment of action in the market, followed by 'Power Lunch' – a report of the first half of the trading day – and 'European Closing Bell', a pacy wrap-up of markets across Europe and a review of the business day.

Many of CNBC Europe's presenters have had careers as financial professionals, ensuring they can provide expert in-depth analysis and commentary on the business and financial stories of the day, combined with style, wit and humour.

The channel offers a range of advertising and sponsorship tools, tailored to individual client needs. It offers traditional spot campaigns, promotions, sponsored features and also sponsored programming opportunities. The award-winning 'Advantage Technology', sponsored by Sun Microsystems, is an example of the success in this type of advertiser-funded programming. Another is 'Long Live and Prosper', a six-part series examining the issues of the ageing population. Broadcast on the CNBC network around the world, this was a truly global programme, with the production team taking in ten countries in just 43 days.

CNBC Europe's advertisers, including Airbus, Boeing, Barclays, Chevron Texaco, Cisco Systems, HSBC, Oracle, Rolex, Samsung and UBS, can also take advantage of a special Return on Investment commitment offered by the channel. Using a quarterly survey called Viewertrack, based on a 5,500-strong database of viewers, CNBC Europe measures awareness and perception of an advertiser's product or service and asks their opinion about the quality and effectiveness of their advertising campaign. Awareness and favourability are also tracked throughout the year. If a campaign fails to meet ROI targets set by CNBC Europe, the channel will give the client an incremental discount on any subsequent campaign. CNBC Europe claims it is the only broadcaster to offer this type of service on a continuous basis to its clients.

Recent Developments

CNBC Europe introduced important enhancements to its product in 2004, including redesigning its London studio and introducing a new on-air look. As well as making the studio lighter and introducing new graphics, the identity of CNBC Europe's five business day programmes have also been given a new identity.

The channel also introduced new programming in 2004, including a six-part series covering the media industry, 'Media Talk', and a new daily business round-up show, 'Europe Tonight'.

During 2004, CNBC Europe dedicated significant resources to covering developments with the EU Enlargement process and at the European Central Bank, both of which helped enhance CNBC Europe's

reputation as the destination channel for the most important business stories.

The channel has also increased its industry sector coverage, broadcasting from leading events such as 3GSM, ITU, CeBIT, as well as being the lead broadcaster for the World Economic Forum in Davos.

Elsewhere, CNBC Europe has increased its capacity to provide coverage from other European centres, putting new camera facilities in Madrid and Zurich and also expanding its coverage from Eastern Europe and the Middle East.

Always looking to expand its audience, CNBC Europe is exploring opportunities in new media, developing a broadband streamed video version of CNBC Europe, available on subscription.

CNBC Europe has also invested in making its content available over mobile platforms, launching a live video streaming service to mobile handsets in seventeen European countries. This is the first-ever pan-European 24-hour 'live' broadcast service to mobile phones.

Promotion

CNBC Europe's marketing strategy is to build the brand profile amongst its key audience segments and make it the channel of choice for senior business executives, the financial professional and active private investors.

CNBC Europe's recent trade advertising campaign has used real viewers as the subjects. The campaign focuses on communicating the 'engagement' the viewer has with the channel and the senior business leader profile of its core audience. This campaign runs in a range of publications including M&M Europe, Media Week, the Internationalist and Campaign.

The channel is just embarking on a corporate brand campaign in selected international business media.

To build the brand, CNBC Europe actively participates in some of the world's premier business and industry events. In 2004, it was the official broadcaster at events including the World Economic Forum in Davos, 3GSM in Cannes, CeBIT in Hannover, the World Investment Conference in La Baule and the International Advertising Festival in Cannes.

Other promotional activity includes direct mail shots targeting international media buyers, newsletters and flyers as well as media agency roadshows which take the CNBC Europe sales team around media agencies, twice a year.

Brand Values

CNBC Europe aims to provide its audience with the most relevant, up to the minute news, real-time information, analysis and comment, 24 hours a day. Integrity is at the heart of its business. It is customer-focused and team driven. Its brand is centred on five core attributes: global, real-time, influential, accountable and engaging.

www.cnbceurope.com

THINGS YOU DIDN'T KNOW ABOUT

CNBC Europe

❯ Each year, 3,000 CEOs appear on CNBC Europe, using it as a global forum to deliver their message to an audience of senior decision-makers.

❯ CNBC Europe was the first TV channel to provide 24-hour live streaming to mobile phones.

❯ CNBC Europe reports from ten different stock exchanges across the world.

Market

Corus is an international metals company, providing steel and aluminium products and services to customers worldwide.

With an annual turnover of £8 billion and major operating facilities in the UK, the Netherlands, Germany, France, Norway and Belgium, Corus employs 48,500 people in over 40 countries. Corus comprises four divisions, Strip Products, Long Products, Distribution and Building Systems and Aluminium, and has a comprehensive network of sales offices and service centres worldwide. Corus shares are listed on the London, New York and Amsterdam stock exchanges.

Combining global expertise with local customer service, Corus offers reliability, trust and innovation with the Corus brand representing a mark of quality, loyalty and strength.

Corus is a leading supplier to many of the most demanding markets around the world such as automotive, aerospace, packaging, rail and engineering.

The construction market is one of Corus' most important market sectors accounting for an estimated 30% of the company's turnover. Corus' involvement in construction stretches from research and product development through supply of materials and technical advice. Corus' specialist design team works with architects and consulting engineers across the world to promote the most effective use of its metals.

Achievements

In 2004, Corus made significant progress in terms of turning around financial performance and posted its first ever retained group profit in September 2004.

The brand has also been recognised in its market sectors with various awards for environmental performance, innovation and manufacturing excellence. For example, a Premier Award for Business Commitment to the Environment was awarded to Corus Business, Corus Colors. In addition, two cans co-developed by Corus won Can of the Year Awards in 2004.

The Institution of Mechanical Engineers (IMechE) MX2004 Manufacturing Excellence Award for Resource Efficiency was awarded to Corus Tubes in Corby.

In addition to this, Corus is responsible for some recent impressive projects reflecting its capabilities. Their work includes the production of steel tube for BBL pipeline for gas transportation from the UK to the Netherlands; structural steel for Wembley Stadium in London, World Trade Centre 7 in New York and the prestigious 29-storey Dream Tower development in Jeddah, Saudi Arabia; Kalzip aluminium roof and wall cladding system for the new Grand Theatre in Beijing as well as the supply of inner-body vehicle panel blanks for the new MINI Convertible.

History

Corus was created in October 1999 through the merger of two very strong brands, British Steel (UK steel company) and Koninklijke Hoogovens (Royal Dutch steel and aluminium company).

When the Corus brand was launched it was based on creating one company, with one name, one brand and one vision. The company had a strong ambition to build a metals brand which would be respected worldwide. The name Corus was chosen because it was distinctive, fresh, modern and easily recognisable. It aimed to convey the idea that all the operations within Corus have different strengths but are more powerful when their voices are joined together. This holds as true today as it did when the company was formed in 1999. Corus operates all over the world – but is united by a single brand.

The immediate years following the merger were dominated by financial losses incurred as a result of exchange rate pressures and a declining customer base in the UK. A major restructuring programme was implemented in 2001 which involved job losses and plant closures. However, following the appointment of Philippe Varin as CEO in May 2003, and the implementation of a change programme called 'Restoring Success', Corus announced its first operating profit in September 2004.

Visual identity is defined very precisely in Corus. The re-branding programme after the merger created an opportunity to define a strong identity which would differentiate Corus from its competition. The brand identity is the visual shorthand for recognition, familiarity and loyalty. Corus needs to be seen as one face in a global market, with a strong identity. To achieve this, significant effort was placed in managing brand identity across all Corus operations. Guidelines were produced for work wear,

Understanding is the key to safe behaviour

Competence and behaviour
We will ensure that all our employees are trained so that they are professionally skilled and qualified for their jobs and thereby can contribute to an improved health and safety performance. We will select contractors who can demonstrate competence and effectiveness.

Read the Corus health and safety policy

signage, livery, stationery, literature and merchandise. Consistency was of key importance to avoid confusion and to present a clear, coherent, professional image.

Clarity is the outstanding quality of the Corus mark. It is made up of two elements, a symbol and a wordmark. The large, red 'C' – the symbol – is designed to be instantly recognised.

The key proposition was to 'change the way the world looks at metal'. The challenge was to overturn traditional negative images of the steel industry, which are often associated with pollution, fire and brimstone. The Corus approach focused on the benefits of metal to people in everyday life. The aim was to present metal in a completely fresh way and create a specific photographic style, unique to Corus.

Product

Corus manufactures, processes and distributes many steel and aluminium products for a range of demanding applications. For example, a wide range of construction products and services are available from structural steel for the world's most impressive buildings through to consultancy and advice for architects and engineers; bar and billet is produced for engineering industries; electrical steels for the generation, transmission, distribution and use of electrical power; packaging steels for food, drinks and aerosols, and also for promotional and speciality packaging; rail products and services are supplied to both

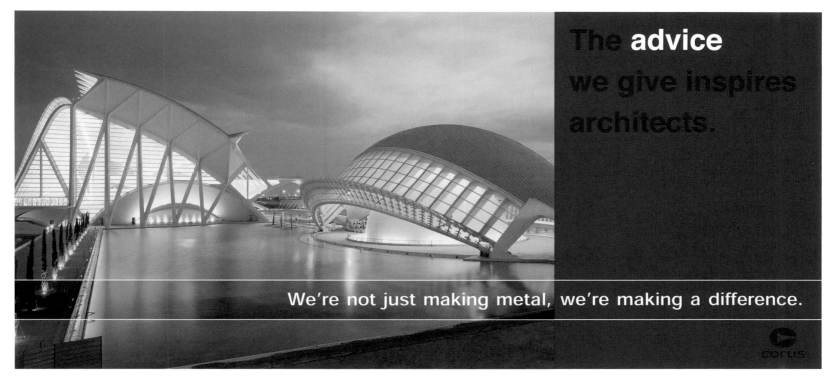

The **advice**
we give inspires
architects.

We're not just making metal, we're making a difference.

corus

nationalised and privatised rail networks; flat and long products are available in a wide variety of specifications for many applications including automotive and domestic appliances; tube products are available for a wide variety of industrial uses. Aluminium products are available for aircraft, vehicle, mould and tool industries. Corus also provides research and development, design and consultancy services across a number of sectors.

Recent Developments
Philippe Varin joined Corus as CEO in May 2003 and a major change programme for Corus named 'Restoring Success' was quickly implemented involving a new leadership team, senior management changes, and a new organisational structure. The objective of Restoring Success is to close Corus' competitive gap by the end of 2006 and create real value for shareholders. The strategic direction was clarified and the main focus is on improved performance, improved health and safety, more efficient customer service and improved profitability. The Restoring Success programme is delivering tangible benefits and improved financial results.

Promotion
Following the initial launch advertising to promote 'The future in metal' campaign in international newspapers, Corus has concentrated its corporate promotional activity on media relations as the main vehicle for its corporate messages. The company has also invested significant effort in ensuring that its internal communications are fully aligned to Company strategy and that all Corus employees are connected to the Restoring Success programme. The communications effectiveness is routinely measured to ensure that employees understand the corporate messages.

Brand values are communicated through poster campaigns e.g. 'we make more than metal, we make a difference', designed to inspire pride and motivation; as well as through the brand's health and safety poster campaign, designed to communicate the importance of the company's health and safety policy.

At the same time the market promotional activity has been targeted at the key market sectors e.g. construction, packaging, rail, oil and gas, and automotive. Corus exhibits all over the world at targeted exhibitions. In addition, it sponsors young designers – for example, the Coventry automotive design awards, the student packaging design awards and young architect of the year awards – to demonstrate its commitment to inspiring young designers to 'Think metal, think Corus'.

In terms of its corporate social responsibility, Corus believes it is an integral part of the communities in which it operates and is passionately committed to ensuring the health and safety of its employees, contractors, visitors and neighbouring communities. A positive health and safety culture is encouraged which does not tolerate unsafe behaviour. Corus aims to continuously improve safety performance and ensure safe operating practices. It also believes that respect for the environment is critical to the success of its business, and therefore strives to continuously improve environmental performance. Indeed, the company has established agreements to improve energy efficiency and reduce emissions of greenhouse gases.

Brand Values
The essence of the Corus brand is about creating value. Its recent promise was to Restore Success by concentrating on Safety, Service and Savings. As the company begins to deliver its promise, it is committed to creating a culture of continuous improvement and achieving a quest for excellence, which will help to

differentiate Corus and position the company as outstanding among its peers.

Corus has behavioural values to support its strategic business objectives and the goal to create value. They include health and safety, passion, teamwork, reliability, trust, openness, respect and integrity.

The market communication values which underpin the brand expression are innovative, proactive and inspiring. The strapline 'The future in metal' encapsulates these values as the brand's promise.

www.corusgroup.com

THINGS YOU DIDN'T KNOW ABOUT

Corus
> In response to growing terrorism and security concerns, Corus has launched 'Surefast'™, a brand new, fast-track modular construction system for high security buildings. With Surefast, explosion resistant buildings can now be built in a fraction of the time usually taken using traditional construction, with build time measured in days instead of months.

> Steel is 100% recyclable.

> The length of steel wire used in the construction of the Akashi Kaikyo bridge in Japan was 300,000km. This would encircle the Earth 7.5 times.

> Corus has reduced its direct emissions of CO_2 by over four million tonnes since 1999. Over the last 30 years, the energy used to make a tonne of steel has reduced by around 40%.

COSTAIN

Market

The construction industry is one of the largest sectors of the UK economy, with a value of £98,298 million in 2004 (Source: MBD).

The market has increased by 63% since 2000, when total construction output was valued at £60,184 million. In fact, construction output has risen for nine consecutive years up to 2004, with the market fuelled by low interest rates and good employment levels.

New construction activity accounted for 54% of the industry's output in 2004, with the balance directed towards repair and maintenance work.

Two areas which have catalysed growth in the construction industry in recent years have been private housing and private commercial construction. According to MBD, the private housing construction market experienced a two-fold increase between 2000 and 2003, with an estimated value in 2004 of £18,285 million. Meanwhile, the private commercial construction sector increased by 18% between 2000 and 2002 to £14,966 million, with the analysts predicting an output for 2004 of £16,713 million.

The supply side of the UK construction industry is highly fragmented, comprising some 167,178 companies (Source: MBD), of which 32% are engaged in specialist trades. It is an industry spanning very small and very large players, with 71% of companies earning less than £250,000 in 2004. According to MBD, only 1% of companies earned more than £5 million from the sector in 2003 and 2004.

With a turnover of £623.5 million in 2003, and employing nearly 12,000 people worldwide, Costain falls into this category of international construction groups, competing against other major players such as Mowlem, McAlpine and Bovis.

In recent times many in the construction industry, clients and contractors, have adopted a more mature approach to the business and opted for best out-turn value rather than lowest tender cost. This has created a disciplined approach to service delivery rather than contractual protection and has produced benefits for both client and contractor alike. Costain has played a major role in this cultural change.

Achievements

Costain's portfolio of projects includes some of the world's largest and most challenging construction projects, including the Channel Tunnel Rail Link, The Thames Barrier, the new headquarters for the Met Office and the Tsing Ma Suspension bridge in Hong Kong –

the world's longest combined road and rail bridge. The 2,170m double-decked bridge, which carries road and rail traffic, received both the Supreme and Civil Engineering Awards from the British Construction Industry. Costain joined a three way Anglo Japanese construction joint venture to build this £550 million contract. Costain is also responsible for the construction of the Diamond Synchrotron – the largest scientific facility to be built in the UK for 30 years. The facility, in Oxfordshire, will enable scientists and engineers to probe deep into the basic structure of matter and materials answering fundamental questions about everything from the building blocks of life to the origin of our planet.

Through projects such as this, Costain has built a reputation for being at the forefront of the construction industry, with an emphasis on high-calibre skills and premier service. It has also become a household name, admired and respected throughout the world of engineering and construction.

History

Costain has a distinct pedigree which dates back to 1865 when Richard Costain – a 26 year old jobbing builder from the Isle of Man with vision – founded the original construction business in Liverpool. For 140 years Costain has been at the forefront of UK and international construction and was floated as a public company in 1933 with a share capital of £600,000.

Costain's achievements have shaped landscapes across the globe. For example, in the mid 1920s Costain

built houses throughout south east England – 1,000 houses were built in Selsdon alone – for £425 each. Furthermore, in 1935, Costain built eleven miles of the Trans-Iranian Railway, seven tunnels and two viaducts in isolated mountainous terrain – a feat for which it got paid just £1 million. Also in the 1930s, Costain owned, developed and built Dolphin Square – then the largest block of flats in Europe and also built Lambeth Bridge House, as the headquarters for the Ministry of Works, which was the largest office block in Europe at that time.

The company has operated continuously in the Middle East since 1935, and in central and southern Africa since 1947. In Asia, it built the 210mw power station for Sri Lanka's Victoria Dam and hydro-electric scheme – at the time, this was Britain's largest overseas aid project.

Costain played an active role in the war effort of the 1940s, with wartime work including 26 aerodromes, part of the Mulberry Harbours, munitions factories and 15,000 post-war prefabricated Airey houses.

The company expanded rapidly in the 1960s and into the 1970s through its successful presence in the Middle East; and during the same period steadily diversified into coal-mining and property in the key markets of the UK, Australia and US.

The decade began well, as in 1971 Costain became the first UK contractor to win the Queen's Award for Export Achievement – and has since won nine further Queen's Awards. Indeed, during the early 1970s, more than half the Group's turnover came from international operations in 25 countries.

The shape of Costain is constantly changing as new markets are embraced, but the unique Costain way of incorporating in-depth attention to detail and service remains.

Product

Costain is one of the foremost civil engineering contractors in the UK, with a comprehensive regional spread of operations and an outstanding reputation for major projects. Its primary markets include marine, public health, road, rail and energy and infrastructure projects. Costain also pursues marine civil engineering on a worldwide basis.

The Building Division of Costain Limited has a renowned reputation for undertaking complex projects throughout the UK, from its five regional offices: London, Southern, Eastern, Midlands and Northern. Costain takes pride in the relationships it has developed within the construction community and seeks to deliver value and quality through

Costain has built 42 Tesco stores in the last 25 years, with a value of more than £100 million. Further to this, in May 2004, the company was awarded contracts by the retailer Tesco worth more than £27 million and, in the same month, Costain won three contracts, worth approximately £15 million, to help rebuild infrastructure in Iraq. The project is a joint venture with the Kurdistan Regional Government.

In November 2004, the Costain Marine division completed work on a major extension to the UK's biggest container port, The Port of Felixstowe. The 270m extension to the Trinity III terminal took four years to complete and underlines Felixstowe's position as one of Europe's most important container ports.

With regard to international marine work, Costain formed a powerful alliance in 2004 with China Harbour Engineering, one of China's largest construction groups. The two companies have a working history of some fifteen years and a complementary skill base. China Harbour has one of the largest marine fleets in the world with access to low cost labour while Costain has an international brand with high calibre civil engineering experience.

Another significant contract awarded to Costain in 2004 was a £22.5 million project to restore and upgrade one of London's most famous landmarks, the Grade I listed St Martin in the Fields Church, in Trafalgar Square. This project will be completed in 2007.

Another of Costain's promotional channels, Building Awareness, also performs an important social role. Building Awareness aims to raise young people's awareness of the construction industry through direct involvement and partnership with a number of schools across the UK. Costain and its partners are committed to providing resources and funding to support events and activities, work placements, sponsorship and much more to give students and teachers the opportunity to find out more about what the company does.

Building Awareness brings together all industry stakeholders – professional institutions, schools, training boards, the business supply chain, and Costain's own staff – together with the common purpose of lifting young people's sometimes inaccurate and unfavourable perception of construction as a career.

innovation and technical excellence.

Costain has established itself as a leader in the Asset Management market. This work involves clients who fully understand the value of partnering relationships and want long-term, expert, building and maintenance care for their valuable assets. Costain has won most of its Asset Management business in the water sector, winning long-term contracts with Thames Water, Yorkshire Water, Wessex Water, Dwr Cymru Welsh Water, United Utilities and Southern Water.

Because of the long-term income that can be derived from this work, Costain wants its Asset Management operation to be 50% of the total Group contracting business by 2006.

Costain Oil, Gas & Process is an international process engineering contractor, delivering safe, cost-effective solutions for investments in the worldwide energy and process sectors.

Recent Developments

Over the last two years, Costain has continued to win major construction and engineering contracts all over the world, whilst incorporating changes in attitudes and culture to ensure management disciplines and continual focus on the right sectors, clients and contracts.

In 2003, the group undertook some £700 million worth of work in the rail infrastructure sector, developing St Pancras and the Stratford tunnels for the Channel Tunnel Rail Link and also redeveloping Kings Cross Underground Station for London Underground.

Promotion

To reach its target audience of construction clients in the public and private sectors, Costain promotes itself in a variety of ways, using national and international trade fairs and events, as well as advertising in key technical titles, such as Contract Journal, and in key business-facing newspapers such as the FT.

Costain also uses its news magazine Blueprint, as a means of raising awareness of current projects and new developments from all over the group. Blueprint was named the UK construction industry's 'Company Magazine of the Year' in 2004.

Brand Values

The key element underpinning Costain's brand is a desire to be Relationship Driven. In pursuit of this, Costain's vision is to be the leader in the delivery of sustainable engineering and construction solutions.

Its mission is to be seen as the automatic choice for projects which require innovation, initiative, teamwork and high levels of technical and managerial skills.

The Costain brand itself can be dissected into seven key values: Customer Focused; Open and Honest; Safe and environmentally aware; Team Players; Accountable; Improving Continuously – with the aim of making Costain the Natural Choice.

www.costain.com

THINGS YOU DIDN'T KNOW ABOUT

Costain

> Costain created the largest and deepest hole ever made in London clay during construction of the Aldergate office complex.

> Costain built the Kariba township in Zimbabwe in fifteen months to house 10,000 people.

> Costain completed Hong Kong's first cross-harbour tunnel in 1972 – a 1,850m steel immersed tube tunnel.

> More than 10,500 drawings were needed to design the £232 million Dubai Dry Dock.

> Specialist precast concrete sleepers were produced by Costain for the rail track through the Channel Tunnel and for rail networks both in the UK and overseas.

> 320m of Hydrotite sealant were supplied by Costain to prevent water from the River Thames flooding the basement of the Houses of Parliament.

A Passion to Perform.

Deutsche Bank

Get in touch
with the future

A Passion to Perform.   Deutsche Bank

Market

Deutsche Bank has established itself as one of the leading corporate and investment banks, providing a full range of services to corporate and institutional clients in all of the world's major markets. It has built an outstanding franchise in sales and trading (both equity and fixed income) and commands a strong reputation for innovation and intellectual leadership in derivatives and other high-value product areas. The bank has also developed a leading global corporate finance platform, together with highly successful cash management, trade finance and other corporate banking services.

Deutsche Bank is also one of the world's leading asset managers. It has significant positions in both institutional and retail asset management and is a leading mutual fund provider both in the US and Europe. The bank has a substantial global Private Wealth Management business, and is the leading private German bank with a remarkable footprint also in Italy and Spain, serving a total of thirteen million private and business clients in Europe.

Achievements

The lean, dynamic, focused, universal Deutsche Bank has a world-class platform with global resources, far-reaching industry insights and excellent know-how. Indeed, the prestigious financial journal 'International

Financing Review' recognised its accomplishments in 2003 by presenting it with eight awards including its coveted 'Bank of the year 2003' accolade. In the same year 'The Banker' elected it as 'Interest Rate Swaps House of the Year' and the bank was also awarded 'Best Fixed Income and Credit Derivatives House' by 'AsiaMoney'.

In 2004 Deutsche Bank again won a raft of awards including several 'IFR Awards', Euromoney 'Awards for Excellence', was rated 'House of the Year' in the Derivatives business by the Banker, Risk Magazine and Asia Risk, achieved number one rankings by Institutional Investor as well as top positions in the Euromoney 'Poll of Polls, 2004'.

History

Founded in Berlin in 1870 to support the internationalisation of business and to promote and facilitate trade relations between Germany, other European countries, and overseas markets, Deutsche Bank has developed into a leading global provider of financial services.

In the early 1870s the first branches were established in Bremen and Hamburg, followed by Frankfurt am Main, Munich, Leipzig and Dresden. As soon as 1873, the first foreign branch was opened in London.

Deutsche Bank M&A transactions started in 1917 and had a first highlight with the merger of the automobile manufacturers Daimler and Benz in 1926.

In the 1970s Deutsche Bank pushed ahead with the globalisation of its business, when today's Deutsche Bank

Luxembourg S.A. was founded and additional offices were opened in locations such as Moscow, Tokyo, Paris and New York. Major deals in the UK included a number of advisory roles for the UK based BP. Deutsche Bank also advised on and financed the £2.6 billion London Underground Financing.

Today, the bank offers financial services in 74 countries throughout the world with roughly €845 billion in assets and more than 60,000 employees. Deutsche Bank is the 'National Champion' in the German banking market, has a leading position in Europe and is part of the 'global bulge-bracket' investment banking league.

Passion: Pursuing excellence.
Performance: The European global powerhouse.

A Passion to Perform.   Deutsche Bank

Product

Deutsche Bank believes that satisfied clients are the key to sustained corporate success, so it offers its clients a broad range of first-class banking products and services.

The Private Clients and Asset Management Division comprises three areas: Private and Business Clients, Private Wealth Management and Asset Management.

Private and Business Clients provides private clients with an all-round service extending from daily banking offers to holistic investment advisory and tailored financial solutions. Private Wealth Management caters to the specific needs of high net worth clients, their families and select institutions worldwide. Asset Management caters to institutional clients as well as retail investors. As a global provider, it offers customised products in equities, bonds and real estate.

The Corporate and Investment Bank comprises two areas: Global Markets and Global Banking.

Global Markets handles all origination, trading, sales and research in cash equities, derivatives, foreign exchange, bonds, structured products and

securitisations and thereby occupies a leading position in international foreign exchange, fixed-income and equities trading as well as in derivatives.

Global Banking comprises the Global Cash Management, Global Trade Finance and Trust & Securities Services business divisions and handles all aspects of corporate finance, advises corporations on M&A and divestments, and provides support with IPOs and capital market transactions. Global Banking also covers global corporations, financial institutions and the German 'Mittelstand' (mid-caps) through strong relationship management teams.

Recent Developments
Deutsche Bank competes to be the leading global provider of financial solutions for demanding clients, creating exceptional value for its shareholders and people. To turn this mission into reality, Deutsche Bank has undergone significant organisational developments over the last few years. Between 2002-2003, it placed the focus on its core businesses – selling margin activities, making divestments and concentrating on revenues – to achieve a reduction of its operating cost base. Deutsche Bank also aimed to optimise the capital base/balance sheet through its share repurchase programme, as well as optimise the Private Clients and Asset Management (PCAM) business by streamlining its structure and increasing efficiency and profitability.

Passion: Long-term relationships.
Performance: Delivering tailored solutions.

A Passion to Perform. Deutsche Bank ☑

Its current restructuring process, which began in autumn 2004, focuses on increasing efficiency in the Corporate and Investment Bank (CIB) by integrating its sales and trading activities, improving client coverage, streamlining the Asset Management Business and strengthening the regional Management within the organisation.

Promotion
Deutsche Bank's communication initiatives leverage its strong and globally renowned brand, which has proven to be a key driver of business and to have a consistent profile across markets and stakeholder audiences.

The communication is targeted at people with a modern mindset, a can-do, achievement-oriented attitude.

Both, the brand's Corporate Campaign 2003/04 as well as its evolution in 2005 rely heavily on the Deutsche Bank logo (which is among the most well known in the financial services industry) and its 'A Passion to Perform' claim, supported by strong visuals and engaging statements.

To ensure impact and brand alignment of communications initiatives Deutsche Bank regularly monitors progress on brand-related key performance indicators in relevant markets.

Deutsche Bank is highly aware of its role as a corporate citizen who bears responsibility not only for business but also for society. With the aim of providing 'More than money' the bank is going far beyond the provision of financial resources alone. For many decades Deutsche Bank has been a dedicated patron of the arts and music, has supported community development projects and educational programmes. With the bank's commitment in these areas, the goal is always to enable individuals to push their limits, to discover their talents and to realise their full potential.

The bank's foundations and charitable institutions play a key role, firmly anchoring its CSR activities around the world. In Great Britain, for example, Deutsche Bank Citizenship UK primarily supports projects in disadvantaged areas of London, through its numerous volunteer programmes and by working closely with over 40 non-profit partner organisations.

The Deutsche Bank Microcredit Development Fund is an exemplary combination of social commitment and professional expertise. In 2003, approximately 600,000 microcredits with a total volume of US$42.7 million were generated from the Fund's assets.

In the US, sponsorship work to safeguard young people's futures is done by the Deutsche Bank Americas Foundation. With the Deutsche Bank Asia Foundation the company wants to create a sustainable base for its commitment to society in Asia. Over the next five years, the Foundation will provide some €5 million, primarily for educational projects.

At the beginning of 2005 Deutsche Bank committed a major donation to Tsunami victims in Asia and co-operated closely with local relief organisations.

'Bank of the Year'
IFR Awards 2003

Last but not least, Deutsche Bank's think-tank, the Alfred Herrhausen Society for International Dialogue (AHS), brings together renowned experts from the fields of politics, business, academia and society. The annual forums it organises are set up to analyze the critical issues, trends and respond to the need for reform in international civil society and initiate debate about possible solutions.

Brand Values
Deutsche Bank has recently emphasised its core positioning as a European global powerhouse dedicated to excellence, constantly challenging the status quo to deliver superior solutions to its demanding clients and superior value to its shareholders and people.

The brand is supported by four key 'pillars' that have a different emphasis in different markets:

Pursuing excellence, leveraging unique insights as a multi-cultural bank, delivering innovative solutions and building long-term relationships at eye-level.

This all goes to show that 'A Passion to Perform' applies not only to the Bank's relationships with its clients, but to every aspect of life at Deutsche Bank – it is the way Deutsche Bank does business.

www.db.com

Value the differences.

Diverse perspectives foster innovation and creativity.
They enable us to build teams with a unique range of capabilities winning the trust of our most demanding clients. They enhance our ability to respond to global business issues and provide innovative, superior solutions.
Diversity matters, because it makes us more successful.
For more information please visit: www.db.com - Jobs & Careers

A Passion to Perform. Deutsche Bank ☑

THINGS YOU DIDN'T KNOW ABOUT

Deutsche Bank
❯ Deutsche Bank opened its first foreign branch in London as early as 1873.

❯ Deutsche Bank listed its shares on the NYSE on October 3rd 2001.

❯ Deutsche Bank has one of the most well-known logos in the industry.

❯ Deutsche Bank's workforce is predominantly located outside its German home market. With more than 7,500 employees in London, Deutsche Bank is one of the largest employers and occupiers of space in the Square Mile.

❯ Deutsche Bank provides substantial funding and additional support for community and cultural projects across the globe.

Market

Outside of the industry, DHL is often still referred to as a courier company – a term that harks back to the days when international packages were accompanied throughout their journey by a single person. To this day, many people still believe that the DHL man who collects a package from their office or front door is the same person who will be delivering it in New York, Tokyo or wherever.

In reality, this image of the company (and the industry) is 20 years out of date. Today, DHL alone handles over 100 million packages a year in the UK and more than one billion worldwide. DHL is no longer a company that just carries urgent documents for those that can afford it – it is an essential partner for thousands of businesses providing fastest possible access to markets and customers around the world. The boom in e-commerce is also widening DHL's traditional customer base to include more and more home consumers who are using the internet to shop around the world. Not surprisingly, the speed and peace of mind that DHL provides is highly valued.

The express and logistics industry is a crucial facilitator of trade, productivity and investment and global revenues are estimated to be over €1.5 trillion. The market is currently extremely competitive, with customers expectations of speed constantly increasing and to survive it is no longer good enough to just move goods from point A to point B.

Achievements

DHL invented the international express delivery industry, pioneering the concept of international door-to-door delivery of time-sensitive documentation and later expanded the concept to include parcels and dutiable items.

The secret behind DHL's growth over the last 35 years has been in delivering what its customers want – a factor supported by the fact that many of the companies that started doing business when it started operating remain customers today.

Throughout its history, DHL has made real break-throughs – political and technological – on behalf of its customers. In the mid 1970s, it was the driving force behind postal reform in the US, championing the vision of tailored value-added services for business that were different to those offered by the postal authorities. The company has also

successfully harnessed technology to keep its service levels at the forefront of the market. In 1979 it developed one of the first word-processing computers in the world, the DHL1000, which greatly increased the efficiency of processing orders and documentation. In 1983, it was the first express delivery company to introduce a 'track and trace' system, helping customers to follow the progress of their deliveries.

DHL's unofficial motto has always been 'first in, last out'. This relates to the company's global reputation for operating in virtually every country in the world and, in particular, for maintaining a presence under difficult and often dangerous circumstances. DHL was the first delivery company to re-open in Afghanistan and was the first air operator allowed to fly into

Recent Developments

2003 marked a 'rebirth' of the DHL brand. The Deutsche Post World Net group concentrated all express and logistics activities under the internationally renowned brand of DHL. The same year DHL substantially strengthened its network inside North America through the acquisition of the US express company, Airborne.

The visual integration of DHL into the corporate design of Deutsche Post World Net is part of the Group's strategic branding decision. DHL adopted the major corporate design elements of the group such as the colour yellow and typography. The DHL logo was slightly modified while keeping its most characteristic and familiar elements.

Baghdad airport following the removal of Saddam Hussein. Not surprisingly, the company's unrivalled delivery network is also relied upon by governments and aid agencies during times of emergency or crisis – the Tsunami disaster in Asia being just one recent example.

The Deutsche Post World Net group has held a stake in DHL since 1998. The full acquisition of this now worldwide market leader by the German global player in 2003 represents a milestone in the company's history.

History

The name DHL was made up from the initials of the three company founders Adrian Dalsey, Larry Hillblom and Robert Lynn. Together they had an ingenious idea: they personally flew shipping documents from San Francisco to Honolulu in Hawaii allowing ship cargoes to be cleared by Customs before the actual ships had even arrived. This saved shipping operators a fortune by substantially cutting down wasted days in port and gave birth to a new industry – international air express.

After that things took off fast. In 1970 DHL obtained a foothold on the US East Coast, expanded into the Pacific rim in 1971, and in 1974 established its first European base in London. Since 1977 DHL has also had a presence in the Middle East, and in 1978 DHL leased its first office space in Germany. Realising early on that the transfer of data via fax significantly reduced the business potential of classic document delivery, the year 1980 saw the addition of express shipping of dutiable goods as a new service. In 1983 DHL was the first express services provider brave enough to venture into the Eastern block and the first to enter the People's Republic of China in 1986.

Product

DHL has five strong brand areas: DHL Express, DHL Freight, DHL Danzas Air & Ocean, DHL Solutions and DHL Global Mail.

DHL Express provides express and time definite shipping – but much more than traditional international air services. A brand new road express service to mainland Europe and one of the largest same day delivery networks in the UK and Ireland are just two features of the new DHL Express portfolio.

DHL Freight handles partial, full and special deliveries for all of Europe, moving goods by road, rail and combined transport.

DHL Danzas Air & Ocean specialise in airfreight and sea transport along with freight forwarding for major industrial projects.

DHL Solutions operates in the realm of storage and procurement logistics.

DHL Global Mail offers international outbound letter mail to business customers.

What makes DHL unique in 2005 is its ability to offer any type of delivery for any size of shipment to virtually anywhere in the world. With a fleet of 250 aircraft, 75,000 vehicles, 5,000 offices in 227 countries and more than 170,000 staff, DHL is a formidable operation.

Promotion

DHL is one of the best-known business brands in the world, which is partly due to a number of memorable marketing campaigns. (Ten years after the event, many still recall the DHL campaign featuring the Diana Ross song 'Ain't No Mountain High Enough'.)

The global DHL re-launch campaign focused around the statement 'More': DHL can now do even more than before with more speed, more power, more efficiency, more services and more products. The 'More' message was translated into the various individual national languages of Europe, Asia and Africa. The globally run 'Pyramid' television advertisement reflected DHL's comprehensive logistics expertise. The message: The ancient Egyptians would have relied on DHL when they were building the pyramids.

Another important promotional platform for the company – certainly as an internal marketing and team building tool – is the long-standing DHL EuroCup football tournament. Founded in 1982, the competition started life as a small friendly competition between colleagues from the Netherlands, Belgium and the UK. Nowadays, it is an annual tournament with 3,000 employees from over 20 countries competing.

Brand Values

Perhaps the greatest testament to the DHL brand is that 'to DHL' something has become a generic term around the world for sending an item in the fastest possible way.

As a pioneer and continual innovator in the logistics sector, DHL capitalises on the extensive experience of its specialised divisions Express, Freight, Danzas Air & Ocean, Solutions and Global Mail to refine its unique product portfolio. The brand stands for enduring attributes such as speed, reliability, transparency, professionalism, flexibility and most of all closeness to the customer. DHL knows precisely the wishes and needs of its customers by virtue of its local presence throughout the entire world.

www.dhl.co.uk

THINGS YOU DIDN'T KNOW ABOUT

DHL

> DHL is the ninth largest airline in the world.

> More than 90% of the world's top companies use the services of DHL.

> DHL delivers 80% of all movie reels to UK cinemas – and the popcorn.

> DHL invented the world's first word processor capable of operating in both English and Arabic.

> DHL's annual employee EuroCup event is the largest non-professional football tournament in Europe.

Market

Dunlop is a renowned name in the world of tyres. The brand is synonymous with driving in every major market in the world.

Dunlop is a leader in supplying tyres to the world's most prestigious car manufacturers. This close co-operation enables Dunlop to anticipate the needs and requirements of the car industry, which reflects the needs and requirements of the entire market. Dunlop is a major partner to the likes of Audi, BMW, Lexus and Mercedes-Benz in developing tyres that meet the exact needs of these cars.

Dunlop is also a major player in the diverse and growing motorcycle arena, translating unparalleled race success into road tyre performance. In the road haulage market, Dunlop is the choice of companies who need guaranteed performance to ensure they meet their targets.

Achievements

Motorsport has always been where Dunlop pushes boundaries, develops technologies and builds partnerships. In addition, 34 victories have been won in the Le Mans 24 Hour race using Dunlop tyres. No other tyre manufacturer even comes close. Indeed, almost every major touring car championship in the world used Dunlop tyres, including the British Touring Car Championship and the spectacular German DTM.

Dunlop has also seen similar success on two wheels, ever since the Motorcycle Grand Prix World Championships were started in 1949. Dunlop riders have won more than 50% of all the Grand Prix held, collecting over 100 World Championship titles along the way.

History

From its very beginnings it is obvious what Dunlop set out to do – to deliver a better driving experience for drivers and a better riding experience for riders.

The story does not start on four wheels or even on two, but on three. In 1888 Dunlop's founder, John Boyd Dunlop provided his son with a smoother ride and better handling tricycle by inventing the first practical pneumatic tyre.

Dunlop immediately patented his idea and started to develop his invention into a commercial venture, founding what quickly became known as the Dunlop Pneumatic Tyre Co Ltd. In 1890 Dunlop opened its first tyre plant in Dublin, Ireland and three years later its first tyre factory in mainland Europe in Hanau, Germany. By 1895 Dunlop tyres were also being sold in France and Canada, and manufactured in Australia and the US. By 1898 the business had outgrown its Dublin base, and production was transferred first to Coventry and then in 1902 to the 400 acre site in Birmingham – later known to the world as Fort Dunlop.

In 1910 Dunlop planted its flag in Malaya, establishing 50,000 acres of rubber plantation. In 1913 the first

Japanese tyre factory opened its gates in Kobe. In 20 years, Dunlop had made the solid tyre obsolete and grown from pioneer to the first global multinational company. It manufactured worldwide and sold worldwide.

Its founding father's entrepreneurial spirit became the ethos of the company, obviously realising that to be a successful multinational corporation the company would have to remain a pioneer in research and development as well as in business. Dunlop's objective was, and still is, to continuously produce better products to enhance the performance of vehicles and the driving experience of their drivers.

By the start of World War II, Dunlop was the byword for success in a range of activities – not only tyres where it reigned supreme on and off the racetrack, but also brakes, wheels, golf and tennis balls, flooring, and other industrial rubber products. It was a supremacy that was to last until the end of the 1960s.

In 1984 came the consolidation of Dunlop's European and US tyre operations with its Japanese business, as part of the Sumitomo group. In 1999 Sumitomo and The Goodyear Tyre & Rubber Company formed a global alliance, becoming the world's biggest tyre producer.

THE WORLD'S TOP CAR MANUFACTURERS
HAVE ONE THING IN COMMON.

BESIDES BUILDING CARS.

Dunlop tyres are original equipment
on many of the world's finest cars.

DUNLOP DRIVERS KNOW.

The company's technicians and designers in Europe, the US and Japan are committed to sharing their expertise with each other. This knowledge aids product development and helps maintain trust in the brand amongst drivers.

Product

The current Dunlop range is winning plaudits from the motoring press. Autocar described the recently launched Dunlop SP Sport Maxx as its 'best handling tyre' in its gruelling annual tyre test.

The Dunlop SP Sport 01 is renowned as being a quiet running tyre thanks to its unique construction and tread design. As a result it is the choice of many executive car manufacturers seeking comfort as well as high performance.

On two wheels, Dunlop's latest D208RR tyre has proven itself as a track and road star. The same tyre that is used in the national Yamaha R6 Cup is also available for superbike riders wanting an uncompromised road legal track tyre.

Recent Developments

Dunlop is a pioneer in 'Run Flat' tyre technology and its innovation continues to this day with DSST (Dunlop Self Supporting Technology). The technology can support a vehicle's entire weight when the tyre is flat for up to 50 miles at 50mph, even if there is no tyre pressure. DSST tyres allow drivers to get home or to a tyre dealer, instead of pulling over, delivering more peace of mind. The tyres are simple and convenient; they can

MAKE YOUR MOVE AND
LEAVE YOUR MARK

be used on all standard wheel rims and be fitted without special tools or equipment, whilst at the same time living up to the demands of high performance cars. BMW has decided to equip many of its cars with tyres featuring 'fail-safe' technology. On the new BMW 5-series, more than 50% of all cars with the 'fail-safe' system are now equipped with the Dunlop SP 01 DSST tyres as original equipment and the latest BMW 1-series has this technology across the range.

Promotion

Dunlop's iconic status has been earned through product innovation and quality, and reinforced with creative advertising and promotions.

Dunlop drivers, in the main own premium cars, are in-the-know about driving and have an extraordinary passion for performance.

The Dunlop Race Academy is a good example of how the brand connects with its audience. Thousands of hopefuls will be whittled down to a single winner at the Academy. The winner will encapsulate everything that Dunlop stands for – driving passion, knowledge and flair.

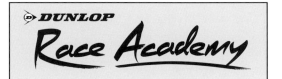

Drivers know that extreme performance is not the only attribute that matters. Ride comfort and noise levels can also be affected by tyre choice. The Dunlop SP Sport 01 continues a long tradition of refinement, and has been hailed by What Car? as a tyre that can reduce in-car noise.

To communicate this benefit, Dunlop ran a major radio campaign focusing on in-car noise. The brand's 'music lovers' promotion struck a chord in the minds of drivers who enjoy sophisticated hi-fi equipment in the car – and don't want to suffer with noisy tyres. Compelling creative helped Dunlop win its first New York Festival Award.

Tread, the lifestyle supplement produced bi-monthly in association with The Independent focuses on igniting the style and lifestyle elements of the brand presenting Dunlop as a cool and urban credible lifestyle brand.

In 2004, Dunlop launched www.driversknow.co.uk, a groundbreaking news, knowledge and information portal for Dunlop's premium audience. An intelligent, inspiring lifestyle content delivers the Drivers Know proposition online. A brand development that will confirm Dunlop as 'the' online tyre branc, leveraging the 'in the know' set.

This typifies the creativity that Dunlop has within its organisation. A creative approach that reaches the public in a way that conventional tyre advertising sometimes doesn't.

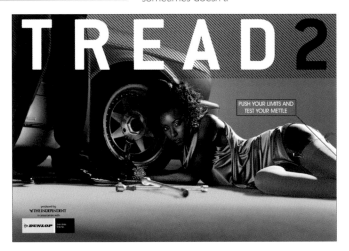

PUSH YOUR LIMITS AND
TEST YOUR METTLE

Brand Values

The challenge remains to push the limit. That attitude rests at the heart of the Dunlop philosophy and design group, and it ensures that Dunlop will continue to set trends – creating new tyres to harness the potential of extraordinary and powerful vehicles – to answer the needs of those drivers who know.

In that process of partnership with Original Equipment Manufacturers (OEMs), Dunlop employs the latest manufacturing and management techniques and works only to the highest standards as set out in international guidelines, such as ISO 9000. Dunlop also continues to meet the demands of the environment by adopting sustainable practices and using resources more efficiently.

From expert to expert, from driver to driver, Dunlop works together with the aim of ensuring the greatest possible performance is achieved.

www.driversknow.co.uk

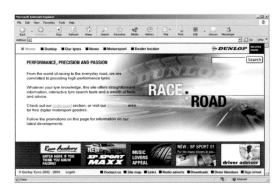

THINGS YOU DIDN'T KNOW ABOUT

Dunlop

> Dunlop's technical team discovered a phenomenon unexplained until then – aquaplaning. Their demonstrations of this phenomenon caused a worldwide sensation and led to numerous awards for the Dunlop team in the mid 1960s.

> Run Flat tyres are a recent addition to the options list on many vehicles. However, the first fitment of Dunlop Run Flat tyres was over 30 years ago – on the iconic Mini 1275GT.

> Over a century ago, Fort Dunlop opened, producing a wide range of tyres and other rubber products. Since the 1980s different companies have marketed the Dunlop non-tyre products and brands, but Dunlop Tyres continue to manufacture race winning motorsport tyres at the famous Birmingham plant.

> More motorsport competitors choose Dunlop than any other tyre brand. With an outstanding record in single seater, touring car, club level racing, motorcycle racing, karting, motocross and all other disciplines of the sport Dunlop are an integral part of the motorsport industry.

> The famous Dunlop Bridge at Le Mans is just one of a family of iconic Dunlop bridges around the world, including a similar bridge at Donington Park.

EARLS COURT AND OLYMPIA LONDON

Market

The UK exhibitions industry is worth tens of billions of pounds to the UK economy each year both through income generated directly at shows and also the indirect tourism income generated through hotels, restaurants, bars and other services. Exhibitions held at Earls Court and Olympia (EC&O) alone generate approximately £1.27 billion each year. Additionally, the industry supports more than 50,000 jobs, both full and part-time. Companies operating within the industry include exhibition organisers, hospitality providers, venues, contractors, stand manufacturers, designers, registration companies, high street food retailers and market research organisations.

In 2003 exhibitions and shows in the UK attracted 10.3 million visitors (a 14% improvement on 2001 figures), with 9.6% of those from overseas (Source: Association of Exhibition Organisers: The UK Exhibition Industry 2003).

Between them these two London venues offer almost 100,000m of floor space.

Broadly speaking the sector is divided between consumer exhibitions, which have seen significant growth over the last six years, and trade shows. The former such as The Daily Mail Ideal Home Show, which has been held at either Earls Court or Olympia since its inception 97 years ago, comprised approximately 55% of the sector in 2004. Trade shows like the Amusement Trades Exhibition International, which has been staged at EC&O for 22 years, account for approximately 45% of all major industry events at Earls Court and Olympia.

EC&O has two dedicated Conference Centres at Earls Court and Olympia which have seen a dramatic shift in their market since 2000. In 2000, approximately 70% of the conferences which took place in the centres were exhibition-led, compared to 2004 where around 70% of conferences are now stand-alone.

Achievements

In 2004, EC&O welcomed 48 new shows through its doors and to date already has 29 new shows lined up for 2005 which range from entrepreneurial launches such as The Guardian Summer Graduate Fair and Classicalive, an event for music enthusiasts, to trade shows Mediacast and Procurement Solutions & Government Computing.

EC&O is not only renowned for hosting exhibitions; première parties, award ceremonies and large banquets also regularly take place in the venues. Concerts in the Earls Court arena in the last twelve months, which include Madonna, Morrissey and Muse, demonstrate the versatility of the venues.

In 2004, EC&O won several awards. At the AEO (Association of Exhibition Organisers) Awards Olympia received the Best Venue Management award for the third time in five years and an Earls Court Event Manager was presented with the Venue Employee of the Year Award. Furthermore, at the Event Awards EC&O was awarded silver for Best Venue Management; a testament to all the concerts and entertainment that were held at EC&O during 2003/04. The entry 'Cars, Stars and Guitars', used case studies of motoring spectacular MPH, The BRIT Awards and Justin Timberlake in concert to demonstrate the flexible nature of the venues and also how departments within EC&O work in close partnership with external partners to provide excellent customer service.

In October, EC&O was short listed for the Marketing Effectiveness Awards alongside other household brand names such as British Gas, for its comprehensive business to business 'venuelicious' marketing campaign.

2004 saw EC&O's relationships with suppliers, organisers and customers greatly improve, with independent research consistently proving that EC&O offers excellent levels of customer service, which is renowned throughout the exhibitions industry.

History

Since Olympia's Grand Hall first opened in 1886, some of history's most famous figures have taken to the stage at the two central London venues together with a cast of millions at the trade fairs, consumer shows, concerts and entertainment that make up the history of these world famous centres.

The venues' story began on Boxing Day 1886 when the Paris Hippodrome Circus opened to the public in the Grand Hall at Olympia. The following year Buffalo Bill and his Wild West show drew the crowds in their thousands.

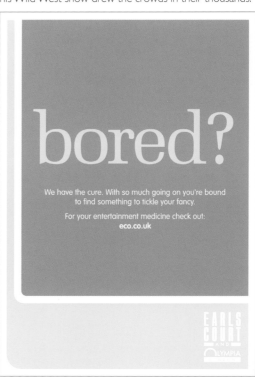

bored?

We have the cure. With so much going on you're bound to find something to tickle your fancy.

For your entertainment medicine check out:
eco.co.uk

I ❤ EC&O

Royal approval of the Grand Hall coupled with such spectacular events served to increase the venue's popularity and the first show jumping event, held there in 1907, pulled in huge crowds. Between 1923 and 1929 two halls were added to Olympia; the New Hall (later renamed the National Hall) and the Empire Hall (later renamed Olympia Two). Olympia's exhibition space was completed in 1959, with the addition of the West Hall. In 2003 the Grand Hall became a Grade II listed building.

In 1937 the attention of the events world was focused on a new centre in West London when the ground breaking Earls Court One was opened. One of the earliest shows, Winter Cavalcade, attracted 250,000 visitors and featured a 100ft high ski slope packed with hundreds of tonnes of crushed ice, a feat closely mirrored in 2004 by the 51ft high and 170ft long ski ramp at the Daily Mail Ski and Snowboard Show. In 1974 Earls Court and Olympia were combined under the common ownership of the Sterling Guarantee Trust which subsequently merged with P&O in 1985. In 1991, Earls Court One was joined by Earls Court Two which offered 17,000m² of column-free space beneath Europe's biggest unsupported roof-span. Conference centres were opened at Olympia and Earls Court in 1987 and 1993 respectively.

The latest chapter of EC&O's history began in May 2004 when St James Capital, leisure and property specialists, and investment bank Nomura International bought the venues from the Morris family and Candover Investments for £245 million. The successful sale of event organiser Clarion Events for £45 million signalled the first step towards EC&O's vision for the future, to further build on its success and create world class exhibition and leisure destinations for London.

Product

Earls Court has been hosting world-class, legendary events and exhibitions for more than 67 years, earning a worldwide reputation for delivering high attendance figures and excellent organisation. The impressive art-deco architecture venue, which boasts 60,000m² of prime space and attracts two million visitors annually, makes it one of the capital's major attractions.

Earls Court One offers more than 43,000m² of floor space with thirteen hospitality rooms and eleven high street catering brands making it the venue of choice for many leading trade and consumer shows.

Earls Court Two, which can be joined to Earls Court One, offers 17,000m² of floor space, six hospitality rooms and four high street catering brands on site.

Olympia, which features original Victorian architecture, has three halls, comprising more than 40,000m² of floor space and attracts more than one million visitors a year. Olympia's space, height and viewing galleries give it the edge for many sports events. Première parties, gala awards and new product launches have also been staged within the venue.

The Earls Court conference centre is a modern and flexible venue, which can accommodate between 90 and 250 delegates. It can also be used for training courses,

corporate roadshows, seminars, product launches and presentations. Olympia's state-of-the-art conference centre can cater for between 250 and 449 delegates. In addition to a purpose-built auditorium with stage, it offers two breakout and five seminar rooms, a 988m² exhibition hall and a modern and contemporary reception area.

Each centre provides specialist in-house audio-visual, telecommunications and catering services which are co-ordinated by a dedicated manager.

Recent Developments

EC&O has a customer focused approach and has introduced a wide range of service initiatives across the company. These moves have seen the Company become more entrepreneurial in style with a flatter management structure, where the voice of all employees is heard.

Quality high street brands such as Pret A Manger, Crussh, Pizza Express and Costa Coffee have opened outlets on the premises. Leith's, part of the Compass Group, bring a modern and innovative approach to banqueting and on-stand catering at both venues.

2005 will see EC&O launch new parties and seated events packages, as the venues are fully equipped to cater for any special event in terms of having excellent customer service, a wide range of halls, a central location and good transport links.

The new ownership by St James Capital has brought a dynamic new approach to EC&O with leisure and property expertise, as it moves towards offering more leisure opportunities such as restaurants, entertainment and gyms wrapped around the core business of exhibitions. EC&O is currently looking at several opportunities that will make the best use of available space within the venues whilst still maintaining excellent standards of service.

Promotion

Although the legendary Earls Court and Olympia brand names often act as a magnet for shows and exhibitions and enjoy approximately 90% brand recognition throughout the UK, tough competition means that considerable resources are placed behind marketing activities.

As well as promoting the venues themselves, EC&O have a dedicated Customer Marketing Manager who works exclusively with customers (exhibition organisers) using the EC&O website www.eco.co.uk and electronic newsletter ENews to help promote their shows, providing a halo-effect for the events. Established in October 2003, to date ENews has well over 14,000 subscribers who regularly receive information on consumer events at Earls Court and Olympia. Examples of other successful marketing activity include a National Rail advertising campaign which was carried out in conjunction with four exhibitions taking place at the venues. The posters appeared across a number of National Rail stations predominately in the South East under the EC&O umbrella branding and demonstrated EC&O's commitment to building stronger relationships with show organisers and emphasising its easy public transport links.

In addition to VENEWS, a quarterly magazine which keeps business abreast of what is happening at EC&O, customer support includes regular events listings in the form of quarterly 'what's on?' postcards and a community newsletter 'The London ECHO' which are distributed to homes and businesses in the local area. EC&O also produces a quarterly wallet-sized leaflet which lists consumer shows at the venues and is currently distributed through 50 London hotels, with the

distribution to be increased to cover a larger area of London in 2005.

2004 also saw the completion of EC&O's new visual identity for its literature, advertising, direct mail and website culminating in new brochures for the conferences, banqueting and exhibitions market.

Over the past three years, EC&O has placed exhibiting at the core of its marketing strategy, regularly exhibiting at trade shows to promote the Earls Court and Olympia conference centres with great success. In the past the conference centres tended to be slightly overshadowed by the renowned exhibition halls and a large part of EC&O's marketing has been focused on challenging the preconception that Earls Court and Olympia are too large to cater for conferences. The focus has been on increasing their profile by emphasising the excellence of the facilities on offer.

Brand Values

EC&O Group provides versatile venues which are capable of creating exciting settings for an array of events. Clients feel reassured that at Earls Court and Olympia they receive the full benefit of the brand's strong reputation and considerable expertise in hosting first class events. From stunning theatrical experiences to glamorous exhibitions, Earls Court and Olympia are the ultimate venues.

Earls Court and Olympia provide the backdrop for a wide range of stylish, glamorous, iconic and imaginative events, proven by the legendary history of the venues. The brand also trades on the venues' 118 years worth of history, having witnessed some of the UK's most spectacular and legendary moments.

The future is bright for EC&O, looking forward to creating more memorable and legendary experiences for years to come.

www.eco.co.uk

THINGS YOU DIDN'T KNOW ABOUT

Earls Court & Olympia

〉 The first ever event held at Earls Court was the Chocolate and Confectionary Exhibitions from September 1st-9th 1937.

〉 The first International Horse Show was held at the Olympia Grand Hall in 1907 and in 2004 1,200 bottles of champagne, 2,390 bottles of wine and eight tonnes of ice were served at the event by over 200 catering staff which included butlers, waitresses, bar persons and chefs.

〉 Earls Court has starred in a number of popular films and television programmes including The Saint, Richard III and Z-Cars to name a few.

〉 Ladies were given free admission to the opening day of the 1937 Motor Show because, according to the Daily Express, most men choosing cars wanted the 'advice of their womenfolk.'

Eddie Stobart

Market

Eddie Stobart is the UK's largest independent logistics company with a turnover of £130 million, a fleet of well over 750 trucks and 25 depots. During its 35 years of existence, Eddie Stobart has steadily increased its market share and developed internationally.

Within the UK haulage industry, 80% of companies have less than 20 vehicles so there are a relatively small number of large operators. The current trend in the industry is toward consolidation and rationalisation. Over the last few years the industry has faced challenges like never before for example the introduction of the working time directive, rising fuel costs, competition from overseas and a national shortage of skilled drivers.

The intense competition, low margin and high level of investment required are typical characteristics of the haulage market. Delivery lead times especially to the national retailers have reduced to twelve hours which has forced a high level of specialist equipment and systems. What Eddie Stobart has is a unique brand status symbolised by its commitment to offering its customers a one stop solution to all their distribution needs.

Achievements

There comes a stage in the story of any rags-to-riches success when you think you might perhaps have missed something, a sleight of hand that hides the reason behind enormous growth. One moment Eddie Stobart has 50 trucks and was turning over £4.5 million and, a few years later, the company had 1,000 trucks and a turnover of £150 million.

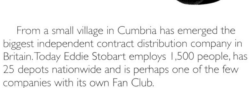

From a small village in Cumbria has emerged the biggest independent contract distribution company in Britain. Today Eddie Stobart employs 1,500 people, has 25 depots nationwide and is perhaps one of the few companies with its own Fan Club.

As to why the Company has succeeded one might consider the following reasons: Principally it has built a reputation for running clean trucks, with smart Drivers who arrive on time at their destination. Also the naming of the trucks after girls names caught the publics imagination, the Drivers compulsory shirt and tie uniform turned the publics image of a truckie from a hairy macho man into a smart, disciplined professional and Eddie Stobart respond to public enquiries which all became the foundation of the present Fan Club with its awesome range of merchandise and members who come from all over the world, ranging from children to pensioners.

Eddie Stobart's other achievements have been recognised in a number of high-profile awards including the 'Supplier of Excellence Award' by the Institute of Transport Management and the 'Middle Market Award' from PricewaterhouseCoopers LLP but perhaps its most prestigious to date is 'Haulier of the Year' in the national Motor Transport Awards.

History

Eddie Stobart established an agricultural contracting business in the 1950s, in the Cumbrian village of Hesket-Newmarket. In 1970 the business was incorporated as Eddie Stobart Limited. During 1976 Eddie Stobart re-located to a new depot in Carlisle with eight trucks

and twelve staff. Increased demand for an integrated storage and distribution service meant that the Company was on the move again to new premises just off the M6. The Company continued to gain new business during the late 1980s and early 1990s resulting in additional depots being opened.

Throughout the 1990s growth continued at around 25% each year and in 2004 Eddie Stobart Limited was acquired by WA Developments International Limited, an investment company part owned by William Stobart. Today the company has depots the length and breath of the UK and an international base located in Belgium.

Product

Collection and delivery is the core function of Eddie Stobart. The company operates 365 days a year throughout the UK and Europe transporting a diverse range of products from manufacturing to consumer goods. Eddie Stobart has vast experience in handling every type of consignment and load combination, offering a single or multi-drop option to and from any location. The service is backed by efficient vehicle planning and modern communication systems to ensure accurate tracking of vehicles and to maintain time-sensitive delivery schedules.

Eddie Stobart's refrigerated transport service offers a next day delivery into Europe using state-of-the-art temperature controlled facilities. Satellite tracking and precise scheduling maintains consistently achievable time-sensitive delivery levels.

Contract distribution affords the customer a highly reliable level of service with fixed costs, which in turn bring long-term benefits through the ability to plan effectively with pre-determined routes and volumes.

The International division has been an area of growth for Eddie Stobart over the past decade. Vehicles operate cross channel and throughout Europe. This diverse work is carried out by seasoned professionals with years of continental driving experience, supported by a highly experienced planning and management team with first hand knowledge of the industry. This combines to present a reliable service to inter-continental traders at efficiency-led costs.

Storage and distribution is a fast moving highly skilled discipline within the logistics industry. Eddie Stobart operates over three million square feet of warehousing, strategically located throughout the UK and Europe, with a huge variety of storage options.

Each warehouse is serviced by a range of the very latest equipment, including articulated and 'man-up' fork lift trucks for the rapid movement of goods. 'Paperless' warehouses use a range of sophisticated bar coding and tracking systems that are able to locate batches or individual pallets quickly. Customers can access their stock levels in real time via electronic communication.

Process management is an added-value service offered by Eddie Stobart, enabling manufacturers to 'contract-out' all logistics related activities, allowing them to release resources to concentrate on their core business.

Recent Developments

Like every other industry, technology has had a huge impact on logistics. Eddie Stobart is investing heavily in in-cab technology comprising of Personal Digital Assistants (PDA) which have the benefits of satellite navigation for better routing of the vehicle. The latest vehicles are fitted with on-board computers using GPS and RDS technology to provide Drivers with vital operating data. Route, fuel and engine diagnostics are also combined in these units, which ultimately leads to more efficient use of the vehicle, generating greater cost savings for the customer as well as the Company.

Large on-screen planning boards allow the real time monitoring of accurate vehicle utilisation and efficiency, keeping empty vehicles to a minimum and enabling the company to better plan peaks and troughs.

The company has four key sites in the UK where Proof of Delivery (POD) can be scanned to allow the customer and supplier to receive up-to-date information regarding the delivery.

'Paperless' warehouse management systems use progressive technology. Pallet barcodes are read on receipt allowing product and location data to be fed to mainframe computers resulting in a highly efficient track and trace capability. Vital stock and location information is made available to the customer in real time through EDI, internet or ISDN links.

Following its takeover by WA Developments International, a substantial investment programme has been put in place which will see 200 new vehicles added to the fleet, each of which will be adorned in the striking new livery. The internationally famous Eddie Stobart truck livery has played a key role in helping make the company 'the' name in European distribution. The Company's trucks stand out from the crowd with their bold colours and punchy graphics, which is key in increasing recall of the brand.

In June 2004, Eddie Stobart revealed a new corporate identity to build on the solid, traditional style – rather than discarding it, heralding a bright new era within

Stobarts. The impressive graphics utilise the latest sign making technology to present a powerful new image in the highly competitive market. It is an opportunity that will further enhance the brand image and capture the qualities and personality of the Company.

Drivers will also receive a new livery in the form of a contemporary new uniform to compliment the new identity. A further development has been a focus on recruitment and training to ensure that a constant supply of highly skilled Drivers is readily available to the Company.

Building the brand and business, Eddie Stobart is also expanding its profile in quite a different area of transport. It is venturing into motorsports, competing with a five car rally team in the 2005 British and World Rally Championships and sponsoring three bikes running under the banner of 'Stobart Honda' in the 2005 British Superbike Championship.

Promotion

Eddie Stobart is one of the best-known haulage businesses in Europe, which is partly due to the immaculate presentation of the Company's trucks and drivers which transcends into the attention to detail and quality of service Eddie Stobart provides its customers. The Eddie Stobart brand name acts as a magnet for clients looking to contract their distribution needs and it enjoys 95% brand recognition throughout the UK, but tough competition means that the Company can not afford to rest on its laurels.

Brand Values

Eddie Stobart places great importance on keeping the brand fresh and exciting for both customers and fan club members alike, whilst maintaining the brand's core values of honesty, respect for people and commitment to what the brand says and what it delivers.

www.eddiestobart.co.uk

The principle marketing channel used to promote the Eddie Stobart brand are the trucks themselves, as they carry the distinctive green livery and contact details. This approach helps the Company keep prices low by saving on expensive media costs.

Much of Eddie Stobart's promotional activity is to build brand awareness through trade publications, press releases, brand merchandising and sponsorship including motorsport, horseracing and it has been the main sponsor of Carlisle United for over ten years. Eddie Stobart's own marketing is focused on the Account Managers who are in charge of fostering new clients via direct contact, events and face to face meetings. The Company produces a quarterly magazine to keep existing and prospective clients and employees informed about Eddie Stobart as well as the website, www.eddiestobart.co.uk which has been designed to be of use to both customers and fans of the Company.

Eddie Stobart has won several high profile awards over the years for its marketing these include the SWOT Marketing Excellence and Marketeer of the Year awards.

THINGS YOU DIDN'T KNOW ABOUT

Eddie Stobart

› The mileage done by Stobart trucks in a year is the equivalent to doing 2,000 laps of the earth.

› One of Stobart's biggest single contracts, worth over £10 million a year, is delivering pet food for Friskies Petcare.

› Every truck is 'wrapped' with transparent highly conformable self-adhesive vinyl which offers maximum versatility and durability.

› All lorries are named by their drivers or by lucky fans who can wait years for their chance to christen a truck.

› Stobart's vast Daventry warehouse complex covers 60 acres – equivalent to 20 Wembley stadiums.

› Eddie Stobart lorries are Corgi's best selling line – they sell 500,000 every year.

› Each week Eddie Stobart delivers over eleven million cans of Coca-Cola.

FINANCIAL TIMES

Market

As the business world continues to battle with the worst advertising recession for 30 years, the ever present global threat of terrorism, corporate scandals abound, along with turbulent stock market movements and the ensuing loss of business confidence, the demand for independent, authoritative and accurate business and financial news is greater than ever.

Achievements

Whether the FT is targeting its readers, its website users and subscribers or its corporate clients, the FT's reach has never been stronger. The combination of the FT's newspaper circulation, FT.com traffic figures, and the number of people viewing FT content via corporate content sales and syndication services, ensures that more people than ever before now rely on the FT brand.

FT journalists were widely acclaimed in 2004, winning 23 awards for editorial excellence. Chrystia Freeland, Richard Waters, John Gapper, Dan Roberts and James Kynge were all winners in the Business Journalist of the Year Awards, whilst the British Press Awards saw Neil Buckley named Business Journalist of the Year. In the same awards, How To Spend It, the FT's glossy luxury goods magazine was named Supplement of the Year against stiff competition. Judges commented:"How To Spend It is utterly distinctive and has such great verve. It manages to do what it does without being pretentious, but with wonderful style and originality." In addition, Gillian de Bono, editor of How To Spend It magazine, was named Editor of the Year in the newspaper magazine category of the annual British Society of Magazine Editors Awards. Presented with the award on November 22nd 2004, this is the second time Gillian has been named Editor of the Year. Other awards include Pension Writer of the Year for Pauline Skypala in the Headline Money Personal Finance Awards, Young Journalist of the Year for Stephanie Kirchgaessner in the Harold Wincott Press Awards, Outstanding Contribution to Pension and Investment Journalism for Norma Cohen, the David Watt prize for James Blitz and AIM Journalist of the Year for David Blackwell. The FT was named winner of the Excellence in Newspapers Award – the top prize for newspapers – in the 2004 Society of Publishers in Asia (SOPA) Editorial Excellence Awards. This is the first time the FT has entered the awards since the launch of the Asia edition in September 2003. The FT also won the Excellence in Newspaper Design and the Excellence in Business Reporting categories. FT.com was named Best Website for Global Markets Coverage in the Barron's awards, and FT.com's Tracy Corrigan was named Editor of the Year in the AOP awards. With two awards in the BVCA Private Equity and Venture Capitalist Journalist Awards for Simon Targett and Sundeep Tucker, the FT's features team also received praise with a Media Award for its in-depth coverage of diversity and work-life issues.

History

The Financial Times launched in 1888 as the 'friend' of the 'Honest Financier and the Respectable Broker'. However, it wasn't until 1893 that the FT began printing on pink paper. This was due to a stroke of marketing genius by Douglas Macrae to distinguish the paper from its rivals.

In 1919, Berry Bros, owners of The Sunday Times, and later The Daily Telegraph, took control of the FT. Developments took place over the course of time. For example, in 1935 the 30-share index was introduced to the Financial Times for the first time.

The Financial News, which was established in 1884, finally merged with the FT in 1945 when its chairman Brendan Bracken bought the company. The paper did however retain the name Financial Times as well as its signature pink paper.

In 1953 the 20,000th issue of the FT was celebrated. To reflect the increased scope of the newspaper an arts page was launched and 'Industry' 'Commerce' and 'Public Affairs' were added to the masthead.

Four years later the paper was taken over by Pearson and the business moved in 1959 to Bracken House, Cannon Street, London. Following this, further improvements were made and in 1960 the Technical page Executive's World page and the Saturday paper's 'How To Spend It' page were all introduced. By the following year, average circulation exceeded 132,000. Developments continued, with the European edition being printed in Frankfurt for the first time in 1979.

Circulation of the FT in the UK had increased significantly and in 1986 passed the 250,000 mark with the aid of the 'No FT…No Comment' ad campaign. In the same year,

technological advancements also took place when printing processes moved from hot metal to cold set printing.

In 1987, the FT published the first world share index and, two years later, the FT Group Head Office relocated to Number One Southwark Bridge. Under the new editor, Richard Lambert who joined the company in 1991, several new initiatives were introduced, including the first edition of 'How To Spend It' magazine in 1994. One year later, the international edition was re-launched and FT.com, the Financial Times website, was created.

In 2000, Creative Business was introduced as a supplement with the UK edition and the European edition of the newspaper was re-launched. 2001 saw the launch of Global Investing pages in the US edition, Richard Lambert named Business Journalist of the decade and the FT reached the 500,000 copies mark. Andrew Gowers, former founding editor of Financial Times Deutschland, was appointed editor of the FT.

In 2002 significant events for the newspaper included the launch of the FT Fund Management supplement as well as the re-launch of FT.com with additional features such as subscription services. Unique monthly users of the site reached 3.2 million and page views exceeded 50 million by December of that year.

In terms of the FT's international development, its first move abroad took place as far back as 1979 when a European edition, printed in Frankfurt, was launched. In fact, the FT celebrated the 25th anniversary of its presence in Europe in 2005, with a series of celebratory events and special publications to mark the occasion. The past two years have been crucial in terms of the FT's global expansion, with the launch of a dedicated edition both in print and online for the Asia-Pacific market in September 2003. The FT expanded its network of journalists across Asia, and established a news editing operation in Hong Kong, which now forms part of the company's global editing process alongside London and New York. The new Asia edition enables the FT to cover Asia in-depth, but more importantly, within its global context. The new Asia content is also channelled through to the FT's other editions, providing a valuable insight into the remarkable rise of China, for example, whether readers are based in San Francisco or Stockholm. The FT also launched its first local language business website for China's fast rising business community, www.Zhongwen.FT.com. The site attracts over 50,000 registered users and is now the leading international source of daily international business news and analysis for Chinese executives.

Since the launch of the Asia edition, the FT has continued to develop its presence across Asia-Pacific. In keeping with its global strategy of investing in leading local business titles, the FT has taken a 13.85% stake in the Business Standard, one of India's leading financial dailies. Continuing this theme, the FT started printing in Sydney recently, providing an essential global perspective for Australia's increasingly internationally-focused business community.

The FT is now printed in 23 sites across the world: London, Leeds, Dublin, Paris, Frankfurt, Stockholm, Milan, Madrid, New York, Chicago, Los Angeles, San Francisco, Dallas, Atlanta, Miami, Washington DC, Tokyo, Hong Kong, Singapore, Seoul, Dubai, Johannesburg and Sydney.

Product
The FT is firmly established as one of the world's leading business information brands and is internationally recognised for its authoritative, accurate, and incisive news, comment and analysis. Whether in print or online, the Financial Times is essential reading for the global business community.

Following the launch of a print site in Sydney in September 2004, the newspaper is now printed in 23 cities across the world. With a daily circulation of over 439,000, the Financial Times has a readership of more than one million people and is available in 140 countries.

The internet partner of the Financial Times, FT.com, is one of the world's leading business information websites, reflecting the values and authority of the Financial Times newspaper, with the immediacy and interactivity of the internet. Since its re-launch in May

2002, the website has continued to be the definitive home for business intelligence on the web, providing an essential source of news, comment, data and analysis for the global business community.

FT.com's 3.6 million unique monthly users generate over 58 million monthly page views,

delivering a premium audience to advertisers. On top of this FT.com also has over 76,000 subscribers. The website combines agenda-setting editorial content with in-depth comment and analysis, as well as interactive tools, financial data, and a significant archive. At the core of the site is authoritative news and analysis, updated throughout the business day by journalists in the Financial Times' integrated newsroom and by the FT's large network of correspondents around the world.

Recent Developments
The FT extended its Saturday UK magazine throughout Europe in 2004 for a number of special editions, including What Europe Means which marked the FT's 25th anniversary in Europe. The FT also launched a residential property magazine, In Residence in September 2004, which is published four times a year. Stapled inside the FT Magazine with the UK edition of the weekend FT, the magazine is also re-published the following Wednesday as a stand-alone supplement. The magazine offers thought-provoking coverage of a wide range of property-related issues, with an intelligent and informative look at issues such as the rise of the elite property developer, the inside story on television property shows and an analysis of issues currently affecting the industry and its consumers.

The FT's award-winning How To Spend It luxury lifestyle magazine celebrated its tenth birthday in 2004, with a special edition dedicated to the theme of celebration. Over the past ten years, How To Spend It has become essential reading for the educated, the affluent and the influential. Unashamedly glamorous, it holds real appeal for discerning, cultured consumers who like to stay ahead of the game outside of the boardroom. The magazine's origins lie in the How To Spend It pages which were formerly published exclusively in the weekend FT newspaper. From an initial Europe-only monthly circulation in 1994, the magazine published nineteen issues in 2004, the majority of which are distributed worldwide. Regular themed issues include A Passion for Fashion, Superior Interiors, Travel Unravelled and Christmas Unwrapped. Since January 2005, all editions of How To Spend It have been published worldwide, following the successful launch of the magazine in Asia in 2004.

Promotion
The FT ran two online polls to support the 25th anniversary of its European edition, and the results were featured in a promotional campaign which ran across Europe. The marketing campaign included full page advertisements in the FT, The Economist, Time, Business Week, and trade marketing titles. Focusing on the results of the 'Most influential European' and 'Most influential European business figure' polls, the campaign emphasised the FT's rapid global growth.

The launch of the FT's Asia edition in 2003 was marked by a highly creative marketing campaign across the region, which culminated in an impressive marketing first: the wrapping of Hong Kong's newest and tallest skyscraper, Two ifc, in a mock up of the FT's front page. Using over 20,000m² of mesh fabric, the wrap was 400m high, 226m from top to bottom and covered 50 floors of the Two ifc building. Installed by a team of eighteen spiderman-style climbers, the wrap secured the FT a place in the Guinness Book of World Records, for 'The world's largest advertisement on a building.'

Brand Values
The FT aims to be the world's leading business information brand. Its goal is to become essential reading – both in print and online – for business leaders and other decision-makers, through the quality of its editing and reporting. The FT is now a truly global news organisation, seeking to explain how events in one area of the world are likely to have an impact on institutions and economies in other regions, looking for trends and common patterns, context and connections.

The FT is distinct by virtue of its commitment to accurate, impartial and authoritative reporting, which is always of the highest quality.

www.ft.com

THINGS YOU DIDN'T KNOW ABOUT
FT

> The FT turned pink in 1893 – a stroke of marketing genius by Douglas Macrae to distinguish the paper from its rivals.

> The Financial Times is believed to be the only daily newspaper with a greater circulation outside of its home market.

> The FT is the only non-US newspaper to be delivered to the White House on a regular basis.

> The Financial Times and FT.com are read in more than 140 countries.

> The FT has 500 reporters worldwide, all writing for each edition of the newspaper and FT.com.

> The FT earned its place in the Guinness Book of World Records in 2004, for its building wrap in Hong Kong.

> James Bond masqueraded as a Financial Times reporter in 'A View To A Kill'.

GE imagination at work

WORLDWIDE PARTNER

wherever there's a way

finding every opportunity to support the Olympic Games

GE imagination at work

Market

GE is a dynamic, multi-faceted organisation that operates across diverse, advanced markets in all four corners of the globe. It is not an exaggeration to state that the company today touches the lives of the majority of the world's businesses and the billions of its consumers through its presence in no fewer than eleven markets. These range from financial services, medical imaging and aircraft engineering, to power generation, television programming and plastics. As a diversified technology, media and financial services company which proudly places research and development at its centre, GE is resolute in its commitment to creating products and services that anticipate and fulfil the needs of the industrialised and developing worlds.

Achievements

GE has grown from a small company that dates back to the late 19th century into a global conglomerate whose annual revenues for 2004 amounted to US$152.4 billion. The world's biggest company by market value, GE can also pride itself on being consistently recognised amongst the most respected and admired of its peers – in 2004 the FT placed GE first in its World's Most Respected Companies Survey for the seventh consecutive year; and in April of the same year Fortune Magazine ranked

GE number two in its Global Most Admired Companies list. Other accolades include Chief Executive magazine ranking GE in third place in its Top 20 Companies for Leaders, Working Mothers Magazine naming GE in its 100 Best Companies For Working Mothers, and Business Week naming GE as the fourth most valuable brand worldwide.

Behind GE's commercial success are its 320,000 employees worldwide who pioneer and power the breakthrough technologies that are instrumental in the company's technological achievements. These include the world's most powerful commercial jet engine (GE90), the world's largest and most advanced gas turbine (H Turbine), a cutting edge medical imaging system that eliminates the need for invasive surgery, and a plastic film that will replace the need for paint on cars and can withstand scratches, sun damage and fading (LEXAN SLX).

History

In 1878, Thomas Alva Edison established the Edison Electric Light Company. Inspired, like many of his compatriots, by the Centennial Exposition in Philadelphia, USA, and living during the period when alchemy gave way to science and logic, Edison fearlessly imagined the future and set about exploring the possibilities that lay ahead.

His company grew rapidly through mergers with competitors, critically amongst them, the Thomas-Houston Electric Company that, in 1892, led to the creation of the General Electric Company. With these mergers came patent rights and the opportunity to combine technologies, placing the newly merged company in a position of dominance in the electrical industry, which it maintains to this day.

The first appliances product for GE, the electric fan in the 1890s, was followed in 1907 by a full line of heating and cooking devices. GE's Aircrafts Engines division was established in 1917 in response to the US Government's quest to find a company to pioneer technology for the fledgling US aviation industry, specifically the first airplane engine booster. Thomas Edison's early experiments in 1893 with plastic filaments for light bulbs led, some 40 years later, to the creation of GE's Plastics Department.

Well over 100 years later, GE continues to keep alive Edison's vision: stretching the boundaries of imagination to create innovative technologies that deliver revolutionary solutions across many industries and markets to billions of customers worldwide.

Product

'Imagination At Work' is an ethos that permeates GE worldwide and one that its people live and breathe as they help solve some of the world's toughest problems. Unfettered thinking is transformed into real-life, workable solutions, made manifest in products and services delivered across global markets.

Improving diagnosis and treatment in medicine is at the heart of GE Healthcare, whose comprehensive range of services helps doctors and hospitals worldwide to deliver faster diagnoses and advanced treatments to patients, with a variety of conditions including cardiovascular, cancer and Alzheimer's. Technology is underpinned by expertise in the fields of disease research, drug discovery, biopharmaceuticals, and in the creation of products such as medical imaging, medical diagnostics, and patient monitoring systems. Following the acquisition of Amersham plc in 2004, GE is a world-leader in medical diagnostics and life sciences.

GENERAL ELECTRIC

GENERAL ELECTRIC
G. E. CO.   GENERAL ELECTRIC

GENERAL ELECTRIC

      GENERAL ELECTRIC

1890s   1900   1930 1934   1942   1950 1969   1986   1992   2003   2004

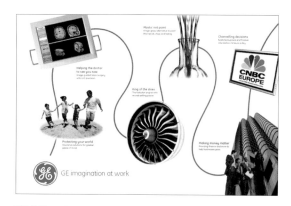

GE's technology can also be found in the home, in the everyday modern products and services that consumers buy and use to run time and energy efficient households. Refrigerators, such as the ClimateKeeper 2, feature a dual-evaporator system that cools fresh food and freezer compartments separately. It does so by using light-bulbs from GE Consumer & Industrial that use less energy; security systems, from GE Infrastructure, which provide audio alarm verification/two-way voice as a standard feature to help combat false alarms. GE is helping consumers by minimising the time and energy expended on the tasks that are an integral part of daily life.

GE provides its technologies to industries far and wide and in many forms. For example, GE Energy is one of the world's leading suppliers of power generation and energy technology, delivering equipment, service and management solutions across the power generation, oil and gas, transmission and distribution, distributed power and energy rental industries. Silicon-based products, thermoplastics and fused quartz are produced by GE Advanced Materials for many markets. GE Transportation combines aircraft engines and rail, and spans the aviation, rail, marine and off-highway industries by supplying jet engines for military and civil aircraft, freight and passenger locomotives, and gas turbines for marine and industrial applications. GE Infrastructure comprises the company's fastest-growing high-tech businesses that offer a set of protection and productivity solutions to some of the most pressing issues that industries face, such as pure water, safe facilities, plant automation, and sensing applications for operating environments.

In the financial sector, GE Insurance Solutions offers a range of insurance and investment products for businesses and consumers, including insurance and reinsurance products for insurance companies, and personal wealth creation and preservation plans for

consumers. GE Money is a leading provider of credit services to consumers, retailers and car dealers. Private label credit cards, personal loans, bank cards, car loans and leases, mortgages and debt consolidation are among the many products that the company provides to help its customers with their financial planning and management. GE Equipment Services provides operating leases, loans, sales and transportation asset management to help medium-sized and large businesses around the world manage, finance and operate their varied and numerous business equipment products. GE Commercial Finance is one of GE's largest 'growth engines'. With lending products, growth capital, revolving lines of credit, equipment leasing of every kind, cash flow programmes, asset financing, and more, GE Commercial Finance plays a key role for client businesses in over 35 countries. The industries served include healthcare, manufacturing, fleet management, communications, construction, energy, aviation, infrastructure and equipment, as well as many others. GE has also made great strides in the field of media and entertainment through another of its companies, NBC Universal. America's number one television network and the USA's fastest growing Spanish-language network, it was formed in 2004 through the combination of NBC and Vivendi Universal Entertainment. Today, NBC Universal delivers a valuable portfolio of news and entertainment, and includes a motion picture company, television production operations, a leading television stations group, Universal Theme Parks, CNBC and Bravo cable channels.

Recent Developments

GE goes from strength to strength and is committed to technology and innovation to fuel its future growth. Today, GE's vision for growth through pioneering innovation and technology is made possible by its 2,300 researchers at four global research centres in Niskayuna, New York; Bangalore, India; Shanghai, China; and, its newest centre in Munich, Germany, which opened in June 2004. Growth is further underpinned by the acquisition in June 2004 of Amersham plc, a world-leader in diagnostic imaging agents and life sciences; in the formation in May 2004 of NBC Universal; and in the strengthening of its security offering with the acquisition in November 2004 of Edward Systems Technology, the fire detection systems business, and in December 2004 of Invision Technology, the leading supplier of explosive detection systems for the US Civil Aviation Authority.

Promotion

Continuing Edison's vision, GE echoes the themes of progress, exploration, discovery and accessible science through its campaigns which include: 'We Bring Good Things To Life', 'Progress Is Our Most Important Product', and 'Live Better Electrically'.

In 2003, GE evolved these themes to 'GE Imagination at Work' communications strategy, which is used to this day. In the same year, GE became a worldwide sponsor of the Olympic Games, with rights to use the Olympic symbol from January 2005-2012. As a member of the

TOP, The Olympic Partner programme, GE is the preferred supplier for no less than fifteen product and service categories, including power generation, modular space, lighting systems and security systems, and has plans afoot to support the next Olympic Games in a variety of innovative ways.

Brand Values

For over 125 years, GE has been admired for its spirit, for its performance and for its imagination. In 2004 Business Week magazine ranked GE the fourth most valuable brand worldwide in the annual Interbrand list, BtoB placed GE in the Top Ten business to business brands, and CoreBrand named GE as having the Most Valuable Brand Equity in the third quarter.

www.ge.com/en

THINGS YOU DIDN'T KNOW ABOUT

GE

> Thomas Alva Edison's first, and possibly greatest, invention was the incandescent electric lamp in 1879.

> GE is the only company listed in the Dow Jones Industrial Index today that was also included in the original index in 1896.

> In 2004, NBC Universal won fourteen Golden Globes Awards, at the 62nd annual event that recognises achievements in television and film.

> GE has been home to two Nobel Prize winners, including in 1973 Dr Ivar Giaever, a Norwegian who received the prize for his 1960 discovery of superconductive tunnelling.

> GE supplied 10 megawatts of electricity – sufficient to power all the lighting, sound and video – for Rock in Rio, the world's largest music festival.

> GE Consumer & Industrial was recognised for its outstanding contributions to environmental protection when it won the 2004 ENERGY STAR Partner of the Year Award.

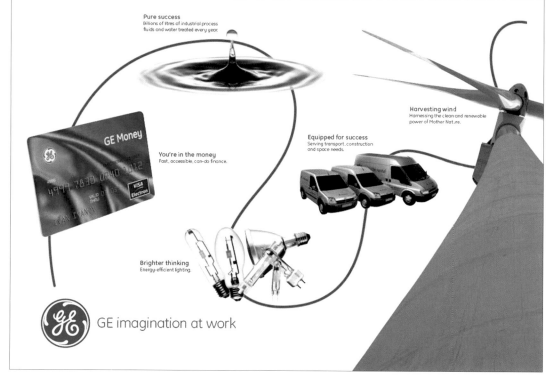

GOOD**YEAR**

Ten years later Goodyear introduced the first all weather tyre, with its famous diamond tread design. In 1912, Goodyear launched its first ever airship, or blimp. These became an icon of the skies, aerial ambassadors for a proud brand.

In 1927, Goodyear started making tyres in the UK. This was Goodyear's first non-US plant, and in the years to follow the company expanded in every corner of the globe. By 1963 the company had made its one billionth tyre but kept a handle on its conservational concerns. In 1978, Goodyear pioneered new uses for old tyres as construction materials for more than 2,000 artificial reefs and floating breakwaters, protecting harbours and providing habitats for marine life. For its innovative and highly successful work in hazardous waste disposal, Goodyear received the Environmental Industry Award from the White House.

In 1999, a global strategic alliance with Sumitomo Rubber Industries, owners of the Dunlop tyre brand, confirmed the organisation's global leadership.

Product

On road, off road. From race track to mud track to mountain track. On tractors, on earthmovers, on trucks. Whatever the vehicle, whatever the terrain, Goodyear prides itself on offering high performance tyres for all applications.

Goodyear led the way to improved wet-weather safety with its V-Tred tyre designs, culminating in the all-new HydraGrip, which won best family car tyre in its very first independent tyre test. Autocar described HydraGrip as 'exceptional'. Goodyear scored firsts with 'Run Flat', 'Bio-Tred' eco-friendly and weather reactive tyres. Goodyear tyres are rigorously tested on track to deliver maximum performance off track. From drag racing, the fastest motorsport on earth, to the gruelling NASCAR race series, Goodyear tyres are put through their paces.

The Goodyear Eagle F1 brings race proven technology to the street. A stunning directional tread pattern gives the road holding of a racing slick in the dry and new levels of security and traction in the wet. Eagle F1 has more independent tyre test wins than any other tyre, with accolades from Evo, Which? Autocar & Auto Express.

Goodyear lead the way in developing Run Flat tyres. Manufacturers as diverse as MINI, BMW, Chrysler, Land Rover, Ferrari, Maserati, Mercedes-Benz and Rolls Royce offer models with Goodyear Run Flat tyres – an incredible technological development that allows the driver to continue for up to 50 miles after a puncture.

Market

Goodyear is a truly global tyre and rubber company marketing word class products in a number of different market sectors. Best known for its leading position in tyre development, with some 200 million tyres sold every year. Goodyear are also a major retailer with a network of fast fit outlets across the world, as well as being a major producer of chemicals and industrial rubber components.

As market leader in farm, 4×4 and run-on-flat technology, as well as award winners in high performance and family car tyres, Goodyear are the discerning choice of car manufacturers across the world. Globally, Goodyear are chosen by vehicle manufacturers; in Europe Goodyear are selected by VW Group, Peugeot, Citroën, MINI, Ford, General Motors, Saab and Volvo, to name but a few. Epitomising quality, Goodyear are suppliers to BMW, Mercedes-Benz, Land Rover, Ferrari, TVR and the new Rolls Royce Phantom. Holding a leading position in all market sectors, Goodyear is working in conjunction with vehicle manufacturers in the development of new tyre technologies, such as Run Flat.

In the world of farming, Goodyear is selected by leading manufacturer's including Caterpillar, JCB, McCormick, CNH and John Deere.

Achievements

All tyres may be black and round, but the level of technology contained within is staggering. Goodyear have led the way in tyre development for over a century. The company took only 28 years to become the world's largest tyre and rubber company and have made a habit of passing milestones ever since.

Goodyear led the way in the use of nylon, synthetic materials and more recently introduced the run flat tyre to the mass market, bringing safety and peace of mind to a new generation of motorists.

Goodyear believes in proving its ability at the cutting edge. The result? More Formula One Grand Prix victories than any other tyre manufacturer and a road tyre range that developed from this success.

With 28 manufacturing bases across the world and sales operations in most countries, Goodyear prides itself on its diverse team of some 90,000 associates and its commitment to quality. In the UK alone, the company employs over 3,000 people, with three UK group factories.

History

Charles Goodyear was a man who changed the world. In 1839, he discovered 'vulcanisation', the process that turns rubber into a versatile, weatherproof material. Goodyear died a pauper, but his name lived on when Frank Seiberling immortalised his name when founding the Goodyear Tyre and Rubber Company in 1898 in Ohio.

With just thirteen workers, Goodyear production began on November 21st, 1898, with a product line of bicycle and carriage tyres and horseshoe pads.

A tyre has to cope with many demands. It has to reduce road noise, provide passenger comfort, offer maximum grip and, of course, be durable and safe. Goodyear's experience in research and development, at the forefront of racing and working with all major car manufacturers means that Goodyear products can be trusted, day in, day out.

Off the road, the latest Goodyear Wrangler MT/R is a real tough act. It was developed to withstand the most extreme off road driving – and was chosen by Land Rover as the official tyre for the inaugural Land Rover G4 Challenge; one tyre for 4,000 miles, over 33 days, in three continents, over four time zones.

In the UK, Goodyear is the market leader in the agricultural tyre market. British farmers can rely on Goodyear not only for durability and traction but also for innovative technology that reduces soil damage and compaction – which results in greater productivity and yields.

In the fleet market, Goodyear know that fleet managers require good service as well as quality tyres. Truck Force is Goodyear's pan-European service network for truck operators, and keeps fleets moving day and night.

Recent Developments
Environmental initiatives are an integral part of Goodyear's strategy. Policies for responsible tyre disposal and recycling are part of the ethic behind a major manufacturer and leading retailer of tyres across the world.

A commitment to discovery is part of the brand's mindset. The Goodyear GT3 tyre features a constituent developed from ordinary corn. This revolutionary tyre development from Goodyear is a benchmark in the world of eco-friendly engineering.

Goodyear is also committed to delivering the highest service levels to its customers. The company's recent multi million pound investment in the TyreFort building in Birmingham has created the largest tyre distribution centre in the UK, capable of holding one million tyres for nationwide next day delivery. TyreFort contact centre builds on Goodyear's philosophy of a sales and service support second to none, and the two second e-business ordering system provides an industry benchmark.

Promotion
The Goodyear brand has built its strength through consistent investment and innovation in integrated marketing campaigns. Periodic heavyweight advertising campaigns have reinforced the brand message supported by regular promotional activity in tyre dealerships. Indeed, the brand's first television advert was as early as 1948.

Goodyear believes that the best way of promoting its products is to show them perform. Following years of unparalleled success in Formula One, Goodyear is still at the forefront in motorsport, as the tyre of choice for NASCAR, the world's fastest saloon car racing championship.

In addition to above-the-line advertising campaigns, Goodyear regularly exhibit at major UK exhibitions, are involved in a diverse range of sponsorship and promotional programmes including football internationals and HydraZorbing (a new and exciting watersport imported to the UK by Goodyear) and communicate the brands portfolio in print and online. Consumer and business to business strategies maximise investment in a highly competitive industry. And, of course, one can't forget that Goodyear has a distinctive brand icon in the form of the Goodyear Airship which performs a powerful advertising role for the brand around the world.

Brand Values
Brand Values are not just a superficial afterthought for Goodyear. At the heart of Goodyear is its total obsession with innovation. Millions of pounds go into developing new technologies for the passenger vehicle, truck and farming communities; delivering the very best performance under the most challenging of conditions. Innovation in product excellence brings passenger vehicle tyres that maximise ever increasing new vehicle

technologies, farm tyres that optimise farmer's capital investment whilst taking care of the environment and truck tyres that are reliable, durable and long-lasting.

This is brought to life through a developing culture in which a committed and competitive team can excel.

www.goodyear.co.uk

WINNER
Auto EXPRESS
TYRE TEST 2003

Which? Magazine
TYRE TEST 2004
RECOMMENDED AS
BEST BUY
17" CATEGORY

evo MOTORING MAGAZINE
TYRE TEST 2002 WINNER

BEST HIGH PERFORMANCE
AUTOCAR
TYRE TEST
2004 WINNER

BEST FAMILY CAR TYRE
AUTOCAR
TYRE TEST
2004 WINNER

THINGS YOU DIDN'T KNOW ABOUT
Goodyear

- The famous Goodyear winged foot logo is based on the famous god of mythology known to the ancient Romans as Mercury and to the Greeks as Hermes.

- Goodyear manufactured blimps for commercial and military use.

- Over the years, Goodyear built more than 300 airships, more than any other company in the world.

- During World War II, in addition to tyres, Goodyear produced rubber rafts and flotation vests.

- Goodyear Run Flat tyres are fitted to many bulletproof vehicles, offering celebrities and dignitaries the highest levels of security.

- The first vehicle to top the 600mph land speed record was on Goodyear rubber.

- Goodyear had the first tyre prints in space. The Apollo 14 'moon buggy' relied on Goodyear for its first journey on the moon.

- Goodyear are the choice tyre for drag racing, the fastest motorsport on earth (0-100mph in two seconds), and the NASCAR race series (average speeds of 200mph at Daytona).

Heathrow express

Market

Serving the world's busiest international airport, Heathrow Express is one of the most successful high-speed rail-air links in the world. The service carries over 15,000 passengers a day on the fifteen minute journey between Heathrow Airport and central London and offers an additional transport option for passengers travelling between Heathrow Central (for Terminals 1, 2 and 3) and Terminal 4.

Heathrow Express is part of BAA's commitment to increasing the use of public transport to Heathrow and caters for a proportion of the airport's 63 million passengers who pass through each year. Tailored to the specific needs of the airport passenger, the Heathrow Express fleet has special design features and the service operates in line with the airport, offering a fifteen minute frequency service, 365 days a year. The service also provides a valuable means of transport for over 41,000 airport employees.

The continuing success of Heathrow Express depends on its delivery of a fast, frequent and reliable service which has been designed to support the flight patterns for Heathrow's business and leisure passengers.

Achievements

Since its launch in June 1998, Heathrow Express has gained market share over both the London Underground and taxi travel to the airport from central London, firmly establishing itself as a favoured route for both business and leisure passengers. The service removes approximately 3,000 journeys from the regional roads every day, and has made savings to the UK economy in terms of time, compared to the use of tube, taxi or bus of over £444 million.

History

In 1987, the Government commissioned Heathrow Access Surface Study concluded that a main line rail link from Paddington would provide the best option for increasing public transport to Heathrow and, in 1991, the Heathrow Express Railways Act was brought in, giving BAA the power to construct the Heathrow Express.

The Prime Minister, the Rt Hon Tony Blair MP, officially launched Heathrow Express on June 23rd 1998. A wholly owned subsidiary of BAA, the service is a £550 million investment which supports the airport operator's.

Heathrow Express also introduced its Taxi Share scheme in 1998, in conjunction with the Licensed Taxi Drivers Association to enable passengers to share a taxi on their onward journey from Paddington Station. The lower fares and shorter waiting times generated by the scheme allow 40-75% more people to leave Paddington by taxi during peak hours. Over 305,000 travellers have shared a taxi so far, saving about 775,000 taxi miles and so helping to ease the pressure on London's roads during the rush hour.

Product

Heathrow Express is a dedicated, non-stop, high-speed rail-air link operating between Heathrow Airport and central London, with a journey time of only fifteen minutes. There are two dedicated stations at Heathrow: Heathrow Central (serving Terminals 1, 2 and 3) and Terminal 4, which is a further 6-8 minutes away. The Inter-Terminal Transfer service also provides an additional option for passenger movement around the airport, offering free travel between the two stations.

The design of the Heathrow stations ensures that they offer customers swift, convenient access to the ultra-modern train service. For passengers with disabilities, the service includes dedicated seating areas in trains. The dedicated platforms at Heathrow and London Paddington are level with train floors to ensure completely step-free access.

The purpose-built trains, capable of travelling at 100mph, run between 5.10am and 11.30pm from Paddington Station 365 days a year (the only exception being on Christmas Day when the service usually runs every 30 minutes). The carriages are air-conditioned and have ergonomically designed seating, generous luggage areas and exclusive Express TV keeping passengers up to date with international news issues. There are Quiet Zones on the trains where the use of mobile phones is prohibited and Express TV is not in use.

Heathrow Express enjoys a loyal customer base and carries approximately 15,000 customers each day. Research by the company indicates a high awareness level among potential users of the service, with the majority of these travellers stating they would consider using Heathrow Express in the future.

Heathrow Express is a key member of Airport Express, a joint alliance between BAA plc and National Express Group which promotes and markets the Heathrow, Gatwick and Stansted Express rail services. The alliance brings together the sales and marketing activities of all three operations to create a single point of contact for travel trade agents and tour operators.

Recent Developments

Steadily increasing passenger numbers, totalling over 22 million in the past six years, has led to further investment to provide increased capacity on-board.

In July 2001 Heathrow Express placed an order for five new carriages, costing a total of £6.5 million, which has resulted in an additional carriage to each Heathrow Express train set-up providing a 14% increase in seat capacity. The new nine-car trains were brought into service in a rolling programme which is now fully complete.

In addition to the purchase of additional rolling stock, Heathrow Express also announced details of a multi-million pound project aimed at delivering a robust ticketing and revenue system using the latest ticketing system technology. The project involved the replacement of 23 Automatic Ticket Vending Machines (ATVMs) and eight Ticket Office Machines (TOMs) at Paddington and Heathrow Airport. It also included sales of tickets over the internet and the introduction of SMART card technologies.

Heathrow Express had already implemented many of the recommendations detailed in the Cullen Inquiry into the 1999 Paddington rail disaster, including the introduction of photoluminescent marking around emergency evacuation windows and an evaluation of a low-level escape lighting system, as part of a fleet wide refurbishment of its rolling stock.

Timing is everything

Don't take any chances. There's no faster way from central London to Heathrow Airport.
Just 15 minutes, every 15 minutes* from Paddington Station.

Heathrow express
www.heathrowexpress.com

Save your crawl for the hotel pool.

The fastest way from central London to Heathrow Airport 15 minutes, every 15 minutes.†

†Timetabled journey time for trains from London Paddington to Heathrow terminals 1, 2 and 3 (approx 8 minutes more to terminal 4) between 05.10 and 23.10. Last train departs 23.30.

 Heathrow **express**

Timing is everything

Other upgrades introduced in the refurbishment included the upgrading of the flat screen televisions, incorporating state-of-the-art technology to provide a clearer, sharper picture; new reinforced luggage shelves; improved lighting system and the refreshment of interior fabrics throughout the trains.

In 2003 Webtod was introduced, which enables customers to book and pay online in one simple transaction. Customers are given a reference number, which they simply type into one of the Heathrow Express ticket machines or insert the credit card used to make the booking to retrieve their ticket at the point of departure.

Promotion

Heathrow Express primarily uses press, outdoor and online to execute its promotional strategy. The company launched an advertising campaign called Back to Business for 2004/05, which highlights the convenience and speed of the Heathrow Express service. The campaign is directed at the business market, particularly within the UK, and aims to communicate the key benefits of the service. The objective is to encourage trial among prospective business passengers by focusing on the core business messages – speed, frequency, and convenience.

The campaign was based around the 'Timing is everything' message and included dramatic and engaging images of time crucial activities such as cricket and baseball. To encourage interaction with the brand, a number of online creative executions were developed. These were placed on a number of large corporate systems in the City of London and on investment trading sites.

Responding to the change of markets at Heathrow Airport, Heathrow Express launched its first leisure campaign in July 2004. The aim was to communicate the key benefits of use and to portray the feeling of 'your holiday starts as soon as you board the train'. A number of different mediums were used including press, underground 48" sheets, door drops and banners on sites such as lastminute.com and Expedia.

The focus for below-the-line activity is working and developing relationships with airlines at Heathrow Airport. Frequent travellers are the focus of joint initiatives run in conjunction with key airlines. Heathrow Express is a partner within the Virgin Atlantic Flying Club programme, whereby Silver and Gold members receive

Timing is everything

Central London to Heathrow Airport in 15 minutes, every 15 minutes†.

Heathrow **express** ⊗

www.heathrowexpress.com

an allocation of First Class upgrades to use on Heathrow Express. This has proved extremely successful since its launch in July 2003, adding value to both brands. The partnership is communicated within membership packs, statements and email newsletters.

To stimulate the leisure market, Heathrow Express uses 'two for one' style promotions which are executed

through a number of channels including Time Out magazine, Visit Britain and airline frequent flyer programmes.

Two successful leisure campaigns with British Airways were also developed in 2004, and communicated through The Evening Standard. Heathrow Express complemented the British Airways low cost leisure fare campaigns with a two for one offer which was fulfilled through a specially set-up website, which allowed customers to pick-up their train tickets from the ticket machines on the platforms at Paddington Station.

In 2005, Heathrow Express will focus on customer relationship marketing, ensuring consistent and frequent communication with the Heathrow Express customer base, giving news, promotions and information about new products. An awareness campaign also exists across all four terminals at Heathrow Airport communicating key benefits of use and directional 'way finding' which steers customers in the direction of the Heathrow Express platforms.

Heathrow Express has listened to and met the needs of their loyal customers by offering convenience in the form of a new product called Carnet, which offers travellers twelve single tickets for the price of eleven in a credit card sized wallet to fit in your pocket. Other activities include advertising in in-flight media and in-flight promotions.

Brand Values

The key brand values are speed, frequency and certainty. Recent research by Heathrow Express has shown that these key benefits are recalled most by its customers.

For both business and leisure customers, Heathrow Express aims to provide the excellent levels of comfort and customer service that air travellers have come to expect. However, different aspects of the brand's personality are highlighted for the business and consumer markets to reflect the most desirable aspect of the brand for each of these segments.

For the business traveller, the brand is portrayed as fast, frequent, reliable and convenient. When speaking to the leisure market, the brand is reflected as not being overly formal or austere while being fast, reliable, convenient, approachable, and family friendly.

www.heathrowexpress.co.uk

THINGS YOU DIDN'T KNOW ABOUT

Heathrow Express

❯ Every year, almost one million miles are travelled by Heathrow Express, the equivalent to almost four times the distance to the moon or 37 times around the world.

❯ Since the service was launched in June 1998, it has carried over 22 million people.

❯ Up to 2,500 pieces of luggage per day or 13,000 tons per year are handled by Heathrow Express. This is the equivalent of 34 jumbo jets or 3,000 elephants.

❯ There is a special Meeter/Greeter fare for those travelling to the airport to see friends and family off, or to meet them on arrival.

HEMSCOTT

Market

Hemscott is a leading supplier of high-quality business and financial information solutions to professional, retail and corporate customers. It has three key divisions: Global Business Information, which comprises data sales in the UK and North America; Global Investor Relations business; and UK Media, comprising advertising and online publishing.

Hemscott owns and manages a proprietary database of regularly updated company information which has been built and developed over 20 years and which includes data from as far back as 1983. The company uses this proprietary data to deliver tailored information and research resources to individuals, companies, their clients and their staff, including integrating data and analysis tools into a customer's own website. Hemscott Company Guru is a regularly updated online knowledge management tool for business professionals, offering in-depth data and extensive search capabilities. Hemscott's Premium and Premium Plus services are online

investment research resources for the consumer, offering a wide range of fundamentals, price and trading data, broker forecasts and easy-to-use analysis tools. Hemscott is also a leading player in the online corporate communications and investor relations market, with over 315 clients, including more than 35 FTSE 100 companies, choosing Hemscott to provide these vital services.

Hemscott is exploiting new confidence in financial and business markets by selling more innovative products to a wider range of blue-chip customers. The mergers with leading US data providers CoreData and bigdough.com in late 2004 takes the number of UK, Irish, US and Canadian companies on the combined database to around 13,000.

Achievements

The company has acquired a number of awards and accolades over the last few years but probably the most significant, certainly as regards the quality and integrity of the company's data, was when The Department of

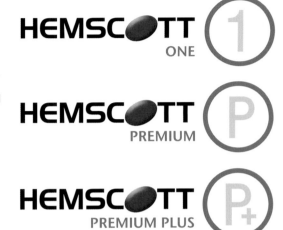

Trade & Industry used the Hemscott database to help produce the Higgs Report into the role and effectiveness of non-executive directors, published in January 2003. Data, including detailed information on the size, composition and membership of the boards of the UK's 2,200 listed companies, was analysed by the Higgs team to build up a detailed picture of the population of non-executive directors in UK listed companies.

Hemscott's investment portal, Hemscott One, was voted Investor's Chronicle Best Research and Information Provider three years running and, in a recent survey of captains of British industry was visited by over a third of those polled and was the fourth most popular website visited. Hemscott also won ProShare's Award for Excellence for Services to the Private Investor in 2004. Hemscott also deserves credit for the awards won by clients of its Online Investor Relations practice at the Investor Relations Society Awards in both 2003 and 2004. British American Tobacco won the IR Best Practice Website Private Investor Award in 2004. Countryside Properties won the Grand Prix Award or Best Smaller Company Investor Relations and Best CSR Practice Award (non FTSE 100) at the Investor Relations Magazine UK Awards 2004. And, most recently, BT won Best Website for Individual Shareholders and Best Overall Performance in Meeting the Needs of Individual Shareholders.

History

Hemscott's origins lie in Hemmington Scott, a publishing company established in 1985 by Jill Meiring (nee Hemmington) and Peter Scott. The company started with eight people and produced the first edition of The Hambro Company Guide, which became The Hemscott Company Guide, eight months later.

In 1989 Hemmington Scott launched The Corporate Register and the next year took its first tentative steps into electronic data sales with its first sale of fundamental data.

In 1995, Hemmington Scott became the first organisation to provide information on quoted companies over the internet. Four years later, it became an Internet Service Provider (ISP) and was the first content provider to supply information for free to ISP customers.

Hemscott itself was formed in December 1999 when Hemmington Scott split into a publishing company and a data provider. It was the start of a period of intensive product innovation, rapid development and growth.

In 2000 it identified target markets and products, undertook a reverse acquisition of Bridgend Group plc and obtained a listing on the Alternative Investment Market (AIM). It also raised £18 million in cash, recruited a new management team, invested in a new IT infrastructure and moved into its current offices at Finsbury Tower in the City of London.

Still Attracting Visitors

Make sure your business really appeals to investors online. Hemscott will design and build you engaging corporate website solutions that last.

Hemscott is the corporate communications and investor relations specialist with the knowledge and infrastructure to get it right first time. We work closely with you to develop and maintain every aspect of your online presence as your business grows.

HEMSCOTT
The Home of Online Investor Relations Solutions

CORPORATE WEBSITES | IR CENTRES | DATA | TOOLS | DESIGN | HOSTING | PROACTIVE MAINTENANCE

CALL : +44 (0)20 7847 0017   EMAIL : IRHOME@HEMSCOTT.CO.UK   WEB : WWW.HEMSCOTTPLC.COM

Later in 2000 Hemscott launched Company Guru, the online research resource for people and listed company information and the Hemscott Analyst newsletter, a subscription service whereby Hemscott emails users with share advice, trends and major company news.

In 2001 Hemscott was named Best Research Provider at the Investor's Chronicle annual awards. The company's turnover was £5.1 million.

In 2002 Company Guru was expanded to include private company data and Hemscott launched Hemscott Premium, an online research resource providing up-to-date information on listed companies for individual investors. The product rapidly became heavily subscribed. ShareSpeak, a phone service for real-time share price information, was launched. By the end of the year the Business Information division, which included a rapidly growing Investor Relations practice, continued to expand.

In 2003 Hemscott acquired the Directory of Directors from Reed Business Information and published it in May. FinMedia Ltd acquired a major shareholding in Hemscott, and Hemscott launched Guru Academic especially for the academic research market and Premium Plus, an advanced online research resource offering exclusive data management tools and real-time streaming prices for serious private investors.

Product

Since its flotation on AIM in August 2000, Hemscott has grown and diversified its business to the point where it is established as a leading provider of corporate information in the UK and now North America.

Hemscott Company Guru is one of Hemscott's most important products in the Business Information division. An online company research resource for business, it provides continuously updated financial data and biographical information on directors. Its intuitive search capabilities and results captured in charts, graphs and reports make it an invaluable and simple to use research tool. Clients can choose from a variety of modules, including quoted company, private company and news cuttings.

The service has recently been enhanced with new search functionality, redesigned data screens and new facilities to download search results and profit and loss, balance sheet and cashflow data to Excel.

In 2003 Company Guru Academic was developed to deliver in-depth research information for students and alumni. Academic institutions across the UK now offer the service to both staff and students.

The Directory of Directors is also part of the Company Guru service. It provides detailed biographical information of 40,000 directors from 12,000 leading UK companies. The directory is also available in print form.

Hemscott Premium, launched in 2002, is a subscription website service, providing a comprehensive online investment research resource for private and corporate investors. Hemscott Premium Plus also offers an even greater range of tools and data aimed at more sophisticated investors and those managing larger portfolios. Key features include PDF Company Facts reports, news event graphing to evaluate the effect of news on share prices, Excel downloads of data and real-time prices, and trade and news information.

Hemscott also offers bespoke data services. The proprietary database comprises around 21 years of detailed and comprehensive information about the financial activities and directors of UK and Irish listed companies. Hemscott provides bespoke sets of this data, which can be integrated into clients' databases, websites and intranets or developed into products for resale.

The database also affords clients access to detailed and timely interim and preliminary results.

Hemscott also provides tailored online investor relations solutions and corporate websites to public companies.

New developments include the Hemscott Desktop Analyst, which allows investors visiting client sites to compare and contrast key information about a company using a variety of charts and analysis options. In addition, News Publisher allows clients to selectively publish company news from over 170 key sources on corporate websites or intranets.

The Interactive Annual Reports Service delivers reports to clients online in HTML, while the Hemscott Total Shareholder Return charting tool allows visitors to a client website to view changes in share price and dividends received over the past five financial years. Hemscott also offers US Securities and Exchange Commission filings data, allowing dual-listed companies to display this information on their websites.

Hemscott operates an award-winning financial website – www.hemscott.com, providing information for private investors, business executives and professional investors. Users are typically high net worth individuals and accordingly companies seeking to target this audience advertise on the Hemscott website. Companies marketing sophisticated financial services and exclusive or luxury products and services of many different categories use the site as a direct route to this market.

Many professional advisers publicise their services by placing advertisements and paying for enhanced entries for their own businesses in the Corporate Advisers area of the www.hemscott.com service. The site supplies in-depth data on corporate advisers.

Hemscott Analyst is another Hemscott service which delivers share recommendation and analysis by email directly to the desktops of subscribers at least three times a week.

Recent Developments

In 2004 Hemscott plc became a global organisation when it expanded into the US, first by acquiring CoreData, a company that builds and maintains databases of historical financial and stock price technical information on North American publicly traded companies, industry groups and major equity markets.

Hemscott also merged with another US company, bigdough.com.inc, which has a powerful database of institutional money managers and their stock holdings, as well as a robust contact management and communications software platform.

With these impressive assets, combined with its new geographical reach into the US, Canada and Europe, as well as its

- UK & North American Data
- Capital Markets Data
- Listed & Private Company Data
- Extensive Director Data
- Company Fundamentals
- Broker Estimates

traditional markets in the UK, Hemscott's continued success as a leading international data and applications provider looks assured.

Promotion

All Hemscott's marketing design work, ranging from press ads to websites to direct mail shots, is done in-house by its own designers and programmers. The company uses the full mix of marketing tools, including advertising, PR, direct mail and email, sponsorship and conferences but while those are successful tactics for profile raising and gaining new business and subscribers, the most potent marketing tool at its disposal is word of mouth.

Users regard Hemscott's products highly and much of the company's expansion during recent years is as a direct result of the loyalty of existing clients, and their positive recommendations to others.

Brand Values

Hemscott's vision is to be the high-quality specialist business and financial information provider of choice in the UK, Europe and North America.

Hemscott's success comes from a combination of presenting its customers with flexible, innovative, 'client led' products and service solutions that enhance their experience; operational excellence, where it provides reliable products and services at competitive prices and exceptional customer service.

www.hemscottplc.com

THINGS YOU DIDN'T KNOW ABOUT

Hemscott

> Hemscott delivers at least 50 share tips a year to subscribers' desktops.

> Hemscott broadcasts company presentations and events over the internet through audio and video websites.

> The Directory of Directors contains profiles of over 41,000 directors of 12,000 companies. It was first published in 1879.

Market

In the global business market, business people have to travel around the world more and more, increasing demand for the services of well-known and dependable hotels. Whether it is just providing a bed for a night, or a full range of meeting, dining and conference facilities, hotels serve the business market in a wide variety of ways, often acting as an essential link in the chain of global business meetings, dealings and transactions.

With this in mind, it is no wonder that international hotel chains derive around 70% of their revenue from business customers, with money not only generated from room nights but also from the usage of facilities, including conference and meeting rooms.

In the UK, KeyNote Research estimates that the total hotel market generated a revenue of £10.18 billion in 2002, which means that business custom accounted for around £7 billion of this total. Large though the market is, rapid growth experienced in the late 1990s has given way to a slow-down since 2001. International events, such as the September 11th attacks in the US, the SARS virus in Asia, the war in Iraq and a downturn in the US and Japanese economies all contributed to the decline, particularly in the corporate sector. Many companies cut back their travel budgets. Advances in video conferencing technology has also had a small adverse effect on hotel demand, meaning more business people do not have to travel to meet.

Business hotel users tend to focus on the major global brands that they know offer a reliable consistent service and range of products, and also that they can negotiate global deals with. InterContinental Hotels Group, which owns Holiday Inn, is one of the foremost players in this global elite, along with major competitors such as Hilton, Marriott and Best Western.

Achievements

Holiday Inn can claim to be one of the world's best-known hotel brands and, from its foundation in 1952, has become synonymous with innovation, spearheading the development of the hotel industry around the globe.

Some of its many innovations include the introduction of the first computerised reservations system, known as 'Holidex', in 1965 and, in 1985, Holiday Inn became the first hotel brand to introduce a frequent guest loyalty programme – 'Priority Club' – which is now the largest in the hotel industry, with 24 million members worldwide.

Holiday Inn has also led the way with its early adoption of internet technology, becoming the first hotel group to take direct reservations on the internet, in 1995. It has also led the industry with its pursuit of simpler, more transparent pricing, designed to reduce the number of price points and deal options so that business customers can budget their costs more easily.

With almost 50 years of expertise in meeting and conference services, Holiday Inn has also earned an enviable reputation for providing high standards of product and service to business customers, whilst offering value for money.

History

The founder of Holiday Inn, Kemmons Wilson, opened the first Holiday Inn in Memphis, Tennessee in 1952, after he returned from a family road trip discouraged by the lack of value and service in family hotels. This has consequently become known within Holiday Inn as the 'road trip that changed the world'. When the doors of this first Holiday Inn opened, it was the first hotel to offer free accommodation and free meals for children, the first to provide air conditioning, free ice, parking and telephones as standard and also the first hotel brand to offer twin double beds in guest rooms.

Today, Holiday Inn is one of the most famous and widely recognised hotel brands in the world, with more travellers having stayed at Holiday Inn hotels than at any other hotel in the world. The brand is committed to innovation and will continue to drive the hotel industry forward for the next 50 years and beyond.

Product

In the UK, Holiday Inn is one of the largest mid-market hotel chains, with over 100 properties offering a full range of services and located close to city centres and attractions. Holiday Inn properties typically have over 120 rooms.

For business customers, Holiday Inn prides itself on its flexible meetings and conference product offering. As different types of businesses have different requirements, Holiday Inn's conference and meeting facilities offer a personalised service in planning, a wide choice of food and on-the-ground support.

All Holiday Inn hotels in the UK & Ireland offer a 'Meetings Network' package. In addition, selected locations have an enhanced offering – the Academy, which offers a full range of state-of-the-art facilities. Whether customers plan a small meeting, training course, major conference or product launch, Holiday Inn's meeting services can meet all needs.

The Meetings Network is a standardised range of meetings services, allowing business customers to easily plan their meetings at any Holiday Inn location. For example, Holiday Inn promises a two-hour response

to all enquiries, a proposal sent within 24 hours and a dedicated meeting host to ensure all elements of the meeting are delivered. This complete meetings package also includes tea and coffee, soft drinks, refreshments, lunch, overhead projector, flipcharts and stationery. In addition, all meeting rooms are also equipped with data ports and most have ISDN lines.

The Academy is a superior range of meeting, conference and training suites from Holiday Inn designed as a purpose built self contained space that comes with its own separate reception area, break-out space, an array of technology and a dedicated support team. Currently, more than 30 hotels in the UK offer the Academy.

Holiday Inn has a total of 434 meeting rooms in 100 major city, town and airport locations throughout the UK and Ireland.

Another important product offering for Holiday Inn business customers is its frequent guest loyalty programme, Priority Club, with 900,000 members in the UK and some 24 million worldwide. Members can earn and redeem points at 3,500 locations worldwide and also with a variety of partners, including airline and car hire firms.

Recent Developments
Holiday Inn further invested in its meetings services during 2004, with conference and meeting facilities in over 30 Holiday Inn hotels in the UK and Ireland benefiting from a multi-million pound refurbishment programme.

A new range of food and drink concepts for Holiday Inn's UK & Ireland conference and meetings offering has also been recently introduced, including choices from international and healthy menu options, branded coffee and themed 'Chocoholics' and 'Healthy' breaks. Holiday Inn meetings will also have the additional choice of Starbucks following a new agreement with the successful coffee brand. Other recent improvements include the addition of light working lunch menu options with healthy choices and a selection of international menus serving Italian, Spanish, British and Oriental dishes.

During 2004, Holiday Inn has also invested heavily in its facilities to ensure it meets all requirements for disabled customers. The company now claims to lead the industry in the provision of facilities for disabled people.

Promotion
In order to reach current and prospective business customers, Holiday Inn advertises in a range of specialist press titles, often using professional magazines covering key sectors such as law, accountancy and medicine.

The hotel group's global sales force is another important marketing tool, looking after the needs of important customers and also chasing new business. These efforts are supported by a local sales team for each Holiday Inn hotel.

Holiday Inn also invests in sponsorship, being the title sponsor of the Seat Cupra touring cars championship for 2003 and 2004. This is Britain's most lucrative one-make saloon car motor racing series, attracting almost 100,000 spectators to six racing circuits in 2003, including a record breaking crowd of 44,000 at the Rockingham Motor Speedway in Corby.

Extensive Holiday Inn branding was featured on all racing cars, with branded banners distributed around the tracks, including Silverstone and Brands Hatch.

As part of the deal, Holiday Inn also sponsored a television docu-soap of the championship, called 'Racing Rivals' which follows the behind-the-scenes exploits of drivers taking part in the Holiday Inn SEAT Cupra Championship. 'Racing Rivals' was aired nationwide on Channel 4, Bravo and Motors TV.

The partnership delivers the Holiday Inn message to a mass audience on two different levels. Firstly TV viewers of motorsport racing are a perfect fit for the company's business audience, while the family racing days out reinforce the Holiday Inn leisure offering, which is all about giving consumers a reason to travel around the UK.

Brand Values
Holiday Inn aims to consistently provide a warm welcome, friendly service and high standards of quality, value and comfort. Success in the provision of these targets have been instrumental in the brand's success. The Holiday Inn offering is also based on its 'Can-do' attitude to service, its dependability, affordability, convenience of location, wide choice of location, and the fact that it is a reassuring choice for the business customer.

www.holiday-inn.co.uk

THINGS YOU DIDN'T KNOW ABOUT

Holiday Inn

> Globally, Holiday Inn has 284,897 rooms at 1,500 hotels.

> Some 139 new Holiday Inn hotels are in the pipeline.

> Holiday Inn is the second largest provider of sit-down restaurants in the world, serving 67 million people every year.

> Holiday Inn was the first hotel company to advertise on US television, in 1966.

Market

The IT market in the UK is currently worth billions of dollars, with continued growth forecast. But it's not the figures that define the market as much as the pressures that drive it.

Customers and consumers grow ever more demanding – and ever more value conscious. The result is an unending spiral of innovation and evolution, with even the most breakthrough new products soon facing the prospect of possible commoditisation. Profit margins get eroded, awaiting the next innovation.

To differentiate themselves from their competitors, companies seek new ways to meet the changing needs of their customers. And as companies seek to become ever more competitive, a number of high-value opportunities are created for IBM.

Driving much of the growth in the IT industry over the last decade is the realisation that technology can be a true enabler of business transformation. Organisations, enterprises and institutions of all kinds understand that they can apply technology to completely re-engineer the way they work.

Inherent in that is the requirement to make all the separate parts of the value chain function as one system. Integrating the company infrastructure with those of its suppliers, partners and customers, while even more challenging, promises even greater rewards. And further efficiencies can be realised by outsourcing non-core day-to-day IT processes.

But foremost, there is a growing market for the key business insights from which the re-engineering process – and the subsequent value – can flow.

Achievements

Innovation credentials include IBM's 3,248 patents in 2004 alone, the twelfth consecutive year that IBM received more US patents than any other company. This was the fourth consecutive year that IBM received

more than 3,000 US patents and IBM remains the only company to receive more than 2,000 patents in one year.

However, it's the results that IBM achieves for its customers that make it the world's third most valuable brand – and gaining in value each year (Source: Business Week, Interbrand 2004).

History

The story of IBM is one of how a series of massive leaps of confidence left rival brands trailing in its wake, again and again. It's also the story of how the 20th century's most prominent supplier of technology has emerged in the 21st century as the leading provider of technology-enabled business solutions.

Establishing the International Business Machines Corporation in 1924, Thomas Watson exploited new technology to provide companies with the latest in typewriters and calculating machines.

Then, with enormous foresight, he expanded production during the Great Depression: with the result that when the new Social Security Act required the US Government to keep employment records, only IBM was able to meet the huge demand for punch card data-processors.

The next giant step was the development of a range of IBM mainframes, compatible with multiple printers, drives and other peripherals. The biggest privately financed commercial project ever, this established IBM's industry leadership for decades.

Another market-changing development was the unveiling in 1981 of the IBM Personal Computer – an overnight sensation. However, relentless commoditisation by a horde of competitors diffused the PC market after only a few years.

By 1993, a similar trend was under way in the mainframe market. So the company switched its strategic focus to what its customers kept saying was its greatest strength: the ability to provide total, integrated solutions.

Flowing from this insight, IBM worked on new technology to make its mainframes compatible with all leading hardware, operating systems and applications. The newly created IBM Global Services could now offer any

company the best possible solution in any situation, even if that meant including a competitor's applications or hardware.

But the next step made all the difference.

IBM recognised the potential of the internet for business in 1995. While the market tentatively experimented with 'shop window' websites, IBM made network computing – later to be called e-business – the company's overarching strategy.

It was phenomenally successful. By redefining the market, IBM re-established its leadership. With its open standards approach to computing, IBM was able to benefit from almost every new technological innovation. And even though the 'dot.com' boom became notorious for many unviable start-ups, many companies that used the internet in conjunction with a sound business model never looked back.

A powerful example of this is IBM itself. Five years ago, it printed around five million paper invoices a year. Today, it has reduced that number dramatically with e-procurement and internet sales resulting in efficiencies of billions of dollars a year.

Of course, IBM's On Demand Business strategy further propelled it from being a product provider to a provider of business solutions. Adding momentum to this was the creation of IBM Business Consulting Services in 2002. No longer organised around product lines, IBM's customer focus saw its client teams become aligned to customers by industry: Small Medium Enterprises, pharmaceuticals and healthcare, retail, government and banking, for example.

Product

IBM remains at the forefront of technological innovation. By the time you read this, the company will have launched a computer capable of one quadrillion (10^{15}) operations per second. IBM software solutions number in the hundreds, IBM chips power games consoles and rival computers, and IBM ThinkPad notebooks win awards for ergonomic excellence.

Yet, as companies realise that their continued success depends on completely re-engineering the way they work, the real role of the technology is to enable business transformation.

Furthermore, at the heart of each transformation there has to be a core business insight – and increasingly it's this that is IBM's most important capability. In fact, such an insight drove IBM's own restructuring process, with IBM Business Consulting Services also aligned to meet specific customer requirements.

Here are a few examples of what this customer-focused approach has achieved.

Boots, the UK's largest health and beauty chain, faces competition from every possible corner: supermarkets, discount shops, upmarket chains and e-tailers. Added efficiency could only begin to counter the threat. So today, IBM not only manages Boots' entire IT infrastructure, experts from the IBM retail consulting unit are also working with Boots to develop fresh uses for advanced technologies. A wireless shelf-edge stock management system and intuitive tills that provide information on promotional products are just the beginning.

The All England Lawn Tennis Club hosts one of the world's most important sporting events, The Championships at Wimbledon. And every year, IBM makes the action more and more accessible to the media, players and public. Courtside tennis experts input every point on IBM ThinkPad notebooks. The data is instantly fed to hundreds of commentators and journalists around the courts and billions of TV viewers around the globe. Players use statistical reports to analyse their games and those of their next competitors. Millions of office workers follow the games via web scoreboards and remote-controlled 'slamcams', and perhaps even purchase a few souvenirs from the online shop. It's pure On Demand Business.

Eurotunnel, market leader for cross-Channel travel, receives more than half its consumer business online. However, with that figure growing steadily, the original website needed to be totally reconstructed to handle

In the new on demand operating environment, different legacy operating systems interoperate seamlessly via 'middleware'. New systems employ open standards software to make it as easy as possible to interact with anyone in the world. Paper-based systems are 'virtualised', making them easy to access and use, by anyone, anywhere. And 'autonomic' self-diagnosing and self-correcting capabilities ensure that businesses aren't held hostage to the system's growing complexities.

But it's no quick fix. And on demand solutions take far more than IT. They depend on core business insights upon which the solution can be based. It is this requirement for business-transforming insight that makes IBM, with its independent software vendor partners, Business Partners and Business Consultancy Services, uniquely positioned to fulfil the growing demand for on demand business.

Promotion

Between 1993 and 2004, IBM moved from the 282nd position in Interbrand's league table of the world's most valuable brands to number three (Source: Financial World Interbrand 1994 and Business Week, Interbrand 2004).

capabilities, IBM sees it as its responsibility to create opportunity and hope for businesses, industries, society and the world.

Each year, IBM Corporate Community Relations invests over US$140 million globally in a range of large scale, global programmes focusing primarily on innovative uses of technology in educational contexts to help raise standards of achievement.

In the UK, programmes include: Reinventing Education – working in partnership with the Department for Education & Skills to encourage the use of technology to share effective practices between schools; KidSmart – providing access to IT in marginalised communities by donating more than 500 computers to nurseries; MentorPlace

WIMBLEDON IS ON DEMAND

ON DEMAND BUSINESS

traffic spikes and to support the latest functionalities. The infrastructure solution provided on time and on budget by IBM and its Business Partner, Pasporte, has made access to information and booking quicker and easier, provides unlimited scalability for unpredictable peaks and allows Eurotunnel to respond quickly to new market conditions and opportunities.

The Ministry of Defence needed to turn its 60 year old Whitehall HQ into a connected, collaborative, 21st century workspace for 3,300 people, and turned to IBM for support. The solution involved IBM Business Consulting Services and in-depth project management, change management and PFI procurement advisory services. And in spite of the scale of the project, it went live on budget, two months ahead of schedule.

ON DEMAND BUSINESS

Recent Developments

Today, leading companies can no longer afford to use the internet merely to exploit new business opportunities. They are actually transforming themselves around its potential – embracing what IBM calls On Demand Business.

The concept was recently summarised by current IBM CEO Sam Palmisano: "More and more businesses are facing escalating expectations from customers and suppliers. They are demanding increased levels of customisation, responsiveness and efficiency. This is the on demand era. It requires real time capabilities in your business processes and technology to meet these challenges."

The company's restructure wasn't the only reason. In 1993, IBM was using 70 different advertising agencies. With no central theme and a mixture of layout styles, typefaces and even logos, the brand identity had been severely eroded.

Reflecting its own restructuring process around the core idea of customer service, IBM made the pioneering strategic decision to consolidate its communications with one core communications partner, around the world.

Ogilvy & Mather was appointed to develop IBM's first global advertising campaign. The result, 'Solutions for a small planet', ran in 47 countries and 26 languages. It was the first step in repositioning IBM as a market-focused, service-orientated solutions provider.

But it was the next development that helped the brand reclaim its leadership. As IBM became aware of the enormous benefits that the internet could provide to businesses of all kinds, the company's solutions and communications had to reflect and deliver this new vision. Into a component-orientated marketplace, IBM launched its second integrated global campaign, alerting and educating the market about the potential of 'e-business'.

The 'e-business' campaign was so successful that any mention of internet-enabled business solutions by any IT company, effectively helped to promote IBM.

But in the meantime, at IBM, 'e-business' continued to evolve faster and further than competitors could follow. In 2005, with 'On Demand Business' now part of the IBM DNA, the brand journey has gathered more momentum, with the benefits of sense-and-respond business permeating every communication channel in an integrated campaign backed by US$800 million.

Brand Values

IBM has a fundamental belief in progress, science and the improvability of the human condition. With its unique

– providing virtual mentoring using e-mail to over 800 students, in partnership with Manpower and Adecco; TryScience – a highly stimulating, interactive science based website designed to encourage interest in science amongst 8-14 year olds.

Finally, IBM launched a new model and standard for community volunteering, the On Demand Community programme, which is supporting 25,000 IBM employees worldwide in providing their time and skills in schools and community groups.

www.ibm.com/uk

THINGS YOU DIDN'T KNOW ABOUT

IBM

> IBM has employed five Nobel Prize laureates. Two still work at the company.

> In 1996, as IBM scientists experimented with ways to add ever more processing power to a microchip, they used the tip of a scanning tunnelling microscope (STM) to form the letters 'IBM' out of 35 individual atoms. The STM has since evolved into the IBM Atomic Force Microscope (AFM), an essential tool of the nanotech era.

> IBM's most high-flying intranet is 220 miles above our heads, in the International Space Station. IBM has been computing in space since Explorer I in 1958 – participating in the Mercury, Gemini and Apollo missions, as well as the Mars Rover expedition.

> IBM recycles 96% of its computer equipment worldwide.

Market

During the last 25 years, Intel® has become the world's largest chip manufacturer; Intel is also a leading manufacturer of computer, networking and communications products, the power of the Intel brand in part demonstrates how computing and IT-based solutions have become a driving force, not only in business, but through almost every aspect of modern society. Intel is now setting the pace for the digital world, from wireless networking to home entertainment.

A classic expression of how Intel's business taps into wider social trends, is its success in becoming a pioneer in the field of wireless (or wi-fi) computer technology with its Intel® Centrino™ mobile technology brand. The world is becoming increasingly mobile, with business and consumer users needing to access the internet or use IT devices on the move. Research firm Gartner estimates that by 2007 there will be more than ten million frequent users of European public WLAN hot spots, and over twelve million infrequent users.

Intel is also at the heart of another trend sweeping the market – the blurring boundary between home computers and home entertainment. Intel is introducing products that are revolutionising the way people experience entertainment in their homes. With soaring sales of digital cameras, MP3 players, CD/DVD players, digital TVs, personal video recorders and a slew of other digital devices, Intel sees the 'Entertainment PC' as being the media 'command centre' of the digital home.

At the high-end of the business market, Intel is also leading the way. According to the 24th edition of the TOP500 list, nearly two-thirds of the world's fastest supercomputers now use Intel® Itanium® or Intel® Xeon® processors. Three years ago, Intel had only three systems on the list.

Intel's market is increasingly international, with non-US sales rising from 57% of worldwide revenues in 1998 to 75% in 2004. Intel's presence in emerging markets like China, India and Russia is extremely strong. For example, the company generated sales in China of US$3.7 billion in 2003.

Achievements

Intel is one of the greatest business success stories of the modern age. Founded in 1968 with just twelve employees and revenues in its first year of just US$2,672, Intel has grown into a giant, with record annual revenues in 2004 of US$34.2 billion and ranked 53rd in the Fortune 500. As of January 2005, Intel had been profitable for 66 consecutive quarters.

By 1993, Intel had introduced its first Pentium® processor. Since then, the company has continued

to render its own products obsolete almost every year – a strategy unheard of in any other business. As founder Gordon Moore comments; "If the auto industry advanced as rapidly as the semiconductor industry, a Rolls-Royce would get half a million miles per gallon, and it would be cheaper to throw it away than to park it."

Intel's track record gives it a brand more valuable and powerful than many classic 'business' brands. Indeed, according to the influential Interbrand/Business Week survey of The Best Global Brands, Intel's brand value of US$33 billion makes it the world's fifth most valuable brand – not bad, considering it makes products that most people don't touch or feel for themselves. With an 8% increase in brand value compared to 2003, Intel remains one of the strongest performers in the league, demonstrating that it remains on the pulse of business and consumer needs.

History

In 1968, computer boffins Robert Noyce and Gordon Moore created Intel with the aim of creating a more efficient computer memory, based on semiconductor technology. They came up with the 1103 in 1970 and it became the world's biggest-selling semiconductor device by the end of 1971.

Their most significant breakthrough came when a Japanese company called Busicom asked them to design twelve chips for a range of calculators. At the time, each electronic product required its own individually tailored chip. But Intel engineer Ted Hoff felt that it might be possible to create a single chip capable of carrying out a wide range of different functions – an advanced computer 'brain'.

The invention worked, and Intel realised that it had created a product with almost limitless applications. There was a problem, however – under the terms of the original contract, Busicom held the rights to the product. Moore and Noyce therefore bought them back for US$60,000.

Originally known as a 'microcomputer', Intel's first microprocessor went on the market in 1971. By the time the company introduced the 8008, a few years later, its early predictions had begun to materialise: the chip revolutionised supermarket cash registers, traffic lights, petrol pumps, airline reservation systems and arcade games. As fast as its chips were installed, Intel created smaller and more powerful versions.

In the early 1980s, IBM began tentative talks with Intel over the possibility of using its 8088 processor for an undisclosed new product. Only when the deal was finally struck did Intel realise it was providing the brain of the first PC.

Ingredient #1 for building business.

Business grows on smart IT solutions. And powerful solutions are built on Intel technology. From desktop PCs to laptops and servers, Intel technologies are designed for performance and reliability. So your company can maximise its competitive advantage, improve customer responsiveness and keep growing. For more details, visit www.intel.com/business

Intel continued to develop ever more efficient microprocessors, including the Pentium processor in 1993. In 1997 it made another breakthrough by deciding to market itself as the brain behind a number of electronic products.

Product

Intel offers more than 450 products and services, from 294 offices and facilities around the world. To remain at the cutting edge and create products that continue to push the boundaries of new technology, Intel invests massively in research and development, spending US$4.4 billion in 2003, accounting for approximately 33% of the entire US semiconductor industry's R&D expenditure. In 2004, Intel's investment in R&D rose to US$4.8 billion. The company's R&D is conducted from 75 labs and by more than 7,000 researchers and scientists.

Intel's product range is organised into seven areas: processors; motherboards; chipsets; networking and communications; handheld and handset; network connectivity; embedded components and flash memory as well as software. These components are the architecture on which the digital world is built.

However, through its 'Intel Inside®' campaign, Intel is primarily known for producing microprocessors. These tiny 'brains' are constantly pushing the boundaries of technology, getting smaller, faster and more multi-functional.

The Intel Pentium processor remains its best-known product. The latest incarnation of the Intel Pentium processor is the Intel® Pentium® 4 Processor with Hyper Threading Technology Extreme Edition 3.73 GHz. Designed specifically for those who crave high performance, it meets the most demanding applications. The processor can work on two sets of tasks simultaneously using resources that otherwise would sit idle, getting more work done in the same amount of time.

Intel's other main processor brands include the Intel Itanium family and the Intel Xeon family brands, designed for use in servers. The Intel® Itanium® 2 processor, Intel's highest-performing and most reliable server platform, is designed to help businesses meet their critical computing needs with mainframe-class reliability.

NASA is using 10,240 Intel Itanium 2 processors to power its planned Space Exploration Simulator, which

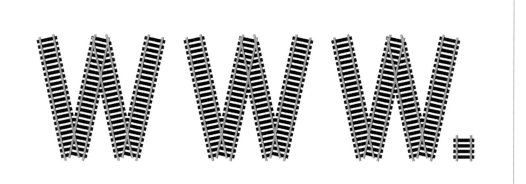

Loads of mainline stations now have **wireless hotspots**. With built-in wireless connectivity, laptops powered by **Intel® Centrino™ mobile technology** make it easier than ever to get online when you're out.

Laptops online.

With **Intel® Centrino™ mobile technology,** getting online wirelessly is really simple and with so many **wireless hotspots,** in places like railway stations, **it's now easier than ever.**

will be among the world's largest Linux OS-based supercomputers.

Intel Celeron® processors are designed for use in desktop and laptop PCs, offering exceptional value and reliability for everyday computing tasks.

The Intel Centrino™ mobile technology brand marks the first time Intel has brought together a whole set of technology under a single brand name. The Intel® Pentium® M Processor, in conjunction with the Intel® 855

MOBILE
TECHNOLOGY

chipset family and the Intel® PRO/Wireless network connection, is a new and key component of Intel® Centrino™ Mobile Technology, delivering enhanced mobile performance for sleeker, lighter notebook designs.

Intel is also a major player in flash memory, with revenues growing by more than 40% in the first half of 2004. The company believes it gained several points of market segment share during that time.

Recent Developments
Intel recently launched new software tools to help developers design, analyse and optimise applications running on Intel-based platforms supporting Intel® Extended Memory 64 Technology. This is in addition to software products Intel already offers to support its Intel® Itanium® 2 processor family.

Intel software products with support for Intel EM64T allows computing platforms to access larger amounts of memory, helping developers easily create the fastest software possible on Intel architecture.

Intel is also using its know-how to help improve the everyday quality of life for elderly people, building and testing wireless sensor networks for the home. Intel is catalysing research into this area and, in March 2004, participated in a demonstration to Congress in Washington, to showcase future technologies for aging adults and their carers.

This initiative is another example of Intel's continued community involvement. Its established Teach to the Future programme has so far helped train 1.5 million teachers around the world, recently launching in Australia, Chile, Turkey, the Ukraine and Vietnam.

At a corporate level, Intel recently elected a new chief executive officer, Paul S Otellini, the former president and chief operating officer, succeeded Craig R Barrett who became chairman of the board of directors.

Promotion
Intel has spent almost US$8 billion promoting the brand since 1991 and continues to invest. Intel's incredible rise to the world's fifth most valuable brand began in 1989, with a campaign aimed at promoting its 386SX microprocessor to IT managers. This was successful, but consumers remembered the processor and not the company's name. The problem was that Intel was a component, buried deep inside another device. Its advertising agency Dahlin, Smith and White came up with part of the solution – the slogan 'Intel. The computer inside.' This later became the famous 'Intel Inside®'.

At the same time, Intel began approaching computer manufacturers with the idea of a co-operative marketing programme whereby Intel would share the cost of any ads that showed its logo. In the first year, 300 companies took it up on the offer. Meanwhile, in 1995, Intel unveiled TV ads using the familiar five-note melody.

Together with the launches of the Pentium and Pentium Pro processors, the campaign achieved strong results. According to research, only 24% of European PC buyers were familiar with Intel's logo in 1991, rising to 94% by 1995.

With the Intel Centrino mobile technology brand now high on its list of priorities, Intel is building an

infrastructure of wireless 'hot spots', backed by a high-profile TV, Radio, PR and print advertising campaign. Intel is also educating corporate users about the benefits of wi-fi, and has deployed wireless technology across its own network. It has also been involved in helping to deploy public networks in Europe and Brussels airport.

Intel also promotes its brand through alliances like Toyota Motorsport. The racing team has joined forces with Intel to reduce its computer-aided design time. Using Intel® Itanium® 2 processor-based servers, Toyota can achieve faster and more accurate design simulations, allowing it to achieve a ten-fold reduction in car development time. The technology also allows Toyota to redesign up to 15% of the car in only two weeks between grand prix races, continually improving speeds and road-holding ability.

Brand Values
Intel's external brand values emphasise groundbreaking technology, quality and reliability. But Intel has always striven to underline its corporate culture, and is conscious of presenting itself as a forward-thinking company – a giant with the soul of a start-up.

Intel also aims to be open, egalitarian and disciplined. When Robert Noyce and Gordon Moore were building Intel, they were keen to banish hierarchies within the organisation. They preferred a company with no executive suites, no pinstriped suits and no reserved parking spaces. Intel aims to keep the spirit of its founders alive.

www.intel.com

THINGS YOU DIDN'T KNOW ABOUT

Intel

› The 90-nm based Pentium® M processor has 140 million transistors and the Pentium 4 processor has 125 million. By comparison, in 1999 the leading mobile, desktop and server processors each had only 28 million.

› Intel plans to spend approximately US$4.8 billion on R&D in 2005, which is about equal to the US Government's annual budget for basic research in physical science and engineering.

› Montecito a future processor for the Intel® Itanium® processor family will have over 1.7 billion transistors and will be the first dual core processor for this family.

› If your feet were as quick as the Intel® Pentium® 4 processor with Hyper-Threading Technology at 3.6 GHz, you could walk to the moon in less than a quarter of a second and to the sun in about 91 seconds. You would be travelling at about 4.8 million times the speed of sound.

Market

The Institute of Directors (IoD) is one of the UK's leading business membership organisations. With approximately 55,000 individual members from companies of all sizes, types and geographical locations, membership spans the whole spectrum of business leadership, from the largest companies to the smallest private firms.

Membership of the IoD is on an individual rather than corporate basis. It represents individual directors and ensures that it caters for all their needs in terms of development, professionalism and integrity. A respected authority on corporate governance issues, the IoD champions professionalism in the boardroom and as such offers a wide range of training and development services designed to ensure that individual directors are fully equipped to fulfil their role, and to therefore drive the success of their organisations.

The IoD has members on 92 of the FTSE 100 boards and also represents a large number of SME directors. It is dedicated to championing the entrepreneur, and is committed to ensuring that good practice is being observed by directors, no matter how large or small their organisation.

Achievements

Over the past five years, membership of the IoD has grown substantially and now includes directors from many sectors – from media to manufacturing, e-business to the public sector.

The IoD has been running courses for directors since the early 1980s. The success and popularity of these professional development products increases year on year, and the IoD filled a record 4,500 course places in 2004.

In March 1999 it was granted approval from the Privy Council for new by-laws to enable it to establish a professional qualification for directors, Chartered Director. The IoD's Chartered Director qualification is fast being considered to be a prerequisite by many companies for all directors employed on the board, having been endorsed by high-profile organisations such as the Confederation of British Industry, Investors in People and the Centre for Tomorrow's Company.

The IoD runs a full programme of business events each year which attract high-profile speakers. Jack Welch, Ronald Reagan, Sir Richard Branson, Bill Gates and Baroness Thatcher have been a few of the business community role-models to grace past IoD platforms.

Its flagship event held at the Royal Albert Hall every year, the Annual Convention, is not only the biggest business event in the UK, it is arguably also one of the most important events of the business calendar.

As a result of its relationship with the private members' club, France-Amériques, IoD members and their guests can now use their exclusive premises in the heart of Paris, a short distance from the Champs Elysées. As the scope of IoD International grows, members will be able to access similar facilities in many different countries over the coming years.

History

When the IoD was founded in 1903, to support and promote the interests of directors, the head of a family run accountancy firm became the first founding member of the IoD. W. A. Addinsell set up the Institute on his company premises and brought together ten other directors well-known in the City from a range of

The IoD's policy team is highly successful and influential in representing the views of its members to Government and in providing comment on significant events in business. It responds to more than 80 Government consultation documents a year, which help in shaping the business environment. It provided valuable input into the Higgs review – a review of the role and effectiveness of non-executive directors – which was published in January 2003 and called for positive measures to spread best practice.

As part of the work it is doing within IoD International, the organisation has recently opened new premises in Paris.

disciplines including law, banking and insurance. It went on to receive 334 applications for membership in its first year and gained a Royal Charter in 1906.

The stimulus to the IoD's creation came from the company legislation of 1900-1901, which included details of concern regarding the responsibilities and liabilities of directors. Their initial objective was to inform directors about the legal implications of the directorial role and to exchange experiences. A legal committee was also established to scrutinise legislation and liaise with MPs in order to develop a legal framework conducive to an ethical and profitable economy.

The success of this initiative has enabled the Institute to be a forerunning advocate of best practice in corporate governance across the globe today. Director magazine was first published in 1947, providing information, inspiration and best-practice advice to Britain's business decision makers.

The London headquarters of the IoD is at 116 Pall Mall, a Grade 1 listed building. This landmark of London's great Georgian heritage is now one of the country's most popular business venues, with thousands of IoD members visiting the premises every week.

In the interest of meeting the needs of its growing number of younger members, the IoD opened a second London premises at 123 Pall Mall in 2001. The interior, designed by Wayne Hemingway, has a much more contemporary feel than the more traditional surroundings at 116, and includes facilities that make use of all the latest technology. The premises were officially opened by the Right Honourable Prime Minister Tony Blair on July 26th 2001.

Product

The IoD is dedicated to creating an environment in which business can flourish. It represents the business community to Government, regulatory bodies and the media. Through IoD Policy, the organisation exerts its influence in a number of different ways: by taking a position in the media (both nationally and locally); through direct discussions with senior Ministers; through detailed discussions with civil servants; through written responses to various consultation documents; through the production of research and policy papers. The IoD concentrates on those issues that are of most concern to business, examining them in depth and drawing substantially on its members' experience.

The IoD is committed to offering training and development products and services that bring benefits both to the individual member and the organisation. These divide into four distinct product groups: courses and qualifications covering leadership, strategy, finance and personal skills; conferences covering topical issues affecting all businesses; executive one-on-one coaching; board development services provided in-company and tailored to the needs and situations of the individual company. There is also a full calendar of events, which include a range of dinners and lunches and the Annual Convention.

Hospitality is a very big part of the IoD's core product offering. The facilities available in its two Pall Mall premises include a restaurant, brasserie, wine bar, cocktail bar, rooms available for functions and meeting rooms.

Recent Developments

UK based business leaders now have a dedicated HQ in the heart of Paris, following the opening in October 2004 of the Institute of Directors' first European premises. IoD Paris is the first IoD facility of its kind in Europe, with others planned for the future. It follows on from similar ventures throughout major cities in the UK, including Belfast, Bristol, Edinburgh, Manchester and Nottingham, with 2005 seeing new premises in the City of London and Thames Valley. All premises provide a full range of services for members, whether they are just dropping in to catch up on emails or require full board meeting and conferences facilities. The regional premises are open to all 55,000 members.

The organisation has also been making strides on the technology front, promoting the adoption of new website functionality, for example, ICOM – a web-based print and production facility for regional offices that enhances brand consistency across all branches. It has also introduced e-support tools for delegates taking IoD qualifications which are intended to support them through their learning and revising.

The IoD Policy Unit regularly meet with senior politicians and civil servants and significantly in April 2004, the entire IoD Board and Council were granted an invitation to Downing Street for a private meeting with Tony Blair. The Prime Minister answered questions on many of the key issues facing IoD members in the current economic and political climate. The IoD's role is to represent the views of its members and to bring about change, not to support one particular political party, and this was an ideal opportunity to ensure that those views were being communicated directly. The Council have since had similar sessions with the leadership of the Conservative and Liberal Democrat parties.

Promotion

The Institute makes full use of a comprehensive portfolio of media. Via direct marketing, both paper-based and electronic, members and non-members are kept abreast of major developments in the Institute's product portfolio.

Its successful and reputable in-house publication, IoD News keeps members abreast of all developments within the IoD, while the organisation uses email to the full by building an email community on an opt-in basis and sending out the monthly 'e-News' bulletin.

The organisation designs high-quality direct mail literature in-house with its brand values in mind. The IoD team works hard to create a suite of literature covering all products, instantly recognisable under the IoD umbrella brand.

Direct sales of membership itself have increased substantially via a strategic integrated acquisition campaign to targeted directors. One of the most successful recruitment channels the IoD enjoys is word-of-mouth, where members consistently recommend the Institute to colleagues and friends.

Perhaps one of the most significant promotional messages benefiting the Institute is its consistent presence in the nation's editorial space. The IoD distributes regular press statements on a variety of business issues with a view to representing its members' surveyed views on relevant issues. Local and national coverage in all media is generated on a daily basis, keeping the Institute's brand and identity in the forefront of the business arena.

Brand Values

Originally formed to protect the interests of directors and to support and set standards for all directors, the IoD brand has been built – and is now promoted – on the three cornerstones of professionalism, integrity and heritage.

This is especially relevant in the boardroom, where the IoD works to ensure that directors are aware of all their duties and responsibilities and are equipped to uphold them.

Lord Avebury, the first President, defined the Institute's objective in 1904 as:

". .to protect the interests of directors. It is much more important that it should enable directors to carry out the great responsibilities which they have undertaken; that it should be the centre from which they might obtain

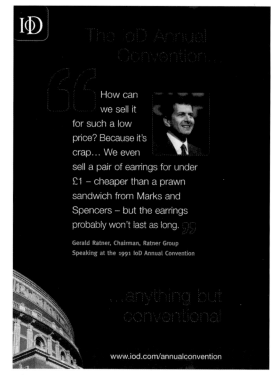

> How can we sell it for such a low price? Because it's crap... We even sell a pair of earrings for under £1 – cheaper than a prawn sandwich from Marks and Spencers – but the earrings probably won't last as long.
>
> Gerald Ratner, Chairman, Ratner Group
> Speaking at the 1991 IoD Annual Convention

www.iod.com/annualconvention

information upon various points of interest; that it should be the meeting ground on which they might consult together."

This still holds true today, but to enhance the Institute's perceived relevance in the 21st century, while maintaining these core strengths, the IoD's corporate identity was refreshed in 2001. All promotional collateral was revamped and standardised, with the introduction of contemporary imagery and simple, clean typefaces to maintain a consistent, meaningful presence in the business market.

The brand's repositioning is reflective of British business: incorporating past successes with innovation.

www.iod.com

THINGS YOU DIDN'T KNOW ABOUT

IoD

> Every Conservative Prime Minister has spoken at the IoD Annual Convention since 1957, including Harold MacMillan, Edward Heath and Margaret Thatcher.

> The architect who designed 116 Pall Mall, John Nash, also designed the Brighton Pavilion and Marble Arch.

> In 1939 the IoD supported the war effort by allowing the Institute's premises to be transformed into air-raid shelters.

> In 1955 the IoD's Annual Convention had one of the largest ever lunches eaten under one roof in London.

Market

JCB is a household name in most parts of the world. People point at a piece of construction equipment and refer to it as a JCB. In terms of non-consumer brands, JCB has one of the highest brand recognition of all business to business brands.

JCB is Europe's largest manufacturer of construction equipment, with manufacturing plants on four continents. JCB exports more than 70% of its UK production, a considerable feat given the strong pound. The market for construction equipment is a cyclical market and when there is talk of a downturn, purchasers of capital equipment always get nervous. The big markets for construction equipment are the US, Europe and the developing world. JCB has over 500 dealerships worldwide to spread the risk of any one economy slowing down.

JCB has a business objective to achieve 10% of the world market for construction equipment, no small task when you consider there are over 500 manufacturers in the industry.

Achievements

The proper name for a 'digger' is a backhoe loader, first introduced by JCB in 1953. Since then it has become the brand leader virtually the world over and its yellow machines are a familiar part of the landscape and language. The JCB name even appears in the Oxford English Dictionary.

The backhoe loader is part of a rich heritage of innovation. Another major achievement was the introduction of the Loadall machine in 1978. This revolutionised aspects of the building industry, allowing bricks to be lifted in pallets instead of being carried in a hod by a labourer. JCB also developed the first and still the only high-speed tractor, the Fastrac. Designed to combine all the benefits of a normal tractor with road versatility, the Fastrac has won numerous awards, including the Prince of Wales Award for Innovation in 1995. Another design classic was the Teletruk – the only forklift truck not to use cumbersome double masts at the front. Instead, it employs a single lifting arm which gives the driver greater flexibility.

JCB has won many other awards over the years for innovation excellence, exporting and design. Among

them there are fifteen Queen's Awards for Technology and Export Achievement.

JCB recently brought all its advertising and creative design in-house, combining engineering design, industrial design and graphic design all under one roof – JCB DesignWorks. JCB DesignWorks has won many accolades for in-house design and has recently designed work for the brand extension side of JCB – including power tools, work wear, garden equipment and a range of JCB Toys, DVDs and clothing for kids.

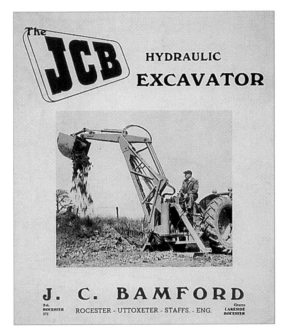

History

JCB started as one man's dream. It is the classic entrepreneurial story. Joseph Cyril Bamford (Mr JCB) was one of Britain's finest innovators who died in 2001. Mr JCB started business in 1945 manufacturing a tipping trailer with a £1 welding set in a lock-up garage he rented in Uttoxeter, Staffordshire. He sold it at the local market for £45 and went back immediately to make another one. A great British success story was born.

By 1948, Joe was employing six people. It was then that he turned his attention to making a hydraulic machine – Europe's first hydraulic tipping trailer. This developed into a hydraulic arm for tractors – called a Si-draulic, one of JCB's earliest commercial hits.

The first product to carry the JCB logo as we know it was in 1953. This was a backhoe loader which people nowadays call a 'JCB'. In the 1960s JCB introduced the famous 3C machine. This was a massive seller in its day, selling over 3,000 in 1964. Joseph Cyril Bamford was a brilliant marketer and was next to become famous for a marketing feat. The new 3D machine provided the operator of the machine with the facilities for boiling a kettle in the cab. Joe visited every purchaser of the new 3D himself and presented them personally with the JCB kettle. Joe's visits in his Rolls-Royce (number plate JCB1) became legendary and the 3D was an overnight success.

Joe's publicity skills were also evident when he began the tradition of JCB 'stunts' in the 1960s. Elaborate manoeuvres performed for the TV cameras – such as driving a car under a machine raised up on its hydraulic arms – showed the versatility and power of the machines and began the tradition of the famous 'Dancing Digger' shows which continue to this day.

Mr JCB was quick to realise that to be a good exporter, the potential customer had to get a feel for why JCB was special. He realised that the only way to do this was to show them the care and detail that went into making the machine but he had one problem – JCB was right in the heart of the midlands, making the journey for foreign customers unattractive because of the long journey. Joe solved it by buying JCB its own aircraft and helicopter which was branded with the JCB logo. To this day, visiting customers are still flown to Rochester by jet and helicopter.

In the 1970s the company began expanding its product range, such as the hugely successful Loadall telescopic handler. Later, JCB expanded into wheeled and tracked excavators and, in 1991, signed a joint venture with Japan's Sumitomo Construction Machinery and has since gone on to produce its own range of excavators. By 1994, JCB's product diversification had paid off, with £140 million of its £565 million sales coming from products launched in the previous five years.

Product

JCB now produces over 180 types of machines for uses spanning construction, industrial and agriculture. Sales have reached the £1 billion mark and much of this growth is coming from new products.

Products range from a micro machine that can all but fit through a normal hall door to machines that are as big as houses. In industry terms they range from Mini Excavators, Backhoe Loaders, skid steers, tractors,

telescopic handlers, wheel loading shovels, to dump trucks. JCB's sub-brands within the industry are Fastrac, Loadall and Robot.

Recent Developments

Following the completion of a factory in Georgia, USA in 2000, JCB opened a new facility in Brazil in 2001. In addition, a second factory in India is planned, to

complement the existing production facility near Delhi – which today produces more than 5,000 machines each year.

Other developments have been nearer to home: the World Parts Centre in Uttoxeter which provides more than 1,000 dealerships worldwide with a 24-hour, seven day a week service, and which is supported by the European Parts Centre near Paris.

After building a transmissions and axle production facility in Wrexham, a multi-million pound investment in a new factory near Derby has seen the first JCB diesel engines roll off the production line.

Promotion

JCB has a rich heritage of striking promotional activities, with the company's founder, Joseph Cyril Bamford setting the standard. JCB brings a sense of excitement to the industry that people more readily associate with the car industry.

The company has invested heavily in advertising, promotion and sponsorship over the years. Although the primary target market is not a consumer market, the general public nevertheless have a good recall of JCB advertising.

Many of the techniques now familiar in consumer advertising were being used by JCB's ad agency, Brookes and Vernons, in the technical press over 25 years ago. The lavishly photographed ads have won the agency and manufacturer many awards over the years and set new standards in heavy equipment marketing.

The company's PR brilliance has been demonstrated by its JCB Dancing Diggers, which have become renowned worldwide. Diggers can rise up on their buckets only and role over like an elephant in the circus. Something that is most definitely not advisable to do on the normal building site. The company also has a JCB GT – a digger fitted with a V8 Chevrolet engine, capable of doing an incredible 100 mph. In addition, JCB has expanded into a number of new areas – work wear, power tools, garden equipment and a range of toys, DVDs and clothing for kids. This approach into consumer markets will be developed further in the future.

Brand Values

JCB is a company that is committed to its core brand essence, the DNA of JCB – hard work. Mr JCB's son – Anthony Bamford continues the standard set by his father. The company's machines too,

have to be hard working to meet the demands put on them by the JCB customers.

JCB has always been known for its attention to detail. A JCB machine is seen as world class, innovative, high performance, strong and stylish. JCB carries out business with a sense of style and being family-owned, JCB has a great sense of community and pays particular attention to helping those who are underprivileged.

In addition, JCB machines have been provided for disaster areas, after earthquakes in Turkey, Iran and the recent Tsunami in Asia.

www.jcb.co.uk

THINGS YOU DIDN'T KNOW ABOUT

JCB

> The JCB logo is instantly recognisable – however, it does cause some communication problems because of its unique shape. From 1960 the company resorted to fitting typewriters with special keys to accurately render the logo. This practice continues today with all computers having pre-set logo's for faxes, letters and memos.

> In 1958, Joe Bamford bought ten scooters with the number plates JCB1 to JCB10. JCB over the years has purchased registration plates for all company cars, which incidentally are all white. JCB owns number 1-14 and 17-20 but JCB 15 and JCB 16 are still missing.

> A JCB has been the subject matter of many songs. In 1958, Lenny Green had a song called JCB and Me and in Ireland, the singer Seamus Moore who calls himself The JCB Man has recorded a song called The JCB Song.

> JCB bucks the general trend in the UK. Since 1975, UK manufacturing employment has fallen from 7.7 million to under four million. In this time, JCB's workforce has doubled.

JWT

Market

JWT's ambition is to be the UK's biggest and most creative network agency. In line with this goal, JWT has closed in on the market-leader in the Nielsen billings league and is now number two in the UK, with billings in excess of £341 million, just £16 million behind the number one position. Furthermore, JWT is ranked number four in the world (Source: Advertising Age).

Achievements

Since Simon Bolton took over the leadership of the agency in 2001, with a very clear agenda for change, much has come to fruition in 2004/05 in terms of creativity and new business, and the broadening and strengthening of JWT's through-the-line capability.

JWT had an extraordinary new business year in 2004, gaining over £100 million of new business and has been, without doubt, the most successful big network agency in new business terms. HSBC and Samsung joined the fold as global clients following triumphs in the two biggest pitches of the year and JWT also won the global assignment for Tourism Ireland.

On a domestic level JWT won Nik Naks, Kingsmill, Bulldog (C&W) Bishop's Finger and Brinton's carpets. As importantly, JWT also gained more work from existing clients; Vodafone gave JWT the task of developing the launch campaign for its 3G consumer offer across the globe and Unilever awarded JWT the Knorr assignment globally.

In 2004 JWT joined The Sunday Times' list of the Top 100 UK companies to work for. This was, in part, a reflection of JWT's continued commitment to leading the field among UK agencies for its policies on work/life balance and maternity and paternity benefits. In addition, the agency was praised for the respect and courtesy with which it deals with employees and its stimulating creative working environment.

For the third time in five years JWT was declared Consumer Agency of the Year at the annual GRAMIA Awards, sponsored by The Grocer.

JWT continues to lead training within the advertising industry. This year the agency won two IPA Continuous Professional Development (CPD) Awards to add to their Gold, a record unsurpassed by any other agency.

JWT continues to be at the forefront among agencies that create work that works. JWT now has 41 IPA Effectiveness Awards – nineteen more than the next ranked agency.

History

JWT is the world's oldest advertising agency. It was founded in 1864 when William J Carlton and Edmund A Smith set up a business in New York selling advertising space in religious journals. James Walter Thompson joined the business two years later as a bookkeeping clerk. He later bought the business for US$500 and put his name over the front door. A London office was set up in 1899. By 1916, when Thompson sold the business on, it had five offices and billings of US$3 million.

JWT was the first agency to focus on in-depth market research for clients. It was also the first to have its own recording studios. During World War II, JWT was responsible for many of the morale-boosting 'home front' campaigns. In 1944, it moved into 40 Berkeley Square – originally a block of luxury flats popular with showbiz legends including Frank Sinatra.

With the arrival of commercial television in 1955, JWT was the first agency to have its own casting department and the first to persuade top film and TV directors to make commercials. On the opening night of commercial TV, it produced spots for Kraft Cheese Slices and Lux toilet soap.

JWT became part of the WPP Group in 1987 and its media department merged with that of Ogilvy & Mather in 1997 to create MindShare. The agency moved from its Berkeley Square home to new premises at One Knightsbridge Green in 2002.

Nick Bell joined in May 2003 to work alongside Chief Executive Simon Bolton on the creative regeneration of the agency. The change has become obvious – in 2004 alone there were sixteen new hires in the creative department. Notable new work in 2004 included the new Kit Kat campaign, 'Make the most of your break' which replaced 'Have a Break, Have a Kit Kat' and Smirnoff Red's 'Not the Usual' campaign. The first ad for new client HSBC, 'Flowers' also earned creative praise as did JWT's work for Allied Bakeries' brand Kingsmill and Nik Naks.

JWT's press work was particularly strong in 2004 with admired campaigns for, among others, the RNIB, Kellogg's Crunchy Nut, Persil and Reckitt Benckiser's Pledge.

The agency continued to invest in creativity in 2004. This included the development of a Worldwide Creative Council made up of creative directors in key markets to continue to drive creative improvement across the network.

Product

JWT's creativity has always been driven by its understanding of the consumer and today's consumer is savvy, time conscious, easily distracted and in control. Time is the new currency.

JWT believes, therefore, that successful brands are the ones consumers choose to spend time with, and successful communications are those that provoke an involvement well beyond the duration of the message.

JWT's role is quite simply to ensure more people spend more time with its clients' brands.

Its purpose is to create ideas that people want to spend time with.

Its belief is that the best ideas buy more of consumers' time.

Its ideas can, and do, manifest themselves across the multitude of communication channels, wherever and whenever they will generate the greatest relevant impact.

Recent Developments

In 2003 JWT stated its commitment to become the most creative of the 'big' agencies. 2004 has seen a new level of creativity in work from the London agency. Highlights of the year include acclaimed work for Kit Kat, with a new 'Make the most of your break' line, a development from one of JWT's most famous, 'Have a Break, have a Kit Kat.' This particularly demonstrates the agency's ability to maintain a brand's relevance and impact over time: Kit Kat has enjoyed a year on year rise in sales of 18% since the new campaign was launched.

A new campaign ,'Not the Usual' for Diageo's Smirnoff Red has been hugely admired both by the target audience and within the creative community, including winning a number of European awards. Likewise, building on the success of the cultural collisions strategy for HSBC, but aiming to increase the emotional appeal, JWTs latest film, Chrysanthemums, has been similarly praised.

JWT has also revamped its integrated offer – in 2004 it merged its CRM company rmg:connect with sales promotion agency Black Cat to form RMG Connect. The company also got a new UK management team: CEO Jonathan Harman and Chief Creative Officer, EMEA Trefor Thomas. Central to JWT's belief in collaboration and application of relevant expertise across all channels to deliver effective truly integrated programmes, RMG Connect were part of the successful HSBC pitch team. Other key clients include Vodafone, Mercedes-Benz, Shell, Avis, Yell and ITV.

marketing trends are also a key feature. These include 'Fab Fifties' – understanding marketing to the over 50s, and 'From Under the Mattress to over the Internet' exploring changing attitudes to money across Europe. JWT also enjoys just having some fun with clients and prospects, whether hosting a live broadcast of an England game with sports celebrities and guest TV soccer pundits; pre release film screenings or the much anticipated annual children's Christmas party.

relationship it has with its own people and with so many of its clients. For example, Unilever celebrated its centenary with JWT in a memorable celebration at Tate Modern in 2002.

JWT offers its staff innovative contracts to support a better work/life balance and, on a day to day level, little 'extras', from the Hyde Park running club through to the weekly in-house massage, themed bar evenings and comedy nights.

www.jwt.co.uk

JWT Specialised Communications has acquired award-winning graduate marketing and digital solutions agency Empower Communications. The new agency joined JWTSC in their Richmond offices at the beginning of the month. Empower Communications brings with it a client list that includes the British Army, PricewaterhouseCoopers, Clifford Chance, ICI, the Metropolitan Police and the DfES Fasttrack.

Promotion

JWT's Marketing and New Business department is led by the ebullient Peter Cowie, known within the industry as Top Banana. The focus of the department is on developing individual relationships with prospective clients.

Beyond this, JWT regularly hosts exclusive events which, in line with the brand's values, bring together inspiring thinking from a wide range of sources. Past speakers have included Estelle Morris, Adam Crozier, CEO of Royal Mail, Greg Dyke, Ex-Director General of the BBC, Virgin's Richard Branson and Olympic gold medallist Lord Coe. Original research and insights into

Brand Values

JWT has always led the way through combining powerful and rigorous planning (Stephen King of JWT was one of the founding fathers of the account planning discipline) with imagination and creativity. This marriage of planning with creativity is even more evident today given the agency's belief in transparency and the effectiveness of true collaboration, which physically manifests itself in the open plan workspace at 1KG without walls and departments. This leads to truly collaborative multidiscipline brand teams, tailor made to individual clients' needs.

Consumer insight coupled with an unrelenting expectation of the very highest levels of creativity are the core values that drive the JWT brand today and enable the agency to create work that consumers choose to spend more time with, to the benefit of the brand.

JWT values openness, collaboration and creating a supportive and secure atmosphere for staff and clients. It is proud to be thought of throughout the industry as a 'clever' agency but, just as importantly, as a nice agency to work for and with. This is reflected in the long-standing

THINGS YOU DIDN'T KNOW ABOUT

JWT

- The first interactive TV ad in the UK was produced by JWT for Kellogg's Frosties.

- JWT makes a TV commercial nearly every working day of the year.

- Many famous people have worked at JWT at some point in their lives. These include Martin Amis, Julie Christie, Ken Done, Adrian Lyne, Faye Weldon, Alan Parker and Bob Payton. And rumour has it that David Bowie used to work in the mailroom.

- Among its diverse staff, JWT has an ex-England Ladies' footballer on reception, a British Thai Boxing champion in the creative department and a British Judo champion in IT as well as an ex British Olympic rower in New Business.

- During the war, on behalf of the Government, JWT declared war on rats too. Every man woman and child was asked to become a rat reporter. This may well have been the origin of the expression 'to rat on someone'.

LandSecurities

Land Securities, which invests in, manages and develops commercial property around the UK, is a market leader that provides office accommodation to more than 2.6% of the UK office workforce and owns retail space visited over 300 million times every year by UK shoppers. Some 55% of the Group's investment portfolio is in the retail sector, with 37% in the central London office market.

In terms of size, the nearest competitors include Prudential, Legal and General, Standard Life and Morley ('institutions'); British Land and Hammerson ('quoted property companies'); Grosvenor and Crown Estates ('traditional institutions').

In the last few years the main change to the market structure has been the emergence of the limited partnership market that has grown from virtually nothing five years ago to represent 3% of the total investment market.

The other core focus of Land Securities' business is property outsourcing, enabling organisations to transfer their short and/or long term property needs to a single specialist provider (Source: IPD using ONS).

History
Land Securities celebrated its 60th anniversary in 2004. It all began in 1944, when Harold Samuel, Land Securities' founder and chairman, bought Land Securities Investment Trust Limited, which at the time owned three houses in Kensington together with some Government stock.

After World War II, Land Securities partnered with many local authorities around the UK to help them rebuild city centres which had suffered damage during the war.

Market
The UK commercial property market, like many other areas of the economy, has enjoyed mixed fortunes in recent years, but still remains strong and growing. According to the Royal Institute of Chartered Surveyors (RICS), commercial property has outperformed shares over the last decade, giving investors a 174% return against 81% for equities. Although the sector was hit by low occupancy and falling rents in the post-dotcom downturn, particularly in London and the south east, future prospects for the market are looking brighter – the RICS expects rents and capital values to rise in the office, retail and industrial sectors.

Achievements
From modest beginnings, Land Securities has grown steadily to become the UK's leading commercial property company. A member of the FTSE index since it was created in 1984, the Group manages more than ten million square metres of property across the UK. Having begun with just three houses in Kensington, the Group's investment portfolio is now worth nearly £9 billion.

With over 60 years of careful investment, development, management and more recently property outsourcing, Land Securities has developed a strong heritage and enjoys one of the strongest reputations in the property business.

The group has attracted numerous awards for its performance in many areas of its activities including winning Property Week magazine's 2004 Office Developer of the Year and 2003 Property Company of the Year awards and BCSC Gold Awards for the partnership development of the Bullring shopping centre in Birmingham and its White Rose shopping centre in Leeds.

Furthermore, Land Securities' excellence in environmental initiatives has been recognised through its membership of the FTSE4Good and Dow Jones indices, which acknowledges commitment to environmental protection and community involvement. The company has also been awarded seven 'Green Apple' awards by The Green Organisation, an independent environment group dedicated to promoting the positive side of environmental endeavour.

The Group's strength in corporate governance helped it win awards from the European Property Real Estate Association and BDO Stoy Hayward for the 2004 Land Securities Annual Report.

Land Securities established itself as the UK's leading property company by a mixture of postwar development, prudent purchases of London property and the acquisition of property companies. This position was underlined in 1968, when Land Securities took over City Centre Properties, with assets of £155 million – marking one of the biggest property deals of the time.

By 1973, the group's portfolio of property topped the £1 billion mark for the first time and, growing rapidly for the next decade, reached £2 billion by 1983. Around this time, the name of the company was changed, from The Land Securities Investment Trust Limited to Land Securities PLC.

Product

Land Securities is a commercial property company, undertaking property investment, development and outsourcing activities. It is market leader in three key areas of the UK property market: retail; London offices and property outsourcing. It also has projects outside of these areas, including mixed use regeneration. This long term regeneration is demonstrated by Land Securities' plans for Kent Thameside, where there is the potential for up to 13,000 new homes and 300,000m² of supporting retail, leisure and community facilities.

In London, Land Securities owns some £3 billion of office accommodation stretching from the City to Earl's Court in the west. The portfolio includes almost one million square metres of retail and office space, and provides accommodation for over 650 organisations. The Group also has the potential to create 500,000m² of new space in London over the next ten years.

In retail, Land Securities owns and manages £4.5 billion of retail property throughout the UK, including shopping centres, designer outlets and retail parks. Over the next five years, the company will create 340,000m² of new space, transforming the landscapes of towns and cities around the UK.

The outsourcing area of the company's business is undertaken by Land Securities Trillium. Land Securities Trillium created the property outsourcing model in the late 1990s, and it now has a range of tailored long-term outsourcing contracts with diverse public and corporate sector clients. These clients, depending on their business needs, can benefit from a wide range of services, including property financing, estates strategy and asset management, provision of services, through to capital projects delivery, property acquisition and development. Land Securities Trillium applies its expertise to its clients' properties, taking the risk and cost away from the client, leaving them free to concentrate on their own core business. An example of an outsourcing partnership in practice is with the Department for Work and Pensions (DWP). The DWP has around 125,000 employees working in more than 1,700 properties throughout the UK. Under the terms of the 20 year contract, which was agreed in two phases, Land Securities Trillium is responsible for the ownership and management of the DWP's entire estate of 2.5 million square meters. All freehold premises transferred to Land Securities Trillium,

plus responsibility for rental costs, dilapidation liabilities on leased buildings and the cost of upgrading the buildings. In addition, all surplus space was transferred to Land Securities Trillium for disposal. This is a fully integrated service contract encompassing assets, Facilities Management and Life Cycle Maintenance.

Land Securities Trillium has enabled its clients to unlock over £3 billion in capital previously tied up in property.

Recent Developments

Since 2000 the Group has been through a period of substantial change including the acquisition of Trillium, which added the fast-growing property outsourcing arm to the Land Securities business. During this period Land Securities has re-engineered its business, rationalising its property portfolio, expanding its development activities, acquiring major new projects – including the land at Kent Thameside – and introducing a new leasing product – Landflex.

Another important event for Land Securities was the September 2003 opening of the Bullring Shopping Centre in Birmingham. Developed by the Birmingham Alliance – a partnership between Land Securities Group PLC, Hammerson plc and Henderson Global Investors Ltd, the landmark scheme transformed the eleven hectare site of the former 1960s shopping centre into a benchmark for city centre regeneration.

More recently following the appointment of Francis Salway (who joined the company in 2000), formerly the

Group's Chief Operating Officer, as Land Securities new Chief Executive, taking over from Ian Henderson, the Group has restructured its business to concentrate on the core markets of retail, London offices and property outsourcing. At the same time, the Group decided to exit the industrial sector.

Promotion

Land Securities does not undertake above-the-line corporate advertising, but it does have a very active public relations, media and investor relations programme. It also invests in activities specific to properties, developments or sectors in which the Group operates. Examples of its recent activities include the lead sponsorship of the Local Government Association Annual Conference, sponsorship at the OGC Conference and Exhibition 'Government Relocation – Making it Happen' sponsor of the Architect of the Year Award and one of the sponsors for the Royal Institute of Chartered Surveyors Property Management Awards 2004.

The Group also runs marketing campaigns targeting specific B2B customer groups. An example of which is its retail marketing campaign which included the creation of a new magazine title called 'A1', aimed directly at retailer customers. To target Central London office occupiers it has created the Capital Commitment campaign.

The Group is a keen proponent of Corporate Responsibility and published a report called 'No Hot Air' in January 2004 to communicate its corporate responsibility activities. This was the first dedicated report of its CR work, encompassing the vast array of initiatives, schemes and contributions to the environment and communities undertaken by the Group, all over the country.

Brand Values

Land Securities' vision is to be recognised as the UK's leading property company. In order to achieve this it stands by a set of core values, which embody the way in which everyone at the company works and the way they treat each other. These are: Customer Service; Respect for the Individual; Excellence; Integrity and Innovation.

The company runs a programme called Values into Action (VIA), which recognises and rewards employees whose behaviour reflect these core values. VIA has been a part of Land Securities for some time and is considered to be very important to the Group's people and the organisation as a whole.

www.landsecurities.com

THINGS YOU DIDN'T KNOW ABOUT

Land Securities

❯ Lord Samuel, the Group's founder, coined the phrase 'Location, Location, Location'.

❯ Some of Land Securities' famous properties include The Home Office, New Scotland Yard and Piccadilly Lights.

❯ Land Securities manages over ten million square metres of property – equal to 1,500 football pitches.

❯ There are over 750 cleaners at the BBC's premises in London. Every day they clean 100 acres of BBC accommodation, walking the equivalent of London to Bombay every week.

www.lycra.com

Market

LYCRA® is a brand that since its invention 40 years ago has become an integral part of the fashion industry. Invented by DuPont, the LYCRA® fibre gives fabric added comfort and flexibility in a wide range of clothes across all garment categories. Although LYCRA® has been around for over four decades, demand for the product from clothing manufacturers continues to grow. Leading designers claim fibre technology to be their most fundamental inspiration as they strive to make garments with the flexibility and high performance values needed to match the lifestyle of the 21st century consumer. People today expect more from their clothes than style alone; market research highlights that comfort, ease of care, durability, breathability and lightness are all extremely important. Today LYCRA® is the leading brand within the portfolio of INVISTA brands, including STAINMASTER®, ANTRON®, COOLMAX®, THERMOLITE®, CORDURA®, SUPPLEX®, TACTEL®, Polarguard®, ESP® and Avora® FR.

In September 2003 INVISTA became the new name of DuPont Textiles & Interiors (DTI). The name change represented a step towards separating from the parent company DuPont. This was completed in April 2004 with the purchase of INVISTA by Koch Industries Incorporated.

Achievements

A fabric ingredient and not a fabric itself, the fact that LYCRA® is such a well-known name all over the world, bears testament to INVISTA's marketing efforts. LYCRA® boasts a global awareness of over 90% and, according to

Interbrand, is among the top ten clothing and textile brands in the world, sitting alongside names like Levi's and Armani.

And it is not just a famous name – it is also an invention of great significance, being cited by the Council of Fashion Designers of America as one of the 20th century's most important fashion innovations.

Over the years, INVISTA has constantly kept abreast of developments in fashion and fibre technology, launching products that have maintained the fame and market-leading position of LYCRA®. Where some brands die when fashions change, INVISTA has consistently reinvigorated and reinterpreted LYCRA® to answer changing consumer needs especially in the ever changing world of fashion.

History

LYCRA® was invented in 1959 by a team of scientists at DuPont, originally as a replacement for rubber in corsetry. Before LYCRA® was invented, consumers endured saggy, baggy, stretched and bunched clothes. But when the DuPont scientist Joe Shiver perfected a revolutionary new fibre – code named K – that all changed.

In the 1960s LYCRA® revolutionised the way in which fabrics could be used. In beachwear it replaced thick and heavy swimsuits with light, quick-drying garments like the bikini. In 1968, the medal-winning French Olympic ski team became the first high-profile sports personalities to wear ski suits with LYCRA® – a trend that soon spread to other sports. By 1972 Olympic swimmers swore by the sleek, lightweight suits contoured with LYCRA®. The fibre

soon became an integral part of performance wear for millions of amateur and professional athletes.

In the 1970s, the brand started to make an impact on the fashion scene, as disco fever and interest in fitness made leggings and figure-hugging leotards the look of the moment. Leggings and stretch jeans with LYCRA® are among the defining looks of the decade. By the mid 1980s, over half of all women's hosiery and underwear relied on LYCRA® for a close, comfortable fit.

During the 1990s, LYCRA®'s position in the sports market strengthened through the development of hi-tech fibres such as LYCRA® POWER in compression shorts, which helped reduce athletes' muscle fatigue. This decade also saw the rising popularity of the fibre not just in women's fashion but in men's too. President Clinton gave the brand an important endorsement by sporting a suit made with LYCRA®, not to mention the interest sparked by the England football team's decision to don business suits made with LYCRA®.

HAS IT.

When jeans and tops have LYCRA®, you get a great fit. (If the tag doesn't say "has it", it doesn't have it.)

You either have it or you don't.

LYCRA

Product

LYCRA® is a man-made elastane fibre. Never used alone, but always blended with other fibres, it has unique stretch and recovery properties. LYCRA® adds comfort, fit, shape retention, durability and freedom of movement. This is achieved thanks to the unique properties of the fibre, which can be stretched up to seven times its initial length before springing back once tension is released.

Any natural or man-made clothing fibres can be mixed with LYCRA®. Very small amounts of LYCRA® can transform the performance of a fabric – the amount of LYCRA® in a material can be as little as 2%. There are various ways of integrating LYCRA® with other fibres to provide fabrics for all needs.

INVISTA carries out continual research and development in fibre technology. This is supported by an understanding of the market and ever changing fashion trends coupled with an awareness of developing consumers wants and needs.

An example of this brand development was the launch in 2001 of the campaign Jeans with LYCRA®. This garment marketing concept brought enhanced fit and freedom to denim and was welcomed by designers and manufacturers who were looking for new directions in which to develop denim in a race to gain market share and brand recognition. The denim market has gone from strength to strength in recent years.

In 2001, LYCRA® set the scene for the future of leather with the launch of breakthrough technology: Leather with LYCRA®. Using proprietary techniques, the technology fuses layers of leather with layers of LYCRA®. This new structure gave the natural leather a 'memory' which enables it to stretch and recover without losing any of its original quality or natural appearance.

Leather with LYCRA® was launched to the fashion world by Randolph Duke in Los Angeles, Carlos Miele in São Paulo, and Lawrence Steele in Milan who all featured collections which showcased the versatility of LYCRA®.

INVISTA™ has also made important contributions to the hosiery sector in recent years. LYCRA® Curves are designed to flatten the stomach and lift the bottom comfortably. The LYCRA® LegCare range has been proved in tests to help prevent tired and swollen legs – a common symptom among busy women who spend their

When legwear has LYCRA®, you get to be whoever you want to be. (If the legwear package doesn't say "has it", it doesn't have it.)

You either have it or you don't.

LYCRA

days standing and walking. LegCare hosiery has a 'massaging' effect, which allows the blood to flow more easily in the leg, reducing swelling and feelings of heaviness and fatigue.

INVISTA™ has continued to innovate to keep LYCRA® at the cutting edge of sports and fashion technology. LYCRA® POWER is specially designed to reduce muscle fatigue and increase endurance; Soft Comfort LYCRA® offers improved comfort for hosiery garments and LYCRA® 3D is a knitting technique that further improves appearance, comfort and fit.

Recent Developments

Throughout 2003 and 2004, INVISTA™ launched a completely new innovation that delivers specific well-being benefits in clothes: LYCRA® Body Care. The LYCRA® Body Care collection uses textile finishes and specially engineered yarns to deliver freshness, moisturising and massaging benefits to clothes. Freshness is delivered by technologies that inhibit the growth of odour-causing bacteria as well as trapping odour-causing molecules that are then released in the next wash. Micro-encapsulation means moisturising agents are stored in the fibre structure which break open and release their contents to continuously hydrate the skin. Compression technology and temperature management in high-tech hosiery yarns offers massaging action.

The launch of LYCRA® elastic fibre T-400 represents another significant development. This completely new fibre under the LYCRA® umbrella has a dimensional stability which gives it superior dyeability and colourfastness. It is ideal for applications such as denim, shirts and other woven fabrics that require moderate stretch.

INVISTA has also introduced a revolutionary new scanning technology to safeguard the LYCRA® brand against fraud and ensure customers can have confidence in the integrity of the product. LYCRA® BrandScan™ is a sophisticated scanning system, which determines whether a fabric or garment labelled as containing LYCRA® really does contain the brand.

The ability of the LYCRA® brand to respond to consumer needs via innovation was reinforced in 2004 through strategic partnerships with other global brands such as Rimmel and Coca-Cola. In February, Rimmel LYCRA® Wear was launched in the UK following an exclusive licensing agreement with parent company Coty Inc, one of the world's leading manufacturers and marketers of personal fragrances and colour cosmetics.

Rimmel LYCRA® Wear is an addition to the brand's nail product portfolio; a longer lasting shockproof nail varnish. The partnership is the first collaboration of the science between cosmetics and textiles, and for the first time introduced LYCRA® in liquid form. In April 2004, LYCRA® and Coca-Cola commissioned Colcci to design their first joint collection. Colcci is a major Brazilian casual and jeanswear company. The collection, named Coca-Cola by Colcci is now available throughout stores in Brazil.

INVISTA's commitment to innovation is evidenced in its prolific launch of new products over the last twelve months. Black LYCRA®, launched in September 2004, is the world's first truly black elastane. It offers reduced elastane 'grin through' in dark fabric shades and remains black even after repeated wash cycles. The colour integrity of Black LYCRA® helps reduce fabric returns, can achieve simplifications in fabric manufacturing and is suitable for wovens, circular knits and seamless constructions.

LYCRA® 275B was created to meet the needs of serious swimmers and pool lovers alike. Both have high expectations of their swimwear and LYCRA® 275B offers a longer lasting fit and shape retention. Using INVISTA proprietary technology, swimwear made with LYCRA® 275B keeps its fit and shape five to ten times longer than those which contain unprotected elastane.

Promotion

The promotional strategy of LYCRA® is essentially two-pronged. Its most important audiences are retail and manufacturing partners who include the fibre in their garments and fabrics. But to do this, designers and retailers have to be convinced that there is strong consumer demand for clothes containing LYCRA®. Consequently, INVISTA™ invests US$1 million annually in research to understand consumer behaviour, to better target its audience and generate LYCRA® demand at retail.

INVISTA™ co-ordinates trade and consumer advertising to increase awareness of the brand among trade partners and end-users alike.

HAS IT.

When underwear has LYCRA®, it knows how to stay in place. (If the tag doesn't say "has it", it doesn't have it.)

You either have it or you don't.

LYCRA

INVISTA™ has always invested heavily in marketing the LYCRA® brand, a fact which explains why it continues to enjoy such strong awareness among business and consumer customers. In 2002 INVISTA™ launched a US$40 million global advertising and promotion campaign, part of a US$200 million three-year investment in the brand. The 'Has It' campaign illustrates the benefits of LYCRA® by associating the brand with a confident and stylish lifestyle attitude – 'you either have it or you don't'. The aim of the campaign is to engage consumers with the LYCRA® brand in order to motivate them to actively look for garments with the LYCRA® label. INVISTA™ has also introduced new 'LYCRA® Has It' hang tags to further drive awareness in store.

LYCRA® ownership of 'style' continued with its innovative sponsorship of a unique TV experience in Asia. LYCRA® My Show was a nationwide talent competition. Over twelve episodes, the programme was aired on the Oriental TV Channel as well as three other local TV channels in different parts of China. The show supported individualism, talent and hidden potential thus embodying some of the aspirational brand values that LYCRA® has become synonymous with. The investment in LYCRA® My Show recognises INVISTA™'s commitment to Asia both as a business partner and a market opportunity.

2004 saw LYCRA® continue their dedication to high-end fashion, teaming up with designers Zac Posen and Sebastien Pons. The highly anticipated LYCRA®-sponsored 'Western Gypsy Love Story' collection by Pons showcased denim with LYCRA®, whilst Zac Posen's Spring 2005 collection presented a number of garments using the latest LYCRA® technology to give traditionally rigid fabrics a sexy fit, stretch and comfort.

Brand Values

INVISTA's marketing for LYCRA® focuses on a key product promise – that LYCRA® equals comfort, fit, shape retention and freedom of movement.

Whilst this is the functional brand promise, recent marketing has aimed to establish the brand's lifestyle appeal. These include projects like the sponsorship of a 20-page pan-European supplement with Elle magazine.

www.lycra.com

THINGS YOU DIDN'T KNOW ABOUT

LYCRA®

❯ It is possible to buy LYCRA® tights which contain a mosquito-repellent.

❯ Tests carried out by INVISTA at the Pennsylvania State University and Free University Hospital of Amsterdam proved that LegCare hosiery reduces fatigue and leg swelling.

❯ LYCRA® is now one of the world's top ten fabric brands and among the top five ingredient brands.

❯ Pound for pound, LYCRA® has more holding power than rubber.

McCann Erickson

● ● ● ● ● ● ●

NUROFEN | PAIN BARRIER

Market

The UK is generally recognised as one of the most important, creative and buoyant advertising markets in the world. However, it has suffered turbulent times in recent years, enduring a recession between 2000-2003 when global economic uncertainty led to a cut in advertising expenditure. In 2004, the industry finally began showing strong signs of recovery. Having seen UK advertising expenditure steadily fall from £14,355 million in 2000 to £13,810 million in 2003, the market was forecast to bounce back to £14,362 million by the end of 2004 (Source: WARC World Advertising Research Centre).

The grand total of advertising expenditure at constant prices has been recovering since the fourth quarter of 2003 and the forecast from The Advertising Association is that the recovery will continue with real growth of 4% for 2004 against 2003 and 3.4% in 2005.

McCann Erickson has long been a major force in the UK and global advertising industry. In the most recent rankings by Advertising Age (2004), McCann Erickson was ranked number one agency, both in the number of multinational accounts handled and in the total number of brand assignments.

It has agencies in 205 cities in 131 countries and holds a majority interest in agencies in 77 countries. Together, these territories account for 99% of the world's advertising expenditures. In the world's ten largest countries, McCann has agencies in an average of five to six cities with deeper roots than any other agency network.

In the UK, McCann Erickson is the second largest agency with billings of £303 million (Source: Campaign Magazine February 2004).

Furthermore, it has the UK's strongest regional network with offices in London, Manchester, Birmingham, Bristol, Leeds and Dublin.

Achievements

Thanks to its impressive reputation and global reach, McCann Erickson has built one of the best client lists in the industry, working with the world's biggest and best-known brands, such as GM, Nestlé, Coca-Cola, MasterCard, Microsoft, UPS and L'Oréal.

In an industry where client relationships are notoriously short, McCann Erickson has developed

extremely deep bonds with some of the blue-chips it works for. For instance, Nestlé has been a client since 1940, with McCann Erickson responsible for iconic work such as the Nescafé Gold Blend soap opera campaign – the most effective coffee campaign ever produced. Its relationship with another key client, Coca-Cola, dates back to 1955.

The agency was among the first to respond to the demands of globalised business, creating the first global advertising campaigns for UPS, Microsoft, Strepsils, Acuvue and L'Oréal. McCann Erickson's campaign for MasterCard is the world's largest, running in 96 countries and translated into 48 languages.

The agency's work has earned the respect of clients across the industry. In August 2004 McCann Erickson was named in the FT as the 'UK's best advertising agency to work with' (Source: Richmond Research Sample of 200 Marketing Directors). The annual Agency Reputation Survey by Marketing Week saw McCann Erickson voted by clients as the number one agency for strategy and effectiveness (Source: Marketing Week Agency Reputation Survey 2004 Sample of 152 Marketing Directors). It has won other prestigious awards, including winning 'Agency of the Year' at The Euro Effies 2004 (European Effectiveness Awards) and named by Adweek magazine as 'Global Agency of the Year' for three consecutive years.

McCann Erickson has also been named 'US Agency of the Year' by Advertising Age.

History

McCann Erickson has grown consistently since it opened its doors in the UK in 1927. Reflecting the agency's consistently-held core aim to create advertising that effectively influences people and sells products and services, the company's founder Harrison McCann once said, "If we don't move people to move goods out of the store, we have failed you."

Some highlights of the agency's history include winning its first Nestlé assignment in 1940 and, in 1955 being appointed to the US$15 million US assignment for Coca-Cola. One of the agency's best-known early campaigns for the company was in 1963 when the 'Things go better with Coke' campaign was launched.

Other famous campaigns created through McCann Erickson's history include some of the best-known lines in advertising history, such as the 'Put a Tiger in Your Tank' ads launched for Esso in 1964, and the 'I'm Worth It' campaign introduced for L'Oréal in 1972.

It was in 1987 that McCann Erickson first unveiled the long-running award-winning 'soap opera' campaign for Nescafé Gold Blend. The 'Gold Blend couple' survived in various incarnations for over ten years, before the ads took a new creative direction in 1998.

AmericanAirlines®
Up to 40% off flexible business fares at www.americanairlines.co.uk

In 1997, the McCann Worldgroup was formed as the world's first truly integrated global agency network, expanding the company globally into marketing communications that embrace more than advertising alone.

Also in 1997, McCann Erickson launched the 'Priceless' advertising campaign for MasterCard, and, in 1999, it began working with another prize account in world advertising – Microsoft.

Product

McCann Erickson's first aim has always been to create advertising that helps sells products and services. As such, it is dedicated to helping its clients achieve top-line growth, beyond what they can squeeze from supply chain efficiencies alone.

This means an advertising agency's principle job is to influence consumer behaviour in a way that creates demand. This requires innovation, the ability to come up with new answers to old questions, and a single-minded focus on consumers' needs and desires.

McCann Erickson is in the business of 'supplying demand' to many of the fastest-growing companies in the world, companies such as UPS, MasterCard, Pfizer and Johnson&Johnson. These companies are at the forefront of the 'demand economy', helping to shape the consumer desires of the future.

There are three factors that McCann Erickson believes make it unique. Its key differentiation lies in its creativity, driving the agency to think beyond the obvious, to mistrust the tried and tested and to create powerful connections between the business and the customer.

The second key part of its product offering is delivery. As the largest advertising agency in the world, and the second largest in the UK, McCann Erickson offers industry-leading resources, expertise and talent to bear on any client issue. It is also part of Worldgroup, combining seven best-in-class communication agencies working under common management, working as a team.

The third pillar of McCann Erickson's product offer is demand. The agency believes it is not enough for consumers simply to know about and desire brands –

demand means that they actually have to do something. To stimulate this, McCann Erickson has developed a proprietary process, the Demand Chain, which ensures that it focuses its planning and creativity on one simple goal, action.

Recent Developments

During 2003 and 2004, McCann Erickson put together a new management team for the UK office, which includes some of the industry's most accomplished advertising professionals.

The team includes the Chairman, Rupert Howell, who founded and ran HHCL, named by Campaign magazine, as 'Agency of the Decade' for the 1990s.

Also in the new team is Executive Creative Director Robert Campbell, who founded the advertising agency Rainey Kelly Campbell Roalfe, and Executive Planning Director Damian O'Malley, who founded Woollams Moira Gaskin O'Malley. Also joining McCann Erickson in London as Chief Executive is Stephen Whyte the former CEO of the advertising agency Leo Burnett, which, under his leadership, became the most creatively awarded agency in Europe in 2001.

Promotion

McCann Erickson promotes itself through a business development and corporate communications department that is responsible for internal and external communications.

It runs an issues-led marketing programme, aimed at existing and potential clients, which highlights the agency's commitment to thought leadership, creativity and effectiveness. The programme is supported by public relations and mailing activity.

In addition, McCann Erickson produces a range of materials to keep clients and prospects informed of agency developments. These include a website, regularly updated showreels and award mailings.

McCann Erickson also successfully raises its profile by entering all the major award schemes for the advertising industry. Its achievements in these make it one of the most awarded agencies in the UK.

Brand Values

McCann Erickson's brand values are summed up in its long-standing and well-known mantra, 'truth well told'.

Truth is a demanding standard, but the agency aspires to it in all aspects of its work. Truth in terms of building trust with clients by providing them with honest and impartial advice, and truth in terms of developing communication strategies built on essential truths about brands, the companies behind them and the customers that buy them.

Another differentiating value for the agency is its meritocratic working environment.

McCann Erickson promotes teamwork, openness, imagination, and respect for the ideas and craft skills that are necessary to produce memorable and persuasive communication.

Above all, as the market leader in the advertising industry, McCann Erickson seeks to exercise the highest ethical standards in everything it does.

www.mccann.co.uk

THINGS YOU DIDN'T KNOW ABOUT

McCann Erickson

> The agency's Chairman, Executive Creative Director and Executive Planning Director all founded, built and sold their own, highly successful agencies before joining McCann Erickson.

> McCann Erickson's building is the only Grade II, listed, art-deco, ex-car park in London.

> The McCann New York agency has seventeen floors, 1,466 offices, 40 conference rooms, 42 coffee machines, 35 refrigerators and five cafés.

> McCann Erickson works with three of the top five brands in the world (BusinessWeek 2nd August 2004).

> The best-known of the male partners in the Nescafé Gold Blend couple, Anthony Head, went on to star in the hit series, Buffy the Vampire Slayer and as the Prime Minister in the BBC comedy Little Britain.

"Shall we go back to mine for a crabstick?"

The British coffee Association

Coffee. Irreplaceable.

Michael Page

INTERNATIONAL

Market

Recruitment consultancies play a vital role in keeping the wheels of business turning, acting as the intermediary between companies and prospective job candidates. Identifying and finding suitably qualified people for job vacancies, either for permanent or contract positions, is a highly valuable service for employers, and also for the appointees whose careers progress as a result.

The value of the global recruitment market is currently estimated at over £100 billion per year, and is estimated to have grown by 14% annually over the last decade. Such is the demand for recruitment consultants' skills, whose knowledge and connections can boost their clients' business by finding the right person for the right job, that spend on their services is set to double in the UK over the next ten years.

As a world leader in the recruitment of qualified and skilled professionals for organisations across a broad spectrum of industries and professions, Michael Page International has been one of the fastest-growing brands in this increasingly competitive market. In particular, it has performed strongly in the specialist professional services recruitment sector, which has rapidly developed in recent years, thanks in part to the efforts of Michael Page International.

While it has embraced the internet to develop its business, the company fully realises that the industry remains a relationship-based experience for clients and candidates alike. It is this personal approach that has helped Michael Page International gain a healthy slice of the multi-billion pound recruitment consultancies market worldwide.

Achievements

Michael Page International has grown from a small London consultancy to become an international company based in sixteen countries, with 109 offices and 2,435 staff. It is among the most widely recognised brands in the global professional recruitment industry – a strength which provides a competitive advantage for the group in attracting clients, candidates and employees.

It boasts a client base including all of the companies in the FTSE 100 Index and over 80% of the companies included in the FTSE Eurotop 300 Index, serving their needs with a database of over 1.8 million suitably qualified candidates around the world.

After 27 years of operation, Michael Page International can lay claim to a considerable number of industry 'firsts'. It was, for instance, the first executive recruitment firm to be floated on the London Stock

Exchange. The company was also among the first to establish an in-house consultant training programme covering the operational and management aspects of the recruitment business. Furthermore, it was the first in the recruitment industry to develop an international computerised applicant network – a system that provides consultants with instant access to a database of job vacancies and applicants the world over. The company has continued to invest heavily in the development of IT systems, gaining recognition as among the most innovative in the business.

Michael Page International has won numerous awards in recognition of its many achievements. As well as being awarded Business Superbrand status since 2000, it has been regularly honoured by the industry, including the Recruiter Awards, where it won Best Accountancy/ Financial Recruitment Firm in 2003 and 2004. It was also named Best Recruitment Consultancy Website at the Chartered Institute of Management Accountants Awards (CIMA) in 2003, and the online service was also named Best Recruitment Website by PQ Magazine in 2004.

History

Bill McGregor and Michael Page, who came from the oil and brewing industries, established Michael Page International in London in 1976. The company was founded principally to recruit accountants for industrial clients. It grew rapidly, and by 1979 had opened offices in Manchester, Birmingham, Glasgow, Leeds and Bristol. By now, it was already the largest advertiser in the Financial Times – a position it has held ever since.

In 1985, it marked its ambitions for international expansion by opening an office in Australia and, in the same year, expanded its UK offering by establishing Michael Page City, providing a specialist service to the banking and financial markets.

By the end of its first decade, Michael Page International had built a network of offices throughout the UK and continental Europe, and also expanded to cover recruitment in the legal, marketing, sales, consultancy, taxation, information technology, engineering, human resources, retail and corporate treasury sectors.

In 1988, the company was admitted to the London Stock Exchange, opening the door for further expansion, as Michael Page International opened offices in Germany and, in 1992, established a sub-brand, Accountancy Additions, and a specialist Public Sector division in the UK.

Following a major investment in IT in the early 1990s, the company introduced its national recruitment database in 1993 and its first generation website in 1997.

Other milestones in its history include the creation of Michael Page Human Resources in 2000 and the opening of offices in Tokyo in 2001 and Shanghai in 2003. More

specialist divisions have continued to be added as Michael Page International broadened its expertise, with an Engineering Recruitment Division starting in 2001, a Health Recruitment Division in France in 2002, and, in 2003, a Secretarial Recruitment Division in the UK and a Real Estate & Construction Recruitment Division in France.

After initially opening US offices in Manhattan and New Jersey, Michael Page opened a third office in Connecticut in 2003 and continued expanding into 2004 opening offices in Boston and Chicago.

Sleeveless Body Warmer, Zip Up Cardigan, Denim Jeans all by Esprit Hair & Make-up by Denise Lilley Styling by Jo Harris Photography by Bob Komar Career as a Temporary Management Accountant arranged through Michael Page Finance

www.michaelpage.co.uk

Michael Page
FINANCE

Opinio juris sive necessitates

A selection of current opportunities within London Industry & Commerce

Setting the precedent in Legal recruitment

Michael Page LEGAL

Product

The product of Michael Page International is based on the '4Cs': consultants, candidates, clients and care. Michael Page International wholeheartedly believes that professional consultants come first, without them nothing can be achieved. This is wholly reflected in the organic growth of the company, whereby nearly all the current management is the result of internal promotion. Bill McGregor is still involved in the business day-to-day and the CEO, Terry Benson, started life as a consultant in the Birmingham office. And to ensure that consultants are professional in the way they work, they are not paid by commission.

The company believes that if you provide a sincere and genuine service to candidates everything will fall into place. Michael Page International has long realised that the creation of loyalty stems from finding out about a candidate's career aspirations and then showing them how they can realise their vision. Many candidates come to the company's door by way of referral or recommendation, or often, they already have a history of being placed into previous roles via the consultancy.

Michael Page International also recognises that by having a pool of quality candidates, clients will be drawn to the business. Coupled with this, the provision of a personal service to all clients, taking the time to find out how they can provide a bespoke recruitment solution, creates a powerful incentive to secure repeat business.

Finally, care and consideration always has a way of rewarding in the future.

With the 4Cs as guiding principals, Michael Page International has developed its brand to signify efficiency and quality in recruitment services. The brand has been developed along two central and associated fronts.

Firstly, the company has focused on developing specialist consultancy teams to recruit for the disciplines in which they are often personally qualified. Thus the company has bankers recruiting for banks, salesmen recruiting sales professionals and so on. Secondly, the business operates on a global basis to facilitate the international movement of skilled management.

Its people are clearly the company's most important asset and have helped Michael Page International to achieve an unrivalled level of expertise and market penetration.

The company's breadth of experience is reflected in the twelve specialist divisions in which it is now structured. These comprise: Accounting, Tax and Treasury; Banking and Financial Markets; Marketing; Retail; Sales; Legal; IT and Technology; Human Resources; Engineering & Manufacturing; Procurement & Supply Chain; Consultancy and Secretarial.

To communicate all of these activities, Michael Page International has also created its own in-house marketing department.

Recent Developments

As well as its recent expansion into Japan, Brazil, and China, Michael Page International's continued expansion into the US, with new offices in Boston and Chicago, is an important development for the company.

The Chicago office in particular represents an exciting opportunity, as the local market there experiences an economic revival. As a major commercial and financial centre, Chicago is key to the company's continued growth in North America and the office there has received a strong response from the company's existing clients who have operations in the area.

Promotion

The recruitment industry, while rapidly adapting to the digital revolution, continues to utilise traditional methods of recruitment. As such, Michael Page International promotes itself to both clients and candidates using recruitment advertising in national newspapers, magazines and industry journals. The company is a market leader in the classified advertising pages of the national and trade press worldwide and, in the UK, it is the recruitment industry's biggest advertiser, significantly ahead of its nearest rival. It also holds a leading position in Australia, France and the Netherlands.

The company's global office network, which has established close relationships with local organisations, also promotes the recruitment services of Michael Page International to a wide audience. This regional presence helps the company to achieve an extremely high level of local market penetration. The internet also helps the company to target new candidates, especially in places such as South Africa where it has no offices. The website is an extremely useful resource for candidates in those countries looking for international job opportunities.

Michael Page International also promotes its brand through sponsorship of events and professional conferences as well as providing corporate hospitality for clients and candidates at Ascot, Warwick and Twickenham.

It also helps reinforce its position as a leader of the industry, through publishing information such as booklets with specific career information and salary surveys.

Distinguishing itself in what is a highly fragmented industry, the Michael Page International brand promises 'a world of possibilities'.

It has invested more in brand marketing than any rival in the recruitment industry, recently unveiling its 'Fashion' campaign. The campaign helps Michael Page International stand out in an environment dominated by bland 'shopping list' job advertising, and reflects candidate and client career and lifestyle aspirations, in a charming rather than a crude or brash way.

Brand Values

The quality and expertise of its consultancy and support staff are the best expression of the brand values of Michael Page International. The company's policy is to recruit and train its staff to be the best in the business – to be passionate about their work and make the best matches possible between candidates and clients – and above all, to uphold the philosophy of the '4Cs'.

The Michael Page International brand is identified as a specialist with individual businesses operating in specific markets and disciplines. It is a global brand, which sets common standards of service excellence, entrepreneurial spirit, continuity and operational effectiveness throughout its worldwide operations – a network of offices that operate at national, regional and local levels.

www.michaelpage.co.uk

Leather Handbag, Satin Trenchcoat by Esprit
Leather Gloves, Silk Scarf by TopShop
Personal Organiser by Filofax
Micromesh Tights by Falke
Career as a Financial Analyst arranged through Michael Page Finance

www.michaelpage.co.uk

Michael Page FINANCE

THINGS YOU DIDN'T KNOW ABOUT

Michael Page International

› Every year since 1992, Michael Page International has been the largest recruitment advertiser in the Financial Times. In 2000 it accounted for more than double the volume of advertising of the next three largest recruitment advertisers.

› Every nine minutes Michael Page International helps professionals by placing them into new roles.

› In 1988 Michael Page International produced a training video for candidates featuring 'Mr Bean' played by Rowan Atkinson. This was two years before the first Mr Bean show appeared on TV and fourteen years ahead of the film, Bean: The Movie.

MINTEL

Market

Investment in market research is always top priority. It will identify the most lucrative path to take, in good times and bad. Market research is the one business constant. In an era of information overload, it is essential to obtain the right research to drive a business forward; it must not complicate the road to success.

Mintel has experienced tremendous growth and expansion by providing a complete research revolution to clients for over 30 years, and is now a business and household name. Consistently high levels of service, clear branding and a focus on quality have resulted in unprecedented client growth and investment. Expansion has been exceptional, with the US operations leading the way. Staff turnover is low, with today's more mature company based upon organic growth and experience. While the group has retained its head offices in London and Chicago, Mintel has an established satellite office in Sydney and a successful sales agency in Ireland. As a leading supplier of market research, Mintel's reputation remains unmatched. It goes beyond being a research supplier by becoming a research consultant for its clients, enhancing development plans and using detailed insights to propel organisations to the next level. A reputation for high quality, reliable market, consumer, product and media research, coupled with the most effective delivery mechanisms, has earned Mintel Business Superbrands status consistently since the awards began.

Achievements

Mintel's accomplishments reach far and wide, surpassing just the immediate research community. From being the American Marketing Association's first corporate sponsor, to sponsoring the Chartered Institute of Marketing's graduate scheme, as well as being their preferred supplier for market research. In support of Mintel's continued commitment to the US, the company was recently

37% of US adults bought food or drink to consume when commuting or driving to work in the last month.

gnpd
part of Mintel Group

presented with the prestigious BABC (British American Business Council) award. Although these awards recognise Mintel's success, the company's achievements are most evident by its consistent growth both in revenue and the size of the global team. This is an accomplishment that represents how dedicated Mintel's employees are to the core business. The company's organic business model has resulted in impressive company-wide growth of more than 50% in the past two years.

Mintel's core report range is now interactive, meaning that updated information and analysis are continuously pushed through the website and passed onto clients, so that at any point the data they use is both topical and relevant. In addition, Mintel now supplies clients with graphing, analytical and presentational tools to ensure its data is used comprehensively throughout its clients' organisations. Its more detailed consumer analysis highlights the very best way to reach consumers from a marketing perspective.

History

Mintel began over three decades ago by providing food and drink research in the UK. Now the brand spans all corners of the world, with leading analysts who are renowned experts in areas as diverse as leisure, consumer goods, retail, financial services, sales promotion and social trends. Traffic to the group website is testament to Mintel's success, with hits exceeding 2.3 million every month.

Mintel's ability to predict market changes and developments has inevitably driven the company's own strategic direction. Furthermore, the ability to analyse data and deliver it using the latest technology, has allowed Mintel to stay one step ahead of its competitors. By identifying opportunities, the company has expanded accordingly, both in the products supplied and the geographical areas of operation. Its portfolio has grown from supplying published research to offering a full-service research solution, giving clients the tools they need to surpass all of their business objectives.

The Chicago office, which opened just seven years ago, now rivals the London office in terms of size as well as revenue. Over the last few years Mintel's reach has been extended into exciting new areas such as Israel, China and South Korea. The continuing support and loyalty of its clients, many of whom had their first Mintel experience while studying at university and have maintained that relationship throughout their working life, is obviously an integral part of its branding success. Mintel has rewarded that loyalty with constant innovation and improvement to the product and level of service.

Product

Mintel's product portfolio spans many arenas such as consumer goods, financial services and retail. The company's offerings are the result of years of client feedback and the innate ability to sense exactly what the market needs. Global reach allows clients to depend on Mintel for anything: from delivering the latest household wipe in Malaysia to the office in a matter of days, providing access to a direct mail campaign in

shedding light on the bottled water market

MINTEL

IBWA members save 15% on market and consumer research from Mintel. For free information about Mintel's new bottled water report, call **312.943.5250** or email **info@mintel.com.**

reports.mintel.com

Alberta within minutes, or offering intelligent insights on an emerging food trend in Europe within seconds. Extensive commitment to the instantaneous delivery of information has given Mintel's clients immediate access to exclusive global information, with all products available through the industry-leading interactive website, www.mintel.com.

From the newest ketchup in Seattle, to the latest window cleaner in Stockholm, Mintel's Global New Products Database (GNPD) is the premier global consumer packaged goods database. By tracking when and where products are hitting the shelves, Mintel's information allows clients to see what competitors are offering and the opportunities which are surfacing in over 50 countries, every hour of the day. The database highlights over 500,000 products featuring information such as ingredient, packaging, and pricing details. Clients are able to delve into areas that they never before had

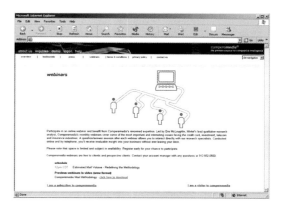

access to from Kazakhstan to Madagascar. In addition, Mintel's network of worldwide shoppers allows customers to have a product in their hands in a matter of days to touch, feel, and examine.

Comperemedia is another of Mintel's key product-monitoring tools. This powerful system highlights marketing campaigns customers are receiving in their mailbox each day using an extensive panel of households in both the US and Canada. From top financial service providers, to the largest telecommunication operators and national airlines, Comperemedia provides unprecedented access to over two million high resolution direct mail pieces. In addition, Comperemedia provides monitoring of three quarters of a million print advertising campaigns in top consumer and trade press in a whole host of fields.

The flagship product, Mintel Reports, gives a comprehensive exploration into a variety of different industries. Information such as market size, segmentation, advertising and promotional activity within a sector, as well as Mintel's exclusive consumer research, allows Mintel to provide market projections for the next five years. Topics such as functional foods, luxury automobiles, and DVRs are just some of the industries that have been examined this past year. Analysis gives clients the insight needed to make the right business decisions.

Recent Developments

Mintel's portfolio of offerings is always evolving in response to the marketplace. Just recently, the company launched Mintel Premier, an enhanced and interactive tool that delivers the ubiquitous Mintel report in a way never before approached by a research supplier. Clients can use Premier to communicate within their organisation, create customised charts and graphs based on their search criteria, and get up-to-the-minute research information instantly instead of waiting for the

latest version to be published. In addition, Premier cross-references Mintel's other relevant reports to give clients an accurate portrait of the market and how it relates to other industries.

New in 2004, Mintel's Menu Insights was the direct result of a need in the marketplace. Clients such as ingredient companies and foodservice providers were seeking information on how restaurants were using their products, and in response, Mintel created Menu Insights. Menu Insights is a menu-tracking database, which compiles information from over 500 restaurants ranging from mainstream restaurants to high-end establishments. It also includes menu analysis of the nation's top 50 chefs in addition to insightful editorial and quarterly trend reports.

Mintel ECLIPS was created as a result of Mintel having been frequently asked to facilitate primary research such as focus groups for clients. Produced in conjunction with Innovation Focus, Mintel ECLIPS is an exciting new product that is unlike anything currently being offered in the market research industry. It gives clients an unprecedented look at the consumer's habits and attitudes, allowing them to actually see and hear consumers' opinions on market activity. This revolutionary qualitative research tool compiles hundreds of video clips into a searchable online database, revealing the most current and prevalent attitudes among consumers today.

Promotion

Mintel has recently set itself a goal to provide both 'insight and impact' in everything that it does. This aim is not only carried through the research it provides, but through the work that it carries out with its clients to obtain the best possible results for their business.

Mintel communicates this message through countless media – the newly enhanced website, the company's concise and educational marketing literature, informative client webinars, and continued presence at top industry trade shows.

The company's consistent image to clients is essential to the Mintel brand. In fact Mintel's logo has remained virtually untouched over the past fifteen years. With the exception of the introduction of the electronic 'e' which heralded Mintel's industry leading e-commerce facilities and now stands for Mintel's commitment to remaining at the forefront of technological developments. The colours of yellow and black are synonymous with Mintel. In fact, Mintel account managers have now started a programme where they like to 'leave a little yellow on every client's desk' in order to keep the brand fresh in the customer's mind.

Every team member at Mintel is a brand ambassador and Mintel employees depend on each other to create the best possible impression. Each contact point with a Mintel employee leaves clients with a consistent message of how Mintel can help them make informed business decisions.

Mintel has always been at the forefront of new communication techniques

and has recently successfully implemented a programme of client webinars, combining web conferences and training. This has proved to be the ideal tool to help clients maximise Mintel data.

Mintel's superior research boasts daily coverage on television, radio and top consumer and trade press including The Wall Street Journal, FT, USA Today, The New York Times, BusinessWeek, Investors' Business Daily and The Times, just to name a few. Journalists find Mintel information indispensable to support and create their stories. The endorsements they provide on the Mintel website speak volumes.

With press circulation exceeding 35 million in any one month in the UK alone, journalists have described the reports as being invaluable in terms of "emerging trends and forecasting the future". Others acknowledge the "strong relationship" they have with Mintel's press office, describing this of "critical importance when working to tight deadlines".

In addition, Mintel's credibility lies with the governing associations for many of the markets it examines. Partnerships with trade associations provide members with information that will take their industry to the next level.

Although everyone at Mintel enjoys reading about its latest research findings in the press, the best endorsement comes directly from satisfied clients who met and surpassed their business objectives.

Brand Values

Mintel's brand values have been condensed into one simple phrase – insight and impact. To all of Mintel's clients the company provides insight into their markets, consumers and products and Mintel also provides it with impact, questioning the status quo, challenging established concepts and ultimately having a positive impact on clients' profits. Equally, internally everyone aims to find insight in everything they do and ensure that their output makes maximum impact upon their clients' business.

www.mintel.com

THINGS YOU DIDN'T KNOW ABOUT

Mintel

> According to Mintel's Menu Insights the true American dish is not a hamburger, hot dog or southern fried chicken, it is in fact the Italian pizza.

> Since the year 2000, Mintel's GNPD has picked up over 530,000 new products worldwide, with as many as 150,000 new products being picked up in 2004 alone.

> Some of the more unusual products which Mintel's consultancy service has been asked to send to clients include US tap water to Japan and cold takeaway fish & chips for UK quality control.

> Mintel has always been an influential force. Back in 1972, when Mintel's World in a Shopping Basket was published, it was revealed that Iceland was the most expensive country of the fifteen surveyed. As a result, questions were asked in the Icelandic parliament.

> The most unusual new products highlighted by the GNPD innovations team include curry flavoured toothpaste, collagen soup, banana mayonnaise, green tea cereal and sweet smelling CDs.

> An iconic pop star once refused to go on tour without the right brand of water. Mintel was called in to source the water and save the tour – the pop star shall remain unnamed.

500k[1]

npower

In only three years the npower brand went from 0 to 90% national awareness with an estimated value of £200 million. The brand has successfully shed heritage associations with regional monopoly supply, but maintained the loyalty of the customer bases it has acquired. It has avoided the 'fly-by-night' tag attached to many new brands that can put off risk-averse customers, and it has developed the flexibility to allow expansion beyond the core products of gas and electricity.

Market

The UK energy retail market is today worth £25 billion (Source: DTI). It is dominated by six major suppliers of which npower is consistently ranked in the top three by industry analyst Datamonitor.

The market has gone through radical change since deregulation began in 1992. Previously electricity was provided by twelve regional suppliers while gas was supplied, nationwide, by British Gas. Customers could not choose their supplier and prices were set by the regulator. Following deregulation we now have a fiercely competitive national energy market.

The business energy sector is particularly complex. Large industrial and commercial customers' needs and buying patterns differ vastly from those of small and medium sized enterprises (SMEs) who, at the low end, are more akin to domestic customers. Meanwhile there is a large overlap in the middle-market which includes, for instance, big single site customers, or small groups.

Deregulation brought challenge as well as opportunity. Companies with an eye on the long game needed to establish scale to survive. Around five million customer accounts was seen to be the minimum for most companies to succeed. This meant both organic growth and acquisitions were important. It also meant keeping existing customers happy and loyal.

Pace of change led to a volatile market and huge integration challenges for merged companies. Along with the organisational and HR issues, decisions had to be taken regarding the IT systems for storing huge customer databases and swapping customers between suppliers. Designed in isolation, these now needed to be integrated or to communicate with each other.

In the market today these practical hurdles still exist alongside tough strategic questions about branding. Energy companies have been grappling with issues like the value of existing regional brands, versus the value of adopting and building a single, new national brand. Equally important is the issue of how 'broad' a brand can stretch beyond traditional energy, without snapping.

Achievements

In less than four years npower integrated five companies into a single, national whole. It now employs around 12,000 people and has over six million customer accounts and provides gas, electricity and home related services. npower business holds 20% of the business to business energy market – serving over half a million customers.

To achieve this npower has had to become very adept at change management and growth, but the key to success has been keeping the customer as the centre of attention. In a commodity market, price is always a key factor, but the careful development of the npower brand, in a traditionally low-interest sector, has been vital in maintaining customer relationships.

History

In 1999 the domestic electricity market fully opened up to competition and the company National Power began to build a 'retail' business with the purchase of gas company Calortex and the Midlands Electricity Board.

In October 1999 it created the npower brand as a collective name for its customer businesses. In 2000 it added new entrant Independent Energy to the npower stable. Later that year National Power demerged into International Power and Innogy plc. Innogy kept npower along with power generation, trading and engineering assets.

In 2001 Innogy plc acquired the Yorkshire Electricity Group and swapped the distribution business (the wires) of Yorkshire Electricity for the customers of Northern Electric and Gas.

In May 2002 Innogy was acquired by the German multi-utility company RWE and later renamed RWE npower while the customer-facing brand continued as npower.

Product

Energy is a low interest product, which is difficult to differentiate. At the most basic level the pricing is the product, but npower took the view that marketing needed to be more innovative than a series of pricing skirmishes. These would be counterproductive and costly, encouraging customers to come and go regularly with maximum disruption and minimum return.

npower believed simple clever product innovations would help attract loyal customers. Examples of this include an unprecedented partnership signed with Greenpeace to develop and sell 'npower Juice', a domestic, non-premium priced green electricity tariff. Although a niche product for now, 'npower Juice' attracts users who are significantly more loyal than mainstream electricity consumers.

A further innovation helping cement loyalty has been npower's diversification into home moving products. These range from providing simple home move information through to conveyancing.

On the business to business front product innovation has tended to mean introducing flexibility to help meet the needs of business customers, which vary widely in their consumption habits and patterns. At the SME end this will never stray far from the basics of accurate and timely billing, but npower has looked to develop size and sector specialisms. A classic and popular example of a simple improvement on multiple billing is a collated service for group sites where head office receives collated statements and a summary invoice, while individual sites receive energy statements.

At the industrial and commercial end of the spectrum the financial stakes are incredibly high. In the current market structure, predicting demand and tracking consumption are vital for major energy users. npower has met this trend with a Half Hourly Online product, which allows customers to track usage securely via the internet, and receive alerts when consumption is breaking pre-set thresholds.

Meanwhile npower's Renewables and Consolidation Service helps major business customers bear the growing burden of statutory environmental obligations, and protects them from the market risk of over-reliance on a single power generator.

Recent Developments

At the end of 2003, npower added to the momentum created by 'npower Juice' with the launch of North Hoyle the UK's first major offshore wind farm and the 'npower Juice fund' – designed to boost fledgling renewables

projects. npower stepped up the 'green' offer to businesses as well with the acquisition of two high profile customers, BT and the new Wembley Stadium. The contract with BT is the world's biggest green power supply deal while Wembley is the first UK stadium to be supplied by renewable energy. npower is now offering green electricity to all business customers.

2004 saw npower welcome a new corporate charity partner in Macmillan Cancer Relief. This two-year relationship involves a raft of fundraising activities for the cancer care charity including cricket legend Phil Tufnell's 500 mile money raising walk around the cricket grounds of England and TV support for Macmillan's biggest fundraiser the 'World's Biggest Coffee Morning'. The npower 500 and other initiatives have so far raised £300,000 for Macmillan.

Promotion
npower's approach to promotion and marketing has evolved with the company. At launch npower was a challenger, competing with established brands and the immediate goal was to gain awareness and promote the, still novel, idea that energy customers had a choice of supplier. From the outset it was clear that mass marketing was needed to put npower on the radar for business customers as well as domestic users.

Early television advertising included a campaign using the strapline 'There are some things in life you can't choose, your energy supplier is not one of them'. A controversial execution featuring a ginger-haired family was instrumental in putting npower on the map. Awareness was sustained and improved through a simple but daring two-year sponsorship deal with ITV's 'The Bill' and associate sponsorship of the FA Premiership.

Following a two-year gap npower returned to the small screen in 2004 with a major TV campaign and a new direction. The new adverts featuring the strapline 'Are you npowered', show a young couple celebrating a wedding anniversary under a canopy of fairy lights and a husband's valiant attempts to cook baked beans on toast. As customers become more confident about the relationship they want from their energy supplier these adverts serve to highlight npower's more personal focus.

A real watershed in npower's brand development was achieved with its decision to take over sponsorship of English Test Cricket. The cricket sponsorship built the stature and reputation of the brand by linking it with an established, national, experience. The demographics of cricket followers meant the sponsorship registered from the outset with business users – something npower capitalised on by extending its sponsorship and developing business to business marketing tie-ins with the successful county cricket Twenty20 Cup competition, promoting 'after work' fun for business customers. This approach is also working with npower's sponsorship of premiership rugby team Worcester Warriors, utilising corporate hospitality and networking opportunities for business customers. Cricket sponsorship continues to reach new audiences with the addition of the npower village cricket championships and a new agreement with the ECB for cricket fans who sign up for a dual fuel domestic deal – npower will pay their membership costs towards the England Supporters' Cricket Club. 2005 promises to be a highlight in npower's sponsorship

with activity centred around the biggest event in the cricket calendar – the Ashes Test Series.

In the residential market, npower built on widespread awareness with sponsorships linking the brand to 'home' related properties, for instance the Daily Mail Ideal Home Show, BBC Good Food Show and Channel 4's strand of home programmes.

For business customers the mass-marketing approach was supported by bespoke communications. npower broke new ground with the award-winning customer

magazine 'The Hub' aimed at major business users, mixing business and lifestyle features. Alongside The Hub, npower also produced 'Insider' – an objective round up of topical energy issues supporting the 'industry expertise' positioning valued by specialist energy buyers.

At the SME end npower has struck a balance between sector-focused marketing, for instance title Sponsorship of the Pub Show in 2003, and building links with business 'communities of interest'. Tie-ins with Durham University's SME research department and with the Sunday Times Enterprise Network, for example, helped position npower as an expert in the growing 'middle market' business sector and guaranteed regular national media exposure as well as valuable access to SME databases.

Looking forward – the new relationship with Wembley Stadium as first official supplier opens up a whole new audience for the npower brand. npower will be offering six ten-year seat licences at the stadium – that's a seat at every major event from the opening in 2006 to 2016. This will take place over the next three years via a nationwide promotion that was launched in a high profile TV campaign around football's Euro 2004.

Brand Values
npower has been created from a variety of companies, each of which joined with a specific culture and a different business plan. The creation, and more importantly adoption, of a clear and specific set of brand values was as vital in guiding the company's internal behaviour as it was in creating a personality for the brand.

In 2004 npower adopted new brand values of personal, rewarding and forward thinking and refreshed the brand with brighter colours and re-proportioned letters to give a more contemporary, friendly, up-to-date feel.

With literally millions of customer interactions per year, these brand values are demonstrated in daily dealings with customers as well as in headline marketing activity.

Externally, the values are reflected in the feel of npower, which market research consistently indicates is fresh and innovative, without sacrificing the warmth element needed to build loyalty.

www.npower.com

THINGS YOU DIDN'T KNOW ABOUT

npower

> Well known customers of npower include Argos, BT, Sainsbury's, Wembley Stadium and the English Test Cricket Squad.

> npower can speak to customers in five different languages other than English: Urdu, Punjabi, Welsh, Gujerati and Chinese.

> npower's metering business 'MeterPlus' makes 22 million visits a year, driving twelve million miles and walking three million miles.

> All of npower's customer call centres are based in the UK. They receive nearly twelve million calls and three-quarters of a million letters a year.

o2.co.uk/business

O₂ Business Zones
40% off all calls to two chosen area codes.
Call 0800 781 0202

0121

02410

O₂

Market

O₂ (UK) is one of five licensed operators competing in the UK's mobile communications market. O₂ competes principally with Vodafone, Orange, T-mobile and 3.

The mobile communications market place is as competitive as it has ever been following liberalisation some 20 years ago. Against this market context, where there is a strong emphasis on the delivery of new products and services to deliver short term differentiation, O₂ has remained focused in its strategy of customer centricity by putting the customer first and only delivering products and services that are genuinely based upon customer needs. O₂ has recognised that while voice services remain the key driver in the use of business mobiles, customers are increasingly comfortable with new mobile data services and increasingly demanding of efficient and effective service.

Text messaging is now a widely used service and the market is seeing signs of growth in new areas of mobile data. New applications such as mobile email, picture messaging (MMS) and music over mobile are increasingly used by customers as the benefits become more apparent and the functionality of new devices improves.

Talk to a person not a recorded message

Join Best for Business 0800 781 02 02

O₂

The launch of services over 3G, much hyped by the marketing press, was approached with deliberate caution by O₂, which, true to its customer centric principles held off 3G launch until technology and handsets were ready, before introducing Wi-Fi and GPRS through O₂ Connection Manager.

Effectiveness Awards

Achievements

A look at the awareness ratings of O₂ and key competitors since launch demonstrates just how far the brand has come in terms of establishing a recognisable and salient identity in the business market. Just eight months after launch, O₂ had achieved a staggering 62% spontaneous brand awareness amongst all business decision makers despite a comparatively small share of voice. A year later, in December 2003, O₂ overtook the two key players, Orange and Vodafone, to lead the market in spontaneous brand awareness amongst corporates with 81%.

Tracking shows that strong awareness is being translated into purchase intent. Latest data (September 2004) shows that O₂ also leads the field in network consideration, with more business decision makers agreeing that O₂ is either the only network or one of a few that they would sign to.

O₂ has made progress on many other fronts too. During the course of 2004, the customer base of the UK business grew by 10%, taking its total to approximately fourteen million. Significantly, the UK business' service revenue also grew by 20%.

In addition, O₂ has received a number of high-profile accolades from within the telecoms and marketing industries. Between April-October 2003, O₂ achieved the best call success rate figures ever published by Oftel, strengthening the brand's position as a serious contender in business mobile telecoms, as network performance is a critical driver in the business market. The following month – November 2003 – the Two Minute Challenge won Best Campaign of the Year at the National Business Awards.

More recently, the No IVR campaign was shortlisted for the 2004 National Business Awards, and in November 2004, O₂ picked up the most coveted prize in the advertising industry: the IPA Advertising Effectiveness Awards

Grand Prix. Judges cited the "astonishing level of (communications) integration" as a principal reason for O₂'s success.

History

O₂ was officially launched on May 1st 2002, following the demerger of mmO₂ from BT the previous November. mmO₂ comprises a number of wholly owned European subsidiaries, formerly belonging to BT's wireless portfolio and now trading collectively under the O₂ brand. These include O₂ UK (formerly BT Cellnet), O₂ Germany (formerly Viag intercom) and O₂ Ireland (formerly Esat Digifone). The Group has operations in the Isle of Man (Manx Telecom) and owns a leading internet portal, formerly known as Genie, now also trading under the O₂ brand.

Product

Whatever the finer details of the approach, an objective shared by most mobile operators is to attract high value business customers, and to encourage them to take up mobile data solutions. However, before moving the customer through to using data, it is important that they are comfortable and confident in using their mobile.

That is why in 2004 O₂ put significant investment into its network and into its service for small business and corporate customers, all of whom can speak to a person 24/7, getting a more personal service, so queries can be answered quickly and effectively and customers can make the most of their mobile while having the time to get on with their day.

In mobile data O₂ maintains its lead. Within the business market mobile internet and mobile email are key applications.

Following its launch in 2001 Blackberry has gone from strength to strength. A wireless 'always on' email device, that can integrate with corporate IT systems or act as a stand alone for small businesses, Blackberry enables users to send and receive email whilst on the move without ever having to dial up to receive messages.

Xda, a personal handheld device, combines an advanced mobile phone and touch screen PDA into one device. A winner of many accolades including What Cellphone 'Award of Excellence 2004', the Xda has been key to O₂'s drive to get business customers using mobile data, in the corporate market having helped businesses to build relationships with their customers.

On the back of the success of Xda, new and faster devices have been launched. Xda II, an enhanced version of the original, has Bluetooth giving wireless connectivity to other Bluetooth enabled devices and tri-band functionality enabling seamless usage within the US as well as other countries across Europe, Asia & Australia.

Recent Developments

The strategic challenge for O₂ in the business market was to establish the brand as a credible challenger to the big business players; Orange and particularly Vodafone. Trust is all important for businesses whose day to day workings hinge on telecoms solutions that are efficient and utterly reliable.

However, gaining trust takes time and, most importantly, proof. The O₂ strategy is to focus on consistently delivering tangible substantiation that the brand understands and can deliver on business needs. Hence the development of a number of service innovations that cut through competitive clutter of tariffing shouts.

The Two Minute Challenge offering was developed in direct response to a key insight – that time is a critical barrier to switching amongst SMEs. A new interface was required that listened to SMEs' needs and delivered against them simply and quickly; hence the Two Minute Challenge, which saw O₂ pledging to find the right mobile solution for SMEs in under two minutes. This was a genuine service innovation which cut to the heart of SMEs' needs. The Two Minute Challenge led to a 6% increase in O₂'s SME market share, moving O₂ from 3rd to market leader in under two months. SBA amongst SMEs increased to an all-time high of 69% and PAA to an all-time high of 72%.

Following the success of the Two Minute Challenge, work was undertaken by O₂ to determine how else the potent time insight could be leveraged. The subsequent No IVR pledge saw the

brand promise that when a Best for Business customer contacts O₂, they will always speak to a person and not a recorded message. Since the launch of No IVR, O₂ has seen a rise of 4% in network preference to become the most preferred network. Imitation is supposedly the sincerest form of flattery, and July 2004 saw an Orange press campaign copying O₂'s No IVR proposition.

2004 brought two new campaigns which further illustrated O₂'s understanding of business needs. The Business Zones campaign ran in March, driven by the insight that a large number of calls made by business users are to suppliers and customers in their surrounding area. This campaign communicated a simple value for money proposition while proving O₂'s ability to cater for business on a region-specific, localised scale.

In September 2004, O₂ ran its Network Performance campaign, promoting awareness of its success in the Oftel survey. With both an empathic approach to working with business customers and a high-performing network to offer, O₂ continues to strengthen its position as one of the leaders in the business mobile telecoms market.

Promotion

Since its launch in May 2002, O₂ has moved rapidly to generate strong awareness of the brand, with an emphasis on reaching the high value, technology-accepting business and personal customers that it most wants to attract.

One of O₂'s key strengths is its striking brand identity – with its instantly recognisable blue grad and bubble properties – which is consistent across all customer touchpoints. The O₂ brand provides a serene and calming antidote to the shouty sales messages that flood the market.

In the business sector, following on from the corporate launch, O₂ has run product-based advertising; most recently launching the XDA IIi with a campaign that equated the new, higher-spec handset with a fine piece of automotive machinery. O₂'s business advertising in 2004 has been focused primarily on communicating its understanding that business users have specific needs – it is essential their network performs well and that their mobile service provider shares an empathy with the way they work.

To further enforce the service messages of its creative advertising, O₂ has also experimented with different media usages to communicate a particular message. For example, the media bookings for the Two Minute Challenge were planned specifically to catch SME users when they had two minutes to spare. Similarly, 'top' and 'tail' TV spots were booked, so that two short ads – one introducing the proposition and one signing it off – surrounded two minutes of other advertising.

O₂ has also worked hard at stimulating positive editorial, through engagement in sponsorship to build awareness of the brand and, more unusually for a sponsorship deal, to stimulate immediate use of its products. A classic example of this is the range of mobile media services O₂ has developed to complement its partnerships with the Zurich Rugby Premiership, Arsenal Football Club and the England Rugby Squad.

Brand Values

Branding involves more than simply projecting a new image. For service businesses in particular, it means changing the inner world – how people on the inside of the business see the brand, how they think and how they behave. This was the challenge that faced O₂ when it parted with BT – to reinvent the brand both internally and externally.

The best part of four years on, O₂ possesses a fresh and distinctive personality, resting on the four core values that have been set out to define the brand. Firstly, O₂ is a bold company that is full of surprises and continually producing practical and relevant business solutions; it creates for its subscribers a world of 'clear blue space'

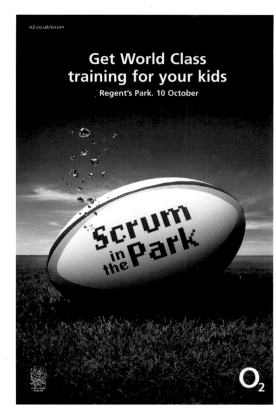

full of exciting possibilities. Secondly, O₂ is clear and straightforward. It is a company with the ability to communicate complex technologies and propositions in a way that is simple and easy to understand. Thirdly, it is an open and candid brand: it is fresh in a way that entirely sets it apart from its key competitors. Finally, O₂ is a trustworthy brand. It is responsive in listening to the needs of its customers, and it is honest in both its branding communications and its conduct as a company. Above all else, O₂ is an enabling brand which constantly invites its audience to try new things with its consistent 'See what you can do' message.

Today, O₂ projects a modern, attractive and internationally persuasive brand identity, capitalising on its extensive networks, depth of experience and customer centric approach.

www.O2.co.uk

THINGS YOU DIDN'T KNOW ABOUT

O₂

〉 O₂ is the UK leader in non-voice services including, data connections via GPRS, 3G and Wi-Fi.

〉 The England rugby squad and their coach use O₂ Xda to keep in touch with each other.

〉 In 2002, O₂ UK handled more than ten million texts from viewers of Channel 4's Big Brother.

〉 Manx Telecom, part of the O₂ group, piloted Europe's first live 3G network in December 2001.

〉 Each month O₂ customers send more than three quarters of a billion text messages.

officeangels
RECRUITMENT CONSULTANTS

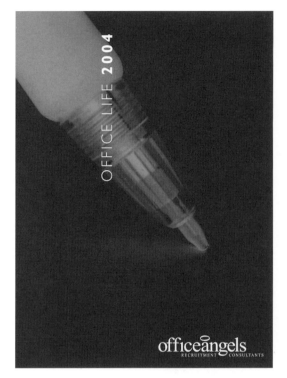

OFFICE LIFE 2004

officeangels
RECRUITMENT CONSULTANTS

Market

The UK recruitment market is growing rapidly year on year and is currently worth £24.5 billion – marking a 6.6% increase since 2003 (Source: REC Annual Recruitment Industry Survey 2003/04). Agencies big and small are not only vying for the best clients, but the finest candidates. To succeed in such a competitive marketplace demands a unique and clearly differentiated offering and Office Angels excels in delivering such a service.

Office Angels is the UK's leading recruitment consultancy specialising in secretarial and office support staff for assignment and permanent positions. A multi-site company with over 80 branches and a rapidly expanding network of satellite offices, Office Angels is an authority on recruitment issues and is distinct in the services it offers to both clients and candidates. Each week, it finds 8,000 people short-term assignments and places more than 9,000 people in permanent jobs every year.

The business boasts a prestigious range of clients, including 90% of The Times top 100 companies in the UK. Office Angels helps organisations grow their businesses from scratch or realise their ambitious expansion plans.

Achievements

Office Angels is recognised as the UK's leading secretarial and office support recruitment consultancy because it has earned the reputation of offering the very best recruitment solutions.

Seven years ago Office Angels coined the term 'Executary', to give recognition to senior secretaries and PAs as well as highlighting the

increased responsibilities within their role. Supported by The Guardian newspaper, the Office Angels Executary of The Year Award has become a high profile national event, achieving recognition and prestige for both winners and their companies.

Office Angels has been praised for a progressive approach to age diversity in its placement of both over 45's and the younger generation of school and college leavers in work. An Age Positive Employer Champion, Office Angels acknowledges that today's workforce is made up of a diverse range of age groups and therefore embraces a non-discriminatory approach to recruitment.

The brand enjoys a highly creative and effective national and regional PR campaign that results in a higher media profile than any other recruitment consultancy. In 2004 alone, Office Angels generated over 1,000 media hits, reaching 600 million people. Office Angels has maintained and developed its position as an authority on human resource issues and has generated stories on appraisal techniques, team building trends and office etiquette. The brand also analyses human interest and work-related stories through a range of press releases including interview faux pas, spicing up meetings and the escapist jobs that office-workers are dreaming about.

This combined range of activity ensures that recall of the Office Angels name is arguably significantly higher among job seekers and clients than any other recruitment consultancy.

History

Established in 1986, Office Angels has expanded to over 80 branches nationwide, employing around 600 people.

The brand has built its reputation on putting people first by matching individual skills to individual needs. The Office Angels mission is to offer the very best recruitment solutions to clients and job seekers by enabling their employees to make it happen.

Office Angels is part of Ajilon, a global leader in consulting, managed services and speciality staffing. Its associate businesses – OAexec, Computer People, Ajilon Executive, Ajilon Finance, Jonathan Wren, Ajilon Consulting, Roevin and Ajilon Learning – provide an integrated approach to company-wide resourcing.

Product

Office Angels' areas of expertise enable clients to use one supplier for all their office support requirements. Both assignment and permanent staff are assigned across a range of secretarial, administrative, financial, call centre and customer service positions.

All Office Angel's consultants undergo intensive training and development throughout their career, to ensure they are equipped with first class skills to work in the 'people business'.

The service provided to job seekers is free and each candidate follows a thorough and formal procedure from registration through to assignment, which includes an in-depth interview and skills evaluation.

To assess candidates' skills, Office Angels uses Ajilonresult, a bespoke skills

officeangels
RECRUITMENT CONSULTANTS

evaluation system, which allows consultants to assess the fundamentals, like standard PC packages, but can also create tailored tests to reflect a client's exact requirements. Office Angels also provides online training courses for candidates, which can be tailored to the individual's specific needs. Typical courses include business writing, call centre management, software packages such as PowerPoint and Excel and time management.

Through working closely with candidates and providing them with continued support, Office Angels lives by its belief that it is in the business of finding 'jobs for people' rather than 'people for jobs.'

Integral to Office Angels' commitment to its assignment staff is its ongoing candidate care programme. Initiatives such as regular social and networking events, Angel of the Month Awards, savings schemes, competitions, training and free Friday lunches help ensure that candidates are rewarded for their dedication and professionalism.

Office Angels is totally committed to promoting diversity across the business, not only as an employer but also as a supplier of staff to its clients.

The company is improving awareness by explaining how diversity impacts on business performance. As a member of Race for Opportunity (RfO), Office Angels has participated in a UK-wide benchmarking exercise on their current race initiatives and will use the results of the survey to shape future equality and diversity initiatives. This year Office Angels were placed in the top five most improved organisations regarding race and diversity strategies.

Building on the information unearthed by 2003 research 'Generation X', which focussed on 16-19 year olds, Office Angels conducted more in depth research in 2004, this time highlighting the experiences and opinions of 18-65 year old office workers, to provide a snapshot of office life in 2004. Key findings from the report revealed today's office workers are likely to be highly motivated, driven by money and status, work beyond the statutory state pension age and are likely to be making their own provision for the future.

Office Angels regularly arranges business seminars for clients in order to identify and react to key recruitment issues, and the commissioning of original business research helps clients to understand on-going employment dynamics.

Recent Developments

The Office Angels website (www.office-angels.com) is being redeveloped to enable candidates to register quickly with the branch of their choice and view all current vacancies online. Importantly, this facility is not a substitute for the personal, one-to-one service that is the cornerstone of the Office Angels philosophy. Rather, it is designed to help potential and existing candidates and clients access information quickly and efficiently.

Promotion

Office Angels has developed a highly effective marketing strategy which aims to capitalise on the brand's position as an industry leader. Activity encompasses press, outdoor and radio advertising, direct mail, event marketing, public relations, sponsorship, corporate social responsibility, internal communications, research, the internet and an extensive programme of client and candidate care.

The business also has regular link-ups with leading consumer brands for local and national promotions including Filofax, Braun, Pringles, Berlitz, Travelocity and Twinings.

Office Angels is committed to conducting regular research studies and publishing reports on a range of employment-related issues including flexible working, employee benefits and managing communications in the modern office. These gain editorial recognition in both the national and regional press, as well as broadcast, recruitment and lifestyle media.

Talk to the Angels!

Laura   **Emma**   **Julia**   **Liz**

Since opening its door in 1986 the Slough branch of Office Angels has provided thousands of job-seekers and employers with the answer to their recruitment prayers. Having established a successful reputation in the local area for offering a quality recruitment service, the team are constantly striving to provide an unrivaled personal service to all their candidates and clients. By taking the time to get to know people and carefully assessing their skills, experience and personalities, they can make perfect matches time and time again for both candidates and clients.

We are delighted to announce Julia Swallow as the new Branch Manager with her team, Emma, Liz, Laura and Clare. (Hurry back from holiday Clare – the Temps Desk needs you!).

So whether you are thinking of changing jobs or would like to try temping – talk to the Angels.

We currently have a huge amount of temporary and permanent vacancies

★ PAs ★ Secretaries ★ Administrators ★ Call Centre Agents ★
★ Accounts Clerks ★ Receptionists ★ Office Juniors ★

So come in and see us or give us a call!

Office Angels Ltd, 274 High Street, Slough, Berks SL1 1NB.
Tel: 01753 691484 Email: slough@office-angels.com
(Employment Agency)

Part of the Ajilon Group
www.office-angels.com

officeangels RECRUITMENT CONSULTANTS

Brand Values

The maverick style and personality of the Office Angels brand attracts both clients and candidates alike. Office Angels has a passion for recruitment and is dynamic and forward thinking. Its clients are not industry or sector specific as they buy 'personalities' rather than 'processes' and therefore want an attentive, personal service. Clients are also keen to discuss issues, as they have the assurance that the Office Angels name signifies that there will be a real difference in the service they receive.

www.office-angels.com

THINGS YOU DIDN'T KNOW ABOUT

Office Angels

> A survey conducted by Office Angels in 2004 revealed that the average office worker meets 832 people during their working life and will work with or meet at least five of these again in different jobs.

> Working closely with the Royal National Institute for the Blind (RNIB), Office Angels has introduced technical testing equipment that blind and visually impaired candidates can use to give them access to work opportunities with its clients.

> Each year the 600 staff of Office Angels nominate a charity to be the main focus for fund-raising activities.

> Office Angels has a broad spectrum of candidates, of which one in four are male, one in five are over 45, and nearly one in three are women returning to work after a career break.

> Brits are usually known for their reserve and politeness, yet Office Angels research reveals six out of ten (61%) office workers admit to displaying bad manners on a regular basis. 63% admitted to arriving late at least twice a week, and 76% confessed they regularly swear at work but wish they could kick the habit.

P&O

Market

P&O operates in a truly global market, with services – ports, shipping and logistics – that are integral to the smooth-running and growth of international trade. Although many people in the UK might associate P&O most closely with shipping, especially through its P&O Ferries division, its fastest growing business is container ports.

Traffic at the world's biggest container ports has grown exponentially over the last 20 years. Driving the growth has been the trend towards unitised cargo handling, an increase in global trade and, over the last decade in particular, rapid economic growth in Asia. According to figures from Ocean Shipping Consultants (OSC) and P&O, world container port volumes increased from 112 million TEU (20ft equivalent units – the industry term used to measure the number of containers a port handles) in 1994 to 300 million TEU in 2002. This represents an increase of 168%. By 2015, OSC estimates that world container port volumes are set to reach 620 million TEU.

Driven by the explosion in trade to and from China, East Asian ports are growing fastest, having increased their share of the global market from 37.6% in 1990 to 46.4% in 2002. Hong Kong and Singapore are the world's largest container ports, handling 20.8 million and 18.4 million TEU respectively in 2003. Shanghai in China is the third largest.

Economic liberalisation has resulted in many container terminals around the world being transferred to private operators. P&O has been a key player in this fast-growing and profitable market, investing over £1 billion in facilities at key ports in Asia, Europe, North and South America and Australasia. With 27 container terminals, and logistics operations in over 100 ports, it has a presence in eighteen countries. Other players in this private terminal operator market include Hutchison Group of Hong Kong, Port of Singapore Authority and APM Terminals.

Having handled 11.3 million TEU in 2003, P&O Ports can claim around a 5% share of world container port handling volume.

Although important, there is more to the international ports market than containers. Roll-on roll-off (ro-ro), general cargo, bulk cargo, cruising and maritime services are other areas of business in which P&O Ports has significant interests.

P&O still remains a substantial player in the shipping market. P&O is a household name in the UK for ferry travel carrying freight and tourist traffic between the UK and France, Spain and Holland. The Anglo-Continental ferry market is highly competitive, facing fierce pressure from low-cost airlines and the Channel Tunnel. However, P&O is realigning its business to take advantage of the growing freight market and specific areas of the tourist market. In total, P&O Ferries carried 13.3 million passengers in 2003.

P&O also retains a 25% stake in one of the world's largest container shipping lines, Royal P&O Nedlloyd.

Achievements

Over its long history, P&O has established itself as one of the world's pre-eminent and most respected maritime brands. From its roots as a mail carrier, it has established itself at the hub of world trade, leveraging its powerful heritage, brand recognition, knowledge of global markets and expertise in port development and logistics. This has served it particularly well in Asia, where P&O has had a strong presence since the early 1940s, and which is now a powerhouse of growth.

The company has also successfully restructured itself, changing its business to suit current economic conditions and business trends. The transformation during the 1990s from multi-faceted conglomerate to a leaner organisation focused on ports, shipping and logistics has left P&O well-placed to move forward by funding more investments in its vital ports business.

The strategy is paying dividends. Container throughput at P&O's terminals was up by 27% in 2003 compared to 2002. Operating profit in 2003 was £129 million, some 70%, of P&O's total operating profit.

History

P&O has a unique heritage. Chartered as The Peninsular and Oriental Steam Navigation Company in 1840, it started running steamers between England, Spain and Portugal but soon extended eastwards to India, the Far East and Australia. Beginning in the 1960s, it diversified into a wide range of businesses, making acquisitions such as the Bovis group of companies in 1974 and acquiring London's Earls Court and Olympia exhibition halls in 1985 when the group merged with SGT.

In 1996, its container shipping line, P&O Containers, merged with rival Dutch line Nedlloyd to form P&O Nedlloyd. Another merger in 1998 saw its Dover-Calais ferry operations combine with Stena Line, in a bid to fight competition from The Channel Tunnel. (Later, in 2002, P&O acquired Stena's stake to take full control of this business).

In 1999 more rationalisation occurred with P&O selling Bovis Construction. Then in 2000 the company demerged its highly successful cruise businesses to form a separate listed company, P&O Princess Cruises, which was subsequently acquired by Carnival Corporation. After also exiting from bulk shipping, contract logistics and dramatically thinning down its investments in

property, and reducing its stake in P&O Nedlloyd to 25%, this left the remaining P&O focused on ports, shipping and logistics. Much of the asset sales were carried out to fund its investments in ports, particularly in Asia. Port development is a capital-intensive business, with P&O committed to investing around £200 million a year between 2004 and 2007.

Product
Although the shape of P&O has changed, the business of the company remains fundamentally the same – connecting the world.

P&O's activities – P&O Ports, P&O Ferries, P&O Cold Logistics and P&O Properties, plus its shareholding in Royal P&O Nedlloyd, all put P&O at the heart of international transport and logistics.

In 2003, £350 million was invested in ports, via acquisitions and the expansion of existing facilities.

P&O has port interests all over the world, often owning a shareholding in a terminal along with other partners, but taking on the management and day-to-day operations of the terminal itself. All of these terminals are common-user, as opposed to the dedicated terminal model whereby particularly large shipping lines have their own container handling facilities.

With trade growing particularly fast in Asia, the company has invested heavily in the region. In China, its container terminals at Qingdao and Shekou grew by 89%

and 68% respectively in 2003. Its portfolio in Asia also includes terminals in Mumbai, Mundra and Chennai, India; Laem Chabang, Thailand; and Colombo, Sri Lanka. In the Americas, P&O Ports assets include terminals in New York and Buenos Aires, Argentina and a new investment in Vancouver, Canada. Amongst its port assets in Europe, P&O operates container terminals at the ports of Antwerp, Belgium; Marseilles and Le Havre, France, and Southampton and Tilbury in the UK. In Australia, P&O operates terminals in the four major ports.

P&O Ferries is a household name in the UK for ferry travel. It operates routes carrying freight and tourist traffic between the UK and France, Spain, Belgium and Holland with P&O Irish Sea operating routes between Ireland and the UK. P&O has a fleet of 25 ships. P&O Ferrymasters, the European road haulage and freight management business, is also part of P&O Ferries. P&O Cold Logistics provides a full range of services, ranging from refrigerated warehousing to complex retail supply chain management for temperature controlled products. It is one of the world's few expert companies in temperature controlled logistics and is a strong player in the US, Australasia and Argentina.

P&O has for some time had a valuable property portfolio. Over the past few years, as part of the company's strategy of reallocating capital to its strongest growth areas, P&O has been disposing of its property

assets. In 2004, P&O set a target of realising £250 million of property sales which it exceeded and it has set a similar target for 2005. The funds raised will help P&O invest further in its ports business.

Recent Developments
P&O Ports has made some significant investments, further boosting its capacity. Its largest was the £120 million acquisition of a new container terminal in Mundra, in the Indian state of Gujarat. In 2003, the company also opened additional capacity built at its Qingdao Qianwan container terminal (QQCT) in China. QQCT is the subject of a major expansion plan, which will ultimately boost its capacity from 1.3 million to 6.4 million TEU. Another major development was the acquisition of a new 300,000 TEU terminal at the Port of Vancouver – this is the company's first investment in Canada, which is a strategically important port for trans-Pacific trade with Asia.

In 2004, P&O also introduced new capacity in China, France, Thailand and in the UK. Longer term, P&O hopes to gain permission to build a major new container terminal on the Thames estuary. The so-called London Gateway will involve an investment of some £750 million.

2004 was also a pivotal year for P&O Ferries as it faced continuing challenging market conditions. Towards the end of the year P&O Ferries announced the conclusion of its fundamental business review. This included proposals to have a simplified, customer focused product operated on fewer routes with fewer ships and a substantially lower, more flexible cost base.

Another important recent development was the decision to reduce the 50% shareholding in the container line P&O Nedlloyd and create a new independent company, Royal P&O Nedlloyd, in which P&O retains a 25% stake.

Promotion
P&O's business to business promotion is driven via its different divisions. The brands, are united under the strapline P&O uses for its Annual Report – 'International Strength, Local Focus'. This phrase also reflects P&O's strong community involvement. The company is committed to carrying out its work in a way that contributes to the well-being and development of the societies in which it operates. Putting this principle into practice, P&O's community involvement ranges from direct charitable donations through to supporting infrastructure projects in the communities where it operates.

Often the P&O name is used in a secondary branding capacity. In many major port projects, P&O is one of the shareholders in the development, although it may manage the port. Consequently, it is common for the port to be promoted by its name, such as the Qingdao Qianwan Container Terminal (QQCT), but supported by the P&O brand.

The P&O Ferries brand has a very high profile in the UK. Its promotional activity is consumer focused as well as targeting freight companies on the business to business side. The brand embraces all forms of promotional activity, from above-the-line advertising to online and digital promotions. The high quality of its service and product is widely recognised throughout the industry. This is illustrated by the number of awards the business consistently wins. Most recently P&O Ferries received the award for 'Best Short Sea Crossings' and 'Best Operator All Other Routes' at the 2005 Travel Weekly Globe Awards.

Brand Values
The P&O name and flag are recognised throughout the world. P&O's identity embodies over 160 years of history from which the company's flag and initials are drawn.

The brand stands for professionalism, commitment and high standards. P&O's reputation relies on its employees delivering first class service throughout every business in every location where it operates.

www.pogroup.com

THINGS YOU DIDN'T KNOW ABOUT

P&O
› P&O employs 25,000 people around the world.

› In 2003, P&O Ports handled over eleven million containers. In the time it takes to read this page, over 30 containers will have transited through the company's terminals.

› P&O Ferries carried over thirteen million passengers last year – more than the entire population of Greece.

› P&O is one of a few independent commercial companies that is governed by a Royal Charter. Incorporated in 1840 P&O's name therefore includes neither 'plc' nor 'Limited'.

› The P&O house flag is the Company's oldest symbol, incorporating the Royal colours of Portugal and Spain, the countries of the Iberian Peninsula to which its earliest services ran in the 1830s.

Market

From the newspapers, books and magazines we read, to the packaging that covers the goods we buy, the products of the printing industry are all around us. This is why the printing industry is often regarded as an indicator of the economy as a whole.

According to the research company Key Note, the UK market for sales of printed products in 2002 was £12.52 billion and Key Note forecasts that this is rising at around 1.8% a year until 2007. As for UK printing companies themselves, a Business Ratio report by Prospect Swetenhams states that among the UK's 126 largest printing companies, average sales were £22.4 million in 2002/03, with profits of £1.3 million. With annual sales in 2003 of £92 million, and pre-tax profit of £4.6 million, Pindar is well ahead of this median, and is around the 16th largest printing company in the UK (Source: PrintWeek 500 2004 Survey).

The printing industry is fragmented, with thousands of small and medium-sized suppliers. Although there have been many mergers, there are still more small companies competing in the UK industry than elsewhere in Europe.

With increased demand for more advanced communication routes, faster turnarounds, greater personalisation and improved targeting, companies require hi-tech solutions from computer-to-plate (CTP) systems, sophisticated print ready file techniques using pre-flight software, and a wide variety of individualised online collaborative proofing.

Achievements

Throughout its history, Pindar has always maximised its competitiveness by adopting the latest technology. For example, it took full advantage of the opportunities uncovered by the technical revolution-taking place in the 1970s, revolutionising its processes by introducing image and text databasing. This was a major breakthrough for the time, which helped Pindar secure the hugely important contract for the typesetting of Yellow Pages telephone directories for British Telecommunications (BT).

Prior to 1979, directory production in the UK was a state monopoly. Through the vision and drive of the then chairman, Tom Pindar, Pindar was able to transform a manual production methodology into a digital process, which had, by 1984, encompassed all of Yellow Pages' pre-press operations.

As well as investing in cutting-edge technology being the first in the UK to install a web large format 48 page A4 press and the first commercial web printer to be 100% CTP, the company has also continually invested in the training and development of its employees – a commitment that has resulted in so many of them staying with the company. This is demonstrated through the various training and development programmes across the businesses, from online training for new software to apprenticeship schemes, NVQ training initiatives and tailored induction programmes for new recruits. In addition, Pindar's imaginative approach to multiskilling, team working and twilight shifts led them to succeed in winning the Chartered Institute of Personnel Directors (CIPD) People Management Award in 2000. More recently Pindar received the People in Print award for people development at the inaugural Print & Paper Europe 2004 event.

Today, Pindar remains a leading light in the application of new technologies and prides itself in being able to predict the waves of change in order to harness them to the benefit of customer needs. Investment in software and electronic media has placed the company in a strong position to be able to respond quickly to new opportunities being created.

Pindar's strength in new technology has always been notable. However the organisation has also built its reputation by adopting a marketing and customer-led approach to transforming the business of communications. While many printers like to highlight their latest investments in plant, Pindar's approach is quite different. For the last two decades, its vision for business has been to provide a stream of integrated services,

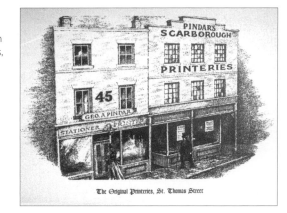

The Original Printeries, St. Thomas Street

adding value with its ability to partner with its customers, as opposed to focusing only on its technical abilities.

History

Pindar was founded in 1836, when George Kyte Grice established a business in Scarborough. In those days, the sales territory stretched as far as a horse could draw a wagon load of paper – about 20 miles.

In the early 1870s, George Arthur Pindar, the present chairman's great grandfather, joined the company and subsequently purchased the business from Mr Grice for just £500. Today, Pindar remains a family-owned business.

Having revolutionised its processes by introducing image and text databasing in the 1970s, the next big technological leap was the adoption of desktop publishing in the late 1980s. This provided the company with a further opportunity to enhance its product range and outshine competitors through the innovative creation of bespoke software systems for catalogues and other content rich customers and markets. Pindar has installed over 2,000 systems within customer locations – resulting in cross media applications from print to the internet.

While much of the industry saw desktop publishing as a threat, it was seized upon by Pindar. This period has seen huge growth, as the company has expanded in the UK through high-end databasing and in printing from digital to massive web presses, as well as overseas through its software business and in rapid response printing.

The market for rapid response printing is well served by Pindar's acquisition of AlphaGraphics, a chain of business to business 'quickprint' franchise operations. Back in the 1980s Pindar became the master licensee for AlphaGraphics UK and Ireland. More recently Pindar became the major shareholder of this US based company, AlphaGraphics Inc, which is one of the leading franchise operations in the US and increasingly so across the world.

Product

The Pindar businesses work with thousands of customers, in hundreds of locations, across four continents. Behind every local customer relationship, and supporting every local initiative are shared resources, shared technical capabilities, and shared beliefs in what is important in business. Each is recognised as a leader in its field. In any competitive marketplace, it helps to have a strong brand and Pindar is committed to building two: Pindar and AlphaGraphics. Each means something strong in its own market, and has developed a real presence that is reinforced with every customer experience.

Beneath these two brands, Pindar has built three successful, distinct yet mutually supportive businesses. Pindar Set works with a unique commitment to one customer Yell Group across three continents and from eight centres. Pindar Graphics has hundreds of

customers across its range of activities and UK centres, and is developing an ever-stronger basis of collaboration with customers who are now practically strategic partners.

AlphaGraphics, collectively, has more customers than either of the Pindar businesses. Each of the stores is a business in its own right, playing a vital part in the local economy and community.

Pindar Set is dedicated to one customer, Yell Group. Its imaginative approach to helping Yell work better has led to a relationship that is now in its 25th year. Pindar Set is one business consistently working across three continents in a common and shared framework transforming the business of directories.

Pindar Set is responsible for processing all the ads and classified pages that go into making up all the Yellow Pages and Business Pages directories in the UK and the Yellow Book directories in the US.

In 1999 Yell acquired Yellow Book USA. Following a successful bid Pindar Set began creating ads for Yellow Book in 2000. This heralded the start of Pindar Set's growth into the US marketplace. Pindar Set today has two service centres in the US and two studios in Bangalore, India enabling the company to process ads in real time across three continents. This provides Yell with a dedicated global service network in the production of ads and pages.

Pindar Graphics origins as a local printer can still be seen in everything it does today, even though the business is now one of the most advanced and sophisticated in its market. It has built a unique capability in making complex communications work better. Its main focus has always been to help its customers make better use of their printed communications, to help them achieve their commercial objectives.

Government departments and education authorities recognise its standards in accuracy and timeliness. They truly appreciate Pindar Graphics' ability to maintain the total confidentiality that is required for their work. The range and depth of output extends into areas like security coding and logistics, because these extra dimensions bring extra reward. In catalogues, it has developed strong capabilities in content management, enabling it to ensure that the incredible complexities involved in putting together such huge volumes run smoothly. In travel, it has demonstrated how it understands the intricacies of that information, and how even the most apparently simple job contains layer upon layer of detail.

AlphaGraphics is a printshop, a design centre, a retail store, a partner for local business, a factor of the local economy and a part of the local community. AlphaGraphics plans, produces and manages the full array of visual communications for all of its customers. As a franchise operation, it has a unique view of business life. It is constantly looking for new locations, and new people to become the owner-managers that have a wide appeal in the marketplace.

Today, Pindar has the competence and capability to produce one copy to one million copies, or any number in between.

Reflecting its customer-led approach, Pindar puts great emphasis on listening to its customers and potential customers. Where possible, the company strives to be involved from the earliest concept stage, right through to the end product. This consultative approach helps Pindar understand its customer's goals and strategies, and to develop its role in helping them achieve these.

Recent Developments
In 2004 Pindar Set's business doubled in size as a result of supporting Yell's growth in the US.

Also during 2004, Pindar developed a new state-of-the-art bindery in Scarborough, equipped with associated mailing and fulfilment capability. These new binding and mailing lines brought fresh benefits and efficiencies for existing customers and also satisfied the demands of major new customers, including a flagship contract from Avon Cosmetics.

Promotion
Pindar is committed to building two brands: Pindar and AlphaGraphics and these brands are visible in one of Pindar's highest-profile promotional investments through its sport marketing initiatives. This includes the sponsorship of Emma Richards who, in 2002, became the first British woman to complete the solo round-the-world race – Around Alone – and subsequently a number of high-profile transatlantic races. As well as sponsoring Emma, Pindar sponsor Hannah Mills, a talented sixteen-year-old sailor who joined the team in 2003 and Sophie Luther who was the winner of a competition designed to find and support new talent in the world of ocean racing.

In addition Pindar are sponsoring a 2005 Global Challenge yacht, crewed by seventeen amateurs battling it out in an around the world yacht race against the prevailing winds, tides and currents. This is one of sport's most prestigious yacht races, with the deserved reputation as 'the world's toughest yacht race'.

Pindar uses its sponsorship to provide opportunities for all employees and customers to experience sailing. The company sees strong parallels with the ethos of the inclusiveness of sailing as a sport for the motivation of its employees, enabling ordinary people 'to achieve extraordinary things'.

Brand Values
In all of its business activities, Pindar strives to look for new ways to share knowledge, to transfer and build capability, and to continually look at things from a fresh perspective. In building lasting relationships with its customers, Pindar hopes they choose to work with Pindar because they want to, and not because they have to.

www.pindar.com

THINGS YOU DIDN'T KNOW ABOUT

Pindar

❯ Tom Pindar, Lifetime President was awarded an OBE by the Queen in 1986 and became a Deputy Lieutenant of North Yorkshire in 1993.

❯ Tom Pindar, who joined the company in 1949, became a high profile figure within the industry and is recognised as being one of the principal pioneers of photo typesetting and computer-driven phototypesetting.

❯ Depicted in Pindar's logo the Arctic Tern is a hard working, tenacious and loyal creature. The Arctic Tern travels further than any of its rivals when migrating, and although peaceable, will ferociously defend its territory when threatened.

RIO TINTO

Market

As one of the biggest names in the mining industry, Rio Tinto produces a broad range of metals and minerals, sold in a variety of markets with differing characteristics and pricing mechanisms. Markets for metals and minerals reflect business cycles in the global economy. Metal prices, for example, are set every day by the London Metal Exchange, and these provide the basis of prices for metals sold all over the world. Fluctuations in prices inevitably affect Rio Tinto's financial results, though the company in recent years has enjoyed record profits due to buoyant markets.

The big story in the global mining industry is China's phenomenal appetite for minerals – especially iron ore, copper and aluminium – as the country rapidly undergoes its own industrial revolution. In 2003, China accounted for nearly 8% of Rio Tinto Group sales and 9% in the first half of 2004. This has come from minimal levels only a few years ago and now represents growth at a time when demand elsewhere in the world has been relatively subdued. The indirect effect of China's mineral supply and demand on global markets is considerable.

Achievements

Rio Tinto owns long life operations producing coal, copper, gold, aluminium, industrial minerals and iron ore. In addition, it continues to research and develop new projects, and has a clear and focused exploration programme to seek out opportunities for further expansion.

When we go shopping, almost everything we buy can be traced back, either directly or indirectly, to the mining industry – and often to Rio Tinto itself. The company provides the minerals and metals that are the building blocks of everyday life, including iron, copper, aluminium, titanium dioxide, borates, gold, diamonds, coal, uranium, nickel, zinc, silver, lead and salt.

Rio Tinto is also a significant energy producer, providing low-sulphur steam coal to power stations that supply homes, businesses and industries in the US, Australia and Asia. It provides metallurgical coking coal to iron and steel mills in Asia and Europe. It also mines the uranium oxide that, when enriched into fuel rods, enables nuclear power stations to generate electricity in Europe, the US and Asia-Pacific. Growing internet use and ever more sophisticated forms of consumer electronics are increasing the demand for power in the developed world, as is electrification in developing countries.

Rio Tinto has a consistent record of outperforming its sector in total shareholder returns. Indeed, the company points out that in the period from 1995 until December 2004, it comfortably outshone the Morgan Stanley Capital International (MSCI) Mining and Metals Index as well as the FTSE 100 in the UK and the ASX All Share Index in Australia.

Rio Tinto also has strong credit ratings: Standard & Poor's A+ and Moody's Investor Service Aa3.

History

British entrepreneurs founded Rio Tinto in 1873 to buy and reopen an ancient copper mine in Rio Tinto, southern Spain which the Spanish Crown was willing to sell to provide much needed money for a country weakened by 50 years of civil strife. The payment was made in gold bars, transported to Madrid by train and oxcart in wooden cases. The founding Spanish business was however later sold to fund expansion elsewhere.

In 1905, another company, The Consolidated Zinc Corporation, was created to treat zinc-bearing mine waste at Broken Hill in New South Wales, Australia – later expanding into mining and smelting there and in the UK. The British parents of these two companies merged in 1962, creating Rio Tinto plc. At the same time, the Australian interests of both companies were merged, creating Rio Tinto Ltd. The pair effectively operated as separate entities until 1995, when they finally became a single company.

After the 1962 merger, Rio Tinto plc embarked on a number of new mining projects, extracting copper at Palabora in South Africa, uranium at Rössing in Namibia, and copper and tin at Neves Corvo in Portugal. Between the late 1960s and the mid 1980s it also developed significant interests in cement, chemicals, oil and gas and manufactured products for the construction and automotive industries.

However, after a major strategy review in 1988, the company decided to refocus on its core mining and related activities. In the late 1980s and early 1990s it sold off non-core businesses, while acquiring more mining interests.

In parallel, its sister company Rio Tinto Ltd grew through the development of important mineral interests, such as iron ore in Australia, copper in Papua New Guinea, bauxite and aluminium smelting in New Zealand and Australia, as well as coal, diamonds and gold in Australia and Indonesia.

Since the two sister companies merged in 1995, Rio Tinto's exploration and technology efforts have been refocused to guarantee efficiency and exploit the Group's full potential. Capital expenditure has been at record levels as it develops its wide range of projects. Rio Tinto completed US$4 billion worth of acquisitions in 2000, covering aluminium, iron ore, diamonds and coal, and adding further strength to an already exceptional base of resources. During 2004 the Group sold off non-core assets for US$1.2 billion and made investments of about US$4 billion in development projects.

Product

Rio Tinto's mines provide some of the world's most vital materials, from the superstars of the commodities industry – like iron, copper, silver, diamonds and gold – to little-known yet vital substances like ilmenite, rutile, zircon, bauxite, and boron.

Ilmenite, for example, with its ability to scatter light, imparts brilliance and opacity to paints, plastics and paper. Rutile is used in the manufacture of titanium metal, which is used to make jet engines. Zircon is a mineral

used in the production of ceramic tiles and sanitary ware. Refined to zirconia, it is used in advanced ceramics, computers, spacecraft, clothing, jewellery and electronics. As an ingredient of TV screens and computer monitors, it protects us from harmful x-rays. Rio Tinto is one of the world's leading suppliers of these vital minerals.

Bauxite is refined into alumina, which is smelted into aluminium. Rio Tinto is a major producer of all three.

The Group is also a top supplier of boron. Boron-based minerals are called borates, a vital ingredient of many home and garden products. Rio Tinto Borax's mine in California's Mojave Desert is the world's largest borates mine.

Rio Tinto's gold production comes mainly as a by-product of copper mining. The Group produces 7% of world copper, ranking it fourth in the world, and 4% of mined gold, making it the fifth largest producer.

Gem diamonds share the stage with gold as a luxury commodity. With the opening of the Diavik diamond mine in Canada in 2003, Rio Tinto is able to offer diamond products across the colour spectrum, including the most spectacular flawless whites.

Rio Tinto is among the world's largest producers of iron ore with production of about 74 million tonnes per year. In energy, Rio Tinto accounts for 7% of traded thermal coal and 13% of uranium, ranking the company fourth and third respectively in world terms.

Recent Developments
Rio Tinto has a number of projects under construction, representing an increased interest in certain commodities. The US$900 million Diavik diamond mine in northern Canada produced its first diamonds in early 2003. Diavik is expected to deliver the greatest value, per tonne of ore, of any diamond mine in the western world.

The US$750 million Comalco alumina refinery project at Gladstone in Australia will make Rio Tinto a major player in the traded alumina market. Alumina is an intermediate product for the manufacture of aluminium. The new refinery will start in 2005 with an initial capacity of 1.4 million tonnes per year and with options to expand to 4.2 million tonnes.

In energy products, the US$255 million Hail Creek project in Australia, together with the expansion of its existing Kestrel mine, will make Rio Tinto a significant supplier of hard coking coal. The first shipments of coal were expected in October 2003.

Also in Australia, in April 2002 Rio Tinto committed itself to the construction of a commercial size iron smelter at a cost of US$200 million. Using new technology, it is more efficient than conventional processes and reduces greenhouse gas emissions.

A wholly owned Rio Tinto subsidiary, Kennecott Utah Copper in the US, owns 37,000 hectares of land adjacent to its mining and smelter complex at Salt Lake City. It has formed a spin-off company, Kennecott Land, to develop 4,000 hectares for residential use. The first stage, Project Daybreak, is costing US$50 million.

Rio Tinto is also in the process of expanding and developing many of its existing mining projects, and raising production to meet market demand.

Promotion
Rio Tinto recognises the importance of maintaining a spotless reputation, while being seen as a leader in the field of sustainable development. All activities linked to this area are grouped under one line manager, the head of communication and sustainable development – who reports to the chief executive.

The department's communications are primarily aimed at shareholders, opinion leaders and key media. Among other duties, it conducts corporate auditing and reviews for 'The way we work', Rio Tinto's statement of business practice. This statement is crucial to the company's conduct, as it describes the manner in which it works closely with local communities and adopts safety and environmental policies that go beyond requirements. 'The way we work' has been translated into eighteen languages to spread the word, including Oshidonga (Botswana), Farsi (Iran), Welsh, Japanese, Russian, Chinese, Indonesian and Zulu.

In addition, the communication unit works closely with Rio Tinto's health, safety and environment (HSE) department, which plays a key role within the Group.

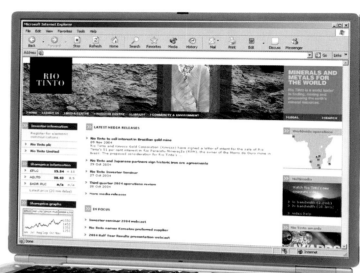

Building from a foundation of compliance with existing health and safety rules, Rio Tinto seeks to improve its performance by setting targets, implementing effective management systems, and operating the best possible practices. Its goal is zero injuries in the workplace and the elimination of occupational disease.

Brand Values
The company's strategy has been substantially unchanged for well over a decade. The underlying principle is simple: it is in business to create value for its shareholders, in a responsible and sustainable manner.

In order to deliver superior returns to its shareholders over many years, it takes a long term, responsible approach to all its activities. It helps meet the global need for metals and minerals that contribute to improved living standards, as well as making a direct contribution to economic development and employment in those countries where it invests.

Rio Tinto seeks world class, large-scale, low-cost operations. It does not invest on the basis of product or geographical location. Instead, it looks for projects that will create shareholder value and generate strong cash flow, even when prices are depressed. By consistently pursuing this strategy over many years, Rio Tinto has established a spread of commodity exposures that serve this goal well.

www.riotinto.com

THINGS YOU DIDN'T KNOW ABOUT

Rio Tinto

> In 1873, £400,000 in gold bars was smuggled by oxcart over the Pyrenees through lines of warring factions to the hard-pressed Spanish Government in Madrid. British businessmen sent the bars as a down payment on the Rio Tinto copper mines, suggested to have been the original 'King Solomon's Mines'.

> British managers at the Rio Tinto mines introduced football to save Spanish workers from the taverns and brothels, and thereby founded Spain's oldest football club, Recreativo de Huelva, now in the first division La Liga.

> Rio Tinto operations around the world hold annual bird watching events for staff and families in partnership with BirdLife International. Participants gather information about bird species relevant to environmental management.

> Talc from different deposits has such a variety of textures that Christian Dior alone uses more than 20 different Rio Tinto talcs in its formulations.

> Sodium borohydride, derived from the mineral borates mined by Rio Tinto, is being used to develop technology that can safely store hydrogen fuel in emission free cars.

Market

Thames Water's utility business in London and the Thames Valley provides water and wastewater services to some thirteen million customers in over five million premises – around a quarter of the population of England and Wales.

Thames Water is part of the Water Division of RWE, one of the largest water companies in the world serving over 70 million customers in 20 countries.

The company transfers the skills and capabilities developed from its utility operation to the competitive market, successfully developing its non-regulated business in three ways: water industry outsourcing, Government sponsored initiatives and the extension of its services to other industries.

Achievements

Since privatisation, Thames Water has hugely increased investment in services and its infrastructure, improving the quality and reliability of water supplies and embarking on a major wastewater facilities upgrade programme.

One of its major investments was aimed at maintaining reliable supplies by improving the flow of water around London. Thames Water conceived, designed, constructed and now operates the £250 million 'Thames Water Ring Main', which provides up to 1,300 million litres of water a day to customers in the capital. Despite working at depths of up to 65m below ground level in a major city, the project was completed two years ahead of schedule and within budget.

In anticipation of new European standards for drinking water, a programme to upgrade 44 treatment works has been completed which covers 90% of the company's water supply. This will greatly reduce, and in some cases eliminate trace elements in water exceeding the European standard of 10ug/1 that comes into force in 2013.

As part of a £1 million a day investment in sewage treatment, Thames Water has also helped transform the river Thames into the cleanest metropolitan river in the world. From being biologically dead, the river is now home to 120 species of fish.

In addition a £350 million investment in advanced water treatment works has helped the company achieve the highest ever levels for drinking water quality.

Other major improvements included a £40 million customer services centre, which opened in 1993 and operates all year round, 24 hours a day.

2004 saw the completion of a new £80 million state-of-the-art sewage treatment works in Reading, which is amongst the most advanced in the UK and has been specifically designed to comply with new EU directives.

As part of its commitment to the environment, in 2002 RWE Thames Water produced 135.1 gigawatt-hours (GWh) of renewable electricity – 12.7% of our total electricity consumption during the year. The company has also worked to protect the environment and wildlife in other ways. For instance, a ground-breaking partnership with The Wildfowl and Wetlands Trust transformed a redundant reservoir complex in Barnes, West London, into The Wetlands Centre, a major new wildlife sanctuary for the capital, spanning over 100 acres.

History

The company's history dates back over 400 years, when water supplies were first provided to the growing city of London. The modern company was formed in 1989 when the existing Water Authority was split and the water and wastewater operation was privatised. Following privatisation in 1989, the company expanded its business overseas under a series of acquisitions, competitive bids and private outsourcing contracts. In 2000 Thames Water was bought by RWE, the 5th largest industrial services company and 2nd largest multi utility in Germany. At that point Thames Water became the Water Division of RWE and the third largest water company in the world.

Product

Thames Water offers a comprehensive range of services including: providing water and wastewater treatment; the supply of high quality water treatment products and services; water process engineering; the design and construction of major infrastructure; planning and asset management; project management; customer services; and specialist consultancy. It is also able to assist clients in developing sources of finance for major projects.

The company's Asset Data Services team provides a range of conveyancing searches for both residential and commercial properties including the CON29DW, Commercial Drainage and Water Searches and Environmental Reports. Thames Water's Developer Services team provides over 24,000 new connections to the network a year by managing the design and installation of new water and wastewater assets. The team also offers a range of other utility infrastructure services including, network analysis, building water provision and multi utility.

Through its Affinity Sales team Thames Water exercises strategic partnerships to capitalise on its domestic customer relationships, which have delivered a significant portfolio of non-core products and services. Several hundred thousand water customers chose to purchase additional products from the brand, the majority of these on an ongoing basis.

The company's Commercial team has successfully tendered for opportunities to manage an element of other water companies' operations through water industry outsourcing. Recent contracts awarded to Thames Water include the operation of Dwr Cymru Welsh Water's Income and Billing, an essential business function that receives over one million telephone calls from customers a year and sends over 1.5 million bills to customers a year. Under Thames Water, Dwr Cymru Income and Billing has been recognised by OFWAT as the best performing customer services operation in the UK water industry.

Thames Water also forms part of Scottish Water Solutions, a consortium that won the contract to deliver 70% of Scottish Water's £1.8 billion capital investment programme. Particular focus of the contract is the upgrade of water and wastewater treatment works, which will guarantee a quality water supply for the residents of Scotland in the future. Together with its partners, Thames Water is managing five wastewater treatment works, nine storm works and part of the sewerage network in and around the city of Edinburgh as part of the Seafield PFI (public finance initiative) Contract, under an 'upgrade, operate and maintain' contract. A key aim is to ensure compliance with regulatory (European Urban Wastewater Directive, European Bathing Water Directive, Waste Management License) and contractual requirements. Initial works enabled the cessation of the disposal of sewage sludge in the North Sea. Treated sludge

is now recycled to land. As a result of Thames Water's investment, radical improvements have been made to the quality of discharged wastewater, improving the quality of the Almond and Esk rivers. The 30-year contract was signed in 1999 and is worth over £94 million. The company's consortium arranged the financing of the scheme and won the Project Finance award for 'European Water Deal of 1999'.

Thames Water has also been able to contribute its skills of asset management, change management, major projects and the experience of running a complex underground network in the nations capital to the

Metronet Consortium which delivers maintenance and capital improvements to 70% of the London Underground network through a 30-year £30 billion contract. The maintenance and refurbishment of track, civil assets and station assets will directly benefit millions of commuters who use the London Underground every day.

Through a PPP/ PFI contract structure, Thames Water also provides clean and wastewater services to the MOD at Tidworth Garrison, Wiltshire to approximately 10,000 military personnel as part of a contract to upgrade and operate the incumbent assets. Thames Water in partnership with EdF, will provide a multi-utility service to the MOD project through Allenby Connaught. This involves the provision of new and refurbished living accommodation, dining facilities and technical buildings for a substantial proportion of the British Army stationed at Aldershot and across the Salisbury Plain, a population served of around 50,000 military and non-military personnel.

Recent Developments

One of the biggest challenges faced by Thames Water is to be able to continually provide a reliable supply of clean water to its customers. As well as the ageing Victorian infrastructure, population expansion in the South East is putting pressure on water supply and on the capacity of Thames Water's sewerage network. Climate change is also leading to a bottleneck in the amount of water that can be captured for treatment. Despite the wet weather last summer, London receives less annual rainfall per capita than in Madrid or Istanbul. A third of the water mains network in the capital is more than 150 years old; over half is more than 100 years old.

Extreme weather conditions (such as the heavy rainfall of autumn 2000/01 and the prolonged summer dry spell in 2003) have since further damaged the ageing pipes.

The corrosive nature of clay soils in inner London also damages water mains, as does the capital's pounding 24-hour traffic.

Thames Water has therefore put replacing over 1,025 miles of London's Victorian water mains at the centre of its business plan for 2005-2010. The planned work is essential to reduce leakage and ensure that the capital's growing population continues to receive the water it needs.

Promotion

Since 2001 Thames Water has used the RWE Corporate Design style, including adopting its parent company's endorsement – the RWE Group logo – which appears next to each one of Thames Water's brand marks. The RWE Corporate Design style includes: Corporate colours – Blue and Grey as primary colours, with each Division having their own unique secondary colour; Unique company typeface; Pixels and Photography style.

The implementation of the RWE Corporate Design style was a massive project, centrally co-ordinated by the Thames Water brand team in Reading, with over 70 brand ambassadors worldwide. This was the first time all of its companies around the world had used a common design style, and the result has been not only a tremendous improvement in the quality and creativity in its marketing communications materials, but also a reduction in costs as more of its offices share materials. In order to encourage this further, Thames Water developed an online marketing portal called Watermark, which aims to help staff create and access marketing, communication and business development materials and resources, from one single source. The site received 5,500 hits during the first three months of its launch. Watermark also provides a link to the RWE Brand Management System (BMS), which hosts the most up to date Corporate Design guidelines.

Excellence in **customer service and operational support.**

Thames Water is the largest water and wastewater company in England and Wales, serving over thirteen million customers, including a quarter of a million businesses. We are also one of the world's largest water enterprises, managing resources to serve 70 million people in 46 countries around the globe.

In the UK our focus for major commercial customers is on delivering excellence in customer service and operational support. Our experience has shown that what customers require above all else is that we get the fundamentals right, particularly in account management and supply. This means a constant dialogue with our customers to ensure that our services, and the way in which they are delivered, match customer expectations.

For further information please call 0845 641 0000 or e-mail us at key.customer@thameswater.co.uk

Thames Water's design style can now be seen across all of its marketing communications materials, such as bill inserts, advertising and brochures, as well as on its silver company vans as well as on corporate signage.

Brand Values

Thames Water's vision is to be the leading water and wastewater company in the UK. This approach is underpinned by its Brand Values, which characterise the brand's emotional and functional strengths. They are: in partnership – it works together with its customers to understand their needs; reliable – it builds on its heritage and experience to offer unique solutions to its customers; performance orientated – it is passionate about delivering exceptional results for its customers; caring – the brand is committed to acting in a socially and environmentally responsible way; forward thinking – Thames Water is always striving to be better; and locally involved – it is committed to providing lasting benefits for the communities in which it operates.

www.thameswater.com

THINGS YOU DIDN'T KNOW ABOUT

Thames Water

❯ Each day 2,700,000 cubic meters of water is pumped in London. This is equivalent in volume to seven times the daily production of the North Sea oil field.

❯ Tap water is over 1,000 times cheaper than bottled water. Drinking water supplied to its customers is tested against stringent national and European standards. In 2003, over half a million tests were carried out to check its quality.

❯ With over 150,000km of water mains and 90,000km of sewers, the pipes that Thames Water currently operate, if placed end-to-end, would span nearly two-thirds of the distance to the moon.

❯ Human waste can in fact be turned into fuel. At Thames Water's UK plants, 90% of the sludges treated are used to produce methane fuels, or electricity.

THOMSONLocal

Market

In today's busy and confusing world, information is in demand. The average consumer is becoming increasingly savvy about how to get hold of the data that they need and now need to be able to access it quickly, conveniently and in a wide variety of formats.

The need to find suppliers of goods and services is particularly acute, with people searching for information in many different ways: in print, online, by phone, on mobile phones as well as via digital television. The need for information remains constant; the choices in finding it can only grow. Businesses, in turn are responding to this need and becoming increasingly multi-channel in their route to servicing their customers and reaching their potential customers.

Reflecting this, the classified directory market, in which Thomson Directories is a leading player, continues to grow strongly and was worth just over £1 billion in 2003. (Source: Advertising Association).

Achievements

Throughout its history, Thomson Directories has been energetic in predicting market demands and flexible in its response to consumer needs. For example, in the late 1970s, it was early to spot a need in the marketplace for a local directory.

Its market-driven approach has ensured that it has constantly and successfully delivered a range of advertising, marketing and information solutions in support of customers' business objectives.

Today, Thomson Directories delivers information products using a regularly updated database of over two million business listings. This is the basis for a range of powerful database products and services, including the printed Thomson Local directories.

The company has won several awards in recognition of its achievements, being awarded the ISO:9001 quality standard in 2004 for the Thomson Directories' Database Quality Management System. In 2003, its Business Search PRO was named Best CD Rom by the European Association of Directory Publishers and also by the Directory Publishers Association. The DPA also named Thomson Local 'Champion Directory' in 2002.

History

The brand can trace its roots back to 1965 when the predecessor of the company was first established as 'Thomson Yellow Pages' which first introduced the Yellow Pages to the UK a year later as sales agents for the Post Office. The Yellow Pages quickly took off, with the increasing consumer need for information being realised. In 1980 Thomson Directories Ltd was set up as an independent publisher of local directories and trials were undertaken in six regions. Following this initial success, near-national rollout of the Thomson Local followed in 1981.

After a couple of changes of ownership in the 1990s, Thomson was acquired in August 2000 by SEAT Pagine Gialle, the leading European publisher of telephone directories.

Since then, investments and enhancements in the Thomson Directories product have continued, with www.thomsonlocal.com going online in 2002, followed by the introduction of www.webfinder.com in 2003. Later in the same year, full colour was rolled out to the majority of Thomson Local directories.

Today, Thomson Directories is based at Farnborough in Hampshire, with over 500 head office staff and a further 500 employees located throughout the UK at ten regional sales offices.

Product

Thomson Directories is best known for the famous Thomson Local blue book, used by six million people every week, generating fifteen million business referrals. There are 173 different editions, covering over 85% of the UK's business and residential population. Each year, 22 million copies are distributed free of charge.

However, there is more to the business than the blue book. Online products are another important aspect of the Thomson offering, such as www.thomsonlocal.com – an easily searchable online information source providing all the information, and more, from 173 editions of the Thomson Local Directories. This site also includes WebFinder, a search engine that enables users to make location specific web searches online. This site generates over fourteen million page impressions every month. The company also partners with other leading internet site owners to distribute its search engine and content on these sites.

Thomson Directories also has a variety of products designed to help companies conduct direct marketing. These include the award-winning Business Search PRO, a database of two million UK businesses, available online or on CD Rom, which can be used to search and build direct mail and telesales lists.

Business users looking for sales leads can take advantage of New Connections, a monthly subscription

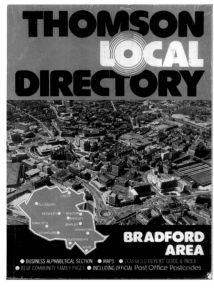

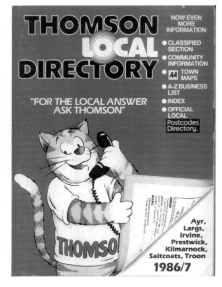

service providing sales leads on companies who are new, relocated, or have a new branch or new owner. Another sales lead service is Fastest Growing Companies, a database of growing companies based on turnover, compiled by matching financial data from Companies House with the Thomson Database of verified trading businesses.

Further business to business services include Email Marketing Solutions for Business. Providing over 350,000 opt-in B2B email addresses, this service is a highly useful and cost-effective one-to-one communication tool, allowing users to easily track results.

Customers can also take advantage of The Thomson Database, one of the UK's largest business databases with over two million business listings. This can be utilised under licence by organisations to offer additional products and services.

Recent Developments

New products recently developed by Thomson Directories to meet customers' changing needs include a new section within Thomson Local called Localplus. This is a new lifestyle section providing users with relevant and up to date information to meet their needs.

Another new inclusion is a 64-page NHS Direct Self-Help Guide in all 154 English titles – equating to some eighteen million copies. Thomson Directories is the only third party distributor of this guide in the UK.

The www.thomsonlocal.com website has also been added to, with the inclusion of the Localplus lifestyle section. Information on cinemas, restaurants, motoring, hotels and travel etc can be found and refined to the local user.

The website is continually enhanced to improve the look, feel and user experience to make searches easier and quicker.

The successful and popular Business Search PRO product has been re-positioned as an annual subscription service. Now available as an online version or a two CD package, this is designed to ensure users are working with the most up to date data.

Another important development has been the launch by Thomson Directories of an Email Marketing Service. This provides marketers with 350,000 email addresses, of people who have 'opted in' to providing their information. Aware that this is a sensitive area regarding data protection and 'spam' prevention, Thomson Directories is driving best practice by protecting those using the service and those receiving the emails.

Promotion

Since the early 1980s, Thomson Directories has advertised on television, using cats as its distinctive brand icon. Originally, a ginger cat called Thomson was the 'face' of the brand, making a string of on-screen celebrity friends. The tagline of those advertisements, 'For the Local answer, ask Thomson', is still remembered by many users.

In 1996, the blue cat was first introduced to both TV and print work and the strapline changed to 'The Answer Comes out of the Blue'.

TV advertising continues to drive usage of both Thomson Local and www.thomsonlocal.com, and, in 2004, the 'Cat Lady' was introduced. Lean, fast and smart, the Cat Lady has been designed to embody the qualities which underpin the Thomson Local Directories.

Brand Values

The heart of Thomson Directories' business is about helping buyers and sellers find each other, whatever their circumstances, making the Thomson Local the 'Smarter Choice' for both.

Its products are designed with the user in mind, enabling them to find information, quickly, easily and directly. Thomson prides itself on providing information for people relevant to where they are and how they want to search, be it in print or online.

Thomson Directories always seeks to innovate, yet remains a dependable, helpful brand which people can rely on for their information needs, wherever that may be.

www.thomsonlocal.com

THINGS YOU DIDN'T KNOW ABOUT

Thomson Local

> Each week Thomson Local Directories are used by six million people and generate fifteen million business referrals.

> There are 173 different editions of the Thomson Local.

> The Thomson Database has two million business listings.

> Two million calls are made every year to maintain the accuracy of the Thomson Database.

> There are over 1,800 headings in the Thomson Local, with Restaurants being the most referred to.

> All businesses are entitled to a free listing in their local directory.

Market

With businesses needing ever-more market, competitor and consumer intelligence to guide them in their strategies, investments and decision-making; market research and information is a service in great demand. An integral part of marketing and business development services, market information can offer tangible results, giving businesses insights on which they can base meaningful decisions. Not only used by companies to assess current trends, market information is increasingly being used to predict what the future may bring.

Businesses have an array of market research agencies to choose from, in a fragmented supply base with many different specialisms, such as FMCG, retail, automotive, political, online and healthcare. For its part, TNS sets itself apart from the competition by providing the 'sixth sense of business', which demonstrates its ability to provide insight and understanding into markets, rather than just research findings.

The wide scope of suppliers in the UK market research and market information industry alone is reflected by Marketing magazine's annual league of the UK's 65 biggest market research agencies. This shows TNS to be the biggest player in the market, with a turnover in the UK of £160 million.

Worldwide, the market information industry was worth US$17.5 billion by turnover in 2004. This is an impressive total, considering that the industry measured US$6 billion by turnover in 1990. To put its position in context, TNS' global turnover in 2004 was US$1.5 billion, making it the world's second largest market information company.

From 1995 to 2001, strong demand for market information saw the industry grow at 8-9% per year, but this slowed as economic conditions toughened in 2002 and 2003. As the world economy recovers, there is a corresponding increase in demand for market research and information, with analysts currently predicting growth rates of 4-5%.

Some of the factors driving this growth include the trend towards globalisation, which creates demand for consistent international data, and the introduction of new technology, which allows suppliers to add more value to their services and produce faster results.

As with many marketing agency sectors, recent years have seen a lot of consolidation among market research firms, with TNS being involved in one of the most high-profile deals when it acquired NFO Worldgroup Inc in 2003.

Achievements

TNS has built itself into the second largest market information company in the world. In terms of customised research, TNS is the global leader, and is also market leader in a number of key markets, such as France, Spain, the Netherlands, Norway, Finland and Denmark.

Its global network, spread of sector expertise and business mix gives the group a unique position in the industry, which is reflected by its steady revenue and profit growth. TNS has a track record of achieving profitable growth, with its operating profit more than doubling over the last five years. It has delivered consistent improvement in operating margin and also maintained a steady growth in earnings each year in line with, or ahead of growth in the overall market.

The TNS group has successfully expanded its business through a combination of organic growth and acquisitions, most significantly the acquisition of NFO Worldgroup Inc in July 2003, further strengthening its existing network in North America, Europe and Asia and creating a major force in market information.

The Group can offer expertise on a truly impressive scale. For example, it is the world leader in conducting

consumer panel research, running panels in 31 countries and has a presence in a further seventeen through alliances.

TNS' hi-tech services have also put it at the top of the market information sector. InfoSys TV, its advanced TV audience analysis system is used in fourteen countries and is the system of choice for all but one of the broadcasters in the UK. TNS technology is used to measure TV viewing and radio listening habits in 21 countries.

The group's expertise and innovation in market information has helped it become a key partner to major clients. For example, in 2003, IBM appointed TNS as its primary corporate research provider, while in the same year, the FMCG giant Unilever awarded TNS a contract to become its global preferred supplier of consumer panel data.

In 2004, BSkyB appointed TNS to develop and operate an innovative audience research system, designed to deliver new insights into the benefits of advertising to satellite TV viewers. The system involved the creation of a research panel comprising 20,000 households with digital satellite TV – four times larger than any comparable audience panel in the UK. Also in 2004, TNS secured a major contract with the European Commission to run its Standard Eurobarometer – the largest study of its kind in the world evaluating into public opinion on social, political and economic issues in 33 European countries.

Also significant was TNS' recent joint win, with Information Resources Inc (IRI) of a multi-million pound three-year deal with Premier Foods. TNS and IRI won the contract to replace the food giant's incumbent market information provider, starting in January 2005. Working together, TNS and IRI will provide advanced market insight, sophisticated reporting and responsive account management, providing the company with accurate and insightful knowledge to support its business.

TNS' work has helped it win numerous important awards, such as being named Market Research Agency of the Year by Marketing magazine in 2003. In 2004, TNS won six of the thirteen categories in Marketing magazine's Research Awards, winning media, retail, telecoms, leisure, international and financial. It was commended in a further three categories.

tns™   the sixth sense of business™

Who wants a glimpse of the future, when you can take a long hard look at it?

These days, knowing the facts about what's happening in your market just isn't enough.
You need to know what's going to happen, and, more importantly, what to do about it when it does.

As a world leading market information company, that's exactly what we deliver – insight.
Insight that can guide you through the ups and downs of the future, combined with a little inspiration that only a company committed to looking at things differently can deliver.

It's because we don't just stop at delivering the data. We look behind the numbers, beyond the trends and use our imagination to add real value to every solution we deliver. Which is why more and more companies are turning to us for strategic and tactical advice.

So the next time you want to know what the future has in store for you, email **enquiries@tns-global.com** or visit **www.tns-global.com**

History

TNS has expanded rapidly since 1997 when UK listed company Taylor Nelson AGB acquired the French operation Sofres. Through a series of strategic acquisitions it has reinforced its global network and strengthened its specialist sector presence and now operates from more than 70 countries. Some of these key acquisitions have included TNS Nipo in 1999 – the largest market information group in the Netherlands – and CMR, the largest provider of advertising expenditure measurement in the US – in 2000.

In April 2003 the operation, which was known as Taylor Nelson Sofres, re-branded as TNS. Then in July 2003 TNS completed the acquisition of NFO Worldgroup Inc further strengthening its existing network in North America, Europe and Asia Pacific. Its membership of the Gallup International Association, means it has partner offices in a further sixteen countries.

TNS has introduced a wide and increasingly sophisticated range of products to enable it to make use of the latest technological developments and experience significant growth, such as the launch of TNSInfo – a web portal information tool – in 2001, and the first commercial application of Portable People Meters, in conjunction with Arbitron, in 2003. Portable People Meters are pager-sized devices that 'hear' codes from the TV and radio, allowing super-accurate measurement of broadcast audiences. TNS has identified this as the future of TV audience measurement, allowing broadcasters to measure the person, not the TV set.

TNS continues to grow its business organically and through acquisition. In 2004, it acquired TNS Data in Central America and announced that it would increase the size of its consumer panel in France from 8,000 to 12,000.

Product

TNS' business is unique in the industry by having considerable experience in both syndicated and custom research. Key to the continuous side of the business is the TNS Worldpanel service. Using technology such as barcode scanners, internet and till receipt scanning, Worldpanel provides continuous measurement and analysis of consumer purchasing behaviour. Worldpanel clients tend to be multinational and local FMCG brands and own-label manufacturers, fresh food suppliers, retailers and market analysts.

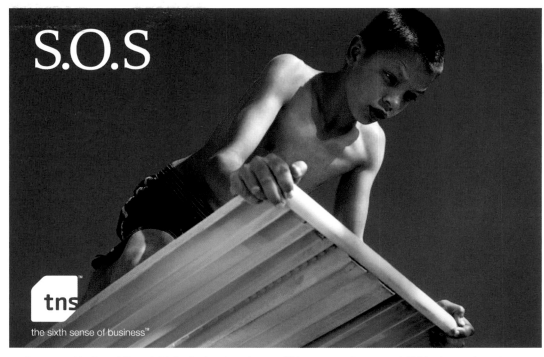

S.O.S

tns

the sixth sense of business™

TNS also offers a mixture of continuous and custom research services across the following key business sectors. Its media intelligence unit measures advertising spend across TV, radio, print and internet, and also tracks sports sponsorship and cinema trailers. The TV and Radio Audience Measurement division uses leading-edge technology to measure TV viewing and radio listening habits.

In Healthcare, TNS offers a range of custom and multi-client services to help major pharmaceutical, biotech and medical supply clients define market opportunities develop brands and track performance.

TNS's Technology sector offers a range of services to help high-tech clients identify the appropriate marketing strategies to deal with such a rapidly changing and developing marketplace.

Every year, TNS's Polling and Social division conducts millions of surveys and is the world's leading political polling organisation, tracking public opinion on political campaigns, as well as legislative and policy issues.

Consumer, Media and Financial & Professional services are the remaining key business areas with tailored research strategies, analysis and insight developed by TNS to satisfy clients' information demands.

In 2005, TNS is further developing this broad range of custom service expertise under four core Areas of Expertise: New Product Development (product and concept testing, forecasting and brand tracking); Motivational Research (e.g. brand portfolio management and competitor analysis); Brand Advertising and Research (advertising pre-testing and advertising testing) and Stakeholder Management (customer retention and employee commitment).

Recent Developments

An important new development from TNS was the launch, in February 2005, of a multi-country online service, called the European Access Panel. Branded '6ᵗʰdimension', the service will give TNS' clients access to a managed panel in which they can identify their exact target research group as well as ensuring that consistency of responses is maintained and the integrity of the data is safeguarded.

TNS sees 6ᵗʰdimension as a key component of driving future growth in Europe. The service will respond to increasing client demands for an online panel with fast turnaround times and high response rates. As well as providing turnaround times several weeks shorter than conventional research methods, 6ᵗʰdimension will provide clients with enhanced cross-market consistency in data collection and analysis.

The UK FMCG consumer-tracking arm of Worldpanel is being significantly expanded from 15,000 to 25,000 households over a period of two years, completing the recruitment drive by 2006. The expansion will deliver a groundbreaking advance in integrated consumer understanding, utilising greater depth and breadth of data analysis to realise complete consumer profiling.

This means an increase of 60% in the products that can be tracked and analysed by TNS.

Promotion

TNS uses a variety of marketing vehicles to raise awareness and generate business opportunities for its products and services worldwide. These include advertising, public relations, direct mail and e-marketing as well as attending trade shows, delivering papers at conferences and sponsoring or organising key industry events. In addition, TNS has a strong online presence via its global website.

The brand has also been raising its awareness through a partnership with television news channel CNN and TIME magazine. The deal provides feedback on current affairs and world issues which feature in CNN programmes as well as regular news items in the European edition of TIME magazine. In 2004, TNS extended its deal with CNN and TIME so that it now also includes the Asia Pacific region.

Brand Values

TNS sees itself as providing 'the sixth sense of business'. The brand is the eyes and ears of business, looking beyond the numbers, beyond the trends and reading between the lines. TNS believes that this 'sixth sense' of business enables it to understand the world in which clients operate, interpreting the opportunities and dangers they face and providing them with a window on the future. It means understanding what is happening today and what will happen tomorrow by providing intelligence that cuts through the noise and clutter of the 21st century. The company's brand values are summed up in four words: wit, intelligence, attitude and imagination.

www.tns-global.com

THINGS YOU DIDN'T KNOW ABOUT

TNS

❭ TNS' global network and advanced technology allows it to monitor the behaviour of 81,650 households around the world, providing information on over 80 million purchases every year.

❭ TNS' access panel is one of the largest in the US, with 500,000 households available for mail and phone surveys and 2.54 million individuals available online.

❭ TNS is the world's largest custom research company.

❭ TNS runs media intelligence services in 20 countries, covering over 1,600 TV stations, 11,300 press titles, 4,500 radio stations, and over 3,000 websites. In 2004, this translated into 150 million TV Spots, over fourteen million press ads, 20 million radio spots, 100 million web banners, and three millions brands monitored worldwide.

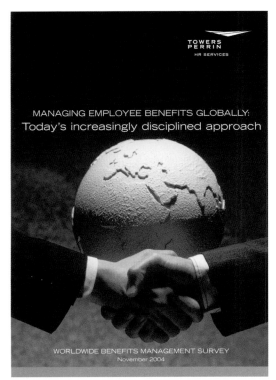

MANAGING EMPLOYEE BENEFITS GLOBALLY:
Today's increasingly disciplined approach

WORLDWIDE BENEFITS MANAGEMENT SURVEY
November 2004

Market

Towers Perrin is a global professional services firm that helps organisations around the world optimise performance through effective people, risk and financial management.

The firm provides new answers to the challenges clients face in the areas of human resource consulting, management and actuarial consulting to the financial services industry and reinsurance intermediary services.

With revenue in excess of US$1 billion, Towers Perrin is one of the world's largest independent consulting firms.

Achievements

Towers Perrin's market-leading pedigree began with the development of the world's first private pensions plan by founder, H Walter Forster, earning him the nickname 'the father of pension planning'. Later, in the mid 1940s, the firm published its first 'TPF&C Pension Tax Manual', which

To some people, it's just string.

To others, it's possibility.
Innovation means seeing things for what they could be.

For 70 years, Towers Perrin has been known for innovation – in human resources, risk management, financial services management and reinsurance intermediary services. We focus on getting results for our clients. And that means understanding the strength – and the infinite possibilities – in every organization.

See more about us at www.towersperrin.com

TOWERS PERRIN

quickly became the standard US Internal Revenue Service reference on pension law. The result of Towers Perrin's determination on behalf of clients to blend quality with fresh thinking has been an enviable client list. Today it includes three quarters of the world's 500 largest companies. In the UK, Towers Perrin serves approximately 720 clients, of which 74 are from the FTSE 100. The firm also plays a key role across the UK's public sector, working with government departments to more efficiently and effectively deliver public services.

Across Europe, over 80 of the Financial Times' 100 top European companies are clients and in the US three-quarters of the Fortune 1000 corporations are Towers Perrin clients. Given the international nature of many of its clients, Towers Perrin has to excel in delivering professional services that are genuinely global.

History

In 1917, a Towers Perrin founder developed the first private pension plan for Union Carbide and Carbon Corporation. Thirteen years later Towers, Perrin, Forster & Crosby (TPF&C) opened for business in Philadelphia with reinsurance and life divisions. Employees numbered 26, and the company's first year income was less than US$200,000. The reinsurance practice was instrumental in developing syndicates to provide additional capacity in London as a way of offsetting a worldwide reinsurance shortage.

The mid to late 1940s saw the life division become the pension division, which published the first TPF&C Pension Tax Manual, which in turn quickly became a standard US Internal Revenue Service reference on pension tax law. The company began producing the TPF&C Letter to inform clients of trends and regulations in the areas of pensions and benefits. At the close of the 1940s, TPF&C opened its second office, in Chicago, and a third in New York City, as employees reached 120.

In 1952, the firm's first communications consulting unit was formed and total income reached US$2 million. Four years later, the first non-US office opened in Montreal, and the pension division became the employee benefit plan practice as a first step toward marketing a wider range of consulting services.

The end of the 1950s saw income reach US$4 million as TPF&C produced the first personnel manual, which became the prototype for companies wanting to develop formal benefits descriptions for their employees. Tillinghast, the company's actuarial and management consulting subsidiary, developed a prize-winning paper on discounted cash-flow methodology that became an industry standard for pricing life insurance products and companies.

The 1960s was a decade of expansion for TPF&C as it introduced compensation and organisation consulting services, established a centralised, six-month training programme

for new consultants, and began a formalised research programme for clients. In 1965 Brussels became the firm's first office outside North America, and four years later the company opened its first office in London. Income more than tripled during the decade to US$14 million, while staff more than doubled to almost 500.

Growth and prosperity continued in the 1970s and early 1980s, with offices opening in Caracas, Hong Kong, Brisbane, Melbourne, Sydney and Tokyo. By 1987, Towers Perrin was established as the umbrella name for the firm as revenues exceeded US$500 million, staff numbers rose to 4,000 and the number of clients around the world reached 8,500.

In the run up to the new millennium, Towers Perrin Administration Services (TPAS) was formed to handle the strain that benefit and vendor administration activities have placed on clients and it quickly became one of Towers Perrin's fastest growing businesses. In 1995 the firm acquired Kinsley Lord, a British change-management consulting firm. The following year the company's income passed US$1 billion.

Product

Towers Perrin provides human resource consulting to public and private sector organisations, as well as management and actuarial consulting to the financial services industry, and reinsurance intermediary services to clients. Its businesses comprise HR Services, Reinsurance and Tillinghast.

The HR Services business provides human resources consulting around the world. The advice it offers lies in the fields of employee benefits, rewards and performance management, communication, change management,

RECONNECTING WITH EMPLOYEES
Quantifying the value of engaging your workforce

UNITED KINGDOM

employee research and the delivery of HR services. In short, HR Services helps organisations effectively manage their investment in people.

The Reinsurance business of Towers Perrin provides reinsurance intermediary services and consulting expertise, combining a creative blend of traditional and non-traditional risk transfer vehicles. It offers clients help with reinsurance strategy and programme review; claims management and programme administration; catastrophe exposure management; contract negotiation and placement; and market security issues.

Tillinghast provides actuarial and management consulting to insurance and financial services companies, and advises other organisations on risk financing and self-insurance. It helps clients with challenges in connection with mergers, acquisitions and restructuring; financial and regulatory reporting; risk, capital and value management; products, markets and distribution; and financial modelling software.

Moses and TAS:P/C together defining a new paradigm in financial modelling for the UK general insurance market

Recent Developments

The dawn of the new millennium saw Towers Perrin acquire Pegasus, a specialist designer of reinsurance products, with clients around the world. A year later, the firm formalised strategic relationships with nine leading organisations, including JP Morgan/American Century and MEDSTAT Group.

In 2002 Towers Perrin opened an office in Shenzhen, China. In the UK, it acquired Denis M Clayton & Co, a British insurance and reinsurance intermediary and consultancy. It also acquired Classic Solutions, a financial modelling software company and two HR software integrators Working Concepts and Delphi.

The following year, Towers Perrin launched Executive Compensation Resources, a data collection, analysis, research and information services unit within the Executive Compensation practice.

Building its presence in China in 2004, Towers Perrin opened offices in Beijing. The same year, it formed an alliance with Marcu & Asociados to provide consulting services for both the HR Services and Tillinghast

businesses in Argentina, Bolivia, Chile, Paraguay and Uruguay. Tillinghast has recently analysed market-consistent valuations and embedded value as methods for determining the true value of insurance companies. In late 2004, Towers Perrin launched the European Engagement Study, a new method to determine employees' feelings about their jobs, their workplace and the measurable impact that engaged employees have on company performance. The newest addition – in spring 2005 – to the Towers Perrin portfolio is a jointly-owned business with EDS, a new company to deliver a comprehensive range of HR outsourcing services to enterprises, HR departments, employees and pensioners. The newly created company, with US$600 million in global revenues, will combine the market-leading technology and business process capabilities of EDS with Towers Perrin's knowledge of benefits administration and the HR domain experience of Towers Perrin.

Promotion

For Towers Perrin, marketing means understanding business issues and customer needs, and then delivering services that entirely satisfy clients.

The Towers Perrin brand is well known in its target markets in the UK, but the company is aware that its competitors' names are also prominent. Buyers don't differentiate simply on the basis of services offered but on professional reputation; how the company serves its clients; how it delivers its work; and the impact that work has on its clients' success.

Understanding clients and their issues is fundamental to Towers Perrin's success and it takes a holistic approach to client relationship management. Through continuous, classic marketing programmes such as surveys and workshops, the company tests hypotheses and listens to clients. It supports these initiatives with a rigorous programme of client and prospect interviews, as well as market research that enables it to target individual clients. Towers Perrin is intensely proud of the number of its clients who have remained so for many years, who treat the company as a trusted advisor.

But winning new clients is also a clear priority, and Towers Perrin aims to grab their attention by publishing points of view and genuine thought leadership on topical issues, by demonstrating depth of knowledge, often around technical subjects and presenting to prospects in fresh and creative ways.

The company has set up client forums, where large groups of clients come together to share experience, new ideas and thinking. Latterly, these large meetings have been replaced by smaller workshops where clients can work through their issues 'live', a potentially risky approach, but one that is immensely rewarding.

Towers Perrin believes the key to the success of its promotional strategy is an appropriate balance between strategic in-house marketing expertise and outsourcing for all aspects of direct marketing: databases, events, surveys, thought leadership, market intelligence and media relations. It has built all these in-house capabilities over the past ten years and resisted short-term savings from outsourcing to agencies except during peak periods. The approach offers better control of quality and delivery time-schedules and, most important of all, develops the depth of knowledge that comes from experience. These facets are vital to keeping Towers Perrin at the leading-edge of a constantly-evolving market and ahead of its competitors.

Brand Values

Towers Perrin's mission, vision and values are the principles by which it operates. Its brand strategy is embedded in these principles.

The firm's mission is to make significant contributions to improving its clients' business performance and thereby to create value for stakeholders. Its brand personality – practical, innovative and committed to its clients' success – is at the heart of this mission.

Towers Perrin's vision is to be a pre-eminent global consulting firm that business and professional communities hold in the highest regard. It aims to achieve marketplace leadership by building businesses with the best-in-class capability to deliver measurable results for clients. Its brand attributes reflect its global goal to be an outstanding business that provides clients with superlative work through fresh and creative thinking.

Towers Perrin is dedicated to the values of integrity, respect and professionalism. It embraces warmly such attributes as honesty, fairness, agility, innovation, high performance and discipline that, in combination with its values, will help it realise its vision.

www.towersperrin.com

THINGS YOU DIDN'T KNOW ABOUT

Towers Perrin

> In 1917, H. Walter Forster, one of the company's founders, developed the first private pension plan for Union Carbide and Carbon Corporation.

> In the mid 1980s, Towers Perrin first developed the concept of employee total rewards: expressing an employer's deal with the workforce that incorporated tangible pay and benefits with workforce environment and learning and development opportunities.

> Towers Perrin introduced flexible benefits to the UK in 1989.

> Towers Perrin created the people processes and organisational structures that have made the FSA and Ofcom the world-class regulators that they are today.

> Tillinghast published a seminal paper on the effects of terrorism after 9/11 for the insurance and reinsurance industries, as well as many other groundbreaking industry papers, such as on asbestos liability projection.

Market

Yellow Pages is part of Yell, a leading international directories business which is the biggest player in the £4.2 billion UK classified advertising market (Source: The Advertising Association 2003). The market consists of a range of media, including other printed directories, local and national newspapers and online directories. In the financial year 2004, Yell published 90 regional editions of Yellow Pages in the UK, containing more than one million advertisements, and distributed almost 28 million copies.

Yell has an integrated portfolio of products across printed, online and telephone-based media. Its business proposition is putting buyers in touch with sellers through a range of simple-to-use, cost-effective advertising solutions.

Achievements

Since Yell's first Yellow Pages was published almost 40 years ago, the directory has become a part of everyday life and both consumers and advertisers trust Yellow Pages to deliver the results they require year after year. Consequently, Yellow Pages is used 1.2 billion times a year, with more than £240 million generated daily for businesses that appear in the directory, or £88 billion annually (Source: Saville Rossiter-Base 2004).

Yellow Pages is well known for its award winning and memorable advertising campaigns, which have contributed to keeping the directory at the forefront of people's minds for many years.

Yell is very aware of environmental and social issues and its impact on the wider community. For instance, Yellow Pages works with local councils to encourage the recycling of old directories; 83% of UK councils have the facilities to recycle Yellow Pages directories and 51% of people say that they recycle their directories (Source: FDS International Ltd, 2004). In addition, all of its new directories are made from 48% recycled fibres.

As part of its commitment to excellence, Yell has achieved and maintained registration to ISO9001, ISO4001, and ISO18001, the international management, environmental and health and safety standards.

Both in 1999, and again in 2004, Yell won the prestigious European Quality Award, the coveted pan-European business excellence award created and managed by the European Foundation for Quality Management (EFQM). Yell is the first company ever to win the award on two occasions.

Yell also won a Queen's Award for Enterprise for its integrated approach to sustainable development in 2002. It was acknowledged for demonstrating outstanding commercial success, whilst at the same time ensuring that work practices benefit society, the environment and the economy.

In the same year, Yell won a Green Apple Environmental Award for its directory recycling scheme, and in 2003 won a further Green Apple Award for environmental best practice.

Yell was also, in 2003, awarded a BIG TICK by Business in the Community, the independent organisation which helps businesses to improve their positive impact on society. The BIG TICK recognises companies that have reached a measurable standard of excellence in the field of corporate responsibility. Yell was also a finalist in the 'Business in the Environment' category of the Business in the Community Awards for Excellence.

History

The first directories date as far back as Elizabethan times, when street directories were published detailing the names and addresses of local residences and businesses. But the forerunner of modern day directories did not properly emerge until the 1840s, with the publication of Kelly's London Post Office directories. These contained information on local gentry and traders, listed by county.

The growth of the telecommunications industry offered further potential to publishers of directories. Yell's first Yellow Pages directory appeared in 1966, bound into the standard Brighton telephone directory. From 1973, Yellow Pages were rolled out across the UK and existed as a product in its own right, becoming a registered trademark in 1979.

Over the years Yellow Pages has continued to improve and enhance its product, as well as extending into new areas to keep up with the developing directories industry. Aside from Yellow Pages, Yell's products in the UK also include the following:

Business Pages, a specialist directory covering business to business suppliers introduced in 1985.

Yell.com, a leading site for finding businesses, shops and services in the UK that was launched in 1996.

Yellow Pages 118 24 7, a telephone-based information service providing in-depth classified business information, and business and residential listings. It was launched in 2003 following the deregulation of 192 directory enquiries and replaced the Talking Pages service that had been introduced in 1988. In 1999 Yell expanded into the US with the purchase of Yellow Book USA, the largest independent publisher in the US. Since then there has been further expansion in the US. The most significant development was the purchase of the McLeod directories business in April 2002, which doubled Yell's geographic US footprint. With the additional purchase in December that year of National Directory Company, Yell consolidated its position as the largest independent publisher of yellow pages directories in the US. In March 2004, the acquisition of Feist took Yell's US presence to 42 states and Washington DC.

In July 2003, having been sold by BT to a private equity consortium in 2001, a new milestone in Yell's development was heralded with the company's listing on the London Stock Exchange – the biggest flotation in the London market for two years.

Product

Yell is committed to supporting the growth and development of businesses in the UK. It aims to understand, anticipate and meet the changing demands of advertisers and users, and to take advantage of new technologies and communication methods in the development of world class products and services.

New customers are shown the value of Yellow Pages advertising packages with attractive pricing schemes. Customers are retained year after year through the provision of excellent service and products. Over the past four years, Yellow Pages has won more than

100,000 new advertisers a year in the UK and has a high customer retention rate, reflecting strong satisfaction. By proving the value of its advertising and building on its relationships with customers, Yellow Pages also encourages existing advertisers to expand their advertising programmes.

Today there are more than 2,200 classifications in the Yellow Pages directory and these are reviewed on a regular basis to ensure that it is as easy as possible for Yellow Pages users to find the products and services they need. By classifying businesses under the most relevant and up-to-date headings, Yellow Pages makes life simple for its users. Alongside more traditional classifications such as Builders and Plumbers, recent additions include Fair Trade Goods (2004) and Graffiti Removal (2005), reflecting current social and market trends.

Yell.com now features approximately two million UK business listings, searchable by business type, name and location. In September 2004 the site generated more than 69 million page impressions. The information that Yell.com provides can now be accessed through the website, mobile internet and via text message.

Yellow Pages 118 24 7 offers callers a classified business directory service, including additional details such as opening hours and store locations, as well as residential directory listings. In the financial year 2004, 3.9 million enquiries were received and it carried advertisements for nearly 64,000 paying advertisers.

Information'. In March 2005, Yellow Pages will launch for the first time in Hull, completing Yellow Pages' coverage of the entire UK. Other developments across the Yell portfolio include the launch of Yell.com mobile in 2004. It is the first mobile business information service of its kind in the UK, enabling users to access Yell.com's business information from a mobile handset. Yell.com mobile also helps users to get where they want to go by offering full colour street maps and walking and driving directions.

Recent Developments
Yellow Pages is constantly looking at new and innovative ways of attracting new advertisers and retaining existing ones, as well as ensuring the directory is easy to use and relevant to local needs.

In October 2001 full-colour advertisements were published in Yellow Pages for the first time. It is an innovation which has proved to be popular with advertisers, allowing them more flexibility in the style of their advertisements.

A significant and striking redesign of the Yellow Pages directory was launched in June 2004 to highlight to users the 'added value' content within the directories. The design uses a new colour coding system flagged on a new-look front cover and incorporates iconography supported by vibrant colour imagery. The design creates a more contemporary look and feel to increase the appeal of the directory to users.

The 'added value' content has been refreshed and features expanded information sources such as a 'Your Area Guide' that highlights community, leisure, travel, sports and shopping information, and 'Consumer

Promotion
Yellow Pages has consistently used strong advertising campaigns to build and reinforce awareness of the brand. The famous JR Hartley TV advertisement, 'Fly Fishing', where an elderly man used Yellow Pages to search for a book that he had written years before, aimed to remind consumers that Yellow Pages is 'Not just for the nasty things in life'. The advert won a British Television Silver Award in 1983, and in 2000 'Fly Fishing' came 13th in a Channel 4 poll of the '100 Greatest TV Ads of all Time'. Other advertising awards include a British Television Gold Award for the 'Cleaners' advert in 1998, and an award for Best Taxi Design at the 2003 Campaign Poster Awards.

The latest wave of Yellow Pages TV advertising features James Nesbitt of TV's 'Cold Feet' and 'Murphy's Law' fame, who turns to Yellow Pages in a variety of humorous real-life situations. James Nesbitt has also fronted a television and radio advertising campaign for the new Yellow Pages 118 24 7 service.

Brand Values
The Yellow Pages brand is built on its reputation for accessibility, trustworthiness, reliability and warmth. Yellow Pages is ubiquitous, with 97% of adults having a copy at home and 64% of workers having a copy in the workplace (Source: Saville Rossiter-Base 2004). Research shows that Yellow Pages is well ahead of the classified advertising competition on value, with the vast majority of advertisers saying they feel it offers good value for money (Source: Saville Rossiter-Base 2004). Similarly, research has also shown over a number of years that users are more satisfied with Yellow Pages directories than any other information source such as local newspapers, TV text services, local libraries, classified magazines and even friends and neighbours (Source: Consensus Record 2002).

In keeping with the brand's friendly and helpful personality, Yellow Pages' involvement with charity and environmental projects reflects its concern with issues that affect individuals and communities throughout the UK.

Yellow Pages has worked with Marie Curie Cancer Care since 1999, supporting the annual 'Daffodil Campaign', which has raised more than £11 million for the charity to date.

Yellow Pages' support of the Directory Recycling Scheme (DRS) forms part of the company's ongoing commitment to the environment. A major schools recycling initiative – The Yellow Woods Challenge – was launched in October 2002, with Kirk, a woodland creature, as its mascot. Its aims are to educate children about recycling and conservation, and to encourage them to recycle old Yellow Pages directories.

www.yellgroup.com

THINGS YOU DIDN'T KNOW ABOUT

Yellow Pages

❯ Yellow Pages is used 3.3 million times per day in the UK and 100 million times a month (Source: Saville Rossiter-Base 2004).

❯ Almost 28 million Yellow Pages directories were distributed in 2004 to households and businesses in the UK.

❯ New classifications include Fair Trade Goods (2004) and Graffiti Removal (2005). Recently deleted classifications include Anchor Makers, Sword Makers, and Braces, Belt & Suspender Manufacturers (2003).

❯ The most popular classifications for users are Restaurants, Insurance (all), Garage Services, Plumbers, Builders and Car Dealers & Distributors (Source: Saville Rossiter-Base 2004).

❯ In 1991, following popular demand, the book 'Fly Fishing' was written – eight years after the commercial featuring the JR Hartley character first aired. It became a Christmas bestseller.

❯ Yellow Pages can be recycled into animal bedding, fake snow, stuffing for jiffy bags, egg boxes and cardboard.

ZenithOptimedia
The ROI Agency

Market

ZenithOptimedia is one of the largest agencies operating in the UK media agency sector.

ZenithOptimedia is a full service agency in the broadest sense of the word, providing not only the traditional services of strategic media planning and buying, but also diversified services including sponsorship, consumer research, marketing consultancy and modelling, direct marketing and digital communications.

ZenithOptimedia's positioning as the ROI agency seeks to help marketers realise better returns on their marketing communications investment.

Achievements

ZenithOptimedia was created as a result of a merger between Zenith Media and Optimedia in January 2003. On creation of the new company the new proposition 'The ROI Agency' was born. The agency has been widely credited with driving industry debate on the need for greater accountability in marketing communications.

The agency has received numerous industry awards over the last two years including Media Week Awards, Campaign Media Awards, PPA Awards and this year was the only media agency to receive an IPA Effectiveness Award for its work for British Airways. The IPA award is a ringing endorsement of the ROI agency positioning. The agency performs consistently well in Marketing Week's annual survey of clients and is a regular top player in the category for 'best media planning, buying and placement' as well as being consistently cited as one of the best media agencies delivering 'value for money'.

Over the past twelve months the agency has had an impressive run of new business wins valued in excess of £80 million.

History

The current agency was formed from the merger of Zenith and Optimedia in 2003, when it also became part of the Publicis Groupe.

Zenith was a pioneer in the UK media industry, blazing the trail for the media independent sector. Formed in 1988 Zenith brought a wholesale change to the way that media was planned and bought and retained a market leading position for the next ten years. Zenith was also the first agency to recognise the importance of building an international network, opening offices in Asia and the US before any of its competitors.

Optimedia was the media independent arm of Publicis with a strong focus on communications planning and with a strong reputation for launching brands into the marketplace. Internationally Optimedia like Zenith built a strong network based around the client needs of brands such as British Airways, L'Oréal and HP.

The companies brought complementary skills to the merger as well as geographic compatibility allowing an ever stronger network offering to be created.

Product

ZenithOptimedia's traditional core competencies were in the fields of strategic media planning and buying. The agency aims to deliver best in class thinking in these areas via the ROI Blueprint. This process is designed to ensure a focus on its client's business objectives, brand attributes and consumer insights throughout the planning and buying process. The process ensures that all possible touchpoints with the consumer are considered in the planning process. This process is standardised across markets and is utilised on all client business. In anticipation of changes in the marketplace the company has successfully built up a range of diversified services as new core competencies over the years.

ZenithOptimedia's 'Alliance' offers expertise across all areas of sponsorship and brand partnership. This encompasses work in the more traditional areas of broadcast sponsorship as well as event marketing and consulting.

Sponsorship Intelligence, the evaluation arm of Alliance, also work for a number of the major sporting bodies such as FIFA and the IOC.

Zed Media, wholly owned by ZenithOptimedia is one of the UK's leading direct and digital agencies. It was formed in 2003 by bringing together digital and direct capabilities of the ZenithOptimedia group in the same company under the proposition of 'Where all lines meet'. Zed have specialists in digital planning and buying, search marketing, internet partnerships and affiliate marketing, interactive television, mobile marketing, data list broking, direct planning, inserts, door to door together with DRTV and traditional press buying teams. Zed was recognised as the leading direct and digital agency in the UK by Marketing Weeks Reputations Survey, in 2004.

ZenithOptimedia acquired Ninah in 2001. Ninah offer advanced marketing consultancy services including marketing mix modelling and investment to profit modelling as well as advance econometrics. Ninah's approach to the discipline is based on a consensus approach which involves all the stakeholders both internal and external to a business.

Pay & Go™

Free texts and picture messages 7-8pm

Simply register your postcode and top-up £20 or more each month on your O₂ Talkalot tariff.

Valid for 6 months when you join between 1 July – 30 September 2004.

O₂

united international pictures

BRITISH AIRWAYS

Lloyds TSB

hp invent

mfi

WOOLWORTHS

Yaris. You could love it too much.

Now available in three shades of special edition blue with metallic finish, blue interior trim and CD player. Make sure it looks its best. Call 0845 275 5555 or visit toyota.co.uk

TODAY **TOMORROW** **TOYOTA**

Yaris 1.0 VVT-i manual, Official Fuel Consumption Figures in mpg (l/100km): Urban 41.5 (6.8), Extra Urban 57.6 (4.9), Combined 50.4 (5.6). CO_2 Emissions: 134 g/km.
Calls to Toyota will be charged at local rate and may be monitored and recorded.

Consumer Research is a key area of investment for the agency. As the communications world becomes ever more complex, bespoke approaches to research are essential in creating a better understanding of consumers and their interaction with the media. The agency has pioneered a number of ground breaking research programmes including the Persistence study which allows a better understanding of what generates recall from TV understanding, and MediaDNA which provides advertisers with a better understanding of how to leverage media brands values.

Recent Developments

The Open Village at ZenithOptimedia was created in response to the need to connect with consumers in an engaging way that differentiates its client's brands and delivers competitive advantage. It is the means by which it can identify, recommend and execute non traditional communication solutions. To this end, relationships have been developed with a range of specialist partners that enable the agency to go beyond conventional media into areas such as product placement, sponsorship (sports, event and broadcast) programme production, advertiser funded programming, event creation and contract publishing.

The value of these relationships falls into two key areas. Firstly, ZenithOptimedia planners are trained by each specialist to understand the relevance of each communication solution. Knowing when to make a recommendation is a critical aspect of holistic planning. Secondly, the implementation of integrated strategies requires specialist skills and additional resource, which is provided by the Village partner working alongside the client, ZenithOptimedia and other relevant agencies.

This entails a disciplined approach and briefing process, which guarantees that a comprehensive range of communication opportunities have been considered for every single brand in response to individual objectives.

As a media specialist, ZenithOptimedia applies the same rigorous targeting approach to Open Village communication opportunities as it does to traditional media. Furthermore, it collaborates with all relevant contributors to ensure that consistent brand equity leads the identification of relevant channels. ZenithOptimedia aims to choose the right opportunity at the right price, and ensure that the deal is effectively evaluated. In addition, it makes sure that all the media work together as an integrated whole.

The Open Village is staffed by a number of strategists that come from both traditional media agencies as well as sales promotion, account planning and television production.

It forms part of the wider creative thinking team which is headed up by the UK media agency sectors first Creative Director.

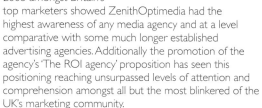

Promotion

ZenithOptimedia actively markets its services through a variety of both traditional and non-traditional business to business approaches. Research conducted in 2003 amongst Britain's top marketers showed ZenithOptimedia had the highest awareness of any media agency and at a level comparative with some much longer established advertising agencies. Additionally the promotion of the agency's 'The ROI agency' proposition has seen this positioning reaching unsurpassed levels of attention and comprehension amongst all but the most blinkered of the UK's marketing community.

Brand Values

ZenithOptimedia has three clear brand values, which speak for themselves. These are Energy, Excellence and Enterprise.

www.zenithoptimedia.com

THINGS YOU DIDN'T KNOW ABOUT

ZenithOptimedia

> ZenithOptimedia has invested in excess of £7 billion of advertising on behalf of its UK clients since launch.

> If you combined the time of all the ad spots ZenithOptimedia TV and Radio has bought since inception it would take 450 years to watch them.

> On average a ZenithOptimedia brand will be in every ad break on television.

> ZenithOptimedia has 160 offices in 60 countries worldwide.

> ZenithOptimedia are the only UK media agency to have built a freestanding rocket in Trafalgar Square on behalf of their client UIP for the launch of Thunderbirds the movie.

ZURICH

Market

Zurich Financial Services is an insurance-based financial services provider with headquarters in Zurich, Switzerland. Its core business is insurance – general and life. Its global network focuses on key markets in North America and Europe.

Basing its business on a tradition of innovative financial solutions, Zurich is one of the world's major players in insurance and offers its customers a broad range of insurance-related products.

Using local expertise backed by an international network, it provides insurance and risk management products and services for small to medium sized enterprises, corporations and multinational companies. Zurich also offers a comprehensive range of insurance products for individuals – such as property and car insurance – as well as financial products such as life cover, investment and pensions.

Europe is one of the Group's core markets and the UK is a significant contributor to Zurich's overall profits in Europe.

In the UK, Zurich works across many market sectors, either selling direct to customers or distributing its products and services through intermediaries.

Achievements

As an indication of Zurich's success in its chosen markets, in 2004 gross written premiums and policy fees were US$49.3 billion. The General Insurance segment recorded gross written premiums of US$37.6 billion, and the Life Insurance segment gross written premiums and policy fees of US$11 billion. Net income at Farmers Management Services rose 14% to US$686 million. In the same period, Zurich's business operating profit increased by 36% to US$3.1 billion.

Zurich is the number one player in the market for corporate business, gaining market share, while delivering market leading combined ratios. Meanwhile, Zurich has upheld its premier position as the largest provider of insurance to solicitors in the UK market.

Recent research has shown that overall, Independent Financial Advisor's (IFA's) satisfaction with Zurich Independent Financial Advisor (ZIFA) sales support, has reached an unprecedented high. Indeed, 94% of IFAs were satisfied with the support and a promising 67% were very satisfied. This result was the best achieved by any of the twelve benchmarked companies.

The Insurance Times Awards are some of the most sought after in the industry. Zurich's outstanding insurance claims service won it the Claims Award in 2004, while for its achievement of quality customer focused cover, it was made Motor Insurer of the Year. This award, voted by brokers, demonstrates their confidence in recommending Zurich to their personal and commercial customers. Zurich asserts that its business should be managed in a responsible way and takes corporate social responsibility very seriously. Having completed the Business in The Community (BiTC's) Corporate Responsibility and Business in the Environment indices, Zurich qualified for the Dow Jones Sustainable Development Index, one of the leading indexes tracking performance of companies committed to responsible business and long-term growth from the day it began. Zurich Cares, the community arm of Zurich in the UK, helps disadvantaged people build an independent future for themselves and has a lasting effect within communities. The programme is delivered through The Zurich Community Trust (UK) Ltd, a separate registered charity funded from pre tax profits which leverages further donations from employees. One thousand local, national and international charities benefit from the programme each year through a combination of financial support, employee volunteering and the sharing of business skills.

History

The roots of the Zurich Financial Services Group go back to the 19th century, with the founding in 1872 of Zurich Insurance Company. Within eight years, the company was already servicing a large clientele beyond its native Switzerland. This growth continued, with the business reaching all continents by the end of the 1970s. In September 1998, Zurich Financial Services Group was created from the merger with the financial services business of B.A.T Industries plc – bringing together Zurich, Allied Dunbar, Threadneedle, Sterling and Eagle Star under one roof in the UK – together with major consumer and small business insurer, Farmers, in the US.

The insurance business is often influenced by the welfare and social policies of the country it operates in. Zurich has had to make major adjustments over the years to respond to these changes. Its historical agility and adaptability has served it well as it has found plenty of opportunities and financial successes in change.

Product

Zurich UK offers a wide range of products within each of its market sectors. Its commercial insurance and services products help businesses – from sole traders to large commercial

International insurance and risk management network
Global thinking for local markets

115% of any growth in the FTSE 100 Index

The security of a 100% money-back guarantee

businesses – to keep running should the unexpected happen. Some products are suitable for a wide variety of businesses – such as fleet insurance, employers' liability cover and property insurance – while others are tailored to specific types of businesses. For example, Zurich has a wide range of products and services aimed at businesses operating in the construction industry.

'The London market' serves the needs of the FTSE 250 and the FTSE 100 multinational companies who need an insurance company that can manage relationships and deliver multiple products and services similar to the above, but on a global scale.

Zurich's insurance for professionals offers professional indemnity plans, which cover the advice given by solicitors, accountants and other people in service professions.

Meanwhile, Zurich's 'risk services' include audits, surveys and advice to help customers reduce the levels

of risk within their business. It focuses particularly on the areas of health and safety, property protection, motor fleet risk, business continuity, occupational health, strategic and engineering risk.

Zurich has a wealth of expertise in working with public sector risk management and insurance needs. This spans helping those involved in education, health, social housing, community services and local authorities.

Zurich helps customers, through its range of personal consumer products, from protection for themselves and their possessions (including car, boat, and home insurance) to planning for their short and long-term financial future through pensions, investments, mortgages and life insurance.

Many of Zurich's products are sold through intermediaries and the brand offers extensive support in recognition of their importance to the business such as marketing consultancy, including the unique Marketing Toolkit. In its position as the UK's fourth largest general insurer, the brand offers high levels of support to general insurance brokers working in a variety of markets. both personal and commercial. This support focuses or building relationships with brokers and their customers and ensuring they find it easy to do business with the company. Recent initiatives include a revamped website

for its commercial business, which makes it easier and quicker for brokers to conduct business online.

Zurich, via its franchised adviser network, provides face-to-face advice on a range of financial services and helps to create a complete financial package to suit individual needs. As franchises, these businesses are run by the franchisee with support from Zurich. This includes compliance services, business development and marketing support.

Zurich also offers support to all other intermediaries through the Zurich Intermediary Group which offers first class dedicated point of contact service and a range of added-value services for IFAs. These services include training and development, online investment information, business continuity and access to industry experts.

As well as distributing its products through intermediaries, Zurich also deals directly with business customers in the public and private sectors. Again, it goes further than just selling its services, by offering information and assistance. An example of this is Riskline, a telephone helpline offering expert risk management advice for the cost of a phone call.

In the UK, Zurich has worked with a number of strategic partners to develop products specifically for target audiences.

Recent Developments

Last year the Health and Safety Executive (HSE) warned the insurance industry of the dangers in entering confined spaces. In response, Zurich acquired the capability of offering and carrying out Remote Visual Inspections (RVI). The equipment involved includes a hand held manipulator with camera and light source, which can be inserted into any confined space, feeding back images of the inside. RVI reduces the need for man access, thus lowering risks and repeatable images provide a more accurate inspection into previously inaccessible areas.

Zurich is in the process of transforming its business to compete in the changing financial services marketplace. In line with their strategy to strengthen the Global Life Insurance business. In turn, Zurich announced its intention to split the manufacturing and distribution arms of its UK Life business and, as a result has founded Openwork, currently known as Zurich Advice Network, which will be launched in the summer of 2005. Openwork will be directly authorised by the Financial Services Authority as an independent multi-tied distribution network who will distribute life, pensions, investment and mortgage products. The aim is to create the largest, most profitable and most respected adviser-based distribution network in UK financial services. It will be a key business partner for the manufacturing arm of Zurich who will provide Openwork with protection and investment products

(under the Sterling brand). Zurich Assurance intends to be a major player in the protection market and has applied rate reductions to three products – Adaptable Term Plan (ATP), Decreasing Mortgage Cover (DMC) and the Lifestyle Critical Illness plan, with further enhancements and rate reviews planned for the Income Protection Plan (IPP) and Adaptable Life Plan (ALP) during the second half of the year. Offering competitive products will enable Zurich to compete effectively in the marketplace as a product provider, offering its products to the whole spectrum of intermediaries.

Promotion

Zurich is the official shirt sponsor of the British & Irish Lions' Tour to New Zealand in 2005. As an obvious extension of its support for the domestic rugby game, the brand will be the sole sponsor of the shirts and training kit with the Zurich logo displayed prominently.

Zurich will also be continuing its association with the World Economic Forum (WEF), which is an independent, international organisation incorporated as a Swiss not-for-profit foundation. Zurich achieves its promotional goals through a variety of other channels including technical articles and advertising in specialist trade press, industry representation at Government level, membership of industry bodies, event sponsorship, newsletters and websites. This type of activity allows it to share its expertise with customers and represent their views.

Brand Values

Managing the brand in a responsible way is fundamental to Zurich's business approach. It has therefore created an environment that is permeated by value and trust. Pragmatic in its approach, Zurich is looking towards the future without losing sight of its core values and loyal customer base.

Zurich is an ambitious and vigorous but fair player, aiming to treat people as individuals and offer products and services that people really want and need.

Zurich places great importance on being a good corporate citizen, in consideration of its employees as well as the wider community.

www.zurich.co.uk

THINGS YOU DIDN'T KNOW ABOUT

Zurich

❯ 1886 Herman Hollerith invented a punch-card counting machine (a milestone on the way to digital data processing). Zurich starts its computer age by introducing Hollerith machines for statistics and accounting in 1928.

❯ 1912 Zurich became the first European insurance company in the US.

❯ Zurich insures the majority of Fortune's Global 100 companies.

❯ Over 50,000 hours have been volunteered by 30% of Zurich's employees through its CSR programmes.

CHARLIE HOULT
Chief Executive Officer
Loewy

LOEWY

About Loewy

Loewy delivers brand communications in business to business sectors including tech, telecom, professional services, corporate and public sector as well as consumer marketing in food, fashion and retail. The firm employs 100 people at two locations in London – and continues to grow by acquisition.

Current clients include Eurostar, Computacenter, Kimberly-Clark, Reed Exhibitions, BAA, Welsh Development Agency, Pfizer, Oxford University and AOL.

Loewy is the creative business behind iconic brands of the 20th century including the Coca-Cola bottle, Lucky Strike packaging, Shell corporate identity, Greyhound buses and Concorde interior.

www.loewygroup.com

Loewy has been in the business of brands for 75 years. This activity was called 'industrial design' when we covered Gestetner copiers or Greyhound buses in streamlined casings that hid the ugly workings. It was called 'product differentiation' when we created elegant styles for Frigidaire fridges or the Philishave. It was called 'packaging' when we reshaped Coca-Cola's bottle to the icon it became. And, it was called 'corporate identity' when we redesigned the Shell logo in 1973 which is still used today.

Whatever the activity was called, it is 'creativity' added to 'customer-centric thinking' which made these businesses into famous brands. With a modicum of vision and some management bravery…

It's fantastic to see the rise of branding in the business community, a field where differentiation is so important but branding still immature.

In fact, it's easy to put together an argument that says branding activity is a much tougher challenge in business to business sectors than in consumer sectors, because there are less physical entities to plaster with 'stuff', less turnaround of traded units, less investment in profile and promotion.

As we go global in business services – software development, call centres, legal work, internet, communications – it is ever more difficult to define a range of 'uniques' for your business, as against a panoply of competitors. There are just so many people doing the same thing.

Paradoxically, this drives the big brands still bigger and could be said to further polarise the market, rather than acting for diversity. In a world where trust needs to be earned, it is the badge of a trusted brand that can lift a product or service, old or new. Witness Microsoft, for instance, which fuels not so much a business as a mid-sized economy with its power to build and grow.

So, how do we find differentiators? In analysis, it often happens that jettisoning a broad brush approach at one level, descends into niche definitions that become equally crowded and difficult to 'own'. A solution of the moment is the intuitive response – gut instinct is very fashionable.

We also see much debate within business about the difference between building a brand and building a reputation. Do business brands only differentiate on the customers and relationships they have developed? Or, are there more intangibles which need to set into play?

A brand should do more than a reputation.

Here and now

For the Business Superbrands in this book, it's great to see them seizing the opportunity and delivering such strong marketing propositions. They prove the value of managing their reputation, the emotional asset, the goodwill of colleagues… their brand.

The Business Superbrands shame the vast business to business market that is missing out. The tools of branding, marketing, advertising, communications, design are the tools of our trade and are so well advanced that it is staggering how anyone can be left behind. And, yet, so many business to business brands are left behind.

There are many factors for this. Let's pick on ugly design (for which, read: haphazard, inconsistent, random, cliché). Today's digital design tools can be very harmful if they fall into the wrong hands. Not only can different designers get hold of briefs from a company and go off in different directions which create inconsistencies in the delivery of brand communications, but also computers are everywhere – offering different colleagues the chance to toy with templates, styling and even 'get creative' themselves.

Careful control and management of your brand asset is imperative – and communicating this requirement to the board of directors needs a strong respect for the marketing department. Here, too, come the challenges. So many firms have strong personalities in management, finance and sales who talk tough to the marketing 'cost centre', so it takes a confident soul to run this department.

One test we deploy for awareness of this challenge is the 'Reception Test'… Do the receptionists get away with creating their own signs for their lobby area, sign-in book or cranky swinging door? Or, does the marketing team have a handle on this most important of showcases for brand consistency? And, even in the most outer-lying offices of a business empire? Do you have anarchy?

I think you know the symptoms. The cure starts from the top, not the bottom.

Best practice will out

Competition is coming! The competitive threats of globalisation, free trade, expanding Europe give rise to low cost alternatives. Prosperity in major markets has provided the resources for many organisations to expand head-to-head in new markets… Technology is driving cheaper product into the mass market. The media is diversifying across numerous new channels, making it harder to reach a clear target. All these will continue to drive the pressure higher for the leaders and harsher for the losers.

And, the 'free form economy' is going to stretch and flex the business of brands. ebay today, retailing tomorrow. Business relationships are changing as the internet matures and every business tackles the global channel that is open to them. And, all our roles as middlemen are being redefined.

Response to brand building

We see that pressure coming through in managing the Return On Investment in brand building. ROI is the all important indicator of marketing effectiveness and business stewardship. CEOs are hiring procurement specialists to track all expenses across a business and Marketing Departments are not immune. The business of branding and creativity is now coming under strict scrutiny for its value creation.

For us, we have redefined ROI. In Loewy terms, this stands for Return On IDEAS.

It's not about the investment input, it's how ideas perform. In a world where so much competition is bringing so many similar business models head-to-head, it's distilling the intellectual property into liquid gold, which will pay the dividends.

Cost effectiveness is one key performance indicator, but branding needs to be judged on CREATIVE effectiveness. The right creative idea can deliver exponential impact to a business. And, managed tightly across a multi-disciplinary team, creative ideas can be ramped up with only marginal extra expense so that the idea can play out across the whole range of media and communications options. Here, too, is a crucial area where the new world of creative services can leverage branded communications.

To understand effectiveness, we must understand a business's growth strategy. The bright agencies need to be business gurus first and marketing supremos second – because it's the empathy with a client's challenge which is paramount. This is where our agency's key directors spend most of their time with the clients. Our 'delivery team' has the depth and breadth to turn their hand to any brief and come back with a really tight, impactful response. So, we need to make them think entrepreneurially, understand the sales process, tune their antenna to the business challenges.

Thoughts on delivery

Business to business marketing budgets aren't the largest in the business. Some of the businesses are far more complex in their products or services than consumer-facing companies, be they for FMCG brands, travel or car companies. This makes it even more imperative for an agency to invest up-front in the thinking and the creativity. It is ever more important to distil the 'Iceberg Principle'… the one-eighth of the business story that we put 'above the waterline', which gives the lie of the seven-eighths that provide the foundations, albeit out of sight.

Most of all, the best business to business brands offer a rock of stability, but scope for significant flexibility. Today's businesses need to flex and stretch as they keep pace. The survival of Business Superbrands depends on a heap of strategic research, a bold reading of gut feel and some well directed creative fireworks.

3M

PIP FRANKISH
General Manager, Corporate Marketing & Communications

Pip is General Manager, Corporate Marketing & Communications for 3M's UK/Ireland operations and previously held other B2B communications roles at Texaco and ABB as well as within 3M. In her current assignment, she is responsible for the protection and enhancement of 3M's corporate reputation, including all brand assets.

ANDREW LOCK
Marketing Communications Manager

Andrew is Marketing Communications Manager for 3M UK and local leader for the 3M Global Brand Asset Management programme. Andrew has held a number of sales and marketing roles at 3M on a UK and European basis, Marketing Communications positions at XEROX and Synopsys together with some agency side experience.

Allied Irish Bank (GB)

JOAN MULCAHY
Chief Operating Officer

Joan joined AIB in 1973. As a qualified accountant she has gained experience in industry as well as in a wide range of banking areas including corporate and retail banking, treasury and financial control. In 2000 Joan moved from her role as Financial Director for the Bank's UK operation, AIB Group (UK) plc, to the role of Chief Operating Officer. This role has a wide remit which includes strategic marketing and brand management. Joan is a graduate of University College Dublin, holds ACCA and MBA qualifications and is a member of the Board of AIB Group (UK) plc.

AMEC

TANIA HORTON
Global Brand

Tania joined AMEC in 2001. She was promoted to brand guardian in 2004 and is responsible for AMEC's global brand activities. Tania has over eight years experience in a variety of business to business marketing and communications roles.

JULIET SYCHRAVA
Communications Director

Juliet joined AMEC in October 2003 from UK top ten law firm Norton Rose, where she was Head of Communications. Having started out as a financial analyst and then journalist for Euromoney and the Financial Times, Juliet was previously at Brunswick, and Dewe Rogerson, the leading London PR firms, and spent four years working for Accenture.

Arriva

JULIAN EVANS
Director of Corporate Communications

Julian joined Arriva as Director of Corporate Communications in 1999. He has been employed in the private, public and voluntary sectors. Holding senior communications positions in the retail, utility, finance and transport sectors he has worked for a number of organisations including the Co-op, Thomas Cook, Christian Aid and East Midlands Electricity.

CATHERINE MASON
Marketing & Customer Services Director

Catherine, a University of Liverpool graduate, gained her MBA from Henley Management College. She has held a series of consumer marketing roles with top UK companies including GlaxoSmithKline and Dairy Crest. Currently Marketing and Customer Services Director with Arriva's UK Bus business, which she joined in 2000, she has been involved in brand building and marketing activities.

Barclays

JIM HYTNER
Marketing Director

Jim joined Barclays in October 2004 and is responsible for developing the Barclays brand and all UK marketing activity. Prior to joining Barclays, Jim spent twelve years in TV, spanning BSkyB, Channel 5 and ITV, having learnt his trade at Kraft and Coca-Cola. He is also a visiting lecturer at Wharton Business School.

BASF

CHRIS WILSON
Corporate Communications Manager

Chris has been helping to promote and protect BASF's corporate brand for 27 years. As well as being responsible for advertising and media relations in the UK, he is the company's European Brand Champion, helping to implement the worldwide branding project which BASF introduced in March 2004. A former journalist, he moved into PR with a new town development corporation before joining BASF in 1977.

Basildon Bond

MARK BEAUMONT-THOMAS
Marketing Communications Manager

Mark has spent his whole career in the stationery industry. He has worked in various marketing and sales management roles at John Dickinson. Prior to this he worked at Spicers, the market leading office products wholesaler, also in a variety of marketing and sales management roles, and as general manager of their Birmingham regional distribution centre. Currently, Mark is responsible for all marketing communications at John Dickinson Stationery.

DEBORAH MUNRO-WILKINSON
Brand Manager

Debbie has worked for thirteen years in the stationery and office products industry and has gained a wealth of experience in product management in this marketplace. She has been responsible for developing many of John Dickinson's market leading brands, including Black n' Red, Challenge and Lion Brand. In the last four years she has been expanding the presence of Basildon Bond in both new and existing markets.

Blue Circle

MIKE LOMAX
Marketing Communications Manager

Mike has been in Marketing and Brand Communications for 25 years, working with blue-chip brands such as Pilkington, GE and GEC, Baxi and Owens Corning. Since May 2001, Mike has been in charge of Marketing Communications for Blue Circle cement products. Blue Circle is a brand of Lafarge, the largest building materials manufacturer in the world.

BMRB

RICHARD ASQUITH
Managing Director

After gaining a BA (Hons) degree in Economics, Richard joined RSGB rising to Board Director in 1990. In January 1999 he joined BMRB to run TGI, custom media research and BMRB's omnibus services. In August 2004 he was made Managing Director of BMRB. He has managed many high profile UK industry media research projects and proprietary strategic research for a wide range of press, broadcast and agency clients.

STEVE COOKE
Marketing Director

Steve is responsible for the marketing communications strategy for BMRB and the KMR Group. He headed up the rebranding of BMRB, resulting in the new identity launched in March 2005. Steve has BA (Hons) in Geography and Management Studies and a post graduate diploma in Marketing. He has previously worked for television sales house TSMS and media independent BBJ.

Bosch

ROBERT MEIER
Managing Director

Robert was appointed to head up the UK headquarters of Bosch in July 2004 bringing with him over 22 years experience of working with the global Bosch Group to the role. Previously commercial director for the Diesel Systems division in Feuerbach, Germany, one of Bosch's largest plants, his responsibilities involved worldwide ventures. He spent time at Bosch's headquarters in Germany, in the area of planning and controlling with overseas subsidiaries such as the UK, and was also advisor for Bosch sites in Scandinavia and South America.

BEVERLEY DANIELS
Corporate Affairs Manager

Beverley's long career with Bosch started in 1979 and her experience includes working in the original equipment division and as project support manager. She was appointed corporate affairs manager in March 2004 and in her current role she is responsible for internal communications, brand management, corporate PR and PR for the original equipment division. Beverley also sits on the SMMT's (The Society of Motor Manufacturers and Traders) Public Affairs Committee.

BSI

DAVID BROWN
Corporate Development Director

As a member of the BSI Group Executive, David is responsible for strategic planning, mergers and acquisitions, and Group Marketing (including Corporate Branding, PR/Communications and the Group's web presence). David has held senior appointments in both the US and the UK, with specific responsibility for strategy and M&A in KPMG, Arthur D Little, Morgan Crucible, TRW/Lucas Varity and Rolls-Royce.

PUNIT SHAH
Group Marketing Manager

Punit is responsible for the implementation of BSI's global branding strategy across 110 countries. Punit started his career agency side and joined the BSI Group in 1997. He became Group eBusiness Manager in 2000 leading the team that developed BSI's highly successful online presence.

Business Post

PAUL CARVELL
Chief Executive Officer

Paul joined Business Post Group as CEO in 2001 and immediately initiated a detailed review of Group strategy. He was instrumental in steering through a three year plan that saw the company move successfully from 'single product' status to its present position as a broad based supplier of a full range of branded express delivery services. Paul led negotiations for a licence to operate mail services and presided over the successful launch of UK Mail, the first alternative postal service in over 350 years. His earlier career included senior positions with TNT, Christian Salvesen, Transport Development Group and GE Capital.

CASIO

TOMOKI SATO
Director

Tomoki is Director responsible for Corporate Strategy and Marketing at Casio UK. He has previously worked as a product planner both in the UK and Japan for several years and has also been responsible for new business development, where he gained significant experience working with manufacturers across Europe on joint programmes. He was assigned his current role in February 2003 and has worked to deliver the future CASIO Brand Strategy for UK.

Caterpillar

STUART LEVENICK
Caterpillar Group President & Executive Office member

Stuart is responsible for Asia Pacific marketing and operations, global purchasing and human services. With broad experience in North America, Russia, Southeast Asia and Japan during his 28 years with the company, he currently chairs Caterpillar's global brand nomenclature committee.

JENNIFER WILFONG
Manager of Caterpillar's Marketing & Brand Management

Jennifer is Manager of Caterpillar's Marketing & Brand Management department, with responsibility for marketing communications, corporate identity, Trademark Licensing, Cat.com web strategy, customer events and product demonstration venues. Her eighteen-year career with Cat has included roles in marketing, product development, distribution, order fulfillment, and Cat Financial.

CIM

ANNABEL PRITCHARD
Corporate Brand Manager

Annabel is the Corporate Brand Manager of The Chartered Institute of Marketing, the world's largest professional marketing body, managing all aspects of brand communication and reputation worldwide. This ranges from brand strategy to design, website, PR and events. She has relaunched CIM's membership magazine 'the marketer', and rebranded CIM's conference centre, Moor Hall. Previously, Annabel led the marketing for PA Consulting Group's Strategy and Marketing Practice and was a researcher at Nestlé UK.

CIMA

HELEN DAWSON
Brand Marketing Manager

Helen joined CIMA in 1999 and has worked in the Brand Team for five years. Helen's role involves all brand development work including the more recent brand engagement project with CIMA's staff and has responsibility for the corporate identity across all marketing material. Helen played an integral part in the development of CIMA's new brand identity.

RAY PERRY
Director of Brand

Ray joined CIMA as Director of Brand in April 2002. Prior to joining CIMA, Ray was Director of Corporate Marketing at the Chartered Institute of Marketing. He is a Fellow of CIM and holds an Executive MBA from Henley Management College. Ray championed CIMA's new corporate identity and re-branding process in 2004.

IoD

ANDREW MAIN WILSON
Chief Operating Officer

Andrew has 20 years experience building and transforming premium quality service industry brands, as Marketing Director of Thomas Cook and Sales and Marketing Director of Citibank Diners Club. Andrew joined the Institute of Directors in 1996 to transform the brand, commercial activities and significantly expand membership. Membership has since increased 50% to 54,000, and revenues have increased 100%.

JCB

CHRIS WRIGHT
Worldwide Marketing Director

Chris has responsibility for all JCB marketing activities worldwide. Chris has an MBA from INSEAD, and was previously Creative Director at St Luke's advertising agency, where he created campaigns for IKEA, BT, Peperami and the BBC. JCB is Europe's largest manufacturer of construction, industrial and agricultural machinery with manufacturing operations in the UK, US, Brazil and India.

JWT

NICK BELL
Executive Creative Director

Nick took up the role of Executive Creative Director for JWT London in May 2003 and has overseen the development of some of JWT's most successful campaigns of recent years. He is a highly experienced and awarded creative – his personal role-call of honours includes a Cannes Grand Prix, four Cannes Gold Lions, two D&AD Silver Awards, ten Campaign Press Silver Awards, two New York Clio Gold Awards and a US Andy Award of Excellence.

SIMON BOLTON
CEO UK & Ireland

Simon's professional career has taken him to India, Malaysia, Thailand and the US. He became Group Chief Executive of JWT UK in 2001. Since then he has overseen the move of the agency to 1 Knightsbridge Green, driven the development of JWT's integrated communications offering and grown the 600-strong agency to its top two position in the UK. Major new business wins under Simon's leadership include Axa, HSBC, Samsung, Kingsmill and Knorr.

Kall Kwik

JOHN BLYTH
Head of Marketing

John has been Head of Marketing at Kall Kwik UK since 2000 where his remit is to guide and protect the brand. A repositioning of the business based on its ability to deliver tailored solutions has increased its salience to corporate clients, and reinforced its market leading status.

Land Securities

EMMA DENNE
Director of Corporate Communication

Emma joined Land Securities in 2000 to the newly created role of Head of Corporate Communication, since then she has been responsible for developing the Group's corporate communication strategy and team. Prior to this she was Account Director at Financial Dynamics, a leading business communication consultancy, where she headed FD's property sector specialist team.

FRANCIS SALWAY
Group Chief Executive

Francis was appointed Group Chief Executive in July 2004. Since joining Land Securities in 2000 he has been instrumental in developing the Group's product range and was the driving force behind the decision to focus Land Securities activities on three core sectors of the UK property markets. He is committed to the Group's brand values which he believes sustain its market leading position.

McCann Erickson

ROBERT CAMPBELL
Executive Creative Director

Robert began his advertising career as a copywriter and has since worked at many of the best agencies in London. He started two major London advertising agencies: Rainey Kelly Campbell Roalfe and before that, the Banks Partnership (now Banks Hoggins O'Shea FCB). Robert has been chairman of British Television Awards, British Radio Awards, Campaign Press Awards and Campaign Poster Awards, and has served on a number of the major global and domestic awards juries.

RUPERT HOWELL
Chairman & President EMEA

Rupert began his career at Ogilvy in 1979, and later joined Grey and Young & Rubicam where he became London's most successful New Business Director, winning over £100 million of business. He founded his own agency, Howell Henry Chaldecott Lury in 1987 which sold ten years later for £24 million to Chime Communications plc and in January 2000 was voted UK Agency of the Decade by 'Campaign' magazine. After a year's earnout, Rupert became Joint CEO of Chime, but left exactly five years after selling HHCL.

Mediaedge:cia

MAINARDO DE NARDIS
Worldwide Chief Executive

With 25 years communication experience behind him, Mainardo has led Mediaedge:cia as Worldwide CEO from its creation in January 2002. He has also been an integral part of the brand's heritage, having managed some of the businesses which would later become Mediaedge:cia since 1987. Mainardo is responsible for the Mediaedge:cia brand positioning, a task he is particularly passionate about.

Michael Page International

MICHAEL STEVENSON
Marketing Director

Michael has overall responsibility for global marketing across the Group. His early career started at Lever Brothers before moving into the agency world with Ogilvy & Mather and Bates Dorland, and onto Mazda Cars UK before joining Michael Page in 2000. Michael firmly believes in the accountability of marketing and is committed to providing simple, business-focused branded solutions.

Mintel

JENNY CATLIN
European PR Manager

Having joined Mintel three years ago, Jenny initially focused on PR campaigns solely in the UK, but she is now using her formal training as a European linguist to further develop the European operations. Alongside her PR role, Jenny works to improve internal communications throughout the company, encouraging everyone at Mintel to be an ambassador of the brand.

AMANDA LINTOTT
UK PR Manager

Amanda joined Mintel ten years ago, and has worked in a variety of roles. Having settled in public relations, Amanda has been closely involved in growing the communications enterprise from a UK to a global operation. She is based in the London office and plays an integral part in Mintel's brand development.

npower

GIUSEPPE DI VITA
Head of Sales & Marketing

Giuseppe has been with npower since 2000 and prior to his new appointment held the role of Head of Product Management and Commercial, responsible for e-commerce, pricing and change management. Giuseppe took up his new role in July 2004 and his role unites the brand, marketing and sales activities, ensuring customers receive clear and consistent messages across the board.

KEVIN PEAKE
Head of Customer Marketing

Kevin joined npower in May 2000 as Head of Brand. He became Head of Customer Marketing in 2004 and is now responsible for brand strategy, internal marketing, market research, advertising and sponsorship. Previously he worked in marketing and brand at Comet, TSB and Abbey National. Kevin is instrumental in the npower cricket sponsorship and Wembley stadium sponsorship.

O₂

CATH KEERS
Customer Director

Cath became Customer Director at O₂ in January 2004 where she is responsible for the Brand Vision and the Customer Strategy which defines how O₂ differentiates itself in the market place. Prior to this appointment Cath was O₂ UK Marketing Director where she was responsible for all of O₂'s marketing activity in the UK for both the business and consumer sectors. She successfully launched the O₂ brand in the UK, including the development of the innovative interactive sponsorship of Big Brother which firmly positioned O₂ as the leader in text messaging.

Office Angels

SARAH EL-DOORI
Associate Director, Marketing & Public Relations

Sarah was promoted to her current role in 2003. She manages all elements of the marketing strategy for the nine brands in the Ajilon portfolio, including Office Angels, Computer People, Jonathan Wren, Ajilon Finance, Ajilon Executive, OAexec, Roevin, Ajilon Consulting and Ajilon Learning.

P&O

PETER SMITH
Director, Communications & Strategy

Peter joined P&O in 1994 and joined the main board in 1999. As well as being responsible for communications and strategy his remit also includes human resources, corporate risk and government relations. Peter has a team of five who manage P&O's corporate communications activity.

Pindar

DAVID JESSON
Group Marketing Director

David joined Pindar in September 2003 and is responsible for the Pindar Organisations marketing and communications strategy and implementation. David has responsibility for the successful sports marketing campaigns supporting the UK's top professional sailors. Before joining Pindar he held senior marketing positions with Marlow Foods, McCain Foods and American Home Products.

ANDREW PINDAR
Chairman

Andrew, a 25-year veteran with the company, has been a Director since September 1982 and succeeded his father Tom as chairman of the Pindar Organisation in November 1997. He continues to build on Pindar's position as one of the UK's leading printing specialists, creating new value from more complex and integrated communication opportunities.

PricewaterhouseCoopers LLP

JON GELDART
Marketing Director

Jon is PricewaterhouseCoopers' UK Marketing Director responsible for the Middle market and regions. He sits on the firms' Global Middle Market marketing leadership group and has additional responsibilities encompassing Knowledge Management, and CRM within the UK. Jon is a Business Superbrands Council member.

Prontaprint

KEITH DAVIDSON
Head of Marketing

Keith was appointed Head of Marketing at Prontaprint in 2000 and oversaw a major rebranding exercise designed to reflect the company's positioning as the premier provider of print-on-demand, business to business communication solutions across the UK and Ireland. Two years on, Prontaprint became the first print industry brand to be acknowledged as a Business Superbrand. Davidson, who is responsible for all aspects of Prontaprint's marketing and brand management, maintains a strong focus on Prontaprint's brand development strategy and commissioned a brand review programme in 2004.

LAIRD MACKAY
Managing Director

Laird was appointed Managing Director of Prontaprint Limited in June 2004 with the remit of overseeing all company operations. One of his key objectives is focusing on opportunities to further leverage the brand's positioning in the business to business marketplace. Before assuming his current role, Laird was Operations Director with Initial City Link and the world renowned Federal Express Company. Laird also served in the RAF as flight commander on a helicopter squadron, and navigator.

Reed

JAMES REED
Executive Chairman

James is Executive Chairman of Reed, the UK's recruitment, HR and training specialist. He became Operations Director of Reed Employment in 1994, and was appointed Chief Executive in 1997. Since then, through organic growth, Reed has more than doubled in size, reed.co.uk has become the UK's leading private sector recruitment site, currently carrying over 200,000 job opportunities, and Reed in Partnership has become a leading private sector provider of Welfare to Work services. Before joining Reed, James worked for the Body Shop, Saatchi & Saatchi, Afghanaid, Help the Aged, and latterly as a producer of documentaries and factual programmes for BBC TV. James graduated from Oxford in 1984 with a degree in Philosophy, Politics and Economics (PPE) and he subsequently gained an MBA from the Harvard Business School.

Rio Tinto

CHERRY DEGEER
Manager Corporate Communications

Cherry joined Rio Tinto in 1997 and is responsible for Rio Tinto's corporate communications activities and global visual identity, promoting design, editorial and brand consistency across the company's business units. Cherry's role includes the co-ordination of all internal and external corporate communication projects: websites, intranet, video, multimedia, advertising, printed literature and she is also editor of Review, Rio Tinto's corporate magazine.

ANDREW VICKERMAN
Head of Communication & Sustainable Development

Andrew has overall responsibility for corporate communications, health, safety and environment activities for Rio Tinto. His corporate communications responsibilities encompass, media, sustainable development, public affairs and community relations in addition to communications strategy and brand management. Andrew has a BA, MA and PhD from Cambridge University and prior to joining Rio Tinto in 1991 he worked as a development economist and as a consultant for international organisations, including the World Bank.

Samsung

IN SOO KIM
CEO & President of Samsung Electronics Europe

In Soo Kim joined Samsung Corporation in 1976. He is now Head of the European and UK operations of Samsung Electronics. Prior to this, he was an Executive Vice President of Corporate HR and has held a number of other strategic roles during his career at Samsung Electronics. Increasing the Samsung brand power further in Europe and enhancing Samsung's standing as a premium consumer electronics company are In Soo Kim's main objectives and he is focusing his organisation and efforts on achieving this target.

HADRIAN BAUMANN
Senior Manager, European Marketing

Hadrian was appointed to his current position in 2002. He is responsible for implementing the company's European brand and retail marketing strategy. Extensive working experience with Samsung Electronics in Korea, a two-year stint at a consultancy and an MBA provide Hadrian with a strong background to help building Samsung into a household name in Europe.

SDL International

MARK LANCASTER
Chairman & CEO

Mark progressed his career through to international Development Director with Ashton-Tate before founding SDL in 1992 to provide services for the globalization of software. He is responsible for the strategic development of SDL, driving it to market leadership with annual revenues over £60 million. He has been instrumental in defining, reinforcing and supporting the SDL brand.

TERRY LAWLOR
VP Worldwide Marketing

Terry is responsible for marketing strategy and execution worldwide and since joining SDL has helped strengthen the SDL brand. Prior to SDL he spent over 20 years in IT with more than ten years marketing software and service solutions at SupportSoft and Informix Software. He has held senior management positions in marketing, sales, customer services and R&D.

Shell

VENETIA HOWES
Vice President Global Brands

Venetia has responsibility for the strategic development of the Shell brand. Her experience includes business to business marketing in chemicals, shipping and lubricants, and she was previously the Marketing Manager for Shell's global aviation business. She took the CIM post-graduate Diploma mid-career and is an active member of the Worshipful Company of Marketors.

RAOUL PINNELL
Chairman, Shell Brands International AG

Raoul developed an early interest in business whilst at school, Bradfield College, leaving to pursue Business Studies, subsequently followed by a post graduate Diploma in Marketing. Following seventeen years with Nestlé, five years at Prudential and three years at NatWest, Shell International appointed him to head its Global Brands & Communications division in 1997.

Thames Water

JOHN EVANS
Marketing & Strategy Director

John joined the company in July 2003 as Global Marketing Director, having previously been Marketing Director of Powergen since May 1999. His current role as Marketing and Strategy Director includes global strategy and brand management, championing customer management and supporting business development. John has been a member of ISBA since October 2000, firstly on the Council and now as a member of the Executive Committee.

MELANIE HARRIES
Brand Manager

Melanie joined the company in September 1999, working in the International Business Development team, where her work took her to Thailand, Indonesia and China. She has worked in the brand team in the divisional centre for three years, and her current role includes managing brand and marketing communications activities, primarily in the UK and US.

The Red Consultancy

MIKE MORGAN
Chief Executive

Mike joined red in 1996 and was promoted to chief executive in 2004. Together with managing directors Andrew Baiden and Amanda Duncan, he heads a seven strong board reporting to parent company Incepta. Mike's clients include McDonald's, DHL and Maxxium.

TNS

CHRIS GOARD
Group Marketing Director

Chris has 25 years of marketing experience within the consumer, industrial and business to business sectors across Europe, the US and Asia Pacific. He began his career in client services at ACNielsen, followed by international FMCG marketing and business development roles within Quaker, Purina, Hermesetas and Beatrice Foods. For the past twelve years Chris has worked as Group Marketing Director for the Market Information group TNS which operates a global network spanning 70 countries. Chris' responsibilities include managing the corporate brand, driving TNS' philosophy of the sixth sense of business globally and co-ordinating marketing internationally.

Towers Perrin

Our role is simple: to understand our clients' needs and create marketing and sales campaigns that meet those needs. Marketing is an integral part of the firm which enables the unit to play a pivotal role in research, CRM programmes and pitches and proposals. In parallel, our marketing services team creates some of the most innovative professional services programmes around. Our strong brand means two things: it reduces the cost of sale – people know who we are and what we stand for. Secondly, it means a great place to work.

Travis Perkins

IAN GOLDSMITH
Group Planning Director

Ian has been in planning roles for Blue Circle and Travis Perkins for more than fifteen years, having previously worked in strategy and management consulting. Ian joined Travis Perkins five years ago and within the Group Planning role has responsibility for Corporate Strategy, Property, Facilities Management, Environment and Marketing.

Voca

PHIL KENNEDY
Head of Brand Marketing & Communications

Phil's primary objective is to create, deliver and market the new brand identity that will reflect and enhance the commercial mandate Voca is pursuing in the UK and Internationally. Prior to this, Phil has worked for Prudential, Royal Bank of Scotland, Direct Line Financial Services and N.A.G. He was part of a team that set up a new D2C financial services and his experience also includes working on the agency side, including Saatchi & Saatchi and J.Walter Thompson.

DAVID SEAR
Chief Marketing Officer

David joined Voca in 2003 and plays a key part in the new commercial vision of the business. Previously Chief Operating Officer at WorldPay Group plc, part of RBS, David ran the company as it established its position as a major global player in the adoption and development of e-commerce. David also spent seven years as European Managing Director at Equifax Cheque Services – the world's largest cheque guarantee company. Prior to that David worked with WH Smith Group.

XEROX

RICHARD WERGAN
European Head of Brand & Marketing Communications

Richard was appointed to this position in November 2001. He is responsible for developing communications strategy and implementing marketing activity in 22 European countries across all disciplines – Corporate Brand and Product Advertising, Direct Marketing, e-Marketing, Sponsorship, Events, Internal Communications and Marketing Collaterals. Richard is also the European Representative on the Xerox Global Executive Marketing Board, responsible for marketing across the Xerox Corporation.

Richard joined Xerox from the Y&R Group where he was Account Managing Director of IBM for EMEA. He has spent the last fifteen years working in the marketing communications industry, working in agencies and multinationals. Passionate for integrated marketing, strategic planning and measurement, he co-founded a direct communications agency in London in the mid 1990s. Richard started his career in Marketing at Unilever in sales and brand management.

Yellow Pages

PHILIPPA BUTTERS
Head of Design

Since joining Yell in 1997, Philippa has worked on the creation and implementation of all the product brand identities, including the transformation of the Yellow Pages and Business Pages directories, the Yell group corporate identity and most recently the design implementation for the new Yellow Pages 118 24 7 service.

ZenithOptimedia

GERRY BOYLE
Managing Director

Gerry began his career at Leo Burnett before joining Michaelides & Bednash as a media strategist. Gerry joined Zenith Media in August 1999 as Communications Director with responsibility for bringing a greater level of consumer insight and qualitative understanding to client's business, and building the planning proposition. In January 2000 he was promoted to Managing Partner and Head of Planning. The ZenithOptimedia merger in 2003 saw a change in management structure where Gerry became Deputy Managing Director, before being recently promoted to Managing Director.

ANTONY YOUNG
Chief Executive UK Group

Originally from New Zealand, Antony started his career at Saatchi & Saatchi NZ, before moving to Hong Kong as Regional Media Director for Saatchi & Saatchi Asia. He was appointed Chief Executive of Zenith Media, launching the network across Asia, including establishing the biggest agency in China. After six successful years which included twice winning 'Agency of the Year', Antony moved to London in 2003 to lead the merger of ZenithOptimedia in the UK. He has been instrumental in launching ZenithOptimedia as 'The ROI Agency'.

Zurich

JAMES HILL
Corporate Marketing Director

James is a marketing graduate, Chartered marketeer and holds an MBA in strategic marketing. For the last ten years his responsibilities have been in corporate marketing. As Zurich's Corporate Marketing Director James manages all central aspects of brand development. This includes advertising and sponsorship, corporate hospitality and events, corporate identity, research, brand portfolio positioning and transition projects and aspects of the businesses web interface.

CHARLOTTE THURSZ
Worldwide Head of Brand

Charlotte joined Zurich in 2001 to help develop the brand in the UK as the company started its transition from Eagle Star and Allied Dunbar. She now has responsibility for establishing Zurich as a strong and compelling brand globally. Her time at Zurich follows a decade of classic domestic and international consumer marketing with fmcg giants P&G, GSK, and The Coca-Cola Company.

Directory

3M
3M United Kingdom PLC
3M Centre
Cain Road
Bracknell
Berkshire
RG12 8HT

Adecco
Adecco UK Ltd
Adecco House
Elstree Way
Borehamwood
Hertfordshire
WD6 1HY

Allied Irish Bank (GB)
Allied Irish Bank (GB)
Bankcentre
Belmont Road
Uxbridge
Middlesex
UB8 1SA

AMEC
AMEC plc
65 Carter Lane
London
EC4V 5HF

Arriva
Arriva plc
Admiral Way
Doxford International Business Park
Sunderland
SR3 3XP

Barclays
Barclays Bank PLC
1 Churchill Place
London
E14 5HP

BASF
BASF plc
PO Box 4
Earl Road
Chadle Hulme
Cheadle
Cheshire
SK8 6QG

Basildon Bond
John Dickinson Stationery Limited
Sawston
Cambridge
CB2 4XD

BDO Stoy Hayward
BDO Stoy Hayward LLP
8 Baker Street
London
W1U 3LL

BG Group
BG Group
Thames Valley Park
Reading
Berkshire
RG6 1PT

Blue Circle
Lafarge Cement UK
Manor Court
Chilton
Oxfordshire
OX11 0RN

BMRB
BMRB
Ealing Gateway
26-30 Uxbridge Road
London
W5 2BP

Bosch
Robert Bosch Ltd
PO Box 98
Uxbridge
Middlesex
UB9 5HN

BSI
BSI Group
389 Chiswick High Road
London
W4 4AL

BT
BT
BT Centre
81 Newgate Street
London
EC1A 7AJ

Business Post
Business Post Ltd
Express House
Wolseley Drive
Birmingham
B8 2SQ

Cable & Wireless
Cable & Wireless
Lakeside House
Cain Road
Bracknell
RG12 1XL

CASIO
Casio Electronics Co.Ltd
Unit 6
1000 North Circular Road
London
NW2 7JD

Caterpillar
Caterpillar Inc.
100 NE Adams Street
Peoria
IL 61629-6150
USA

CIM
The Chartered Institute of Marketing
Moor Hall
Cookham
Berkshire
SL6 9QH

CIMA
CIMA
26 Chapter Street
London
SW1P 4NP

CNBC Europe
CNBC Europe
10 Fleet Place
London
EC4M 7QS

Cohn & Wolfe
Cohn & Wolfe
30 Orange Street
London
WC2H 7LZ

Coley Porter Bell
Coley Porter Bell
18 Grosvenor Gardens
London
SW1W 0DH

Conqueror
Arjo Wiggins
Fine Papers House
Lime Tree Way
PO Box 88
Chineham
Basingstoke
RG24 8BA

Corus
Corus
30 Millbank
London
SW1P 4WY

Costain
Costain Group PLC
Costain House
Nicholsons Walk
Maidenhead
Berkshire
SL6 1LN

Datamonitor
Datamonitor plc
108-110 Finchley Road
London
NW3 5JJ

Deutsche Bank
Deutsche Bank AG
Taunusanlage 12
D-60325 Frankfurt/Main
Germany